INTERNATIONAL FINANCE

An Analytical Approach

2ND EDITION

McGraw·Hill Australia 
A Division of The ***McGraw·Hill*** *Companies*

National Library of Australia Cataloguing-in-Publication Data

Moosa, Imad A.
International finance: an analytical approach.

2nd ed.
Includes index.
For tertiary students.
ISBN 0 07 471228 4.

1. International finance—Econometric models. 2. International economic relations—Econometric models. 3. Australia—Foreign economic relations—Econometric models. I. Title.

332.042

Published in Australia by
McGraw-Hill Australia Pty Limited
Level 2, 82 Waterloo Road, North Ryde, NSW 2113, Australia
Director of Editorial: Michael Tully
Senior Sponsoring Editor: Ailsa Brackley du Bois
Developmental Editor: Valerie Reed
Production Editor: Amber Cameron
Permissions Editor: Colette Hoeben
Senior Marketing Manager: Sharon-Lee Lukas
Marketing Manager: Susan Talty
Director of e-Learning: Cameron Craig
Editor: Caroline Hunter, Burrumundi Partnership
Cover and Internal Design: Lucy Bal
Typesetter: Kim Webber, Southern Star Design
Proofreader: Tim Learner
Indexer: Diane Harriman
Printed by Best Tri Printing and Packaging Co. Ltd

INTERNATIONAL FINANCE

An Analytical Approach

2ND EDITION

Imad A. Moosa

La Trobe University

Boston Burr Ridge, IL Dubuque, IA Madison, WI New York
San Francisco St. Louis Bangkok Bogotá Caracas Kuala Lumpur
Lisbon London Madrid Mexico City Milan Montreal New Delhi
Santiago Seoul Singapore Sydney Taipei Toronto

Text at a glance

Chapter introduction

Each chapter starts with an introduction, which provides the 'big picture' context of the topic as well as the specific aspects covered. See Chapter 2, p. 28.

Learning objectives

These cover the important components of each chapter. See Chapter 8, p. 226.

In Practice

There are many of these boxes in each chapter. They contain interesting background information—for instance, international currency symbols and nicknames—as well as relevant, topical items in the news. See coverage from *The Economist* in Chapter 4, p. 99, 'Depreciation of the world's second biggest currency'. *(And what was the world's second biggest currency in 2002? You'll never guess. Frequent Flyer points!)*

Research Findings

This is another boxed feature that provides empirical evidence to support the theory. Don't be misled into thinking that these are dry and dusty academic arguments—they are relevant and interesting. For instance, see Chapter 1, p. 19, 'Is globalisation good or bad?', which covers a report published by the World Bank in 2001.

Insight

These features are used to add fascinating background information or elaborate on points in the text. For instance, see Chapter 5, p. 151, where the different types of financial crises that have been experienced by Mexico, Asia, Russia, Brazil and Argentina are classified and explained.

Flow charts

These are used to explain the sequence of international operations. For instance, see Figure 14.18 in Chapter 14, p. 411, 'Using a currency swap as a hedge'.

Examples

Numerous examples in every chapter explain the theory and relate it to readily understandable situations. See Chapter 10, pp. 276 and 279 or Chapter 12, p. 319.

Chapter summary

This useful section at the end of each chapter reviews the key points covered and is a handy revision aid. See Chapter 2, p. 59.

Key terms

These are bolded, listed at the end of each chapter and defined in the comprehensive, end-of-book glossary.

End-of-chapter material

A variety of review questions and problems are provided to reinforce and test your understanding of the material covered. Use these to ensure you are prepared for your exams and assignments.

Appendixes

These add in-depth information and are an excellent reference. For instance, the appendixes to Chapter 2 help you 'talk the talk' by explaining foreign exchange jargon. See p. 65–6.

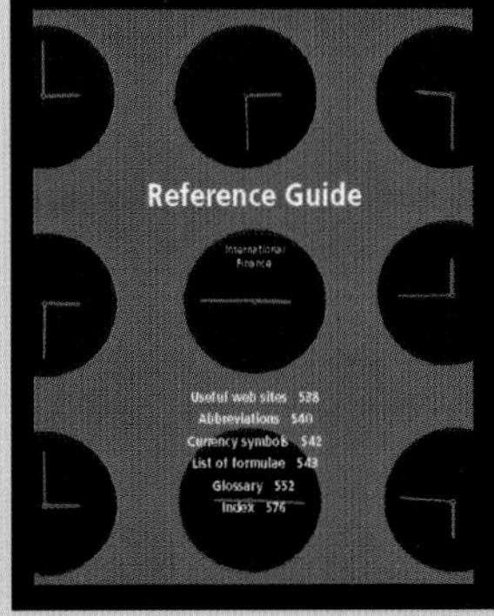

International Finance Reference Guide

This handy section at the back of the book (go to p. 537) brings together a wealth of invaluable reference material for International Finance students, including:

E-Student

www.mhhe.com/au/moosa2e

MaxMark (Premium content)

Unique to McGraw-Hill, MaxMark is a self-paced learning tool that consists of approximately 30 interactive, multiple-choice questions, with extensive feedback for every chapter of the book. MaxMark is designed to help you maximise your marks by allowing you to set time limits, randomise questions and switch the extensive feedback on or off.

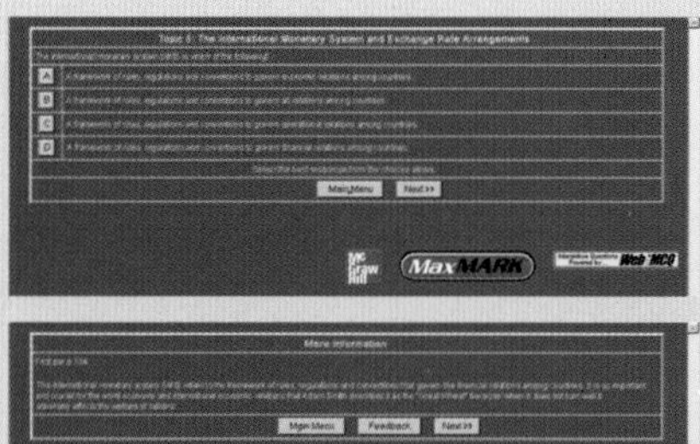

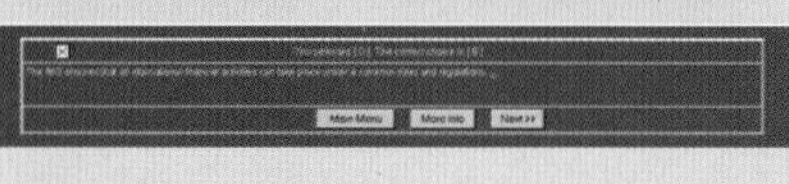

New to this edition, the *International Finance* MaxMark was prepared by Tiffany Hutcheson, University of Technology, Sydney.

PowerPoint Slides

Downloadable PowerPoint slides, written by Afaf Moosa, summarise the key points of each lecture. They can be downloaded as a revision aid.

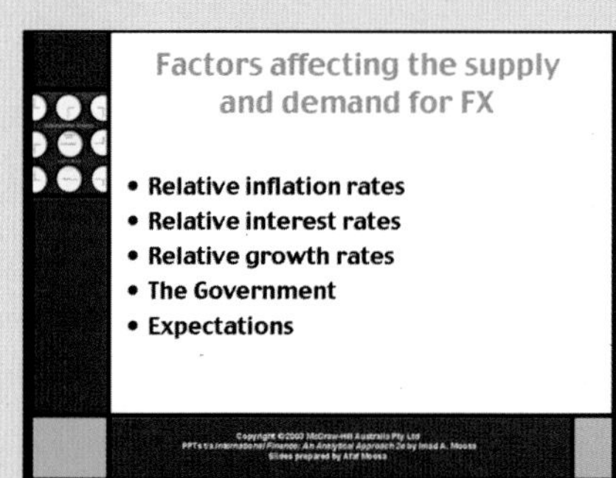

PowerWeb (Premium content)

PowerWeb has been built into your Online Learning Centre to give you smoother access to this powerful product. PowerWeb is exclusive to McGraw-Hill and gives you online journal articles and news items related to your course. These international articles are specific to the chapter of the text that you are studying.

The PowerWeb articles are available in full and have been selected by a team of international academics to give you exposure to current events and ideas in International Finance. The articles are up to date and updated annually.

Quizzes can be taken after reading each article. PowerWeb articles are selected to help you develop a level of knowledge that your peers and future employers are bound to respect.

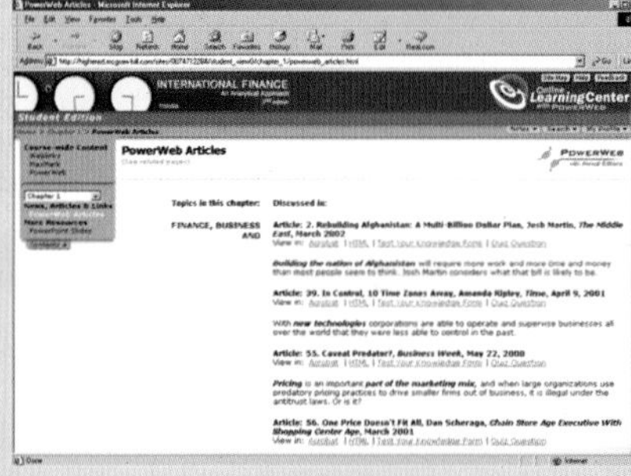

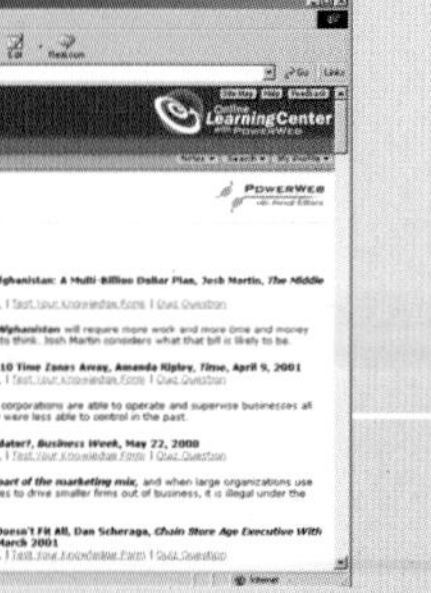

PowerWeb and MaxMark are Premium content items and access to both is via registration of the code at the front of this text. If you need to purchase another Premium content code, you can do so at your campus bookstore or on the book's web site.

The new Online Learning Centre with PowerWeb that accompanies this text is an **integrated online product** to assist you in getting the most from your course.

As a leading publisher of electronic material, McGraw-Hill has been producing a variety of online tools to assist in course-work for many years. This is the first time that they have been integrated into the one area for easy student access.

The Premium content areas, which are accessed by registering the code at the front of this text, provide you with excellent online resources. Once you have registered, you will have seamless access to PowerWeb articles, the MaxMark revision program and subject-specific news feeds. Each component of the Online Learning Centre is described below and can be found in both the *student edition* and the *instructor edition*. The *Information Centre* provides you with additional text information.

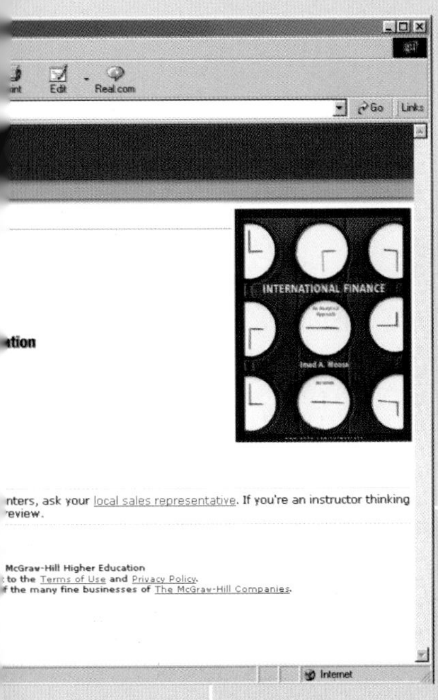

E-Instructor

www.mhhe.com/au/moosa2e

Test Bank

(for instructors only)

The Test Bank has been expanded and revised, and contains 30 multiple-choice questions for each chapter. It can be fully customised and loaded into McGraw-Hill's exclusive online testing tools for secure delivery. Prepared by Greg Jamieson, La Trobe University.

WebMCQ

(for instructors only)

You can set up your own online assignments and exams using our powerful and flexible online quizzing tool. Sophisticated tracking and reporting capabilities allow you to determine topics where students are weakest so that you can target and address these in tutorials.

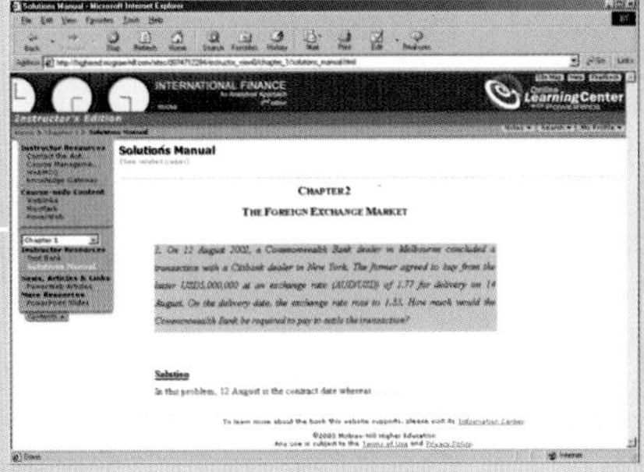

Solutions Manual

(for instructors only)

Comprehensive Solutions Manual prepared by the author.

Contact the author

Imad Moosa welcomes your feedback and comments on the text. An email link is provided for instructors.

To Nisreen and Danny

Whose favourite multinational firm is McDonald's

your course
Text:
International Finance: An Analytical Approach 2nd edition
Text supplements for academics:
Instructor's CD-ROM, PowerPoint Presentations, Solutions and Instructor's Manual
Text web site:
Online Learning Centre
Cases & News Online:
PowerWeb and Online Newsletters
Revision online:
MaxMark
your way
Online testing & revision:
WebMCQ and Test Bank
Online course delivery:
WebCT, Blackboard and PageOut
Custom Publishing & Cases

Contents in brief

Contents

About the author

Imad Moosa obtained a BA in economics and business studies, an MA in the economics of financial intermediaries and a PhD in monetary economics from the University of Sheffield (United Kingdom) in 1975, 1976 and 1986, respectively. He has received formal training in model building, exchange rate forecasting and risk management at the Claremont Economics Institute (United States), Wharton Econometrics (United States) and the International Center for Monetary and Banking Studies (Switzerland). Until 1991, Imad had worked as a financial analyst, a financial journalist and a professional economist in banking and finance. As a result, he gained practical experience in foreign exchange, money market operations, new issues, securities portfolios and corporate finance. He was also an economist at the Financial Institutions Division of the Bureau of Statistics at the International Monetary Fund (Washington, DC).

In 1991 Imad started an academic career by lecturing in Economics and Finance at the University of Sheffield (United Kingdom). In 1994 he joined La Trobe University, where he currently holds a Chair in Finance. He has published seven books and over one hundred papers in academic journals. His work has appeared in the *Journal of Futures Markets, Journal of Applied Econometrics, Quantitative Finance, Journal of Financial Studies, American Journal of Agricultural Economics, IMF Staff Papers, Southern Economic Journal, Journal of Development Economics, Journal of Comparative Economics* and *Journal of Economic Behavior and Organisation*. He has also written for professional magazines such as *Euromoney*.

In May/June 2003, Imad was a member of the US Treasury team visiting Baghdad to rebuild the financial sector of Iraq. He joined a group of economists and bankers with the specific assignments of designing a new currency and exchange rate arrangement.

Acknowledgments

I would like to thank all of those who contributed to the first edition of this book (with their affiliations at that time):

Nabeel Al-Loughani	*Kuwait University*
Dean Arden	*La Trobe University*
Prasad Bidarkota	*La Trobe University*
Chongwoo Choe	*La Trobe University*
Kevin Dowd	*University of Sheffield*
Pauline Kennedy	*La Trobe University*
Liam Lenten	*La Trobe University*
Julie McNab	*McGraw-Hill Australia*
Rod Maddock	*La Trobe University*
Bob Sedgwick	*Sheffield-Hallam University*
Khalifa Shoshan	*University of Sheffield*
Lee Smith	*La Trobe University*
Rabee Tourky	*La Trobe University*

In preparing the second edition I have received assistance and support from a number of colleagues, friends, students and reviewers, as well as family members. First and foremost, I must thank my best research assistant (who also happens to be my wife, Afaf) for producing all the figures shown in this book by utilising her expertise in Excel and Microsoft drawing. Then I must thank my second-best research assistant, Sean Patterson, who read the whole manuscript and updated the problems. Two of my former students who studied the first edition, Suzanne Glavas and Anette Todorovski, read the manuscript or parts of it and came up with numerous suggestions for improvement. As usual, Lee Smith was extremely helpful, reading the whole manuscript and detecting some errors that I would have overlooked. I must also thank my good friend, Ron Ripple, for accepting to read the manuscript despite his other commitments.

I would like to thank the following friends and colleagues who assisted me in one way or another: Liam Lenten, Georgina Luck, Xiangkang Yin, Samantha Booth, Judy Harrison, Jill Addison, Liz Telford, Georgina Eagle, Monica Hodgkinson, Brigitte Carrucan, Brien McDonald, Buly Cardak, Greg Jamieson, Gunky Kim, Robert Waschik, Michael Harris, Hasan Tevfik, Razzaque Bhatti, Bob Sedgwick, Kevin Dowd and Nabeel Al-Loughani.

I would like to join McGraw-Hill Australia in thanking the following people, who provided feedback on the first edition and the second edition manuscript:

Carol Barry	*Swinburne University of Technology*
Christopher Bilson	*Australian National University*
Michael Burrows	*University of South Australia*
Y.H.Cheung	*Edith Cowan University*
Craig Ellis	*University of Western Sydney*
Victor Fang	*Monash University*
Vince Hooper	*University of New South Wales*
Tiffany Hutcheson	*University of Technology, Sydney*
Leong H. Liew	*Griffith University*
K-B. Oh	*La Trobe University*
Isaac Otchere	*University of Melbourne*
Subhrendu Rath	*Curtin University*
Hazbo Skoko	*Charles Sturt University*
Mark Tucker	*Swinburne University*
Henry Yip	*University of New South Wales*

The ancillary authors are:

PowerPoint slides	Afaf Moosa
MaxMark	Tiffany Hutcheson *University of Technology, Sydney*
Test Bank	Greg Jamieson *La Trobe University*

Last, but not least, I would like to thank the McGraw-Hill team, particularly Valerie Reed, Ailsa Brackley du Bois, Yasminka Nemet and Amber Cameron, who were instrumental in encouraging me to write the second edition of this book, an experience that I have enjoyed thoroughly. I must also thank Caroline Hunter, whom I had the pleasure of working with on both editions, for her excellent editing of the manuscript.

Preface

Since the first edition of this book appeared in 1998, I have received feedback and comments from users, students and colleagues, either directly or through McGraw-Hill staff. In particular, the first edition has been criticised on the following grounds: *(i)* it is difficult and too mathematical; *(ii)* there is too much economics; and *(iii)* it lacks real-life examples. Writing the second edition of this book was a great challenge, as I had to introduce some changes to meet the perceived loopholes in the first edition without oversimplifying the content.

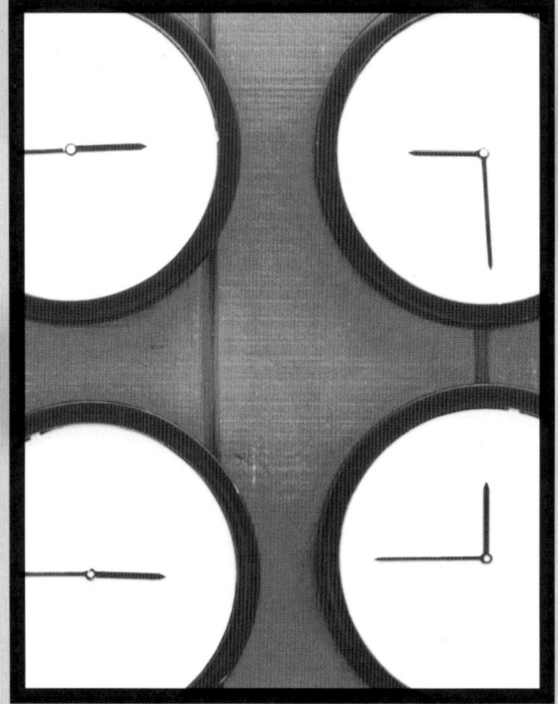

I would like to explain why I wrote the first edition in the way I did, although, in retrospect, I realise that I might have taken things a bit too far (and I acknowledge the validity of the criticism). To start with, whereas the use of algebraic manipulation could have been avoided in certain places, it was made necessary by introducing bid-offer spreads into the operations and the relations underlying these operations (for example, covered interest parity). I felt, and many people agree with me, that it is a unique feature of this book to introduce such an explicit role for the bid-offer spread, which makes the treatment of the subject matter more realistic and practical than in other books. Furthermore, the mathematic representation is important for the preservation of the generality of the underlying principles.

As far as the economic content is concerned, it is my firm belief that economics provides the necessary tools to analyse the relationships used as the basis of international financial operations. How can we talk about the factors affecting exchange rates without the supply and demand model? And how can we understand hedging and other international financial operations without a good grasp of international parity conditions? I must admit, however, that I went too far by using more economics than is necessary for understanding international financial operations. Finally, I have no excuse for not using more practical examples and for depending almost entirely on fictitious case studies.

I have tried to deal with these issues as effectively and comprehensively as I can in the second edition. While I have endeavoured to keep the role of the bid-offer spread, I have deleted all unnecessary mathematical manipulation. The economics has been reduced significantly. For example, Chapter 12 and the section on the effect of

speculation in Chapter 10 from the first edition have been deleted completely and the theories of foreign direct investment have been re-written in a user-friendly style. And I have introduced a large number of practical issues and examples to illustrate certain points. These major changes are explained in detail later on.

In writing the second edition, I have asked three students who used the first edition to read the whole manuscript. They came up with a large number of suggestions, for which I am grateful. I have also received good comments from some colleagues who used the first edition and from a number of reviewers. It is the combination of these inputs that has produced the second edition. However, I am the only person responsible for any remaining errors and omissions in this book (hopefully none).

Imad Moosa
June 2003

The organisation of this book

This book contains 18 chapters covering seven topics in International Finance. The topics can be broadly classified as follows:

1. Introduction and overview *(Chapter 1)*
2. Basic concepts and relationships *(Chapters 2 and 3)*
3. Exchange rate arrangements, determination and forecasting *(Chapters 4, 5 and 12)*
4. Currency derivatives, Eurobanking and international banking *(Chapters 6, 7 and 8)*
5. International parity conditions *(Chapters 9, 10 and 11)*
6. Hedging and foreign exchange risk management *(Chapters 13 and 14)*
7. International financing and investment operations *(Chapters 15, 16, 17 and 18).*

The following is a brief description of these topics and an explanation of the logic of the ordering of the chapters. The sequence is determined by the basic criterion that if a chapter presents concepts that are essential to the understanding of the material in another chapter, then the latter should follow the former. For example, **Chapter 5** is placed where it is because the discussion depends crucially on concepts and tools introduced in **Chapters 2** and **4**. And **Chapter 3** is placed where it is because it is inappropriate to introduce the concept of the effective exchange rate without knowing what the bilateral exchange rate is (**Chapter 2**).

Chapter 1 deals with an overview of International Finance, setting the background for studying the material presented in the following chapters. The chapter discusses why finance has become international and how international financial operations have changed following the developments that have taken place since the end of World War II. The discussion gives rise to concepts and relationships that are studied in detail in the chapters that follow. The second topic, covered by **Chapters 2** and **3**, deals with the basic concepts and relationships pertaining to the exchange rate and the balance of payments. **Chapter 2** deals with the organisational aspects of the foreign exchange market and various concepts of the exchange rate. **Chapter 3** describes the structure of the balance of payments and its relationship with the foreign exchange market. The chapter introduces more exchange rate concepts, including the real effective exchange rate.

Knowledge of the basic concepts of the exchange rate and the balance of payments prepares students for studying the determination and forecasting of exchange rates. **Chapter 4** deals with the determination of flexible exchange rates in a free market as portrayed by the supply and demand model. **Chapter 5** describes various exchange rate arrangements and therefore the determination of exchange rates under various systems. **Chapter 12** looks at why exchange rate forecasting is needed and surveys the methods employed to do this. Some of the models presented in **Chapters 2, 9, 10** and **11** are used as the basis of the econometric forecasting models.

The fourth topic deals with currency derivatives and some institutional features of the major players in the spot and derivative markets: Eurobanks and international banks. **Chapter 6** covers currency swaps and currency futures contracts. Both of these topics follow from the discussion of forward contracts in **Chapter 2**. **Chapter 8** deals with some aspects of Eurobanking and international banking since these activities form the backbone of the spot and derivative currency markets.

International parity conditions are covered in **Chapters 9, 10** and **11**. The reason for placing these chapters here rather than earlier is that an understanding of these conditions is crucial for understanding the international operations of hedging, financing and investment, which are covered in the remaining part of the book. This topic is dealt with more extensively than in any other comparable book because of the belief that these conditions are crucial for international financial operations. Thus, **Chapter 9** deals with purchasing power parity and **Chapter 10** deals with covered interest parity, whereas **Chapter 11** deals with uncovered interest parity and real interest parity.

The topic of hedging foreign exchange risk follows in **Chapters 13** and **14**. Whereas **Chapter 13** deals with the definition and measurement of risk and exposure, **Chapter 14** covers the management of the exposure using products studied earlier in the book (futures, options, etc.), as well as some operational techniques. This topic has become so extensive that there is now a tendency for teaching it in Risk Management rather than International Finance courses.

Finally, international financing and investment operations are covered in the last four chapters. **Chapter 15** covers short-term financing and investment, whereas **Chapter 16** and **Chapter 17** examine long-term financing and portfolio investment. **Chapter 18** deals with foreign direct investment.

It may or may not be possible to cover the material presented in this book in one (13-week) semester or one (10-week) term. The ultimate choice depends on the instructor's preferences and the background of the students taking the subject. Given these parameters, the instructor can mix and match various topics.

Features of the second edition

The second edition has been revised to ensure that this new text is less technical and unnecessarily detailed, and that it includes more practical examples and reduced economics. The general changes can be summarised as follows:

1. The text contains **three kinds of boxed features**: In Practice, Research Findings and Insight. The In Practice boxes contain practical examples and cases. The Research Findings boxes summarise important pieces of research, written in a simplified language. The Insight boxes are used to elaborate on certain points or concepts.

2. The **case studies** as they appeared in the first edition have disappeared. This is because some of them were more like long problems than case studies. Those that qualify as real case studies now appear as In Practice boxes, in addition to numerous new ones. Those that are more like long problems now appear as problems.

3. The book has been **reduced to 18 chapters** by deleting Chapter 12 (too much economics) and by merging the two chapters on short-term investment and financing into one chapter (the new Chapter 15).

4. The body of the text does not have citations. The **citations** and **references** appear in the boxes. Hence, there is no reference list at the end of the book.

5. There are no **footnotes** in the text. They only appear in boxes to refer to relevant studies that are cited.

6. There are numerous **new flow charts** that explain international financial operations.

7. The difficult material has been cut back and the number of equations has been reduced significantly.

8. **New additions** include a list of formulae and a list of useful web sites at the end of the book, and a list of key terms at the end of each chapter (the key terms are bolded at first mention).

9. The **key terms** are defined at the end of the book in the most comprehensive glossary in any book of its kind, with over 800 entries.

Chapter-by-chapter highlights

The following are specific changes introduced to each chapter.

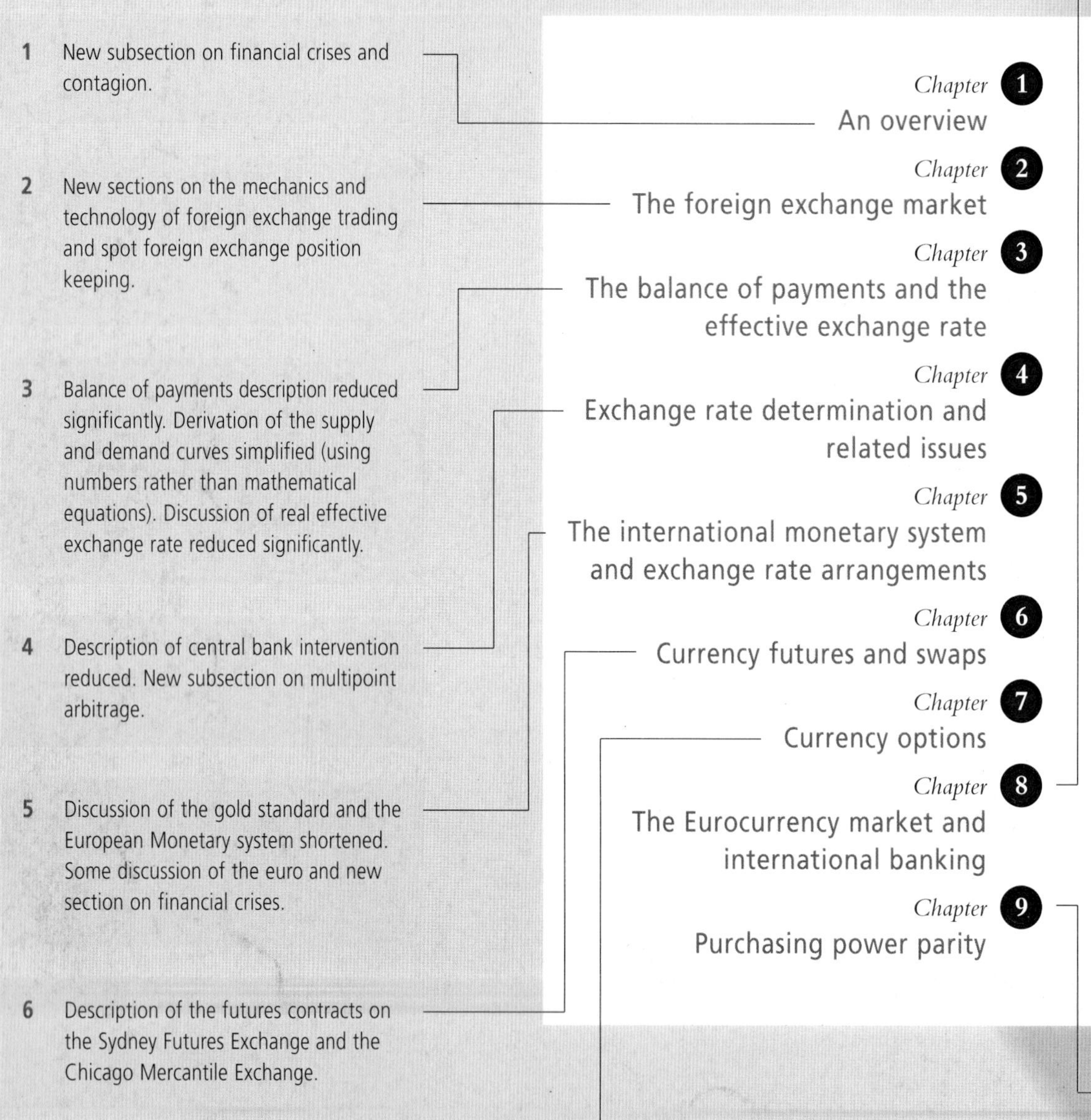

1 New subsection on financial crises and contagion.

2 New sections on the mechanics and technology of foreign exchange trading and spot foreign exchange position keeping.

3 Balance of payments description reduced significantly. Derivation of the supply and demand curves simplified (using numbers rather than mathematical equations). Discussion of real effective exchange rate reduced significantly.

4 Description of central bank intervention reduced. New subsection on multipoint arbitrage.

5 Discussion of the gold standard and the European Monetary system shortened. Some discussion of the euro and new section on financial crises.

6 Description of the futures contracts on the Sydney Futures Exchange and the Chicago Mercantile Exchange.

7 New option terms added. Description of the currency options listed on the Chicago Mercantile Exchange and the Philadelphia Stock Exchange. More user-friendly description of option positions. Discussion of the Black–Scholes formula deleted (we are not concerned with option pricing but rather with how they are used for hedging and speculation).

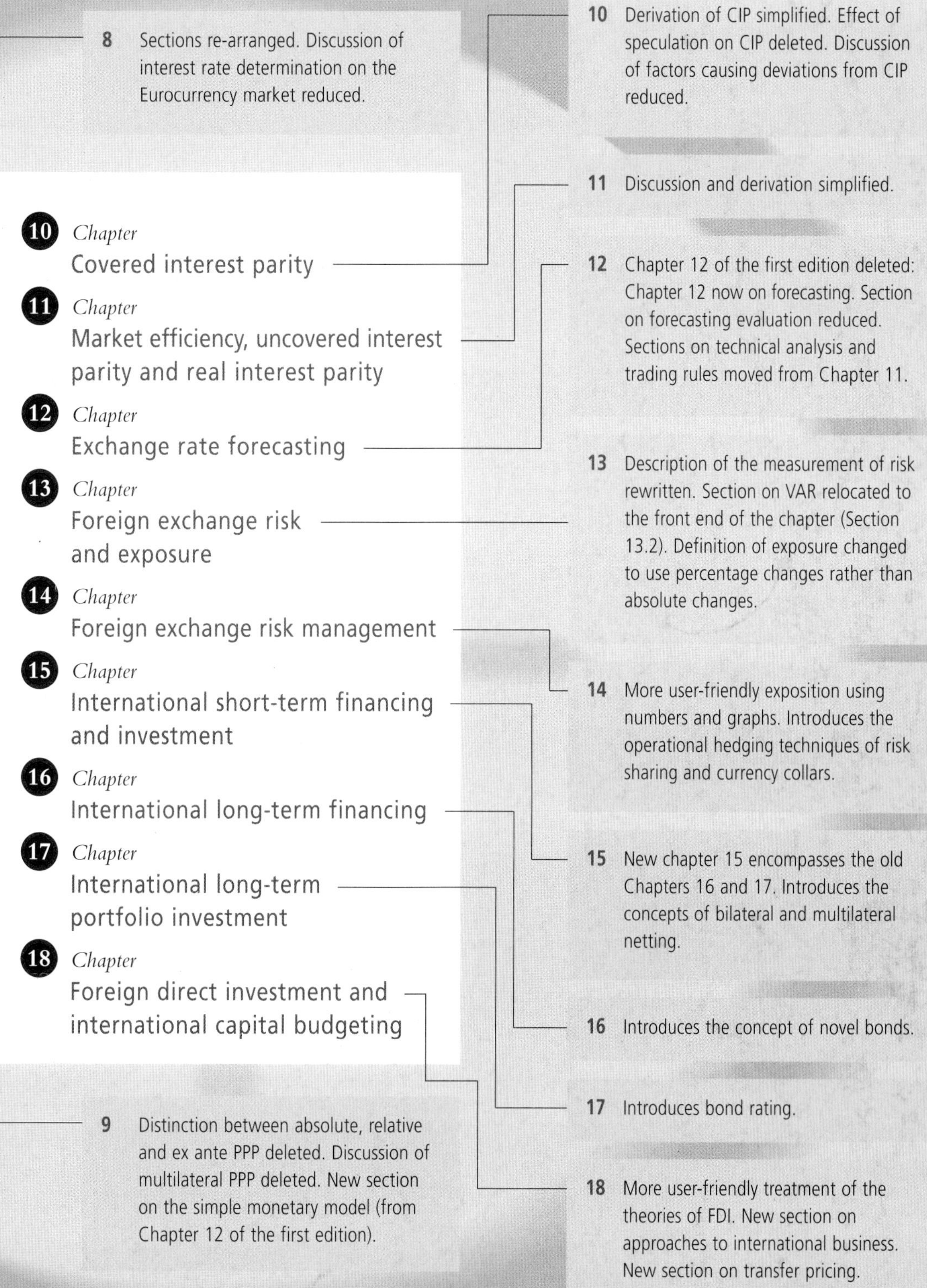

8 Sections re-arranged. Discussion of interest rate determination on the Eurocurrency market reduced.

9 Distinction between absolute, relative and ex ante PPP deleted. Discussion of multilateral PPP deleted. New section on the simple monetary model (from Chapter 12 of the first edition).

10 *Chapter* Covered interest parity

11 *Chapter* Market efficiency, uncovered interest parity and real interest parity

12 *Chapter* Exchange rate forecasting

13 *Chapter* Foreign exchange risk and exposure

14 *Chapter* Foreign exchange risk management

15 *Chapter* International short-term financing and investment

16 *Chapter* International long-term financing

17 *Chapter* International long-term portfolio investment

18 *Chapter* Foreign direct investment and international capital budgeting

10 Derivation of CIP simplified. Effect of speculation on CIP deleted. Discussion of factors causing deviations from CIP reduced.

11 Discussion and derivation simplified.

12 Chapter 12 of the first edition deleted: Chapter 12 now on forecasting. Section on forecasting evaluation reduced. Sections on technical analysis and trading rules moved from Chapter 11.

13 Description of the measurement of risk rewritten. Section on VAR relocated to the front end of the chapter (Section 13.2). Definition of exposure changed to use percentage changes rather than absolute changes.

14 More user-friendly exposition using numbers and graphs. Introduces the operational hedging techniques of risk sharing and currency collars.

15 New chapter 15 encompasses the old Chapters 16 and 17. Introduces the concepts of bilateral and multilateral netting.

16 Introduces the concept of novel bonds.

17 Introduces bond rating.

18 More user-friendly treatment of the theories of FDI. New section on approaches to international business. New section on transfer pricing.

CHAPTER

An overview

Introduction

International finance as studied in this book deals with the financial operations of business firms in an environment of open and integrated financial markets. These operations include arbitrage, financing, hedging, investment and speculation. The basic question that is addressed is the following: Given the macroeconomic and macrofinancial environment of the present time, how do business firms operate with respect to their financial operations? We will therefore tackle the macro aspects first and then concentrate on the micro, firm-level aspects of the subject matter. This chapter presents an overview of the broad issues of concern to students of international finance.

Objectives

The objectives of this chapter are:

- To identify the factors that have led to the prominence of international finance as an academic discipline and a business activity.
- To explain the role of the financial manager in the present global environment.
- To verify the internationalisation of finance by several indicators.
- To describe the economic, financial and institutional developments that have led to the formation of the present global environment.

1.1 The importance of international finance

International finance has assumed increasing importance at an accelerating rate, both as an academic discipline and as an activity in which business firms get involved. The period extending between the end of World War II and the early 1970s was characterised by the operation of a system of fixed exchange rates, the presence of stringent **capital controls** and the segmentation of financial markets. As a reflection of this setting, international finance was taught not as a separate subject but as part of international economics, more precisely as the financial counterpart of international trade. At that time, students (including the present author) concentrated on the benefits of international trade resulting from the utilisation of **comparative advantage**, while international finance was treated only as an ancillary topic, needed because international trade must be financed. Emphasis was placed upon the mechanisms and settings of international settlements and the consequences for the balance of payments. As for business firms, there was little desire or ability to engage in international or cross-country financing and investment. International transactions predominantly took the form of financing exports and imports, and international firms were those trading with the outside world. Furthermore, hedging foreign exchange risk was not a major problem under a system of fixed exchange rates and relatively limited cross-country financial transactions.

Things, however, started to change with the collapse of the **Bretton Woods system** of fixed exchange rates in August 1971, when the US President, Richard Nixon, announced that his country was no longer prepared to convert the US dollar into gold. After a period of chaos and uncertainty, major countries shifted to a system of flexible or floating exchange rates in 1973, and by the onset of the 1980s exchange rates had become volatile and misaligned. This shift was accompanied (at least in developed countries) by a trend towards the abolition of capital controls and the implementation of **financial deregulation**, a trend that is still continuing at the present time.

These developments have given prominence to international finance. As an academic discipline, the field has become concerned with the very important issues of exchange rate determination and the sources and consequences of **exchange rate volatility**. These issues are significant for **international firms**, now that the economic and financial environment makes it viable and desirable for them to expand the scope of **international operations**. Thus, the term international operations has changed from the limited scope of trading with the outside world to the wider scope of carrying out part of the production operations abroad and considering financial decisions from an international perspective. This has led to the emergence of **multinational firms** and **transnational firms**.

Exchange rate volatility has also brought with it the need to hedge foreign exchange risk. In the kind of environment where we live today, this risk is relevant not only for business firms with international operations, but also for firms whose operations are purely domestic. For example, **appreciation** of the domestic currency could induce foreign competitors to enter the domestic market, threatening the market share of purely domestic firms. In the present environment, firms simply cannot insulate themselves from events that occur across national frontiers.

What happens in the financial markets of other countries is bound to show up in the domestic markets. A decision by the **Federal Reserve System** (the US central bank) to change the US interest rate will very likely

International, multinational and transnational firms

The term 'international business firms' traditionally referred to firms engaged in the cross-border activities of importing and exporting, such that goods were produced in the home country and then exported abroad, and vice versa. The financial implications of these transactions pertain to the payment process between buyers and sellers across national frontiers. As international operations expand, the international firm may feel that it is desirable, if possible, to expand in such a way as to be closer to foreign consumers. Production will then be carried out both at home and abroad. Thus, a multinational firm carries out some of its production activity abroad by establishing a presence in foreign countries via subsidiaries and joint ventures. The financial implications of this activity are more significant than those of exporting and importing. The foreign 'arms' of a multinational firm (subsidiaries, affiliates and branches) normally have different base currencies, which are the currencies of the countries where they are located. This set-up results in a greater currency and financial risk in general.

As cross-border activity expands even further, the distinction between 'home' and 'abroad' becomes blurred, and difficulties arise as to the identification of the 'home country'. What is created in this case is a transnational firm. In this book, the term 'international firm' is used to refer to a firm that indulges in international cross-border operations in the modern sense without necessarily being a multinational firm (that is, without necessarily indulging in foreign production). However, the term 'multinational firm' will be used particularly in conjunction with foreign direct investment, an activity that involves foreign production.

affect the mortgage payments of Australian home owners. The Asian crisis of 1997/1998 affected the operations of several Australian companies with exposure to the region, forcing investors to dump stocks of these companies. Thus, Coca-Cola Amatil, which obtained 40 per cent of its profit from the Philippines and Indonesia, saw a steep drop in its market value over a short time in the second half of the 1990s. The end of the 1990s bull market (when stock prices rose persistently) in April 2000, with the collapse of technology stocks, took place in the United States, Australia and other countries around the same time. The US accounting scandals of Enron (2001) and WorldCom (2002) caused a worldwide slump in stock markets in 2002.

The transmission of effects across national frontiers may be more pronounced on the sectoral or individual firm level. For example, the WorldCom accounting scandal is believed to have had a special effect on Australian telecommunication stocks. This is because WorldCom, the second largest US telecommunication company, owned Australia's second largest Internet service provider, Ozemail, and 10 per cent of the Australia-Japan submarine cable, in which Telstra owned a 40 per cent interest.

International finance has both macro and micro aspects. The macro aspects include exchange rate determination and volatility, the joint determination of the exchange rate and the balance of payments, the role of the exchange rate in macroeconomic equilibrium and fluctuations, and exchange rate policy. These topics, particularly the policy aspects, are studied in international monetary economics or open-economy macroeconomics. This book deals with, or rather concentrates on, the micro aspects by examining the behaviour of business firms, given the global economic and financial environment within which they operate. In particular, the book presents a comprehensive treatment of the financial operations of business firms in the present international environment.

RESEARCH FINDINGS

Chain reaction in world stock markets

The issue of whether or not a crash in a major stock market leads to crashes in other markets has been investigated by financial economists. In particular, these economists have repeatedly investigated the validity of the proposition that 'when America sneezes, the world catches cold'.

Eun and Shim conducted empirical research to answer three questions:[1]

- How much can the movements in one stock market be explained by developments (particularly unanticipated events) in other stock markets?
- Does the US stock market indeed influence other markets?
- How rapidly are the price movements in one market transmitted to other markets?

Their investigation produced the following answers:

- There is a substantial amount of multilateral interaction among national markets.
- The US market is by far the most influential with respect to its effect on other markets.
- Developments in the US market are rapidly transmitted to other markets.

Richard Roll investigated the great crash of October 1987, which he attributed to 'the normal response of each country's stock market to a worldwide market movement'.[2] Out of the 23 markets that he studied, 19 declined more than 20 per cent.

1 C. S. Eun and S. Shim, 'International Transmission of Stock Market Movements', *Journal of Financial and Quantitative Analysis*, 24, 1989, pp. 241–56.

2 R. Roll, 'The International Crash of October 1987', *Financial Analysts Journal*, September–October 1988, pp. 19–35.

Before these operations can be studied, we must look at the global environment, making it necessary to study some macro and institutional aspects, but only in so far as they impinge upon our understanding of how business firms operate. International business operations under a system of fixed exchange rates with capital controls and market segmentation can be very different from the situation under a system of flexible exchange rates with free capital movement and **market integration**. Thus, we need to start with an examination of the global environment, as shaped by the international monetary system and other international arrangements. The objective is to find out what the existing set-up allows, what it does not allow and what constraints it imposes. We also need to study how the key variables of exchange and interest rates are determined in such an environment. Finally, we need to find out what instruments are offered by financial markets to carry out these functions. Using this knowledge as a foundation, we can proceed to study the operations of international firms.

1.2 International finance and the role of the financial manager

Let us look at the matter from the perspective of a financial manager who tries to run a business in the present environment. Business firms engage in international operations so that they can reap the benefits of the internationalisation or **globalisation** of trade and investment, subject to the costs of doing so. One obvious benefit of international trade is the extension of the market for the firm's products beyond the national frontiers. The costs arise from foreign competition, **foreign exchange risk** and **country risk**. Foreign exchange risk results from uncertainty about future exchange rates that affects sales, prices and profits. Country risk, on the other hand, results from economic, political and social factors that may have adverse implications for sales, prices and profits. The advantage of the globalisation of finance is to enhance the ability of business firms, and market participants in general, to diversify their financing and investment portfolios. Once again, this endeavour is subject to the same risks mentioned above, as well as the **financial risk** arising from changes in foreign financial variables such as interest rates.

Given this background, the financial manager needs to be concerned about several issues that can be detected easily by reading the financial press. These issues include fluctuations in exchange and interest rates, balance-of-payments difficulties, and the **international debt problem**. But why would the financial manager be concerned about these issues? Simply because they have ramifications for the firm's profitability and performance. Exchange and interest rates determine the firm's cost of financing and the return on investment. The volatility of exchange and interest rates implies volatility of profitability and raises the need for managing financial risk, which is not cost-free. Balance-of-payments difficulties affect interest and exchange rates and the economic performance of countries, since they are often viewed as a constraint on economic policy. The international debt problem has not only caused some major international banks to incur huge losses or allocate massive provisions against bad loans, but has also made international business firms in general think seriously about country risk before taking any decision about doing business with a particular country.

It is useful at this stage to present some classic real-life examples to demonstrate why exchange rate fluctuations can demolish a business. The first example is that of a British company, the Beecham Group, which in 1971 raised a Swiss franc loan of CHF100 million at a time when the exchange rate between the Swiss and British currencies was about 9.87 CHF/GBP (see list of currency symbols). At this exchange rate, the value of the loan in pound terms was GBP10.13 million. When the repayment of the loan became due in 1976, the pound had depreciated against the Swiss franc, as the exchange rate had plunged to 4.4 CHF/GBP. At this exchange rate, the value of the principal that had to be repaid was GBP22.73 million. Thus, the depreciation of the pound gave rise to an additional cost of GBP12.86 million in principal repayment alone.

The second classic example is that of another British company, Laker Airlines, which provided cheap transatlantic flights for British holiday-makers. During the 1970s this company borrowed US dollar funds to purchase several US-made DC10 jet planes. As the pound started to depreciate against the dollar in 1981, the demand for transatlantic flights by British holiday-makers declined, whereas the value of the company's debt in pound terms increased. The outcome of this chain of events was inevitable: Laker Airlines went into bankruptcy.

There are other examples of the effect of appreciating currencies. The appreciation of the US dollar in the first half of the 1980s caused a sharp loss of domestic and foreign market shares for US companies such as Caterpillar and Eastman Kodak. The latter's pre-tax earnings were reduced by USD3.5 billion over the period 1980–1985. The subsequent appreciation of the yen led to a 69 per cent reduction in the 1986 pre-tax profit of Canon, the Japanese camera firm.

The **depreciation** of the Australian dollar in the early years of the twenty-first century has adversely affected the performance of Australian trading firms engaged in retailing imported foreign goods. This is because the depreciation of the Australian dollar made imported goods more expensive (in Australian dollar terms), which put these firms in a dilemma: either passing on the increase in cost to the consumer, risking declining sales or accepting a cut in profit margins. Such a dilemma would normally arise unless the Australian importers were billed in Australian dollars with long-term contracts ensuring stable domestic currency prices. In this case, the foreign producer of the imported goods bears the cost. On 23 April 2002, the *Australian Financial Review* reported a potential loss of AUD4.8 billion to be faced by the federal government on its loan portfolio, resulting from changes in exchange rates. It was also reported that although importers budgeted for currency movements within their profit margins, no one expected the fall of the dollar to 48 US cents, and 'not even the fattest margin can trade successfully on those levels'. It seems that Australian importers squeezed their portfolio margins in response to the Aussie dollar's weakness, unless they had been smart enough to negotiate contractual agreements to be invoiced in Australian dollars.

Now that we have identified some of the issues that the financial manager needs to be concerned with, we must identify the knowledge to be acquired so that the underlying tasks are executed effectively and efficiently. To start with, the financial manager needs to be acquainted with the macroeconomic environment in which the firm operates. This requires knowledge of: (i) major economic indicators such as growth, inflation, unemployment and the balance of payments; and (ii) government policies, including monetary, fiscal and structural policies. Within the macroeconomic environment, the microeconomic environment relates to specific decisions at the firm's level. The financial manager must have the skills necessary to handle such problems as: (i) the management of foreign exchange risk; (ii) analysis of capital budgeting that pertains to direct investment in projects; and (iii) factors affecting the demand for the firm's products.

Studying international finance is important for the financial manager for at least the following two reasons. First, it helps the financial manager to decide how international events affect the firm and which steps can be taken to exploit positive developments and insulate the firm from harmful ones. Second, it helps the manager to anticipate events and to make profitable decisions before the events occur. Such events include: (i) changes in exchange

The effects of the appreciation and depreciation of the Aussie dollar

IN PRACTICE

After falling to a low of 48 US cents in 2001, the Australian dollar rose to a 15-month high of over 55 cents by mid-May 2002. Although the Australian currency was undervalued by many measures at this level, some Australian companies (with exports and foreign currency earnings) felt the negative impact of the appreciation.

One such company was the National Australia Bank (NAB), which started to feel the pressure of currency appreciation on its offshore earnings (most notably its British operations) from which the bank derives pound-denominated earnings. A weak Australian dollar produces larger Australian-dollar earnings from a given amount of pound-denominated earnings. In a report published by J.B. Were in May 2002, it was estimated that NAB's earnings would drop by AUD20 million for every penny the Australian dollar appreciated against the pound. This was so much the case because the British and Irish subsidiaries had become key earnings drivers, as pointed out by NAB's managing director in an interview with Channel Nine on 12 May 2002.

In its issue of 29 January 2003 the *Australian Financial Review* reported concerns about the Australian exports sector. The paper stated explicitly that 'exporters, particularly to the US, will have to cope with the nasty reality that their goods are now more expensive for overseas buyers'.[1] The most immediate impact, however, was felt by those who had invested in equity funds, particularly those who invested in US or non-Japanese Asian equities. According to Alex Schuman, the Commonwealth Bank's senior currency strategist, '40 per cent of all net gains in offshore equity funds for the past few years have originated from the $A depreciation'.[2]

1 C. Lim, 'Winners and Losers in $A Stakes', *Australian Financial Review*, 29 January 2003, p. 23.

2 ibid.

rates; (ii) changes in interest rates; (iii) changes in inflation rates; (iv) changes in national incomes; and (v) changes in the political environment. These events are intricately linked. For example, exchange and interest rates are linked via **uncovered interest parity**; exchange rates and inflation rates are linked via **purchasing power parity**; interest rates and inflation rates are linked via the **Fisher equation**; changes in national incomes affect the exchange rates and inflation rates; and changes in the political environment affect almost everything else. We will come across these concepts in various parts of this book.

1.3 Indicators of the internationalisation of finance

The internationalisation (or globalisation) of finance has been driven by advances in information and computer technologies, the globalisation of national economies, the liberalisation of national financial and capital markets, and competition among the providers of financial intermediary services. There are several factors that indicate the ever-increasing degree of the internationalisation of finance. These indicators include: (i) the volume of international bank lending (including cross-border lending and domestic lending denominated in foreign currencies); (ii) the value of securities transactions with foreigners; (iii) the flows of **portfolio investment** and **foreign direct investment**; (iv) the value of daily turnover (trading volume) in the global foreign exchange market; and (v) the percentage of foreign exchange trading conducted with cross-border counterparties.

These indicators can be put into perspective by noting that in 2001 the US GDP (the total value of goods and services produced in the United States that year) was about USD10.7 trillion. In its *Quarterly Review* of March 2002, the **Bank for International Settlements (BIS)**, which acts as the central bank of central banks, reported some staggering figures that indicate the extent of the internationalisation of finance. By the end of 2001, cross-border claims of banks on other banks worldwide were USD11.3 trillion, compared with just over USD3 trillion for local claims. At the same time, the value of outstanding international debt securities was USD7248 billion, of which USD398 billion were short-term money market instruments. Between 2000 and 2001, the gross new issues in the international bond and note market increased from USD1708 billion to USD2025 billion.

In its 2001 *Triennial Central Bank Survey*, which aims to measure the size of the global foreign exchange market, the Bank for International Settlements estimated the value of daily trading involving spot and forward transactions to be USD1200 billion, compared with USD188 billion in 1986. Needless to say, this amount reflects international operations involving goods, services and (predominantly) financial assets. About 58 per cent of the volume was related to transactions with cross-border counterparties.

Consider Figure 1.1, which shows the growth of foreign direct investment (FDI) **flows** and **stocks** as reported by UNCTAD in its annual publication, *World Investment Report*. FDI flows increased from an average of USD225 billion a year during the period 1990–1995 to USD735 billion in 2001, having reached the staggering level of USD1492 billion in 2000. The outstanding value of FDI stocks was USD636 billion in 1980, but at the end of 2001 the figure was up to USD6846 billion.

Figure 1.1 Foreign direct investment flows and stocks (USD billion)

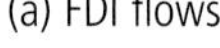
(a) FDI flows

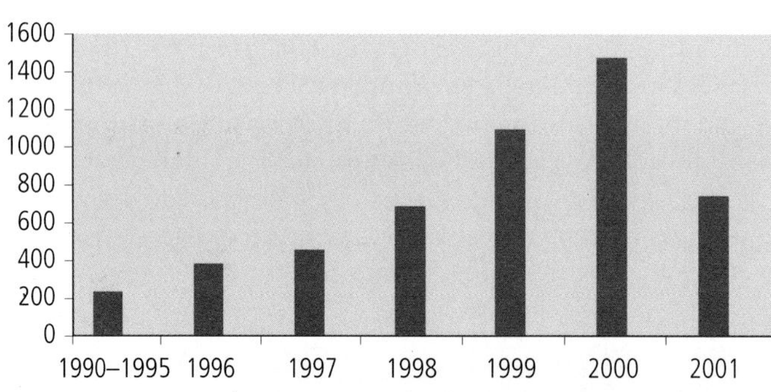

(b) FDI stocks

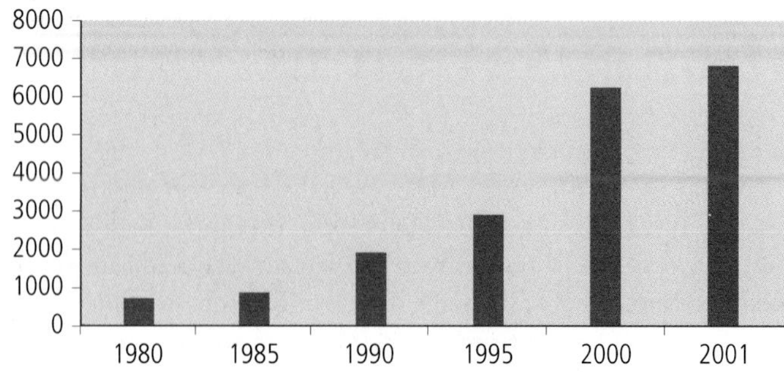

Source: World Investment Report, UNCTAD, 2002.

Post-war economic, financial and institutional developments

The economic and financial environment within which business firms operate at present is the product of a number of developments that followed the end of World War II. These developments took place initially under the Bretton Woods system of fixed exchange rates, and subsequently under the present system of predominantly managed and independent floating (see Chapter 5).

The emergence of the Eurodollar market

The **Eurodollar market** emerged in London in the late 1950s due to a combination of factors. This market, a symbol of capitalism, was ironically initiated by the Soviet Union, motivated by the Soviet's desire to maintain their dollar balances but keeping them outside the United States. The market has since grown rapidly, encompassing non-dollar currencies, such that it is presently known as the **Eurocurrency market**. Related markets have also emerged, including the **Eurobond market** and the **Eurocredit market**. In general, these are markets for assets and liabilities denominated in currencies other than that of the country in which they are held.

Currency convertibility

Because of the damage inflicted on Europe in World War II, the Bretton Woods Agreement of 1944 allowed for the inconvertibility of the currencies of the European countries while they were rebuilding their economies. It was not until the late 1950s that European currencies became convertible again. The Japanese yen did not become convertible until the early 1960s.

The European Economic Community and the European Union

The **European Economic Community (EEC)**, which is currently known as the **European Union (EU)**, was established by the Treaty of Rome in 1957 to promote economic and financial cooperation among European countries. Since 2002, 12 of the 15 EU countries have given up their national currencies in preference for the euro, the new European currency. These countries are Austria, Belgium, Finland, France, Germany, Greece, Ireland, Italy, Luxembourg, the Netherlands, Portugal and Spain. In April 2003, the EU enlargement took place when 10 more countries, including Estonia and Malta, became EU members.

Changes in relative economic size

There has been a trend towards greater symmetry in economic size among industrial countries (as measured by their shares of world output and trade). The relative size of the United States has declined significantly, whereas the shares of the EU and Japan have risen. In terms of output, the US share was 41.5 per cent in 1962. In 2001, Japan's output (measured by GDP) was 38 per cent of that of the United States, whereas the euro zone produced more than 75 per cent of the US output. One result of this change is that a system of the Bretton Woods type with a single hegemon (the United States) is no longer viable.

IN PRACTICE

Will the euro make the EU a single market?

The introduction of the euro as a hard currency in January 2002 is thought to be a major step towards the creation of a single market for European business. A single currency should boost intra-European trade, a proposition that many academic economists (but not all of them) agree with. Although a single currency is an important factor, it is not sufficient for boosting trade. The very existence of borders creates some other factors that affect adversely the environment in which businesses operate. These factors include administrative rules and standards, social and religious phenomena, capabilities (including geography and natural resources), and information differences (including language). While a single currency makes it easier to compare prices, Europe currently has heterogeneous customers who buy heterogeneous products. Although prices in the euro zone will converge, they will do so more slowly than most observers anticipate and most politicians hope for.

The same goes for capital markets. A quick look at the banking system or the financial services industry in general suggests that there are significant differences. In particular, European stock markets remain fragmented with little cross listing (that is, listing companies from one country on the stock exchange of another country). The introduction of the euro is certainly a necessary but not a sufficient condition for the creation of a single European market.

Deterioration of the US external position

The US external position has deteriorated, turning the United States from a surplus to a deficit country. Following the end of World War II, the United States emerged as the supreme economic and financial power. Until the beginning of the 1970s, the US current account of the balance of payments was in surplus, but trouble started then as the current account sank into deficit because of the cumulative effect of the Vietnam War. This change in the external position forced the US government to abolish the **convertibility** of the dollar into gold in 1971, which signalled the collapse of the Bretton Woods system of fixed exchange rates.

Although the US current account recovered subsequently, a persistent deficit started to appear in the 1980s, continuing until the present time. The reason for the re-emergence of the deficit in the 1980s was the massive military expenditure program of the Reagan Administration. Since the total expenditure of the US government was in excess of its total revenue, the US budget was in deficit and had to be financed. Because of the low saving ratio in the US economy, the budget deficit had to be financed by borrowing abroad (that is, by selling US Treasury bonds to foreigners). This borrowing led not only to an increased level of foreign indebtedness but also to a current account deficit, since interest payments are recorded on the current account. The occurrence of both a current account deficit and a budget deficit is known as the **twin deficit problem**. Although the US budget deficit was eliminated during the Clinton era, it re-emerged following the expansion in military spending after the events of 11 September 2001.

The budget deficit (implying an expansionary fiscal policy) coupled with a contractionary monetary policy, led to a high level of US nominal and real interest rates, appreciation of the dollar, and the emergence of the international debt problem in 1982. Contrary to the US position, both Japan and Germany registered current account surpluses for most of the period. These two countries used their surpluses in part to finance the US deficit by acquiring US Treasury bonds.

The current account developments over the period 1968–2001 are illustrated in Figure 1.2. It is interesting to note that the relatively small US deficit in 1991 was a temporary phenomenon resulting from the transfers associated with the Gulf War. Also interesting is the observation that Germany turned into a deficit country in 1991 because of the reunification with East Germany. The case for Australia has been one of deficit throughout the period.

Figure 1.2 Current account balances (USD billion)

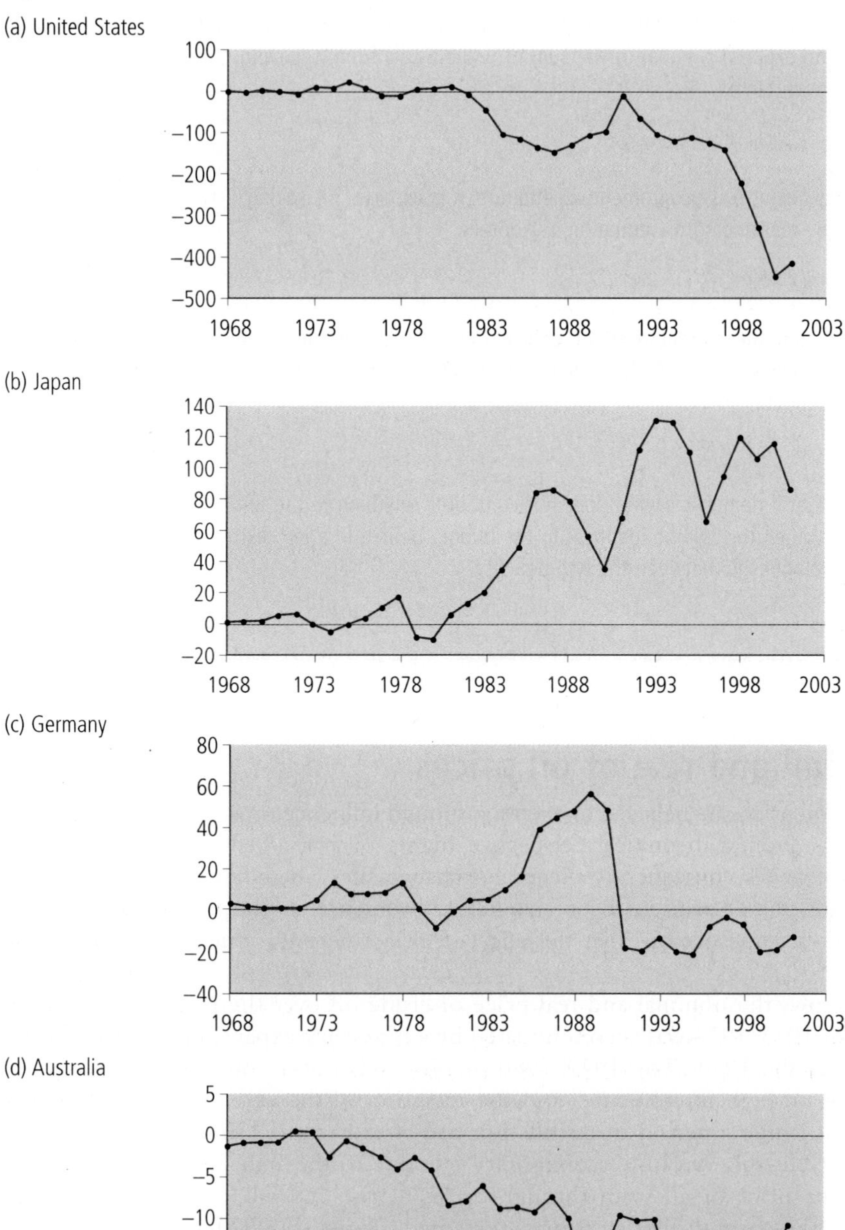

Source: Main Economic Indicators, OECD.

INSIGHT

The concept of the 'twin deficit'

The twin deficit phenomenon can be illustrated by resorting to elementary macroeconomics. In equilibrium the sum of injections into the circular flow of income (investment, government expenditure and exports) is equal to the sum of withdrawals from it (saving, taxes and imports). This equality is written as

$$I + G + X = S + T + M$$

where I is investment, G is government expenditure, X is exports, S is saving, T is tax revenue and M is imports. By rearranging the equation, we obtain

$$(X - M) = (S - I) + (T - G)$$

Which means that the current account deficit, $(X - M)$, is the sum of the domestic saving-investment balance, $(S - I)$, and the budget deficit, $(T - G)$. If saving is just adequate to cover investment, we obtain

$$(X - M) = (T - G)$$

which shows that if domestic saving does not contribute anything to the financing of the current account deficit, then this will be identical to the budget deficit. In a less extreme case, there will be a positive relationship between the two deficits.

The rise, fall and rise of oil prices

Fluctuations in oil prices are believed to exert a profound influence on economic activity and financial markets. From a theoretical perspective, higher oil prices reduce output and raise prices and interest rates, consequently affecting exchange rates. These relationships are highly controversial, and there seems to be a significant divergence in the views on the issue. However, it has become obvious that the effect of prices depends crucially on the policy response.

Figure 1.3 shows the nominal and real price of crude oil over the period 1971–2001. The increase of 1973/1974 was accommodated by a monetary expansion, resulting in the high inflation of the 1970s. The 1979/1980 increase was not accommodated by such a policy, resulting in high interest rates and the recession of the early 1980s. In 1986 oil prices collapsed, while a period of disinflation had already started. In 1990 the price of oil rose sharply, but this was only a temporary rise due to the Iraqi invasion of Kuwait. In the 1990s the price of oil went through cycles of rise and fall, but it has, since the beginning of the twenty-first century, remained above USD20/barrel (just over USD26/barrel in May 2002). In early 2003 the price of oil went above the USD30/barrel mark as tension rose and military action loomed with no diplomatic solution in sight to the Iraqi weapons crisis, but the price fell following the end of combat operations in April. The real price of oil (the nominal price adjusted for world inflation, which is what is important for economic activity) has, however, increased less dramatically than the nominal price: in May 2001, the real price was actually lower than what it was in 1974.

Figure 1.3 Nominal and real price of oil (January 1971 = 100)

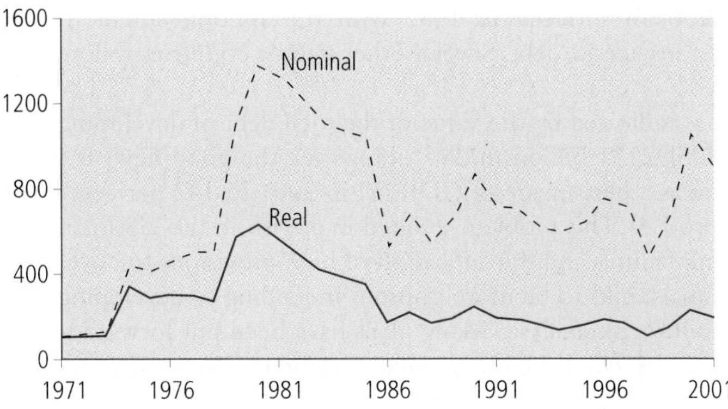

Source: International Financial Statistics, IMF.

RESEARCH FINDINGS

The economic and financial effects of fluctuations in oil prices

The rise and fall of oil prices have triggered controversy in the academic literature and the media. There does not seem to be a solid agreement on what effects oil price fluctuations have on economic activity, prices, interest rates and exchange rates. Although there is no magic formula that automatically calculates the effects of changes in oil prices, it is generally believed that a rise in oil prices leads to (i) a negative supply-side shock, (ii) a transfer of income from oil-importing countries to oil-exporting countries, and (iii) higher inflation.

A significant amount of empirical research has been done on this issue. One of the most important pieces of work was done by Hamilton, who concluded that there was secular as well as cyclical correlation between oil prices and US economic activity in the post-war period.[1] Similarly, Burbridge and Harrison concluded that a large part of the high inflation and lower growth in 1974 and 1975 could be attributed to oil price shocks.[2] But Gordon gave a small weight to the contribution of higher oil prices to the 1973/1974 inflation, by arguing that inflation in that period was a combination of an underlying 'hard core' inflation inherited from the 1960s and aggravated by a rapid pace of economic expansion between 1971 and 1973.[3] Moosa argued, on the basis of empirical testing, that there is no long-run relationship between oil prices and macroeconomic variables in OECD countries, but he acknowledged the existence of a short-run causal effect from oil prices to output and inflation.[4] More recently, Hooker argued that oil prices did not exert any effect on US macroeconomic indicators after 1973.[5]

One thing that seems plausible is that the impact of higher oil prices is unlikely to be as severe as it was in the 1970s. This is because OECD countries use only half as much oil relative to GDP as in the past, and because the real oil price is much lower than what it was in the late 1970s and early 1980s, as shown in Figure 1.3.

1 J. D. Hamilton, 'Oil and the Macroeconomy Since World War 2', *Journal of Political Economy*, 91, 1983, pp. 228–48.

2 J. Burbridge and A. Harrison, 'Testing for the Effects of Oil Prices Using Vector Autoregressions', *International Economic Review*, 25, 1984, pp. 459–84.

3 R. J. Gordon, 'Alternative Responses of Policy to External Supply Shocks', *Brookings Papers on Economic Activity*, 1, 1975, pp. 183–204.

4 I. A. Moosa, 'Can OPEC Cause Inflation and Recession?', *Energy Policy*, November 1993, pp. 1145–54.

5 M. A. Hooker, 'What Happened to the Oil Price-Macroeconomy Relationship?', *Journal of Monetary Economics*, 38, 1996, pp. 195–213.

The international debt problem

The international debt problem surfaced in 1982 with the announcement that Mexico would no longer be able to service its debt. Several other debtor countries followed Mexico by defaulting.

The size of the problem is indicated by the value of the total debt of developing countries, which reached a level of USD2131 billion in 2001. However, the good news is that debt as a percentage of exports and as a percentage of GDP fell in 2001 to 142 per cent and 34 per cent, respectively (see Figure 1.4). This problem resulted in a crisis in the US financial system in the 1980s, involving bank failures and the allocation of high provisions to cover bad loans. It has also forced international banks to be more cautious in lending to developing countries, emphasising the use of country risk analysis. Many plans have been put forward to deal with this problem, which has also triggered the emergence of **debt-equity swaps** and secondary markets in developing countries' debt.

Figure 1.4 Indicators of developing countries' debt

(a) Developing countries' external debt (USD billion)

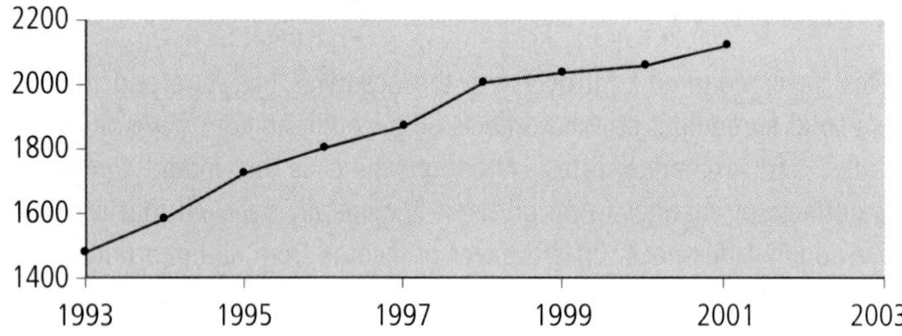

(b) Debt as a percentage of exports

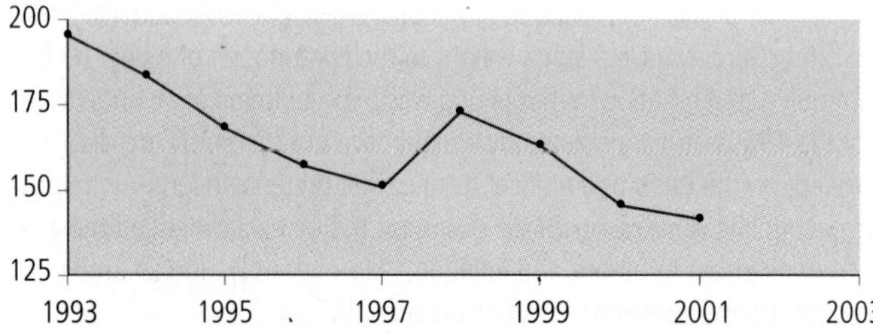

(c) Debt as a percentage of GDP

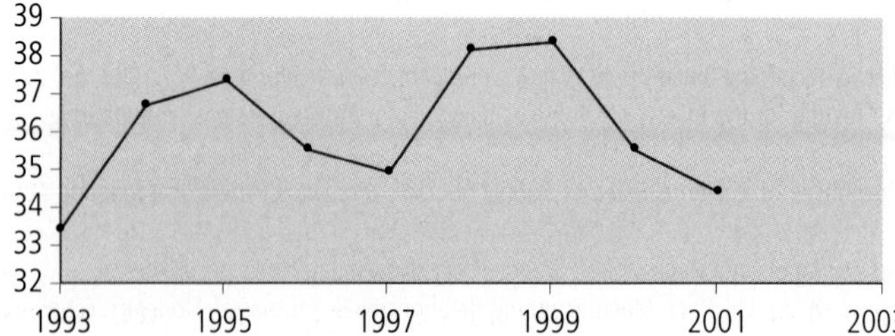

Source: World Economic Outlook, IMF, various issues.

The international use of non-dollar currencies

There has been a trend towards increasing international use of currencies other than the US dollar in both **current account transactions** (imports and exports) and **capital account transactions** (financial transactions and capital flows). This shift is indicated by changing currency composition towards a lower share of the dollar in: (i) trading volume in the foreign exchange market; (ii) the invoicing of exports and imports; (iii) holdings of foreign exchange reserves; (iv) Eurocurrency deposits; (v) international bond issues; and (vi) international bank loans. Things have changed significantly since the period extending between the end of World War II and the late 1950s, during which the dollar was the only convertible currency and, therefore, was used almost exclusively to finance international trade.

While many observers believed that the emergence of the euro would undermine the role of the US dollar as an international currency, this has not materialised, and it is unlikely to materialise in the near future. One cynical view on this issue is that the dollar will remain important as long as it is used to settle drug dealings (the 'drug currency', as some call it). It is also obvious that the international use of the yen does not reflect the emergence of Japan as the world's largest creditor country or its position in the world economy. It is undeniable that the dollar is still the most important international currency. In 2001, the US dollar commanded almost half the international bond issues, whereas the euro accounted for only 35.6 per cent. Figure 1.5 shows the currency composition of international bond issues.

Figure 1.5 The currency composition of international bond issues

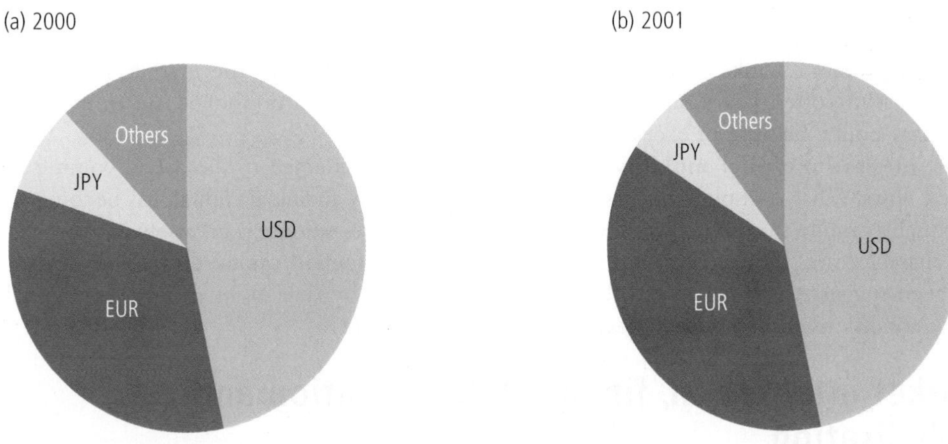

Source: BIS.

Increased capital mobility

The 1980s witnessed the start of a sharp expansion in the volume of net and gross capital flows in major industrial countries. **Gross capital flows** have increased as a reflection of increased cross-border banking and flows of securities, the development of the Eurocurrency market, and the entry of foreign institutions into domestic markets.

In contrast to **net capital flows**, gross flows do not necessarily correspond to a transfer of real resources across countries. Most gross flows arise as investors (mainly institutional investors such as insurance companies and pension funds) diversify their portfolios internationally. Gross flows also tend to take the form of short-term capital movements from one financial centre to another for the purpose of currency speculation. These movements intensify during periods of turbulence in the foreign exchange market, such as the episode of speculation against some European currencies in September 1992.

The increase in capital flows is undeniable, even though they cannot be measured precisely. The recent financial history of the world shows several indicators of this phenomenon. For example, it is believed that one of the reasons for the shift from a system of fixed exchange rates to a system of flexible exchange rates is the increased volume of capital flows, with Eurobanks serving as a conduit to that effect. As capital controls started to be less stringent, speculative capital movements made it difficult to maintain fixed exchange rates, and the system eventually collapsed. The more recent experience of the **European Monetary System (EMS)** is similar. Towards the end of 1992, capital controls in the countries of the European Community were completely dismantled. When some currencies (the British pound and the Italian lira) fell under pressure, there were heavy speculative capital flows out of these currencies, leading to their depreciation to levels below those allowed by the **Exchange Rate Mechanism (ERM)** of the EMS. Despite efforts by the Bank of England (the British central bank) to halt the slide of the pound by direct intervention, coupled with higher interest rates, the pressure was immense and the pound (as well as the lira) had to leave the ERM. Speculative capital flows resulted in renewed pressure on the system later on, leading to its *de facto* collapse in March 1993. The monetary authorities of Thailand went through a similar bitter experience in 1997 as speculative attacks against the baht took place.

Another indicator of this phenomenon is the failure of central bank intervention to halt the rise of the dollar in the first half of the 1980s, more precisely between early 1981 and February 1985. The reason is simple: with limited resources (compared to the sheer volume of trading), central banks cannot in general reverse the direction of the market. Finally, an indicator is the often-heard outcry by central banks that they can no longer run an effective monetary policy because of excessive capital flows.

The increase in **capital mobility**, however, may not be reflected in the actual volume of capital flows. What is implied here is that capital, particularly financial capital, has become so potentially mobile that any divergence in cross-country rates of return on assets with similar risk characteristics tends to be eliminated by (actual or potential) capital flows. Therefore, it has been suggested that capital mobility is best measured by deviations from international parity conditions, which will be dealt with in Chapters 9–11.

Market integration, financial deregulation and globalisation

There has been a growing trend towards the integration of the financial markets of major industrial countries. Market integration may be defined as follows: a country's financial markets are integrated with the world financial markets if (i) capital is free to move into and out of the country and (ii) domestic assets are close substitutes for foreign assets. This tendency has been fostered by the relaxation of capital controls and financial deregulation as well as new technology that facilitates cross-border transfer of funds. Financial deregulation has been motivated in part by the desire to improve financial efficiency by encouraging competition in domestic financial markets and to reduce risk by allowing residents to hold internationally diversified portfolios. Another factor is the need to finance large fiscal and current account deficits. It is noteworthy that financial market integration is a necessary but not a sufficient condition for capital mobility or, more precisely, for capital flows to occur.

RESEARCH FINDINGS

Is capital mobile?

The issue of capital mobility and the related issue of market integration provide one of the most pronounced cases of contradiction between casual empiricism and conventional wisdom, on the one hand, and the results of formal empirical testing on the other. In an influential paper, Feldstein and Horioka found domestic saving and domestic investment to be highly correlated.[1] This result is interpreted to mean that countries do not resort to foreign savings to finance domestic investment because of the lack of capital mobility. This conclusion has given rise to the so-called 'Feldstein-Horioka puzzle'. Because it is often the case that the terms 'capital mobility' and 'market integration' are used interchangeably, the Feldstein-Horioka results are taken to imply lack of financial market integration.

To reconcile various claims, Moosa made the following observations:[2]

- Capital mobility is not a necessary condition for market integration.
- Equalisation of real interest rates across countries is not a necessary condition for market integration.
- Market integration is conducive to capital mobility, or it leads to increasing 'potential' capital flows.
- Capital mobility is a sufficient condition for market integration, or at least a high level of capital mobility indicates a high level of market integration.
- Equalisation of real interest rates does not preclude the effect of a shortfall in domestic saving on domestic investment.

Some economists have tried to resolve the Feldstein-Horioka puzzle by using econometric reasoning. Moosa resolved the puzzle by arguing on the following lines: (i) saving-investment correlation is not an appropriate measure of capital mobility; (ii) international parity conditions are more appropriate measures of capital mobility (see Chapters 9–11); and (iii) different kinds of capital have different mobility.[3] He concluded that casual empiricism and formal evidence are supportive of the hypothesis that capital is mobile.

1 M. Feldstein and C. Horioka, 'Domestic Saving and International Investment', *Economic Journal*, 90, 1980, pp. 314–29.

2 I. A. Moosa, 'A Note on Capital Mobility', *Southern Economic Journal*, 63, 1996, pp. 248–54.

3 I. A. Moosa, 'Resolving the Feldstein-Horioka Puzzle', *Economia Internazionale*, 50, 1997, pp. 437–58.

Deregulation has taken the form of reducing or abolishing restrictions on external and domestic financial transactions. For example, the most common restrictions on external transactions include exchange controls (quantitative restrictions on capital movements), dual or multiple exchange rate arrangements (for example, using a fixed exchange rate for transactions involving exports and imports and a flexible or free-market rate for financial transactions) and taxes on external transactions. The integration of financial markets has proceeded much more rapidly than the integration of goods markets, in part because the latter has been inhibited by **protectionism**. In 1994, the World Trade Organisation (WTO) succeeded GATT in its efforts to reduce non-tariff barriers and protectionism. One of the consequences of financial deregulation has been the re-emergence of investment banks as leading financial institutions.

RESEARCH FINDINGS

The meaning of financial liberalisation

While abolishing capital controls is essential for **financial liberalisation**, the latter requires more than the former. In a survey of financial liberalisation, Williamson and Mahar identified six dimensions of financial liberalisation:[1]

- abolishing credit controls
- deregulating interest rates
- allowing free entry into the banking and finance industry
- privatising banks
- making banks independent of government control
- freeing international capital flows.

They examined 34 (rich and poor) economies using a four-point scale of financial liberalisation: 'repressed', 'partly repressed', 'largely liberal' and 'liberal'. The results showed that while there were 24 financially repressed economies in 1973, none was present in 1996. The number of largely liberal economies has gone up from two to 18, and the number of liberal ones from 4 to 10. The study recognises the benefits of liberalisation as: (i) leading to greater efficiency in the allocation of resources; and (ii) the promotion of saving, which is essential for economic growth. Against these benefits there is the cost of being susceptible to financial crises.

[1] J. Williamson and M. Mahar, *A Survey of Financial Liberalisation*, Princeton Essays in International Finance, No. 211, 1999.

The increasing integration of markets for goods, services and capital has led to the emergence of the phenomenon of globalisation. The term refers to the growing economic interdependence of countries worldwide through the increasing volume and variety of cross-border flows, and also through the more rapid and widespread diffusion of technology. While globalisation presents new opportunities and challenges, there is no consensus view on its desirability or its optimal extent.

Regional cooperation

There has been a trend towards regional cooperation. In Europe this tendency started in 1957 with the establishment of the European Economic Community. Since then membership of the EEC, or the European Union as it is presently known, has increased from the original six countries to 15, 12 of which have decided to give up their national currencies in favour of the euro (at the time of writing, the United Kingdom, Denmark and Sweden were out).

There are other schemes of regional cooperation. In June 1989, an agreement was signed to establish the **North American Free Trade Agreement (NAFTA)**. Another example is the **Asia–Pacific Economic Cooperation Council (APEC)**, which includes economically diverse and geographically dispersed countries. Such a scheme also exists between Australia and New Zealand in the form of the **Closer Economic Relations (CER)** Agreement, implemented on 1 January 1983 to replace the **New Zealand–Australia Free Trade Agreement (NAFTA)**, which had been in operation since 1966.

RESEARCH FINDINGS

Is globalisation good or bad?

We have all seen the demonstrations and protests against globalisation whenever there is a meeting of international organisations (the IMF, the World Bank, the WTO), business leaders (for example, the World Economic Forum) and politicians (for example, the summits of the largest industrial countries and those of the EU). The protesters (as well as their advocates and sympathisers) argue that globalisation is good for rich countries but only at the expense of poor countries, which are exploited in the process. Is this claim justifiable? Maybe for some, and maybe not for others.

A report published by the World Bank in 2001 claims that globalisation is good for poor countries, just like it is good for rich countries.[1] The report divides poor countries into those that are 'less globalised' and those that are 'more globalised', measured by the ratio of external trade to national income. The calculations show that the more-globalised poor countries (including China, India and Mexico) experienced an average growth rate in per capita GDP of about 5 per cent in the 1990s. This compares with about 2 per cent for rich countries and a decline of 1 per cent for the less-globalised poor countries (including much of Africa). The report concludes that 'poor countries that are in the biggest trouble are those that have globalised the least'.

While these figures are indisputable, the conclusion of the report remains controversial. First, it is arguable (according to the **catch-up hypothesis**) that poor countries tend to grow faster than rich countries because they start from a low level of national income. Second, it is also arguable that the distribution of income within each country and among countries, which is also important, has been deteriorating. The counterarguments are as follows. First, why is it that more-globalised poor countries are on the way to catching up with rich countries (because they are growing faster), whereas less-globalised poor countries are not? Second, if Bill Gates moved his business and his wealth to Darwin, the distribution of income in the Northern Territory and in Australia would deteriorate sharply, but such a move would be great for Darwin, the Northern Territory and Australia.

[1] *Globalization, Growth and Poverty*, World Bank Policy Research Report, December 2001.

Further developments followed when in June 1988 a ministerial review of the agreement put forward a comprehensive package to enhance the process of the free trade area. On 1 July 1990, free trade in commodities was achieved when all tariffs, import licensing and quantitative restrictions were removed. On some occasions, the idea of a common currency for Australia and New Zealand, the **Anzac**, was discussed, even at the prime ministerial level in New Zealand. This scheme, however, failed to win the approval of commentators for at least two reasons: (i) the percentage of trade between the two countries relative to their total trade is rather low; and (ii) their terms of trade often move in different directions.

Similar attempts have been made by the former communist countries, particularly the Baltic countries and the countries of Central and Eastern Europe. For example, the **Central Europe Free Trade Area (CEFTA)** includes the Czech Republic, Hungary, Poland, the Slovak Republic and Slovenia, and the **Baltic Free Trade Area (BFTA)** comprises the three Baltic republics of Estonia, Lithuania and Latvia. In 2002, there was some talk about a North Asian free trade agreement comprising China, Japan, Korea and Hong Kong. This idea was debated in a conference that was held in Tokyo in April 2002.

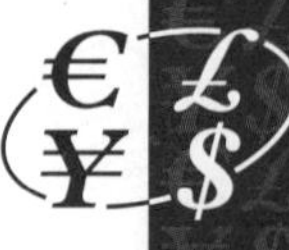

IN PRACTICE

The pros and cons of a currency union between Australia and New Zealand

In the 14 October 2000 issue of *The Economist* (p. 104) it was reported that more than 80 per cent of 400 New Zealand firms surveyed were in favour of a **currency union** with Australia, which could take the form of New Zealand using the Australian dollar rather than the New Zealand dollar being the domestic currency. It was also reported that Helen Clarke, the New Zealand prime minister, had suggested that a currency union with Australia might be desirable and even inevitable.

Arguments for a currency union between the two countries include the following:

- By eliminating exchange rate uncertainty, a currency union would boost trade and investment.
- Transaction costs for trading firms would fall.
- By reducing the currency risk premium (required to hold one currency by the citizens of the other), interest rates would be brought down.

On the other hand, the arguments against a currency union are the following:

- The trade benefits would be negligible, given that trade between the two countries comprises a small percentage of their total trade.
- A currency union would lead to the loss of the ability to pursue independent monetary policy, which may be required to respond to adverse shocks.
- While both countries are commodity exporters, the composition of their exports is different. This would create a problem if, for example, the prices of minerals rose while the prices of farm products fell.
- The New Zealand interest and exchange rates track the Australian ones very closely. Hence, a currency union would not make much difference anyway.

It is therefore believed that any currency union between the two countries would bring small benefits to New Zealand and almost nothing to Australia.

Increased volatility of financial markets

Since the late 1970s and the early 1980s, financial markets (including the foreign exchange, bond and stock markets) have been highly volatile. Volatility is the short-term (day-to-day or month-to-month) variability of financial asset prices (including exchange rates) around their long-term trends. This increase in volatility has led to the emergence of **risk management** as a separate discipline, both in the academic and professional worlds.

Increased volatility of exchange rates can be traced back to the collapse of the fixed exchange rate system in the early 1970s, obviously because flexible exchange rates are more volatile than fixed exchange rates. Figure 1.6 shows that the exchange rates of the yen and the pound against the US dollar were less volatile in the 1960s before the switch to flexible exchange rates (the big jump in the GBP/USD exchange rate during the fixed exchange rates era represents the 1967 devaluation of the pound). More recently, the volatility of exchange rates has been due to the erratic movements of speculative capital flows. It is believed that the introduction of the euro will increase exchange rate volatility because the European Central Bank will be less concerned about the EUR/USD exchange rate than individual national central banks were about their exchange rates. This is because the economy of the Euro zone as a whole is more closed and inward looking than the individual members' economies.

Figure 1.6 Exchange rate volatility

(a) JPY/USD exchange rate

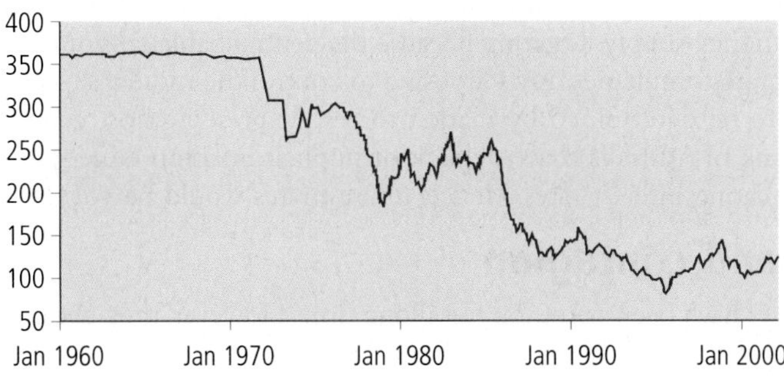

(b) GBP/USD exchange rate

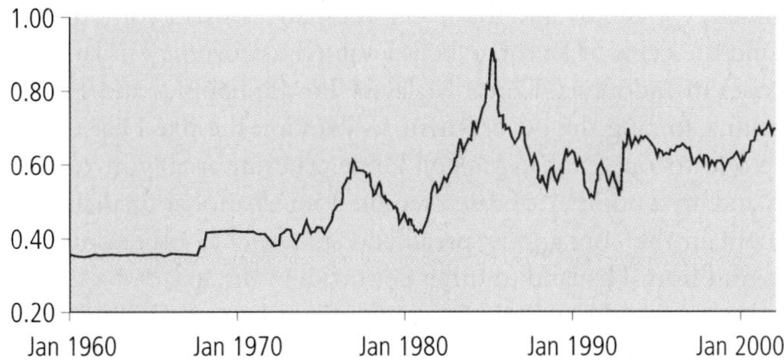

(c) Percentage change in the JPY/USD exchange rate

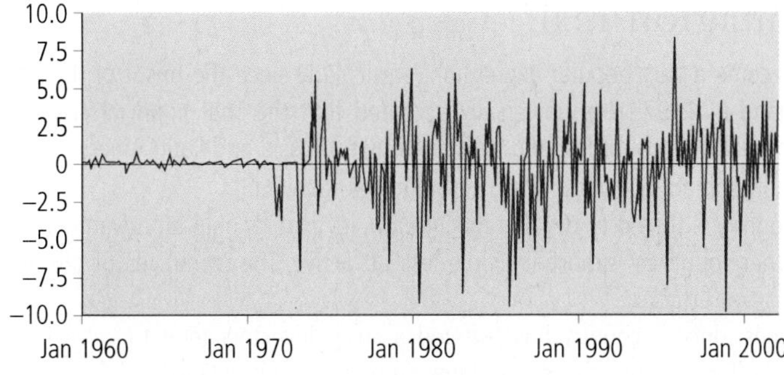

(d) Percentage change in the GBP/USD exchange rate

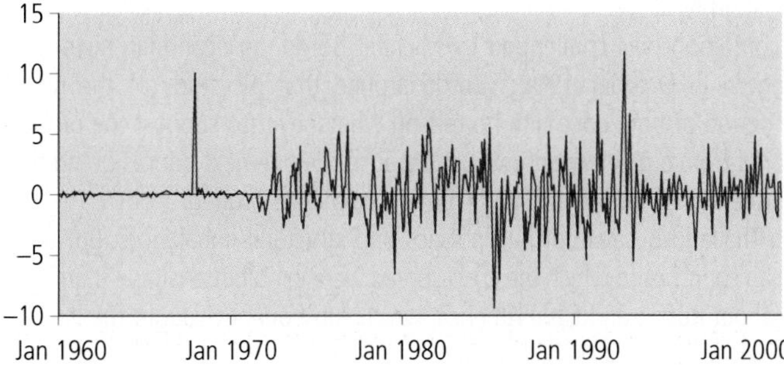

Source: Main Economic Indicators, OECD.

Volatility of interest rates, which is related to the volatility of exchange rates, can be traced back to 1979 when the Federal Reserve System (the US central bank) shifted from a policy of controlling interest rates to a policy of controlling the money supply. Interest rates are more volatile under a policy of money supply targeting because the central bank cannot control the money supply and interest rates simultaneously. Choosing to control the money supply implies that interest rates are left to be determined by market forces. At present, most central banks (including the Reserve Bank of Australia) have explicit or implicit inflation targets, which are pursued mainly by manipulating interest rates. Hence, interest rates would be volatile.

Financial crises and contagion

Financial and currency crises have been common for a long time. However, they became widespread in the post-war period, particularly since the 1980s because of the increased interdependence of financial markets, giving rise to **contagion** (the process whereby a financial crisis moves from one country to another). In the 1990s **currency crises** occurred in Europe (the 1992/1993 crisis in the European Monetary System and the 1998 Russian crisis), Latin America (the 1994/1995 Mexican crisis and the crisis of Brazil, which devalued its currency in January 1999) and Asia (the 1997/1998 crises in Indonesia, Korea, Malaysia, the Philippines and Thailand). In 2001/2002 a crisis hit Argentina, forcing the government to abandon the fixed parity exchange rate with the US dollar (the one-to-one exchange rate). These crises invariably involved significant international spillovers and, in a number of cases, required international financial assistance to limit their severity and contain the contagious spread and spillovers to other countries. The **Asian crisis**, for example, spread from Thailand to other countries in the space of a few months. The spillover covered countries in Asia, Latin America, Central and Eastern Europe, Russia and South Africa. All of these countries experienced capital outflows starting in late 1997.

RESEARCH FINDINGS

Is financial contagion real?

Financial contagion has become a very popular expression, particularly since the onset of the Asian crisis that started in Thailand in 1997. It is universally accepted that the Thai financial crisis was contagious, spreading to other Asian countries, and subsequently to Russia and Latin America.

Currency crises presumably spread in several ways, including the following:

- Trade links: when one country is forced to devalue its currency, its exports gain an advantage over competitors, whereas other countries' exports become less attractive. The currencies of the latter may be subject to speculative attacks.
- Macroeconomic similarities: once a country has suffered a crisis, investors tend to worry about others in similar situations (for example, those with large current account deficits).
- Portfolio behaviour: when investors lose heavily in a particular country, they may sell in other markets just to maintain liquidity.

The consensus view on contagion was challenged by Michael Bordo, an economic historian, in a conference held in Washington in October 1998.[1] Bordo argued that his study of the history of financial crises over a long period of time gave him no reason whatsoever to support the proposition that investors withdraw capital from a given economy just because the one next door is going through a financial crisis. There must be something wrong with that economy, he argued.

The Asian crisis started in Thailand because of bad policies and structural imbalances. But then, the argument goes, the other Asian countries to which the crisis spread were in no better shape than Thailand. The same thing can be said about Russia and Latin America, which subsequently caught the 'flu'.

1 'Is Contagion a Myth?', *The Economist*, 31 October 1998, p. 92.

Securitisation and financial innovation

Securitisation refers to the tendency to raise funds in capital markets via marketable securities rather than bank loans. In the 1970s, the surpluses of oil exporting countries were deposited mainly with Eurobanks and recycled via syndicated loans. But towards the end of the 1970s and the beginning of the 1980s, the trend started to change by giving preference to bonds and other negotiable (that is, marketable or tradeable) securities. Securitisation is still fashionable. In a survey of global investment banking, *The Financial Times* (31 January 1997, p. 6) reported that 'asset securitisation was one of the fastest growing sectors in the international capital markets in 1996' and that 'bankers remain optimistic on the prospects for 1997'.

There are both demand-side and supply-side reasons for this change. On the demand side, borrowers found it easier to raise big loans by issuing bonds and selling them to thousands of small investors than to raise the whole amount from one bank or a small number of banks. On the supply side, lenders found it more attractive to hold liquid, marketable and divisible financial assets, which allow the possibility of making capital gains.

Financial innovation refers to the creation of new financial instruments and the recreation of old instruments in a new form. Financial innovation was motivated by the need for new instruments to manage financial risk and by the increased sophistication of investors. In the 1980s, we started to hear about **financial engineering** producing things like options on swaps, swaptions, caps, collars, floors, and so on. This trend is continuing until the present time. By the end of June 2001, the value of the notional amount outstanding of derivative instruments was USD99.7 trillion, up from USD72.1 trillion at the end of June 1998. Over-the-counter instruments are not traded on organised exchanges (for example, the Sydney Futures Exchange) but are rather negotiated between two counterparties. They include foreign exchange derivatives, interest rate derivatives, equity derivatives, commodities derivatives and credit-linked derivatives. We will study some currency derivatives in subsequent chapters.

Summary

- International finance has assumed increasing importance as an academic discipline and a business activity. This is partly due to the collapse of the Bretton Woods system in 1971.
- This book studies the financial behaviour of business firms, given the global economic and financial environment within which they operate.
- The financial manager needs to be acquainted with the macroeconomic environment defined by (i) major economic indicators and (ii) government policies. The microeconomic environment pertains to such problems as (i) foreign exchange risk management and (ii) capital budgeting.
- Finance has been internationalised. Indicators of this phenomenon include: (i) increasing international bank lending; (ii) growing securities transactions with foreigners; (iii) flows of portfolio investment and foreign direct investment; (iv) trading volume in the foreign exchange market; and (v) foreign exchange transactions with cross-border counterparties.
- A number of post-war developments have shaped the present environment. These include: (i) the emergence of the Eurodollar market; (ii) currency convertibility; (iii) the birth of the EEC; (iv) changes in relative economic size; (v) the deterioration of the US external position; (vi) the rise and fall of oil prices; (vii) the international debt problem; (viii) the international use of non-dollar currencies; (ix) increased capital mobility; (x) market integration and financial deregulation; (xi) regional cooperation; (xii) the increased volatility of financial markets; (xiii) financial crises; and (xiv) securitisation and financial innovation.

Key terms

Anzac 19
appreciation 3
Asian crisis 22
Asia–Pacific Economic Cooperation Council (APEC) 18
Baltic Free Trade Area (BFTA) 19
Bank for International Settlements (BIS) 8
Bretton Woods system 3
capital account transactions 15
capital controls 2
capital mobility 16
catch-up hypothesis 19
Central Europe Free Trade Area (CEFTA) 19
Closer Economic Relations (CER) 18
comparative advantage 2
contagion 22
convertibility 10
country risk 5
currency crises 22
currency union 20
current account transactions 15
debt-equity swaps 14
depreciation 6
Eurobond market 9
Eurocredit market 9
Eurocurrency market 9
Eurodollar market 9
European Economic Community (EEC) 9
European Monetary System (EMS) 16
European Union (EU) 9
Exchange Rate Mechanism (ERM) 16
exchange rate volatility 3
Federal Reserve System 3
financial deregulation 3
financial engineering 23
financial innovation 23
financial liberalisation 18
financial risk 5
Fisher equation 7
flows 8
foreign direct investment 7
foreign exchange risk 5
globalisation 5
gross capital flows 15
international debt problem 5
international firms 3
international operations 3
market integration 5
multinational firms 3
net capital flows 15
New Zealand–Australia Free Trade Agreement (NAFTA) 18
North American Free Trade Agreement (NAFTA) 18
portfolio investment 7
protectionism 17
purchasing power parity 7
risk management 20
securitisation 23
stocks 8
transnational firms 3
twin deficit problem 10
uncovered interest parity 7

MaxMARK

MAXIMISE YOUR MARKS! There are 30 interactive questions for this chapter available online at **www.mhhe.com/au/moosa2e**

Review questions

1 How are the operations of international firms affected by the exchange rate system, the presence of capital controls and the segmentation of capital markets?

2 How has the nature of international operations changed since the early 1970s and particularly since the beginning of the 1980s?

3 What is the effect of exchange rate volatility on the operations of international firms?

4 Distinguish among international, multinational and transnational firms.

5 Why are we concerned about what happens in the US economy and financial markets and those of other major countries?

6 Describe a scenario whereby a decision by the European Central Bank results in foreign exchange losses for an Australian trading firm.

7 Distinguish between the macro and micro aspects of international finance.

8 What are the issues that the financial manager needs to be concerned with?

9 How has the international debt problem affected the operations of international banks and business firms in general?

10 Describe a scenario whereby a firm is forced into bankruptcy because of unfavourable changes in exchange rates.

11 What must the financial manager be acquainted with?

12 What are the indicators of the internationalisation of finance?

13 What are the major developments that have shaped the present economic and financial environment?

14 What is the twin deficit problem? How did this problem affect interest rates and exchange rates in the 1980s?

15 Why do some people demonstrate against globalisation when it is supposed to be good for the economic welfare of nations?

16 In the 1980s there was a view stipulating that indebted oil-exporting countries, such as Nigeria and Mexico, should rejoice at the collapse of oil prices. This view is based on a hypothetical causal relationship running from oil prices to consumer prices and consequently to interest rates. Explain how falling oil prices may be beneficial for indebted oil-exporting countries.

17 Explain why international business firms faced a different macroeconomic environment in the aftermath of the 1973/1974 rise in the price of crude oil from that which followed the 1979/1980 rise.

18 Give some examples indicating that capital mobility has increased. Why do some economists claim that capital is internationally immobile?

19 What is financial liberalisation? Is it good or bad for economic growth?

20 Define market integration. What is the relationship between market integration and financial deregulation?

21 What is the relationship between market integration and capital mobility?

22 Why has the idea of a currency union between Australia and New Zealand not materialised?

23 'The introduction of the new European currency (the euro) is not a sufficient condition for boosting trade in Europe.' Explain.

24 Risk management as an independent activity emerged in the 1980s due to the increased volatility of interest and exchange rates. Why has volatility increased?

25 What is financial contagion? Are financial crises really contagious? If so, why is it that Australia did not catch the 'Asian flu'?

26 What is securitisation? What factors have led to the popularity of securitisation?

27 Define financial innovation. What is the motivation for financial innovation?

28 Explain how the 1990 upgrading of the Closer Economic Relations (CER) Agreement between Australia and New Zealand might have affected trade between the two countries. Obtain some data (from the Internet or other sources such as the IMF's *Directions of Trade Statistics*) on trade between the two countries and show whether or not trade has increased following the upgrading of the Agreement.

CHAPTER

The foreign exchange market

Introduction

The foreign exchange market is larger, in terms of trading volume, than any other market, financial or otherwise. In fact, it dwarfs all other markets. It is also the most liquid of all markets. Every transaction arising from international trade or investment must pass through the foreign exchange market, since these transactions involve the exchange of currencies. Furthermore, developments in the foreign exchange market determine the levels of and changes in exchange rates, which have significant implications for businesses and economies. This chapter provides a general overview of the institutional aspects of the foreign exchange market and exchange rate concepts.

Objectives

The objectives of this chapter are:

- To describe the basic features of the foreign exchange market.
- To identify market participants and traded currencies.
- To describe the mechanics and technology of foreign exchange trading.
- To introduce some exchange rate concepts.
- To illustrate foreign exchange position keeping.
- To describe the Australian foreign exchange market.
- To introduce some foreign exchange jargon.

2.1 Definition and characteristics of the foreign exchange market

The **foreign exchange market** is the market in which national currencies are bought and sold against one another. This market is called the 'foreign exchange' market and not the 'foreign currency' market because the 'commodity' that is traded on the market is more appropriately called 'foreign exchange' than 'foreign currency': the latter is only a small part of what is traded. Foreign exchange consists mainly of bank deposits denominated in various currencies. Still, the term 'foreign currency' will be used interchangeably with the term 'foreign exchange'.

The foreign exchange market is the largest and most perfect of all markets. It is the largest in terms of trading volume (turnover), which currently stands at over one trillion US dollars per day. It is the most perfect market because it possesses the requirements for market perfection: a large number of buyers and sellers; homogenous products; free flow of information; and the absence of barriers to entry. The foreign exchange market is made up of a vast number of participants (buyers and sellers). The products traded on the foreign exchange market are currencies: no matter where you buy your yens, euros, dollars or pounds they are always the same. There is no restriction on access to information, and insider trading is much less important than, for example, in the stock market. Finally, anyone can participate in the market to trade currencies.

The importance of the foreign exchange market stems from its function of determining a crucial macroeconomic variable, the exchange rate, which affects to a considerable extent the performance of economies and businesses. This market is needed because every international economic transaction requires a foreign exchange transaction. Unfortunately, however, its function of exchange rate determination is not very well understood in the sense that economists are yet to come up with a theory of exchange rate determination that appears empirically valid.

Unlike the stock market and the futures market, which are **organised exchanges**, the foreign exchange market is an **over-the-counter (OTC) market**, as participants rarely meet and actual currencies are rarely seen. There is no building called the 'Sydney Foreign Exchange Market', but there are buildings called the 'Sydney Stock Exchange' and the 'Sydney Futures Exchange'. It is an OTC market in the sense that it is not limited to a particular locality or a physical location where buyers and sellers meet. Rather, it is an international market that is open around the clock, where buyers and sellers contact each other via means of telecommunication. The buyers and sellers of currencies operate from approximately 12 major centres (the most important being London, New York and Tokyo) and many minor ones. Because major foreign exchange centres fall in different time zones, any point in time around the clock must fall within the business hours of at least one centre. The 24 hours of a day are almost covered by these centres, starting with the Far Eastern centres (Sydney, Tokyo and Hong Kong), passing through the Middle East (Bahrain), across Europe (Frankfurt and London), and then passing through the US centres, ending up with San Francisco. This is why the first task of a foreign exchange dealer on arrival at work in the morning is to find out what happened while he or she was asleep overnight. Some banks and financial institutions may for this reason operate a 24-hour dealing room or install the necessary hardware (Reuters' screen, etc.) in their dealers' homes. Others may delegate the task to foreign affiliates or subsidiaries in active time zones.

2.2 Market participants

Market participants are foreign exchange traders who, directly or indirectly, buy and sell currencies. These classes of participants enter the market as **arbitragers**, **hedgers** and **speculators**. Arbitragers seek to make profit by exploiting exchange rate anomalies (for example, when an exchange rate assumes two different values in two financial centres at the same time). Hedgers enter the market to cover **open positions** in an attempt to reduce or eliminate foreign exchange risk (an open position arises, for example, when an importer has to meet a foreign currency payment, which is due some time in the future). This position can be covered, for example, by buying the foreign currency forward. Speculators, on the other hand, bear risk deliberately by taking decisions involving open positions to make profit if their expectations turn out to be correct. A speculator would buy a currency if it were expected to appreciate, realising profit if the currency appreciates subsequently (and realising loss otherwise). We will come across and elaborate on these concepts throughout this book, but for the time being we concentrate on the institutional classification of market participants.

There are five broad categories of participants in the foreign exchange market: customers, commercial banks, other financial institutions, brokers and central banks. Customers include individuals and companies utilising the services of commercial banks to buy and sell foreign exchange in order to finance international trade and investment operations. Thus, customers include, *inter alia*, exporters, importers, tourists, immigrants and investors. Exporters sell the foreign currencies they obtain from foreigners buying their products. Importers buy the foreign currencies they need to pay for the foreign goods they buy from foreign suppliers. Tourists going abroad buy foreign currencies, whereas those coming from abroad (foreign tourists) buy the domestic currency to pay for their living expenses while they are on holiday. Immigrants buy foreign currencies when they transfer funds to relatives in their home countries. Finally, investors buy and sell currencies as part of their acquisition and disposal of assets (bonds, shares, real estate, etc.). Customers are **price takers** in the foreign exchange market, which means that they buy currencies at the exchange rates quoted by **market makers.**

Large commercial banks are market makers in the sense that they stand ready to buy and sell currencies at the exchange rates they declare, acting via their foreign exchange **dealers**. On the retail side commercial banks deal with customers, but on the wholesale side they deal in the **interbank market** or the **wholesale market** (that is, with other banks). Commercial banks participate in the foreign exchange market mainly as speculators, trying to make short-term profit by getting exposed to foreign exchange risk. They also make profit on their dealings with customers from the differences between the buying and selling rates. They execute this function via the **dealing desk** or **dealing room**, which houses a group of dealers. These dealers may specialise in the trading of a particular currency, a group of currencies or a particular type of transaction (for example, **spot transactions** as opposed to **forward transactions**).

Other financial institutions (such as investment banks and mutual funds) and large companies may deal directly by conducting foreign exchange operations themselves and not through banks. Dealers representing commercial banks, other financial institutions and large companies do business with each other in two ways. The direct way is to telephone other dealers directly, or to contact them via an electronic dealing system. Otherwise, dealing can be carried out indirectly via a **broker**, thus preserving anonymity. With the introduction of **online trading systems**, a new (direct) mode of trading has emerged.

The function of a broker is to spread market information and to bring together buyers and sellers with matching needs. Brokers differ from dealers in that they do not take positions themselves, but obtain their 'living' by charging **commission fees**. Major brokerage houses are global in nature, servicing the interbank market around the clock.

Finally, central banks participate in the foreign exchange market because they act as bankers for their governments and also because they run the exchange rate and monetary policies. All of these functions require market participation. For example, under a system of managed floating, central banks often intervene in the foreign exchange market by buying and selling currencies, with the objective of 'smoothing out' exchange rate movements or to prevent the domestic currency from appreciating or depreciating excessively.

The foreign exchange market is dominated by interbank operations, the buying and selling of currencies among banks. The liquidity of the interbank market is due to large-volume transactions, as well as the fact that banks accept an obligation of **reciprocity** in quoting to other interbank dealers. However, it is by no means true that the interbank market is completely homogenous. Furthermore, not all banks are equally active in the interbank market. Thus, participants in the interbank market are classified into: (i) market makers, normally the largest banks; (ii) other major interbank dealers, who are willing to reciprocate quotes in a number of currencies; and (iii) second-tier banks, including banks that are active primarily in their domestic currencies and those unwilling to reciprocate quotes and often dealing in small amounts.

IN PRACTICE

Who are the big players in the foreign exchange market?

In its May 2002 issue, *Euromoney* reported the results of its annual foreign exchange survey. The top 10 institutions in terms of market share were:

Citigroup	11.17
UBS Warburg	10.96
Deutsche Bank	9.79
Goldman Sachs	6.60
JP Morgan Chase	5.86
Chase Manhattan Bank	4.69
Credit Suisse First Boston	4.62
Morgan Stanley	3.70
ABN Amro	3.40
SEB	2.76

In terms of 'who's best where', the Sydney results showed the following (the numbers are votes):

Citigroup	164
ANZ Banking Group	116
Deutsche Bank	114
Westpac Banking Corporation	78
National Australia Bank	62
ABN Amro	60
Commonwealth Bank of Australia	56
HSBC	49
UBS Warburg	49
State Street Bank & Trust	41

2.3 The size and composition of the foreign exchange market

The size of the (global) foreign exchange market is measured by the sum of daily turnover in foreign exchange centres around the world. This is normally done through a survey that is coordinated by the Bank for International Settlements (BIS) and conducted in each financial centre by the domestic central bank (for example, the Sydney survey is conducted by the Reserve Bank of Australia). In this survey, which is conducted every three years in April, banks and financial institutions are asked about their foreign exchange activity, including spot and forward transactions. Since 1995, the survey has been re-designed to cover OTC derivatives activity, including currency and interest rate derivatives (such as currency options). The exposition here is restricted to the so-called 'traditional foreign exchange market', which includes spot and forward transactions only.

Figure 2.1 shows the volume of daily turnover in the global foreign exchange market as measured through the BIS surveys since 1989. The global total is measured by adding up turnover in individual financial markets. In 2001 daily turnover declined, as compared with the previous survey, for the first time. The 19.5 per cent decline to USD1200 billion is attributed to at least two factors. The first is the introduction of the euro and the abolition of the national currencies in 12 European countries. Although the trading of the euro has been more than that of the former German mark, it has also been less than the combined trading of the national currencies. The second reason is consolidation in the banking industry via mergers and acquisitions. As we can see from Figure 2.1, forward transactions (consisting of **outright operations** and **swap operations**) comprise the bulk of transactions in the foreign exchange market.

Figure 2.1 Daily turnover in the foreign exchange market (USD billion)

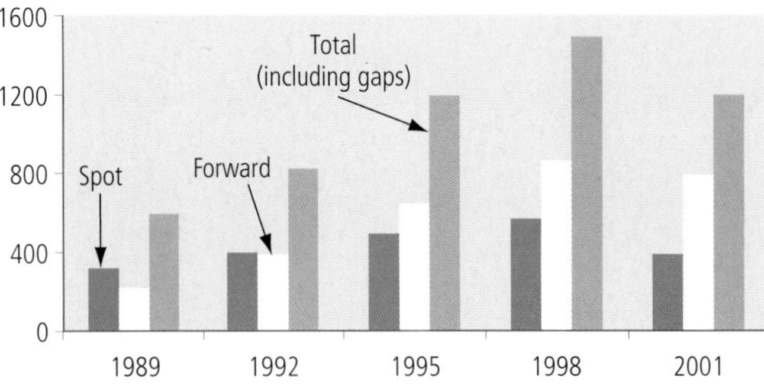

Source: BIS.

Figures 2.2–2.4 are based on information collected from the 2001 survey. As for the geographical distribution of turnover, London remains the most important foreign exchange centre in the world (commanding over 30 per cent of the total daily turnover), as shown in Figure 2.2. This is followed by New York (15.7 per cent) and Tokyo (9.1 per cent). The Australian foreign exchange market is in eighth place with about 3.2 per cent of the total, ahead of France (3 per cent).

Figure 2.2 The geographical distribution of foreign exchange market turnover (per cent)

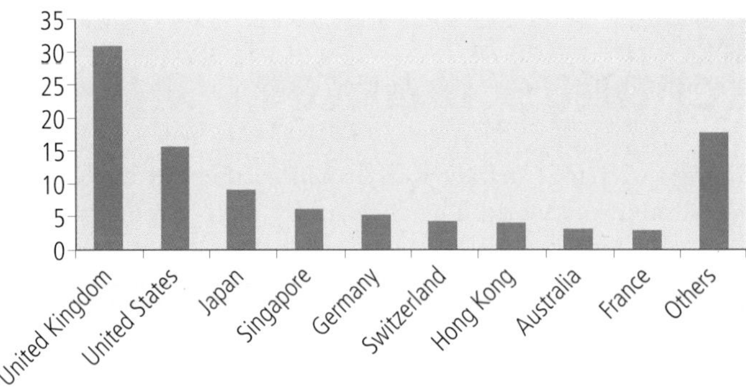

Source: BIS.

Figure 2.3 shows the composition of the interbank market, which comprises more than half of the operations in the foreign exchange market. Dealings of commercial banks with other financial institutions constitute about 28 per cent, whereas the smallest part is attributed to non-financial institutions and other customers. Figure 2.3 also shows that 60 per cent of the transactions are conducted with cross-border counterparties. In Chapter 1, this was taken to be an indicator of the extent of the internationalisation of finance.

Figure 2.3 Foreign exchange market turnover by counterparty (per cent)

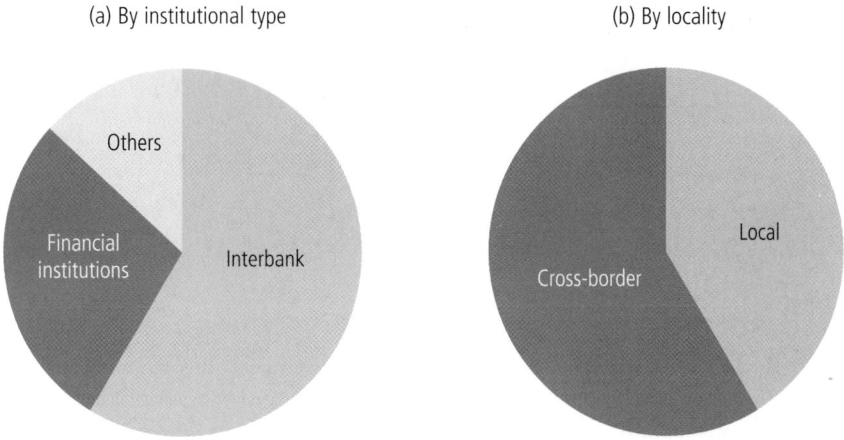

Source: BIS.

Figure 2.4 portrays the currency composition of foreign exchange market turnover. In Figure 2.4(a) the currency composition is shown by single currencies, in which case the maximum percentage would be 200 per cent owing to double counting (a USD100 transaction against the euro is counted for both the dollar and for the euro). Obviously, the US dollar is the most actively traded currency, with over 90 per cent of transactions involving this currency. The dollar is followed by the euro, the Japanese yen and the British pound. The Australian dollar is the seventh most actively traded currency, commanding 4.2 per cent of total trading. Figure 2.4(b) shows the composition in terms of currency pairs, in which case the maximum percentage is 100 per cent. About 30 per cent of total trading consists of buying the US dollar against the euro, and vice versa. This is followed by transactions involving the US dollar and the Japanese yen, and then those involving the US dollar and the British pound. Transactions involving US and Australian dollars come in sixth place, commanding about 4 per cent of total trading. Finally, 17 per cent of the trading involves the US dollar against minor currencies, and only 9 per cent of the transactions do not involve the US dollar, which are sometimes called **cross transactions**.

Figure 2.4 Currency composition of foreign exchange market turnover (per cent)

(a) By single currencies

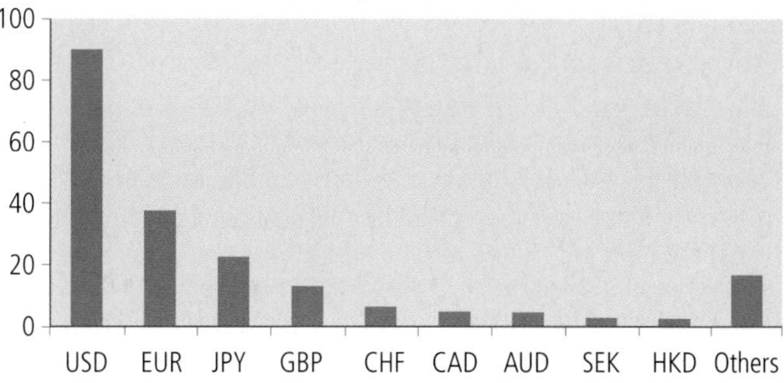

Continued...

(b) By currency pairs

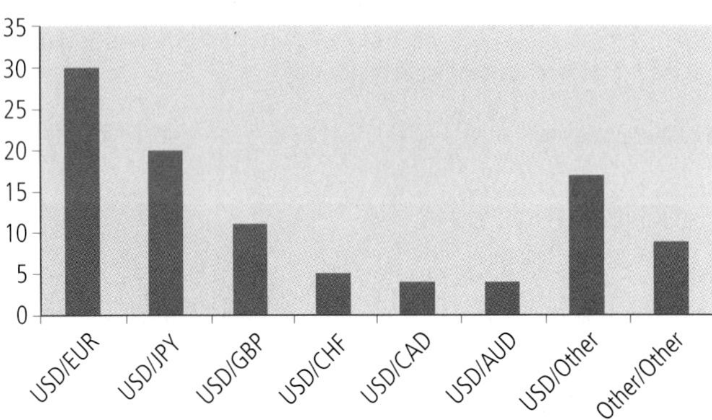

Source: BIS.

Traded currencies may be classified into the following groups:

- The US dollar, which is the most heavily traded currency for the following reasons: (i) the US financial markets are very large; (ii) the US dollar is predominantly used as a means of settling international transactions; (iii) it is a major component of international reserves; and (iv) it is the most widely accepted currency on the retail level internationally.

IN PRACTICE

The international status of the US dollar

In addition to the reasons listed in the text to explain the international status of the US dollar and its heavy trading, there are some less conventional reasons. In a report in *International Currency Review*, two unconventional reasons were suggested for the love affair with the US dollar.[1] The first of these reasons is that the holders of US dollar-denominated assets know that the full faith of the United States underpins the US currency. This, the report says, compares with the euro, which is not issued by a government, but rather by 'a dodgy experimental political collective with dictatorial tendencies' (that is, the EU). The second reason, described as politically incorrect and universally ignored, is that 'the most valuable commodity in the world is drugs; and the drug currency is the US dollar'.

The present author experienced the international status of the US dollar while on a visit to Hanoi, Vietnam, in November 1994. While attending a function in the Australian Embassy, the author failed miserably to convince some Embassy officials (who were working behind the bar) to accept the Australian dollar in payment for two stubbies of VB, and who insisted instead on receiving payment in the US currency. This author felt that the Embassy staff were 'unpatriotic' in refusing to accept the Australian currency in exchange for Australian beer!

Another trivial but interesting incident supporting the international status of the US dollar happened in Japan during the 2002 World Cup soccer tournament. As potential spectators joined long lines to buy tickets for the semi-final match between Brazil and Turkey, they were told (by the Japanese organisers) that only US dollars would be accepted for payment (the Japanese national currency was not accepted). The people waiting in line were furious, because they were supposed to leave their places in the line, change their yens into dollars and rejoin the line. Strangely, it took the efforts of a Brazilian diplomat to make the Japanese organisers change their mind, reluctantly accepting their national currency for payment!

[1] 'The Introduction of Euro Notes and Coins Did Nothing at all to Rescue the Collective Currency', *International Currency Review*, 27, 2002, pp. 3–5.

- The euro and the yen, which are heavily traded because of the economic, financial and trade importance of Europe and Japan. However, the trading of the yen does not reflect the relative size of the Japanese economy or the big role Japan plays in international trade.

RESEARCH FINDINGS

The internationalisation of the yen

Although the use of the Japanese yen in international transactions has been increasing, it is still modest compared to the US dollar and the euro. This does not seem to be consistent with the role of Japan in the world economy.

Two economists at the International Monetary Fund have identified the factors that are necessary for a currency to be used internationally, attempting to apply them to the yen.[1] These factors include the following:

- The notion that the top currency is provided by the top power.
- The need to have confidence in the value of the currency and therefore in the issuing country's inflation performance.
- The issuing country should have deep, open and broad domestic financial markets.
- The greater the country's share of world exports and the greater the extent to which these exports are denominated in the exporter's currency, the greater would be the demand for that currency to pay for imports.

Japan seems to have performed well in relation to these factors:

- Japan's strong economic performance (at least up to the 1990s) has allowed the country to emerge as a world economic and political power.
- Japan has achieved low and stable inflation.
- Japan has carried out a number of measures to broaden its financial markets and to ease the access of foreigners to these markets.
- Japan has achieved a larger increase in its share of world exports than any other major industrial country.

However, some problems remain:

- Despite efforts to liberalise Japanese financial markets, some areas are still subject to restrictions (for example, the Treasury bill market is not very active).
- Japan's exports to developed countries are predominantly denominated in these countries' currencies. The absolute level of Japanese exports to non-Asian developing countries fell during the 1980s, causing a reduced role for the yen in international trade.
- The bankers' acceptances market is not well developed, making it difficult for Japanese firms to obtain trade financing in yen.
- Japan's international intermediary function has not contributed to the willingness of foreigners to hold liquid liabilities denominated in yen.

[1] G. S. Tavalas and Y. Ozeki, 'The Internationalization of the Yen', *Finance and Development*, June 1991, pp. 2–5.

- The pound, which is still heavily traded despite the decline of the United Kingdom as a major economic and financial power. This may reflect the historical importance of the British currency, which played a more important role in the international monetary system under the gold standard than the dollar played under the Bretton Woods system (see Chapter 5).
- Currencies that are heavily traded in certain centres but lack liquidity in others. These include the currencies of Switzerland and Canada.

- Currencies that are heavily traded locally, but are traded internationally for the purpose of financing exports and imports. These include the currencies of Australia, New Zealand and Hong Kong.
- Third World currencies that are traded almost entirely on a local basis. These are sometimes called **soft currencies** or **exotic currencies** to indicate that they are not widely traded or used as common settlement currencies.

IN PRACTICE

Currency symbols and nicknames

Many currencies have traditional symbols that are still used. These include the US dollar ($), the pound (£), the yen (¥) and the Australian dollar ($A). The problem of encoding such symbols for telecommunication purposes has led to the adoption of alphanumeric acronyms (see the list of currency symbols on page 542). These symbols consist of three letters, the first two of which refer to the country of the issue while the last is usually the initial of the currency (the euro being an exception, perhaps because there is no single issuing country). The Swiss franc has the symbol CHF because the first two letters refer to Confederation Helvetia (that is, Switzerland). The former Spanish peseta had the symbol ESP because the first two letters referred to España (Spain). But then the former European currency unit (ECU) had the symbol XEU. The Australian dollar's symbol, AUD, is obvious.

Some of the currencies also have nicknames that are used by foreign exchange dealers. For example, the Australian dollar is Aussie or Oz, the former French franc was Paris, the pound is Cable, the New Zealand dollar is Kiwi, and the Swiss franc is Swissi.

2.4 The mechanics and technology of foreign exchange trading

A foreign exchange transaction consists of the following sequential processes:

- **Price discovery:** the dealer judges the exchange rate at which the transaction can be executed. This requires an assessment of the liquidity of the market and the expectation held by others about future changes in the exchange rate.
- *Decision making:* the dealer seeks information to support the decision to execute the transaction. Execution, which is the transaction itself, is initially conducted via the telephone or other means of telecommunication.
- **Settlement:** this involves completing the transaction by making payments in one currency and receiving payments in another. This function is performed by the so-called **back office** rather than by the dealers to allow an independent check on their activities.
- **Position keeping:** the dealer monitors the resulting position, calculating profit and loss. A decision may be taken to close the position subsequently.

Foreign exchange market technology applies to all of these processes. The following is a brief outline of the historical development of foreign exchange technology. Prior to World War I, the foreign exchange market had physical locations, where pre-transaction processes and execution were carried out manually. Post-transaction processes were also settled manually with a physical delivery of bills. Physical delivery in foreign exchange persisted until quite recently: cheques and mail transfers were used until the 1970s. In continental European centres some form of physical location continued to exist until the 1980s, as commercial banks met daily with the central bank to fix the rate at which to settle customer orders.

The following are the main technological devices used in conducting foreign exchange business:

- The first means of telecommunication used in the foreign exchange market was the telegraph. Some USD/GBP transactions were executed by using the trans-Atlantic cable laid in 1858 between London and New York (hence the pound's nickname, Cable).
- Although telephone deals may be traced back to 1926, it was not until the late 1970s that reliable international networks were installed in banks' dealing rooms.
- Then there was the telex, which is a telephone line with an automatic typewriter. It largely supplanted the telegraph after World War II.
- In decision making and settlement the successor to the telex was the fax.
- A breakthrough for price discovery and decision making was the **screen-based information system** carrying news and prices from other banks. The first was the Reuters' Monitor, which was introduced in 1973. This was followed by other vendors such as Telerate. By 1984, there were some 40 electronic information services in London.
- By the second half of the 1980s the major part of communication in the foreign exchange market had shifted to **screen-based automated dealing systems** (also known as **conversational dealing systems**), which are networks that connect terminals. A dealer with a terminal can use it to call another dealer with a terminal on the same network.
- The next stage in the development of screen-based systems involved the automation of the execution process, which materialised in 1992 when Reuters introduced its automatic matching system. **Automatic order matching systems** are networks of terminals where dealers enter orders in the form of a buying and/or selling price for a given amount of currency. The network selects and displays the best buying and selling orders for each currency pair.
- The Internet is another development. Open access to the Internet removes the need to build dedicated connections to counterparties or customers. In 1997 an Internet-based foreign exchange dealing service (aimed mainly at wealthy individuals) was established in the United Kingdom by the Currency Management Corporation.
- More recent developments pertain to **online foreign exchange trading**, including the emergence of Internet-based multidealer foreign exchange services, such as Currenex (April 2000), Fxall (May 2001) and Atriax (August 2000). For more details, see the box on page 38.

2.5 The spot exchange rate

The function of a market is the determination of the price of the commodity in which it is traded. The commodity that is traded on the foreign exchange market is 'foreign exchange', currencies and bank deposits denominated in various currencies. For simplicity, we will just call them currencies.

The bilateral spot exchange rate

A foreign exchange market participant would normally want to buy one currency and sell another, typically (but not necessarily) the domestic and a foreign currency. The price of one currency in terms of another is called a **bilateral exchange rate**, because two currencies are involved in the transaction. Confusion may arise because the exchange rate is the price of one kind of money in terms of another kind of money.

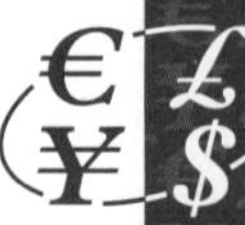

IN PRACTICE

The new technology of foreign exchange trading

The development of online foreign exchange trading has lagged behind the e-trading of other financial assets. Developing online foreign exchange facilities has been held up by a lack of consensus among leading banks as to how to develop the sites and reluctance to undertake the necessary (costly) investment. While some banks believe that online trading could undermine the profitability of their foreign exchange operations, benefits would accrue to customers in terms of easier access to research and analysis, quicker and more comprehensive price discovery, and more efficient processing and transparency. Getting exposed to the information provided by many banks simultaneously (without having to phone each of them, or even log on to their individual web sites) gives customers a choice. This can be done by using multibank portals, which some banks do not view favourably for fear of losing customers to their competitors.

As a result of increasing demand from customers for the introduction of online trading via multibank portals, banks started to feel compelled to respond positively. In August 2000 the three largest participants in the foreign exchange market (Deutsche Bank, Chase Manhattan and Citigroup) teamed up with Reuters (an information provider) to offer a range of foreign exchange services over the Internet. The venture (known as Atriax) collapsed in March 2002. Other ventures have also emerged, including Currenex, State Street's Global Link, FX Connect System, Fxall, Forexster and Northern Trust FX Passport. Still, the pressure remains for the establishment of multibank sites. State Street ran its FX Connect system for more than three years before opening it to other banks. Currenex is such a multibank web site.

As a result of these developments, it is expected that 70 per cent of the market will be e-trading by 2004, and by 2012 it will be about 95 per cent. In this way, e-trading provides disintermediation, allowing users of foreign exchange services to trade currencies directly with each other.

Multibank portals allow the provision of **straight through processing (STP)**, which is the end-to-end automation of the trading process from order to settlement. It is estimated that STP could result in about a USD12 billion cost reduction for the foreign exchange industry as a whole. In the conventional dealing environment, two traders agree on the details of the trade over the telephone. Each one of them types these details into a dealing system and sends a fax to the other. Each one reads the other's fax to check that they have the same record of what was agreed. With STP, the trader begins by uploading the trade requirements from an order management system. Subsequently, the trade record is enriched with additional information and sent electronically to the trader needing it.

When the exchange of currencies takes place immediately, the underlying operation is called a spot transaction, and so we define the **spot exchange rate** as the rate applicable to transactions involving immediate exchange of the currencies. The word 'immediate' means different things. When you use the services of a moneychanger at Melbourne Airport to exchange some Australian dollars for Hong Kong dollars because you are about to board a plane to Hong Kong, you obtain the Hong Kong dollars that you have bought immediately, meaning at once. This is also called a **cash transaction**. In an **interbank transaction**, on the other hand, the exchange of currencies does not take place at once, but rather in two business days (where a business day is a day on which banks and other foreign exchange market participants are open for business). When a transaction between two bank dealers is concluded today, each bank will in two business days credit the other's account with the prescribed currency and amount agreed upon. This is still regarded as an **immediate delivery**, and so the underlying exchange rate is a spot exchange rate. If the delivery takes place some time in the future, then the underlying operation is a forward transaction.

Two dates are involved in a spot transaction. The first (called the **contract date**, the **dealing date**, the **done date** or the **trade date**) is the date on which the transaction is concluded at the exchange rate prevailing on the same date. The second date, which falls two business days later, is called the **delivery date** or **value date**. The exchange rate prevailing in the market may actually change between the two dates, but, no matter what happens, the exchange of the currencies takes place at the exchange rate agreed upon when the transaction is concluded. However, it is often possible to exchange currencies on the business day following the transaction date (a **value-tomorrow transaction** or **next-day transaction**) and sometimes on the transaction date itself (a **value-today transaction** or **same-day transaction**).

Suppose that two dealers, A and B, agree on Monday on a deal whereby A sells to B AUD1 million at a spot exchange rate of 0.50 US cents per Australian dollar. The two dealers nominate bank accounts to which the proceeds of the transaction will be credited. On Wednesday, A credits B's nominated account with AUD1 000 000, whereas B credits A's account with USD500 000. This exchange of currencies is described in Figure 2.5. The settlement of interbank transactions normally takes place via an electronic settlement system such as SWIFT, the **Society for Worldwide Financial Telecommunication**. This system began operations in 1977, connecting over 3000 commercial and investment banks in over 60 countries.

Figure 2.5 A spot foreign exchange transaction

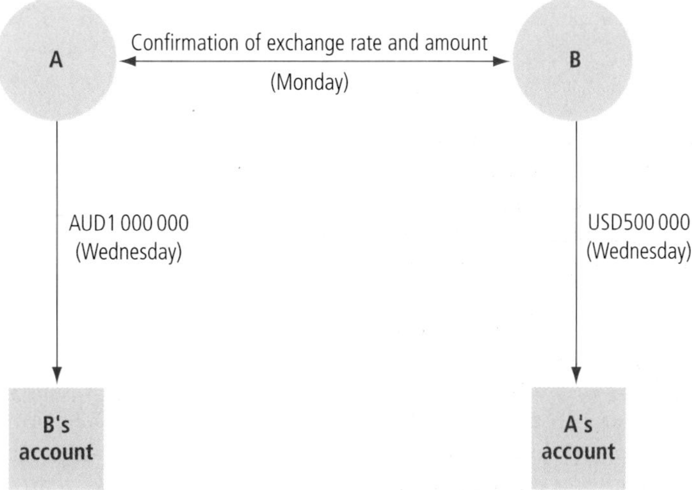

Spot rate quotations

The spot exchange rate is the price of one currency in terms of another for immediate delivery. The commodity that is traded is a currency, but the price is expressed in terms of another currency, which serves as the unit of account or the measure of value. Like the price of any commodity, the exchange rate is an expression of the value of one unit of a currency (the commodity) in terms of another currency (the unit of account). Sometimes, the currency whose unit is being priced is called the **base currency**, whereas the currency doing the pricing is called the **quoted currency**

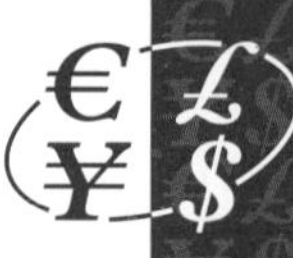

IN PRACTICE

Dealing with risk in foreign exchange transactions

Transactions in the foreign exchange market take place at all hours of the day and night, invariably involving institutions in different national jurisdictions. The cross-border, cross-time zone nature of foreign exchange transactions poses a challenge for the efficient settlement of hundreds of thousands of deals struck on a daily basis.

There are two kinds of settlement risks: **Herstatt risk** and **liquidity risk**, arising from insolvency and liquidity problems, respectively. Herstatt risk got its name from an historical incident involving failure to settle a transaction. In 1974, Bankhaus Herstatt failed to deliver US dollars to counterparties after it was ordered into liquidation by the German authorities. Defaults have since occurred in the cases of the Bank of Credit and Commerce International (BCCI) and Barings Bank.

Liquidity risk arises from the possibility that a counterparty will default because of an operational or system problem that leaves it with insufficient liquidity to make payment. This problem is particularly common in emerging markets where the physical infrastructure for payment and settlement may not be adequate to accommodate transactions that are increasing in size and number.

Default that occurs either because of insolvency or liquidity could trigger system-wide problems. The failure of one large bank may cause a second bank to fail, in turn causing a third bank to fail, such that a 'domino effect' will arise. Two solutions have been suggested to solve

The spot exchange rate between two currencies, x and y, can be expressed as $S(x/y)$. This expression reads as follows: the spot exchange rate measured as the price of one unit of y in terms of x (the number of units of x per one unit of y). Thus, currency y is the traded commodity (the base currency) and currency x is the unit of account (the quoted currency). We will use this notation throughout this book, but sometimes we drop S or x/y for simplicity and convenience.

What is important to remember here is that if $S(x/y)$ rises, then this would indicate appreciation of y and depreciation of x, and vice versa. This is because a larger number indicates that one unit of y after its appreciation is worth more than before in terms of units of x. Thus, we refer to the rise and fall of exchange rates but the **appreciation** and **depreciation** of currencies (never say that an exchange rate has appreciated because any change in the exchange rate involves appreciation of one currency and depreciation of the other). When $S(x/y)$ changes between two points in time (0 and 1) from $S_0(x/y)$ to $S_1(x/y)$, then the rate of appreciation or depreciation of currency y (expressed as a decimal) is given by

$$\dot{S}(x/y) = \frac{S_1(x/y)}{S_0(x/y)} - 1 \tag{2.1}$$

where $\dot{S}(x/y)$ is the percentage change in the exchange rate measured as the x price of a unit of y, and hence it is the percentage change in the value of currency y. Remember that S is the variable whose value changes between time 0 and time 1, but (x/y) is the unit (or units) of measurement.

this problem: (i) eliminating the delay between the two legs of a transaction (simultaneity); and (ii) reducing the number and size of payments requiring settlement. Simultaneity here refers to the delivery of currencies, but this requires closing the gaps in the operating hours of the major wholesale domestic payment systems and the development of some sort of linked payment systems or verification of payments to guarantee intraday 'finality of payment'. Reducing the number and size of payments can be achieved through bilateral and multilateral netting systems. It is estimated that multilateral netting reduces settlement risk by about 73 per cent for a group of about 20 participants and by as much as 95 per cent for a bigger group.[1]

One of the developments in this field was the establishment of the Exchange Clearing House (ECHO) in August 1995. The problem with netting is the difficulty of making the netted amounts legally enforceable. A more recent development is the **continuous linked settlement (CLS)**,[2] which enables member banks to settle foreign exchange transactions through a central service provider, CLS Bank. The idea is that this system would eliminate settlement risk by implementing payment-versus-payment methodology and by providing multilateral netting of foreign exchange transactions. By utilising technology developed by IBM, CLS provides market participants with same-day payments and settlement (T+0 rather than T+2, where T stands for 'transaction').

[1] L. A. Kodres, 'Foreign Exchange Markets: Structure and Systemic Risks', *Finance and Development*, December 1996, pp. 22–5.

[2] Foreign Exchange Revolution, *The Banker Supplement*, September 2000.

The question is, how do we calculate the corresponding change in the value of currency x? This can be done in two ways. The first is to calculate it as the percentage change of the reciprocal rate, $S(y/x)$. The reciprocal rate is expressed as

$$S(y/x) = \frac{1}{S(x/y)} \tag{2.2}$$

which says that the spot exchange rate measured as the price of one unit of x is the reciprocal of the spot rate measured as the price of one unit of y. Then we calculate the appreciation (positive change) or depreciation (negative change) of x as the percentage change of $S(y/x)$ as

$$\dot{S}(y/x) = \frac{S_1(y/x)}{S_0(y/x)} - 1 \tag{2.3}$$

The other method that can be used for the same purpose is to calculate the percentage appreciation or depreciation of x directly from the percentage change in the value of currency y as

$$\dot{S}(y/x) = \frac{1}{1 + \dot{S}(x/y)} - 1 \tag{2.4}$$

Remember that these formulae produce decimals that have to be multiplied by 100 to obtain the percentage changes.

Example

Suppose that currency x is the US dollar and currency y is the Australian dollar. Now assume that the exchange rate between the two currencies measured as the price of one Australian dollar, $S(USD/AUD)$, rises from 0.52 to 0.56. This obviously means appreciation of the Australian dollar and depreciation of the US dollar, because the price of one Australian dollar has risen from 52 to 56 US cents. Thus, we have $S_0(USD/AUD) = 0.52$ and $S_1(USD/AUD) = 0.56$. By employing Equation (2.1) we can calculate the percentage appreciation of the AUD as

$$\dot{S}(USD/AUD) = \frac{S_1(USD/AUD)}{S_0(USD/AUD)} - 1 = \frac{0.56}{0.52} - 1 = 0.077$$

or 7.7 per cent. To calculate the percentage depreciation of the US dollar by using the first method, we have

$$S_0(AUD/USD) = \frac{1}{S_0(USD/AUD)} = \frac{1}{0.52} = 1.9231$$

$$S_1(AUD/USD) = \frac{1}{S_1(USD/AUD)} = \frac{1}{0.56} = 1.7857$$

which means that the value of one US dollar has fallen from AUD1.9231 to AUD1.7857, or by 7.2 per cent.

The same result can be obtained without calculating the reciprocal exchange rates by using Equation (2.3) as follows

$$\dot{S}(AUD/USD) = \frac{1}{1+\dot{S}(USD/AUD)} - 1 = \frac{1}{1+0.077} - 1 = -0.072$$

or 7.2 per cent, which is the same answer as the one obtained by using the first method.

Note that when the exchange rate is expressed as $S(x/y)$, the following rules should be applied to convert an amount of y into x, and vice versa:

- To convert from y to x we multiply the y amount by the exchange rate.
- To convert from x to y we divide the x amount by the exchange rate.

Example

Again, assume that x is the USD and y is the AUD, such that the exchange rate is $S(USD/AUD) = 0.52$. If we convert AUD1000 into USD, we get

$$1000 \times 0.52 = \text{USD}520$$

and if we convert USD1000 into AUD, we get

$$\frac{1000}{0.52} = \text{AUD}1923.08$$

INSIGHT

Exchange rates, physics and mathematics

In the previous examples the exchange rate between the Australian dollar and the US dollar was given two values, depending on how it is measured: 0.52 if it is the price of one Australian dollar; and 1.9231 if it is the price of one US dollar. Both of these values are right, but we have to be very careful as to the expression assigned to the exchange rate. The first value is *S(USD/AUD)*, whereas the second is *S(AUD/USD)*.

A look at the media explains this. In its issue of 4 June 2002, the *Australian Financial Review* reported the exchange rate between the Australian dollar and the pound as 0.3891 ('Wholesale Market', p. 50). This is fine, except for one problem: this exchange rate is portrayed to be *S(AUD/GBP)* (or $A/£, as the table says). This cannot be right, because the number clearly means that one Australian dollar is worth 38.91 British pence, and it cannot mean that the pound is worth 38.91 Australian cents. In other words, the number must refer to the value of one Australian dollar, or *S(GBP/AUD)*.

Now, try to detect the flaw in this argument. It has been brought to the attention of the present author that, in at least one major Australian university, students are told that if the exchange rate between the British and Australian currencies is 0.39, then this corresponds to the expression AUD/GBP (dropping *S* for the purpose of this argument). This is because, the argument goes, if *AUD/GBP* = 0.39, then by manipulating this 'equation' we get *AUD* = 0.39*GBP*, which looks right. Hence, the *Australian Financial Review* must be right in the way it reports the exchange rates, unless we detect the flaw in this argument. The flaw arises because AUD and GBP are units of measurement, not variables. Mathematically, we cannot multiply or divide by units of measurement, and so the manipulation of this 'equation' is wrong (in fact, it is not an equation at all).

We need to remember that the exchange rate is a price, like any other price. We say that the price of tomatoes is five dollars per kilo, the price of labour (the wage rate) is 20 dollars per hour of work, and the price of capital (interest rate) is 5 per cent per one unit of the capital borrowed. In all cases, we are pricing a 'commodity', which is one kilo of tomatoes, one hour of labour and one unit of capital. The exchange rate is a price like any other price: *S(GBP/AUD)* is the price of one Australian dollar in terms of the pound, whereas *S(AUD/GBP)* is the price of one pound in terms of the Australian dollar. Thus, the first expression must assume the value of 0.3891, as reported in the *Australian Financial Review*, whereas the second expression must assume its reciprocal, that is 2.5700.

In physics, things are measured in a similar manner. Density is measured in grams per cubic centimetre (the mass of one cubic centimetre of something, such as beer), and speed is measured in kilometres per hour (the distance travelled in one hour). If we follow the same flawed argument in physics, then we can say that if the speed of a car is 90, then km/h = 90, and by manipulation we obtain the result that one kilometre is equal to 90 hours (or any number of hours, depending on the speed). Obviously, you do not need to be a physicist to realise that this is nonsense! For detailed arguments, see the article by Moosa and Pereira.[1]

[1] I. A. Moosa and R. Pereira, 'Pitfalls in Measuring and Quoting Bilateral Exchange Rates', *Accounting Research Journal*, 13, 2000, pp. 106–11.

What is used in practice?

Obviously, it can be confusing if two foreign exchange dealers trying to conclude a transaction to exchange two currencies express the exchange rate differently from each other. In other markets, prices are expressed as the number of units of money per one unit of the commodity (which could be a dozen, a kilo, a portion, etc.). Therefore, we say that the price of a glass of beer is AUD2. We never say that the price of one Australian dollar is half a glass of beer. In the foreign exchange market, the underlying commodity is foreign exchange or foreign currency. So, it makes a lot of sense to express the exchange rate as the domestic currency price of one unit of the foreign currency, which we may write as $S(d/f)$. This is called a **direct quotation** of the spot exchange rate (the number representing the value of the exchange rate is called a direct quote). It is also called **normal quotation** or **price quotation** because it gives the domestic currency price of one unit of the foreign currency. When the direct quotation is used, a higher level of the exchange rate implies appreciation of the foreign currency and depreciation of the domestic currency. The reciprocal of this exchange rate, $S(f/d)$, gives the price of one unit of the domestic currency in terms of the foreign currency. This is called **indirect quotation**. It may also be called **quantity quotation** or **volume quotation**, because it gives the quantity of foreign currency that can be obtained in exchange for one unit of the domestic currency.

We must bear in mind that the words 'domestic' and 'foreign' are relative. What is domestic relative to one country is foreign relative to another. Thus, a direct quotation from the perspective of one country is an indirect quotation from the perspective of another. For example, if the exchange rate between the Australian and New Zealand currencies is expressed as $S(AUD/NZD)$, then this is a direct quotation from an Australian perspective but it is an indirect quotation from a New Zealand perspective. The opposite is valid if the exchange rate is expressed as $S(NZD/AUD)$. Notice that the indirect quotation is the reciprocal of the direct quotation, that is

$$S(d/f) = \frac{1}{S(f/d)} \tag{2.5}$$

Since the US dollar is the most important currency, exchange rates are normally expressed as the price of one US dollar, which is the number of units of the other currency per one unit of the US dollar, or $S(x/USD)$, where x is any other currency. This is indirect quotation from a US perspective. There are some exceptions to this rule, however. The most notable exception is the pound, whose exchange rate against the US dollar is quoted as $S(USD/GBP)$. There is an historical reason for this anomaly. Before 25 February 1971, the pound was not a decimal currency as it is now (equal to 100 pence). Instead, each pound was equal to 20 shillings and each shilling was equal to 12 old pennies. It would have been rather awkward to express the exchange rate as $S(GBP/USD)$. For example, an exchange rate of 1.60 (USD/GBP) would have been equal to 12 shillings and 6 (old) pennies, which is rather cumbersome. Another story is that expressing the pound exchange rate in this way makes the Brits feel better as it is a reflection of the importance of London, the home of the pound, as the most important foreign exchange centre in the world (this story is less credible).

The Australian dollar exchange rates are also reported in indirect quotation from an Australian perspective, both in the media and in foreign exchange transactions. For example, the exchange rates on 2 May 2002 as reported by the *Australian Financial Review* were as follows: 0.5393 against the US dollar, 68.53 against the yen, 0.5946 against the euro and 0.3679 against the pound. These rates obviously represent the price of one Australian dollar in terms of other currencies, and so they must represent the rates expressed as $S(USD/AUD)$, $S(JPY/AUD)$, $S(EUR/AUD)$ and $S(GBP/AUD)$, respectively. The direct quotations are the reciprocals of these rates. Hence, the values of these exchange rates expressed in direct quotations (from an Australian perspective) are $S(AUD/USD) = 1.8543$, $S(AUD/JPY) = 0.0146$, $S(AUD/EUR) = 1.6818$ and $S(AUD/GBP) = 2.7181$. In this book, both ways of expressing the Australian dollar exchange rates are used. The objective is not, of course, to create confusion but rather to teach and train you to be flexible enough to deal with exchange rates no matter how they are expressed.

The bid and offer rates

When dealers attempt to strike a deal, they quote exchange rates in terms of two numbers, the so-called **two-way quote** or **two-way rate**. For example, a dealer may quote an exchange rate of the Australian dollar against the US dollar in direct quotation from an Australian perspective as 1.8525–1.8575. The first number is the **bid rate**, the rate at which the dealer, or the market maker (who quotes this rate), is willing to buy the US dollar. The second number is the **offer** (or **ask**) **rate**, the rate at which this dealer is willing to sell the US dollar. The offer rate is higher than the bid rate by an amount called the **bid-offer spread**, the **dealing spread** or the **bid-offer margin**, m. It is calculated as

$$m = S_a - S_b \tag{2.6}$$

where S_a and S_b are the offer and the bid rates, respectively. In our example the bid-offer spread is calculated as

$$m = 1.8575 - 1.8525 = 0.0050$$

Alternatively, the spread may be calculated as a percentage of the bid rate, or

$$m = \frac{S_a}{S_b} - 1 \tag{2.7}$$

which in our example is

$$m = \frac{1.8575}{1.8525} - 1 = 0.0027$$

or 0.27 per cent.

We also define the mid-rate as the average of the bid and offer rates. Hence

$$S = \frac{1}{2}(S_b + S_a) \tag{2.8}$$

In our example the mid-rate is

$$S = \frac{1}{2}(1.8525 + 1.8575) = 1.8550$$

The spread is much higher in the retail business than in the interbank business because of the higher costs associated with small retail transactions. You may have noticed that the bid-offer spreads reported by newspapers are significantly narrower than those advertised by moneychangers at Melbourne Airport. In the interbank market, competition keeps the bid-offer spreads narrow.

Now, let us be more specific by referring to Figure 2.6. If Dealer A quotes to Dealer B 1.8525–1.8575 for $S(AUD/USD)$, then this means that:

- A is willing to buy the US dollar at AUD1.8525 and sell it at AUD1.8575.
- If B wants to deal, then he or she can buy the US dollar at 1.8575 and sell it at 1.8525.

This means that A's bid rate is B's selling rate, and vice versa. In this case A is the market maker, whereas B is a price taker. Since buying one currency necessarily implies selling the other currency, the following is also valid:

- A is willing to buy the Australian dollar at the reciprocal of 1.8575 (that is, at USD0.5384) and sell it at the reciprocal of 1.8525 (that is, at USD0.5398).
- If B wants to deal, then he or she can buy the Australian dollar at the reciprocal of 1.8525 (that is, at USD0.5398) and sell it at the reciprocal of 1.8575 (that is, at USD0.5384).

Figure 2.6 A foreign exchange spot transaction with bid-offer spread

IN PRACTICE

How the media report exchange rates

In its issue of 6 May 2002, the *Australian Financial Review* reported the following exchange rates ('Retail Market', p. 38), which were provided by Westpac Banking Corporation on 3 May 2002:

	Buy/sell
US dollar	0.5357/0.5291
British pound	0.3667/0.3592
Euro	0.5959/0.5793
Japanese yen	68.66/67.03
New Zealand dollar	1.2023/1.1791

These quotations are rather confusing. The 'buy' and 'sell' rates should correspond to the bid and offer rates of the Westpac Banking Corporation. Why is it, then, that the bid rates are higher than the offer rates, which is the opposite of what is stated in the text? Surely, a market maker such as Westpac wants to buy low and sell high.

To clarify this confusion, we have to determine how the exchange rates are expressed and to which currency the words 'buy' and 'sell' refer. The exchange rates are obviously expressed as the price of one Australian dollar, *S(x/AUD)*, but the 'buy' and 'sell' rates refer to the other currency, and this is the source of confusion. Thus, 0.5357/0.5291 means that Westpac is willing to buy the US dollar at the reciprocal of 0.5357 and sell it at the reciprocal of 0.5291. The confusion would certainly disappear if the exchange rates were expressed as *S(AUD/x)*, which gives the following:

	Buy/sell
US dollar	1.8667/1.8900
British pound	2.7270/2.7840
Euro	1.6781/1.7262
Japanese yen	0.01456/0.01492
New Zealand dollar	0.8317/0.8481

Hence, the exchange rates now represent the buying and selling rates of one unit of the foreign currency in terms of the Australian dollar (direct quotation). These rates mean that Westpac is willing to buy the US dollar at AUD1.8667 and sell it at AUD1.8900. Now, the bid rates are lower than the offer rates.

Alternatively, the exchange rates can be left as they appear in the first table, provided that the words 'buy' and 'sell' are switched around. It would also be useful if it said 'Sell/buy (Australian dollar)', so that there is no confusion about the rates representing the prices of one Australian dollar.

Now that we have distinguished between the bid and offer rates, we must be very careful when we convert exchange rates from direct into indirect quotations. In general, the following relationships hold:

$$S_b(y/x) = \frac{1}{S_a(x/y)} \tag{2.9}$$

$$S_a(y/x) = \frac{1}{S_b(x/y)} \tag{2.10}$$

Example

If the exchange rate between the US dollar and the Australian dollar is 1.8525–1.8575, then this means the following:

$$S_a(AUD/USD) = 1.8575$$
$$S_b(AUD/USD) = 1.8525$$
$$S_b(USD/AUD) = \frac{1}{S_a(AUD/USD)} = \frac{1}{1.8575} = 0.5384$$
$$S_a(USD/AUD) = \frac{1}{S_b(AUD/USD)} = \frac{1}{1.8525} = 0.5398$$

Now, we come to the definition of a **point** in exchange rate quotations. All major currencies are decimal in the sense that the unit is divided into 100 parts. Thus, a dollar is 100 cents and a pound is 100 pence. A hundredth (1/100) of a cent and a penny is called one basis point, or simply one point. Thus, the spread of Dealer A in the above example is 0.0050 or 50 points (1.8575 minus 1.8525). Because the spread is small, the offer exchange rate may be quoted as the number of points only (the last two decimals). Thus, A's quotation is 1.8525–75. Also, during short time intervals on a trading day, exchange rates move slightly, normally by a small number of points. It may in this case be more convenient to quote both the bid and offer rates in terms of points only (that is, 25–75). This is a shorthand quotation, which leaves out the so-called **big number**. Finally, a dealer may quote an exchange rate as '25–75 on 5'. This means that the dealer is quoting a bid rate of 1.8525 and an offer rate of 1.8575 applicable only to round amounts of USD5 million.

Exchange rates for major currencies, with the exception of the Japanese yen, are usually quoted to four decimal places in the interbank market. This is because the fourth decimal place is a point. Sometimes a fifth decimal place is used and is called a **pip**. The Japanese yen is quoted to two decimal places because it has a small par value. Whether four, five or two decimal places are used depends on the monetary significance involved (that is, the value of the point or the pip in a transaction).

Interbank dealing on two-way rates is carried out on the basis of the principle of reciprocity. When Dealer A asks Dealer B for a price, B may respond in an ascending order of 'generosity' by: (i) not quoting a two-way rate; (ii) quoting a two-way rate with a wide spread; and (iii) quoting a two-way rate with a narrow spread but only for small amounts. Dealer B will get a similar response at another time when he or she asks Dealer A for a quote.

IN PRACTICE

Quoting the Australian dollar exchange rates

The Australian dollar exchange rates are quoted in indirect quotation from an Australian perspective. Thus, the exchange rate between the Australian dollar and the US dollar is quoted as USD/AUD, which takes values such as 0.55. It has been suggested that changing the quotation by expressing the exchange rate as AUD/USD will not only have the benefit of being in line with other currencies, but it will also have two additional advantages: it would reduce transaction costs (the bid-offer spread) and exchange rate volatility.[1]

Let us start with the bid-offer spread. Banks like to quote 10-point spreads. Thus, if the bid rate were 0.5500, the offer rate would be 0.5510. The value of this spread is 0.1 US cents. If the exchange rate were expressed the other way round, the bid rate would be 1.8149. With a bid-offer spread of 10 points the offer rate would be 1.8159, but the value of these 10 points is 0.1 Australian cents. In percentage terms the bid-offer spread is 0.18 per cent if the exchange rate is expressed as USD/AUD and 0.06 per cent if the exchange rate is expressed as AUD/USD.

As for volatility, a similar line of reasoning is used. If a market maker quotes the exchange rate at 0.5500, then the next move (if the outlook for the Australian dollar is unfavourable) is to quote 0.5490, a depreciation of 0.18 per cent. If, on the other hand, the exchange rate was 1.8149, then the next quote would be 1.8159, a fall of 0.06 per cent only.

[1] 'Cut Volatility with New Quoting for $A', *Australian Financial Review*, 18 June 2002, p. 24.

The situation is different when Dealer A acts on behalf of a customer who wants to buy a currency that is not actively traded. Dealer A does not seek a two-way rate from Dealer B because Dealer A does not want to reciprocate in this currency. Here, Dealer B treats Dealer A as a customer, in which case the former is not faced with uncertainty about whether the rate is for selling or buying.

The situation may also arise when a dealer makes a mistake in quoting rates (that is, when there is a **misquote**). In this case, market etiquette suggests that the calling dealer asks the quoting dealer to double-check the quote. If the quoting dealer decides to stand by the quote, the deal will go ahead even if there is a misquote.

Cross exchange rates

A **cross exchange rate** is the exchange rate between two currencies derived from their exchange rates against another currency. If x, y and z are three currencies, then

$$S(x/y) = \frac{S(x/z)}{S(y/z)} \tag{2.11}$$

In practice, z is the US dollar because exchange rates are normally expressed in terms of the US dollar. Thus, the cross exchange rate may be defined as an exchange rate between two currencies, neither of which is the US dollar. Alternatively, the cross exchange rate may be defined as an exchange rate between two currencies, neither of which is the domestic currency (in this case, z is the domestic currency). Analogously, **cross trading** is defined as the exchange of two currencies, neither of which is the US dollar or the domestic currency. This kind of trading is less widespread, and is normally more expensive, particularly if it involves currencies that are not heavily traded. This is because this kind of trading involves two transactions rather than one. In direct trading, x is exchanged for y in one transaction.

IN PRACTICE

The mechanics of foreign exchange trading

The mechanics of trading differs between brokered transactions and direct deals. In direct deals, the dealer receiving the call acts as a market maker for the currency to be traded. Hence, a direct deal between A and B on 12 February involving the Australian dollar and the US dollar may go as follows:

A: Bank A calling. Price on US dollar, please.
B: Twenty-five–eighty-five on five.
A: Five yours at twenty-five.
B: Confirming I buy five million US dollars at 1.8525, sell nine million, two hundred and sixty-two thousand and five hundred Australian dollars, value date 14 February.

The conversation is so brief because things move very quickly in the foreign exchange market. Dealer A identifies the calling bank and asks for a quote on the US dollar against the Australian dollar. Dealer B responds by quoting a bid rate of 1.8525 and an offer rate of 1.8585. Dealer A likes the bid rate of dealer B and accepts to sell USD5 million at this rate. Dealer B confirms the transaction, stating the relevant rate and the amount of Australian dollars equivalent to USD5 million at that rate, as well as the delivery date. On the delivery date (14 February) Bank B will be credited with USD5 million and Bank A with AUD9 262 500.

In a brokered deal the telephone conversation takes place between the dealer asking for a quote and a broker acting on behalf of other dealers. If the broker gets a price that is acceptable to another dealer, the broker confirms the deal and reports the second dealer to the first dealer. Payment arrangements will be made and confirmed separately by the respective back offices. The two dealers share the brokerage fees.

In cross trading, if a direct deal is unavailable, x is exchanged for z and z is exchanged for y. Two transactions are more costly because they involve brokerage fees and bid-offer spreads.

A bid-offer cross exchange rate may be calculated by assuming that two transactions take place, as shown in Figure 2.7(a). Assume that a customer (B) wants to convert x into y via z. This deal involves the following two transactions:

- Buying z and selling x at the rate $S_a(x/z)$ to obtain $1/S_a(x/z)$ units of z. In this case C is the market maker.
- Buying y and selling z at the rate $S_b(y/z)$ to obtain $S_b(y/z)/S_a(x/z)$ units of y. In this case A is the market maker.

This means that:

$$S_a(x/y) = \frac{S_a(x/z)}{S_b(y/z)} \tag{2.12}$$

Assume now that the customer (B) wants to convert y into x via z, which is described in Figure 2.7(b). This deal involves the following two transactions:

- Buying z and selling y at the rate $S_a(y/z)$, to obtain $1/S_a(y/z)$ units of z.
- Buying x and selling z at the rate $S_b(x/z)$, to obtain $S_b(x/z)/S_a(y/z)$ units of x.

This means that:

$$S_b(x/y) = \frac{S_b(x/z)}{S_a(y/z)} \tag{2.13}$$

Figure 2.7 Cross and direct trading

(a) Cross $x \rightarrow z \rightarrow y$

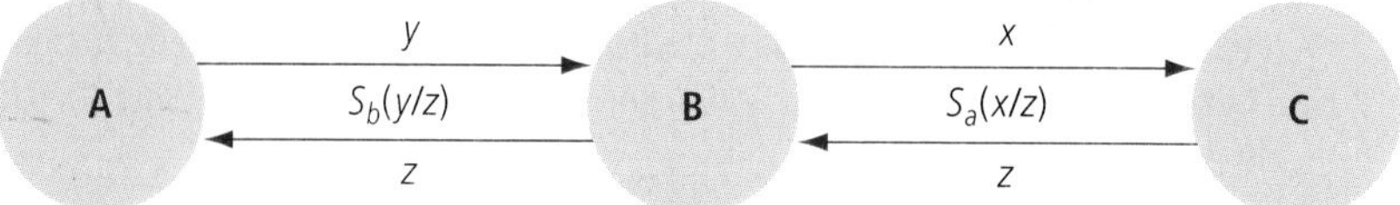

(b) Cross $y \rightarrow z \rightarrow x$

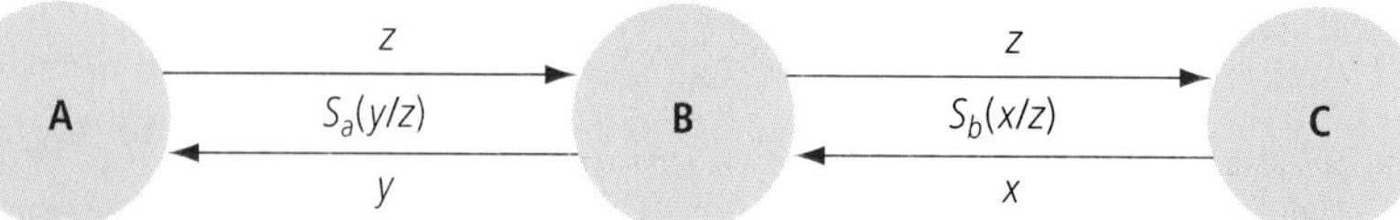

(c) Direct $x \rightarrow y$

A

y

$S_a(x/y)$

x

B

(d) Direct $y \rightarrow x$

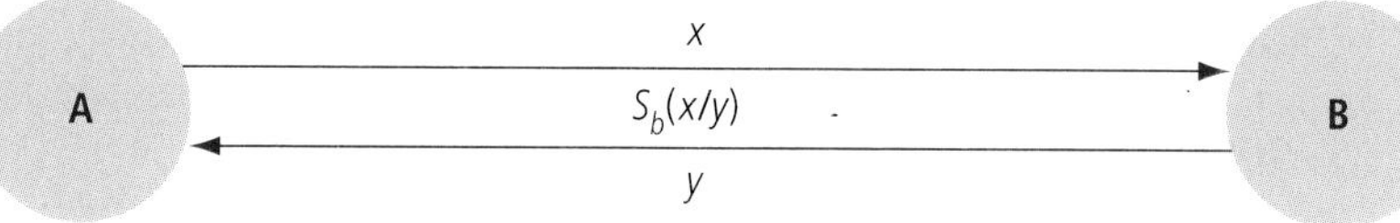

Example

If $S(JPY/AUD)$ = 67.05–68.75 and $S(GBP/AUD)$ = 0.3590–0.3670, then a transaction to convert JPY1 000 000 to pounds via the Australian dollar works as follows:

- Buying AUD and selling JPY at 68.75 to obtain AUD14 546.
- Buying GBP and selling AUD at 0.3590 to obtain GBP5222.

This means that the offer cross exchange rate between the pound and the yen (the rate at which the customer buys) is

$$S_a(JPY/GBP) = \frac{1\,000\,000}{5222} = 191.50$$

On the other hand, a transaction to convert GBP1000 to yen via the Australian dollar works as follows:

- Buying AUD and selling GBP at 0.3670 to obtain AUD2725.
- Buying JPY and selling AUD at 67.05 to obtain JPY182 711.

This means that the bid cross exchange rate between the pound and the yen (the rate at which the customer sells) is

$$S_b(JPY/GBP) = \frac{182\,711}{1000} = 182.71$$

These bid and offer rates can be calculated directly from Equations (2.9) and (2.10) as follows:

$$S_b(JPY/GBP) = \frac{S_b(JPY/AUD)}{S_a(GBP/AUD)} = \frac{67.05}{0.3670} = 182.70$$

$$S_a(JPY/GBP) = \frac{S_a(JPY/AUD)}{S_b(GBP/AUD)} = \frac{68.75}{0.3590} = 191.50$$

which gives the same results.

The *Australian Financial Review* and other financial newspapers report a matrix of cross exchange rates. This matrix is prepared for n currencies as follows. Suppose that we have n exchange rates expressed in indirect quotation against the domestic currency, z. These exchange rates may be written as $S(x_1/z)$, $S(x_2/z)$, …, $S(x_n/z)$. In general, the cross exchange rate $S(x_i/x_j)$ can be calculated as

$$S(x_i/x_j) = \frac{S(x_i/z)}{S(x_j/z)} \tag{2.14}$$

whereas the reciprocal of this rate is calculated as

$$S(x_j/x_i) = \frac{1}{S(x_i/x_j)} = \frac{S(x_j/z)}{S(x_i/z)} \tag{2.15}$$

A matrix of cross rates is a symmetrical matrix with diagonal elements equal to unity because they represent the exchange rates between each currency and itself. The half-matrix below the diagonal reports the reciprocals of the exchange rates above the diagonal.

Example

To see how a cross rate matrix is constructed, consider the following exchange rates:

$$S(NZD/AUD) = 1.2023$$
$$S(GBP/AUD) = 0.3667$$
$$S(EUR/AUD) = 0.5959$$

The construction of the (3 × 3) matrix requires the calculation of three cross rates and their reciprocals, which would be placed in the matrix as follows:

	NZD	GBP	EUR
NZD	1	S(GBP/NZD)	S(EUR/NZD)
GBP	S(NZD/GBP)	1	S(EUR/GBP)
EUR	S(NZD/EUR)	S(GBP/EUR)	1

After calculating the cross rates, the matrix would look like this:

	NZD	GBP	EUR
NZD	1	0.3050	0.4956
GBP	3.2787	1	1.6250
EUR	2.0176	0.6153	1

2.6 Spot foreign exchange position keeping

A foreign exchange transaction is a contract to buy one currency and sell another. As we have seen before, these transactions are settled by the exchange of deposits denominated in the two currencies. The deposits used for settlement are held with **correspondent banks**. A **nostro account** is an account that a dealer holds at a correspondent bank in a foreign country for the purpose of making and receiving payments in the currency of that country (for example, a pound account held by the Commonwealth Bank of Australia with National Westminster Bank in London). A **vostro account** is an account held by a bank on behalf of a foreign dealer. The words nostro and vostro are Latin for 'ours' and 'yours'.

When dealers trade currencies they create short and long positions in various currencies. A **short position** on a particular currency is created when the dealer borrows an amount of that currency and sells it. This is normally done if the currency is expected to depreciate. Eventually, the dealer has to buy back the currency to close or square the position. Conversely, a **long position** is created when a currency is bought because it is expected to appreciate.

Position keeping is the monitoring of positions in each currency, which is the net cumulative total of currency holdings arising from various deals. Over time, dealers record the details of their individual transactions sequentially on a schedule called a **blotter**. The blotter lists the domestic and foreign currency amounts exchanged in each deal, which enables the dealer to calculate the resulting long and short positions in each currency from the individual amounts. A simple blotter (with five deals) may look like this:

AUD deal amount	AUD balance	AUD/USD rate	USD deal amount	USD balance
+10 000 000	+10 000 000	1.6525	–6 051 437	–6 051 437
+20 000 000	+30 000 000	1.6645	–12 015 620	–18 067 057
–10 000 000	+20 000 000	1.6725	+5 979 073	–12 087 983
+25 000 000	+45 000 000	1.6445	–15 202 189	–27 290 172
–50 000 000	–5 000 000	1.6500	+30 303 030	+3 012 858

This blotter records the following items (by column):

- The amounts of the domestic currency (AUD) bought (+) and sold (–).
- The balance of the domestic currency (AUD) after each individual deal.
- The exchange rate applicable to each individual deal.
- The amount of foreign currency (USD) bought (+) and sold (–).
- The balance of foreign currency (USD) after each individual deal.

Position keeping can be used to (i) measure exposure to the risk of future changes in exchange rates, and (ii) measure the potential or unrealised profit/loss that has been made on positions due to past exchange rate changes. Unrealised profit can be realised via **position squaring** at the current market exchange rate. This is done by buying the short position currency and selling the long position currency.

The calculation of unrealised profit/loss is called **valuation**. Currency positions can be valued by calculating the **average rate** at which a long position in the domestic currency has been bought, or a short position has been sold, and comparing this average rate with the current market rate at which the dealer can square these positions. This process of comparison is called **marking to market**. A long position is profitable if the market rate is higher than the average rate, whereas a short position is profitable if the market rate is lower than the average rate.

The average rate is calculated by dividing the domestic currency balance by the foreign currency balance. Thus, at the end of the sequence of deals the average rate is

$$\frac{5\,000\,000}{3\,012\,858} = 1.6596$$

Because there is a long position on the US dollar, this position would be profitable if the market exchange rate is higher than the average rate. If the market rate is 1.700, the unrealised profit per unit of the foreign currency is

$$1.7000 - 1.6596 = \text{AUD}0.0404$$

which means that the overall profit on the long position is

$$3\,012\,858 \times 0.0404 = \text{AUD}121\,720$$

This can be realised by selling USD3 012 858 at the market rate of 1.700.

IN PRACTICE

Allfirst's foreign exchange losses

By January 2002 a rogue trader named John Runsak had piled up losses amounting to USD691 million at Allfirst, the US subsidiary of Allied Irish Bank (AIB). He was hunted down on 30 January when Allfirst controllers called banks in Asia to find out that trades that Runsak claimed to have done with them were fictitious. This piece of news made big headlines in the media, and was considered the largest event of its kind since Nick Leeson brought about the collapse of Barings Bank in 1996. How could this have happened when traders are supposed to observe certain limits on their dealings? This particular trader had a limit of a few million dollars.

A report that was released subsequently showed that the poor structure and mismanagement at Allfirst created ideal conditions for what happened. Runsak was hired in 1993 as a foreign exchange dealer. In 1994 he breached his trading limits, but he was regarded as a star trader to the extent that this incident was dismissed as 'trader error'. The lack of supervision allowed him to hide increasing losses from foreign exchange operations by constructing bogus option transactions that presumably offset the real loss-making transactions. He managed to avoid scrutiny by the back office since these operations did not require net cash transfers. Moreover, he managed to have a 'running tab' with two big trading counterparties, Citibank and Bank of America, which allowed him to trade without having to report each trade internally. He even manipulated the prices at which he traded, not to mention the fact that he traded from home and when he was on holiday.

Bank chiefs everywhere demanded reassurance from their risk controllers that no such fiasco could visit their banks. It was thought that this sort of event was inconceivable, given that controls had been designed (following the collapse of Barings) to catch errors or fraud at every stage.

2.7 The forward exchange rate

The **forward exchange rate** is a rate contracted today for the delivery of a currency at a specified date in the future. This date in the future (called the **forward value date**) must be more than two business days away, otherwise the underlying transaction will be a spot transaction. If the delivery takes place one week after the transaction has been concluded, then the underlying rate is a one-week forward rate. Typically, forward contracts extend up to one year, in maturities of one month, two months, and so on. However, forward contracts of maturities longer than one year can also be found. A special kind of forward contract is called a **break forward contract**. This contract can be terminated at a predetermined date, thus providing protection against adverse exchange rate movements. It may also be called **forward with optional exit**, abbreviated as FOX.

The interval until a forward value date is calculated from the spot value date, not from the transaction date. For example, the forward value date of a sale of one week forward agreed on 16 June would be one week from the spot value date of 18 June, which would be 25 June. The forward value date is usually fixed, not by agreeing on a specific date, but by agreeing on a term, which is a whole number of weeks or months after the spot value date (for example, one month). The specific date is then fixed according to one of two conventions: (i) the **modified following business day convention**; and (ii) the **end/end rule**. The modified following business day convention works as follows: the maturity date is set to be the value date, but if that falls on a non-business day, the date is moved to the following day. If that falls in the next calendar month, it would be moved to the last business day of the current calendar month. The end/end rule is that if the value date is the last business day of the current calendar month, maturity will be the last business day of the final calendar month.

Forward transactions are classified by forward value date into:

- **short dates**: maturity of one month or less
- **round dates** (**fixed dates** or **straight dates**): original terms to maturity of a whole number of months
- **broken dates** (**odd dates**): original maturities of less than round dates.

Forward transactions are of two types: **outright forward contracts** and **foreign exchange swaps** (or **spot-forward swaps**). An outright forward contract involves the sale or purchase of a currency for delivery more than two business days into the future. Hence, the only difference between an outright forward transaction and a spot transaction is the value date. The word 'outright' indicates that no spot transaction is involved. On the other hand, a foreign exchange swap (which is different from a **currency swap**) involves a spot purchase against a matching outright forward sale (or vice versa). For example, a foreign exchange swap transaction is concluded when a trader agrees to sell a currency and simultaneously to repurchase it (thus reversing the operation) some time in the future at an exchange rate determined now (see Figure 2.8). When the reversal is on adjacent days, the term **rollover** is used.

Three kinds of foreign exchange swaps can be distinguished:

- **forward swaps**, which start on the spot value date and end on a forward value date
- **forward-forward swaps**, which start on a forward value date and end on a later forward date
- **overnight swaps** and **tom/next swaps**, which end on or before the spot value date.

The forward spread

Also called the **forward margin**, the **spot-forward spread** or the **forward pickup/markdown**, the **forward spread** is the difference between the forward rate and the spot

Figure 2.8 Outright and swap forward transactions

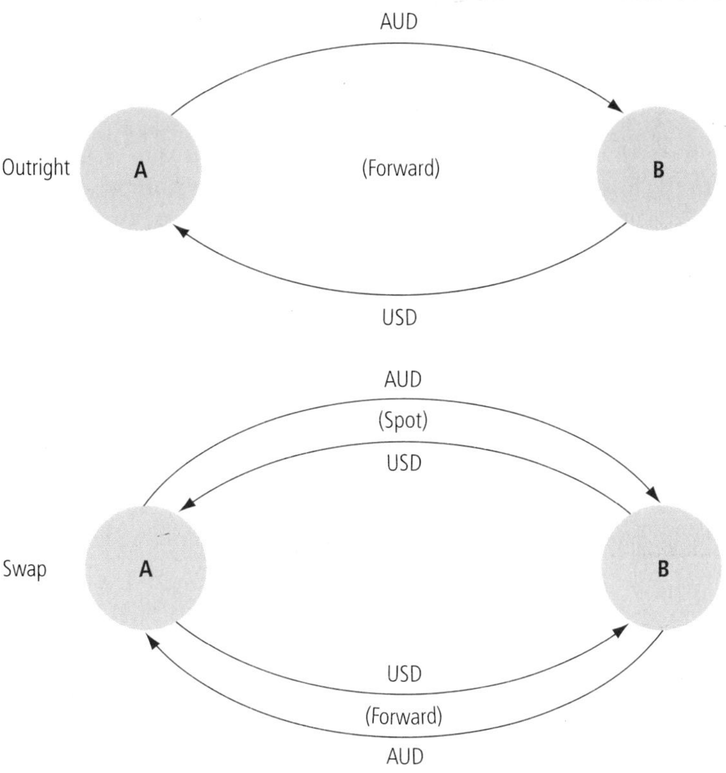

Example

The following example illustrates the mechanics of a foreign exchange swap when a dealer sells USD1 million spot and buys it three months forward. Assume that the spot and three-month forward rates (AUD/USD) are 1.7850–1.7880 and 1.7870–1.7900, respectively. The cash flows involved in this operation are

	USD	AUD
Present	−1 000 000	+1 785 000
Future	+1 000 000	−1 790 000
Net	0	−5 000

If the spot rate changes to 1.7940–1.7970, the three-month forward rate becomes 1.7960–1.7990. The cash flows in this case will be

	USD	AUD
Present	−1 000 000	+1 794 000
Future	+1 000 000	−1 799 000
Net	0	−5 000

Obviously, the net cash flows are unaffected by the change in the spot rate.

rate calculated as a percentage of the latter. When it is measured in per cent per annum, the spread, m, is calculated as

$$m = \frac{F(x/y) - S(x/y)}{S(x/y)} \times 100 \times \frac{12}{N} \tag{2.16}$$

where F is the forward rate, S is the spot rate and N is the maturity of the forward contract in months. Both the forward and spot rates are calculated as the number of units of x per one unit of y. The percentage difference is annualised by multiplying it by $12/N$. This annualisation makes it possible to compare the forward spread on various maturities and also to compare the spread with the interest rate differential.

Obviously, the forward spread can be positive or negative, depending on whether the forward rate is greater than, or less than, the spot rate. A positive spread is called a **forward premium**, whereas a negative spread is called a **forward discount**. Note, however, that the bilateral exchange rate is an expression of the price of one currency against another, and so if one currency is selling at a premium, the other must be selling at a discount. When the spot rate is equal to the forward rate, then the forward spread is zero. In this case, neither of the two currencies sells at a premium or a discount. Rather, they sell at par, or both currencies are said to be flat. To avoid confusion, the following rules summarise all of the possibilities:

- If $F(x/y) > S(x/y)$, then y is selling at a premium and x is selling at a discount.
- If $F(x/y) < S(x/y)$, then y is selling at a discount and x is selling at a premium.
- If $F(x/y) = S(x/y)$, then both currencies are selling at par.

In the previous example, the US dollar sells at a premium, whereas the Australian dollar sells at a discount. This is why the operation results in a negative cash flow (–5000).

Example

If the spot exchange rate between the Australian dollar and the US dollar, $S(AUD/USD)$, is 1.7800 and the three-month forward rate, $F(AUD/USD)$, is 1.7890, then the US dollar is selling at a premium. The forward spread is

$$\frac{1.7890 - 1.7800}{1.7800} \times 100 \times \frac{12}{3} = 2.02\%$$

Forward rate quotations

There are two ways of quoting forward rates. The first is the **outright rate**, which is expressed exactly as the spot rate, using two numbers to represent the bid and offer rates. The second is the **swap rate**, which is quoted in terms of the points of discount/premium (that is, the spread expressed as a–b or a/b).

When the forward rate is expressed as a swap rate, the number of points corresponding to the bid and offer rates are given for a particular maturity. Converting a swap rate into a bid-offer outright rate is simple. Just follow these rules:

- If $a > b$, add the points to the spot bid and offer rates. This indicates that the forward rate is higher than the spot rate.
- If $a < b$, subtract the points from the spot bid and offer rates. This indicates that the forward rate is lower than the spot rate.

Example

Consider the following spot and forward exchange rates (AUD/USD):

Spot	1.7800–1.7860
One month	10–20
Three months	20–30
Six months	50–40

The one- and three-month outright rates are calculated by adding the number of points to the spot rate. Conversely, the outright six-month rate is calculated by subtracting the number of points from the spot bid and offer rates. Thus, the outright bid and offer rates appear as follows:

Rate	Bid	Offer
Spot	1.7800	1.7860
One month	1.7810	1.7880
Three months	1.7820	1.7890
Six months	1.7750	1.7820

The bid-offer spread on a forward contract increases as the maturity of the contract lengthens. The reason for this is that the thinness of the market increases as the forward maturity increases. Increasing thinness means a smaller turnover, and hence it becomes difficult to offset positions in the interbank forward market. The difficulty of offsetting longer-maturity forward contracts makes them riskier than shorter-maturity contracts. The risk arises from uncertainty about the price of an offsetting forward contract immediately after quoting the forward rate.

2.8 The Australian dollar foreign exchange market

The core of the Australian foreign exchange market consists of the banking system and the non-bank dealers authorised by the Reserve Bank of Australia (RBA). The Australian foreign exchange market is highly integrated with the global foreign exchange market. This integration is indicated by the fact that about 40 per cent of foreign exchange transactions are conducted with foreign counterparties, most importantly foreign banks.

On 9 December 1983 the foreign exchange controls on the Australian dollar were lifted and the currency was allowed to float. The floating of the dollar was one of the first steps towards the deregulation of Australian financial markets. Since then the Australian dollar has become one of the most actively traded currencies, having been regarded previously as an 'exotic' currency.

Figure 2.9 shows: (a) the size and growth of the Australian foreign exchange market as measured by daily turnover; (b) the currency composition of the turnover; and (c) the composition by counterparty. In 2001, daily turnover amounted to USD52 billion distributed among spot transactions (USD13.2 billion), outright forward (USD3.5 billion) and foreign exchange swaps (USD35.3 billion). More than half of the turnover (53.3 per cent) involved trading the Australian dollar against the US dollar. Most of the trading was done with foreign banks (USD33.7 billion).

Figure 2.9 The size and composition of the Australian foreign exchange market

(a) Daily turnover (USD billion)

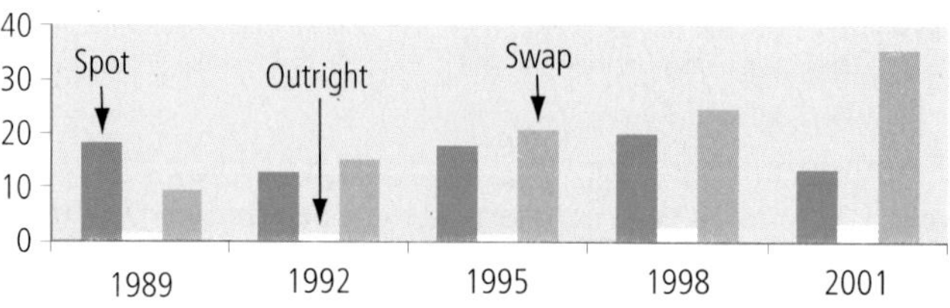

(b) Currency composition (2001)

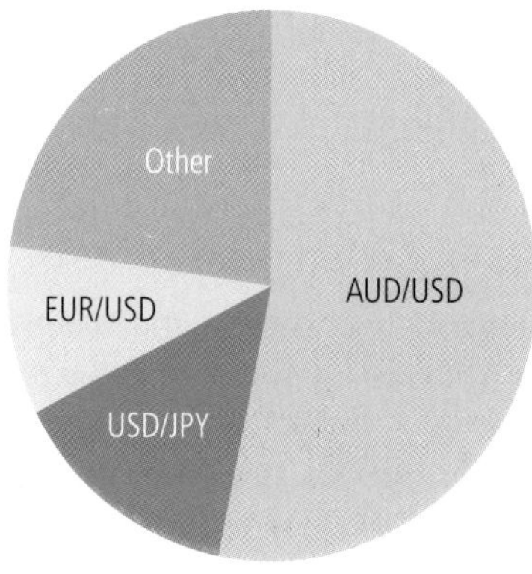

(c) Composition by counterparty

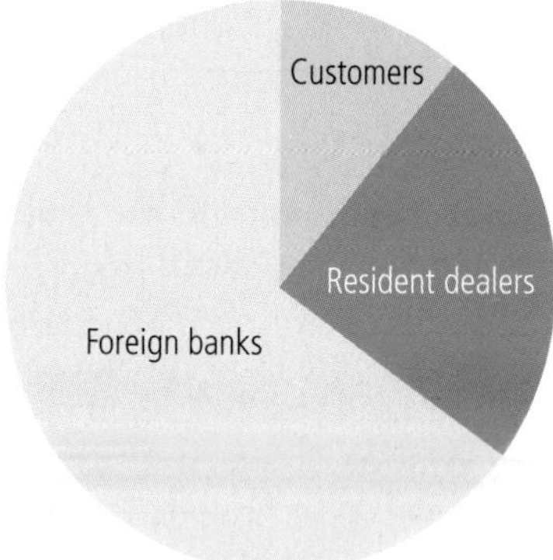

Source: RBA.

There are several reasons for the impressive growth of the Australian foreign exchange market:

- Deregulation provided vast opportunities for foreign investment. This is because with no capital controls, direct investment can take place more readily, and because the resulting financial innovation provided the means of currency risk management.

- Australia's above-average level of real interest rates generated massive capital flows into the country from the mid-1980s onwards.
- Australia's time zone contributed significantly to market growth. Australian trading hours form a link between New York and early European trading.
- The high level of volatility in the Australian dollar exchange rates in the initial years of the float provided opportunities for speculation.

Summary

- The foreign exchange market is the market where currencies are bought and sold. It is the largest and most perfect market.
- Market participants include: (i) customers; (ii) commercial banks; (iii) other financial institutions; (iv) brokers; and (v) central banks. These participants may enter the market as arbitragers, hedgers and speculators.
- The US dollar is the most heavily traded currency, followed by the euro, the yen and the pound.
- A foreign exchange transaction consists of: (i) price discovery; (ii) decision making; (iii) settlement; and (iv) position keeping.
- Foreign exchange technology has developed significantly since the telegraph was first used to settle foreign exchange transactions between London and New York in 1858. More recent developments pertain to online foreign exchange trading.
- The bilateral spot exchange rate is the exchange rate between two currencies applicable to transactions involving immediate delivery. This may be expressed in direct quotation (domestic/foreign) or indirect quotation (foreign/domestic).
- The bid rate is the exchange rate at which a dealer is willing to buy a particular currency. The offer rate is the rate at which the dealer is willing to sell the currency. The difference between the offer and bid rates is the bid-offer spread. The spread may be expressed as a percentage of the bid rate.
- The cross exchange rate is the exchange rate between two currencies derived from their exchange rates against another currency, normally the US dollar or the domestic currency.
- The forward rate is the exchange rate applicable to transactions involving delivery in the future. It may be expressed as an outright rate or a swap rate.
- Position keeping is the monitoring of positions in each currency, which is the net cumulative total of currency holdings arising from various deals. Details of individual transactions are recorded on a 'blotter'.
- The forward spread is the difference between the forward rate and the spot rate expressed in per cent (relative to the bid rate) per annum. A currency sells at a premium (discount) if the forward rate is higher (lower) than the spot rate.
- The Australian foreign exchange market, which is highly integrated with the global foreign exchange market, consists of the banking system and the non-bank dealers authorised by the Reserve Bank.
- The Australian dollar was floated in December 1983 as a first step in the deregulation of financial markets.
- A number of factors have contributed to the growth of the Australian foreign exchange market, including: (i) deregulation; (ii) high real interest rates in the 1980s; (iii) Australia's time zone; and (iv) the volatility of the Australian dollar in the early years of the float.

Key terms

MaxMARK

MAXIMISE YOUR MARKS! There are 30 interactive questions for this chapter available online at **www.mhhe.com/au/moosa2e**

Review questions

1. What is the meaning of 'foreign exchange'?
2. In what sense is the foreign exchange market the most perfect of all markets?
3. The foreign exchange market is an OTC market. Why?
4. Describe the major categories of participants in the foreign exchange market. How do they operate with respect to their attitude towards risk?
5. What is (a) a price taker and (b) a market maker in the foreign exchange market?
6. What is the difference between a broker and a dealer?
7. Explain why each of the following categories of participants enters the foreign exchange market: (a) exporters; (b) importers; (c) tourists; (d) immigrants; and (e) investors.
8. Central banks are not profit-making institutions. Why, then, do they buy and sell currencies on the foreign exchange market?
9. Why is the US dollar the most heavily traded currency on the foreign exchange market?
10. Despite the importance of Japan as a super economic power, the Japanese yen's role in international transactions is limited. Why?
11. The British pound is still heavily traded on the foreign exchange market despite the relative decline of the United Kingdom as a major economic and financial power. Why?
12. What are 'exotic' currencies?
13. What is the role of the 'back office' in settling foreign exchange transactions?
14. What is straight through processing? Why is it expected to reduce transaction costs in the foreign exchange industry?
15. What is the meaning of 'immediate delivery' in foreign exchange transactions?
16. What are Herstatt risk and liquidity risk? How can they be dealt with?
17. Distinguish between the contract date and the delivery date in foreign exchange transactions.
18. Distinguish between direct and indirect quotations of exchange rates. What happens to the domestic currency as the exchange rate rises if it is measured in direct quotation?

19 If the exchange rate between the Australian dollar and the Canadian dollar is quoted as AUD/CAD, what is this quotation from an Australian perspective and a Canadian perspective?

20 In actual trading, the exchange rates between the US and European currencies are expressed in direct quotation from a European perspective. Why is the pound a major exception to this rule?

21 Distinguish between a point and a pip in exchange rate quotation.

22 What is the principle of reciprocity in foreign exchange dealing?

23 Suppose that you are a foreign exchange dealer wishing to buy the Australian dollar against the US dollar. Given the market conditions, you are willing to buy at 0.5820. You phone another dealer who quotes 0.5480–0.5510. What would happen, assuming that you abide by the market etiquette?

24 Distinguish between nostro and vostro accounts.

25 How do you square a short position and a long position?

26 What is the meaning of 'marking to market' in spot foreign exchange transactions?

27 Distinguish between outright forward contracts and swaps.

28 What are the factors that have contributed to the growth of the Australian foreign exchange market?

Problems

1 On 12 August 2002, a Commonwealth Bank dealer in Melbourne concluded a transaction with a Citibank dealer in New York. The former agreed to buy from the latter USD5 000 000 at an exchange rate (AUD/USD) of 1.77 for delivery on 14 August. On the delivery date, the exchange rate rose to 1.83. How much would the Commonwealth Bank be required to pay to settle the transaction?

2 The exchange rate between the British pound and the Australian dollar (GBP/AUD) rose from 0.3780 to 0.3960 in one week.
(a) Calculate the percentage appreciation or depreciation of the Australian dollar.
(b) Using the result obtained in (a) above, calculate the percentage appreciation or depreciation of the pound.
(c) Calculate the corresponding values of the AUD/GBP exchange rate.
(d) Using the result obtained in (c) above, calculate the percentage appreciation or depreciation of the pound.
(e) Using the result obtained in (d) above, calculate the percentage appreciation or depreciation of the Australian dollar.

3 If the exchange rate between the British pound and the Australian dollar (GBP/AUD) is 0.3980, what is:
(a) The direct quote from an Australian perspective?
(b) The indirect quote from an Australian perspective?
(c) The direct quote from a British perspective?
(d) The indirect quote from a British perspective?

4 The USD/AUD exchange rate is quoted as 0.4977–0.5176.
(a) What is the bid-offer spread in points and in percentage terms? What is the monetary value of the point in this case?
(b) Calculate the AUD/USD exchange rate. What is the bid-offer spread in points and in percentage terms? What is the monetary value of the point in this case?

5 Dealer A quotes 0.6030–0.6050 for the EUR/AUD exchange rate to Dealer B. What are the following:
(a) The price at which A is willing to buy the Australian dollar?
(b) The price at which A is willing to buy the euro?
(c) The price at which B can buy the Australian dollar?
(d) The price at which B can buy the euro?
(e) The price at which A is willing to sell the Australian dollar?
(f) The price at which A is willing to sell the euro?
(g) The price at which B can sell the Australian dollar?
(h) The price at which B can sell the euro?

6 If the exchange rate between the Australian dollar and the Japanese yen, expressed in indirect quotation from an Australian perspective, is 70.10–71.60, what is the direct quotation for this rate? What are the mid-rates in both cases?

7 At 9.30 a.m. Dealer A calls Dealer B and asks for a quote on the AUD/GBP exchange rate. Dealer B responds by quoting 2.5500–2.5540. Dealer A decides to buy GBP200 000 at the quoted rate. At 3.30 p.m., Dealer B quotes 50–90. Will dealer A make profit or loss by selling the pound at 3.30 p.m.?

8 The exchange rate between the Australian dollar and the euro, expressed in direct quotation from an Australian perspective, rises from 1.62405 to 1.62808. Calculate:
(a) The appreciation or depreciation of the euro in points and pips.
(b) The appreciation or depreciation of the Australian dollar in points and pips.

9 On 4 June 2002 the following exchange rates were prevailing:

USD/AUD	0.5674
JPY/AUD	70.43
GBP/AUD	0.3891
EUR/AUD	0.6075

Calculate the following cross rates: JPY/USD, GBP/USD, EUR/USD, JPY/GBP, JPY/EUR and EUR/GBP.

10 The following exchange rates are quoted:

GBP/AUD	0.3820–90
AUD/EUR	1.6400–80

Calculate the bid-offer spread on the exchange rate between the pound and the euro expressed in direct quotation from a British perspective.

11 On the basis of the following exchange rates, construct a cross exchange rate matrix that does not include the Australian dollar. All exchange rates must be expressed in bid-offer terms.

GBP/AUD	0.3820–0.3900
EUR/AUD	0.6020–0.6080
CHF/AUD	0.8800–0.8860

12 A German foreign exchange dealer trading the Australian dollar against the euro conducts the following transactions in November 2002:

Date	Exchange rate (EUR/AUD)	Amount (euro)
14 Nov	0.5563–0.5613	+5 000 000
15 Nov	0.5661–0.5711	+10 000 000
18 Nov	0.5581–0.5631	–7 000 000
19 Nov	0.5566–0.5616	+8 000 000
20 Nov	0.5562–0.5612	–12 000 000

(a) Construct a blotter to show these transactions and the positions in both currencies.
(b) Calculate the average exchange rate at which the dealer bought and sold the Australian dollar.
(c) Calculate the unrealised profit/loss on the final position.
(d) What would the dealer do to square the final position?

13 The spot and forward rates between the Australian dollar and the euro (AUD/EUR) are as follows:

Spot	1.6030
One-month forward	1.6260
Three-month forward	1.5920

Calculate the forward spread in per cent per annum for both maturities. State whether the Australian dollar sells at a premium or a discount.

14 The following are the spot and swap forward values of the EUR/AUD exchange rate:

Spot	0.6020–0.6100
One-month forward	20–40
Three-month forward	40–60
Six-month forward	80–40

Calculate the outright forward rate for each maturity. State whether the euro sells at a premium or a discount.

Appendix 2.1

More foreign exchange jargon

This appendix contains some terms that are used in foreign exchange dealing or are related to the foreign exchange market. These terms do not appear in the body of the text.

Bears: Market participants who think that a particular currency is going to depreciate, so they sell it (they take a short position). Hence, bearish.

Book: A foreign exchange trader's book is his or her current position (that is, whether he or she is long or short on particular currencies). Traders 'talk their books' when they speak from a particular position.

Bottomish: The situation when the foreign exchange market has fallen to such a low level that a floor is imminent.

Bulls: Market participants who think that a particular currency is going to appreciate, so they buy it (they take a long position). Hence, bullish.

Fall out of bed: A currency falls out of bed if it depreciates suddenly and substantially.

Hit on the screen: When a dealer is hit on the screen, he or she has to deal at the rate displayed on the screen, even though it may not be the prevailing market rate.

How are you left? A question asked by a dealer to find out whether the counterparty wants to do more business after a sizeable transaction has just been concluded.

One-sided market: This situation arises when market participants hold the same views about future market trends, and so the market will be dominated by buyers with few wanting to sell, or vice versa.

Overbought: A currency is overbought when it has been pushed up to a level that is viewed as being too high to be sustainable.

Parity: One-to-one. An exchange rate of AUD1 = CAD1 indicates parity between the Australian dollar and the Canadian dollar.

Position: To take a position is to take a stand, preparing to execute a deal to become long or short on a particular currency. It also refers to the trader's balance of a particular currency.

Short covering: Buying currencies to cover a short (sold) position.

Technical correction: A discontinuity or a reversal in the market trend without any apparent change in the fundamental factors affecting the market.

Technical rally: A sudden rise in a currency without any apparent fundamental change.

Technical reaction: A sudden depreciation of a currency after appreciation.

Thin market: A market characterised by low activity reflecting lack of demand for and supply of currencies.

Toppy: A market that has lost the tendency to rise, and so the next expected move is downwards.

Upside potential: The amount or percentage by which a currency is expected to rise. The opposite is downside risk.

Appendix 2.2

Types of trading orders

The following table contains a description of the types of orders on which a dealer may execute a customer's transactions:

Order	Description
Limit order	An exchange rate is set at which the order is to be executed.
At-the-market order	The transaction is to be executed immediately at the best available exchange rate.
Stop-loss order	Used to limit potential losses. It is triggered when a certain exchange rate prevails. The exchange rate at which it is executed is the next available.
Take-profit order	The opposite of the stop-loss order.
Open or good-until-cancelled order	Remains valid until it is executed or cancelled.
Good-until-specified-time order	Automatically cancelled if not executed by a certain time.
Day order	Valid until the end of the business day.
Night order	Valid until the start of the next business day.
Fill-or-kill order	All or any part of the order that can be filled at a specified exchange rate must be filled. If the remaining part is not filled within a short time, it is cancelled.
Any-part order	As above except that the remaining part is valid until filled or cancelled.
All-or-none order	At a specified rate either the whole order is filled or it is cancelled.
Either/or order	Two orders are given. If one is executed, the other is automatically cancelled.

CHAPTER

The balance of payments and the effective exchange rate

Introduction

The balance of payments records financial flows that affect financial variables such as interest and exchange rates. These variables, which in turn affect the balance of payments, are the raw material of corporate decision making. Since countries tend to indulge in multilateral rather than bilateral trade, the relevant exchange rate is the multilateral or effective exchange rate. Furthermore, since the balance of payments position is affected by the competitiveness of the economy, the relevant exchange rate is the real rather than the nominal rate.

The balance of payments statistics (and the related trade and indebtedness statistics) are important for decision making, because they allow financial managers to form opinions about the economic and financial conditions in the countries they do business with. For example, the structure of exports may indicate financial vulnerability if they are dominated by a single commodity or a small number of commodities. The position of the current account of the balance of payments is indicative of the ability of the underlying country to service its debt. And the debt statistics can be used to measure the vulnerability of the underlying country to financial crises and the country's ability to raise funds from financial markets.

Objectives

The objectives of this chapter are:

- To outline the structure of the balance of payments.
- To examine the Australian balance of payments statistics.
- To illustrate the relationship between the balance of payments and the foreign exchange market.
- To derive the supply of and demand for foreign exchange curves.
- To identify the factors affecting the balance of payments.
- To introduce the concepts of real and effective exchange rates.

3.1 Definition of the balance of payments

The **balance of payments** of a country is a systematic record of all economic transactions between the residents of the reporting country and the rest of the world over a specified period of time. Several terms in this definition need some explanation.

To start with, the term 'rest of the world' implies that the balance of payments is a record of multilateral **economic transactions**. The labelling of these transactions as 'economic' is essential to stress that what is recorded on the balance of payments are transactions involving the exchange of value. Such transactions include the transfer of ownership of goods, rendering services, and the transfer of money and other assets (predominantly financial assets).

The concept of **resident**, which applies to individuals and institutions, is indeed elusive as residence is often determined on the basis of an arbitrary rule of thumb. For example, overseas students and temporary workers living in Australia are not considered (for the purpose of compiling the Australian balance of payments statistics) as being resident in Australia but rather in their country of origin. The matter becomes more complicated in the case of multinational companies with foreign subsidiaries. The company itself is considered as being resident in the country in which it is incorporated, but its foreign subsidiaries are considered to be resident in the countries where they are located. The importance of the concept of 'residence' follows from the fact that the balance of payments does not record transactions between local residents. For example, transactions arising from trade between Victoria and New South Wales are not recorded on the Australian balance of payments. However, these transactions could affect, and give rise to, transactions that are recorded on the Australian balance of payments. When, for example, the federal government sells bonds to Australian citizens, this transaction will not be recorded on the Australian balance of payments. Nevertheless, this action may lead to an increase in interest rates on Australian dollar assets, which may induce Japanese insurance companies to buy them. If this takes place, the underlying transactions will be recorded on the Australian balance of payments.

An important point is that the balance of payments measures **flows**, not **stocks**. For example, the balance of payments records exports, imports and transfers, which are flows in the sense that they occur over the reporting period (a month, a quarter or a year). Moreover, it also records changes in the holdings of assets and liabilities (which are flows), not their levels (which are stocks). In this sense, the balance of payments of a country is similar to the statement of sources and uses of funds for a firm. The statement recording the levels (or stocks) of assets and liabilities at a particular point in time, which corresponds to a firm's balance sheet, is called the **balance of indebtedness**.

Finally, there is the problem of interpreting monthly or quarterly balance of payments figures. If the balance of payments or one of its components is prepared on a monthly or quarterly basis, then two points must be observed: (i) the figures may be annualised; and (ii) they may or may not be **seasonally adjusted**. The second point is more important, because seasonally unadjusted figures may obscure the true underlying trend. This arises from confusion between the seasonal behaviour and the change in trend. Several factors give rise to seasonality in the balance of payments figures. For example, receipts from tourism and air travel rise during the holiday season and decline otherwise.

3.2 Australian balance of payments statistics

The Australian balance of payments statistics are prepared by the **Australian Bureau of Statistics (ABS)** following international standards. The ABS defines the balance of payments as 'a statistical statement designed to provide a systematic record of Australia's economic transactions with the rest of the world'. The accounting entity is the Australian economy, so that the recorded economic transactions are conducted between the residents of Australia and the rest of the world. For this purpose, Australia's territory is defined to include the territories lying within its political frontiers and territorial seas and international waters over which it has exclusive jurisdiction.

The ABS defines the concept of 'resident' to encompass 'all persons residing in the territory of Australia on other than a temporary basis'. All persons living in Australia for 12 months or more are considered to be resident, with the exception of foreign diplomatic, consular, military and other government personnel, as well as foreign students studying in Australia. Resident enterprises include those engaged in the production of goods and services on a commercial or equivalent basis within the territory of Australia.

The Australian balance of payments consists (following the terminology of the ABS) of the **current account** and the **financial account**. The current account is the sum of (i) the **merchandise account** (or **trade balance**), (ii) **net services**, (iii) **net income** and (iv) **current transfers**. The financial account (alternatively known as the **capital account**) records official and non-official net financial flows. A balancing item representing errors and omissions is added to balance the balance of payments. Remember that the balance of payments is an accounting identity in which a surplus on the current account must be offset by a deficit in the financial account, and vice versa. Because of some missing information and errors in recording trade and financial flows, the two accounts do not match and this is why the **balancing item** (also known as **errors and omissions**) is added.

In the financial year 2001/2002, which ended on 30 June 2002, the Australian balance of payments recorded the following items, as reported by the ABS:

Item	AUD million
Exports	120 302
Imports	120 120
Merchandise account	182
Net services	1 027
Net income and current transfers	−19 705
Current account	−18 496
Financial account	17 077
Balancing item	1 419

The following observations can be made on these figures:

- The merchandise account, which is the difference between the exports and imports of visible goods (not services), was in surplus by about AUD182 million.
- Net services (including such items as shipping, airlines, insurance and consultancy) also recorded a surplus of AUD1027 million.
- Net income and current transfers recorded a deficit of AUD19 705 million. Net income is the difference between the income earned by Australian factors of production abroad and the income earned by foreign factors of production in Australia (these include wages, interest, dividends and rent). Current transfers include such items as foreign aid and transfers by expatriate workers.
- Hence, the current account recorded a deficit of AUD18 496 million.
- The deficit in the current account is partially offset by a surplus in the financial account of AUD17 077 million. The financial account records net financial flows resulting from the operations of the general government, the Reserve Bank of Australia (RBA) and the private sector's direct and portfolio investment operations.
- To balance the balance of payments, a balancing item is added. It is equal to the difference between the current account and the financial account (AUD1419 million).

Figure 3.1 shows the behaviour of the Australian current account, financial account and balancing item over nearly 30 years (quarterly figures).

Figure 3.1 Components of the Australian balance of payments (AUD million)

(a) Current account

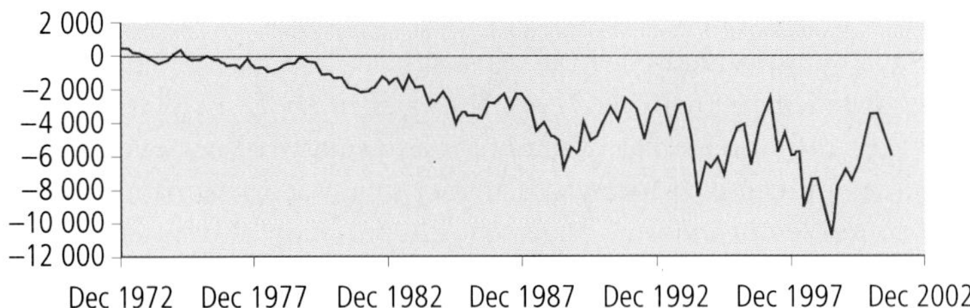

(b) Financial account

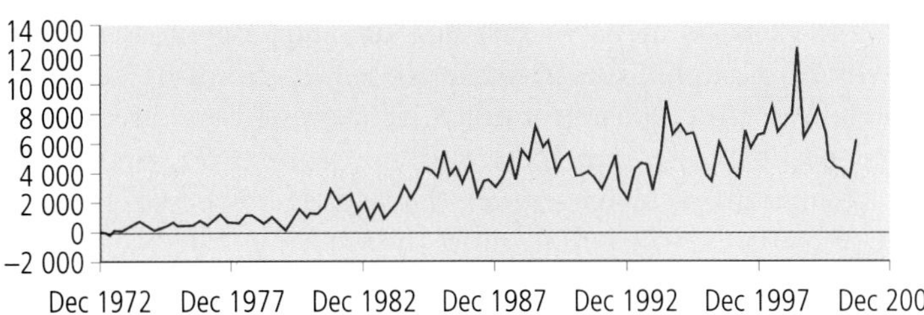

(c) Balancing item

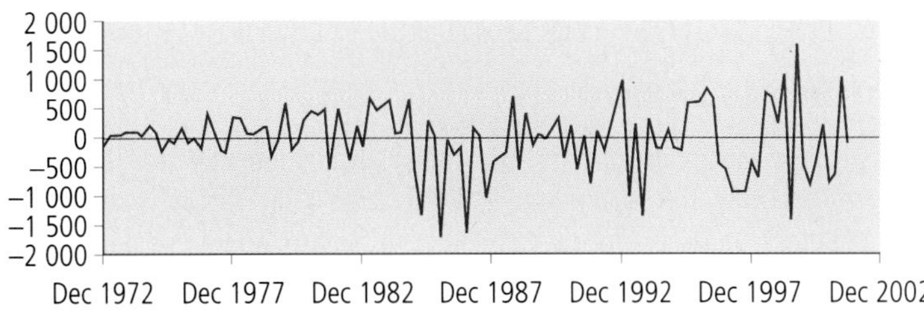

Source: ABS.

3.3 The balance of payments and the foreign exchange market

The demand for foreign exchange is **derived demand**. The demand for a particular currency is derived from the demand for the goods, services and assets denominated in that currency. Thus, the demand for the Australian dollar by foreigners arises because they want to buy Australian goods (for example, wine), services (for example, a flight on Qantas) or assets (for example, Victorian government bonds or an office block on Collins Street in the central business district of Melbourne). By definition, the demand for the Australian dollar is equivalent to the supply of foreign currencies. In general, the demand for a foreign currency is identical to the supply of the domestic currency, and vice versa.

The relationship between the balance of payments and the foreign exchange market arises because the transactions involving trade and capital flows (which are recorded on the balance of payments) give rise to demand for and supply of currencies. Transactions in the market for goods and services (such as imports and exports) give rise to demand for and supply of foreign currencies, respectively. Equivalently, these transactions lead to the supply of and demand for the domestic currency, respectively. Transactions in financial markets (which are recorded on the financial account) also lead to demand for and supply of currencies. The sale of domestic securities and the purchase of foreign securities give rise to demand for foreign currencies (supply of the domestic currency). Conversely, the purchase of domestic securities and the sale of foreign securities give rise to demand for the domestic currency (supply of foreign currencies).

The relationship between the balance of payments and the foreign exchange market is therefore obvious. For each transaction on the foreign exchange market there is a corresponding entry on the balance of payments. For the purpose of illustrating this relationship further we will examine the foreign exchange market from the perspective of the foreign currency, such that the exchange rate, S, is expressed in direct quotation (domestic/foreign). Three possible cases are illustrated in Figure 3.2, which plots the demand for and supply of foreign exchange curves (Df and Sf, respectively). In Figure 3.2(a), the foreign exchange market is in equilibrium at the exchange rate S_0, at which the supply of and demand for foreign exchange are equal. This is equivalent to saying that the balance of payments is in equilibrium (no surplus or deficit). In Figure 3.2(b), there is

RESEARCH FINDINGS

Modelling the balancing item in Australia's balance of payments accounts

Two Australian economists have made an attempt to model the balancing item in Australia's balance of payments accounts, motivated by the belief that it is generated by 'factual and systemic imperfections'. Fausten and Brooks[1] make the following interesting remarks about the interpretation of the balancing item:

- From the perspective of cross-border transaction activity, the emergence of the balancing item can be attributed to the fact that the records of financial and current account transactions are procured from fundamentally different sources.
- Non-zero entries for the balancing item illustrates the unsurprising fact that the real world is not a perfect place.
- If the balancing item is driven by a random process, time series observations on this item should have alternating signs. Persistent positive or negative values indicate systematic measurement and reporting errors.

An attempt was made to explain the balancing item in terms of the exchange rate (as a relative price that affects cross-border transactions) and the extent of economic openness, but the investigators failed to find any conclusive evidence. They concluded that the balancing item has been increasing in magnitude and volatility, violating with increasing frequency internationally agreed acceptability criteria for smallness. They also concluded that whatever the factors that are responsible for its occurrence, the balancing item does exert a non-trivial influence on the compilation of an important set of national statistics, the balance of payments accounts.

[1] D. K. Fausten and R. D. Brooks, 'The Balancing Item in Australia's Balance of Payments Accounts: An Impressionistic View', *Applied Economics*, 28, 1996, pp. 1303–11.

excess demand for foreign exchange at the exchange rate S_1, which is below the equilibrium exchange rate. This excess demand is equivalent to a deficit on the balance of payments. Finally, Figure 3.2(c) shows the case when there is excess supply of foreign exchange, which is equivalent to a surplus on the balance of payments. This occurs at the exchange rate S_2.

A question may arise here concerning the shape of the supply and demand curves for foreign exchange as shown in Figure 3.2. These curves are drawn like the demand and supply curves for any other commodity: the demand curve is downward-sloping, whereas the supply curve is upward-sloping. What we need here is an explanation for why the demand for foreign exchange falls and its supply rises as the exchange rate rises.

Figure 3.2 The relationship between the balance of payments and the foreign exchange market

(a) Equilibrium in the foreign exchange market and the balance of payments

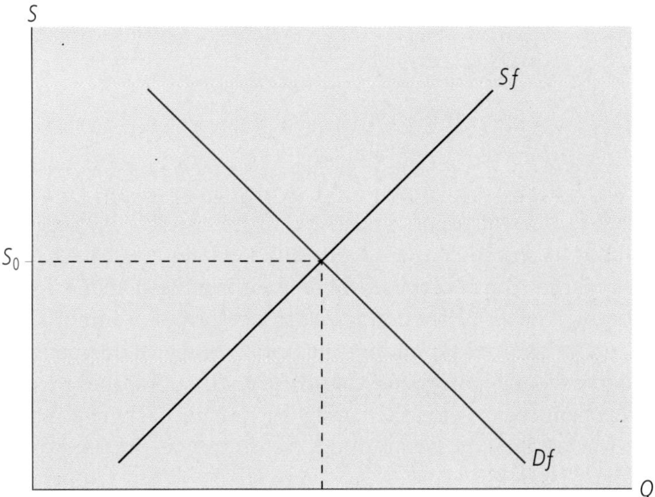

(b) Excess demand for foreign exchange and deficit in the balance of payments

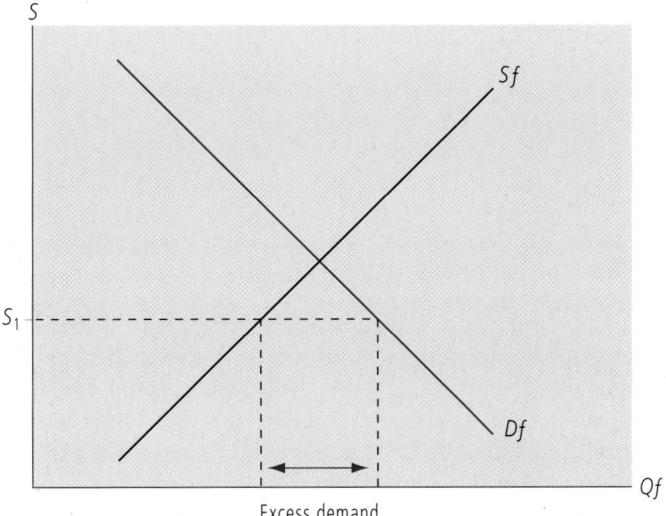

Continued...

(c) Excess supply of foreign exchange and surplus in the balance of payments

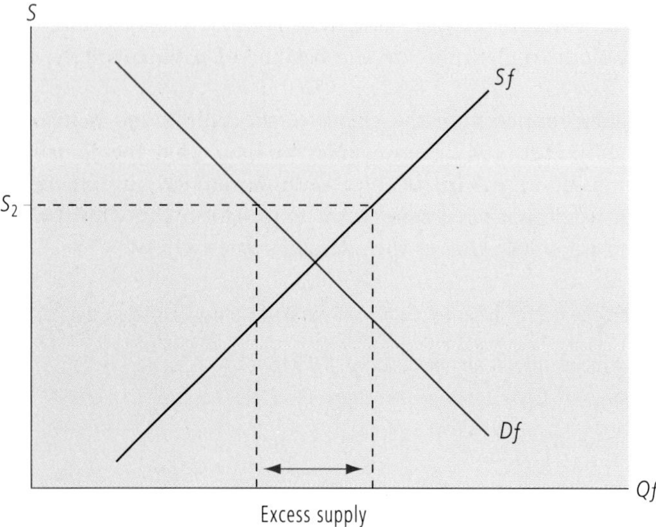

For this purpose, we shall derive the supply and demand curves by concentrating on exports and imports as the sources of supply and demand for foreign exchange. Given this simplifying assumption about its structure, the relationship between the balance of payments and the foreign exchange market can be restated by examining the demand for and supply of imports and exports. Let P_m^* and P_x^* be the foreign currency prices of imports and exports, respectively, and Q_m and Q_x be the corresponding quantities. Since the demand for imports leads to demand for foreign exchange, **import expenditure** ($P_m^*Q_m$) should be equivalent to the demand for foreign exchange. Likewise, the supply of foreign exchange is equivalent to **export revenue** ($P_x^*Q_x$). Bearing these points in mind, we can proceed to derive the demand for and supply of foreign exchange curves by considering what happens to import expenditure and export revenue as the exchange rate changes.

Deriving the demand for foreign exchange curve

The derivation of the demand for foreign exchange curve is based on the following equations:

$$Df = P_m^*Q_m \tag{3.1}$$

$$Q_m = a - bP_m \tag{3.2}$$

$$P_m = SP_m^* \tag{3.3}$$

These equations tell us the following. Equation (3.1) defines the demand for foreign exchange to be equal to import expenditure. Equation (3.2) is the demand for imports function, in which the quantity of imports depends (negatively) on the domestic currency price of imports. And Equation (3.3) relates the domestic price of imports to the foreign price of imports via the exchange rate (measured in direct quotation as the price of one unit of the foreign currency). Remember that imports are foreign goods consumed at home. So, what matters for the demand for imports is the price measured in domestic currency terms.

This depends on the foreign currency price and the exchange rate. A depreciation of the foreign currency (lower S) leads to a lower domestic price of imports, and vice versa.

Now assume that the demand for imports function is $Q_m = 15 - 0.6P_m$. Let us see what happens as the value of the exchange rate, S, varies from 1.00 to 1.60. Since we are examining the effect of changes in the exchange rate on the demand for imports, and consequently for foreign exchange, we will assume that the foreign currency price of imports is unchanged at 10. By using this demand function, we can construct the following table. It can be seen that as the exchange rate rises (the foreign currency appreciates), imports become more expensive (rising P_m), leading to a decline in the demand for imports (lower Q_m) and consequently in the demand for foreign exchange (Df).

S	P_m^*	P_m	Q_m	Df
1.00	10.00	10.00	9.00	90.00
1.05	10.00	10.50	8.70	87.00
1.10	10.00	11.00	8.40	84.00
1.15	10.00	11.50	8.10	81.00
1.20	10.00	12.00	7.80	78.00
1.25	10.00	12.50	7.50	75.00
1.30	10.00	13.00	7.20	72.00
1.35	10.00	13.50	6.90	69.00
1.40	10.00	14.00	6.60	66.00
1.45	10.00	14.50	6.30	63.00
1.50	10.00	15.00	6.00	60.00
1.55	10.00	15.50	5.70	57.00
1.60	10.00	16.00	5.40	54.00

Deriving the supply of foreign exchange curve

Consider now the supply side by using the following equations:

$$Sf = P_x^* Q_x \tag{3.4}$$

$$Q_x = c - dP_x^* \tag{3.5}$$

$$P_x^* = \frac{P_x}{S} \tag{3.6}$$

These equations tell us the following. Equation (3.4) defines the supply of foreign exchange to be equal to export revenue. Equation (3.5) is demand for exports function in which the quantity of exports demanded by foreigners depends (negatively) on the foreign currency price of exports. And Equation (3.6) relates the foreign price of exports to the domestic price of exports via the exchange rate. Remember that exports are domestic goods consumed by foreigners abroad. So, what matters for the demand for exports is the price measured in foreign currency terms. This depends on the domestic currency price and the exchange rate. A depreciation of the foreign currency (lower S) leads to a higher foreign currency price of exports, and vice versa.

Now assume that the demand for exports function is $Q_x = 20 - 1.5P_x$. Like the case of imports, let us see what happens as the value of the exchange rate varies from 1.00 to 1.60.

Since we are examining the effect of changes in the exchange rate on the demand for exports, and consequently for foreign exchange, we will assume that the domestic currency price of exports is unchanged at 10. By using this demand function, we can construct the following table. It can be seen that as the exchange rate rises (the foreign currency appreciates), exports become cheaper (falling P_x^*), leading to a rise in the demand for exports (higher Q_x) and consequently the supply of foreign exchange (higher Sf).

S	P_x	P_x^*	Q_x	Sf
1.00	10.00	10.00	5.00	50.00
1.05	10.00	9.52	5.71	57.14
1.10	10.00	9.09	6.36	63.64
1.15	10.00	8.70	6.96	69.57
1.20	10.00	8.33	7.50	75.00
1.25	10.00	8.00	8.00	80.00
1.30	10.00	7.69	8.46	84.62
1.35	10.00	7.41	8.89	88.89
1.40	10.00	7.14	9.29	92.86
1.45	10.00	6.90	9.66	96.55
1.50	10.00	6.67	10.00	100.00
1.55	10.00	6.45	10.32	103.23
1.60	10.00	6.25	10.63	106.25

Putting things together

Now let us put the supply and demand curves together, as shown in Figure 3.3 (for convenience, the exchange rate is measured on the horizontal axis). As you can see, the demand curve is downward-sloping and the supply curve is upward-sloping. When the value of the exchange rate is somewhere between 1.20 and 1.25, the foreign exchange market is in equilibrium, as the supply of and demand for foreign exchange are equal. By the same token, it means that the balance of payments is in equilibrium because export earnings are equal to import expenditure.

Figure 3.3 The demand for and supply of foreign exchange curves

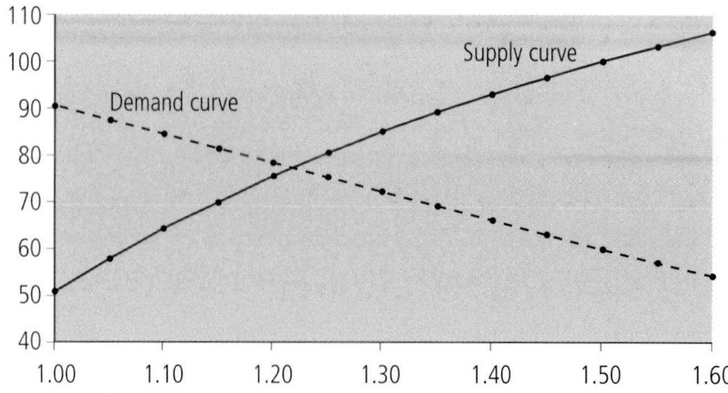

RESEARCH FINDINGS

Exchange rate pass-through

Exchange rate pass-through refers to the effect of changes in exchange rates on the prices of imports and exports as represented by Equations (3.3) and (3.6), respectively. Formally, it is measured by the extent to which exchange rate changes are transformed into changes in the destination-currency prices of traded goods. A full exchange rate pass-through materialises if the change in the exchange rate is reflected in the domestic currency price of imports and foreign currency price of exports. In this case, the effects of adverse changes in exchange rates are passed on entirely to the consumer.

An extensive amount of research has been done on exchange rate pass-through, because the concept triggers many practical questions. For example, the yen appreciated by some 34 per cent during the period January 1994 – April 1995, an episode that gave rise to the following questions:

- Why was there so little change in the US dollar price of imports of Japanese goods to the United States?
- Was the response simply delayed?
- Did Japanese exporters perceive the exchange rate change to be only temporary?
- Does incomplete pass-through imply that Japanese exporters reduced their profit margins on the exports to the United States?

Goldberg and Knetter found that the domestic currency prices of foreign goods do not respond fully to changes in exchange rates.[1] In another study of the effect of changes in exchange rates on Japanese exports, Kikuchi and Sumner identified incomplete pass-through as a transitory consequence of export pricing in currencies other than the yen.[2] They also found that the only long-run effect of the exchange rate on yen-denominated export prices operates through imported material prices.

The same phenomenon was observed in Australia when the Australian dollar depreciated significantly in 2001. Consumers in Australia did not feel any noticeable change in the prices of imported goods because, according to some market sources, Australian imports are predominantly denominated in Australian dollars from the source (this is actually what Microsoft does in dealing with Australian importers). Thus, the cost of the depreciation of the dollar was borne by the foreign manufacturers.

1 P. K. Goldberg and M. M. Knetter, 'Goods Prices and Exchange Rates: What Have We Learned?', *Journal of Economic Literature*, 35, 1997, pp. 1243–72.

2 A. Kikuchi and M. Sumner, 'Exchange Rate Pass-Through in Japanese Export Pricing', *Applied Economics*, 34, 2002, pp. 279–84.

3.4 Factors affecting the balance of payments position

The components of the balance of payments of a country (the current account and the financial account) at a particular point in time can be in equilibrium, deficit or surplus. They could also change from time to time: a surplus could turn into deficit, and vice versa. This change is caused by a number of factors. We start by discussing the factors affecting the current account.

Factors affecting the current account

Economic growth

It is plausible to postulate that imports are positively related to domestic income whereas exports are not, since the latter depend on foreign income. Thus, if a country has a higher growth rate than its trading partners, its demand for goods and services (including imported goods and services) will rise faster than the demand of its trading partners for its goods and services. Assuming that other factors are unchanged, it follows that the country with the higher growth rate will experience a deterioration in its current account.

A plausible question may arise here: why is it that countries like Japan and Singapore have simultaneously experienced rapid growth and current account surplus? The answer is simple: the current account position is determined by the combined effect of all the factors discussed in this section and not just by economic growth.

The exchange rate

The effect of the exchange rate on the current account emanates from the effect of changes in the exchange rate on prices and therefore the demand for domestic and foreign goods (exports and imports). When the exchange rate rises (the domestic currency depreciates), prices of exports in foreign currency terms fall whereas prices of imports in domestic currency terms rise. If the elasticities of demand for exports and imports are sufficiently high, then the demand for imports falls and the demand for exports rises, leading to an improvement in the current account. This chain of reasoning is the basis of using devaluation to correct a balance of payments deficit.

What happens to the current account position depends on the elasticity of demand for exports and imports. Let us deal with this proposition analytically by writing an equation for the current account position in foreign currency terms as

$$B^* = P_x^* Q_x - P_m^* Q_m \tag{3.7}$$

where $P_x^* Q_x$ is export revenue and $P_m^* Q_m$ is import expenditure. Changes in the exchange rate affect the foreign currency price of exports and the domestic currency price of imports (P_x^* and P_m). However, they do not (at least not directly) affect the domestic currency price of exports and the foreign currency price of imports (P_x and P_m^*). Both Q_x and Q_m will also be affected as implied by Equations (3.2) and (3.5). The elasticities of demand for exports and imports allow us to calculate the percentage change in the quantities of imports and exports resulting from exchange rate-induced changes in prices as follows:

$$\dot{Q}_m = e_m \dot{P}_m \tag{3.8}$$

$$\dot{Q}_x = e_x \dot{P}_x^* \tag{3.9}$$

where e_m is the elasticity of demand for imports, e_x is the elasticity of demand for exports and a dot implies the percentage change in the underlying variable. Thus, Equation (3.8) tells us that the percentage change in the quantity of imports is equal to the elasticity of demand for imports multiplied by the percentage change in the domestic currency price of imports. Equation (3.9) describes the corresponding export side.

Example

This example illustrates the proposition that the current account may improve as a result of domestic currency depreciation, depending on the elasticities of the demand for exports and imports. Let $Q_x = Q_m = 100$ and $P_x = P_m^* = 15$. If the initial level of the exchange rate is 1.50, the current account position in foreign currency terms can be calculated by using Equation (3.7) as follows:

$$B^* = 10 \times 100 - 15 \times 100 = -500$$

which shows that at this level of the exchange rate the current account is in deficit. Now consider what happens to the current account position when the exchange rate rises to 1.80 under two scenarios: (i) a low elasticity scenario when $e_x = -0.4$ and $e_m = -0.2$; and (ii) a high elasticity scenario when $e_x = -1.8$ and $e_m = -1.5$. The following calculations need to be performed:

- Calculating the values of $P_x^\star$ and P_m following the rise in the exchange rate (P_x and $P_m^\star$ will not be affected). For example, when $S = 1.80$, it follows that

$$P_x^\star = \frac{P_x}{S} = \frac{15}{1.80} = 8.3$$

- Calculating the values of Q_x and Q_m following the rise in the exchange rate, an outcome that depends on elasticities. Under the low-elasticity scenario, for example, the percentage change in the quantity of exports demanded is

$$\dot{Q}_x = e_x \dot{P}_x^\star = -0.4 \times -17 = 6.8\%$$

which means that the quantity of exports demanded after the change in the exchange rate is 106.8. Once we have the prices and quantities after the exchange rate change, the current account position can be calculated.

The full set of results is displayed in the following table. The results show that when elasticities are low, the rise in the exchange rate brings about a small rise in the quantity of exports and a small fall in the quantity of imports. Coupled with the price changes, export revenue falls more than import expenditure, resulting in a deterioration in the current account. On the other hand, when elasticities are high, export revenue rises more than import expenditure, leading to a surplus in the current account.

	Before the change	After (low)	After (high)
S	1.50	1.80	1.80
P_x	15	15	15
P_x^*	10	8.3	8.3
P_m^*	15	15	15
P_m	22.5	27.0	27.0
Q_x	100	106.8	130.6
Q_m	100	96	70
$P_x^*Q_x$	1000	886.4	1084.0
$P_m^*Q_m$	1500	1440	1050.0
B^*	−500.0	−553.6	+34.0

INSIGHT

What is the J-curve effect?

The effect of elasticities has an important implication for the dynamic response (that is, the response over time) of the current account to a depreciation of the domestic currency. The response is different in the short run (the period immediately following a depreciation) from what it would be in the long run (the period further into the future). This is because the elasticity of demand is lower in the short run than in the long run. It has been found that, for depreciation to have a positive effect on the current account, the sum of elasticities of the demand for imports and exports must be greater than unity (this is called the **Marshall–Lerner condition**). If this condition is satisfied in the long run, but not in the short run, there is a possibility that the current account may deteriorate even further in the short run before recovering in the long run.

This behaviour is described in the diagram below. At time t_1, the current account is in deficit. In the period immediately following the depreciation, the current account deteriorates, registering an even greater deficit. With the passage of time, elasticities increase and once the Marshall–Lerner condition is satisfied, the current account starts to improve. At t_2 the deficit reaches its highest value and from then onwards it starts to shrink. At time t_3, the deficit is eliminated and this is followed by the achievement of a surplus. The time path of the current account position resembles the letter J, and this is why this process is called the **J-curve effect**.

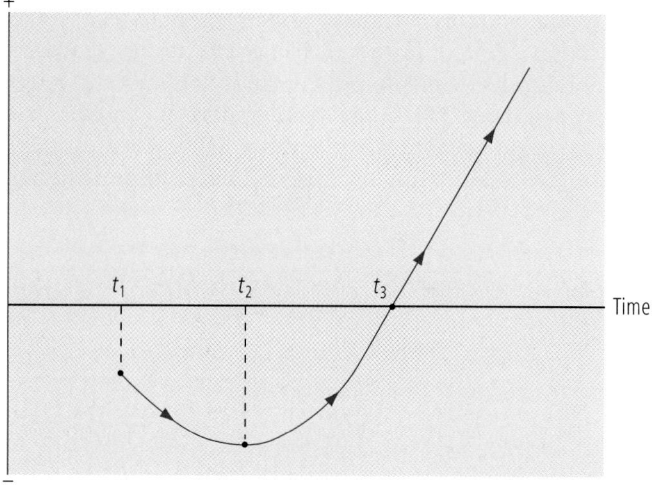

Inflation

A country that has a higher inflation rate than its trading partners suffers from a deterioration of the current account. This is because inflation erodes the competitive position of the economy by making domestic goods less competitive in foreign markets.

In the previous section the effect of the exchange rate on the current account was discussed by making the implicit assumption that the foreign price of imports, P_m^*, and the domestic price of exports, P_x, are unchanged. However, foreign and domestic inflation lead to increasing P_m^* and P_x, respectively. If the domestic inflation rate is higher than the foreign inflation rate, then P_x,rises faster than P_m^*. This leads to a decline in exports and an increase in imports and hence to a deterioration in the current account.

Example

Suppose that a country has a higher inflation rate (5 per cent) than its trading partner (zero) and let us assume that there is no change in the exchange rate (constant at 1.00). Consider the import side. At an inflation rate of 5 per cent the foreign currency price of imports increases by 5 per cent each period. Assuming the same demand function as before ($Q_m = 15 - 0.6P_m$), the quantity of imports and the demand for foreign exchange can be calculated as in the table below. Note that although there is no change in the exchange rate, foreign inflation reduces demand for imports and hence the demand for foreign exchange.

S	P^*_m	P_m	Q_m	Df
1.00	15.00	15.00	6.00	90.00
1.00	15.75	15.75	5.55	87.41
1.00	16.54	16.54	5.08	83.97
1.00	17.36	17.36	4.58	79.55
1.00	18.23	18.23	4.06	74.03
1.00	19.14	19.14	3.51	67.26
1.00	20.10	20.10	2.94	59.08
1.00	21.11	21.11	2.34	49.31
1.00	22.16	22.16	1.70	37.74
1.00	23.27	23.27	1.04	24.16
1.00	24.43	24.43	0.34	8.31

Consider now the export side. Because the domestic inflation rate is zero, the domestic currency price of exports is unchanged at 10. And because there is no change in the exchange rate, there is no change in the foreign price of exports. Hence, there is no change in the quantity demanded (assuming the demand function is $Q_x = 20 - 1.5P^*_x$) and no change in the supply of foreign exchange (export revenue). Thus, we have $P_x = 10$, $P^*_x = 10$, $Q_x = 5$ and $Sf = 50$.

If we calculate the current account as the difference between export revenue (unchanged at 50) and import expenditure (as shown in the previous table), we can plot its position with the passage of time. It is clear from Figure 3.4 that it improves with the deficit turning into surplus. The opposite result would be obtained if the domestic inflation rate were higher than the foreign inflation rate. If we assume that the domestic inflation rate is 5 per cent and the foreign inflation rate is zero, the behaviour of the current account will be as in Figure 3.5. Starting with a deficit, the position will deteriorate even further with the passage of time.

Figure 3.4 Improving current account (zero domestic inflation)

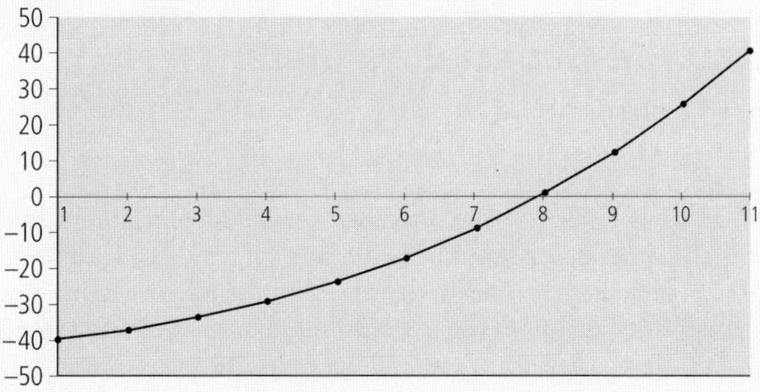

Continued...

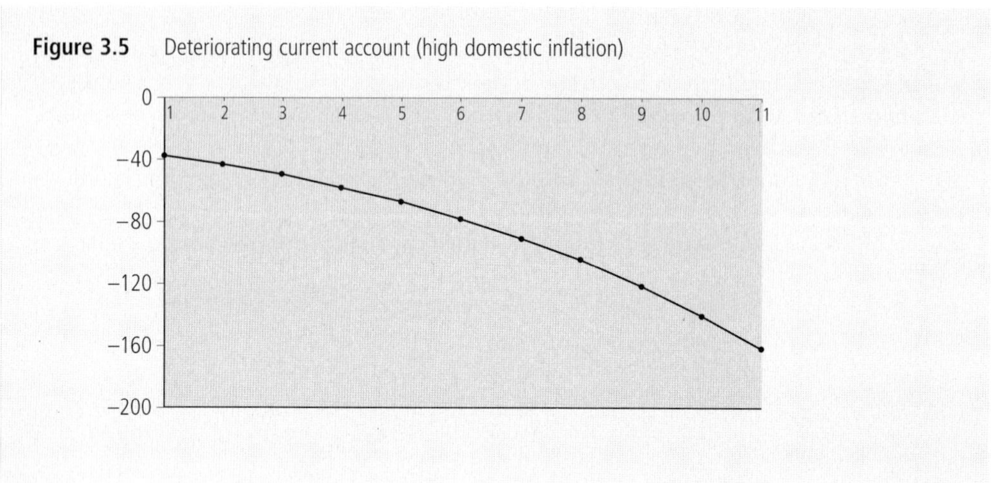

Figure 3.5 Deteriorating current account (high domestic inflation)

Trade restrictions

One reason for imposing trade restrictions, such as tariffs and quotas, is the desire to protect the current account. The effect of these restrictions is to reduce imports and hence produce an improvement in the current account, unless other countries retaliate by imposing similar restrictions, reducing the home country's exports. If such a trade war escalates, the effect is to reduce the volume of international trade, depriving countries of its benefits. Although the general global trend is towards free trade, problems arise every now and then because one country does not like the protectionist policies of another. The media often report trade negotiations aimed at resolving such clashes. In recent years, trade frictions arose between Europe and the United States over bananas and steel. The United States accused Europe of discriminating against its banana exports. Subsequently (in 2002), the United States imposed tariffs on steel imports from Europe and elsewhere.

The causation may go the other way round: trade restrictions may arise out of imbalances in the balance of payments. In its issue of 8 April 1997, the *Australian* reported that 'the second monthly rise in Japanese current account surplus, after four years of falls, has again raised the spectre of growing trade friction with the United States'. During a visit to Japan in April 1997, the then US Treasury Secretary, Robert Rubin, said that 'it is critical that Japan's current account surplus not rise again to a level that is detrimental to global growth, that causes trade frictions with Japan's trading partners and that could fuel protectionist sentiments around the world'.

Factors affecting the financial account

Now we turn to a discussion of the factors affecting the financial account position.

Taxes

Taxes that are imposed on capital gains and/or income from dividends and interest payments may adversely affect the financial account, because foreign investors no longer find it attractive to invest in the underlying country's securities. At the same time, some governments impose taxes to discourage borrowing by foreigners from domestic markets, with the ultimate objective of protecting the balance of payments. Recently, however, there has been a tendency to offer tax concessions to attract foreign direct investment.

Capital controls

Capital controls are imposed typically to deal with a chronic weakness in the balance of payments. Every country has at one time or another imposed capital controls to restrict capital outflows. However, the recent trend has been towards the removal of these controls. A famous example is the US voluntary credit restraint guidelines, which were made compulsory in 1965. They were introduced by the US government to restrict the amount of lending by US banks to foreign borrowers. The United Kingdom started to dismantle capital controls in 1979 with the advent of Margaret Thatcher's Conservative government. Australia started to abolish capital controls in the 1980s with the objective of liberalising and deregulating the financial system.

The expected change in the exchange rate

Investors choose to invest in foreign securities when they believe that the rate of return on this investment is higher than the rate of return on a comparable (in terms of risk, for example) domestic investment. The expected rate of change in the exchange rate, together with the nominal return in foreign currency (interest or dividends plus capital gains), determine the expected rate of return on the foreign security. If a currency is expected to appreciate, the expected rate of return on investment in securities denominated in that currency will be higher, attracting capital flows. Thus, a country's financial account will improve if that country's currency is expected to appreciate.

3.5 The real effective exchange rate

We have seen that changes in the exchange rate affect the price of imports in domestic currency terms and the price of exports in foreign currency terms. We have also seen that changes in domestic and foreign prices affect the competitiveness of exports and imports and therefore the current account. The exchange rate that has been used so far is the nominal bilateral exchange rate (that is, the exchange rate between two currencies unadjusted for changes in prices). We may combine the **nominal exchange rate** and prices to produce a variable, the **real exchange rate**, which affects the competitiveness of the economy and therefore the current account. Furthermore, because trade is normally conducted on a multilateral rather than a bilateral basis, it is more appropriate to consider the **multilateral exchange rate**, or **effective exchange rate**. Let us start with the concept of the (nominal) multilateral or effective exchange rate.

The multilateral (effective) exchange rate

The multilateral (effective) exchange rate is an index (measured relative to a base period) of a weighted average of the nominal exchange rates against the currencies of major trading partners. In one day of trading, the domestic currency may strengthen against one currency, weaken against another and stay unchanged against a third. If this is the case, then we cannot say anything definitive about the overall performance of this currency. It is not straightforward to tell, by observing individual bilateral exchange rates, whether the domestic currency has, in general, weakened or strengthened.

It is normally (but not necessarily) the case that when a currency depreciates or appreciates it tends to do so against all other major currencies, but at different rates. Thus, the domestic currency may depreciate by 2 per cent, 4 per cent and 5.3 per cent against three foreign currencies. The question now changes to the following: how weak is the domestic currency or by how much has it depreciated 'on average'? A simple answer to this question is that the currency depreciated by 3.8 per cent, which is the average of the three rates of depreciation. But this is not appropriate, because a country places more importance on changes in the exchange rates of its currency against the currencies of its major trading partners than against other currencies. For example, Australian policy makers are more concerned about changes in the exchange rate of the Australian dollar against the yen than against the Swiss franc, because Australia trades much more with Japan than with Switzerland.

There is a story that is relevant to this issue. When the pound depreciated to 1.47 against the US dollar in 1976, it was regarded as a disaster by the British authorities. The crisis resulted in a request for the intervention of the International Monetary Fund. Nine years later (at the end of February 1985) the pound depreciated against the US dollar to an all-time low of 1.03, but this was not treated with such alarm as in 1976. Why? The answer lies in the change of the pattern of British trade. In the 1970s the United Kingdom was doing a significant amount of trade with the United States. In the 1980s the pattern changed in favour of trade with Europe. So, more emphasis was placed on changes in the exchange rate of the pound against European currencies.

The implication of the previous discussion is that the effective exchange rate should reflect the geographical distribution of trade. This means that the effective exchange rate should be calculated as a weighted average of the bilateral exchange rates. As such, it summarises the information contained in many of the bilateral exchange rates of a particular currency in order to measure the average value of this currency against others. Because individual bilateral exchange rates are measured in different units, the data is scaled and the units are removed by calculating the **exchange rate relatives** measured as the ratio of a bilateral exchange rate in a particular period of time to its value in the base period. The effective exchange rate is then calculated as a weighted average of the exchange rate relatives. At time t, the effective exchange rate, E_t, of a currency against m other currencies is basically calculated as

$$E_t = \sum_{i=1}^{m} w_i V_{i,t} \tag{3.10}$$

where w_i is the weight assigned to currency i, and $V_{i,t}$ is the exchange rate relative of currency i at time t such that

$$V_{i,t} = \frac{S_{i,t}}{S_{i,0}} \tag{3.11}$$

which is normally expressed in percentage terms by multiplying it by 100. There are several issues associated with the implementation of Equation (3.10). These issues are discussed below in turn.

Determination of the weights

A weight W_i is assigned to currency i, more precisely to the exchange rate relative of the exchange rate of the domestic currency (or the currency for which the effective exchange rate is calculated) against currency i. This weight should reflect the contribution of the country of currency i to the home country's foreign trade. But trade means exports and imports and so this contribution may pertain to exports, imports or total trade. If the weights reflect export shares, then

$$w_i = \frac{X_i}{\sum_{i=1}^{m} X_i} \tag{3.12}$$

where X_i is the value of domestic exports to country i. In this case, we have the **export-weighted effective exchange rate**. Likewise, if the weights reflect import shares then

$$w_i = \frac{M_i}{\sum_{i=1}^{m} M_i} \tag{3.13}$$

where M_i is the value of imports from country i. In this case, we have the **import-weighted effective exchange rate**. Finally, if the weights reflect trade shares, then

$$w_i = \frac{X_i + M_i}{\sum_{i=1}^{m} X_i + M_i} \tag{3.14}$$

in which case we have the **trade-weighted effective exchange rate**.

Export, import and trade weights can be obtained from the geographical distribution of trade as published in the IMF's *Directions of Trade Statistics*. These statistics show, for each country, the destination of exports (where they go) and the origin of imports (where they come from). Obviously, export weights and import weights are different and this is why the export-weighted, import-weighted and trade-weighted effective exchange rates have different values. It is normally the case that export weights are more appropriate for developed countries with diversified exports, whereas import weights are more appropriate for developing countries with a high concentration of exports. For countries like Australia, which has significant two-way trade with the rest of the world, trade weights are more appropriate.

Another important point is the following. Implicit in Equation (3.10) is the assumption that the sum of the weights is equal to one. This means that if a country is involved in international trade with one hundred countries, the effective exchange rate of that country's currency must be calculated from the bilateral exchange rates of one hundred currencies. However, it is normally the case that each country has major trading partners with which it does the bulk of its trade. It makes a lot of sense, both for methodological and practical reasons, to use only the currencies of the major trading partners to calculate the effective exchange rate of the domestic currency. In this case, we use the normalised rather than the actual weights, the $w_i^{\star}$'s. The **normalised weights** are calculated as

$$w_i^{\star} = \frac{w_i}{\sum_{i=1}^{m} w_i} \tag{3.15}$$

which means that they are obtained by dividing each individual weight by the sum of the weights.

Arithmetic versus geometric averages

Equation (3.10) shows that the effective exchange rate is measured as a weighted arithmetic average of the exchange rate relatives. It is well known that the geometric average (or mean) has better mathematical properties than the arithmetic average, particularly in representing rates of change. It may be more appropriate, therefore, to calculate the effective exchange rate as a geometric weighted average of the exchange rate relatives, in which case the effective exchange rate is calculated as

$$E_t = \prod_{i=1}^{m} \left(V_{i,t}\right)^{w_i} = \left(V_{1,t}\right)^{w_1} \left(V_{2,t}\right)^{w_2} \ldots \left(V_{m,t}\right)^{w_m} \tag{3.16}$$

Exchange rate changes and domestic inflation

During the period extending between mid-1999 and mid-2001 the Australian dollar depreciated by nearly 16 per cent on a trade-weighted basis, which resulted in a 19.7 per cent rise in import prices. Yet consumer prices rose by only 9.4 per cent. This has led to the view that the effect of exchange rate changes on inflation has become rather muted.

If this is good news, then the bad news is that appreciation of the dollar would not be accompanied by a fall in the prices consumers pay for imported goods. One reason for this is that retailers try to rebuild their margins when the domestic currency appreciates and when economic growth picks up. Neither the appreciation nor the depreciation effect is passed on completely to the consumer.

Equation (3.16) tells us that the effective exchange rate is calculated as the product of the exchange rate relatives raised to a power equivalent to the assigned weight.

Cross exchange rates

Implicit in Equation (3.10) is the assumption that the bilateral exchange rates are between the domestic currency (or the currency for which we want to calculate the effective exchange rate) and other currencies. If, however, exchange rates are expressed in terms of a numeraire, such as the US dollar, then the exchange rates against the domestic currency must be first calculated as cross rates. The cross exchange rates can be used to calculate the exchange rate relatives and implement Equation (3.10).

Direct and indirect quotations

The effective exchange rate can be calculated from bilateral exchange rates expressed in direct or indirect quotations. If the exchange rates are expressed in indirect quotations, as the foreign currency price of one unit of the domestic currency, then a rise in the value of the effective exchange rate indicates an appreciation of the domestic currency, and vice versa. Alternatively, if the exchange rates are expressed in direct quotation, then it is the other way round. Normally, the first procedure is used because changes in the effective exchange rate become easier to understand.

Changing the weights

As the pattern of trade changes, the structure of the weights used to calculate the effective exchange rate must also change such that heavier weights are assigned to the currencies of the countries with which trade has expanded, and vice versa. The (trade) weights used by the RBA to calculate the Australian dollar's effective exchange rate are reviewed periodically. For example, the weights were revised in October 2001 to reflect the increasing trade with China and Korea at the expense of traditional trading partners such as the United Kingdom.

Example

In this example we calculate the (nominal) effective exchange rate of the Australian dollar against the currencies of Australia's three most important trading partners: Japan (the yen), the United States (the dollar) and Europe (the euro). We will use the same trade weights that are used by the RBA to calculate the dollar's effective exchange rate: yen (0.177), US dollar (0.154) and euro (0.119). Consider the following information about the bilateral exchange rates against the US dollar at the end of January 1999 and the end of January 2002.

Exchange rate	January 1999	January 2002	Percentage change
JPY/USD	113.16	132.80	17.4
AUD/USD	1.5746	1.9507	23.9
EUR/USD	0.8615	1.1329	31.5

The table shows that the US dollar appreciated against the other three currencies in varying degrees. Since we are interested in calculating the effective exchange rate of the Australian dollar rather than the US dollar, we need to calculate the bilateral exchange rates against the Australian dollar in indirect quotation. For this purpose we utilise the formula for calculating the cross rates (Equation (2.11)) to get the results shown in the table below. We can see that the Australian dollar appreciated against the euro, while depreciating against the US dollar and the yen. The table also shows the exchange relatives measured in percentage terms.

Exchange rate	January 1999	January 2002	Percentage change	Exchange rate relative
JPY/AUD	71.87	68.08	−5.3	94.73
USD/AUD	0.6351	0.5126	−19.3	80.72
EUR/AUD	0.5471	0.5808	6.1	106.15

The next step is to calculate the normalised weights, which can be done by dividing the original weights by their sum (0.45). The original and normalised weights are shown in the following table:

Exchange rate	Original weight	Normalised weight
JPY/AUD	0.177	0.393
USD/AUD	0.154	0.342
EUR/AUD	0.119	0.264

Now we are ready to calculate the effective exchange rate. By using an arithmetic mean we get

$$0.393 \times 94.73 + 0.342 \times 80.72 + 0.264 \times 106.15 = 92.95$$

which implies that the Australian dollar depreciated by 7.05 per cent in effective terms. Alternatively, we can calculate the effective exchange rate as a geometric mean as follows

$$(94.73)^{0.393}(80.72)^{0.342}(106.15)^{0.264} = 92.42$$

which is not much different from the rate calculated as an arithmetic mean.

What does the Reserve Bank do in practice?

We have so far discussed the general principles for the calculation of the effective exchange rate. In practice the RBA calculates a nominal effective exchange rate called a **trade-weighted index (TWI)**. As the name implies, the index is calculated on the basis of the (bilateral) trade shares of Australia's major trading partners. Until October 1988 the TWI was calculated as an arithmetic weighted average, but since then the RBA has shifted to using a geometric weighted average. Major trading partners are those accounting for at least 90 per cent of Australia's trade (exports plus imports). The weights are revised annually to reflect or account for changes in the pattern of trade. Figure 3.6 portrays the behaviour of the TWI over a long period of time.

Figure 3.6 The RBA's trade-weighted index, January 1970 = 100

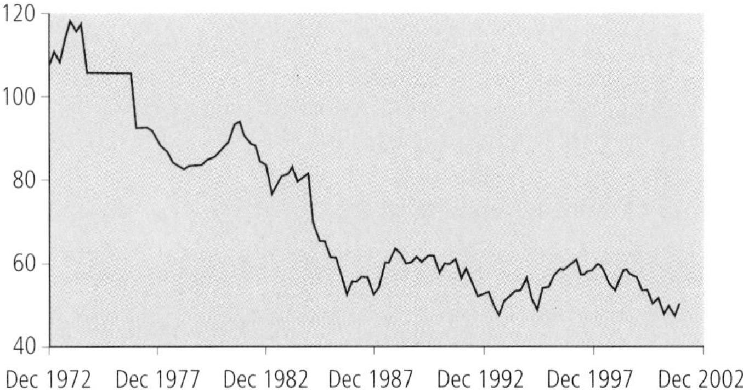

The real exchange rate

The real exchange rate is the nominal exchange rate adjusted for differences in prices or inflation. It is therefore a measure of the purchasing power of currencies in foreign markets. This makes it the relevant rate for measuring the competitiveness of the economy. For a bilateral exchange rate, $S(x/y)$, the real exchange rate, $Q(x/y)$, is calculated as

$$Q(x/y) = S(x/y)\left[\frac{P_y}{P_x}\right] \tag{3.17}$$

where P_y and P_x are the price levels of the countries whose currencies are y and x, respectively. Note that a rise in the real exchange rate Q (real appreciation of y) results from a rise in the nominal rate S (nominal appreciation of y) and/or a rise in the price level in the country whose currency is y (that is, P_y). Both a higher nominal exchange rate and a higher price level erode the competitiveness of the economy. Figure 3.7 displays the behaviour of the Australian dollar's real effective exchange rate.

Just as the nominal effective exchange rate can be calculated from the nominal bilateral exchange rates, the real effective exchange rate can be calculated from the real bilateral exchange rates. Hence

$$Q_t = \sum_{i=1}^{m} w_i\left(\frac{Q_{i,t}}{Q_{i,0}}\right) \tag{3.18}$$

or

$$Q_t = \prod_{i=1}^{m}\left(\frac{Q_{i,t}}{Q_{i,0}}\right)^{w_i} \tag{3.19}$$

In addition to the problems associated with the calculation of the nominal effective exchange rate (choice of weights, etc.), there is the problem of choosing the appropriate price index. For example, should P_x and P_y be represented by the consumer price index, the wholesale price index, the GDP deflator or by another price index?

Figure 3.7 Real effective exchange rate of the Australian dollar (1995 = 100)

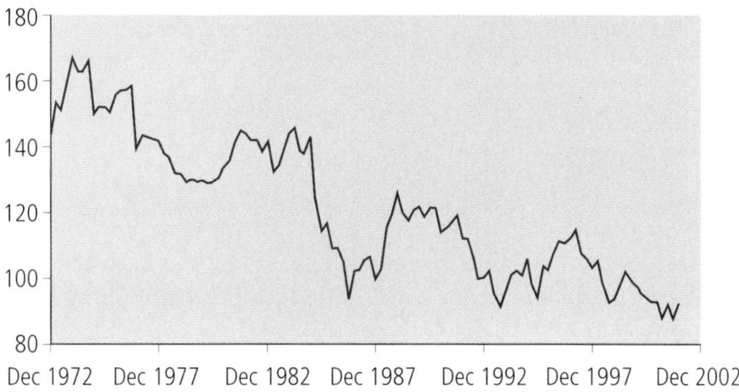

Example

This is an extension of the previous example of calculating the nominal effective exchange rate. To calculate the real exchange rates we need the price levels in the respective countries (areas in the case of the euro). The price levels (measured by the consumer price indices) at the end of January 1999 and the end of January 2002 were as follows:

Country	January 1999	January 2002	Percentage change
Australia	104.41	115.97	11.1
Japan	102.33	99.89	−2.4
United States	107.80	116.20	7.8
Europe	108.80	114.30	5.1

The table shows that Australia experienced a higher inflation rate than the other countries (Japan in fact experienced deflation or falling prices). Because we are using January 1999 as a base period, we need to re-base the price indices to this period, which means giving the price levels a value of 100 in the base period and adjusting the price levels in January 2002 accordingly. This is easy to do: the price level in January 2002 is divided by the price level in January 1999 and then multiplied by 100. We can subsequently calculate the price ratios relative to Australia by dividing the price level in each country by the price level in Australia. This operation gives the following results:

Country	January 1999	January 2002	Price ratio (January 2002)
Australia	100	111.1	—
Japan	100	97.6	0.878
United States	100	107.8	0.970
Europe	100	105.1	0.946

Continued...

We are now in a position to calculate the bilateral real exchange rates by using Equation (3.17), by multiplying the nominal rate by the price ratio. Naturally, the values of the nominal and real exchange rates should be equal in the base period. The results of this operation are as follows:

Exchange rate	Real exchange rate (January 1999)	Real exchange rate (January 2002)	Percentage change
JPY/AUD	71.87	59.82	−16.8
USD/AUD	0.6351	0.4974	−21.7
EUR/AUD	0.5471	0.5492	0.4

This shows that the Australian dollar depreciated in real terms against the yen and US dollar but appreciated slightly against the euro. The difference between nominal and real changes in the three exchange rates is accounted for by changes in prices (that is, differences in inflation).

To calculate the real effective exchange rate of the Australian dollar against the three currencies, we need the weights and the real exchange rate relatives. The latter can be calculated from the previous table by dividing the values of the real exchange rates in January 2002 by their values in January 1999 and multiplying by 100. Hence we have:

Exchange rate	Real exchange rate relatives	Normalised weights
JPY/AUD	83.23	0.393
USD/AUD	78.32	0.342
EUR/AUD	100.37	0.264

The real effective exchange rate is calculated as

$$0.393 \times 83.23 + 0.342 \times 78.32 + 0.264 \times 100.37 = 86.08$$

which implies that the Australian dollar depreciated by 13.9 per cent in real effective terms, which is more than the nominal depreciation. Alternatively, we can calculate the real effective exchange rate as a geometric weighted average as follows

$$(83.23)^{0.393}(78.32)^{0.342}(100.37)^{0.264} = 85.65$$

which is again not much different from the rate calculated as an arithmetic mean.

RESEARCH FINDINGS

The real effective exchange rate and the trade balance

We have previously considered the relationship between the exchange rate and the current account. What matters for the current account is not a particular bilateral exchange rate, but rather the effective exchange rate, because countries deal with a large number of trading partners. And because inflation does affect the foreign currency prices of exports and the domestic currency prices of imports, what matters in this case is the real rather than the nominal effective exchange rate. Hence, studies examining the effect of currency appreciation and depreciation on the trade balance or the current account are based on the real effective exchange rate.

Bahmani-Oskooee examined the effect of changes in the real effective exchange rates of a number of Middle-Eastern countries on the trade balance by estimating a relationship of the form [1]

$$(m/x)_t = a + by_t + cy^*_t + dQ$$

which says that the ratio of imports to exports depends on three variables: domestic income, y; foreign income, y^*; and the real effective exchange rate, Q. By estimating this model statistically (using regression analysis) he concluded that real depreciation has a favourable long-term effect on the trade balance of most non-oil Middle-Eastern countries.

1 B. Bahmani-Oskooee, 'Nominal and Real Effective Exchange Rates of Middle Eastern Countries and Their Trade Performance', *Applied Economics*, 33, 2001, pp. 103–11.

Summary

- The balance of payments is a systematic record of all economic transactions between the reporting country and the rest of the world over a specified period of time. It records trade and financial flows, not stocks.
- The current account records current transactions involving trade in goods and services as well as current transfers.
- The financial account records changes in the levels of foreign assets and liabilities (capital flows).
- The Australian balance of payments statistics are prepared by the Australian Bureau of Statistics.
- The balance of payments is related to the foreign exchange market because the transactions involving trade and capital flows, which are recorded on the balance of payments, give rise to demand for and supply of currencies. For each transaction on the foreign exchange market, there is a corresponding entry on the balance of payments.
- The supply and demand curves for foreign exchange can be derived from the supply and demand for exports and imports.
- Factors affecting the current account include: (i) economic growth; (ii) the exchange rate; (iii) inflation; and (iv) trade restrictions. Factors affecting the financial account include: (i) taxes; (ii) capital controls; and (iii) the expected change in the exchange rate.
- The effective exchange rate is an index of a weighted average of the bilateral exchange rates against the currencies of major trading partners.
- Several issues are associated with the calculation of the effective exchange rate: (i) determination of the weights; (ii) using arithmetic or geometric weighted averages; (iii) calculating the cross exchange rates; (iv) using direct versus indirect quotations; and (v) changing the weights over time.
- The Reserve Bank of Australia calculates a trade-weighted index for the Australian dollar as a geometric weighted average of the exchange rates against a large number of currencies that reflect Australia's trade pattern.
- The real exchange rate is the nominal exchange rate adjusted for differences in inflation.

Key terms

Australian Bureau of Statistics (ABS) 69
balance of indebtedness 69
balance of payments 68
balancing item 70
capital account 70
capital controls 83
current account 70
current transfers 70
derived demand 71
economic transactions 68
effective exchange rate 83
errors and omissions 70
exchange rate pass-through 77
exchange rate relatives 84
export revenue 74
export-weighted effective exchange rate 85
financial account 70
flows 69
import expenditure 74
import-weighted effective exchange rate 85
J-curve effect 80
Marshall–Lerner condition 80
merchandise account 70
multilateral exchange rate 83
net income 70
net services 70
nominal exchange rate 83
normalised weights 85
real exchange rate 83
resident 69
seasonally adjusted 69
stocks 69
trade balance 70
trade-weighted effective exchange rate 85
trade-weighted index (TWI) 88

MaxMARK

MAXIMISE YOUR MARKS! There are 30 interactive questions for this chapter available online at **www.mhhe.com/au/moosa2e**

Review questions

1. What are economic transactions? Give some examples of international economic transactions.
2. Describe a situation in which a transaction that affects the Australian balance of payments is not recorded on it.
3. What is the difference between stocks and flows? Consider the major items on the Australian balance of payments and explain why they are flows, not stocks.
4. Why is it that seasonally unadjusted balance of payments figures may be misleading? What is the problem with seasonally adjusted figures? Identify the balance of payments items that may exhibit seasonal behaviour.
5. What is the balancing item in the balance of payments?
6. In 1992 the International Monetary Fund reported 'a significant deterioration in the coverage and quality of balance of payments data'. Why is this the case, despite the increased sophistication of data collection and refinement methods?
7. In theory, the sum of all countries' capital outflows and inflows must be zero. This, however, is not what is implied by the reported balance of payments statistics. Why is this the case?
8. Describe the relationship between the balance of payments and the foreign exchange market.
9. Why does the demand for foreign exchange rise when the exchange rate (expressed as domestic/foreign) falls?
10. 'The effect of a rise in the exchange rate on the supply of foreign exchange is ambiguous.' Explain.

11 Why do countries that have higher growth rates than their trading partners experience deteriorating current accounts?

12 It is sometimes stated that one of the most important consequences of inflation is its adverse effect on the current account. How does this adverse effect develop?

13 Capital controls are typically imposed to protect the balance of payments. Can we then say that the abolition of capital controls in Australia in the early 1980s led to the deterioration of the Australian balance of payments?

14 Why do countries normally worry more about the effective exchange rates rather than the bilateral exchange rates of their currencies? Why do they also worry more about real than nominal exchange rates?

15 Why did the Reserve Bank of Australia decide in 1988 to calculate the TWI of the Australian dollar as a geometric average rather than an arithmetic average?

Problems

1 The demand for imports function is

$$Q_m = 40 - 1.5P_m$$

Calculate the quantity of imports if the foreign price of imports is 10 and the exchange rate (domestic/foreign) is 1.20. Also calculate the demand for foreign exchange at this rate.

2 Using the same demand function as in Problem 1, calculate the quantity of foreign exchange demanded at the following values of the exchange rate: 1.30, 1.40, 1.50, 1.60, 1.70 and 1.80. Plot the demand for foreign exchange curve.

3 The demand for exports function is

$$Q_x = 40 - 2P_x^*$$

Calculate the quantity of exports if the domestic price of exports is 10 and the exchange rate (domestic/foreign) is 1.20. Also calculate the supply of foreign exchange at this rate.

4 Using the same supply function as in Problem 3, calculate the quantity of foreign exchange supplied at the following values of the exchange rate: 1.30, 1.40, 1.50, 1.60, 1.70 and 1.80. Plot the supply of foreign exchange curve and comment on its shape.

5 Use the demand and supply functions specified in Problems 1 and 3 to demonstrate the effect of inflation on the current account, starting from a situation in which $P_m^* = P_x = 10$ and $S = 1.20$. Plot the path of the current account over several periods of time when:

(a) The domestic and foreign inflation rates are 0 and 5 per cent, respectively.

(b) The domestic and foreign inflation rates are 5 and 0 per cent, respectively.

6 You are given the following information:

Quantity of imports	200
Foreign currency price of imports	20
Exchange rate	1.50

Calculate the foreign currency and domestic currency values of imports. What will happen if the exchange rate falls to 1.20, assuming that the value of the elasticity of demand for imports is −0.5? What if the elasticity is −2.5?

7 You are given the following information:

Quantity of exports	500
Domestic currency price of exports	10
Exchange rate	1.20

Calculate the foreign currency and domestic currency values of exports. What will happen if the exchange rate falls to 0.90, assuming that the value of the elasticity of demand for exports is −0.2? What if the elasticity is −1.8?

8 Assume that Australia trades mostly with two countries only, the United States and the United Kingdom, such that 70 per cent of the trade is conducted with the United States, 25 per cent with the United Kingdom and 5 per cent with the rest of the world. The exchange rates of the Australian dollar in August 1997 and June 2002 were as follows:

	August 1997	**June 2002**
AUD/USD	1.3541	1.7724
AUD/GBP	2.1533	2.5692

(a) Calculate the exchange rates in indirect quotation from an Australian perspective.
(b) Calculate the percentage rates of depreciation or appreciation of the Australian dollar against the two currencies. Comment on your results.
(c) Calculate the exchange rate relatives, using August 1997 as a base period.
(d) Calculate an unweighted effective exchange rate index, using August 1997 as a base period in which the index assumes the value of 100.
(e) Calculate the normalised trade weights.
(f) Calculate the trade-weighted effective exchange rate index. What is the rate of appreciation or depreciation of the Australian dollar in effective terms? Compare this result with that obtained in (b) and (d) above. Comment on your results.
(g) Recalculate the effective exchange rate as a weighted geometric average. Compare the results with the previous ones.

9 Using the information given in Problem 8, calculate the nominal effective exchange rate, using the bilateral exchange rates expressed in direct quotation. Compare the results with those obtained by solving Problem 8.

10 Use the information given in Problem 8 and assume that the price levels in August 1997 and June 2002 were as follows:

	August 1997	**June 2002**
Australia	100	110
United Kingdom	100	105
United States	100	104

(a) Calculate the real bilateral exchange rates.
(b) Calculate the rates of change in the real bilateral exchange rates.
(c) Calculate the real effective exchange rates of the Australian dollar, using the nominal effective exchange rates obtained by solving Problems 8 and 9.

CHAPTER

Exchange rate determination and related issues

Introduction

We have seen that fluctuations in exchange rates could bring about a total collapse of business firms. Identifying, observing and anticipating changes in the factors that affect exchange rates is therefore crucial for managerial decision making in the present environment of globalisation.

In this chapter we present the partial supply and demand model (also called the traditional flow model) as an explanation for the process of exchange rate determination, as well as some related issues. The model is partial in the sense that it considers trade and capital flows to determine the equilibrium exchange rate. In Chapter 3 we derived the curves for the demand for and supply of foreign exchange. In this chapter we consider the factors that cause these curves to shift and, consequently, the exchange rate to change. The related issues covered in this chapter are arbitrage, speculation and the determination of the bid-offer spread.

Objectives

The objectives of this chapter are:

- To present some stylised facts about the observed behaviour of exchange rates.
- To identify the factors that lead to changes in the supply of and demand for foreign exchange and, consequently, the exchange rate.
- To illustrate the effect of arbitrage and speculation on the supply of and demand for currencies.
- To explain how the bid-offer spread and the forward spread are determined.
- To examine the factors that affect the exchange rate of the Australian dollar as implied by the supply and demand model.

4.1 Some stylised facts about exchange rates

We start with some stylised facts (that is, empirical observations) about the actual behaviour of exchange rates and their relationship with other macroeconomic variables. The following stylised facts have been established in the international finance literature.

First, exchange rates appear to follow a **random walk** process. By 'random walk' it is meant that period-to-period changes in the exchange rate are random and unpredictable. This means that the level of the exchange rate tomorrow is as likely to be higher as it is to be lower than its level today. The bottom line is that it is difficult to predict the level of the exchange rate tomorrow and that the best forecast for tomorrow's level is today's level. An interesting analogy is that the best place to look for a drunken person abandoned under a tree the previous day is under that same tree. It is amazing to see how random numbers generated by a computer resemble the observed behaviour of exchange rates (try this for yourself).

Second, the spot and forward rates tend to move in the same direction and by approximately the same amount, particularly if the movements are large. The implication of this observation is that it is not advisable to use the forward rate to predict the spot rate expected to prevail in the future, in the sense that such prediction is unlikely to be better than what is provided by a random walk process (that is, using the most recent value as a forecast). We deal with this issue in Chapter 11.

Third, there is no close correspondence between movements in exchange rates and movements in domestic and foreign price levels. This proposition, which casts doubt on the theory of purchasing power parity, is more valid over a short rather than a long period of time. We deal with purchasing power parity in Chapter 9.

Fourth, there is only a weak general tendency for countries experiencing sharp deterioration in the current account to experience subsequent and consequent depreciation of their currencies. For a counter-example, the US dollar appreciated considerably during the period 1981–1985 while the current account was dipping further into the red (the same phenomenon could be observed in the early years of the new millennium). The empirical evidence on this issue is indeed mixed, but we must warn of the hazards of considering the effect of one factor, such as the current account, in isolation of other factors that change simultaneously.

Fifth, countries that experience rapid expansion of their money supplies also experience rapid depreciation of their currencies. The word 'rapid' must be emphasised here because this proposition seems to be valid for **hyperinflation** countries only (for example, Germany in the 1920s and most Latin American countries in the 1980s). This proposition is a prediction of the monetary model of exchange rate determination, which we examine in Chapter 9.

4.2 Factors affecting supply and demand in the foreign exchange market

In Chapter 3, we derived the supply and demand curves for foreign exchange from trade flows. The equilibrium exchange rate is determined like any other price by the intersection of the supply and demand curves. Figure 4.1 shows the demand for foreign exchange (or currency) curve, *Df*, and the supply curve, *Sf*. The quantity of foreign exchange traded, *Qf*, is measured on the horizontal axis. The exchange rate, *S*, which is measured on the vertical axis, is expressed in direct quotation as the domestic currency price of one unit of the foreign currency (and hence a higher level of *S* implies depreciation of the domestic currency). The intersection of the *Df* and *Sf* curves produces the equilibrium exchange rate, S_0.

Unlike the analysis of the last chapter, the analysis in this chapter does not restrict the sources of supply and demand for foreign exchange to exports and imports. Rather, it extends these sources to capital flows resulting from the buying and selling of financial assets. In other words, the sources of supply and demand are financial account as well as current account transactions.

With this situation in the background, the effect of any factor on the exchange rate is transmitted via shifts in the supply and demand curves. We will now consider these factors in turn, using a two-country model: a home country with a domestic currency and a foreign country with a foreign currency. For the purpose of this analysis, the terms 'foreign exchange' and 'foreign currency' will be used interchangeably. The effect of each factor on the exchange rate is considered by assuming that other factors are unchanged. This assumption, which is not consistent with what happens in reality (where all factors change at the same time), is essential for the purpose of the following exposition.

Figure 4.1 The equilibrium exchange rate

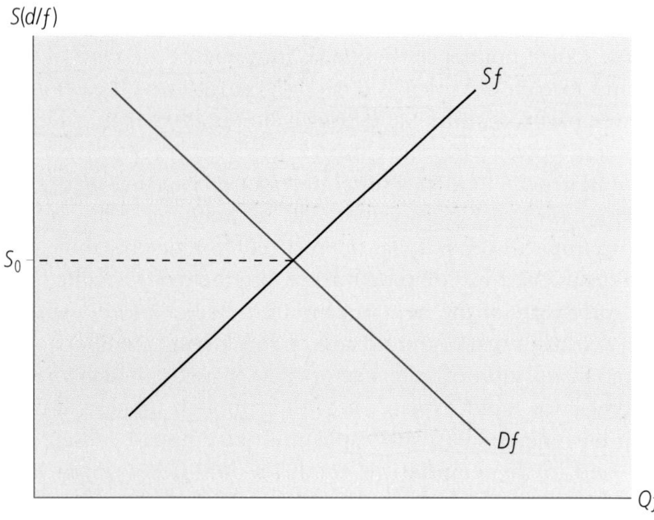

Relative inflation rates

We saw in Chapter 3 that if the domestic inflation rate is higher than the foreign inflation rate, domestic goods will, with the passage of time, become more expensive than foreign goods, leading to an increase in the demand for foreign goods and a decline in the demand for domestic goods. These changes are translated in the foreign exchange market into an increase in the demand for and a decrease in the supply of foreign currency. These changes are represented in Figure 4.2 by a shift of the demand curve to the right and a shift of the supply curve to the left. As a result, the exchange rate moves up from S_0 to S_1 (that is, the domestic currency depreciates). Thus, if a country has a higher inflation rate than its trading partners, its currency will depreciate.

Figure 4.2 The effect of a higher domestic inflation rate

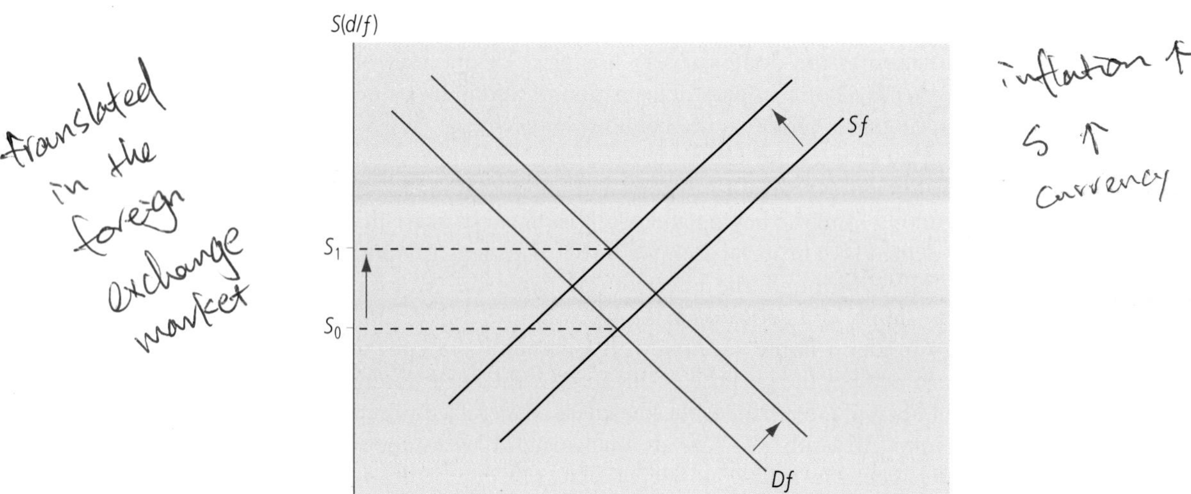

Depreciation of the world's second biggest currency

To start with, try to guess what the world's second biggest currency is. It could be the euro, the yen or the pound. In terms of trading on the foreign exchange market, yes, but not in terms of the amount of the currency issued. In terms of the amount issued, the second biggest currency, as *The Economist* claims, is frequent flyer points.[1] According to the estimates of *The Economist*, the number of outstanding unredeemed frequent flyer points worldwide was 8.5 trillion in early 2002. Valued at an average of 5.5 cents each, the value of the outstanding points is some USD468 billion, surpassed only by the value of US dollar notes and coins.

In a way, frequent flyer points are a currency because they can be used to buy airline seats and, to a lesser extent, other goods and services. Even if you are not convinced by this argument, the value of frequent flyer points can be explained in terms of what has been happening to the supply side, which exactly resembles what happens to a currency when it is in excess supply. Since 1995, the supply of frequent flyer points has increased at an average annual rate of 20 per cent per year, two and a half times as fast as the supply of dollars.

Since there are now too many points chasing too few available seats, the airlines are likely to respond by making free tickets hard to get, which is the same effect as depreciation. This process resembles the causal effect from monetary expansion to inflation to depreciation. The message, therefore, is 'spend your points while you can'.

[1]. 'Fly me to the Moon', *The Economist*, 4 May 2002, p. 62.

Relative interest rates

This factor is more commonly known as the *interest rate differential*. If the domestic interest rate rises relative to the foreign interest rate, domestic financial assets become more attractive than foreign financial assets. This results in a restructuring of portfolios, leading to capital flows out of foreign assets and into domestic assets. In the foreign exchange market, this translates into a decrease in the demand for and an increase in the supply of foreign exchange. The resulting shifts in the supply and demand curves, as shown in Figure 4.3, lead to a fall in the exchange rate from S_0 to S_1 (that is, an appreciation of the domestic currency). It is important to note that, while the effect of changes in relative inflation runs through the current account of the balance of payments, the effect of changes in interest rates runs through the financial account.

On the surface, this prediction is not consistent with the following empirical observation. We have at times observed the existence of triple-digit interest rates in some Latin American countries like Brazil. Yet the direction of capital flows has been out of these countries towards the United States and other countries that have single-digit interest rates. The explanation is simple. High interest rates reflect high expected inflation, which is the case in countries experiencing hyperinflation. While a high interest rate should on its own attract capital, higher expected inflation causes the underlying currency to depreciate, producing a lower expected rate of return. Thus, it may be more useful to consider the effect of changes in relative real interest rates, rather than nominal interest rates. The **real interest rate** is the **nominal interest rate** minus the expected inflation rate (the concept of the real interest rate is discussed in Chapter 11).

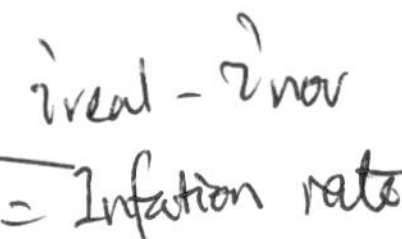

Relative growth rates

If the growth rate of domestic income is higher than that of foreign income, then imports grow faster than exports. In terms of the demand and supply functions described in Chapter 3, a rise in domestic and foreign incomes causes a rise in the demand for and supply of imports and exports, respectively, even with no change in prices. This consequently translates into shifts in the demand for and supply of foreign exchange curves. The demand for foreign exchange, therefore, grows faster than supply. This situation is represented in Figure 4.4 by a bigger shift in the demand curve than in the supply curve. The net effect is a rise in the exchange rate (a depreciation of the domestic currency).

Economic growth may also affect capital flows. Faster growth is normally associated with growing profitability and booming financial markets, which makes domestic assets more attractive for foreign investors, in which case there will be net capital inflows. The supply of foreign exchange will increase more than demand, leading to a fall in the exchange rate. This situation is shown in Figure 4.5.

Figure 4.3 The effect of a higher domestic interest rate

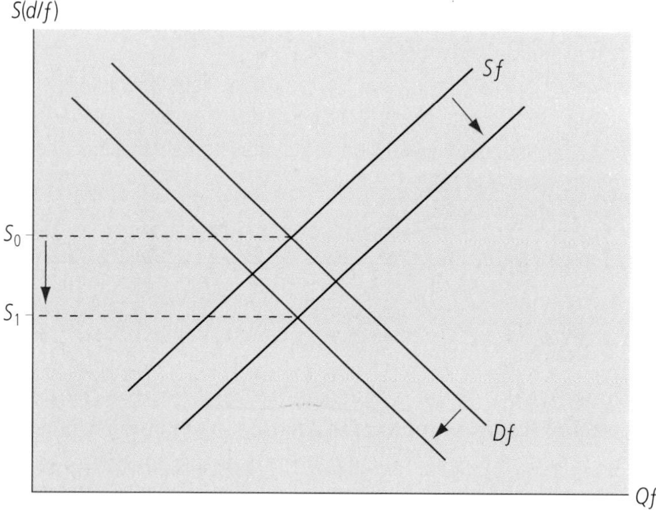

Figure 4.4 The effect of a higher domestic growth rate (current account)

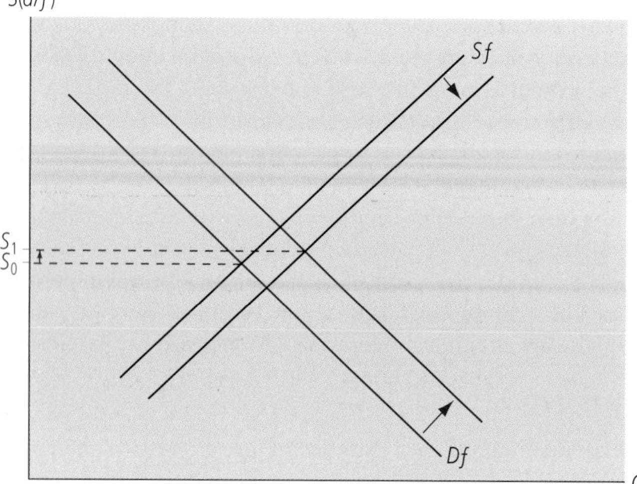

Figure 4.5 The effect of a higher domestic growth rate (financial account)

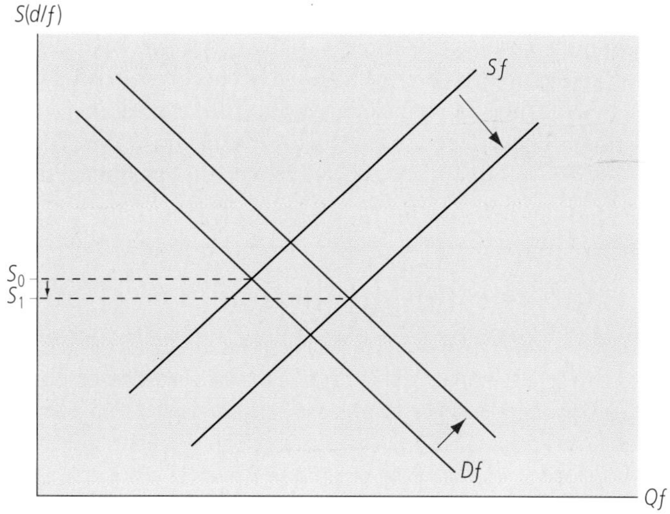

$S(d/f)$

Sf

S_0

S_1

Df

Qf

Capital flows and exchange rate predictive tools

IN PRACTICE

As the volume of cross-border investment activity grows, it is becoming the source of an increasing proportion of all foreign exchange transactions. While international trade has also expanded, its impact on the foreign exchange market has declined to the extent that it now accounts for no more than 1 per cent of all foreign exchange transactions. As a result, it is felt that the traditional explanatory factors (such as growth differentials, inflation differentials and interest rate differentials) are not adequate for explaining exchange rate movements.

Given the importance of cross-border capital flows in the exchange rate determination process, it seems that anyone wishing to find explanations for past movements in exchange rates or predict their future direction must examine capital flows. The Bank of New York has responded to this need by providing for its clients the world's first Internet-based interactive portfolio tool, the Interactive Portfolio Flow Monitor (IPFM), which is based on the daily net cross-border activity within the bank's global custody system. This tool makes it possible to chart net portfolio flows for a particular country or currency zone from three to 24 months, compare the flows with a selection of currency pairs and analyse the statistical relationships between them.

JP Morgan, a US investment bank, has developed two tools that are based on the same idea of emphasising portfolio flows. The first of these tools is the Liquidity and Credit Premia Index (LCPI), which tracks the global risk appetite. When global investors are in the mood to take on risk, cross-border capital flows dominate the balance of payments, with funds moving from low-yielding areas to high-yielding areas. When they are in a risk-averse mood, the opposite is true. Thus, the interest rate differential is unlikely to have an unambiguous impact on capital flows. The LCPI identifies the mood of global investors.

The second tool is the Sentiment and Flow Index (SFI), which is also based on the simple premise that currencies tend to overshoot or undershoot (that is, depart significantly upwards or downwards from their long-term trends). The index allows investors to identify instances when investors are too one-sided about the prospects of one particular currency. By identifying shifts in global risk appetite and extreme positioning in currencies, these tools allow the investor to predict short-run movements in portfolio capital flows.

The role of the government

Apart from **central bank intervention**, the government can affect the exchange rate by influencing, via macroeconomic policy, the three variables that we have considered so far: inflation, interest rates and growth. Moreover, the government can affect the supply of and demand for foreign exchange by imposing or abolishing trade barriers (such as **tariffs** and **quotas**) and taxes. The effect arises because tariffs and taxes change goods prices and the rates of return on financial assets. Hence, the positive effect on the

INSIGHT

Exchange rates and the budget deficit

The exchange rate determination model presented in this chapter seems to suggest the idea that a cut in the budget deficit leads to currency depreciation. This is because a lower budget deficit leads to lower interest rates and hence to a slowdown in capital inflows and currency depreciation. Some eminent economists seem to agree with this proposition, including Laurence Ball of Johns Hopkins University, Gregory Mankiw of Harvard University, Paul Krugman of Stanford University and Martin Feldstein of Harvard University. But central bankers seem to disagree with this view. Alan Greenspan, the chairman of the US Federal Reserve (the US central bank) is quoted as saying that a substantial cut in the US budget deficit will strengthen the US dollar. Hans Tietmeyer, a former president of the former Bundesbank of Germany, argued exactly along the same lines in the mid-1990s. It has also been suggested that countries like Sweden and Italy need to reduce their budget deficits to boost their currencies.

Casual observation does not reveal any systematic relationship between the budget deficit and the health of the currency. In the early 1980s, the US budget deficit was exploding and yet the dollar reached its highest level since the advent of floating exchange rates during that episode (in February 1985, to be precise). But during the first two years of the twenty-first century the dollar was strengthening when the budget was in surplus. Germany's fiscal stimulus (hence, a budget deficit) after re-unification was also accompanied by a strong mark. But, as mentioned earlier, Italy and Sweden had big deficits and weak currencies in the 1990s.

Chris Turner, an economist at Barclays de Zoete Wedd, a British securities firm, analysed 11 episodes of fiscal tightening and found that the domestic currency strengthened in five cases and weakened in the other six cases. So, both casual observation and rigorous empirical evidence tell us that there is no clear-cut relationship between the budget deficit and the exchange rate.

Why is that? One explanation for the absence of a relationship between the state of the budget and the exchange rate is that changes in the deficit affect the exchange rate through more than one channel. Apart from the effect running via changes in interest rates, there may be other channels. For example, a shrinking deficit may imply that there is a lower probability of default by the government, which should be good for the currency. It is also the case that a lower budget deficit reduces the risk premium required by foreigners to hold domestic financial assets, which again is good for the currency. In the October 1995 issue of the *World Economic Outlook*, the IMF considered all these effects and concluded that following a reduction in the budget deficit the currency would appreciate in the long run, but it might appreciate or depreciate in the short run.

The other explanation is more straightforward. Foreign exchange dealers and analysts often reach the wrong conclusions and predictions by concentrating on one factor (which happens to be fashionable) and overlooking the others. In the real world, however, exchange rates are affected by a large number of factors that change at the same time. Examining the relationship between the exchange rate and the deficit in isolation from other factors may be misleading. The domestic currency may appreciate or depreciate on a reduction in the budget deficit, depending on what happens to the other determining factors.

domestic currency of a lower domestic inflation rate and a higher interest rate may be more than offset by the imposition of a tariff on imports and tax on interest income and capital gains.

The central bank plays a role in exchange rate determination by affecting the forces of supply and demand. In the extreme case, the central bank may fix the exchange rate, but this will not prevent the forces of supply and demand from exerting pressure on the exchange rate to change. The central bank can respond to market forces either by imposing capital controls or by intervening in the foreign exchange market by buying and selling currencies at the fixed rate. Obviously, the second alternative is not viable in the long run if, for example, there is a persistent excess demand for foreign exchange (a persistent current account deficit).

Under a system of managed floating, the central bank intervenes by buying and selling currencies. If the domestic currency gets weaker because of an increase in the demand for foreign exchange, the central bank intervenes by selling foreign exchange. This situation is illustrated in Figure 4.6. In Figure 4.6(a), a rise in the demand for foreign currency shifts the demand curve, leading to a rise in the exchange rate from S_0 to S_1. The central bank responds by increasing the supply of foreign currency, causing the supply curve to shift. In an extreme case, if the central bank has adequate resources for intervention, the exchange rate will be brought back to its original level, S_0. Intervention may, however, depend on the **signalling effect**, when the central bank conveys the information that S_1 is not an acceptable level of the exchange rate. In this case, which is illustrated in Figure 4.6(b), market participants may (and only may) respond by selling the foreign currency, taking the exchange rate down to S_2, which is lower than S_1. The signalling effect may be created when the central bank intervenes by selling a small amount of the foreign currency, as shown in Figure 4.6(c). This causes a small shift in the supply curve. Market participants may then respond by selling the currency, causing a further shift in the supply curve. This leads to a decline in the exchange rate to its original level, S_0.

Figure 4.6 The effect of central bank intervention

(a) Foreign currency sales

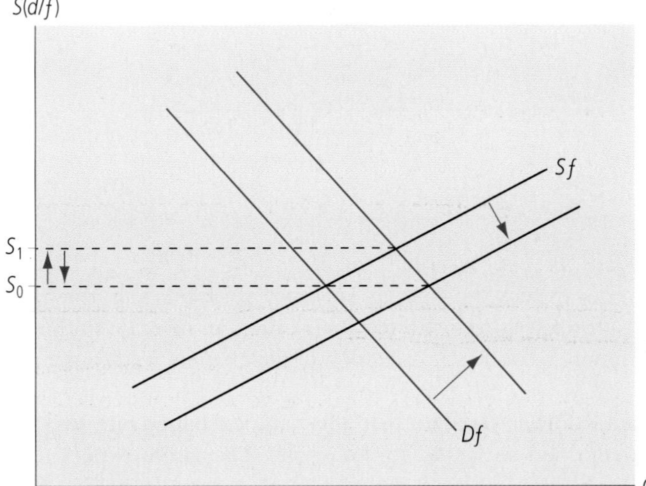

Continued...

(b) Signalling effect without sales

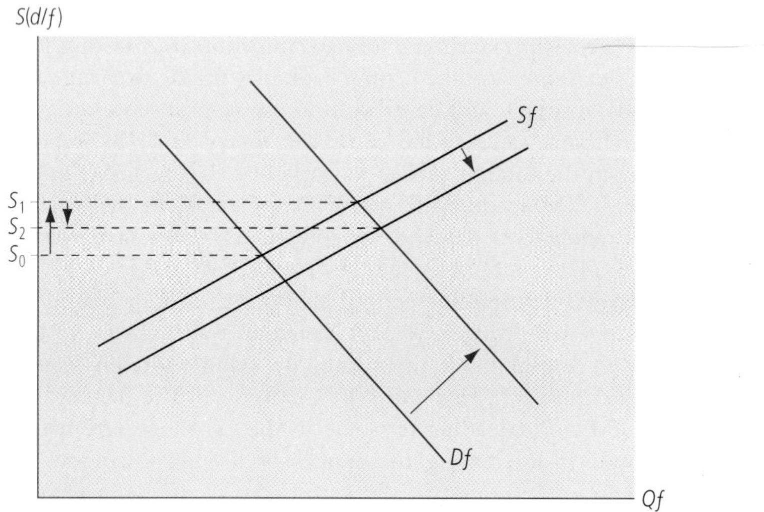

(c) Signalling effect with sales

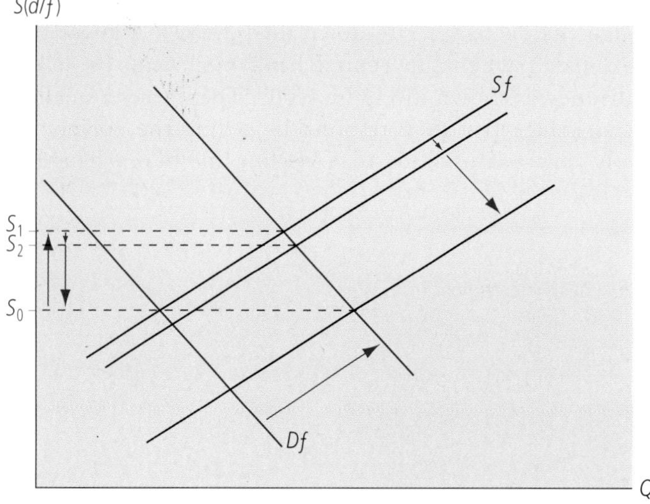

Expectations

Speculators act on the basis of expectations concerning the future path and values of exchange rates. If speculators expect the foreign currency to appreciate, they switch from domestic currency assets to foreign currency assets. This causes an increase in the demand for foreign currency and the supply of domestic currency. These changes lead to the appreciation of the foreign currency.

Expectations may pertain to other variables that affect the exchange rate, including all the factors that have been mentioned so far. If, for example, speculators expect the domestic inflation rate to rise relative to the foreign inflation rate, they react by selling the domestic

INSIGHT

The rationale for and effectiveness of central bank intervention

The answer most frequently given to the question 'Why do central banks intervene in the foreign exchange market?' is that 'intervention is required to smooth out excessive fluctuations in exchange rates in order to avoid the adverse effects of these fluctuations on economic activity'. Sometimes, however, the argument is that central bank intervention should be used to prevent the domestic currency from appreciating and depreciating excessively, as happened to the euro in its early life.

The argument for central bank intervention embodies three propositions:

- Exchange rate fluctuations can be excessive.
- Exchange rate fluctuations have substantial adverse effect on economic activity.
- Central banks can, in practice, smooth out exchange rate fluctuations through the purchase and sale of currencies in the foreign exchange market.

The problem with the first proposition is that it is not straightforward to draw a line between 'excessive' and 'normal' exchange rate fluctuations. The second proposition is theoretically plausible and there is some evidence for the hypothesis that real exchange rate fluctuations discourage international trade. The third proposition on the ability of central banks to smooth out fluctuations in exchange rates leads to two questions: (i) How do central banks determine the timing of intervention? (ii) Are they capable of reversing or even slowing down a market trend?

We start with the first question. The consensus view on this issue is that central banks should intervene in the foreign exchange market to smooth out temporary fluctuations and not to interfere with a fundamental adjustment of the exchange rate (that is, a change in the equilibrium value of the exchange rate as warranted by the underlying economic fundamentals).

As far as the second question is concerned, it is sometimes argued that the sums available for intervention are so small relative to the market size that intervention cannot be effective. However, some economists argue that, although the amounts are small, intervention can be effective because the market watches the central bank. The view that the success of intervention depends crucially on exchange rate expectations is gaining wider acceptance and marks a clear change of thinking about this issue in recent years.

The effectiveness of intervention depends on several factors, the most important of which are the following:

- Intervention is more likely to succeed when the objective is to prolong or reinforce a trend rather than to reverse it.
- For intervention to be effective, it needs to be well publicised after it has taken place.
- Whereas it is useful to publicise intervention after it has taken place, it is not a good idea to announce it beforehand. Intervention is most effective when it is unexpected.
- Intervention is more effective if it is concerted and coordinated.

currency. What is important, however, is not the expected value of the inflation rate *per se*,  but rather its relation to the actual value. If, for example, the domestic inflation rate is expected to be 5 per cent in the next quarter, but turns out to be 4 per cent, this may be taken as a sign of improvement (in the ability of the authorities to control inflation). Hence, the domestic currency may appreciate. If, on the other hand, the actual inflation rate turns out to be 6 per cent, this may be interpreted as a sign of deterioration and hence the currency may depreciate.

RESEARCH FINDINGS

Some survey evidence on the foreign exchange market

Two economists have published the results of a survey that they conducted on the US foreign exchange market.[1] Their results show the following:

- Technical trading (based on charts, for example) characterises about 30 per cent of traders.
- News about macroeconomic variables is rapidly incorporated into exchange rates.
- The importance of individual macroeconomic variables shifts over time, although interest rates always appear to be important.
- Economic fundamentals are perceived to be more important at long horizons.
- Short-run deviations of exchange rates from their fundamentals are attributed to excess speculation and institutional customer/hedge fund manipulation.
- Speculation is generally viewed positively as enhancing market efficiency and liquidity, even though it exacerbates volatility.
- Central bank intervention does not appear to have a substantial effect.
- Traders do not view purchasing power parity as a useful concept, even though a significant proportion (that is, 40 per cent) believe that it affects exchange rates at horizons of over six months.

1 Y. W. Cheung and M. D. Chinn, 'Macroeconomic Implications of the Beliefs and Behavior of Foreign Exchange Traders', NBER Working Paper, No. 7417, November 1999.

Speculative attacks against a particular currency may take place when speculators believe that a currency is overvalued relative to the underlying economic fundamentals. If this is the case, speculators short sell the currency in massive amounts, leading to an increase in its supply and hence its depreciation. An example of this event is the speculative attack against the pound in 1992. The pound was put under pressure by higher German interest rates, and when speculators sensed what was coming up they short sold the currency, eventually forcing it out of the European Monetary System.

Another example is the speculative attacks against Asian currencies (the Thai baht, the Malaysian ringgit, the Indonesian rupiah and the Philippine peso) in the second half of 1997. It all started when currency speculators began to sense that there were clear imbalances in these economies, whose currencies were kept artificially overvalued. This belief initiated speculative attacks against these currencies, starting with the Thai baht. The pressure on the currencies was maintained following the first round of speculative attack for at least two reasons. The first was that hedgers, who had not anticipated this development, had to replenish their foreign exchange balances by selling the Asian currencies. The second was the restructuring of portfolios by those selling assets denominated in these currencies.

4.3 Arbitrage in the spot foreign exchange market

Arbitrage is generally defined as capitalising on a discrepancy in quoted prices as a result of the violation of an equilibrium (no-arbitrage) condition. The arbitrage process restores equilibrium via changes in the supply of and demand for the underlying commodity, asset or currency.

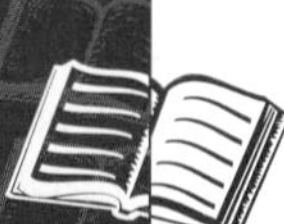

Expectation formation in the foreign exchange market

Expectation formation in the foreign exchange market has been studied extensively, primarily to uncover the nature of the mechanism generating expectations. Foreign exchange traders buy and sell currencies because they expect them to appreciate and depreciate. The question is: how do these traders form expectations? For example, do foreign exchange traders expect a strong currency to keep on appreciating or do they think that it is overvalued, which means that it should depreciate? Another reason for interest in expectation formation is the proposition that exchange rate volatility is the result of the activities of **noise traders** who form extrapolative expectations.

Survey evidence indicates that expectation in the foreign exchange market is extrapolative over a short period of time and regressive over a long period. This means that if a currency is appreciating, most traders would believe that it will keep on appreciating, say, for the next one to three months and then depreciate after that. Takagi obtained what he calls the crucial result that whereas short-term expectations tend to move away from some long-run value, long-run expectations tend to move back towards it.[1]

Pilbeam defined expectation formation mechanisms as follows:[2]

- **Extrapolative expectations** mean that the exchange rate is expected to rise if it rises in the current period, and vice versa.
- **Adaptive expectations** mean that if the exchange rate rises in at least two of the last three periods, then it should be expected to rise in the coming period.
- **Regressive expectations** mean that the exchange rate is expected to rise if it falls in the current period, and vice versa.
- **Rational expectations** mean that expectation is formed on the basis of all available information. If this information is reflected in the forward spread, then a currency that sells at a premium should be expected to rise, and vice versa.
- **Heterogeneous expectations** occur when the trader follows the majority signal.
- **Contrarian expectations** occur when the trader follows the opposite of the majority signal.

Moosa and Shamsuddin examined the expectation formation mechanisms in trading involving the yen against the dollar during the period 1982–1999.[3] By relating the dominance or otherwise of a particular expectation formation mechanism to the profitability of trading based on the underlying mechanism, they found the dominant mechanism to be extrapolative. They also found more evidence for heterogeneous than contrarian expectations, implying some sort of a herd mentality in the foreign exchange market.

In another study, expectation formation was examined under the German hyperinflation of the 1920s.[4] Moosa found that expectations were predominantly adaptive or extrapolative. He also found that expectation was destabilising rather than stabilising, with traders expecting the mark to depreciate further. The importance of expectation as a determinant of the behaviour of exchange rates was confirmed by Moosa, who showed that short-term and medium-term expectation played a more important role than that of non-expectational variables in determining the exchange of four major currencies against the US dollar.[5]

1 S. Tagaki, 'Exchange Rate Expectations: A Survey of Survey Studies', *International Monetary Fund Staff Papers*, 38, 1991, pp. 156–83.

2 K. Pilbeam, 'The Profitability of Trading in the Foreign Exchange Market: Chartists, Fundamentalists and Simpletons', *Oxford Economic Papers*, 47, 1995, pp. 437–52.

3 I. A. Moosa and A. Shamsuddin, 'Expectation Formation Mechanisms, Profitability of Foreign Exchange Trading and Exchange Rate Volatility', unpublished paper, La Trobe University, Melbourne, 2002.

4 I. A. Moosa, 'Testing the Currency Substitution Model Under the German Hyperinflation', *Journal of Economics*, 70, 1999, pp. 61–78.

5 I. A. Moosa, 'A Test of the Post Keynesian Hypothesis on Expectation Formation in the Foreign Exchange Market', *Journal of Post Keynesian Economics*, 24, 2002, pp. 443–57.

In the foreign exchange market, arbitrage is the simultaneous purchase and sale of currencies for the sake of making profit. Profitable arbitrage opportunities arise either because exchange rates differ from one financial centre to another or because they are inconsistent. It must be mentioned at the outset that in today's integrated financial markets, the arbitrage operations discussed in this section rarely, if at all, arise. And even if they did arise, they would be quickly exploited by arbitragers to the point of 'extinction'. It is, however, still important to study these operations because they provide the mechanism whereby the equilibrium relationships are maintained. In fact, the **no-arbitrage conditions** are used for pricing financial assets.

Two-point arbitrage

Also known as **spatial arbitrage** or **locational arbitrage, two-point arbitrage** arises when the exchange rate between two currencies assumes two different values in two financial centres at the same time. Given two financial centres, A and B, and two currencies, x and y, and assuming (for simplicity) no transaction costs and a zero bid-offer spread, arbitrage will be triggered if the following condition is violated:

$$S_A(x/y) = S_B(x/y) \tag{4.1}$$

This condition says that the exchange rate between x and y should be the same in A as in B. If the condition is not satisfied in the sense that the exchange rate between x and y is different in A from its level in B, then one of the currencies is expensive in one financial centre and cheap in the other. Arbitragers in this case buy one of the currencies where it is cheap and sell it at profit where it is expensive.

Let us consider the case when the condition is violated such that $S_A(x/y) > S_B(x/y)$. This violation means that currency y is more expensive in A than in B (or that x is cheaper in A than in B). Let us consider the situation from the perspective of currency y. Arbitragers buy y in B and sell it in A, making profit, $\neq$, that is given by

$$\neq = S_A(x/y) - S_B(x/y) \tag{4.2}$$

The process of arbitrage restores the equilibrium condition via changes in the forces of supply and demand. This is illustrated by Figure 4.7, which shows the supply and demand curves for currency y in financial centres A and B. Initially, the exchange rates in A and B are $(S_A)_0$ and $(S_B)_0$ respectively, such that $(S_A)_0 > (S_B)_0$. As the demand for y increases in B, the exchange rate rises (y appreciates). Conversely, the supply of y increases in A and so the exchange rate falls (y depreciates). This process continues until the exchange rates in both financial centres are equal (that is, until $(S_A)_1 = (S_B)_1$) because this condition eliminates profit and hence the incentive for arbitrage.

Example

Let us imagine that the Reuters' Monitor shows the following information about the exchange rate between the Australian dollar and the US dollar (measured in direct quotation in both centres):

Sydney	1.7800 (AUD/USD)
New York	0.5747 (USD/AUD)

To find out whether or not there is an arbitrage opportunity, we have to check whether the equilibrium condition is violated. When we invert the exchange rate in

New York, we get 1/0.5747 = 1.7400. Thus, the equilibrium condition is violated in the sense that the USD is more expensive in Sydney than in New York. Hence, arbitragers buy the US currency in New York at 1.7400 and sell it in Sydney at 1.7800. Profit in Australian dollar per US dollar bought and sold is

$$\pi = 1.7800 - 1.7400 = 0.0400$$

or 400 points. The effect of arbitrage is to raise the price of the USD in New York and lower it in Sydney until they are equal somewhere between 1.7800 and 1.7400. Suppose that at some stage prior to restoring equilibrium, changes in supply and demand cause the exchange rate in Sydney to fall to 1.7700 and the rate in New York to rise to 1.7500 (or 0.5714 in direct quotation). In this case, profit will be reduced to

$$\pi = 1.7700 - 1.7500 = 0.0200$$

or 200 points. Eventually, the rate falls in Sydney to 1.7600 and rises in New York to the same level (0.5682 in direct quotation). Profit will at this stage be

$$\pi = 1.7600 - 1.7600 = 0$$

and hence arbitrage will not be profitable because the equilibrium condition is restored.

Figure 4.7 The effect of two-point arbitrage

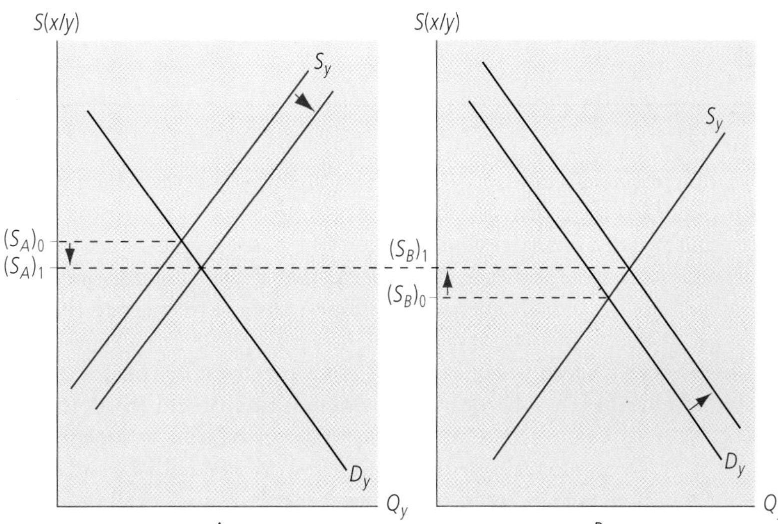

Three-point (triangular) arbitrage

Given three currencies (x, y and z) and making the same assumptions as above, **three-point arbitrage** (also called **triangular arbitrage**) will be triggered if the following condition is violated:

$$S(x/y) = \frac{S(x/z)}{S(y/z)} \tag{4.3}$$

IN PRACTICE

Explaining the weakness of the euro

Following its launch in January 1999, the euro depreciated against the US dollar for the following three years. It even lost ground against the weak Australian dollar. What explains the weakness of the currency of a major trading bloc comprising some of the largest economies in the world? Several explanations have been put forward:

- Economic growth in the United States was stronger than economic growth in the euro area during that period.
- Productivity growth, and hence the profitability of investment, was higher in the United States than in the euro area. In December 2001, Alan Greenspan was quoted as saying that 'the weak euro reflected investors' expectation that America's productivity growth would outpace the euro area's in the years ahead'.
- Investors have more confidence in the US Federal Reserve than in the European Central Bank (ECB). For example, the ECB focuses excessively on price stability and ignores growth. Moreover, some observers believe that the ECB lacks transparency with respect to policy goals and in the way it makes interest rate decisions.
- The US dollar has become a safe haven, so that when investors become more risk averse they hold dollar-denominated assets. This explanation means that investors will accumulate dollar balances even if, and when, the United States goes into recession. The underlying argument is that if the United States enters a recession, the rest of the world will be hurt and so investors pile dollars to avoid risk.
- The euro started life overvalued. Its subsequent weakness was a natural move to a more reasonable (lower) level.

Given these arguments, we can only wonder why the euro appreciated by 20 per cent in the 12 months ending in April 2003.

In this case, the three exchange rates are equal across financial centres, which precludes the possibility of two-point arbitrage (this is why the exchange rates in Equation (4.3) do not have subscripts to indicate the financial centres where they are quoted). This condition tells us that cross exchange rates are consistent in the sense that if we calculate one of them on the basis of the other two, the calculated rate should be identical to the rate that is actually quoted.

Two steps are involved in three-point arbitrage: (i) checking whether or not the condition is violated (that is, whether or not the cross rates are consistent); and (ii) determining the profitable sequence. Let us assume that the no-arbitrage condition is violated such that $S(x/y) > S(x/z)/S(y/z)$. We can determine the profitable sequence with the aid of a triangle, placing each one of the three currencies in one of its corners (in no special order), as shown in Figure 4.8. The idea behind the determination of the profitable sequence is simple. We start with one unit of any of the three currencies and move clockwise as in Figure 4.8(a) around the triangle until we end up where we started from, with the same currency. In this case, we end up with less than one unit of the currency we started with, which gives the unprofitable sequence. The profitable sequence will be in an anti-clockwise direction, as in Figure 4.8(b).

So, let us start with one unit of currency x. Moving clockwise, as in Figure 4.8(a), involves the following steps:

1. Selling x and buying y to obtain $1/S(x/y)$ units of y.

Figure 4.8 Profitable and unprofitable sequences in three-point arbitrage

(a) Unprofitable sequence

(b) Profitable sequence

2. Selling y and buying z to obtain $1/[S(x/y)S(y/z)]$ units of z.
3. Selling z and buying x to obtain $S(x/z)/[S(x/y)S(y/z)]$ units of x.

Since $S(x/y) > S(x/z)/S(y/z)$, it follows that $S(x/z)/S(y/z) < S(x/y)$ or that $S(x/z)/[S(x/y)S(y/z)] < 1$. Hence, we end up with less than one unit of x. The profitable sequence must, therefore, be in an anti-clockwise direction. This sequence, as represented by Figure 4.8(b), involves the following steps:

1. Selling x and buying z to obtain $1/S(x/z)$ units of z.
2. Selling z and buying y to obtain $S(y/z)/S(x/z)$ units of y.
3. Selling y and buying x to obtain $S(y/z)S(x/y)/S(x/z)$ units of x.

Since $S(x/y) > S(x/z)/S(y/z)$, it follows that $S(y/z)S(x/y)/S(x/z) > 1$. Thus, we end up with more than one unit of x and this must be the profitable sequence. The possibilities for three-point arbitrage can be summarised as follows:

- If $S(x/y) = S(x/z)/S(y/z)$, then there is no arbitrage opportunity.
- If $S(x/y) > S(x/z)/S(y/z)$, then there is a profitable arbitrage opportunity by following the sequence $x \rightarrow z \rightarrow y \rightarrow x$.
- If $S(x/y) < S(x/z)/S(y/z)$, then there is a profitable arbitrage opportunity by following the sequence $x \rightarrow y \rightarrow z \rightarrow x$.

Arbitrage restores the equilibrium condition via changes in the supply of and demand for currencies. Let us trace what happens when $S(x/y) > S(x/z)/S(y/z)$. Figure 4.9 shows that the buying and selling of currencies result in changes in the forces of supply and demand, as follows:

1. An increase in the demand for z (the supply of x) and so $S(x/z)$ rises, as shown in Figure 4.9(a).
2. An increase in the demand for y (the supply of z) and so $S(y/z)$ falls, as shown in Figure 4.9(b).
3. An increase in the demand for x (the supply of y) and so $S(x/y)$ falls, as shown in Figure 4.9(c).

These changes in supply and demand restore the equilibrium condition.

Figure 4.9 The effect of three-point arbitrage

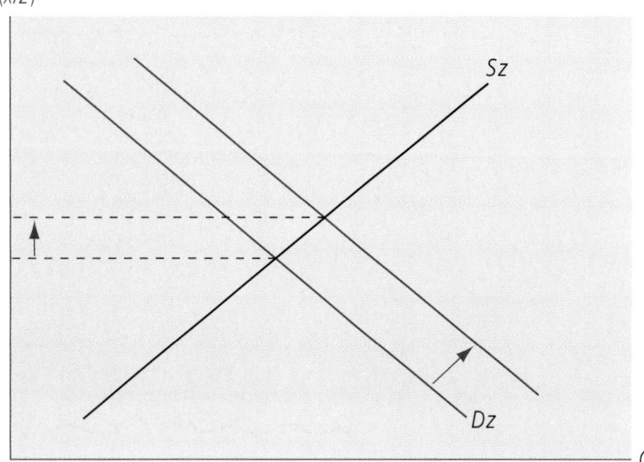

(b) S(y/z)

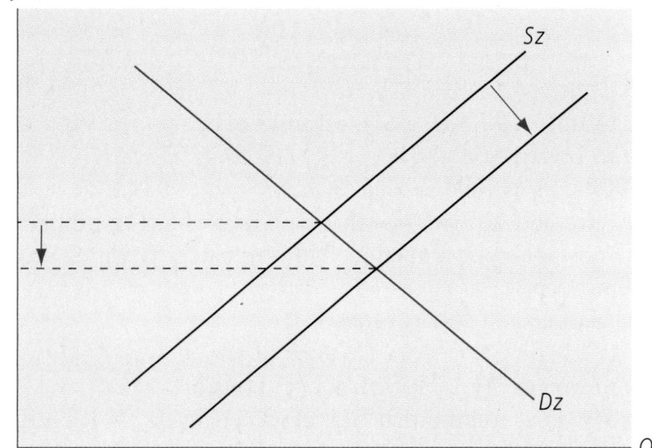

(c) S(x/y)

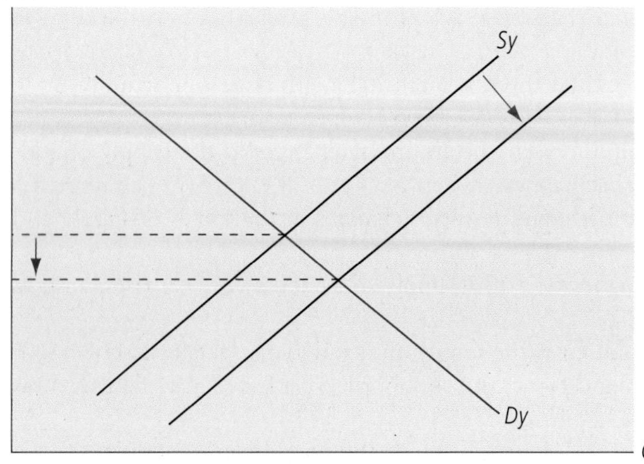

RESEARCH FINDINGS

The profitability of three-point arbitrage

We have presented three-point arbitrage as a risk-free operation, because all of the decision variables (three exchange rates) are known at the time the decision is made. However, Kollias and Metaxas argue that three-point arbitrage involves some degree of risk due to the effect of slippages in the currency quotes.[1]

By using high-frequency, tick-by-tick data on the exchange rates they found that arbitrage opportunities do exist. However, they also found that the exploitation of such opportunities involves a degree of risk that can adversely affect realised returns.

[1] C. Kollias and K. Metaxas, 'How Efficient are FX Markets? Empirical Evidence of Arbitrage Opportunities Using High-Frequency Data', *Applied Financial Economics*, 11, 2001, pp. 435–44.

Example

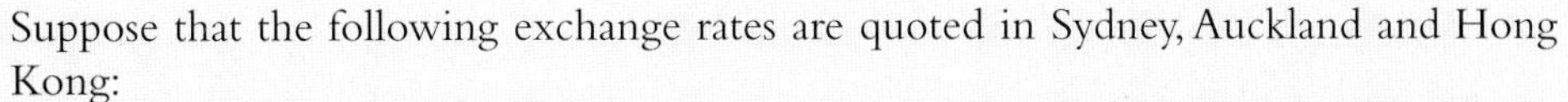

Suppose that the following exchange rates are quoted in Sydney, Auckland and Hong Kong:

$S(HKD/AUD)$ 4.1548
$S(NZD/AUD)$ 1.2052
$S(HKD/NZD)$ 3.5825

To find out whether or not there is a possibility for three-point arbitrage, we have to check the consistency of the cross rates. $S(HKD/NZD)$ can be calculated from the other two rates as

$$S(HKD/NZD) = \frac{S(HKD/AUD)}{S(NZD/AUD)} = \frac{4.1548}{1.2052} = 3.4474$$

Hence, the equilibrium condition is violated, implying a possibility for three-point arbitrage. Let us first try the sequence HKD→NZD→AUD→HKD, starting with one unit of HKD:

1. Sell HKD1.0000 for NZD to obtain ($1/3.5825 = 0.2791$) units of NZD.
2. Sell NZD0.2791 for AUD to obtain ($0.2791/1.2052 = 0.2316$) units of AUD.
3. Sell AUD0.2316 for HKD to obtain ($0.2316 \times 4.1548 = 0.9623$) units of HKD.

Obviously, this is not the profitable sequence. Let us now consider the opposite sequence, starting with one unit of HKD:

1. Sell HKD1.0000 for AUD to obtain ($1/4.1548 = 0.2407$) units of AUD.
2. Sell AUD0.2407 for NZD to obtain ($0.2407 \times 1.2052 = 0.2901$) units of NZD.
3. Sell NZD0.2901 for HKD to obtain ($0.2901 \times 3.5825 = 1.0392$) units of HKD.

This is obviously the profitable sequence. If $S(HKD/NZD) = 3.4474$, then there is no possibility for three-point arbitrage because this rate is consistent with the others. In this case we have:

$$\frac{S(HKD/AUD)}{S(HKD/NZD)S(NZD/AUD)} = \frac{4.1548}{3.4474 \times 1.2052} = 1.0000$$

and

$$\frac{S(NZD/AUD)S(HKD/NZD)}{S(HKD/AUD)} = \frac{1.2052 \times 3.4474}{4.1548} = 1.0000$$

which shows that there is no profitable sequence.

Multipoint arbitrage

Arbitrage involving four, five or more currencies can take place. However, three-point arbitrage is sufficient to establish consistent exchange rates, eliminating the profitability of **multipoint arbitrage**. In the case of three-point arbitrage involving currencies x, y and z, the no-arbitrage condition may be written as

$$S(x/y)S(y/z)S(z/x) = 1 \tag{4.4}$$

If four currencies (x_1, x_2, x_3 and x_4) are involved, then we have four-point arbitrage, in which case the no-arbitrage condition is

$$S(x_1/x_2)S(x_2/x_3)S(x_3/x_4)S(x_4/x_1) = 1 \tag{4.5}$$

and when we have n currencies, the no-arbitrage condition is

$$S(x_1/x_2)S(x_2/x_3)S(x_3/x_4)\ldots S(x_{n-1}/x_n)S(x_n/x_1) = 1 \tag{4.6}$$

Example

Consider the following exchange rates:

$S(AUD/USD)$	1.8811
$S(JPY/USD)$	132.68
$S(JPY/GBP)$	189.24
$S(GBP/EUR)$	0.6125
$S(EUR/AUD)$	0.6086

The no-arbitrage condition in this case is

$$S(AUD/USD)S(USD/JPY)S(JPY/GBP)S(GBP/EUR)S(EUR/AUD) = 1$$

which gives

$$1.8811 \times \frac{1}{132.68} \times 189.24 \times 0.6125 \times 0.6086 = 1.0001$$

Because the no-arbitrage condition is not violated there is no possibility for profitable five-point arbitrage. You may want to check for yourself that there is no possibility for three-point arbitrage either, using all possible currency combinations (taking three currencies at a time). We can actually check that this is the case by working out the process step by step, starting with one AUD and moving as shown in Figure 4.10. In this case, we have a pentagon rather than a triangle. The results of the calculations are displayed in the following table, which shows that starting with one Australian dollar we end up with one Australian dollar no matter which direction we move (try the same exercise by starting with one pound).

Transaction	End currency	Number of units
Clockwise		
AUD→USD	USD	0.5316
USD→JPY	JPY	70.53
JPY→GBP	GBP	0.3727
GBP→EUR	EUR	0.6086
EUR→AUD	AUD	1.0000

Transaction	End currency	Number of units
Anti-clockwise		
AUD→EUR	EUR	0.6086
EUR→GBP	GBP	0.3728
GBP→JPY	JPY	70.55
JPY→USD	USD	0.5317
USD→AUD	AUD	1.0000

Figure 4.10 Five-point arbitrage

(a) Clockwise

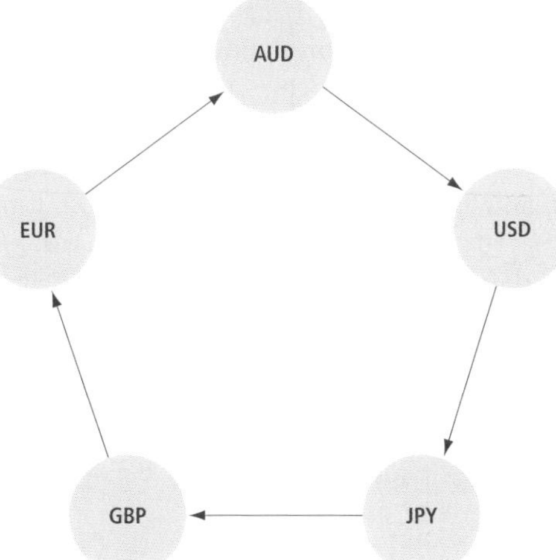

(b) Anti-clockwise

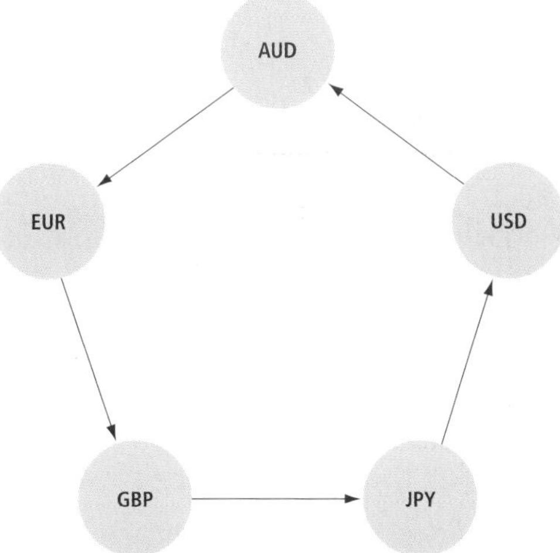

4.4 Speculation in the spot foreign exchange market

Speculators participate in the foreign exchange market, buying and selling currencies by anticipating future movements of exchange rates. Simply stated, speculators buy a currency when they think that it will appreciate and sell it when they think that it will depreciate. If they make the right decision, then they make profit when they sell the currency subsequently at the higher rate. By their actions, speculators affect the supply of and demand for currencies and therefore exchange rates.

Speculation can be *stabilising* and *destabilising*. **Destabilising speculation**, which drives the exchange rate away from its equilibrium value, occurs when speculators buy a currency when it is high and sell it when it is low. This kind of behaviour arises, for example, when speculators believe that there are **bubbles** in the market (a bubble is a sustained rise or fall in the exchange rate without any fundamental reason to justify this behaviour). Thus, when a currency appreciates, speculators think that it will keep on appreciating and so they buy it until the bubble bursts for one reason or another. Conversely, when a currency depreciates they believe that it will keep on depreciating and so they keep on selling it, inducing a run on the currency. Figure 4.11 shows the effect of destabilising speculation in a **bull market**, a **bear market** and over time. In Figure 4.11(a) as the demand for the (foreign) currency rises, shifting the demand curve upwards, the exchange rate rises from S_0 to S_1, reflecting the appreciation of the foreign currency. If speculators believe that the foreign currency will keep on appreciating, the demand curve will keep on shifting upwards and the currency keeps on appreciating. In Figure 4.11(b), as the foreign currency depreciates (because of an increase in its supply, which is initiated for some reason) speculators believe that the currency will keep on depreciating. Thus, they keep on selling it, causing a continuous shift in the supply curve to the right and therefore a continuous fall in the exchange rate. Over time this behaviour causes sharper fluctuations in the exchange rate than otherwise, as illustrated by Figure 4.11(c).

Figure 4.11 The effect of destabilising speculation

(a) Bull market

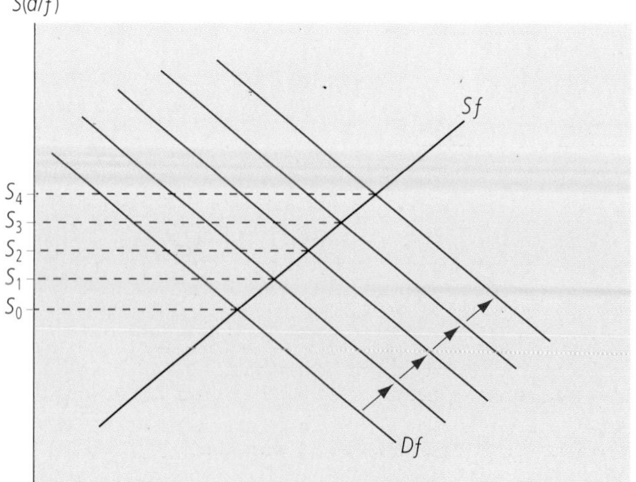

(b) Bear market

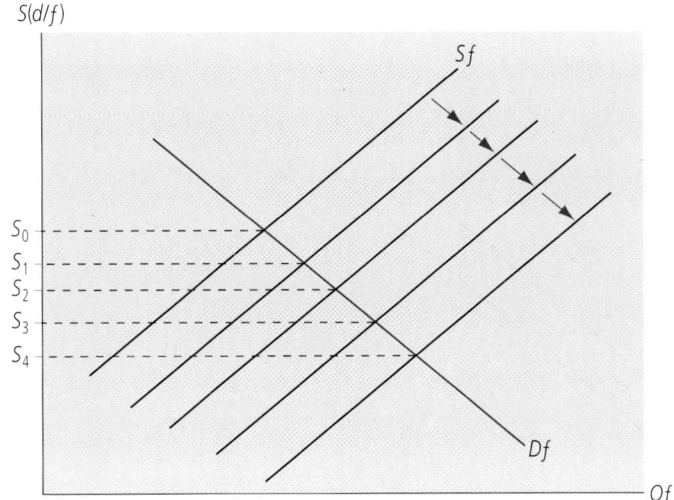

(c) Over time

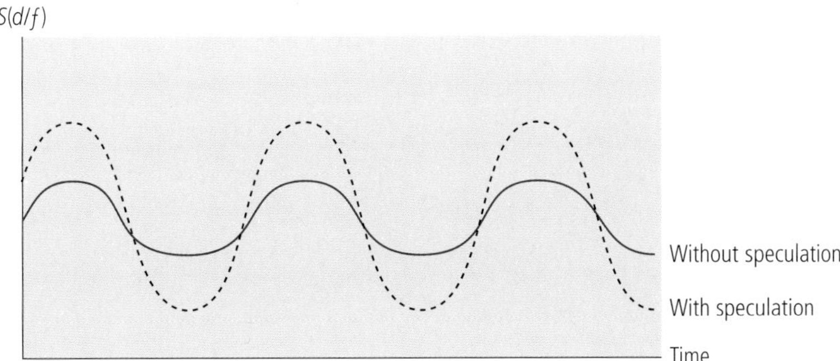

Stabilising speculation works the other way round. When the demand for a currency increases, it appreciates, and as it appreciates further, speculators start thinking that it is overvalued so they sell it, causing it to depreciate. Conversely, when a currency depreciates, because of an increase in its supply, speculators start thinking that it is undervalued and hence it is a bargain. Therefore, they buy it, reversing the trend in the foreign exchange market. The effect of this kind of behaviour is illustrated in Figure 4.12. In Figure 4.12(a) as the exchange rate rises from S_0 to S_1 because of an increase in the demand for the currency, speculators start believing that it is overvalued. Hence, they sell the currency, causing a shift in the supply curve and bringing the exchange rate down to S_2. Figure 4.12(b) shows the situation in a bear market. As the exchange rate falls from S_0 to S_1, because of an increase in the supply of the foreign currency, speculators start believing that it is undervalued. Hence, they respond by buying it, causing a shift in the demand curve. As a result, the exchange rate rises to S_2. The effect of this kind of behaviour is to reduce the sharpness of exchange rate fluctuations over time, as shown in Figure 4.12(c).

Figure 4.12 The effect of stabilising speculation

(a) Bull market

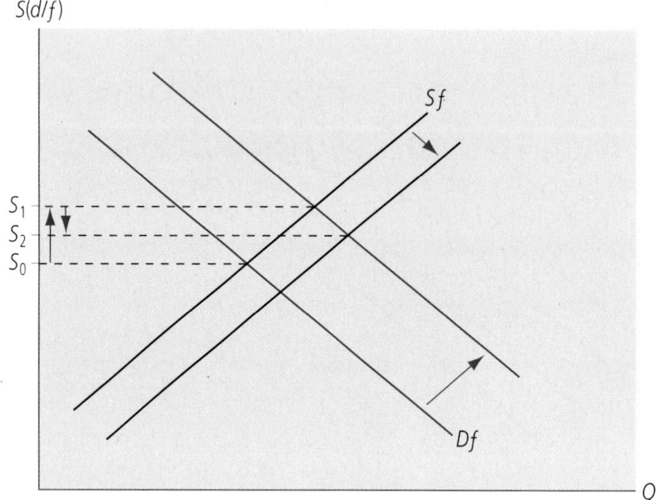

(b) Bear market

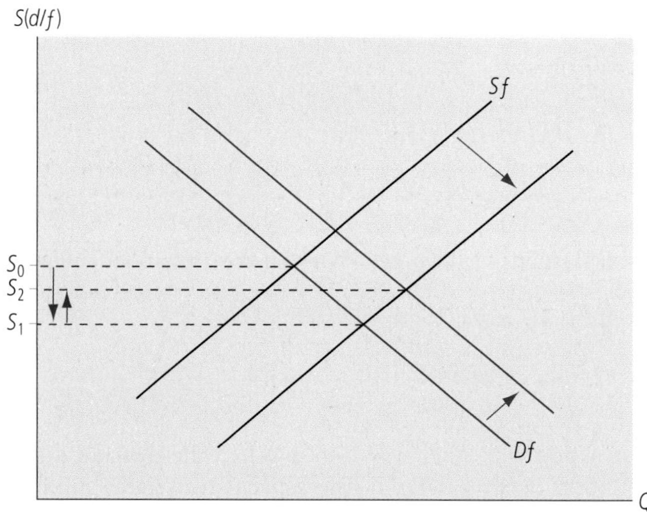

(c) Over time

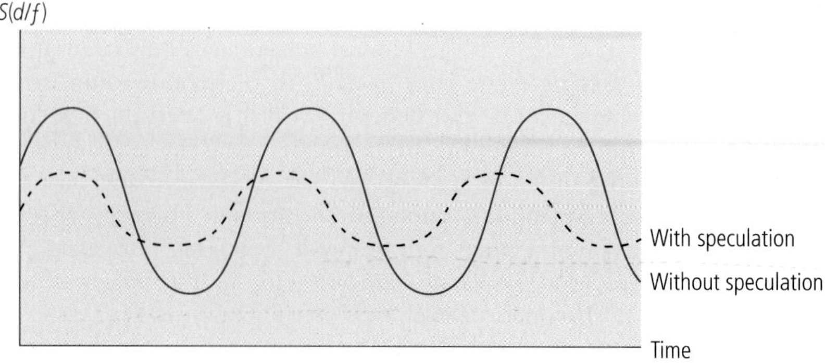

How do speculators speculate?

Speculators in the foreign exchange market try to make profit by buying a currency at a certain rate and selling it subsequently at a higher rate. The question is: how do they decide when to buy and when to sell? Speculators use a variety of methods to generate buy and sell signals. The following are some of these methods (which we study in more detail later in the book):

- *Mechanical expectation formation mechanisms*. Under extrapolative expectations, for example, a currency is expected to appreciate in the coming period if it appreciates in the current period, and vice versa. Hence, a currency is bought when it appreciates and sold when it depreciates.
- *Mechanical trading rules*. A filter rule, for example, indicates a buying opportunity if the currency appreciates by a certain percentage from its most recent low and a selling opportunity if the currency depreciates by a given percentage from its most recent high.
- *Charts*. Chartists buy and sell according to chart formations. For example, the speculator buys when a 'reverse head and shoulders' formation appears and sells when a 'head and shoulders formation' appears.
- *Fundamental models*. The speculator in this case tries to form a view on the appropriate level of the exchange rate, given the levels of the variables (inflation, interest rates, etc.) envisaged by a 'fundamental model', such as the supply and demand model described in this chapter. A buy signal is generated when the exchange rate is below this level by a certain percentage, and vice versa.
- *News announcements*. In this case, the speculator buys when there is a favourable news item and sells otherwise. For example, a speculator would buy the Australian dollar if there were a rise (actual or expected) in Australian interest rates and would sell when an announcement indicated that inflation was heading upwards.

This is not an exhaustive list and each one of these categories has a number of variants. There is no guarantee beforehand that any of these methods will produce profitable trading. Moosa and Shamsuddin experimented with 19 different trading strategies in the trading of the pound against the US dollar and found that some strategies were profitable and others were not.[1] They found filter rules to be extremely profitable, as was trading based on fundamental models. However, they found a trading strategy based on regressive expectations (that is, selling a currency if it appreciates in the current period) to be a loss-making strategy.

1 I. A. Moosa and A. Shamsuddin, 'Heterogeneity of Traders as a Source of Exchange Rate Volatility', unpublished paper, La Trobe University, Melbourne, 2002.

4.5 Determination of the bid-offer spread

In this section we illustrate how the bid-offer spread is determined within the supply and demand model. We then explain how the arbitrage and speculation conditions are affected by the presence of the bid-offer spread.

Determining the bid-offer spread

The bid-offer spread is determined in transactions involving a market maker (say, a bank dealer) and a customer (a price taker). Since the bid rate is the rate at which the dealer buys and the customer sells, it is determined by the intersection of the dealer's demand curve and the customer's supply curve. Conversely, the offer rate is determined by the intersection of the customer's demand curve and the dealer's supply curve. This process is illustrated in Figure 4.13, in which the superscripts d and c refer to the dealer and customer, respectively. In equilibrium, the bid rate is S_b and the offer rate is S_a, whereas the spread is measured by the difference between the two rates.

Figure 4.13 Determination of the bid-offer spread

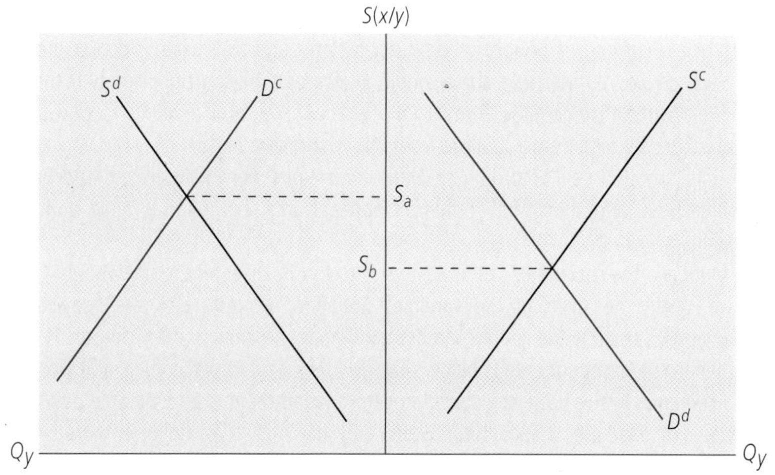

Two-point arbitrage in the presence of the bid-offer spread

So far we have shown how arbitrage works by assuming that there is no bid-offer spread. Let us now relax this assumption in the case of two-point arbitrage. The equilibrium condition in this case is given by the equations

$$S_{b,A}(x/y) = S_{a,B}(x/y) \tag{4.7}$$

$$S_{a,A}(x/y) = S_{b,B}(x/y) \tag{4.8}$$

where $S_{b,A}(x/y)$ is the bid rate in A, and so on. Let us now see what happens if the equilibrium condition is violated, such that $S_{b,A}(x/y) > S_{a,B}(x/y)$. In this case, the arbitrager can make profit by buying y in B at $S_{a,B}(x/y)$ and selling it in A for $S_{b,A}(x/y)$. Arbitrage profit is the difference between the selling rate and the buying rate, or $S_{b,A}(x/y) - S_{a,B}(x/y)$.

Example

Suppose that the exchange rate between the pound and the Australian dollar as recorded in Sydney and London is as follows:

Sydney	0.3750–0.3790
London	0.3700–0.3740

To make profit the arbitrager will buy the Australian dollar in London at GBP0.3740 and sell it in Sydney at GBP0.3750. Profit in pounds per Australian dollar is given by

$$\pi = 0.3750 - 0.3740 = 0.0010$$

or 10 points. Equivalently, profit is made by buying the pound in Sydney and selling it in London.

The effect of the bid-offer spread is to reduce the profitability of arbitrage, since the spread is a transaction cost. If arbitrage is possible at the mid-rates, then we have the following:

Sydney	0.3770
London	0.3720

The arbitrager in this case buys the Australian dollar in London at GBP0.3720 and sells it in Sydney at GBP0.3770. Arbitrage profit in this case is 0.005 or 50 points.

The microstructure approach to exchange rates

The **microstructure approach** has been developed as an alternative to the macroeconomic approach to exchange rates. The microstructure approach to exchange rates can be defined as 'the process and outcomes of exchanging currencies under explicit trading rules'.

A major contributor to the microstructure approach to exchange rates is Richard Lyons, who has written a fascinating book on this subject.[1] At the outset of Chapter 1, Lyons tells the following interesting story: 'Ten years ago, a friend of mine who trades spot foreign exchange for a large bank invited me to spend a few days at his side. At the time, I considered myself an expert, having written my thesis on exchange rates. I thought that I had a handle on how it worked. I thought wrong.'

Lyons identifies three approaches to exchange rate determination: goods, assets and microstructure. Before the 1970s, the dominant approach was the **goods market approach**, whereby the demand for and supply of currencies came from cross-border buying and selling of goods. Hence, a country with a current account surplus would have an appreciating currency, and vice versa. But this approach has failed, particularly now that international trade accounts for no more than 1 per cent of currency trading. In the 1970s, the **asset market approach** emerged. In this approach the demand for and supply of currencies came from cross-border buying and selling of assets. Models based on the asset approach have also failed as predictive and explanatory tools. The problem with this approach is that it is based on the assumption of homogenous beliefs and expectations. The underlying macroeconomic variables, such as growth and inflation, seem to fail to explain exchange rate volatility. Moreover, the huge trading volume in the foreign exchange market cannot be explained by the asset market approach.

In the microstructure approach the demand for and supply of currencies are likewise attributed to cross-border trading of assets. What distinguishes this approach is the fact that it relaxes three unrealistic assumptions of the asset approach by recognising that: (i) some information relevant to exchange rates is not publicly available; (ii) market participants differ in ways that affect exchange rates; and (iii) trading mechanisms differ in ways that affect exchange rates. Lyons argues strongly for the ability of the microstructure approach to explain three puzzles:

- the **determination puzzle**—that exchange rate movements are virtually unrelated to fundamentals
- the **excess volatility puzzle**—that exchange rates are excessively volatile relative to fundamentals
- the **forward bias puzzle**—that excess returns in the foreign exchange market are predictable and inexplicable.

[1] R. K. Lyons, *The Microstructure Approach to Exchange Rates*, MIT Press, Cambridge, Mass., 2001.

Speculation in the presence of the bid-offer spread

Speculation involves buying a currency if it is expected to appreciate and selling it when (or if) it does, making profit of the difference between the selling rate and the buying rate. Let $S_0(x/y)$ be the exchange rate at time 0 (the present time). If the speculator thinks that the exchange rate will be higher at time 1 (that is, $S_1(x/y) > S_0(x/y)$), then he or she will react by buying currency y at time 0 and selling it at time 1. If the speculator is right, then he or she will realise profit amounting to the difference between the selling rate and the buying rate $(S_1(x/y) - S_0(x/y))$. In the presence of the bid-offer spread, the speculator buys at the offer rate and sells at the bid rate, in which case profit realised (if he or she is right) is $S_{b1}(x/y) - S_{a0}(x/y)$.

Example

Suppose that the exchange rate between the pound and the Australian dollar, *S(GBP/AUD)*, is 0.3750–0.3790, which gives a mid-rate of 0.3770. If a speculator thinks that the Australian dollar is going to appreciate against the pound, such that the exchange rate rises to 0.3940–0.3980 (a mid-rate of 0.3960), he or she will buy the Australian dollar at 0.3790 and sell it at 0.3940 to realise profit of 0.0150 or 150 points. If the transactions were conducted at the mid-rates, the buying and selling rates would be 0.3770 and 0.3960, respectively. This gives net profit of 0.0190 or 190 points.

4.6 Determination of the forward spread: the naïve model

The simplest model describing the determination of the spot and forward exchange rates is based on the assumption that there are independent demand and supply forces in the spot and forward markets. It also assumes that there is a separate market with independent supply and demand forces for forward contracts with different maturities. These assumptions are very simplistic and this is why this model is 'naïve'.

Figure 4.14 is a diagrammatic representation of this model. The equilibrium spot exchange rate, S_0, is determined in the spot market, whereas the equilibrium forward rate (for a particular maturity), F_0, is determined in the forward market. Since the forward rate in this case is higher than the spot rate, this implies that the foreign currency sells at a premium and hence the domestic currency sells at a discount. This model, however, is unsatisfactory because of the assumptions of the independence of the two markets and the absence of covered interest arbitrage. Changes in the spot rate can affect the forward rate, for example, by changing the interest rate on one or both currencies, leading to changes in the interest rate differential and therefore the forward spread. This topic is covered in Chapter 10.

4.7 Factors affecting the Australian dollar exchange rate

Since its floating in December 1983, the Australian dollar has been through phases of strength and weakness, but in general it has weakened both against the US dollar and in effective

Figure 4.14 Determination of spot and forward rates when markets are independent

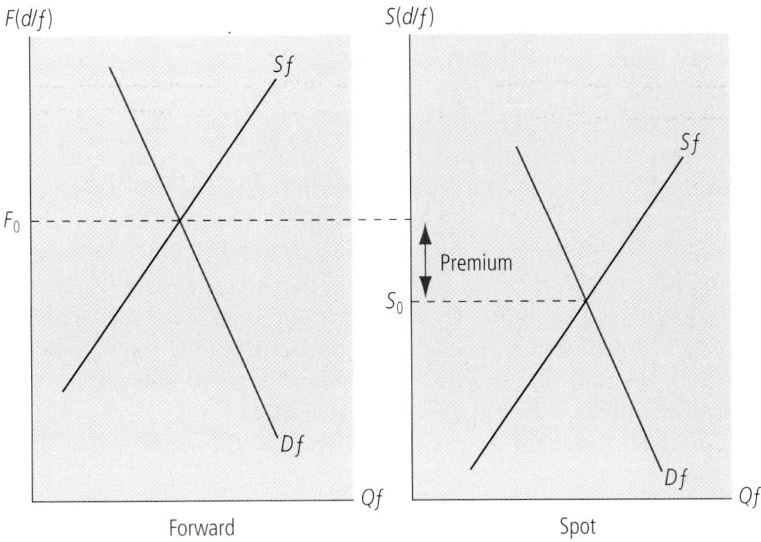

terms. This can be seen from Figure 4.15, which plots the USD/AUD exchange rate as well as the Reserve Bank's trade-weighted index since the floating of the currency in December 1983. In order to plot the two series on the same scale, both are measured relative to December 1983 as a base period in which they assume the value of 100.

Figure 4.15 The Australian dollar exchange rates (December 1983 = 100)

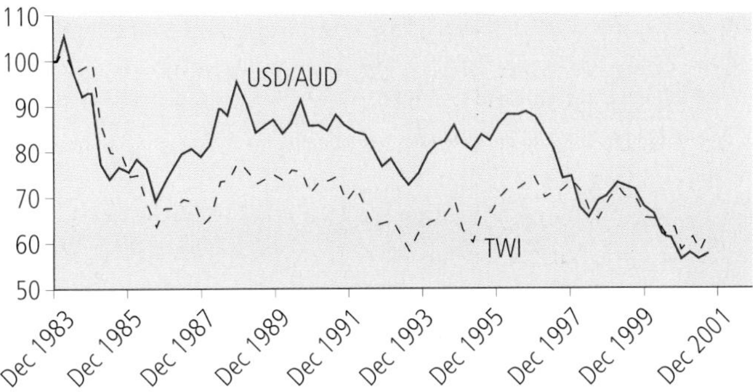

Source: RBA.

Between December 1983 and March 1984 the Australian currency appreciated by 3.7 per cent against the US dollar and by 2.2 per cent in effective terms. This was followed by a phase of sustained depreciation that lasted until July 1986. One of the reasons for this depreciation was the feeling that the Australian dollar was overvalued in early 1984. However, there were also more fundamental reasons for this depreciation, including weak commodity prices, uncertainty about inflation, and rising external debt, all of which led to a speculative attack on the currency. One important event that led to those attacks was the Treasurer's often-quoted remark on the 'banana republic' on 14 May 1986, which instigated a downgrading of Australia as a sovereign borrower. Between July 1986 and August 1988, the Australian dollar restored its strength against the US dollar but failed to regain the losses made in effective terms, appreciating by 25.4 per cent. This appreciation was due to rising commodity prices, which led to an improvement of Australia's **terms of trade** (export prices relative to import prices). Another factor was a rising interest rate differential in favour of the Australian dollar. The following two episodes of depreciation (August 1988 to September 1993) and appreciation (September 1993 to January 1996) seem to be related to the behaviour of commodity prices and hence the terms of trade.

Since 1997, the Australian currency has been predominantly declining both in effective terms and against the US dollar. Several reasons have been presented to explain this decline: (i) the Asian currency crisis of 1997–1998; (ii) the Russian crisis of 1998; (iii) the strength of the US dollar; and (iv) the Australian economy being an old economy. But in general, there has been some uncertainty about the factors driving the exchange rate. Towards the end of 2002, the new economy/old economy argument lost ground, as the US economy showed some weakness. As a result, major currencies appreciated against the US dollar and the Australian dollar followed suit. By early July 2003, the Australian dollar approached 68 US cents, having reached a low of less than 48 US cents in 2001.

Let us now summarise the main factors that determine the behaviour of the Australian dollar exchange rates.

Interest rates and interest rate differentials

Throughout the 1980s Australia had very high interest rates, which attracted massive capital inflows. Figure 4.16 shows the Australian and US short-term (three-month) interest rates. The appreciation of the Australian dollar in the 1980s and its depreciation in the 1990s are related to the behaviour of the interest rate differential.

Figure 4.16 Australian and US short-term interest rates

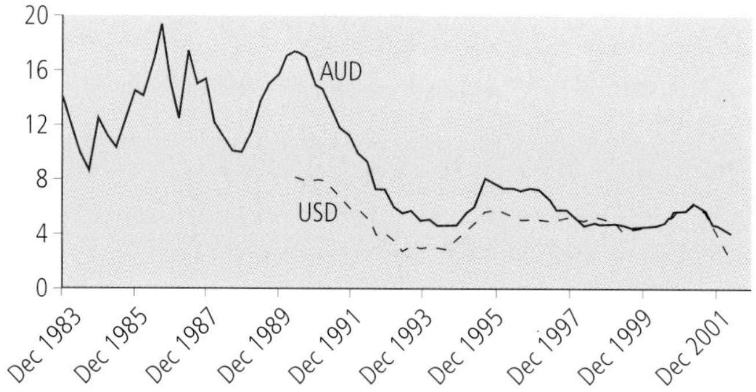

Source: Main Economic Indicators, OECD.

Commodity prices and the terms of trade

Commodity prices have played a crucial role in the determination of the Australian dollar exchange rate. This is due to the fact that Australia is a major commodity exporter (for example, coal, iron ore, alumina, wool). Figure 4.17 describes the behaviour of commodity prices (in US dollar terms) over the period since the floating of the currency. It is expected that the link between the exchange rate and commodity prices would weaken over the coming years as Australia's exports shift in composition away from commodities towards manufactured goods and services. The terms of trade (which are determined in part by commodity prices) play a similar role in the determination of the Australian dollar exchange rate.

Figure 4.17 US dollar commodity price index (1994/1995=100)

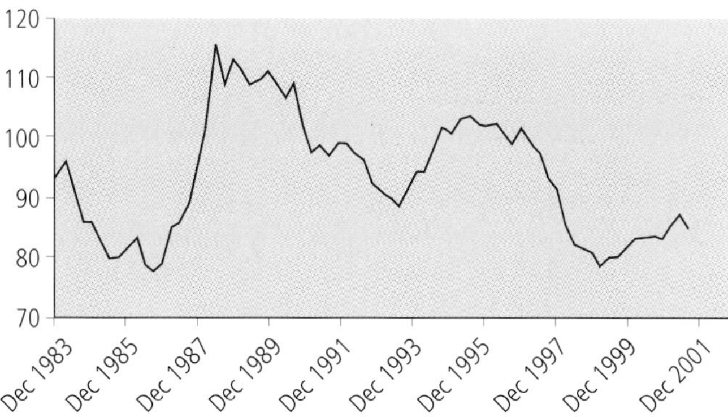

Source: RBA.

Inflation and inflation differentials

Figure 4.18 shows consumer prices in Australia and the United States. It is obvious that the Australian economy experienced higher inflation rates over the whole period. This may explain why the Australian dollar has depreciated. However, inflation differentials cannot explain short-run changes in the exchange rate, which is consistent with the evidence on purchasing power parity (see Chapter 9).

Figure 4.18 Consumer prices (December 1983 = 100)

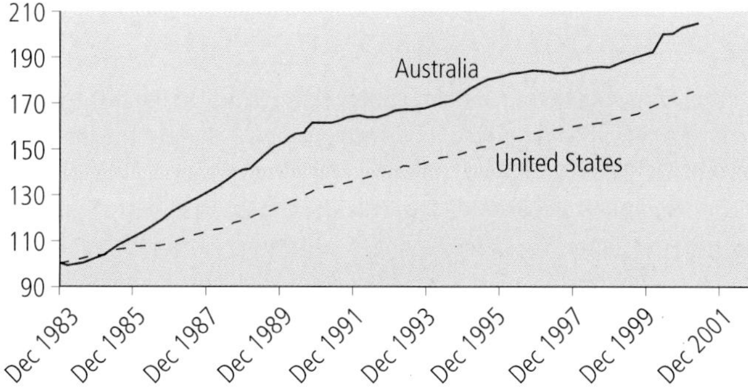

Source: Main Economic Indicators, OECD.

The external account

Australia's **external account** offers a strong intuitive explanation of movements in the exchange rate in certain circumstances. Episodes of weakness in the Australian dollar can be explained by the growing current account deficit and high rates of growth of external debt. The two factors are related because the interest paid on external debt is recorded on the current account. Thus, as external debt grows the current account worsens, unless other components of the current account improve. While there is no consistent relationship between the exchange rate and the external account in the short run, it is obvious that the weak external account must have been a contributing factor to the weakness of the currency since the end of 1983.

The role of the Reserve Bank

The Reserve Bank of Australia (RBA) began operations in 1960, replacing the Commonwealth Bank in its role as the country's central bank. The justification for intervention by the RBA is found in section 10(2) of the *Reserve Bank Act* of 1959, which places 'the stability of the currency of Australia' on the top of the list of ultimate objectives. These objectives, according to the Act, signify the responsibility of the RBA to direct monetary policy to 'the greatest advantage of the people of Australia'.

At different times the RBA has been active on both sides of the market: at times the RBA intervened to support the Australian dollar and at other times it intervened to restrain its rise. The RBA intervenes in the foreign exchange market for three reasons: (i) to calm the market when it tends to become disorderly; (ii) to help reverse **exchange rate overshooting**; and (iii) to give monetary policy greater room for manoeuvre. When the RBA intervenes, it buys or sells Australian dollars predominantly against the US dollar, the latter being the intervention currency. The RBA can deal round the clock with banks all around the world.

Direct intervention by the RBA takes the form of **smoothing** and **testing** transactions. 'Smoothing' transactions aim to ease the volatility of the currency's path in reaction to news to prevent exchange rate overshooting. By 'testing', the RBA tries to discern market volatility from trends.

The RBA prefers to pursue, and has undertaken, **sterilised intervention**. This occurs, for example, when the Bank buys Australian dollars and replenishes cash in the banking system, thereby leaving interest rates unchanged. Replenishment of cash is achieved either by buying Commonwealth government securities in its domestic market operations or by undertaking forward exchange swaps.

RESEARCH FINDINGS

Do fundamentals matter for exchange rates?

The dismal performance of exchange rate determination models with respect to the ability to explain and predict changes in exchange rates has prompted many economists to declare the irrelevance of **macroeconomic fundamentals** (such as growth, inflation and interest rates). These economists argue that macroeconomic fundamentals behave in a less volatile manner than exchange rates and so the former cannot explain the latter. As a result, these economists have been looking for alternative explanations for exchange rate volatility, such as news, nonlinearities and perhaps aliens from outer space (the author made this one up).

So, the question is: do fundamentals, as defined here, matter? Yes and no, depending on how you perceive the meaning of the word 'matter'. Economists claiming that fundamentals do not matter take the issue to the extreme by saying that this is the case because fundamental models do not do a good job of predicting exchange rates. This is asking too much and making the unrealistic assumption that all foreign exchange dealers subscribe to these models and follow them in making buy and sell decisions, which is not the case in practice. Foreign exchange traders follow a variety of techniques, models and tools to generate buy and sell signals and act accordingly. Fundamentals do matter as long as some of the traders observe and act upon them, shifting supply and demand and changing exchange rates in the process. In this sense, economic fundamentals do matter. Moreover, it is the heterogeneity of traders with respect to the techniques they use to generate buy and sell signals that gives rise to erratic shifts in the supply and demand functions and hence in exchange rates.

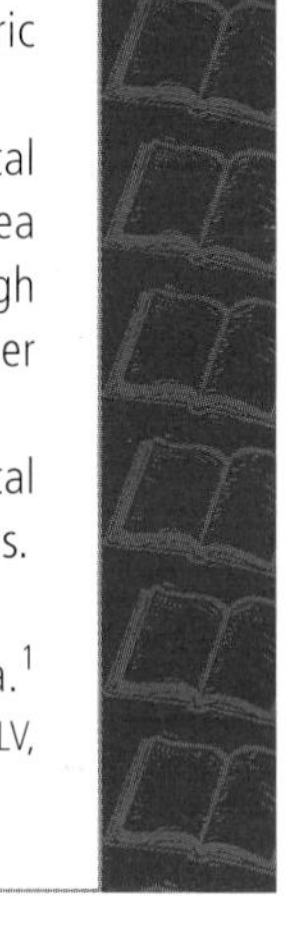

Do currency traders, or at least some of them, pay attention to fundamentals (that is, are there fundamentalists)? The answer is 'yes' and there are many reasons to believe that this is the case. The following points can be made to support this proposition:

- Survey and econometric evidence supports the existence of fundamentalists.
- Business firms subscribe to foreign exchange forecasting services that use fundamental econometric models.
- There are several episodes in which the foreign exchange market was dominated by fundamental factors. The 1979–1980 appreciation of the pound was triggered by the exploitation of North Sea oil. The appreciation of the US dollar in the first half of the 1980s started in response to the high US interest rates. The exit of the lira and pound from the European Monetary System in September 1992 was due to interest rate considerations.
- George Soros, the most successful currency speculator, based his buy/sell decisions on fundamental factors. Soros always talked about equilibrium, disequilibrium and far-from-equilibrium conditions.
- Under extreme conditions, such as hyperinflation, fundamental considerations dominate.

So, fundamentals do matter. For a more detailed discussion of this issue, see an article by Moosa.[1]

[1] I. A. Moosa, 'Exchange Rates and Fundamentals: A Microeconomic Approach', *Economia Internazionale*, Vol. LV, pp. 551–71, 2002.

Summary

- There are some stylised facts about the behaviour of exchange rates. These include the following: (i) exchange rates follow approximately a random walk with little or no drift; (ii) the spot and forward rates tend to move in the same direction and by approximately the same amount; (iii) there is no close correspondence between exchange rates and prices; (iv) there is a weak relationship between the exchange rate and the current account; and (v) countries experiencing rapid monetary expansion also experience depreciation.
- A number of factors cause the supply of and demand for foreign exchange curves to shift and therefore the exchange rate to change. These include: (i) relative inflation rates; (ii) the interest rate differential; (iii) relative growth rates; (iv) government intervention; and (v) expectations.
- Arbitrage in the foreign exchange market is the simultaneous purchase and sale of currencies for the sake of making profit. Two-point arbitrage is profitable if the exchange rate between two currencies is not the same in two financial centres.
- Three-point arbitrage is profitable if the cross exchange rates are inconsistent. If there are no profitable three-point arbitrage opportunities, arbitrage operations involving more than three currencies will not exist.
- Speculation can be stabilising and destabilising, depending on whether it drives the exchange rate towards or away from its equilibrium value.
- Since the bid-offer spread is a transaction cost, the profit derived from arbitrage and speculation in the presence of the bid-offer spread is smaller than otherwise.
- Since its floating in December 1983, the Australian dollar has in general depreciated both against the US dollar and in effective terms, although there have been bouts of strength.
- The factors determining the movements of the Australian dollar include: (i) interest rates; (ii) commodity prices; (iii) terms of trade; (iv) inflation; (v) the external account; and (vi) RBA intervention.

Key terms

adaptive expectations 107
arbitrage 106
asset market approach 121
bear market 116
bubbles 116
bull market 116
central bank intervention 102
contrarian expectations 107
destabilising speculation 116
determination puzzle 121
excess volatility puzzle 121
exchange rate overshooting 126
external account 125
extrapolative expectations 107
forward bias puzzle 121
goods market approach 121
heterogeneous expectations 107
hyperinflation 97
locational arbitrage 108
macroeconomic fundamentals 126
microstructure approach 121
multipoint arbitrage 114
no-arbitrage conditions 108
noise traders 107
nominal interest rate 99
quotas 102
random walk 96
rational expectations 107
real interest rate 99
regressive expectations 107
signalling effect 103
smoothing 126
spatial arbitrage 108
speculation 116
speculative attacks 106
stabilising speculation 117
sterilised intervention 126
tariffs 102
terms of trade 124
testing 126
three-point arbitrage 109
triangular arbitrage 109
two-point arbitrage 108

MaxMARK

MAXIMISE YOUR MARKS! There are 30 interactive questions for this chapter available online at **www.mhhe.com/au/moosa2e**

Review questions

1. 'The exchange rate follows approximately a random walk with little or no drift.' Explain.
2. 'Exchange rates cannot be predicted because they are determined by news.' Explain.
3. Discuss the factors that cause the demand and supply curves to shift, consequently leading to changes in the exchange rate.
4. Why is it that some Latin American countries have (or had at some time in the past) interest rates in excess of 100 per cent and at the same time depreciating currencies?
5. On 7 August 1997, the pound fell in reaction to the Bank of England's decision to raise interest rates. How would you reconcile this event with the predictions of the supply and demand model of exchange rate determination?
6. How do governments affect exchange rates?
7. How do expectations affect exchange rates?
8. Distinguish between stabilising and destabilising speculation. How in practice can we tell whether speculation is stabilising or destabilising?
9. Explain how the bid-offer spread is determined in the spot foreign exchange market.
10. Why does the presence of the bid-offer spread reduce the profitability of arbitrage and speculation in the spot foreign exchange market?

11 Central bank intervention is more powerful when the signalling effect is combined with actual buying and selling of currencies. Why?

12 In 1997, the Thai monetary authorities spent USD12 billion defending the baht. By early August 1997 the currency had lost 17 per cent of its value. Can you explain this failure of central bank intervention?

13 Use the supply and demand model to explain the performance of the Australian dollar since its floating in 1983.

14 Use the supply and demand model presented in this chapter to explain the movements in exchange rates as described in the following stories from 1997, 2002 and 2003:

- 'A growing conviction in financial markets that the Reserve Bank will deliver another interest rate cut next month dominated financial markets yesterday, sending the dollar tumbling to a two-month low.' *Australian*, 9 January 1997.
- 'The [Australian] dollar fell more than half a cent yesterday after the release of Australia's lowest inflation results in two years heightened speculation of another interest rate cut.' *Australian*, 30 January 1997.
- 'Reports that Japanese companies' inward investment strategies might change if Britain stayed out of European monetary union could also have unsettled foreign holders of the pound.' *Financial Times*, 31 January 1997.
- 'Analysts were puzzled by the pound's latest decline yesterday. They linked it to uncertainty about the approaching British election, which must take place by May, to selling by US investment funds.' *Financial Times*, 31 January 1997.
- 'The pound's drop followed sharp falls last week as traders continued to take the view that a British interest rate rise was unlikely before the general election.' *Financial Times*, 31 January 1997.
- 'The hard-pressed Australian dollar will face a big test tomorrow with the maturing of the first substantial Japanese issue of Australian dollar-linked bonds worth JPY20 billion (AUD220 million).' *Australian Financial Review*, 12 February 1997.
- 'The Australian dollar fell against the US dollar on the back of follow-through selling by Japanese, European and US operators. Unloading of dual-currency Samurai bonds and weak commodity prices overcame waning expectations of an imminent interest rate cut following remarks by RBA governor Ian MacFarlane indicating that Australian monetary policy is on hold.' *Australian*, 13 February 1997.
- 'The greenback hit JPY125 yesterday, the first time in more than four years, spurred by expectations of another rise in US interest rates—making US dollar-denominated investments more attractive.' *Australian*, 8 April 1997.
- 'Investors frowned upon the government's Federal Budget, driving domestic bond prices and the Australian dollar lower yesterday.' *Australian Financial Review*, 15 May 1997.
- 'The Australian dollar appears unlikely to benefit from any flow of funds out of Europe in the wake of the French elections because local interest rates are only level with the US rates and there is a prospect of another easing here.' *Australian Financial Review*, 3 June 1997.
- 'French financial markets slumped last night in the wake of the stunning election victory by the Socialist Coalition. The franc fell against the US dollar and the pound on concern that a socialist-dominated French government will undermine the strength of the planned single European currency.' *Australian*, 3 June 1997.
- 'Bank of Tokyo–Mitsubishi foreign exchange manager Makoto Sato said the [Japanese] Finance Ministry has been putting the brakes on the US dollar after it slipped below JPY112 on Monday.' *Australian*, 11 June 1997.

- 'The Australian dollar dived to its lowest point this year and bonds and bank bills surged, pushing three-year yields to three-year lows, after a dismal employment report fuelled speculation about another cut in official interest rates.' *Australian Financial Review*, 13 June 1997.
- 'This year the Australian dollar is an interest rate story, not a commodity story. The big factor not being priced in is a Fed tightening. That would change the whole psychology of the market. If it falls under 56 on the TWI and the yen strengthens, then you get the risk of a lower TWI and higher import prices and inflation.' *Australian Financial Review*, quoting a senior economist at Nomura Australia, 18 June 1997.
- 'The [Australian] dollar's fall was exacerbated by a report that Switzerland would sell half its gold reserves—about 1400 tonnes in the wake of a similar sell-off by the Reserve Bank of Australia.' *Australian*, 27 October 1997.
- 'A still teetering global economy has severely dented the Australian dollar's prospects, prompting market economists to substantially wind back their forecasts for the rest of this year.' *Australian Financial Review*, 1 October 2002.
- 'HSBC expects the $A will be hamstrung by the threat of war [with Iraq] and uncertainty on the global economy ... While the currency initially held its ground in August 1990, the $A tumbled two months after Iraq invaded Kuwait.' *Australian Financial Review*, 12 September 2002.
- 'Strong buying from Asia and an upbeat report [by the IMF] on the domestic economy boosted the Australian dollar.' *Australian Financial Review*, 20 September 2002.
- 'The Australian dollar was stopped in its tracks yesterday and oscillated around US56¢ as the US dollar staged a mild recovery following Iraq's acceptance of the United Nations weapons inspectors resolution.' *Australian Financial Review*, 15 November 2002.
- 'Investors smitten by Australia's high interest rates have gobbled up its currency, pushing it higher against the US dollar this month than most market forecasters predicted.' *Australian Financial Review*, 29 January 2003.
- 'Powering the infatuation with the $A and $A-based assets is a deepening scorn worldwide for all things US dollar-denominated as the United States grapples with myriad economic troubles and geopolitical issues.' *Australian Financial Review*, 29 January 2003.
- 'The star currency performers of the year's troubled first quarter owe their sizzle to old-fashioned interest rates and the American dollar's long-ordained decline.' *Australian Financial Review*, 2 April 2003.

Problems

1 The following exchange rates are quoted in Sydney and London at the same time:

Sydney (AUD/GBP)	2.56
London (GBP/AUD)	0.35

(a) Is there a possibility for two-point arbitrage?
(b) If so, what will arbitragers do?
(c) What is the profit earned from arbitrage?

2 The following exchange rates are quoted simultaneously in Sydney, Frankfurt and Zurich:

AUD/EUR	1.6400
CHF/AUD	0.8700
CHF/EUR	1.4600

(a) Is there a possibility for two-point arbitrage?
(b) Is there a possibility for three-point arbitrage?
(c) If so, what is the profitable sequence?
(d) What is the profit earned from arbitrage?
(e) How do the three exchange rates change as a result of arbitrage?
(f) What is the value of the CHF/EUR exchange rate that eliminates the possibility for profitable arbitrage?

3 The dealers' demand and supply functions are:

$$Qd = 10 - 2.5S_b$$

$$Qs = 5 + 3.5S_a$$

where Qd and Qs are the quantities supplied and demanded by dealers. The customers' demand and supply functions are:

$$Qd = 12 - 2.3S_a$$

$$Qs = 2 + 4.2S_b$$

Calculate the bid-offer spread.

4 The following exchange rates are quoted in Sydney and London at the same time:

Sydney (AUD/GBP)	2.5575–2.5625
London (GBP/AUD)	0.3475–0.3525

(a) Is there a possibility for two-point arbitrage?
(b) If so, what will arbitragers do?
(c) What is the profit earned from arbitrage?
(d) Compare the results with those obtained from Problem 1 above.

5 The following exchange rates were reported by Westpac Banking Corporation on 20 November 2002:

JPY/AUD	67.16
GBP/AUD	0.3484
CHF/AUD	0.8012
CAD/AUD	0.8711

(a) Calculate all possible cross rates.
(b) Using the calculated cross rates, show that there is no opportunity for three-point, four-point or five-point arbitrage.
(c) If the cross rates were 10 per cent higher than those obtained in (a) above, show that there are opportunities for profitable three-point, four-point or five-point arbitrage.

6 The spot exchange rate between the Australian dollar and the Swiss franc (CHF/AUD) is 0.8500–0.8580. A speculator believes that the Swiss franc will appreciate and so buys CHF1 000 000. Two days later, the exchange rate turns out to be 0.8200–0.8280. Ignoring the interest rate factor, answer the following questions:
(a) What will the speculator do?
(b) How much profit will the speculator make?
(c) Assuming that the speculator could buy and sell at the mid-rates, calculate the profit/loss in this case. Comment on your results.

CHAPTER

The international monetary system and exchange rate arrangements

Introduction

The financing of international trade and investment, which financial managers arrange, requires the conversion of currencies from one to another. The conversion takes place in the foreign exchange market in accordance with the rules and regulations set by the international monetary system in operation at the time. This chapter provides a comprehensive treatment of the relevant issues from theoretical, historical and practical perspectives.

The importance of this topic for business decision making stems from the fact that exchange rate regimes affect international financial operations. For example, speculation in the foreign exchange market under a system of flexible exchange rates is different from speculation under a system of fixed but adjustable rates. This is because flexible exchange rates move continuously by small amounts, whereas fixed but adjustable rates move occasionally but by large amounts.

Objectives

The objectives of this chapter are:

- To describe the theoretically possible international monetary systems and exchange rate arrangements according to the degree of flexibility of the exchange rate and the nature of the reserve asset.
- To present an outline of the historical development of exchange rate arrangements, starting with the classical gold standard and ending with the present system.
- To describe the historical development and the status quo of the Australian exchange rate arrangements.
- To outline the pros and cons of fixed and flexible exchange rates.

5.1 Definition and criteria of classification

The **international monetary system (IMS)** refers to the framework of rules, regulations and conventions that govern the financial relations among countries. It is so important and crucial for the world economy and international economic relations that Adam Smith described it as the 'Great Wheel' because 'when it does not turn well it adversely affects the welfare of nations'.

Business firms operating in international markets do so within the framework provided by the international monetary system in existence at the time. The nature of the system affects the sources of financing available to business firms and the countries in which these firms operate. Moreover, the system specifies the role of government and other institutions in the determination of exchange rates when these rates are not allowed to be determined by market forces.

The international monetary system has two components: (i) a public component consisting of a series of governmental agreements among countries and the functions of international public institutions; and (ii) a private component, which is represented by the banking and finance industry. In this chapter we deal with the public component, whereas the private component is dealt with in Chapter 8.

The world has experimented with a variety of international monetary systems that have been through episodes of success and failure. In order to have an idea of the characteristics of these systems, it is useful to classify them according to two criteria. The first of these criteria is the degree of flexibility of exchange rates. This criterion seems logical, given that the prime function of the IMS is to provide arrangements for the conversion of currencies. The second criterion is the nature of the **international reserves** held by central banks. These reserves may be commodities (metals, such as gold and silver, to be precise) or currencies, which presently cannot be converted into gold (fiat currencies). According to these standards, international monetary systems can be classified into the following:

- **Pure commodity standards**, such as the gold standard and the bimetallic standard (gold and silver), which was in operation in France in the eighteenth century.
- **Pure fiat standards**, in which reserves consist entirely of fiat currency.
- **Mixed standards**, in which reserves consist of fiat currency as well as commodities, most notably gold. An example of this system is the Bretton Woods system.

The classification of international monetary systems according to the flexibility of exchange rates is discussed in the following section.

5.2 Flexibility of exchange rates as a criterion for classification

Several systems may arise by restricting or otherwise the movement of exchange rates. Some of these systems have been tried in practice whereas others have not. The following are possible systems.

Fixed exchange rates

Under a system of **fixed exchange rates**, the exchange rate is determined by the central bank or the monetary authorities of the country concerned. It is often the case that under such a system the exchange rate is fixed at a level that makes the domestic currency overvalued. This was probably the problem with the Asian currencies prior to the Asian crisis of 1997.

Perfectly flexible exchange rates

Under a system of **flexible exchange rates**, the exchange rate changes continuously according to the forces of supply and demand in the foreign exchange market, as shown in Chapter 4. Figure 5.1 shows a typical movement of an exchange rate under such a system.

Fixed but adjustable exchange rates

Under this system countries alter the **par value** (that is, the fixed value) of the exchange rate whenever such a measure is necessary. The term **devaluation** is for fixed exchange rates what **depreciation** is for flexible exchange rates. Similarly, the term **revaluation** is equivalent to **appreciation**. However, there are differences. The movements of flexible exchange rates (appreciation and depreciation) are small, continuous and propelled by news, as depicted in Figure 5.1. Conversely, the movements of fixed exchange rates (devaluation and revaluation) are large, discrete and initiated by policy decisions. Figure 5.2 illustrates the movement of fixed exchange rates. The exchange rate is expressed in indirect quotation to show the movements corresponding to the devaluation and revaluation of the domestic currency.

Figure 5.1 Typical movements of flexible exchange rates

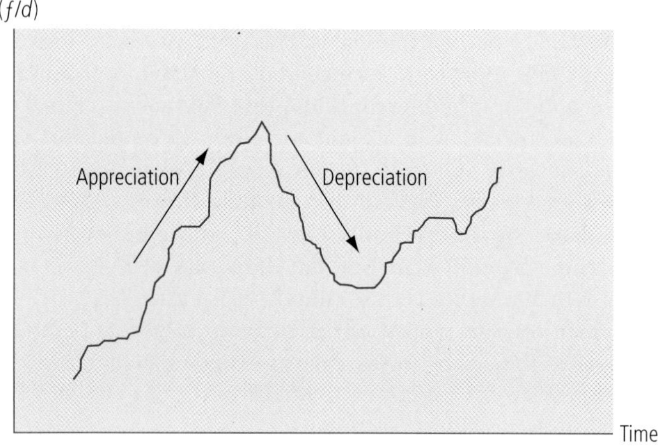

Figure 5.2 Typical movements of fixed exchange rates

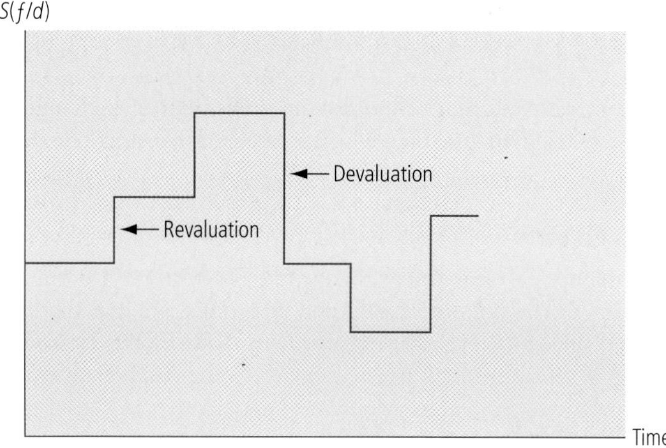

Fixed exchange rates and flexible within a band

Under this system, exchange rates are flexible within upper and lower limits defined by a band around the par value. However, the exchange rates are fixed otherwise in the sense that they are not allowed, by central bank intervention, to move outside the band (below the lower limit or above the upper limit). A typical behaviour of an exchange rate under this system is described in Figure 5.3. The exchange rate is quite flexible within the band but when it breaks through the upper limit (implying weakness of the domestic currency) the central bank intervenes by selling the foreign currency, forcing the exchange rate within the band again. Conversely, when the exchange rate breaks through the lower limit (implying weakness of the foreign currency), the central bank intervenes by buying the foreign currency. Such a system is similar to the **European Monetary System (EMS)** and the **Bretton Woods system**.

Figure 5.3 The behaviour of exchange rates when there is a band

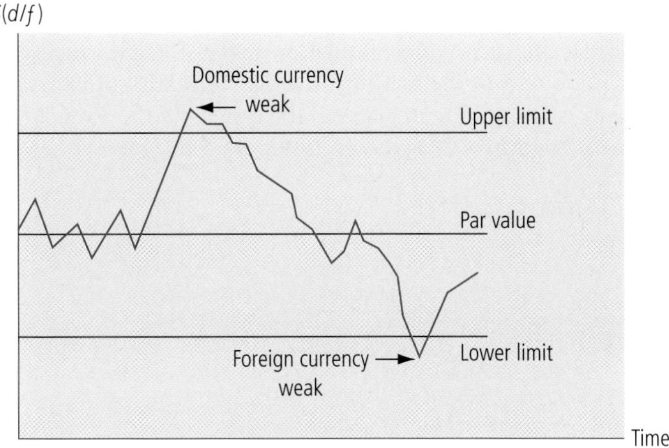

Sometimes, a system of **multiple bands** exists where a currency is allowed to move within a band of certain width against one or a group of currencies and within a wider band against another group of currencies. This system is illustrated in Figure 5.4, which shows three nested bands: A, B and C. Obviously, the currency is allowed a wider variation within band C than within band A. An example of a system with two bands is the **Snake in the Tunnel**, the predecessor of the EMS, where the member currencies were allowed to fluctuate within a narrow band of ±1.25 per cent (the Snake) against each other and a wider band of ±2.25 per cent (the Tunnel) against the currencies of non-member countries as prescribed by the **Smithsonian Agreement**. Within this system, a third, narrower band (called the **Worm**) was in operation, as the currencies of the Netherlands and Belgium were allowed to move against each other by ±0.75 per cent. The EMS was based on the same idea: while most of the member currencies were allowed to fluctuate against each other by ±2.25 per cent, others (such as the Italian lira and the British pound) were allowed to fluctuate against other currencies within the system by ±6 per cent.

Figure 5.4 The case of multiple bands

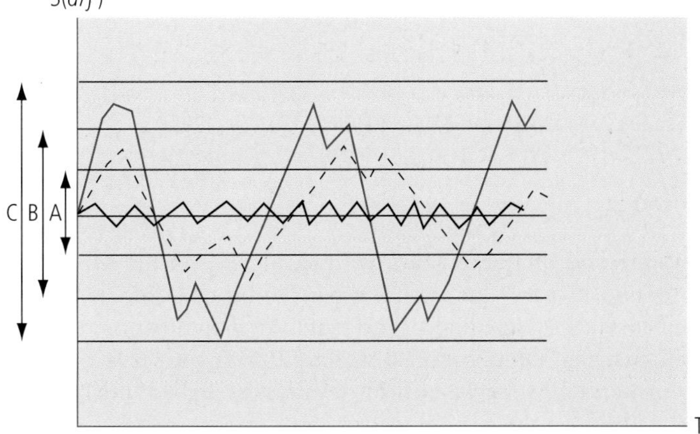

Figure 5.5 illustrates the dynamics of devaluation and revaluation, given the existence of a constant band. Initially, the exchange rate moves within a band around a low par value. The currency is subsequently revalued and starts to move around a higher par value within a band of the same width as the first one. A second revaluation makes the exchange rate fluctuate around a new, higher par value within the same bandwidth. This kind of behaviour resulted from successive revaluations of the German mark (DEM) against the French franc (FRF) within the EMS between 1979 and 1992, as shown in Figure 5.6.

Figure 5.5 Revaluation with constant bandwidth

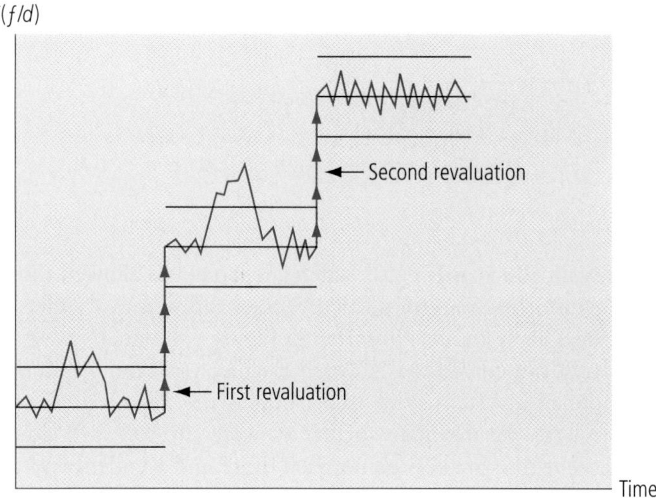

Figure 5.6 The FRF/DEM exchange rate (1979–1992)

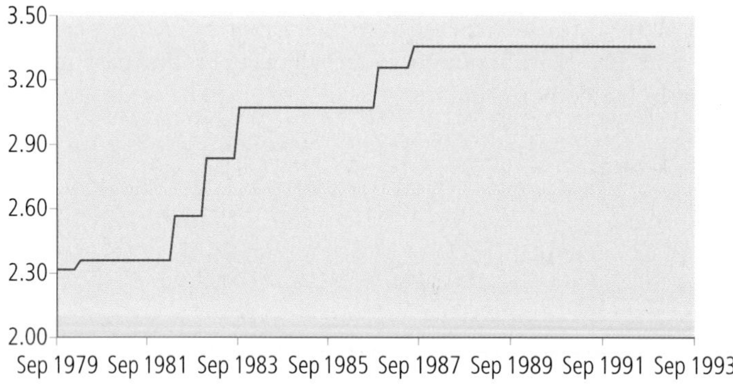

Source: Main Economic Indicators, OECD.

Finally, Figure 5.7 shows the case of a revaluation with an increase in the bandwidth. The currency initially moves around its par value within a narrow band. A decision is made to revalue the currency, coupled with a widening of the band. After revaluation, the currency starts to move around a higher par value within a wider band. To preserve the European Monetary System, European central bankers and finance ministers agreed in March 1993 to revalue the German mark and widen the band from ±2.25 to ±15 per cent.

Figure 5.7 Revaluation with variable (increasing) bandwidth

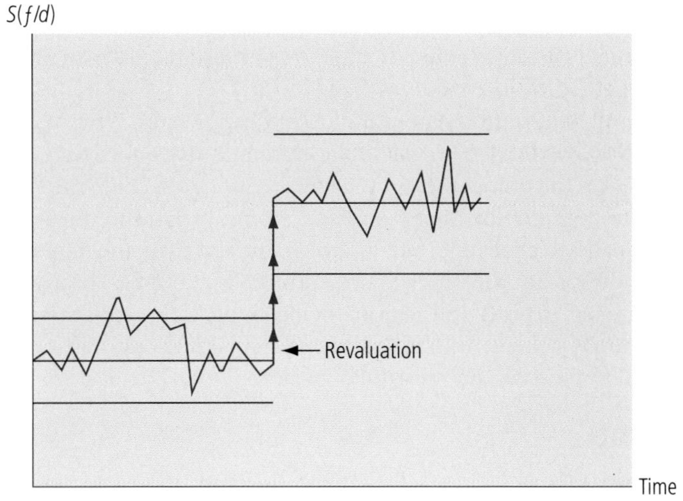

Crawling peg

The word **peg** means the fixed or the par value of the exchange rate. Under a **crawling peg**, the par value is revised periodically according to the average exchange rate over the previous weeks or months or by pegging it to an economic indicator such as inflation. For example, Portugal had a higher inflation rate than its major European trading partners during the 1980s. In order to preserve its competitive position, the domestic currency (the former escudo) was devalued by 0.5 per cent per month. This kind of behaviour is depicted in Figure 5.8.

Figure 5.8 Devaluation with a crawling peg

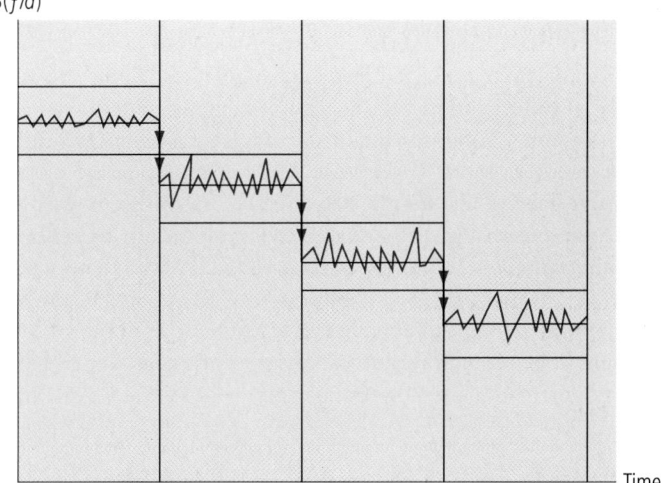

Dual exchange rates

Dual exchange rates represent a mixed system of fixed and flexible exchange rates. A commercial (fixed) rate is used for imports and exports (current account transactions) and a financial (flexible) rate is used for trading in financial assets (financial or capital account transactions). This system is adopted by countries that wish to insulate commercial transactions from exchange rate fluctuations resulting from speculative capital flows. The capital controls introduced by the Thai authorities in May 1997 created a two-tier market with different exchange rates quoted onshore and offshore.

There are at least two problems with a system of dual exchange rates. First, the commercial rate may be fixed at such a low level as to make the domestic currency overvalued, which will have an adverse effect on the competitiveness of the economy. Second, the system works properly only if the two foreign exchange markets (commercial and financial) can be segmented. When the financial exchange rate is much higher than the commercial rate, transactions may (or will) leak from the official market to the free market through fraudulent means such as underinvoicing exports and overinvoicing imports. For this system to work, the two rates must be closely related and, if the financial (floating) rate changes for some fundamental reason, the commercial rate must follow suit.

Managed floating

Under **managed floating**, which is also called **dirty floating**, there are no fixed values because exchange rates are basically flexible. However, central banks intervene in the market to limit the frequency and amplitude of fluctuations in exchange rates around their long-term trends or to keep the exchange rate within a certain range. Central banks do not admit the existence of a **target range**, either because they cannot maintain it or because they do not want to be perceived as tampering excessively with market forces. This system is used by a large number of countries at the present time. It is adopted because countries in general want to see their currencies neither too strong (because of the adverse effect on the competitive position of the economy) nor too weak (because this raises import prices).

Target zones

The system of **target zones** arose out of an attempt by major industrial countries to coordinate their exchange rate policies with the objective of eliminating or at least reducing exchange rate misalignment. According to this system, major countries establish a set of mutually consistent targets for their real effective exchange rates. Thus, the nominal rates would move continuously to reflect differences in inflation rates.

An example of a system of target zones for major currencies was suggested in the 1980s by a famous international economist, John Williamson. This system is based on the so-called **fundamental equilibrium effective exchange rate**, which is consistent with a sustainable current account position. This exchange rate is adjusted periodically to reflect changes in economic fundamentals. The actual exchange rate is then allowed to fluctuate around this level within a **soft-edged band** of ±10 per cent. The band is described as 'soft' because central banks are not committed to buying or selling the currency if it reaches the upper or lower limits of the band. This, the argument goes, would prevent the creation of a one-way bet for speculators thinking that a weak or strong currency will be bought and sold by the central bank.

5.3 The classical gold standard

The **gold standard** is often remembered with nostalgia because the international economy prospered under this system, while the period that followed its collapse was a dark phase in world economic history. The gold standard did not encompass the entire world but only a core of major countries led by Britain. There is widespread disagreement about the years that define the period in which the gold standard was in operation. The gold standard came to an end abruptly at the beginning of World War I in August 1914, when the warring countries abolished the convertibility of their currencies into gold and into each other. While the timing of its end is indisputable, the problem is to identify the year that marks the beginning of the system.

Britain went on the gold standard in 1821, when the Bank of England was legally required to redeem its notes and coins in gold and when the prohibition of the melting of coins and export of gold was repealed. In doing so, Britain formally met the conditions of being on the gold standard. By the mid-1870s France had abandoned bimetallism in favour of gold. In 1870 Germany was still on the silver standard, but war reparations in the form of gold payments from France enabled it to adopt the gold standard. And in 1879 the United States returned to the gold standard after the suspension of gold convertibility during the Civil War. In general, 1870 is regarded as the year in which the gold standard became internationally operational.

Exchange rate determination under the gold standard

Under the classical gold standard, exchange rates are determined as follows:

- The monetary authority in each country fixes the price of gold in terms of the domestic currency, standing ready to buy or sell any amount of gold at that price.
- This establishes a fixed exchange rate between any two currencies called the **mint parity**.
- The exchange rate can vary above and below the mint parity only between certain limits called the **gold points**. The cost of shipping gold between the two countries defines the upper and lower limits on the exchange rate, the **gold export point** and the **gold import point**, respectively.

Example

Assume that one ounce of gold is worth AUD100 and NZD125. The mint parity is calculated as

$$\frac{100}{125} = 0.8000\ (AUD/NZD)$$

Suppose now that the cost of shipping gold between Australia and New Zealand is 1 per cent of the value of the gold shipped. Thus, the cost of shipping AUD0.8000 (80 cents) worth of gold is AUD0.0080 (0.8 cents). From an Australian perspective, the gold export point and the gold import point are calculated as follows:

$$0.8000 + 0.0080 = 0.8080$$
$$0.8000 - 0.0080 = 0.7920$$

This means that (under this hypothetical situation) the residents of Australia would not pay more than AUD0.8080 for one New Zealand dollar. This is because they could buy AUD0.8000 worth of gold in Australia, ship it to New Zealand and sell it there for one New Zealand dollar. The total cost of buying one New Zealand dollar is therefore AUD0.8080 and so there is no reason to pay more than this amount. Likewise, they would not accept less than AUD0.7920 for one New Zealand dollar. This is because they can buy one New Zealand dollar worth of gold, ship it to Australia and sell it for AUD0.8000, obtaining AUD0.7920 net and so there is no reason to accept less than this amount.

Evaluation of the classical gold standard

During the era of the gold standard, world trade and investment flourished, promoting international specialisation and global welfare. Because of such a positive atmosphere, conflicts among countries were extremely rare. So, was the gold standard a success? In retrospect the answer is no. Its apparent success was due to the fact that it was in operation during a rather tranquil period, which means that it was not really put to the test (for example, against the oil shocks of the 1970s).

Irrespective of the pluses and minuses of the gold standard, the system collapsed with the outbreak of World War I as the warring countries suspended the convertibility of their currencies into gold and prohibited gold exports. That was the end of the era of the classical gold standard.

5.4 The inter-war period

In the period between the end of World War I and 1926, a system of flexible exchange rates was adopted. During this period many countries suffered from **hyperinflation**: the German hyperinflation of 1919–1923 was the most notorious case. There was a desire to go back to the gold standard, but there was an obvious shortage of gold at the pre-war levels of the fixed exchange rates. In 1922 the **Genoa Conference** recommended worldwide adoption of a gold exchange standard, whereby the pound would be convertible into gold and other currencies would be convertible into the pound. In 1925 Britain re-established the convertibility of the pound into gold. Soon after, other countries restored convertibility at the pre-war rates. The gold exchange standard was born.

In 1931 the French decided not to accept any more pounds and to exchange their holdings of the British currency for gold. There was little that Britain could do other than to make the pound inconvertible into gold. That was the end of the gold exchange standard, which was followed by the decade of the **Great Depression** (1931–1939), a period of open economic warfare through competitive devaluation.

So, why did the inter-war experiment fail? First, because the 'golden age' of the gold standard was actually a myth. Second, the world economy had experienced significant changes because of the war and the Great Depression, including the following: (i) the pre-war rates were inappropriate because of widely divergent inflation rates; (ii) prices and wages became rigid (particularly downwards); and (iii) countries did not follow the 'rules of the game' because of concern about domestic economic instability.

5.5 The Bretton Woods system

The Bretton Woods system was born in 1944 in Bretton Woods, New Hampshire, endorsed by the delegates of 44 countries. The creation of this system was accompanied by the creation of international institutions, including the **International Bank for Reconstruction and Development** (presently known as the **World Bank**) and the **International Monetary Fund (IMF)**. The IMF was entrusted with the supervision of the new international monetary system and with granting loans to deal with balance of payments difficulties, whereas the World Bank specialised in granting loans for the reconstruction of Europe and for development purposes.

Negotiators at Bretton Woods sought an exchange rate system that would combine the advantages of both fixed and flexible exchange rates (perhaps too good to be true). The choice was a system of fixed but adjustable exchange rates, the **adjustable peg**. Therefore, the dollar was pegged to gold at the fixed rate of USD35/ounce and the United States was prepared to buy and sell unlimited amounts of the metal at this rate. Other countries were required to declare the rates of their currencies in terms of gold or the dollar and to defend the declared rates in the foreign exchange market by buying and selling dollars. Exchange rates could only vary within the **intervention points**, initially fixed at ±1 per cent.

The Bretton Woods system also catered for currency convertibility and multilateral trade. All currencies were to be freely convertible into one another at the official rates. However, because of the consequences of the war, it was agreed that the abolition of controls would be gradual. European currencies did not return to convertibility until 1958.

Some problems with the Bretton Woods system

The Bretton Woods system suffered from a number of problems that led to its eventual collapse. The first of these problems pertains to the adjustment mechanism (of the balance of payments). Multilateral trade and currency convertibility need a real adjustment mechanism, something the system lacked. Governments had to demonstrate the existence of a fundamental disequilibrium in the balance of payments before they could adjust their exchange rates (Britain devalued the pound twice under this kind of arrangement: in 1949 and in 1967). The adjustable-peg system lacked the stability, certainty and automaticity of the gold standard and the flexibility of the free-floating system. The second problem is that speculation can be very destabilising because of the possibility of changing the fixed rates. When a currency is under pressure (perhaps because the country concerned is running out of reserves) it can only be devalued, motivating speculators to sell it.

An important loophole in the system was the defects in the liquidity creation mechanism. In the early 1960s the prospect of a global liquidity shortage caused widespread concern in official circles as attention focused on proposals for new reserve creation mechanisms. This problem has led to the emergence of the so-called **Triffin Dilemma** or the **Triffin Paradox** (after Robert Triffin, the US economist who first recognised the problem). To avoid a liquidity shortage, the United States must run a balance of payments deficit and this would undermine confidence in the dollar. To avoid speculation against the dollar the deficit must shrink, which would create a liquidity shortage. So, it was a vicious circle. One solution to this problem was suggested in 1968, which was the creation of **special drawing rights (SDRs)** as an international currency. The SDR is a composite currency whose value (exchange rate) is calculated as a weighted average of the exchange rates of the currencies to which it is pegged. It is mainly used as a unit of account in transactions involving the International Monetary Fund.

The collapse of the Bretton Woods system

The Bretton Woods era can be divided into two periods: (i) the period of the dollar shortage, 1944–1958; and (ii) the period of the dollar glut, 1958–1971. The second period was characterised by a significant balance of payments deficit at a time when the surplus countries (Germany and Japan) were resisting revaluation of their currencies. In 1962 France began to exchange dollars for gold despite the objection of the United States. Not only were the French doubtful about the future value of the dollar, but they also objected to the prominent role of the United States in the Bretton Woods system. The French action led other countries to worry about whether sufficient gold would remain for them after the French had finished selling dollars. Feeling the pressure, the United States became severely constrained, being unable to change its exchange rate.

On 15 August 1971 the United States responded to a record USD30 billion trade deficit by making the dollar inconvertible into gold, as announced by President Richard Nixon. This action, similar to the action taken by Britain in 1931, marked the collapse of the Bretton Woods system.

5.6 The present system

To help understand the transition from the Bretton Woods system to the present system and track developments since the 1960s, Figure 5.9 displays the US dollar's effective exchange rate during the period 1980–2002. As we can see, the dollar reached its peak in February 1985, then depreciated sharply. Between 1987 and 1996 it was fluctuating within a range. Subsequently, it began to appreciate, propelled by the equity boom and the new economy phenomenon.

Figure 5.9 The US dollar's effective exchange rate

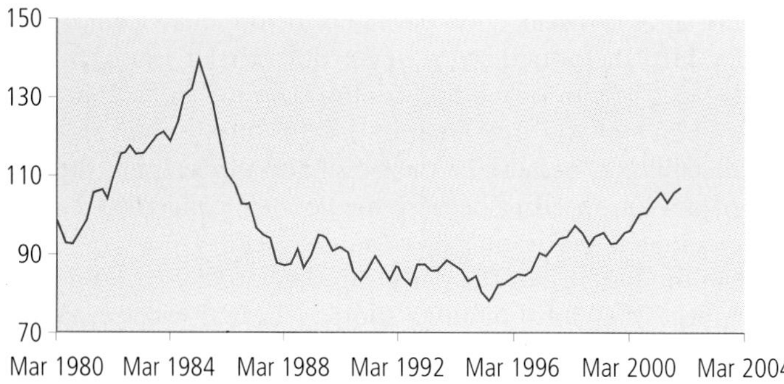

Source: Main Economic Indicators, OECD.

On 18 December 1971 the major 10 industrial countries in the world tried to save the Bretton Woods system by signing the Smithsonian Agreement in Washington, DC. The United States agreed to raise the official price of gold to USD38/ounce but refused to restore the free convertibility of the dollar into gold. Other countries, in return, agreed to revalue their currencies against the dollar. Moreover, exchange rates were allowed to fluctuate within a wider band of ±2.5 per cent, making the change described by Figure 5.7.

This agreement, however, did not solve any of the fundamental defects of the Bretton Woods system. As a result, floating became widespread in 1973, while European countries experimented with the Snake in the Tunnel. The floating exchange rate system was not legalised until January 1976 (with ratification coming in 1978) when the **Jamaica Accord** was signed. The accord allowed countries the freedom of choice of the exchange rate system they deemed appropriate for their economies, encouraging them not to resort to competitive devaluation. There was also an agreement to pursue domestic economic policies conducive to stability. Finally, the official price of gold was abolished, allowing it to fluctuate according to market forces.

Currently, major industrial countries adopt a system of **floating exchange rates**, while 12 European countries have moved to a single currency. The current system has not solved the problems of the Bretton Woods system and has failed in three major areas. The first of these problems is exchange rate misalignments (deviations of exchange rates from their 'fair' values). The second area is that the system has failed to deliver policy autonomy, in the sense that it has failed to cut the policy links among countries. The consequence of these links is that economic policy in one country, particularly if it is a major country, leads to effects that are transmitted abroad. Finally, there is the problem of **protectionism**. Because of financial deregulation, international capital flows have dominated trade flows in determining exchange rates. The resultant misalignments have distorted international competitive positions, leading to strong pressure for protectionism. It seems, after all, that countries have not maintained one of the rules of the game as prescribed by the Jamaica Accord.

In the 1980s and 1990s three major events took place: the **Plaza Accord**, the **Louvre Accord** and the EMS crisis. The first of these was the signing of the Plaza Accord in September 1985 to bring the US dollar down through intervention. As a result of the ensuing intervention, the depreciation of the dollar that started in March 1985 was consolidated and by early 1987 the dollar had depreciated to reach its 1980 levels, at least against the yen and the German mark. In February 1987 the major seven industrial countries signed the Louvre Accord, whereby they agreed to cooperate in order to achieve greater stability in the foreign exchange market. Since then, a major event has been the crisis in the European Monetary System, which is discussed later in the chapter.

Other exchange rate arrangements in the present system

The Jamaica Accord gave countries the freedom of choosing the exchange rate arrangements they deemed appropriate for their economies. However, not all countries opted for floating: some chose other systems encompassing a spectrum with respect to exchange rate flexibility. This is why these arrangements are sometimes described as being 'eclectic'. The choice of the exchange rate arrangement is an issue that has been discussed extensively in the literature. The choice, according to the literature, depends on the characteristics of the underlying economy, such as the degree of openness.

The IMF reports current exchange rate arrangements in every issue of its monthly publication, *International Financial Statistics*. Moreover, a report on exchange arrangements and exchange restrictions is published annually. As at the end of December 2001, the following exchange rate arrangements were in place, as reported in the January 2003 issue of *International Financial Statistics* (the number of countries adopting the arrangement is placed in parentheses).

Exchange arrangements with no separate legal tender (40)

Under this arrangement, the currency of another country circulates as the sole legal tender. Alternatively, the country belongs to a monetary or currency union in which the same legal tender is shared by the members of the union. This includes the 12 European countries using the euro as well as members of other currency unions (for example, Grenada is part of the East Caribbean Currency Union).

Currency board arrangements (8)

A **currency board** is an arrangement that is based on an explicit legislative commitment to exchange the domestic currency for a specified foreign currency at a fixed exchange rate, combined with restrictions on the issuing authority to ensure the fulfilment of its legal obligation. Until early 2002, Argentina opted for this arrangement, exchanging the peso for the US dollar on a one-to-one basis. Following the financial crisis, this arrangement was abolished as the peso was floated. Hong Kong and Estonia follow similar arrangements.

The pros and cons of currency boards

A currency board is a system of fixed exchange rates that was common in colonial territories during the first half of the twentieth century. It is a system whereby the currency board is obliged to supply, on demand and without limit, the foreign currency to which the domestic currency is pegged. The dismantling of colonial regimes led to the virtual disappearance of currency boards. However, interest in currency boards has revived in recent years as financial crises triggered thinking about means of stabilising exchange rates and bringing order to economic conditions in general. Currency boards are believed by some economists to be one of these means.

The first re-introduction of a currency board that has proved to be successful was in Hong Kong in 1983. In 1991 Argentina set up a similar arrangement, whereby the peso was linked to the US dollar at a parity exchange rate (one to one). In 1992 Estonia began to operate a currency board, followed by Lithuania in 1994.

What are the pros and cons of currency boards? The pros are:

- They are an effective means of pegging the exchange rate when a hard peg is required.
- They can be very effective in countries suffering from hyperinflation or in new countries in which financial stability has not yet been established (for example, East Timor).
- They help curb wasteful government spending financed by printing money.
- They are better than the alternatives of weak pegs (for example, Thailand before the onset of the Asian crisis) and free floating.

Other conventional fixed peg arrangements (40)

These arrangements include **pegging to a single currency** and **pegging to a basket of currencies**, such as the SDR. Under these arrangements, the country pegs its currency (formally or *de facto*) at a fixed rate to a single currency or a basket of currencies, allowing the actual exchange rate to fluctuate within a narrow margin of less than ±1 per cent around a central rate (the rate determined by the arrangement). Examples are Bahrain (the US dollar) and Kuwait (undeclared basket until the end of 2002, after which the country switched to pegging to the US dollar).

Pegged exchange rates with horizontal bands (5)

This arrangement is similar to the previous one, except that the band within which the exchange rate is allowed to fluctuate is wider than ±1 per cent. An example is Egypt.

Crawling peg (4)

Under a crawling peg, the exchange rate is adjusted periodically at a fixed, pre-announced small rate or in response to changes in some quantitative indicators (for example, inflation). An example is Bolivia.

Exchange rates with crawling bands (6)

An arrangement of **crawling bands** requires the exchange rate to be maintained within a certain band around a **central rate** that is adjusted periodically at a fixed, pre-announced rate or in response to changes in some indicators. An example is Romania.

Managed floating with no pre-announced path for the exchange rate (42)

Under this arrangement, the exchange rate is determined by market forces but the monetary authority intervenes actively in the foreign exchange market without specifying a path for the exchange rate. Examples are Vietnam and Thailand.

The cons are:

- Governments operating currency boards must accept restrictions on the way they conduct policy.
- Countries on this system must swallow their pride and abandon their monetary sovereignty.
- Governments have to give up **seigniorage**, the implicit profit gained by printing national money (the difference between the face value of a monetary unit and its cost of printing).
- A fixed exchange rate can get excessively out of line with those of the underlying country's trading partners.
- Currency boards are not immune to speculative attacks.

The experiences of the countries that have adopted currency boards recently may provide some evidence in favour of or against this system. While the experience of Hong Kong has been a success, we have not heard much of the experiences of Estonia and Lithuania. On the other hand, the Argentine financial crisis of 2001–2002 was exacerbated by the exchange rate arrangement to the extent that the government decided to abandon it and resort to floating the peso in 2002.

Some economists, such as Rudiger Dornbusch, argue that the demise of Argentina would have happened with or without a currency board.[1] The crisis, according to Dornbusch, was waiting to happen because of the legacy of high debt and earlier deficits, trade unions that have consistently thwarted reform and obsolete industry that would not be competitive at any exchange rate.

[1] R. Dornbusch, 'Fewer Monies, Better Monies', *American Economic Review, Papers and Proceedings*, May 2001, pp. 238–42.

Independent floating (41)

Under **independent floating** the exchange rate is determined by market forces. Any intervention in the foreign exchange market aims at curbing exchange rate volatility. Examples are Australia, the United States and the United Kingdom.

5.7 The European Monetary System

The agreement to establish the EMS as a 'zone of monetary stability in Europe' was reached in the European Council meeting that was held in Bremen, Germany, on 6–7 July 1978. The system started functioning on 13 March 1979, while at the same time the Snake system ceased to exist. All members of the European Economic Community (nine at that time) agreed to participate in all aspects of the EMS, except the United Kingdom, which chose not to join the Exchange Rate Mechanism (ERM).

The heart of the EMS was a system of fixed but adjustable exchange rates whereby each currency had a central rate expressed in terms of the **European currency unit (ECU)**. These central rates determined a grid of bilateral central rates around a band of ±2.25 per cent, except for the Italian lira (6 per cent). If the exchange rates moved above or below these limits, central bank intervention was obligatory.

During its early life, the EMS experienced some turbulence, normally ending up in a **realignment** involving changes in the central rates of the currencies (devaluations and revaluations). The first realignment took place on 24 September 1979, when the German mark was revalued while the Danish krone was devalued. The first realignment that involved all of the currencies took place on 21 March 1983, when the French franc, Italian lira and

Irish punt were devalued while other currencies were revalued. During the period between the inauguration of the system and 11 January 1987, there were 11 realignments.

The period between January 1987 and September 1992 was a period of tranquillity for the EMS, witnessing only one realignment on 5 January 1990. During that period, the pound joined the ERM at a central rate of 2.95 against the mark. The trouble started in September 1992, which was the beginning of the end of the EMS as a fixed but adjustable exchange rate system. The timing of the trouble was not a coincidence, as it occurred at the same time as the removal of capital controls in member countries in the spirit of the 1992 program to unify financial markets within the European Community. Other relevant factors are the following: (i) the fact that the pound became an ERM currency at an artificially high central rate; (ii) German reunification; and (iii) the recession of 1992. The chain of events was as follows. German reunification put upward pressure on German interest rates, as the demand for funds rose to finance the reunification. As a result, the German mark started to appreciate against other currencies, at a time when other countries could not defend their currencies by raising interest rates since their economies were sliding into recession. For the United Kingdom the situation was even more difficult, as the task of defending what was thought to be an overvalued pound was extremely demanding.

When the crunch came in September 1992, the Bank of England tried to keep the pound within the band prescribed by the ERM, by market intervention and also by raising interest rates. This action was ineffective in the face of massive speculative pressure on the pound, providing a classic example of the ineffectiveness of intervention and its inability to reverse a solid market trend. The Italian lira suffered a similar fate. The end result was that these two currencies had to leave the ERM, simply because the exchange rates could not be maintained within the prescribed limits. Three realignments took place on 12 September, 16 September and 12 November. This series of realignments took the exchange rate between the French franc and the German mark from 2.3095 on 13 March 1979 to 3.3539 on 22 November 1992.

This was not the end of the story, however. Speculative attacks against the member currencies (particularly the Irish punt) continued in 1993. On 1 August 1993 it was decided that the band around central rates should be increased to ±15 per cent, in effect terminating the EMS as a system of fixed but adjustable exchange rates. The EMS has thus not provided good evidence for the viability of a system of fixed but adjustable rates in the present environment of open markets and high capital mobility.

In December 1991, members of the European Community signed the **Maastricht Treaty**, which specified a timetable for the move towards the **European Monetary Union (EMU)**. The plan has its origin in the Delors Report of 1989 on the accomplishment of the transition to full monetary union. This report envisaged three stages: (i) removing the remaining exchange controls (completed by the end of 1992); (ii) establishing a European system of central banks and hardening the ERM; and (iii) full implementation of the monetary union when exchange rates become increasingly fixed and the European Central Bank takes charge of running the union's monetary policy.

In January 1999, the common European currency, the euro, was introduced for trading but not in its hard form. In January 2002, the euro notes and coins were introduced, replacing 12 national currencies. For three years after its introduction, the euro lost ground against the US dollar, as shown in Figure 5.10. However, by early 2003 the euro had regained most of its losses against the dollar, but most observers interpreted this as dollar weakness rather than euro strength. Several reasons have been put forward to explain the weakness of the European currency portrayed in Figure 5.10 (see the box in Chapter 4 explaining the weakness of the euro). At the time of writing, it was not clear whether or not the EU members that have opted out of the single currency (such as the United Kingdom) would eventually adopt the currency.

Figure 5.10 The EUR/USD exchange rate

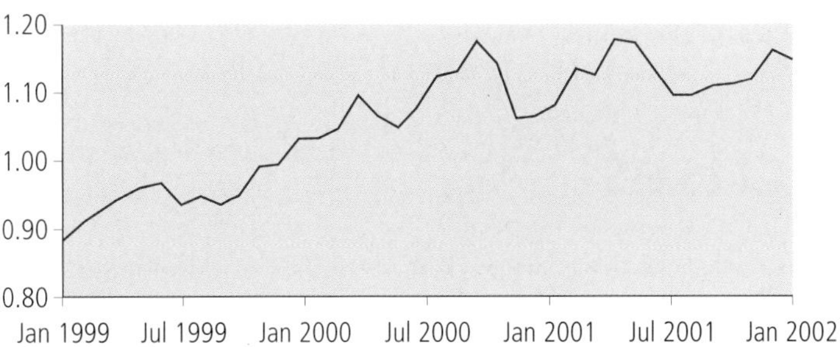

Source: Main Economic Indicators, OECD.

INSIGHT

The euro timetable

June 1989	Delors Report on economic and monetary union
July 1990	Stage one: abolition of capital controls
December 1991	Maastricht Treaty negotiated
January 1994	Stage two: European Monetary Institute created
December 1995	'Euro' chosen as the name of the single currency
May 1998	Euro members chosen, bilateral conversion rates fixed, European Central Bank established
December 1998	European conversion rates fixed
January 1999	Stage three: euro launched
January 2002	Euro notes and coins introduced
July 2002	National notes and coins withdrawn
April 2003	EU enlargement (10 new EU members admitted)

The introduction of the euro and the abolition of national currencies have led to the emergence of a debate about the benefits of the single currency. Supporters of the euro argue that the single currency has substantial benefits for European businesses and economies. Specifically, these benefits are envisaged:

- Currency stability and the operations of the European Central Bank reduce inflation and interest rates.
- Businesses and individuals benefit from reduced transaction and hedging costs. The savings are estimated to be some 0.5 per cent of GDP (about USD40 billion per year).
- The single currency produces efficiency gains, as it is easier to compare prices and wages across the euro area. For example, it is easier to indulge in commodity arbitrage under a single currency by buying commodities where they are cheap and selling them where they are more expensive.
- Transparent pricing boosts competition because it is easier for companies to sell across the euro zone and for consumers to shop around.
- The single currency boosts trade.
- The single currency also boosts the development of a liquid euro-wide capital market, lowering the cost of capital and improving its allocation.

However, these benefits cannot be realised without costs. For the system to work well, the member countries should be similar in terms of reaction to shocks (for example, higher oil prices) and should go through similar cycles. Moreover, the introduction of the euro means that individual countries give up the right to set their interest rates and the option of using the exchange rate as a policy instrument.

5.8 Financial crises

Since the mid-1990s, financial crises have erupted in a number of developing countries in Asia (Thailand, Indonesia, Korea, Malaysia and the Philippines), Latin America (Mexico, Brazil and Argentina) and in Russia. The ramifications have been quite significant as the crises led to bank failures, corporate bankruptcies, unemployment and economic stagnation, increased fiscal burdens on the governments in charge, and depletion of foreign exchange reserves. In a few cases, these crises have even caused political and social turbulence (Argentina, for example). Research on the causes of the crises has highlighted weaknesses in economic fundamentals, excessive short-term foreign borrowing by governments and private sector entities, and volatile short-term capital flows. Another contributory factor is the weakness in the national financial systems.

Before the onset of the Asian crisis in 1997, the countries that experienced the crisis had impressive records of economic performance. It is no wonder then that no one predicted the crisis (just before the emergence of the crisis the IMF was on the verge of 'promoting' these countries from the status of being 'developing'). Asian countries were complacent for a long time because of their success. They did not have the problems that faced Latin American countries in the 1980s (large fiscal deficits, heavy public debt burden and rapid monetary expansion). This complacency prevented the countries from dealing with the problems until it was too late.

The underlying causes of the Asian crisis have been clearly identified. First, substantial foreign short-term funds became available at relatively low interest rates, as foreign investors shifted massive amounts of capital into Asia. The problem was that the domestic allocation of these borrowed foreign funds was inefficient because of weak banking systems, poor corporate governance and limited absorptive capacity. Second, the system of fixed exchange rates gave the borrowers a false sense of security, encouraging them to take on dollar-denominated debt. Third, exports were weak by the mid-1990s because of the appreciation of the US dollar and China's devaluation of its currency in 1994. Thus, the crisis had to happen, producing massive capital outflows, depreciating currencies and collapsing stock markets.

Financial fragility was, however, the main culprit. This factor involved five aspects:

- Many financial institutions and corporations had borrowed foreign currency funds without adequate hedging, making them vulnerable to changes in exchange rates.
- Much of the borrowed funds were short term while assets were long term, creating a maturity mismatch and the possibility of a liquidity attack similar to what happens in a bank run (where bank customers withdraw cash and close accounts on a massive scale).
- Stock and real estate prices had risen substantially, posing the risk of subsequent asset price deflation.
- Credit was often poorly allocated, contributing to the problem faced by banks and other financial institutions.
- Financial fragility reflected ineffective financial supervision and regulation in the context of financial sector liberalisation. Moreover, capital account liberalisation was poorly executed, encouraging short-term borrowing, while limited exchange rate flexibility led borrowers to underestimate foreign exchange risk. Monetary policies allowed domestic credit to expand at a rapid pace.

By mid-1999, the Asian crisis appeared to be over as market conditions stabilised and strong recoveries were under way. And by mid-2002, much of the region seemed to be doing well in terms of macroeconomic and financial indicators. However, some banking and other reforms are still needed.

The Mexican crisis of 1994–1995 was the first in what has now become a long series of financial crises in Latin America. It demonstrated the potential for sharp changes in investor sentiment, which were triggered by an unsustainable external balance, an overvalued currency that is pegged to the US dollar and a fragile financial system. By mid-2002, the crisis in Argentina had not been resolved as the domestic currency's peg to the dollar was abolished. In general, a vicious circle seems to have developed in Latin America. Markets doubt whether Latin American countries are able or willing to continue servicing their debts. As a result, these countries' currencies and financial assets fall sharply, raising the cost of servicing the debt. Markets keep on worrying.

Types of crises

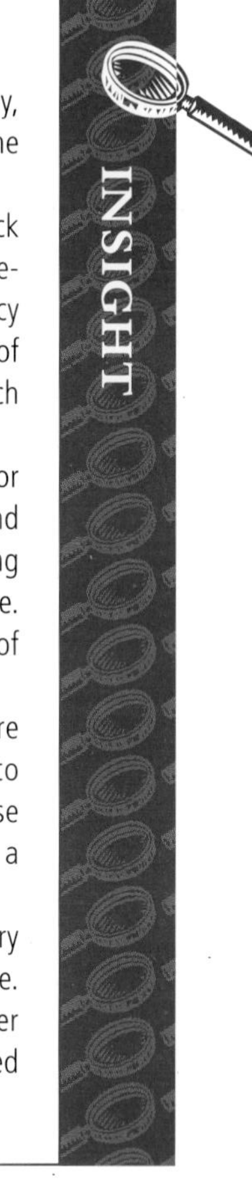

The Mexican, Asian, Russian, Brazilian and, more recently, Argentine crises are invariably mixtures of more than one type of crisis. These types of crises are possible:

- **Currency crises:** these arise when a speculative attack on the exchange rate results in devaluation (depreciation) or forces the central bank to defend the currency by spending a large amount of reserves. The Bank of England and the Thai Central Bank went through such an episode in 1992 and 1997, respectively.
- **Banking crises:** these arise when there is an actual or a potential bank run/failure, inducing banks to suspend the internal convertibility of their liabilities or compelling the government to extend assistance on a large scale. This was definitely a symptom of the Argentine crisis of 2001–2002.
- **Financial crises:** these happen when there are severe disruptions of financial markets, whose ability to function effectively is impaired, exerting an adverse effect on the real economy. The Asian crisis was a financial crisis.
- **Foreign debt crises:** these arise when a country cannot service its foreign debt, sovereign or private. When Mexico announced in 1982 that it was no longer capable of servicing its foreign debt, the so-called international debt problem (crisis) emerged.

5.9 The Australian dollar exchange rate arrangements

Figure 5.11 shows the USD/AUD exchange rate since 1960, which should help us to track developments in the Australian dollar exchange rate arrangements. Since its introduction in the mid-1960s to replace the pound, the Australian dollar has gone through a number of exchange rate arrangements.

Until December 1971, the Australian dollar was part of the **Sterling Area** and so it was pegged to the British currency. Thus, the behaviour of the Australian dollar against other currencies reflected the behaviour of the pound against those currencies. The behaviour of the pound was at that time governed by the provisions of the Bretton Woods agreement, which allowed the currency to move within a narrow band against the US dollar and other currencies.

Figure 5.11 The USD/AUD exchange rate

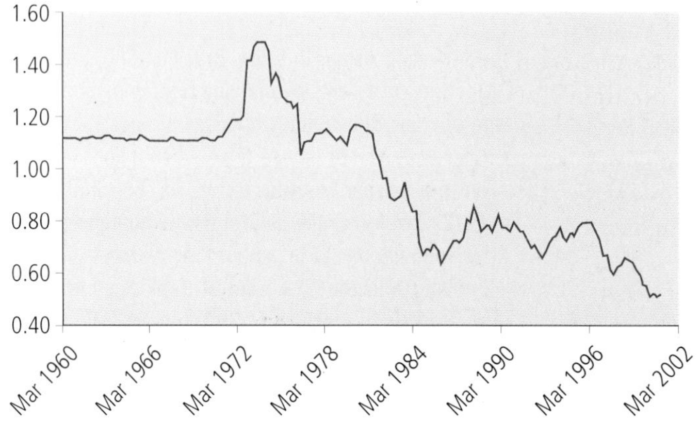

Source: Main Economic Indicators, OECD.

In August 1971, the United States abolished the convertibility of its currency into gold, leading to the collapse of the Bretton Woods system. In order to maintain the stability of the currency, the Australian dollar was pegged to the US currency. This arrangement meant that the Australian dollar had a fixed exchange rate against the US dollar and that the former followed the latter in its movements against other currencies. Following the flotation of major currencies in 1972 and 1973 and in recognition of the multilateral nature of Australian foreign trade, a decision was taken in September 1974 to peg the Australian dollar to a basket of currencies reflecting the trade-weighted exchange rate. This arrangement was changed in November 1976 in such a way as to make the link with the basket of currencies variable rather than fixed. A variable link naturally involves some kind of judgment and, for this reason, the exchange rate was managed by representatives from the Reserve Bank, the Treasury, the Department of the Prime Minister and Cabinet, and the Department of Finance. This arrangement was in operation until the end of 1983, when the decision to float the currency was taken.

The December 1983 decision to switch to a system of floating exchange rates was accompanied by measures abolishing a major part of exchange controls. The decision to float the Australian dollar can be justified by using the same general arguments for floating exchange rates. However, there are two specific arguments. The first is that under fixed exchange rates it is difficult for the RBA to pursue its domestic operations while at the same time being required to clear the foreign exchange market on a daily basis. The second is that Australia is very susceptible to sharp changes in the terms of trade and thus a floating exchange rate is a more appropriate arrangement.

5.10 Fixed versus flexible exchange rates

The debate of fixed versus flexible exchange rates is a prominent issue that international economists have dealt with. No verdict has been reached, but an observer listening to one side of the story can easily be convinced that what has just been heard is the truth. And the 'truth' may be that 'flexible exchange rates are better' or that 'fixed exchange rates are better', depending on which side of the story has just been told.

Let us start with the arguments for flexible exchange rates:

- Under flexible exchange rates, adjustment of the balance of payments is smoother and less painful than under fixed rates. Flexible exchange rates move continuously and in small doses to restore equilibrium.
- Since flexible exchange rates move continuously in reaction to disequilibria in the balance of payments, large and persistent deficits do not arise. This in turn boosts confidence in the international monetary system, resulting in fewer attempts to readjust currency portfolios, and this can only result in calmer foreign exchange markets.
- Liquidity problems do not arise (or at least they are not as acute) under flexible exchange rates, because central banks do not hold foreign exchange reserves for the purpose of market intervention.
- Flexible exchange rates are more conducive to achieving free international trade. The reasoning is simple: because this system maintains equilibrium in the balance of payments, tariffs and other trade impediments will not be imposed.
- Flexible exchange rates are conducive to increased independence of policy, in the sense of allowing a country to follow policies that are different from those of its major trading partners. It is also claimed that, under flexible exchange rates, countries are insulated from what happens in other economies.
- Recent experience shows that developing countries with flexible exchange rates are in a better position to cope with currency crises than those with fixed rates.

The arguments against flexible rates are:

- Flexible exchange rates cause uncertainty and inhibit international trade and investment, because they affect the private sector's decision-making process.
- Flexible exchange rates cause destabilising speculation, accentuating the rise and fall of currencies.
- Flexible exchange rates are not suitable for small economies with undiversified export bases.
- Flexible exchange rates are not appropriate for countries without sophisticated financial systems, because the successful operation of such a system requires developed forward and futures markets.
- Flexible exchange rates are inflationary in a general sense, whereas fixed exchange rates provide discipline.
- Flexible exchange rates are unstable in the sense that small disturbances to exchange rates can grow into extremely large disturbances.
- With flexible exchange rates, serious balance of payments difficulties could lead to a steep fall in the value of the domestic currency, which could adversely affect price stability and output in the short run.

So, what is the verdict? The only answer to this question is that the jury is still out.

5.11 The future of the international monetary system

Obviously, the present international monetary system has its loopholes and weaknesses. The future of the system is a hot topic, in both professional and academic circles, but there seems to be no consensus view on the issue. Several courses of action have been suggested to 'reform' the international monetary system, including a return to the gold standard.

A number of factors have contributed to the revival of interest in the gold standard since the 1980s: (i) dissatisfaction with the instability accompanying floating; (ii) a greater acceptability of the monetarist theories of inflation; (iii) political attitudes supporting balanced budgets and the operation of market forces; and (iv) the election in 1980 of the US president Ronald Reagan, who in pre-election speeches supported the idea of going back to the gold standard. In particular, it is believed that the gold standard provides some sort of discipline against excessive monetary expansion and therefore inflation. However, it is unlikely that the gold standard will solve the current problems of the international monetary system. In today's multi-financial centre world, short-term capital flows are likely to move erratically in a destabilising fashion from one centre to another, hindering the balance of payments adjustment mechanism. We have also seen that the classical gold standard did not really work as envisaged in theory, for reasons including non-conformity to the rules of the game.

The advent of currency crises in the 1990s has led economists and policy makers to seek new designs for the 'international financial architecture'. In 1999, a group of 29 economists (for example, Paul Krugman), former central bankers (for example, Paul Volcker) and currency traders (for example, George Soros) produced a report sponsored by the US Council on Foreign Relations. The report contained the following propositions:

- improving incentives for sound policy by linking IMF loans to crisis-prevention efforts
- encouraging the imposition of holding period taxes on short-term capital flows in countries characterised by financial fragility
- encouraging private-sector burden sharing by introducing collective-action clauses in sovereign bond contracts—this means making the private sector partly responsible for the consequences of sovereign bond issues
- discouraging fixed but adjustable exchange rates in favour of either managed floating or currency boards
- directing the IMF to lend less freely and to distinguish between **country crises** and **systemic crises**
- removing overlapping from the responsibilities of the IMF and the World Bank—the IMF should concentrate on macroeconomic issues, leaving the Bank to deal with the structural aspects of development.

There are obviously problems in implementing these propositions, let alone their adequacy for solving the world's financial problems and for preventing financial crises. Moreover, these views are not universally acceptable, with some advocating the abolition of the IMF after its failure not only to predict but also to deal with the Asian financial crisis.

Another course of action has been suggested, a **global currency**. This is not a new idea, as Richard Cooper of Harvard University proposed it in 1984. The idea has its pros and cons. On the one hand is the undoubted convenience of a single currency, but on the other hand there is the loss of the exchange rate as a policy instrument that can be used if, for example, there is an abrupt fall in the demand for exports. In setting the costs against the benefits, the crucial factors are openness to trade and free movement of factors of production. A small, open economy has more to gain from the convenience provided by a single currency.

IN PRACTICE

Implementing the Tobin tax

In a lecture at Princeton University in 1972, James Tobin, a Nobel Prize-winning economist, proposed what has become known as the **Tobin tax**. This is a uniform international tax payable on all spot transactions involving currency conversion. This would, in theory at least, discourage speculation by making trading more costly, reducing the volume of destabilising short-term capital flows and leading to greater exchange rate stability. Apart from this, it is envisaged that the Tobin tax would reduce 'noise' from market trading while allowing traders to react to changes in economic fundamentals and policy. It would also be superior to protective measures such as capital controls. Moreover, it would enhance market efficiency and financial stability, because it would require the international coordination of macroeconomic policies.

Interest in the Tobin tax was revived as a result of the financial crises of the 1990s. In August 2001, the French Prime Minister hinted at his approval of a tax on cross-border capital movements. Belgium presented a plan to discuss the Tobin tax in the September 2001 meeting of EU finance ministers. And, at around the same time, the German Chancellor, Gerhard Schroder, called for a 'greater debate on speculative financial transactions'.

There are, however, problems with the idea and implementability of the Tobin tax:

- Because of the way it is structured, the Tobin tax would impair the operations of international financial markets.
- The Tobin tax cannot distinguish between normal trading that is conducive to the efficiency and stability of financial markets and destabilising noise trading, which is the target of the tax.
- It is possible to avoid the tax by trading financial derivatives rather than conducting spot transactions.
- There is no clear consensus on who should be entitled to the revenue generated from the tax.
- Speculators can avoid the tax unless every country agrees to implement it.
- It is sometimes argued that most of the trading in the foreign exchange market is motivated by risk management rather than speculation. The so-called 'hot potato theory' stipulates that foreign exchange traders manage their exposure by passing open positions from one to another. Hence, the tax would punish 'disciplined traders'.

An alternative to the Tobin tax is a two-tier structure consisting of a low tax rate for normal transactions and an exchange surcharge on profits from very short-term transactions deemed to constitute a speculative attack on the underlying currency.[1] Under this scheme, an exchange rate would be allowed to move freely within a band, but overshooting the band would result in a tax on the discrepancy between the market exchange rate and the closest margin of the band. Exchange rates could then be kept within a target range through taxation rather than central bank intervention or the depletion of international reserves.

Perhaps easier said than done. *The Economist* seems to think that the Tobin tax is both unwise and unworkable.[2]

[1] P. B. Spahn, 'The Tobin Tax and Exchange Rate Stability', *Finance and Development*, June 1996, pp. 24–7.

[2] 'Roasting an Old Chestnut', *The Economist*, 8 September 2001, p. 81.

Summary

- Business firms operating in international markets do so within the framework provided by the international monetary system. This system has two components: a public component, consisting of the agreements among countries as well as the functions of international public institutions; and a private component, which is represented by the banking industry.
- International monetary systems can be classified, according to the nature of international reserves, into (i) pure commodity standards, (ii) pure fiat standards and (iii) mixed standards.
- International monetary systems can be classified according to the flexibility of the exchange rate as follows: (i) fixed exchange rates; (ii) perfectly flexible exchange rates; (iii) fixed but adjustable exchange rates; (iv) fixed exchange rates and flexible within a band; (v) crawling peg; (vi) dual exchange rates; (vii) managed floating; and (viii) target zones.
- The gold standard of 1870–1914 is often remembered with nostalgia because the world economy thrived under this system. In retrospect, it is believed that the gold standard functioned well because it was not put to the test.
- The inter-war period witnessed an attempt to return to the gold standard but ended with open economic (and subsequently military) warfare.
- The Bretton Woods system was born in 1944 as a system of fixed but adjustable exchange rates. The system collapsed in 1971 when the United States abolished the convertibility of the US dollar into gold.
- Floating became widespread in 1973 while European countries experimented with the Snake in the Tunnel. Floating was legalised by the IMF in 1976 when the Jamaica Accord was signed.
- The present system involves a number of exchange rate arrangements: (i) arrangements with no separate legal tender; (ii) currency boards; (iii) other conventional fixed pegs; (iv) pegged exchange rates with horizontal bands; (v) crawling peg; (vi) exchange rates with crawling bands; (vii) managed floating with no pre-announced path for the exchange rate; and (viii) independent floating.
- The European Monetary Union has replaced the European Monetary System. In 2002, the new European currency, the euro, replaced the national currencies of 12 European countries.
- Several exchange rate arrangements have been used for the Australian dollar. Until December 1971, it was pegged to the pound, then it was pegged to the US dollar. In September 1974, the Australian dollar was pegged to a basket of currencies that reflected Australia's trade pattern. In December 1983, the currency was floated.
- The debate over fixed versus flexible exchange rates is still raging, without any consensus view.
- Several alternative courses of action have been suggested to reform the international monetary system, including a return to the gold standard.
- The advent of currency crises has led economists and policy makers to seek new designs for the international monetary system. Some courses of action include the adoption of a single currency and the implementation of the Tobin tax.

Key terms

adjustable peg 143
appreciation 135
banking crises 151
Bretton Woods system 136
central rate 146
country crises 154
crawling bands 146
crawling peg 139
currency board 145
currency crises 151
depreciation 135
devaluation 135
dirty floating 140
dual exchange rates 139
European currency unit (ECU) 147
European Monetary System (EMS) 136
European Monetary Union (EMU) 148
financial crises 151
fixed exchange rates 135
flexible exchange rates 135
floating exchange rates 144
foreign debt crises 151
fundamental equilibrium effective exchange rate 140
Genoa Conference 142
global currency 154
gold export point 141
gold import point 141
gold points 141
gold standard 140
Great Depression 142
hyperinflation 142
independent floating 147
International Bank for Reconstruction and Development 142
International Monetary Fund (IMF) 142
international monetary system (IMS) 134
international reserves 135
intervention points 143
Jamaica Accord 144
Louvre Accord 145
Maastricht Treaty 148
managed floating 140
mint parity 141
mixed standards 135
multiple bands 137
par value 135
peg 139
pegging to a basket of currencies 146
pegging to a single currency 146
Plaza Accord 145
protectionism 145
pure commodity standards 135
pure fiat standards 135
realignment 147
revaluation 135
seigniorage 147
Smithsonian Agreement 137
Snake in the Tunnel 137
soft-edged band 140
special drawing rights (SDRs) 143
Sterling Area 151
systemic crises 154
target range 140
target zones 140
Tobin tax 155
Triffin Dilemma 143
Triffin Paradox 143
World Bank 142
Worm 137

MAXIMISE YOUR MARKS! There are 30 interactive questions for this chapter available online at **www.mhhe.com/au/moosa2e**

Review questions

1. Why did Adam Smith describe the international monetary system as the 'Great Wheel'?
2. Why is the nature of the international monetary system relevant to international business activity?
3. What are the public and private components of the international monetary system?
4. Into what categories are international monetary systems classified according to the nature of the reserve assets?

5 What is the difference between depreciation and devaluation?

6 What is the Snake in the Tunnel? What is the Worm?

7 Why does the movement of fixed exchange rates go in steps rather than smoothly?

8 What is a crawling peg?

9 Give some actual examples for the following exchange rate systems: (a) flexible exchange rates; (b) fixed but adjustable exchange rates; (c) fixed exchange rates and flexible within a band; (d) multiple bands; (e) crawling peg; (f) dual exchange rates; and (g) managed floating.

10 What are the problems that are likely to be encountered under a system of dual exchange rates?

11 'Every country wants to have a strong currency because it is a sign of economic strength.' Is this a valid statement?

12 'Britain played a more important role under the gold standard than any other country has since played under any system.' Explain.

13 The gold standard is often remembered with nostalgia because it is perceived to have been a big success. Was this really the case?

14 'The collapse of the Bretton Woods system in 1971 resembles the collapse of the gold exchange standard in 1931.' Explain.

15 Why did the Bretton Woods system collapse? Why did the Smithsonian Agreement fail to salvage the system?

16 Has the present system solved the problems of the Bretton Woods system?

17 The US government was not enthusiastic about intervention in the foreign exchange market during the first Reagan Administration (1981–1984). Why did this attitude change during the second Reagan Administration in 1985?

18 Can you think of the reasons for the rise and fall of the US dollar during the 1980s?

19 Why would some countries choose to peg their currencies to a basket of currencies while others peg to a single currency?

20 Why do some countries choose not to reveal the components of the baskets to which they peg their currencies?

21 What are the pros and cons of a currency board? Why did Argentina abandon this arrangement in 2002?

22 What are the different exchange rate arrangements adopted by Australia in the post-war period? Can you find any economic justification for selecting each arrangement and for shifting to a new arrangement?

23 Examine, from an Australian perspective, the fixed versus flexible exchange rates debate.

24 Since 1870, the world has experimented with several international monetary systems. There is, however, no consensus view on the optimal system. Can you think of some measures that could lead to a better international monetary system?

25 Distinguish among the various kinds of financial crises.

26 What are the arguments for and against the imposition of the Tobin tax?

Appendix 5.1

World currencies and exchange rate arrangements

Country	Currency	Exchange rate arrangement
Afghanistan	Afghani	8
Albania	Lek	8
Algeria	Dinar	7
Angola	Readj kwanza	8
Antigua	East Caribbean dollar	1
Argentina	Peso	2
Armenia	Dram	7
Aruba	Florin	3
Australia	Australian dollar	8
Austria	Euro	1
Azerbaijan	Manat	7
Bahamas	Bahama dollar	3
Bahrain	Dinar	3
Bangladesh	Taka	3
Barbados	Barbados dollar	3
Belarus	Rouble	6
Belgium	Euro	1
Belize	Belize dollar	3
Benin	CFA franc	1
Bermuda	Bermudian dollar	1
Bhutan	Ngultrum	3
Bolivia	Boliviano	5
Bosnia Herzegovina	Marka	2
Botswana	Pula	3
Brazil	Real	8
Brunei	Brunei dollar	2
Bulgaria	Lev	2
Burkina Faso	CFA franc	1
Burundi	Burundi franc	7
Cambodia	Riel	7
Cameroon	CFA franc	1
Canada	Canadian dollar	8
Canary Islands	Euro	1
Cayman Islands	Cayman Island dollar	1
Central African Republic	CFA franc	1
Chad	CFA franc	1
Chile	Chilean peso	8
China	Renminbi	3
Colombia	Colombian peso	8
Comoros	Franc	3
Congo	CFA franc	1
Congo (Democratic Republic)	Congo franc	8
Costa Rica	Colon	5
Côte d'Ivoire	CFA franc	1
Croatia	Kuna	7
Cyprus	Cyprus pound	4
Czech Republic	Koruna	8
Denmark	Danish krone	4
Djibouti Republic	Djibouti franc	2
Dominica	East Caribbean dollar	1
Dominican Republic	Dominican peso	7
Ecuador	US dollar	1
Egypt	Egyptian pound	4
El Salvador	Colon	1
Equatorial Guinea	CFA franc	1
Estonia	Kroon	2
Ethiopia	Ethiopian birr	7
Falkland Islands	Falkland pound	1
Faeroe Islands	Danish krone	1
Fiji	Fijian dollar	3
Finland	Euro	1

Continued...

Country	Currency	Exchange rate arrangement	Country	Currency	Exchange rate arrangement
France	Euro	1	Libya	Libyan dinar	3
French Guiana	Euro	1	Liechtenstein	Swiss franc	1
Gabon	CFA franc	1	Lithuania	Litas	2
Gambia	Dalasi	8	Luxembourg	Euro	1
Georgia	Lari	8	Macedonia	Denar	3
Germany	Euro	1	Madagascar	Madagascar franc	8
Ghana	Cedi	7	Madeira	Euro	1
Gibraltar	Gibraltar pound	1	Malawi	Kwacha	8
Greece	Euro	1	Malaysia	Ringgit	3
Greenland	Danish krone	1	Maldives	Rufiya	3
Grenada	East Caribbean dollar	1	Mali Republic	CFA franc	1
Guam	US dollar	1	Malta	Maltese lira	3
Guatemala	Quetzal	7	Martinique	Euro	1
Guinea	Franc	7	Mauritania	Ouguiya	7
Guinea-Bissau	CFA franc	1	Mauritius	Maur rupee	7
Guyana	Guyanese dollar	7	Mexico	Mexican peso	8
Haiti	Gourde	8	Moldova	Leu	8
Honduras	Lempira	6	Monaco	Euro	1
Hong Kong	Hong Kong dollar	2	Mongolia	Tugrik	8
Hungary	Forint	6	Montserrat	East Caribbean dollar	1
Iceland	Icelandic krona	8	Morocco	Dirham	3
India	Indian rupee	7	Mozambique	Metical	8
Indonesia	Rupiah	7	Namibia	Dollar	3
Iran	Rial	3	Nepal	Nepalese rupee	3
Iraq	Iraqi dinar	7	Netherlands	Euro	1
Irish Republic	Euro	1	New Zealand	NZ dollar	8
Israel	Shekel	6	Nicaragua	Gold cordoba	5
Italy	Euro	1	Niger Republic	CFA franc	1
Jamaica	Jamaican dollar	7	Nigeria	Naira	7
Japan	Yen	8	Norway	Norwegian krone	8
Jordan	Jordanian dinar	3	Oman	Omani rial	3
Kazakhstan	Tenge	7	Pakistan	Pakistani rupee	7
Kenya	Kenya shilling	7	Panama	Balboa	1
Kiribati	Australian dollar	1	Papua New Guinea	Kina	8
Korea	Won	8	Paraguay	Guarani	7
Kuwait	Kuwaiti dinar	3	Peru	New sol	7
Kyrgyzstan	Som	7	Philippines	Peso	8
Latvia	Lats	3	Poland	Zloty	8
Lebanon	Lebanese pound	3	Portugal	Euro	1
Lesotho	Maluti	3	Puerto Rico	US dollar	1
Liberia	Liberian dollar	8			

Continued...

Country	Currency	Exchange rate arrangement	Country	Currency	Exchange rate arrangement
Qatar	Riyal	3	Tajikistan	Somoni	8
Réunion	Euro	1	Tanzania	Shilling	8
Romania	Leu	6	Thailand	Baht	7
Russia	Rouble	7	Togo Republic	CFA franc	1
Rwanda	Franc	7	Tonga	Pa'anga	4
San Marino	Euro	1	Trinidad and Tobago	Trinidad and Tobago dollar	7
São Tomé and Príncipe	Dobra	7	Tunisia	Dinar	7
Saudi Arabia	Riyal	3	Turkey	Lira	8
Senegal	CFA franc	1	Tuvalu	Australian dollar	1
Seychelles	Rupee	3	Uganda	New shilling	8
Sierra Leone	Leone	8	Ukraine	Hryvna	7
Singapore	Singapore dollar	7	United Arab Emirates	Dirham	3
Slovakia	Koruna	7	United Kingdom	Pound	8
Slovenia	Tolar	7	United States	US dollar	8
Somali Republic	Shilling	8	Uruguay	Uruguay peso	6
South Africa	Rand	8	Uzbekistan	Sum	7
Spain	Euro	1	Vanuatu	Vatu	3
Sri Lanka	Rupee	7	Vatican	Euro	1
St Christopher	East Caribbean dollar	1	Venezuela	Bolivar	6
St Helena	British pound	1	Vietnam	Dong	7
St Lucia	East Caribbean dollar	1	Virgin Islands—British	US dollar	1
St Pierre and Miquelon	Euro	1	Virgin Islands—US	US dollar	1
St Vincent	East Caribbean dollar	1	Western Samoa	Tala	3
Sudan Republic	Dinar	7	Yemen	Rial	8
Surinam	Guilder	4	Yugoslavia	New dinar	7
Swaziland	Lilangeni	3	Zambia	Kwacha	7
Sweden	Krona	8	Zimbabwe	Dollar	3
Switzerland	Swiss franc	8			
Syria	Syrian pound	3			
Taiwan	Taiwanese dollar	8			

Exchange rate arrangements

1. Exchange arrangements with no separate legal tender
2. Currency board arrangements
3. Other conventional fixed peg arrangements
4. Pegged exchange rates with horizontal bands
5. Crawling peg
6. Exchange rates with crawling bands
7. Managed floating with no pre-announced path for the exchange rate
8. Independent floating

CHAPTER

Currency futures and swaps

Introduction

This chapter deals with currency futures and swaps. These are financial instruments that can be used for both hedging and speculation. Currency futures have evolved because of some difficulties associated with currency forward contracts. Currency swaps, which are different from the foreign exchange swaps encountered in Chapter 2, have in a relatively short time become a very important means of financing and an instrument of risk management.

Objectives

The objectives of this chapter are:

- To describe currency futures contracts.
- To outline the problematic properties of forward contracts and explain how the introduction of futures contracts has solved these problems.
- To compare forward and futures currency markets.
- To describe currency and interest swaps.
- To introduce some swap terminology.

6.1 Currency futures: definition and origin

Futures contracts emerged out of the process of evolution of financial instruments to surmount some problems associated with forward contracts. Like forward contracts, currency futures contracts represent an obligation of the seller to deliver a certain amount of a specified currency at some time in the future at a price (exchange rate) determined now. However, futures contracts differ from forward contracts in several aspects. These differences were introduced specifically to deal with some shortcomings of forward contracts.

Currency futures were first traded on the Chicago Mercantile Exchange (CME) in 1972. Subsequently, they began to be traded on the commodities exchange (COMEX) in New York, as well as other markets such as the Philadelphia Stock Exchange.

The Australian dollar contract was introduced on the CME in January 1987. The Sydney Futures Exchange followed by introducing this contract in February 1988, but it was dropped subsequently because it did not attract sufficient trading volume. However, the contract was re-introduced in February 2001.

6.2 Futures and the problematic properties of forward contracts

The problems with forward contracts

There are at least three problematic characteristics of forward contracts, which have led to the emergence of futures contracts. The first problem pertains to the dimensions of the contract, specifically the size and the settlement date. This problem is similar to the problem of 'double coincidence of wants' often discussed in introductory economics textbooks with respect to the evolution of money as a medium of exchange. In this case, the problem boils down to finding a counterparty who has a matching need.

An example, which is illustrated in Figure 6.1, makes it easier to understand what is meant here. Suppose that an Australian company (A) exports a shipment of goods to Japan worth JPY45.7 million, with the payment due in 42 days. While the Australian company knows the amount it will receive (from the Japanese importer, B) in yen terms, what matters more is the equivalent Australian dollar amount. This amount is conditional upon the spot exchange rate between the Australian dollar and the Japanese yen that will prevail when the receivables are realised in 42 days. This uncertainty can be avoided if the Australian company sells the yen and buys the Australian dollar at a forward rate that is determined now. By doing this, the Australian company will 'lock in' the exchange rate at which the yen receivables will be converted into Australian dollars. Thus, the Australian company wants to sell JPY45.7 million to be delivered in 42 days. The prospective counterparty, C, must be willing to buy the same amount to be received on the same date. This means that the counterparty must agree on the contract dimensions: the size (JPY45.7 million) and the settlement date (42 days from now). This counterparty may prove difficult to find.

Figure 6.1 Using a forward contract

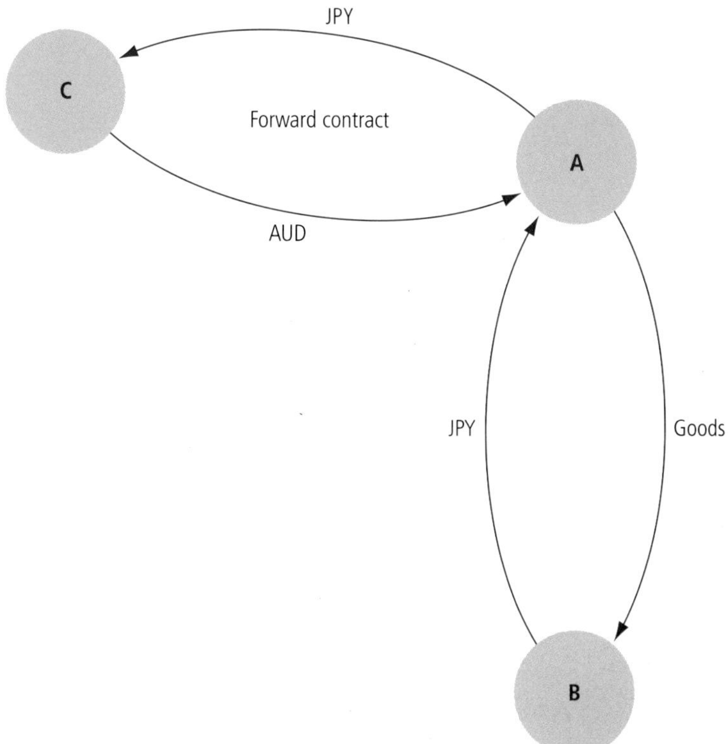

The problem with forward contracts is that they are tailor-made to suit specific needs. Commercial banks are normally willing to offer their customers foreign currency forward contracts that suit their needs. By doing this, banks are exposed to foreign exchange risk and may choose to hedge this risk. In either case, banks charge their customers a fee for bearing this risk, making the transaction more expensive than otherwise.

Another problem with forward contracts is the risk of default. There are two counterparties to a forward contract, a buyer (the long side of the contract) and a seller (the short side of the contract). If, on the maturity of the contract (when delivery of the currencies becomes due), the spot exchange rate is different from the forward rate implicit in the contract, then one of the counterparties will incur losses and tends to default.

Suppose that two counterparties, A and B, entered a forward contract whereby A sells USD1 million at a forward rate (AUD/USD) of 1.80 to receive AUD1.8 million three months later. As the spot rate assumes values that differ from the forward rate on the date of the maturity of the contract, the following would happen (see Figure 6.2):

- At 1.90, A delivers USD1 million in exchange for AUD1.8 million at a time when A could receive AUD1.9 million by selling the US dollar spot to counterparty C. Thus, A will tend to default.
- At 1.70, B delivers AUD1.80 million in return for USD1 million when B can buy this amount spot at AUD1.7 million from counterparty C. Thus, B will tend to default.
- At 1.80, there is no difference. In both the spot and the forward markets, USD1 million costs AUD1.8 million and so neither will tend to default, at least not because of the difference between the spot and forward rates.

Figure 6.2 Tendency to default on a forward contract

(a) A tends to default

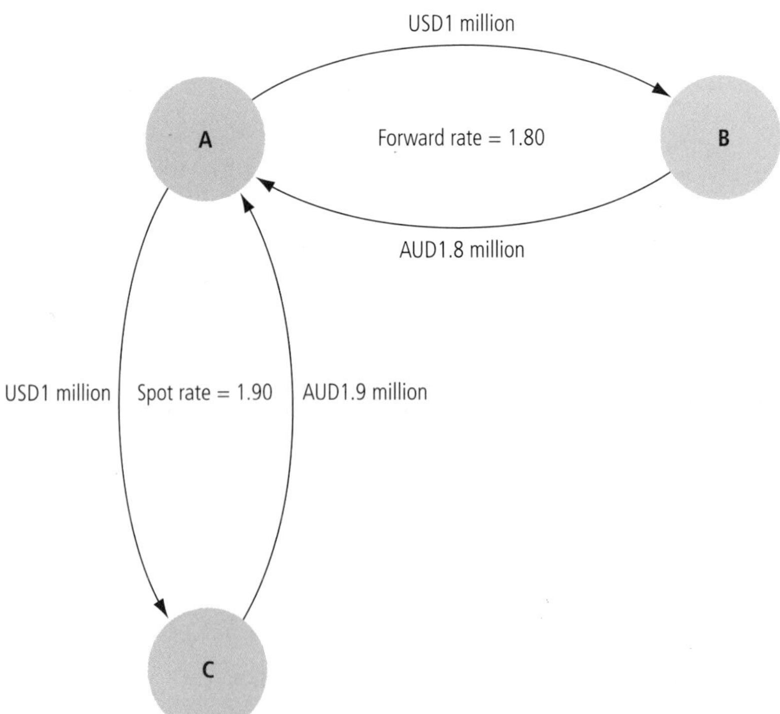

(b) B tends to default

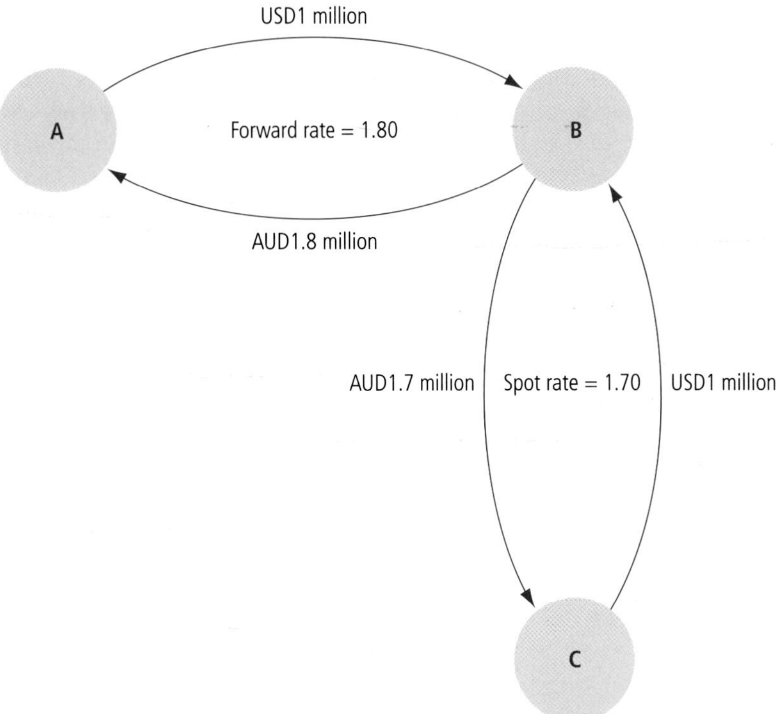

(c) Neither tends to default

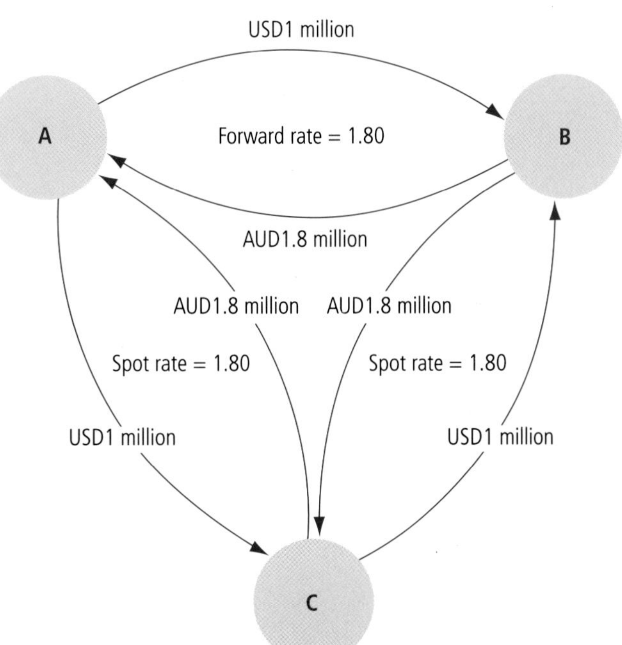

The third problem is the liquidity, or rather lack of liquidity, of forward contracts. Liquidity in this sense is the ability of a counterparty to unwind his or her obligations to a forward contract, which is the delivery of a certain amount of a currency at a certain time. This point can be explained with reference to our example of the Australian exporter. Suppose that, after finding a counterparty who is willing to buy JPY45.7 million, something goes wrong with the transaction with the Japanese importer, leading to the cancellation of the deal. Obviously, the exporter is not going to receive JPY45.7 million in 42 days. So, what is to be done about the forward contract that the exporter now wishes had not been signed?

There are three courses of action, which are described in Figure 6.3. The first is to assign the obligation to another counterparty, D, who wants to sell JPY45.7 million for delivery on the maturity date. If such a counterparty is found, this is not the end of the matter as some costs are involved. The new counterparty may require compensation to take on this deal. The original counterparty may also require compensation because he or she might conceive, or claim to conceive, a higher default risk. The second course of action is to persuade the original counterparty to cancel the contract. The counterparty may agree only if a cancellation fee is paid. The third and final course of action is to enter an offsetting position (that is, another forward contract whereby the exporter buys JPY45.7 from counterparty E for the same delivery date as the original contract). There is bound to be a difference in the forward rates for the two contracts. Moreover, there is the problem of finding another counterparty for the new contract and the problem of increasing risk of default, now that the Australian exporter is exposed to the risk of default of two counterparties rather than one.

Figure 6.3 Unwinding a forward contract

(a) Assigning the obligation to another counterparty (D)

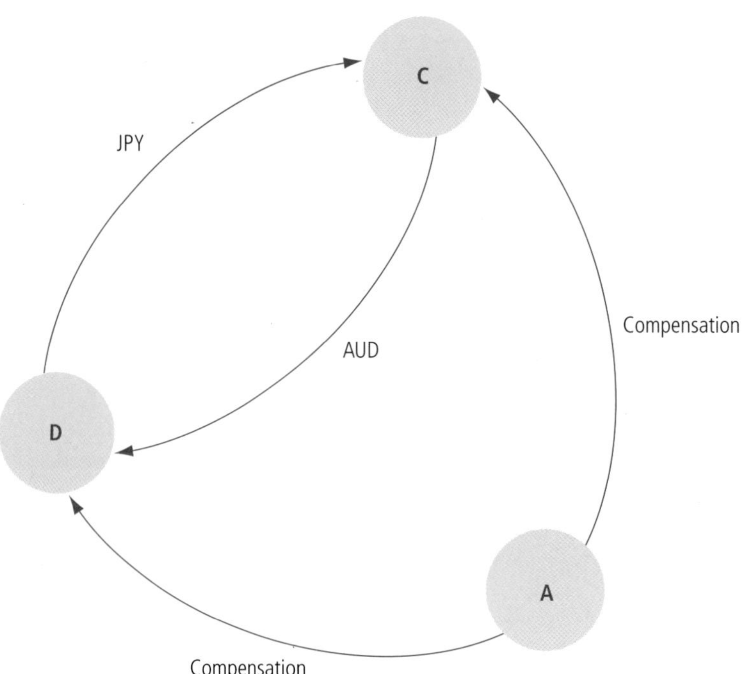

(b) Cancelling the forward contract

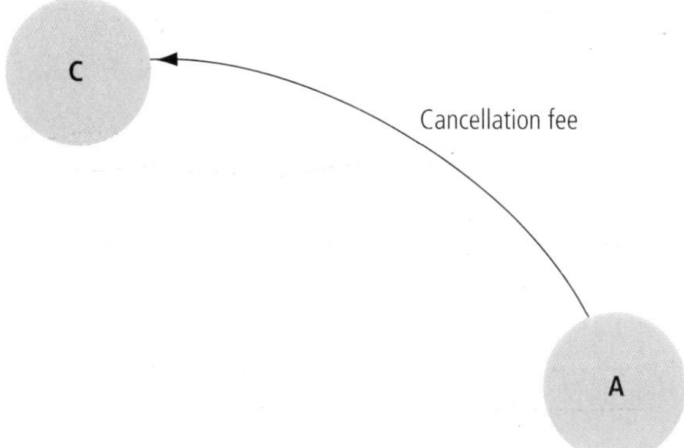

(c) Entering an offsetting position with E

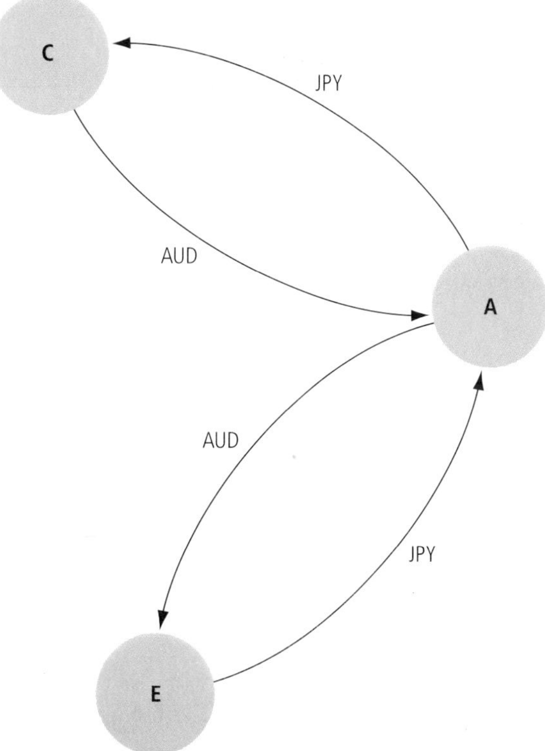

Example

Suppose that, after A and B agree on the AUD/USD contract at 1.80, A decides not to go ahead. A could unwind the obligation to the contract by entering a new contract with counterparty C, whereby A buys USD1 million to be delivered on the same date as the original contract. Suppose that the forward rate for the new contract is 1.85. On the maturity date, the following transactions will take place:

- A receives AUD1.8 million from B in exchange for USD1 million. This transaction settles the first contract.
- A uses the proceeds from the first contract to settle the second contract with C. A receives USD1 million and must deliver AUD1.85 million to C. The difference of AUD50 000 must be bought on the spot market.

How do futures contracts overcome these difficulties?

Now that we have recognised the problems with forward contracts, how do futures contracts overcome the deficiencies of forward trading? The first characteristic of futures contracts is that, unlike forward contracts, they are standardised, which is a necessary requirement for them to be traded on an organised exchange, such as the Sydney Futures Exchange. The contracts are standardised with respect to size and **settlement date** (date of delivery or maturity of the contract). The benefit of standardisation is that it makes it easier to match up orders, promoting a higher trading volume.

In futures trading, default risk is controlled by the operation of a clearing corporation in the exchange where the contracts are traded. The **clearing corporation**, which is normally owned by the exchange, acts as the opposite counterparty to all contracts, as shown in Figure 6.4. This arrangement removes the need to determine the default potential of the counterparty, because the clearing corporation effectively underwrites the default risk of every contract. The presence of a clearing corporation has the additional advantage that it enables counterparties to unwind or liquidate their positions. For example, to unwind a long position on two June Australian-dollar contracts before June, two contracts must be sold. The clearing corporation recognises this and cancels out the two positions.

Figure 6.4 The role of the clearing corporation in futures trading

A legitimate question arises here. If the clearing corporation underwrites the default risk, how does it manage this risk? The answer is simple: by establishing margin accounts and **marking to market** on a daily basis. A trader of futures contracts must establish an account and a margin deposit with the broker who initiates the trader's order on the exchange. The **margin account** is required as a security against potential default. Profits and losses are realised on a daily basis and the account is credited or debited accordingly. The margin account earns interest and therefore does not represent an opportunity cost. There are two kinds of margins: the **initial margin**, which is the amount deposited in the account to open a position in one contract; and the **maintenance margin**, which is the lowest level allowed before the trader is asked to meet a **margin call**. In this case, the trader must pay into the account an additional deposit, called the **variation margin**, to bring the account to the initial margin level.

Example

Suppose that a trader buys one Australian-dollar contract on 1 February at 0.5600 (USD/AUD). The US dollar value of this contract is

$$100\,000 \times 0.5600 = \text{USD}56\,000$$

On successive days the following may happen as the settlement exchange rate changes (in accordance with changes in the spot rate):

Date	Settlement rate	Value of contract	Margin account
2 Feb	0.5800	58 000	+2000
3 Feb	0.5950	59 500	+1500
4 Feb	0.6010	60 100	+600
5 Feb	0.5775	57 750	−2350

For example, as the settlement exchange rate rises to 0.5800 on 2 February, the value of the contract rises to USD58 000. The difference between this value and the value on the previous day (USD56 000) is equal to USD2000. The margin account is credited by this amount.

The combination of daily settlement and margin requirements serves to protect the clearing corporation from the risk of default. The settlement system is designed to avoid a negative balance in the margin account. Another protective feature is the imposition of **daily price limits** designed to keep the lid on losses incurred on a particular day. A limit is the maximum or minimum allowable price (or exchange rate) during a trading session. If the price of a futures contract hits a limit, the market is said to experience a **limit move**, which can be a **limit up** or a **limit down**. The safety feature is that trading is not allowed at prices above the limit up (the maximum) or below the limit down (the minimum). However, these limits may be altered at the discretion of the officials of the exchange. **Position limits**, specifying the number of contracts a trader can hold, may also be imposed as a safety device.

Another important feature of futures trading is the following. When the buyer wants to take delivery of the currency underlying the futures contract, the currency is bought in the spot market at the time of delivery, while the contract is sold back to the exchange. Most of the foreign exchange risk is removed by this operation because, if the currency has appreciated during the time between the initiation of the contract and the delivery date, there will be a gain on the margin account, which compensates for the loss resulting from the appreciation of the currency. We say that most of the risk is removed because the gain on the margin account will not be exactly equal to the loss from the appreciation of the currency. This disparity is due to unpredictable changes in the interest rate on the margin account. For example, if the interest rate is low when the amount in the margin account is high, and vice versa, the margin account will not completely compensate for the appreciation of the currency. This is called **marking-to-market risk**, which makes futures contracts more risky than forward contracts.

Example

Suppose that a US importer of Australian beef bought two Australian-dollar contracts currently priced at 0.5600 (USD/AUD) at a time when the spot exchange rate was 0.5300. The value of the two contracts is

$$2 \times 100\,000 \times 0.5600 = \text{USD}112\,000$$

while the value of AUD200 000 spot is

$$200\,000 \times 0.5300 = \text{USD}106\,000$$

Continued...

Suppose now that during the period between the initiation of the contract and the date of delivery, the Australian dollar appreciates and so the spot exchange rate rises to 0.5800, while the rate implicit in the futures contract is 0.6128. The spot value of AUD200 000 is

$$200\ 000 \times 0.5800 = \text{USD}116\ 000$$

implying an additional cost of USD10 000 resulting from the appreciation of the Australian dollar. The importer sells the two contracts for

$$2 \times 100\ 000 \times 0.6128 = \text{USD}122\ 566$$

making gains equal to USD10 566, which will compensate for the loss on the spot transaction. Notice that this example ignores the marking-to-market risk.

A question that may also arise here concerns the relationship between the exchange rates implicit in forward and futures contracts. These rates must be equal, because otherwise arbitrage will be triggered in the same way as two-point arbitrage in the spot foreign exchange market. Arbitrage ensures that the offer forward rate is equal to the bid futures rate, and vice versa. However, because of the marking-to-market risk, arbitrage does not equate the two rates exactly, in which case we may rephrase the statement by saying that arbitrage ensures that the offer forward rate is not significantly below the bid futures rate, and vice versa.

Example

Suppose that the end of September forward bid exchange rate (USD/AUD) is 0.5800 and that the offer price of the Australian dollar futures contract for September delivery is 0.5675. An arbitrager can make profit by buying the futures contract at

$$100\ 000 \times 0.5675 = \text{USD}56\ 750$$

and selling an equivalent AUD amount forward at

$$100\ 000 \times 0.5800 = \text{USD}58\ 000$$

On the settlement date, the arbitrager realises net profit of

$$58\ 000 - 56\ 750 = \text{USD}1250$$

This operation leads to an increase in the demand for the AUD futures contract and the supply of the forward contract until the rates converge on each other, reducing profit to zero.

6.3 A comparison of forward and futures markets

We now present a comparison between forward and futures markets. These markets differ with respect to the aspects noted below. The following section provides real examples on some of the features of futures contracts, such as size.

RESEARCH FINDINGS

Price discovery and risk transfer in the futures markets

It is arguable that futures markets have evolved and grown rapidly because they contribute to the organisation of economic activity by performing at least two important functions. The first of these functions is **price discovery**, which refers to the use of futures prices to give an indication of spot prices. The second function is **risk transfer**, which pertains to hedging, as futures markets (if they perform this function properly) enable hedgers to shift price risk to others. Most of the following discussion pertains to commodity futures.

The extent to which futures markets perform these functions well can be measured from the (temporal) relationship between spot and futures prices. The price discovery function depends on whether new information is reflected first on futures or spot prices. If information is reflected first on futures prices and subsequently on spot prices, futures prices should lead spot prices, indicating that the futures market performs the price discovery function well. If, on the other hand, spot prices lead futures prices, then the spot market is said to dominate the futures market, in which case the latter is merely a satellite of the former. The ability of the futures market to perform the risk transfer function is measured by the elasticity of arbitrage between the physical commodity (or currency) and the corresponding futures contract: this elasticity determines the correlation of price changes.

The main argument for the hypothesis that futures prices lead spot prices is that the former respond to new information more quickly than the latter due to lower transaction costs and ease of taking short positions. While the futures transaction can be implemented immediately, with little up-front cash, spot purchases require a greater initial outlay and may take longer to implement. It is also arguable that speculators prefer to hold futures contracts because they are not interested in the physical commodity *per se*. Futures positions possess the additional advantage of being easy to offset. Furthermore, hedgers who are interested in the physical commodity and have storage constraints will hedge themselves by buying futures contracts. Therefore, both hedgers and speculators react to the new information by indulging in futures rather than spot transactions. Spot prices react with a lag because spot transactions cannot be executed so quickly.[1]

Futures trading can also facilitate the allocation of production and consumption over time, particularly by providing market guidance in the holding of inventories. If, for example, futures prices for distant deliveries are well above those for early deliveries, postponement of consumption becomes attractive. Thus, changes in futures prices result in subsequent changes in spot prices arising from changes in the spot demand for the commodity.

There is some rationale and empirical evidence for the hypothesis that futures prices lead spot prices and also for the hypothesis that spot prices lead futures prices. However, the case for the first hypothesis is stronger and more compelling. The empirical results reveal that the futures market performs about 60 per cent of the price discovery function and that the elasticity of supply of arbitrage services is adequately high for the market to perform the risk transfer function.[2]

1 P. Silvapulle and I. A. Moosa, 'The Relationship Between Spot and Futures Prices: Evidence from the Crude Oil Market', *Journal of Futures Market*, 19, 1999, pp. 175–93.

2 I. A. Moosa, 'Price Discovery and Risk Transfer in the Crude Oil Futures Market: Some Structural Time Series Evidence', *Economic Notes*, 31, 2002, pp. 153–63.

Market size

The currency futures market is much smaller than the forward market: the latter is almost twenty times as large as the former.

Market structure

The forward market is an **over-the-counter (OTC) market**, comprising a network of buyers and sellers executing transactions by means of telecommunications: telephone, fax and electronic dealing systems (see Chapter 2). Futures contracts, on the other hand, are traded on the floor of an **organised exchange** where buyers and sellers meet face to face. Currently, electronic (online) trading is available for both futures and forward contracts. It remains the case, however, that while there is something called the 'Sydney Futures Exchange', because it is an organised exchange with a physical location, there is no such thing as the 'Sydney Forward Exchange'.

Contract size

Forward contracts are non-standardised and the size is determined by negotiations between the buyer and the seller. Futures contracts have standard sizes, depending on the currency. Market participants can trade multiples, but not fractions, of a contract. For example, the size of the Australian dollar contract on the Chicago Mercantile Exchange and the Sydney Futures Exchange is AUD100 000.

Traded currencies

Because forward contracts are non-standardised and are determined by negotiations, any currency can (at least theoretically) be traded forward. In the futures market, on the other hand, one consequence of standardisation is that only some of the major currencies are traded.

Cross rates

Theoretically, any cross rate can be implicit in a forward contract. For example, it may be possible to negotiate with an Australian bank to buy the Norwegian krone three months forward against the Hong Kong dollar. It is up to the bank to come up with a suitable cross forward rate (which can be calculated in the same manner as a cross spot rate, as shown in Chapter 2). In the futures market, again because of standardisation, currencies are traded predominantly against the US dollar, although a number of cross currency contracts are available on the Chicago Mercantile Exchange (see the following section). If a particular cross currency contract is not available, then trading on the cross rate would require two different contracts.

Example

Assume that futures contracts for the pound (GBP62 500) and Swiss franc (CHF125 000) are priced at 1.45 (USD/GBP) and 0.725 (USD/CHF), respectively. To sell the pound against the Swiss franc, the trader must sell the pound against the US dollar. The value of one contract sold is:

$$62\,500 \times 1.45 = \text{USD}90\,625$$

Simultaneously, the trader buys the Swiss franc against the dollar. The value of one contract bought is:

$$125\,000 \times 0.725 = \text{USD}90\,625$$

The cross rate (CHF/GBP) can then be calculated as:

$$\frac{125\ 000}{62\ 500} = 2.00$$

Needless to say, in practice it never works so perfectly that the value of the contracts sold is exactly equal to the value of the contracts bought. Again, this example ignores the consequences of marking to market.

Exchange rate fluctuations

There are no limits to exchange rate fluctuations in the forward market except for those that apply to the corresponding spot market. In the futures market the exchange sets daily limits on fluctuations and there are provisions to change these limits.

Maturity dates

The maturity dates of forward contracts are fixed by negotiations between the buyer and the seller. Those of futures contracts are set by the exchange.

Maturity lengths

Although forward contracts of short maturities (less than one year) are more common than those of long maturities, forward contracts of maturity as long as 20 years have been dealt. In the futures market, the longest maturity is 12 months.

Credit risk

When a commercial bank offers a customer a forward contract, the bank bears the credit risk arising from the possibility that the customer will default when it is time to deliver. Risk is covered by reducing credit lines to the customer, although the use of margin accounts is gaining acceptance. In the futures market, credit risk is borne by the exchange or, more precisely, by the clearing corporation. It is covered by the margin account, marking to market and daily limits.

Cash flows

In forward trading, there are no cash flows until maturity when the currencies are delivered. In futures trading, there are interim cash flows that take the form of an initial margin and the variation in the margin account, as well as the final payment on the maturity date.

Hours of trading

Like the spot market, the forward market is open around the clock. Trading hours in the futures market are set by the exchange, but some sort of a continuous market can be formed by the global links of exchanges and by electronic trading.

Eligible dealers

In the forward market, any party can be an eligible dealer, since there are no formal restrictions on entry to the market. In the futures market, dealers must be members of the exchange. Non-members can act only via member brokers. For example, the Chicago Mercantile Exchange has a Shareholder Relations and Membership Services Department, which conducts membership purchases and sales, approves applicants for membership and facilitates the transfer of membership between members.

Major users

Forward contracts are used mainly for hedging, whereas futures contracts are used mainly for speculation. Because futures contract sizes and settlement dates are standardised, hedgers using futures contracts face a problem unless: (i) the amount to be hedged is equivalent to the value of one contract or multiples thereof; and (ii) the settlement date is identical to the date on which the payables and receivables are due. For example, a US exporter who wants to hedge an amount of AUD256 000 to be received on 7 May will find it inappropriate to use the futures market because: (i) the value of one Australian-dollar contract is AUD100 000 and hence the amount to be hedged is equivalent to 2.56 contracts, which cannot be obtained; and (ii) the settlement date does not coincide with the maturity date of any futures contract. The hedger will therefore resort to the forward market where the size of the contract and the maturity date can be negotiated. It is the flexibility of forward contracts that makes the forward market much larger than the futures market.

For a speculator, on the other hand, the contract size does not matter. A speculator who believes that the Australian dollar is going to appreciate will buy one or more contracts without there being any reason, for example, to insist on buying AUD165 328 rather than AUD100 000 or AUD200 000, which are the values of one and two contracts, respectively. Moreover, the speculator can realise profit by selling the contracts at any time.

RESEARCH FINDINGS

Why are futures contracts used?

A question that has been dealt with in the academic literature is why futures contracts are traded, which is related to the question of why futures markets have grown spectacularly. Although our previous argument is that futures contracts are mainly used for speculation, survey evidence shows that firms do use futures contacts for hedging.

Financial economists have for a long time been examining the motivation for using futures markets. In the early days of research on futures markets these markets were viewed as straightforward and simple, used mainly for shifting risk or insuring against the risk of price fluctuations. But subsequently a view has emerged that futures contracts are used to maximise the expected utility derived from a portfolio of cash and futures positions. An intermediate view is that taking a futures position is motivated partially by the desire to stabilise income and partially to increase expected profit.

Although all of the motivations stated so far can be accomplished by using forward contracts, organised futures markets are viewed as being superior to informal forward markets. A problem with forward contracts is that they are tailored by means of substantial negotiations, which means that they cannot be offset by identical contracts, and there is no scope for the advantages of clearing houses and settlement by the payment difference.

Another view that has been put forward more recently by Pennings and Leuthold is that the motivation for using futures contracts is contract relationships management.[1] According to this view, futures exchanges provide facilitating services that can be used to establish a successful contract relationship among various parties despite differences in contract-type preferences between firms. It is also argued that the service provided by futures exchanges complements the contract terms such that it yields a communally preferred contracting relationship. Pennings and Leuthold present a model showing that using futures markets can provide preferred contracting arrangements, enhancing relationships between firms.

[1] J. M. E. Pennings and R. M. Leuthold, 'The Motivation for Hedging Revisited', *Journal of Futures Markets*, 20, 2002, pp. 865–85.

6.4 Specifications of currency futures contracts

Futures contracts are traded on the Philadelphia Stock Exchange, the Chicago Mercantile Exchange and other international exchanges. The Australian dollar futures contract is also traded on the Sydney Futures Exchange.

The Philadelphia Stock Exchange

Currency futures contracts on five currencies are traded on the Philadelphia Stock Exchange: the Australian dollar, the British pound, the Canadian dollar, the Japanese yen and the Swiss franc. The following table displays the specifications of these contracts. In addition to this information, the contracts have the following common characteristics:

- *Contract months:* March, June, September and December.
- *Last trading day:* the Friday before the third Wednesday of the month.
- *Settlement day:* the third Wednesday of the month.
- *Daily price limits:* none.
- *Trading hours:* 2:30 a.m. to 2:30 p.m. (US Eastern time), except for the Canadian dollar contract (starting at 7.30 a.m. US Eastern time).
- *Issuer and guarantor:* the Intermarket Clearing Corporation (a subsidiary of the Options Clearing Corporation).

	Currency				
	AUD	GBP	CAD	JPY	CHF
Contract symbol	ZA	ZB	ZC	ZJ	ZS
Contract size	100 000	62 500	100 000	12 500 000	125 000
Quotation	US cents/unit	US cents/unit	US cents/unit	100th US cent/unit	US cents/unit
Minimum price change	USD10.00	USD6.25	USD10.00	USD12.50	USD12.50
Maximum position (contracts)	6 000	5 000	6 000	6 000	6 000

The Chicago Mercantile Exchange

Futures contracts are offered on a number of currencies: the Australian dollar, the Brazilian real, the British pound, the Canadian dollar, the euro, the Japanese yen, the Mexican peso, the New Zealand dollar, the Norwegian krone, the Russian rouble, the South African rand, the Swedish krona and the Swiss franc. The specifications of the Australian dollar contract are as follows:

- *Quotation:* US dollar per Australian dollar (for example, 0.5462).
- *Contract size:* AUD100 000.
- *Minimum price fluctuation (tick):* USD10/contract.
- *Maximum price fluctuation:* there is no price limit.
- *Last trading day:* trading ceases at 9.16 a.m. US Central time on the second business day immediately preceding the third Wednesday of the contract month.
- *Delivery:* physical delivery takes place on the third Wednesday of the contract month in the country of issuance at a bank designated by the Clearing House.

- *Position accountability:* holders of positions of more than 6000 contracts net long or short in all contract months combined must provide, upon request of the exchange, information on the nature of the position.

Futures contracts on the cross rate are also available on the Chicago Mercantile Exchange, mostly involving the euro. The euro contracts (quoted as euro/other currency) are available against the Australian dollar, the British pound, the Canadian dollar, the Japanese yen, the Norwegian krone, the Swedish krona and the Swiss franc. Other cross contracts include the following: AUD/CAD, AUD/NZD, AUD/JPY, GBP/CHF, GBP/JPY, CAD/JPY and CHF/JPY.

The Sydney Futures Exchange

The Sydney Futures Exchange (SFE) and its subsidiary companies provide exchange trade and over-the-counter (OTC) financial services. It offers fully electronic 24-hour trading capability. It also provides other services (such as the dissemination of real time and historical market data) as well as central clearing, settlement and depository services for both derivatives and cash products.

The Australian dollar futures contract was abandoned soon after its introduction in the late 1980s, but was re-introduced in February 2001. The following are the specifications of the contract:

- *Contract size:* AUD100 000.
- *Contract months:* March, June, September and December.
- *Contract code:* AF.
- *Price quotation:* USD/AUD.
- *Minimum price movement:* USD10/contract.
- *Last trading day:* one business day prior to the third Wednesday of the delivery month. Trading terminates at 11.00 a.m. or as determined by the SFE.
- *Settlement day:* delivery is made on the third Wednesday of the month.
- *Settlement method:* holders of bought positions receive AUD and deliver USD on the settlement day (and vice versa for holders of sold positions).

6.5 Currency and interest rate swaps

In Chapter 2 we came across **foreign exchange swaps** when we discussed the concept of the forward exchange rate. In this chapter we deal with currency swaps, which are completely different and should not be confused. **Currency swaps** involve the exchange of interest and foreign currency cash flows or a combination of both.

Swaps have experienced tremendous growth, becoming a very important means of financing. The swap market emerged in the 1980s, starting with currency swaps. As interest rate volatility became a source of concern to international business firms, swaps became more common.

Currency swaps

A currency swap is a transaction in which two counterparties exchange specific amounts of two different currencies at the outset and repay over time in accordance with a predetermined rule that reflects both interest payments and the amortisation of the principal. Normally, fixed interest rates are used for each currency. In some cases, there is no exchange of principal amounts initially and at maturity.

IN PRACTICE

Why were the Kiwi and Aussie popular swap currencies in the 1980s?

Swaps involving the New Zealand dollar were extremely active in the second quarter of 1985. Foreign investors were attracted to New Zealand dollar denominated assets because of a combination of high nominal interest rates and the appreciation of the New Zealand dollar against the US dollar. The problem is that a withholding tax of 15 per cent deterred them from buying domestic government bonds. Foreign borrowers issued New Zealand dollar Eurobonds at yields as much as 300 basis points below comparable New Zealand government bonds, swapping the proceeds into US dollars. The firm issuing the New Zealand dollar bonds obtained cheap US dollars and a New Zealand counterparty, which borrowed abroad and swapped into New Zealand dollars, obtained funds below the rate available in the domestic market.

During the second quarter of 1985, NZD260 million worth of Eurobonds were issued, probably all linked to currency swaps. In early 1986 a similar spate of Australian dollar floating rate notes was issued in the United States, which apparently was motivated largely by withholding tax considerations in Australia. The proceeds of these issues were swapped into US dollars.

Unlike the conventional foreign exchange swaps, which have been used in the foreign exchange market for a long time, currency swaps emerged as a financial instrument in the 1980s. In foreign exchange swaps, only the principal amount is exchanged when the transaction is initiated and again on the maturity of the contract. There is no exchange of interest payments in between these two dates. It is unfortunate, and perhaps confusing, that both kinds of transaction are referred to as 'swaps': no generally agreed terminology has appeared to distinguish between them.

Currency swaps have evolved as a successor to **back-to-back loans** or **parallel loans**. A parallel loan involves two counterparties lending each other loans of equal value, maturing on the same date and denominated in two different currencies. The exchange of the principal amounts is based on the spot rate, whereas the interest payments and the repayment of the principal are based on the forward rates. This kind of financial transaction was developed in the 1970s when exchange controls were in force in the United Kingdom. After the abolition of exchange controls in 1979, parallel loans continued to be used for the purpose of hedging long-term foreign currency exposure at a lower cost than can be obtained in the foreign exchange market.

Currency swaps differ from parallel loans in that the settlement of all payments is carried out on the basis of an exchange rate agreed upon when the contract is initiated. They normally involve an exchange of the principal amounts on the initiation of the contract and the re-exchange of these amounts on the maturity of the contract. Therefore, a currency swap consists of three stages, which can be illustrated by assuming two counterparties, A and B. Counterparty A has a comparative advantage in raising Australian dollar loans but needs Japanese yen funds, whereas B has a comparative advantage in raising Japanese yen loans but needs Australian dollar funds. The implication here is that A can raise Australian dollar loans at a lower rate than B, and vice versa. Thus, it makes a lot of sense if A raises Australian dollar loans while B raises yen loans and then they exchange (swap) the loans. Both, as a result, save on the cost of borrowing. The following stages are then involved in a currency swap:

- The counterparties exchange the principal amounts at the commencement of the swap. A gives B Australian dollars and receives Japanese yen at a mutually acceptable exchange rate,

IN PRACTICE

The World Bank and the origin of currency swaps

The World Bank was a significant contributor to the development of the currency swap market. It was at one time interested in low interest rate loans denominated in the German mark and the Swiss franc, but could not raise the amounts it wanted directly. Thus, it sought to swap dollar loans for loans in these currencies with counterparties who needed dollar loans and having a comparative advantage in raising loans in the other currencies.

A currency swap between the World Bank and IBM in August 1981 was a landmark in the development of the currency swap market. At that time, IBM held the view that the Swiss franc was going to appreciate against the US dollar and hence wanted to replace the Swiss franc debt with US dollar debt. The development of this market was further bolstered by government restrictions on access to some European capital markets.

Government regulations restricting access to some major European capital markets stimulated currency swaps because they can be used to gain indirect access to these markets. Restrictions can also make it more expensive to raise funds in some national markets, in which case swaps overcome this problem.

It is thought that the major step in the evolution of the swap market was the extension of the swap concept from the currency market to credit market instruments denominated in the same currency (that is, interest rate swaps). By 1982 interest rate swaps had grown to a size made it possible to speak of a market.

which could be the spot exchange rate prevailing then. If the principal amount is K Australian dollars, then B receives this amount whereas A receives an amount equal to KS yen, where S is the exchange rate measured as JPY/AUD.

- On the interest payment dates, A pays B the interest due on the yen loan, whereas B pays A the interest due on the Australian dollar loan. If i is the interest rate on the Australian dollar borrowing and i^* is the interest rate on the yen borrowing, then A pays i^*KS, whereas B pays iK on each interest payment date. These amounts, which are valued at the same exchange rate agreed upon at the beginning of the transaction, are channelled to the lenders.
- On the maturity of the contract, the principal amounts are re-exchanged. Thus, A pays B an amount of KS yen, whereas B pays A an amount of K Australian dollars. These amounts are channelled to the lenders. Again, the same exchange rate is used.

This transaction is illustrated in Figure 6.5. Changes in exchange rates naturally affect both counterparties: A benefits from the appreciation of the yen, whereas B benefits from the appreciation of the Australian dollar.

Figure 6.5 A currency swap

(a) Exchange of principal amounts

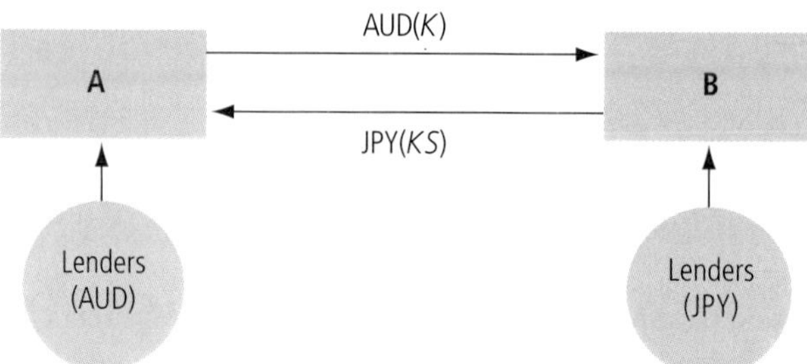

(b) Exchange of interest payments

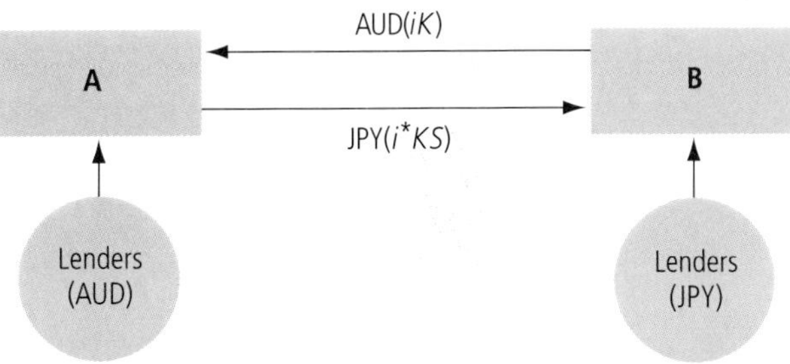

(c) Re-exchange of principal amounts

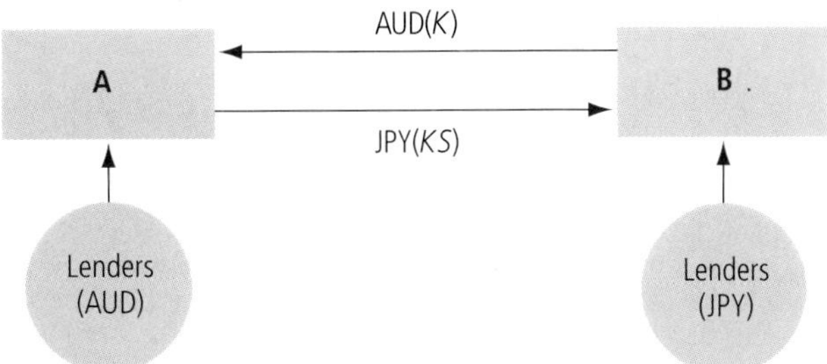

IN PRACTICE

What is the ISDA?

The International Swaps and Derivatives Association (ISDA) is the global trade association representing leading participants in the privately negotiated derivatives industry (that is, OTC derivatives or those not traded on organised exchanges). This business includes interest rate, currency, commodity, credit and equity swaps as well as other related products such as swaptions. The ISDA was established in 1985 and since then it has grown to encompass hundreds of member institutions from more than 40 countries. These members include most of the world's major institutions that deal in, and are leading end users of, privately negotiated derivatives, as well as related service providers and consultants.

Since its inception, the ISDA has accomplished the following:

- developed the ISDA Master Agreement, which governs how swaps and related financial transactions work
- published a wide range of related documentation, materials and instruments covering a variety of transaction types
- produced legal opinions on the enforceability of netting (of payments)
- secured recognition of the risk-reducing effects of netting in determining capital requirements
- promoted sound risk-management practices
- advanced the understanding and treatment of derivatives and risk management from public policy and regulatory capital perspectives.

Example

Assume that A and B agree on a five-year swap, whereby A delivers AUD1 000 000 and receives the equivalent at a spot exchange rate of 65.00 (JPY/AUD). Assume also that the interest rates on the Australian dollar and the yen are 5 per cent and 2 per cent, respectively. The payments made by A to B, and vice versa, under the agreement are shown in Figure 6.6. If in year 1 the market exchange rate is 60, then A benefits because the Japanese yen amount that has to be paid is JPY1 300 000, which is equal to AUD20 000 at the contract rate (65.0), whereas it is worth AUD21 667 at the market rate. If the market exchange rate is 70, then B benefits.

Figure 6.6 A five-year currency swap

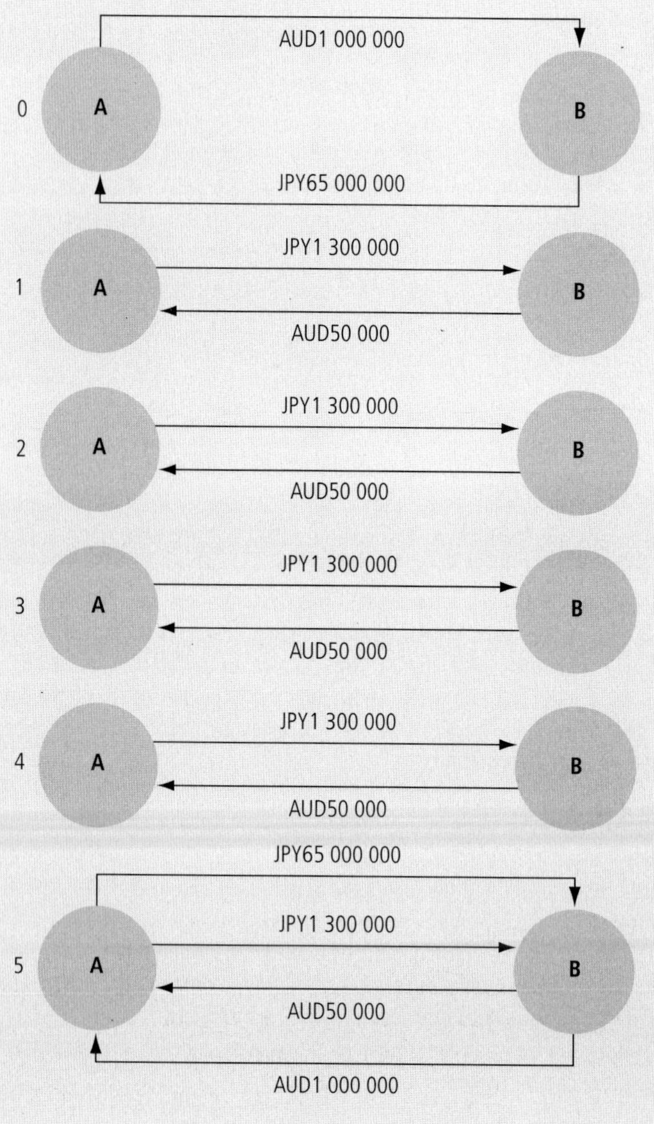

If the principal amounts are not exchanged, then a currency swap resembles a portfolio of forward contracts: the two counterparties agree to exchange two cash flows denominated in two different currencies at a predetermined exchange rate on a sequence of dates in the future. Suppose that counterparties A and B agree on an arrangement whereby A receives a fixed amount of currency y, K, while paying B the equivalent amount of x valued at the contract exchange rate $S_0(x/y)$. What happens on each payment date is illustrated in Figure 6.7, which shows the amount received by A in terms of currency x. In effect, therefore, A receives K valued at a variable exchange rate (the spot exchange rate prevailing on the payment date, S_1), whereas B receives the amount K valued at a fixed exchange rate (the contract exchange rate, S_0). If in period 1, the actual exchange rate, S_1, turns out to be higher than the contract exchange rate, S_0, this would mean that currency y has appreciated and thus the receiver of currency y (the receiver of the variable exchange rate) must benefit. In this case, A receives a net amount equal to the principal, K, valued at the difference between the two exchange rates, which is $K(S_1 - S_0)$. The principal amount itself is not exchanged and this is why it is called the **notional principal**. Conversely, if in period 2 the spot exchange rate turns out to be lower than the contract exchange rate, this would mean that x has appreciated, and so the receiver of x must benefit. In this case, A pays B a net amount of $K(S_0 - S_2)$, and so on.

Figure 6.7 An n-year currency swap not involving the exchange of principals

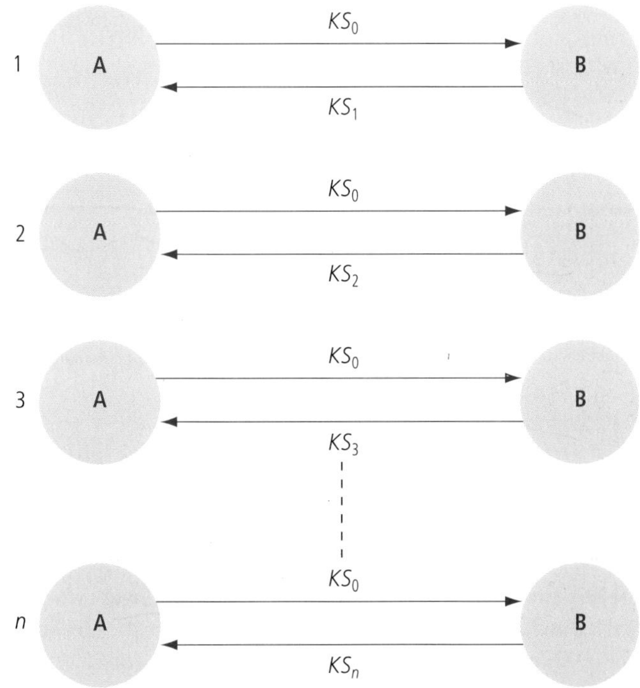

Example

Consider a five-year currency swap with a notional principal of AUD100 000, whereby A receives annual payments in Australian dollars and B receives annual payments in New Zealand dollars at a contracted exchange rate of 1.18 (NZD/AUD). If the exchange rate assumes the values 1.25, 1.15, 1.10, 1.30 and 1.18, then the payments made by A to B, and vice versa, will be as shown in Figure 6.8. In practice, compensatory payments are

Continued...

made. For example, in year 1 a higher exchange rate implies that the Australian dollar has appreciated and so A must be paid a net compensatory amount equal to NZD7000 (125 000 – 118 000).

Figure 6.8 A five-year NZD/AUD swap

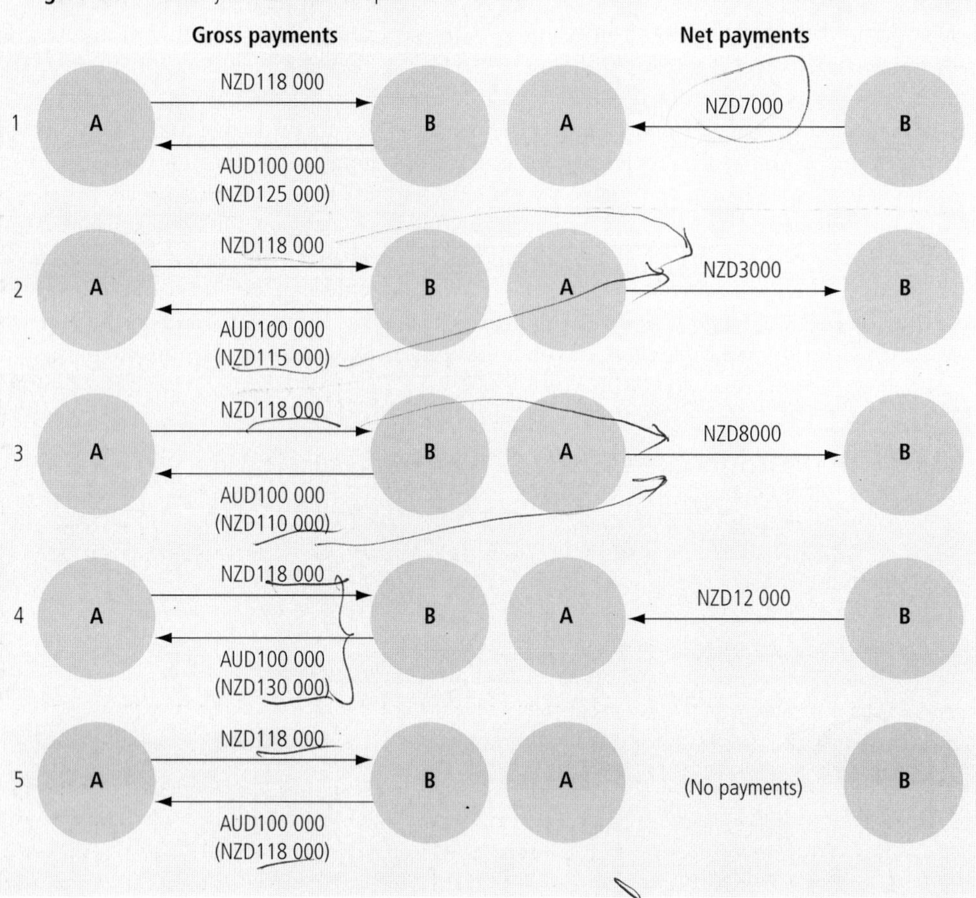

Interest rate swaps

The basic kind of **interest rate swap**, called a **fixed-for-floating swap**, involves the exchange of a notional principal valued at fixed and floating (variable) interest rates denominated in the same currency. Figure 6.9 shows two counterparties, A and B, involved in such a swap, whereby A receives payments based on a fixed rate and B receives payments based on a floating rate (such as LIBOR), both of which are calculated on the basis of a notional principal that is never exchanged, K. Thus, on each payment date, A receives $\bar{i}K$ whereas B receives iK, where $\bar{i}$ and i are the fixed and floating interest rates, respectively. In practice, net compensatory payments are made by one counterparty to the other, depending on whether the floating rate turns out to be higher or lower than the fixed rate. If the floating interest rate turns out to be higher than the fixed interest rate, then B must receive a net compensatory payment from A. This payment is equal to the difference between the two rates applied to the notional principal, $K(i - \bar{i})$. If, on the other hand, the fixed rate turns out to be higher, A must receive $K(\bar{i} - i)$.

Figure 6.9 Fixed-for-floating interest rate swap

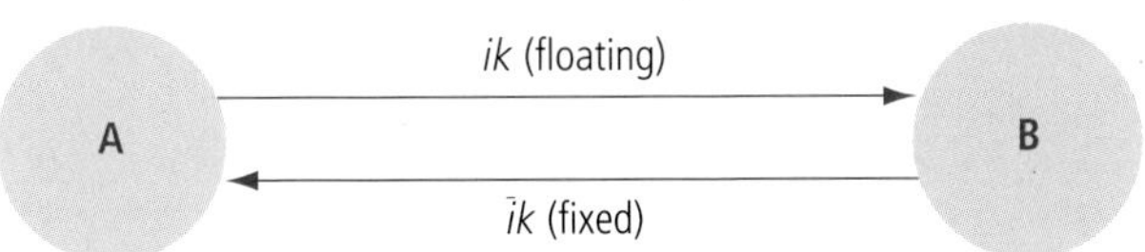

Japanese banks use interest rate swaps to generate income

IN PRACTICE

Japanese banks, which incurred huge losses arising from the write-offs of bad loans in the 1990s, have resorted to using fixed-for-floating interest rate swaps to boost their income. These banks have managed to show better results than otherwise by locking in income from a fixed interest rate in return for paying a lower floating rate. Standard & Poor's, the credit rating agency, reported that income from interest rate swap transactions supplied 80 per cent of the unexpected increase in the revenues of Japan's second largest bank, Sumitomo Mitsui Banking Corporation, in the year to March 2002. *The Economist* estimated that Japanese banks had stocked up some JPY40 trillion of interest rate swaps by mid-2002.[1] Apparently, they managed to do that only because of an accounting loophole that had been closed elsewhere in the developed world.

[1] 'Free Lunch for Now', *The Economist*, 7 August 2002, p. 57.

Other kinds of interest rate swaps include the **basis swap** and the **zero-coupon swap**. A basis swap involves two variable interest rates, such as the deposit rate and the rate on Treasury bills. A zero-coupon swap involves a zero fixed rate, in which case the receiver of the payment based on the fixed rate receives everything on the maturity of the contract.

Example

Consider the following numerical example of a five-year interest rate swap, whereby A receives annual payments based on a floating interest rate and B receives annual payments based on a fixed interest rate. The principal involved is AUD100 000 and the fixed rate is 6 per cent. If, on each payment date, the floating interest rate assumes the values 8.25, 9.75, 5.50, 4.75 and 6 per cent respectively, then the amounts paid and received will be as shown in Figure 6.10. In practice, net compensatory payments are made. For example, in year 1 a higher floating rate implies that the receiver of the floating rate payment must benefit. Thus, A must be paid a net compensatory amount of AUD2250 (8250 – 6000).

Continued...

Figure 6.10 A five-year fixed-for-floating interest rate swap

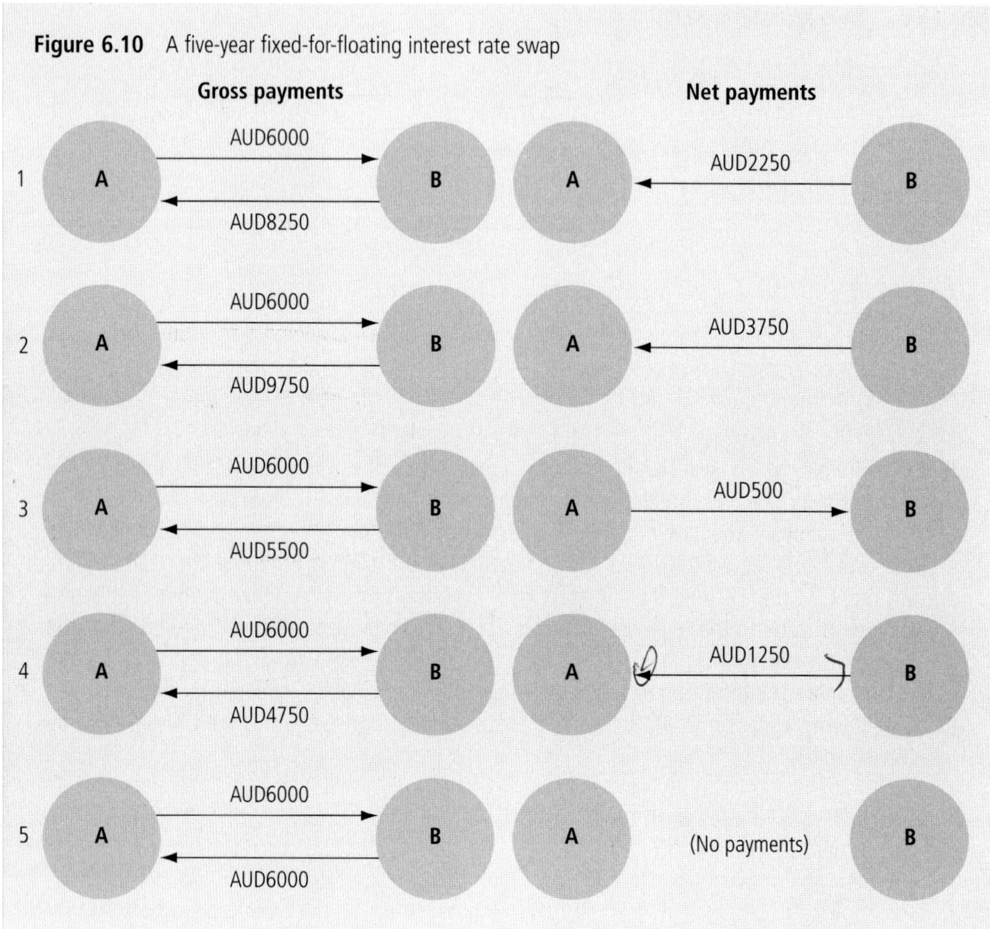

Cross-currency interest rate swaps

A **cross-currency interest rate swap** involves the exchange of payments in different currencies. One set of payments is calculated on the basis of a fixed interest rate, whereas another is calculated on the basis of a variable interest rate. This arrangement can be executed as a single transaction between two counterparties, A and B. Figure 6.11(a) illustrates a swap whereby A receives floating interest Australian dollar payments and B receives fixed interest Japanese yen payments. Figure 6.11(b) shows that counterparty A deals with two counterparties to separate the cross-currency and interest rate components. A pays C the fixed Australian dollar payments received from B, in return for floating Australian dollar payments.

Figure 6.11 Cross-currency interest rate swaps

(a) Dealing with one counterparty

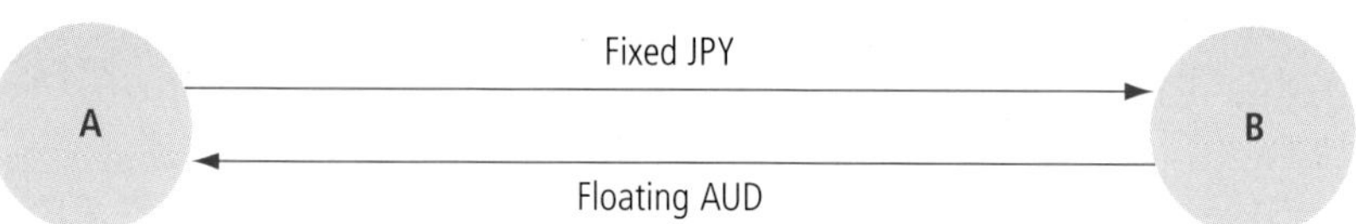

(b) Dealing with two counterparties

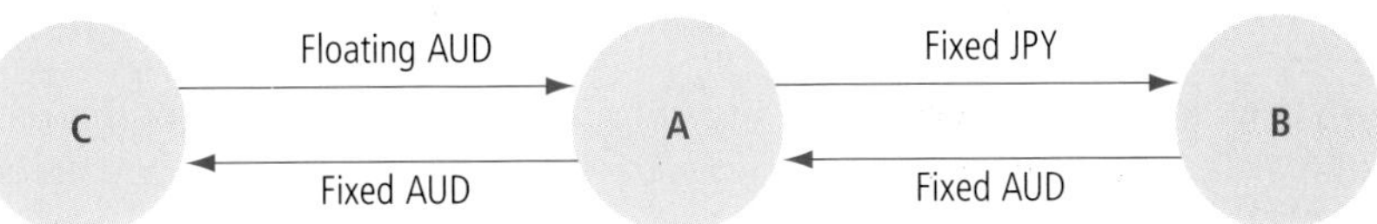

Pricing swap default risk

The meaning of pricing swap default risk in an interest rate swap is adding a premium on the fixed rate to compensate the receiver of the fixed interest payments for the risk arising from the possibility that the other counterparty may default on the payment date. In practice, counterparties may seek to mitigate risk rather than price it. Common methods of mitigating risk include rationing the amount of swaps with any one counterparty, entering into marking-to-market agreements and doing business only with top-rated counterparties.

An alternative to mitigating credit risk is pricing it. To do that it is possible to model the magnitude of potential default risk and estimate a reasonable adjustment to the fixed rate. The magnitude of the adjustment depends on credit quality of the counterparties and existing market conditions (specifically, the shape of the yield curve, or whether short-term interest rates are higher than, equal to or less than long-term interest rates).

Sorensen and Bollier summarised the findings of their investigation of this issue as follows:[1]

- For any yield curve, no adjustment is necessary if the counterparties are high-quality borrowers (that is, they have low credit risk).
- No adjustment is needed if the yield curve is flat (that is, short-term interest rates are not higher or lower than long-term interest rates) and both counterparties have the same credit rating.
- If both counterparties have the same credit rating, the adjustment is not affected by who pays the fixed rate and the shape of the yield curve.
- If the yield curve slopes upwards (long-term interest rates are higher than short-term interest rates), the fixed rate should be reduced, and vice versa.
- If the counterparty paying the fixed rate is of a higher credit rating than the counterparty receiving the fixed rate, the fixed rate should be reduced, and vice versa.

1 E. H. Sorensen and T. F. Bollier, 'Pricing Swap Default Risk', *Financial Analysts Journal*, May–June 1994, pp. 23–33.

Pricing interest rate swaps

Pricing a fixed-for-floating interest rate swap is the process of determining the price or the fixed interest rate on the swap. If the swap market is competitive, then the price or the fixed rate will be driven down until the present value of the fixed rate payments is equal to the present value of the floating rate payments. Moreover, since the fixed rate payments are constant over the life of the swap, they are an annuity. Thus, the pricing process consists of the following steps:

- forecasting the floating rates on each payment date
- calculating the present value of the expected floating rate payments
- calculating the annuity that has the same present value as the expected floating rate payments
- calculating the fixed rate by solving the annuity equation.

6.6 Swap terminology

The following are some of the terms used in association with swaps. Most of this terminology pertains to the kinds of swaps that are derived from the basic kinds described earlier.

Money market and term swaps

A **money market swap** has a maturity of three years or less. This is unlike a **term swap**, which has a maturity of more than three years.

Spot-start, delayed-start and forward swaps

A **spot-start swap** starts (that is, it becomes operational) two days after the contract has been agreed upon verbally. A swap that starts after more than two days but within one year is a **delayed-start swap**. If the starting date is more than one year after the start of the verbal agreement, it is a **forward swap**.

Options on swaps, swaptions and swap buyouts

An **option on a swap** is a contract allowing the holder to exercise, or otherwise, the right to engage in a specified swap. A **swaption** allows one party to the contract (the holder of the swaption) to alter the swap. For example, this party could terminate the swap without paying any penalty. If a counterparty wishes to terminate the swap without holding a swaption, then he or she would indulge in a **swap buyout** (that is, the swap is closed and settled at current prices).

Amortising swaps

Normally, the notional principal on which a swap is based is constant throughout the life of the swap. In the case of an **amortising swap**, the principal declines with time. Another alteration is when the principal takes an irregular pattern.

Summary

- Currency futures contracts represent an obligation of the seller to deliver a certain amount of a specified currency at some time in the future at an exchange rate determined now. They were first traded on the Chicago Mercantile Exchange.
- The Australian dollar contract was introduced on the Chicago Mercantile Exchange in January 1987. In 1988, the contract was introduced on the Sydney Futures Exchange but lack of interest forced it out of the market until February 2001, when the contract was re-introduced.
- Futures contracts emerged in response to three problematic characteristics of forward contracts: (i) non-standardisation of the contracts; (ii) risk of default; and (iii) lack of liquidity.
- Futures contracts solve these problems because they are standardised, while the risk of default is controlled by establishing margin accounts, marking to market on a daily basis and imposing daily limits on price movements.

- Forward and futures markets differ in a number of aspects: (i) market size; (ii) market structure; (iii) contract size; (iv) traded currencies; (v) cross rates; (vi) exchange rate fluctuations; (vii) maturity dates; (viii) maturity lengths; (ix) credit risk; (x) cash flows; (xi) hours of trading; (xii) eligible dealers; and (xiii) major users.
- Futures markets perform two important functions: price discovery and risk transfer.
- A currency swap, which is different from a foreign exchange swap, is a transaction in which two counterparties exchange specific amounts of two different currencies at the outset and repay over time in accordance with a predetermined rule that reflects both interest payments and the amortisation of principal. Currency swaps have evolved as a successor to parallel loans. The World Bank was a significant contributor to the development of the currency swap market.
- If the principal amounts are not exchanged, then a currency swap resembles a portfolio of forward contracts.
- The basic kind of interest rate swap, called a fixed-for-floating swap, involves the exchange of interest payments on a notional principal valued at fixed and floating interest rates denominated in the same currency.
- A basis swap involves two variable interest rates, whereas a zero-coupon swap involves a zero fixed rate.
- A cross-currency swap involves the exchange of interest payments on a notional principal valued at fixed and floating interest rates denominated in different currencies.
- There are other kinds of swap, including: (i) money market swaps; (ii) term swaps; (iii) spot-start swaps; (iv) delayed-start swaps; (v) forward swaps; and (vi) amortising swaps.

Key terms

amortising swap 188
back-to-back loans 179
basis swap 185
clearing corporation 170
cross-currency interest rate swap 186
currency futures 164
currency swaps 178
daily price limits 171
delayed-start swap 188
fixed-for-floating swap 184
foreign exchange swaps 178
forward swap 188
futures contracts 164
initial margin 170
interest rate swap 184
limit down 171
limit move 171
limit up 171
maintenance margin 170
margin account 170
margin call 170
marking to market 170
marking-to-market risk 171
money market swap 188
notional principal 183
option on a swap 188
organised exchange 174
over-the-counter (OTC) market 174
parallel loans 179
position limits 171
price discovery 173
risk transfer 173
settlement date 170
spot-start swap 188
swap buyout 188
swaption 188
term swap 188
variation margin 170
zero-coupon swap 185

MAXIMISE YOUR MARKS! There are 30 interactive questions for this chapter available online at **www.mhhe.com/au/moosa2e**

Review questions

1 What are the problematic characteristics of forward contracts that led to the emergence of futures contracts?

2 'Forward contracts are tailor-made.' Explain.

3 Why does the risk of default arise in forward contracts?

4 What is meant by the 'liquidity' of a forward contract?

5 How do futures contracts overcome the problems associated with forward trading?

6 What is marking-to-market risk?

7 Compare and contrast forward and futures contracts.

8 Explain why forward contracts are used primarily for hedging, whereas futures contracts are used primarily for speculation.

9 How do futures markets perform the functions of price discovery and risk transfer?

10 What is the difference between a foreign exchange swap and a currency swap?

11 'Currency swaps have evolved as a successor to parallel loans.' Explain.

12 Why were the Australian dollar and the New Zealand dollar popular swap currencies in the 1980s?

13 What is the ISDA?

14 How did Japanese banks generate income from interest rate swaps in 2001–2002?

15 Distinguish between a currency swap and an interest rate swap.

16 What is the difference between an option on a swap and a swaption?

Problems

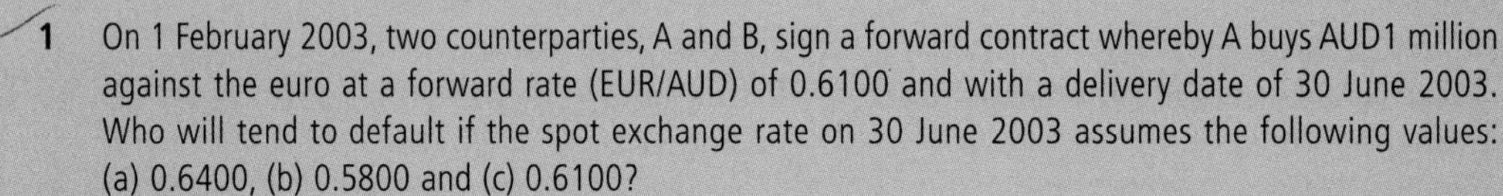

1 On 1 February 2003, two counterparties, A and B, sign a forward contract whereby A buys AUD1 million against the euro at a forward rate (EUR/AUD) of 0.6100 and with a delivery date of 30 June 2003. Who will tend to default if the spot exchange rate on 30 June 2003 assumes the following values: (a) 0.6400, (b) 0.5800 and (c) 0.6100?

2 On 13 March 2003, A (in the previous problem) decides that the AUD1 million amount is no longer required. To unwind the obligation, A decides to enter a new forward contract whereby a new counterparty, C, buys AUD1 million at a forward rate of 0.6000 for delivery on 30 June 2003. Explain what happens on the maturity date by calculating the amounts received and paid by A, B and C.

3 On 25 April 2003 a trader bought two Australian dollar futures contracts at 0.5500 (USD/AUD). Calculate the US dollar value of the two contracts. Assuming no daily price limit and no maintenance margin, calculate the daily variation in the margin account as the settlement rate assumes the following values:

26 April 0.5600
27 April 0.5730
28 April 0.5430
29 April 0.5580

4 On 16 March, a trader bought three Australian-dollar futures contracts at 0.5200 (USD/AUD) when the spot exchange rate was 0.5000. On 14 July, the trader sold the three contracts at 0.5400 and bought the amount spot at 0.5250.
   (a) Calculate the value of the three contracts on 16 March.
   (b) Calculate the spot value of the Australian dollar amount equal to three contracts on 16 March.
   (c) Ignoring marking to market, calculate the net gain (loss) from the transactions conducted on 14 July.

5 In December 1996 two counterparties, A and B, agreed on a five-year currency swap whereby A received payments in Australian dollars and B received payments in Canadian dollars at a contract exchange rate of 1.0892 (AUD/CAD). The notional principal of the swap is AUD500 000. The exchange rate assumed the following values on the payment dates:

Payment date	Exchange rate
Dec 1997	1.0751
Dec 1998	1.0672
Dec 1999	1.0555
Dec 2000	1.1142
Dec 2001	1.0892

Calculate the payments received by A and B on each payment date.

6 In December 1997, two counterparties, A and B, agreed on a three-year fixed-for-floating Australian dollar swap, whereby A received payments based on a floating interest rate and B received payments based on a fixed interest rate. The notional principal is AUD500 000 and the fixed rate is 4.95 per cent. The floating interest rate assumed the following values on the payment dates:

Payment date	Interest rate
Dec 1998	4.62
Dec 1999	5.08
Dec 2000	6.03

Calculate the amounts received by A and B on each payment date.

CHAPTER

Currency options

Introduction

A currency option, like a currency futures contract, is a derivative instrument whose value is contingent upon the value of the underlying currency. But whereas currency futures contracts imply a commitment to deliver the underlying currency, currency options represent a privilege (the right to buy or sell the underlying currency), which may or may not be exercised by the option holder. Like currency futures, currency options can be used for hedging and speculation. This chapter provides an introductory treatment of these important and versatile instruments.

Objectives

The objectives of this chapter are:

- To introduce the basic concepts pertaining to currency options.
- To outline the specifications of exchange-traded currency options.
- To describe frequently used option positions.
- To identify the determinants of option premiums.
- To describe some exotic currency options.

Origin and basic concepts

Currency options emerged mainly in response to customer demand as exchange rates became increasingly unpredictable. Firms became attracted to the possibility of paying a fee to buy insurance against an adverse exchange rate movement but preserving the chance to gain, should the exchange rate move favourably. The use of options also enables firms to retain their competitive positions relative to other firms that have not hedged if rates move in their (the latter's) favour.

The main users of currency options are financial firms holding large investments in foreign assets. Also, limited use of currency options is made by firms bidding on foreign contracts, where forward purchase or sale of the currency for hedging purposes would expose the firm to significant actual loss should the contract not be won. Although some banks offer forward transactions contingent upon winning a foreign contract, these are not options because the firm must fulfil the forward transaction if it wins the foreign contract, even if exchange rates have moved adversely. However, the firm is released from the forward contract if it is unsuccessful in the bidding.

A currency option may be defined as a contract that gives its holder the right (not the obligation) to buy or sell, on or by a specified date, a specified amount of a particular currency at an exchange rate determined at the time of the signing of the contract. In December 1982, the Philadelphia Stock Exchange began trading options on the pound. Currently, options are offered on the pound as well as the Australian dollar, the Canadian dollar, the Swiss franc, the Japanese yen and the euro. Currency options are also traded on the Chicago Mercantile Exchange and other international exchanges.

There are a number of concepts that must be understood in order to see how options are used. Some of these concepts are derived directly from the definition of an option. The starting point is to explain these concepts.

Options writers and holders

An option is a contract between two counterparties. The **writer** (or seller) of the option sells to the **holder** (or buyer) the right to buy or sell the amount of the currency specified in the contract. In return for this privilege, the holder of the contract pays the writer up front a price, known as the **premium**, which will be kept by the writer no matter what happens (that is, irrespective of whether the holder decides to exercise or not). It is essential not to confuse the buying and selling of the option with the buying and selling of the underlying currency. The writer of the option sells the right to buy or sell the currency and hence it is the seller of the option who receives the premium in return. The writer has an obligation to comply with the holder's decision should the latter decide to exercise the right of buying or selling the currency. The holder of the option, on the other hand, buys the right to buy or sell the currency and hence it is the buyer of the option who pays the premium. If the holder chooses not to exercise this right, then the premium will be lost (by the holder).

While writers perceive the key variable in selling options to be the volatility component, buyers feel that they are buying insurance. Commercial and investment banks often write options for their customers. Also, while writers assume **market risk** (resulting from possible adverse changes in exchange rates), buyers assume **credit risk** (resulting from the possibility that the writer will not deliver if the holder chooses to exercise).

IN PRACTICE

The effect of the Asian crisis on Asian currency options

Immediately after the floating of the Thai baht in July 1997, currency options markets for regional Asian currencies virtually vanished as volatilities sky-rocketed. The crisis resulted in no less than the effective closure of the currency options markets in the baht, the rupiah, the won, the ringgit, the Philippine peso, the Singapore dollar, the Hong Kong dollar, the renminbi, the Taiwanese dollar and the rupee for at least 18 months. Long after the end of the crisis, the options markets in these currencies were still stagnant. The following are examples:

- Malaysian ringgit options disappeared following the introduction of capital controls in September 1998.
- The baht options market was adversely affected by the interest rate differential between onshore baht and offshore baht.
- Indian rupee options became very illiquid due to regulatory restrictions.
- The Singapore dollar options market was significantly curbed by the authorities' desire to prevent the internationalisation of the Singapore dollar.

However, liquidity has improved in the won, the Hong Kong dollar, the renminbi and the Taiwanese dollar.

Premium payment and settlement dates

The **premium payment date** is the day on which the premium is due and payable. It is usually the transaction date for exchange-traded options and one or two business days after the transaction date for over-the-counter (OTC) options. The **settlement date** is the day on which delivery of the underlying currency is required and it is always specified in relation to the **exercise date**. For American options the settlement date is generally one or two business days after exercise and for European options it is normally one or two days after the expiry date.

Call and put options

An option gives the holder the right to buy or sell a currency. A **call option** gives the holder the right to buy a currency. In this case, the writer must comply by selling the currency to the holder if the latter decides to exercise. A **put option**, on the other hand, gives the holder the right to sell a currency. The writer must comply by buying the currency from the holder if the latter decides to exercise. Figure 7.1 describes what happens when the contract is initiated and when it is exercised. It is assumed that the currency holder has the US dollar as the **base currency** and the Australian dollar as the **underlying currency** (the currency that is bought and sold according to the contract).

Figure 7.1 The mechanics of call and put options on the Australian dollar

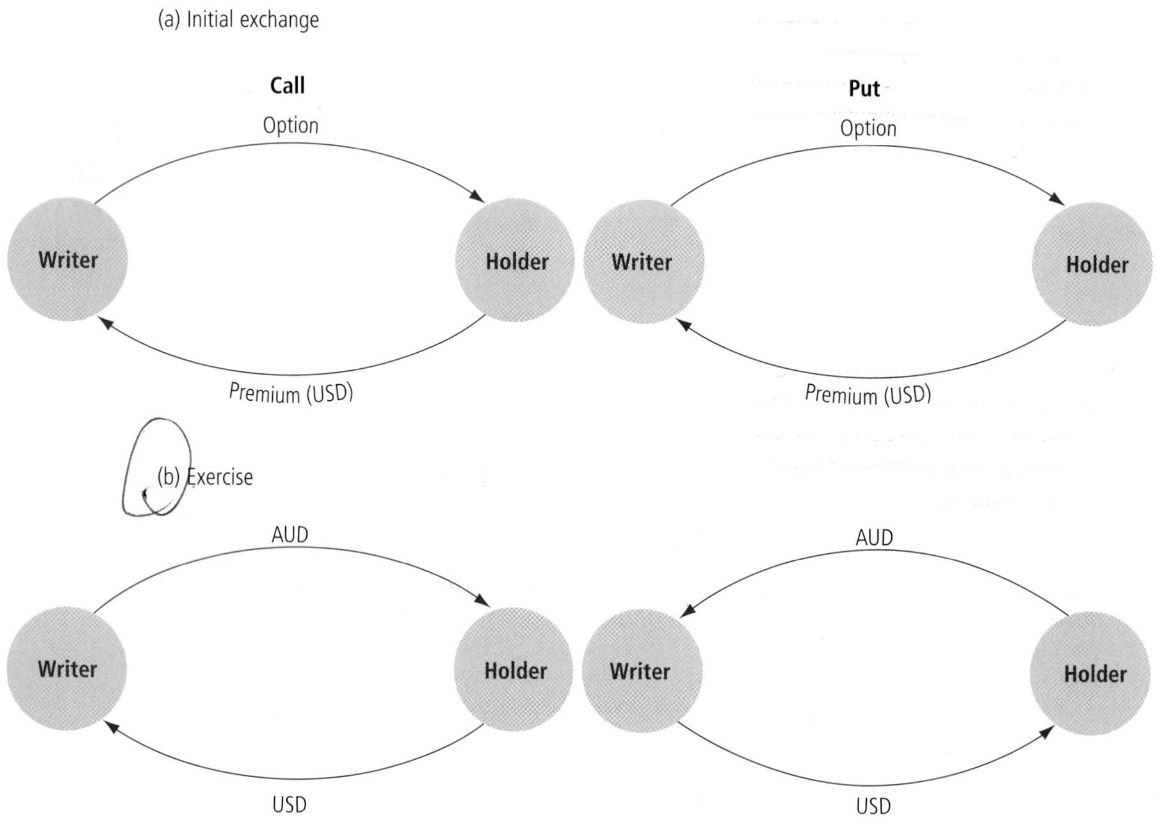

(a) Initial exchange

(b) Exercise

Naked and covered options

A **naked option** emerges if there is no corresponding spot position in the underlying currency (otherwise, we have a **covered option**). For example, if the writer of a Swiss franc call option does not have a spot position in the Swiss franc, the option would be naked. This is because, if the holder of this option decides to exercise, the writer cannot comply unless he or she buys the required amount of the underlying currency (the Swiss franc) on the spot market. The writer of a naked option may be required to deposit a margin.

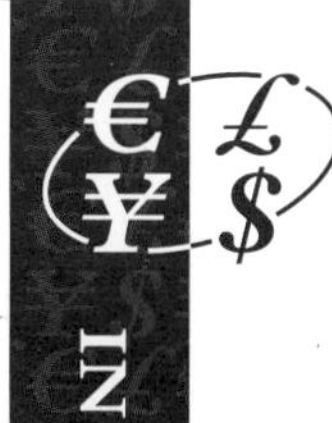

IN PRACTICE

Emerging markets' currency options

The number of currency pairs in which currency options are available has grown dramatically in recent years, predominantly in the OTC market. Chase, for example, is a market maker in over 200 currency pairs. Emerging market currencies have progressively accounted for a growing part of the overall currency options market.

Users of options on emerging currencies must take into consideration various peculiarities of these currencies, including the following:

- Liquidity is more limited outside the underlying country's normal trading hours.
- Official intervention bands have a dampening effect on historical volatility, which is an important determinant of option pricing and strategies.
- When a currency is floated after having been pegged, the information on where the currency might go will be inadequate.
- The risk of devaluation (depreciation) usually outweighs the risk of revaluation (appreciation), leading to a large preference for puts over calls.
- A strong relationship exists between the forward premium and the price of an option.

The exercise exchange rate

Also called the **strike exchange rate** (or price, in general), the **exercise exchange rate** is the rate at which the holder of the option buys (in the case of a call) or sells (in the case of a put) should the decision to exercise be taken. Let E be the exercise exchange rate and S the actual spot exchange rate prevailing when the decision whether or not to exercise is considered. Assume also that these exchange rates are expressed as the number of units of currency x per one unit of currency y, where y is the (underlying) currency to be bought or sold by the holder of the option. Ignoring the premium for the time being, the following rules hold:

- The holder will exercise a call option if $S > E$. Profit is made by buying currency y at E and selling it at S. Gross profit per unit of currency y is $S - E$. If $S < E$, there is no point in exercising a call option, since it is cheaper to buy currency y on the spot market.
- The holder will exercise a put option if $S < E$. Profit is made by buying currency y in the spot market at S and selling it at the exercise exchange rate, E. Gross profit per unit of currency y is $E - S$. If $S > E$, there is no point in exercising the put option, since this will produce a loss.

Figure 7.2 describes profitable exercise of call and put options on currency y when x is the base currency. The difference between the actual and the exercise exchange rates (or vice versa) is called **gross profit**, as opposed to **net profit**, because the premium that is paid by the holder to acquire the option is not considered.

Let us now reconsider the rules by introducing the premium, R. In the case of a call option, net profit per unit of currency y is $S - (E + R)$. In the case of a put option, net profit per unit of currency y is $E - (S + R)$. Note that while the profit obtained by the holder is unlimited, there is an upper limit on the loss, which is the premium. The worst that could happen is that the holder chooses not to exercise, in which case only the premium will be lost. On the other hand, the maximum the writer of an option can gain is the premium, whereas his or her loss is unlimited. Remember that profit/loss is measured in terms of the base currency.

Figure 7.2 Profitable exercise of call and put options on currency y

(a) Call gross profit $= S - E$

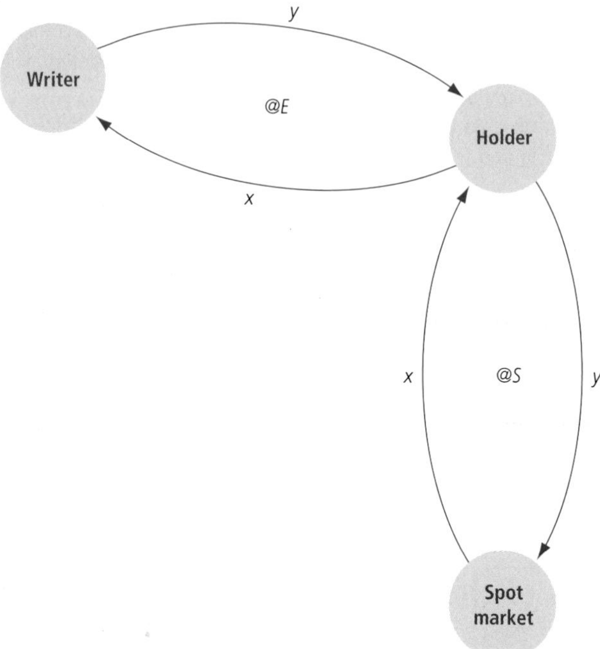

(b) Put gross profit $= E - S$

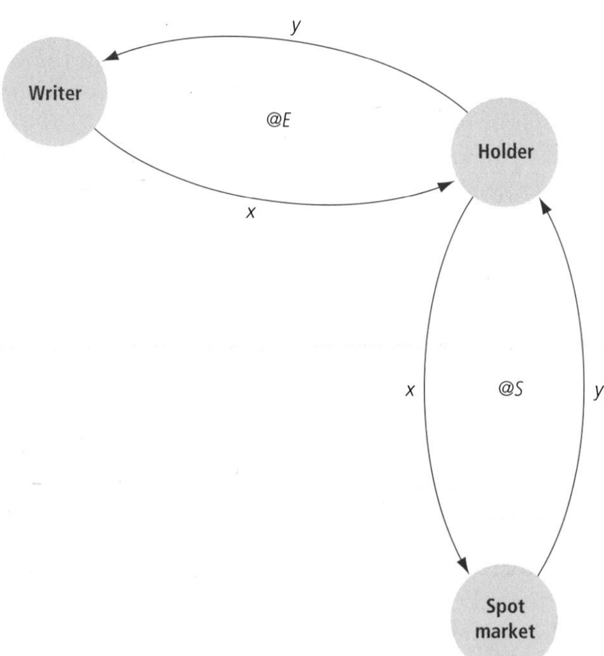

Example

Consider a call option and a put option on the Australian dollar. The call gives the trader the right to buy AUD1 million at an exercise exchange rate (E) of 0.60 (USD/AUD). The put gives the right to sell AUD1 million at the same exercise exchange rate. What will happen if, when the holder can exercise, the actual exchange rate (S) is 0.65 or 0.55?

If $S = 0.65$ then $S > E$. The holder will exercise the call option, buying the Australian dollar at 0.60 and selling it at 0.65. Buying AUD1 million will cost

$$\text{AUD1 000 000} \times 0.60 = \text{USD600 000}$$

By selling AUD1 000 000 at 0.65 the holder will obtain

$$\text{AUD1 000 000} \times 0.65 = \text{USD650 000}$$

Gross profit will be

$$650\ 000 - 600\ 000 = \text{USD50 000}$$

The put option will not be exercised in this case. If, on the other hand, $S = 0.55$, then $S < E$. The trader will exercise the put option but not the call option. The trader will buy AUD1 million spot at 0.55 and sell the amount at 0.60 by exercising the option. Thus, gross profit will be

$$600\ 000 - 550\ 000 = \text{USD50 000}$$

The profitable exercise operations are described in Figure 7.3.

Figure 7.3 Profitable exercise of call and put options on the Australian dollar

(a) Call gross profit = USD50 000

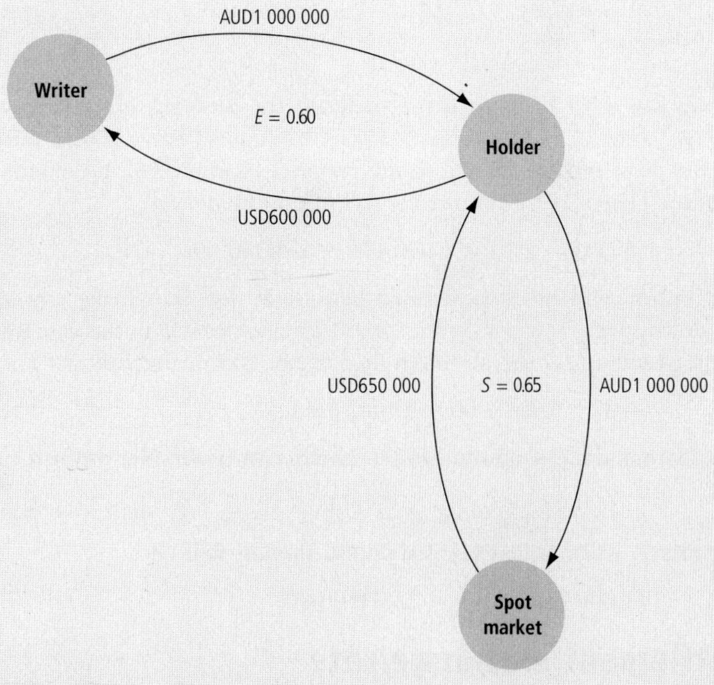

Continued...

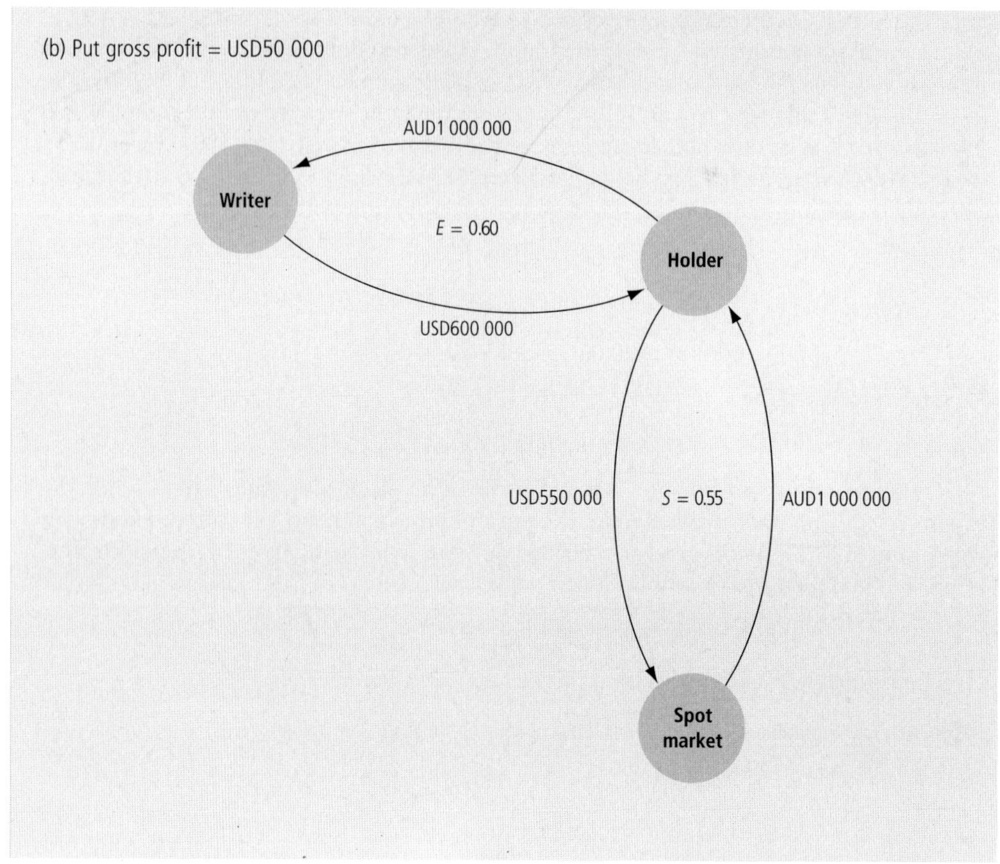

Let us now see what happens if the trader in the previous example pays USD0.01 and USD0.02 (per unit of the Australian dollar) to acquire the call and put, respectively. If S = 0.65, the gross profit obtained in the previous example will be reduced by the cost of the call option. Hence, net profit for the call option holder is

$$50\ 000 - 0.01 \times 1\ 000\ 000 = \text{USD}40\ 000$$

The put option will not be exercised because it does not make any sense to buy the Australian dollar spot at 0.65 and sell it at 0.60. The holder will in this case lose a total amount given by the premium on the put multiplied by the size of the contract:

$$0.02 \times 1\ 000\ 000 = \text{USD}20\ 000$$

If $S = 0.55$, then the put option can be exercised at profit. Net profit is calculated as

$$1\ 000\ 000 \times 0.60 - 1\ 000\ 000 \times (0.55 + 0.02) = \text{USD}30\ 000$$

The call option will not be exercised and so the loss will be

$$1\ 000\ 000 \times 0.01 = \text{USD}10\ 000$$

The settlement exchange rate

The **settlement exchange rate** is the rate at which the underlying currency can be bought or sold when the option is exercised. Most option contracts specify an objective basis on which the settlement exchange rate will be determined, such as the closing exchange rate on the expiry date for exchange-traded options and the market exchange rate at a predetermined point in time on the exercise date for OTC options.

If there is a settlement involving net payment from the writer to the holder, then the following may happen. If the holder exercises a call option, when $S > E$, where S is the settlement exchange rate, then the holder receives (from the writer) a net payment of $K(S - E)$, where K is the amount of the underlying currency (the contract size). If, on the other hand, the holder exercises a put option, when $S < E$, then the holder receives a net payment of $K(E - S)$. This is shown in Figure 7.4.

Figure 7.4 Net settlement payments on successful exercise

(a) Call

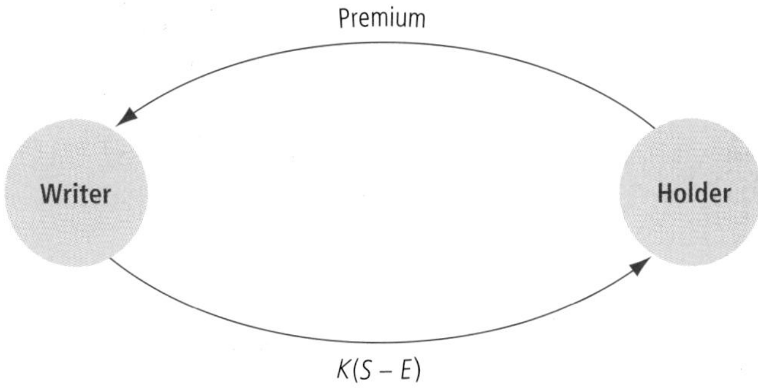

(b) Put

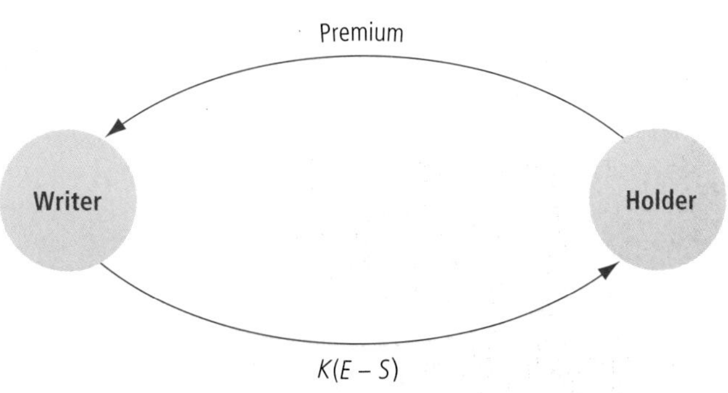

Long and short positions

The holder or buyer of the option is described as holding a long position, whereas the writer or the seller of the option holds a short position on the same option. A long position gives a right, whereas a short position creates a commitment. The following are various possibilities:

- A **long call** position gives the right to buy the underlying currency.
- A **long put** position gives the right to sell the underlying currency.
- A **short call** position implies a commitment to sell the underlying currency to the holder of the option should the latter decide to exercise.
- A **short put** position implies a commitment to buy the underlying currency from the holder of the option should the latter decide to exercise.

A trader who expects a currency to appreciate will take a long call or a short put position. If, on the other hand, a currency is expected to depreciate, the trader will take a long put or a short call position. The pay-off (profit/loss) on a long call (put) is equal to, but has the opposite sign of, the pay-off on the corresponding short call (put) position.

Example

By referring to the previous example, if the holder exercises the call option when $S = 0.65$, the writer must respond by selling AUD1 000 000 at 0.60. To do this, the writer will buy AUD1 million spot at 0.65 and sell it to the holder at 0.60. Gross loss on the short call position is

$$1\,000\,000 \times 0.65 - 1\,000\,000 \times 0.60 = \text{USD}50\,000$$

Since the writer receives the premium (USD10 000) up front, the writer's net loss will be

$$50\,000 - 10\,000 = \text{USD}40\,000$$

which is equal to the profit made by the call holder (that is, the profit on the long call position). Since the holder does not exercise the put at $S = 0.65$, the writer will retain the premium, earning profit of

$$1\,000\,000 \times 0.02 = \text{USD}20\,000$$

which again is equal to the loss incurred by the put holder (that is, the loss on the long put position).

If the holder exercises the put option when $S = 0.55$, the writer must respond by buying AUD1 million at 0.60 and selling this amount spot at 0.55. Net loss will be

$$1\,000\,000\,(0.60 - 0.55) - 1\,000\,000 \times 0.02 = \text{USD}30\,000$$

which is equal to the gross profit on the long put position. At $S = 0.55$, the call option will not be exercised and the writer will gain the premium on the call (USD10 000). The following table summarises the results for net pay-offs:

Position	$S = 0.65$	$S = 0.55$
Long call	+40 000	−10 000
Long put	−20 000	+30 000
Short call	−40 000	+10 000
Short put	+20 000	−30 000

Expiry dates, American options and European options

An option gives the holder the right to buy or sell a currency on or before a certain date, known as the **expiry date** (or **expiration date**) after which the contract terminates—that is, the date after which the holder has no right to buy or sell the currency. An **American option** can be exercised on or before the expiry date, whereas a **European option** can be exercised only on the expiry date. Because an American option gives a greater privilege than a corresponding European option, the premium paid on the former must be higher.

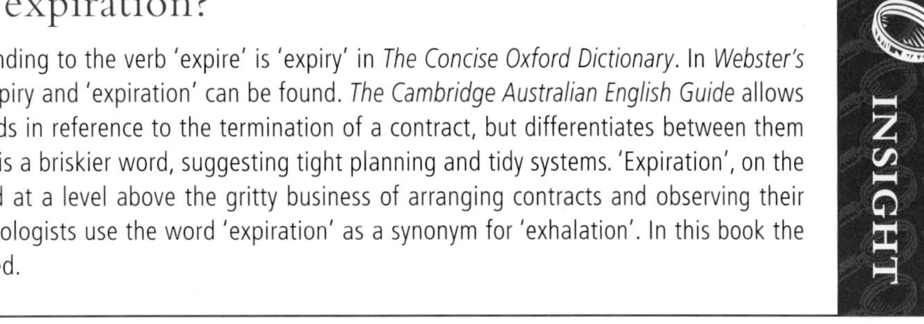

INSIGHT

Expiry or expiration?

The noun corresponding to the verb 'expire' is 'expiry' in *The Concise Oxford Dictionary*. In *Webster's Dictionary*, both 'expiry and 'expiration' can be found. *The Cambridge Australian English Guide* allows for using both words in reference to the termination of a contract, but differentiates between them as follows. 'Expiry' is a briskier word, suggesting tight planning and tidy systems. 'Expiration', on the other hand, is used at a level above the gritty business of arranging contracts and observing their terms. Moreover, biologists use the word 'expiration' as a synonym for 'exhalation'. In this book the word 'expiry' is used.

Example

Suppose that on 1 February, traders A and B hold call options to buy AUD1 000 000 at an exercise exchange rate of 0.60, both expiring on 30 April. Whereas the option held by A is an American option, the one held by B is a European option. Suppose also that the prices of the options are USD0.05 and USD0.02, respectively. Initially, the spot exchange rate is 0.55. B hopes that on 30 April the exchange rate will be higher than 0.60 by an amount greater than the premium so that the option can be exercised at net profit. A, on the other hand, hopes that at any time between 1 February and 30 April, the spot exchange rate will be higher than 0.60 by an amount greater than the premium, because A can exercise at any time.

On 25 March the exchange rate reaches a level of 0.70, representing a protracted appreciation of the Australian dollar. The story going around in the market is that the Reserve Bank believes that this exchange rate is excessively high and so the Bank will intervene to bring it down. Given also that market sentiment indicates that the Australian dollar is due for a downward correction, the expectation is that by 30 April the exchange rate will be down to 0.60. Trader A seems to accept this view and so chooses to exercise, earning net profit of

$$1\,000\,000 \times (0.70 - 0.60 - 0.05) = \text{USD}50\,000$$

Although B seems to accept the same view, there is nothing to do but to wait until the expiry date of 30 April to exercise (of course, B can sell the option itself any time before the expiry date).

On the expiry date, the exchange rate reaches the level of 0.58. B, therefore, chooses not to exercise, incurring a loss of USD20 000. Had B bought an American option, B would have exercised at profit before the expiry date. This added flexibility in American options is the reason they cost more to acquire than comparable European options.

In the money, out of the money and at the money

An option is **in the money** if it can be exercised at (gross) profit. If $S > E$, then a call option is in the money whereas a put option is **out of the money**. Conversely, if $S < E$, then a put option is in the money whereas a call option is out of the money. If $S = E$, then the option (call or a put) is **at the money**. If an option is in the money, this does not necessarily mean that it can be exercised at net profit. This will only happen if it is in the money by an amount that is greater than the premium. A call option is **deep in the money** if S exceeds E significantly (and vice versa for a put). On the other hand, a call option is **far out of the money** if S is far below E (and vice versa for a put).

Example

Consider a call option with a premium of 0.03 and an exercise exchange rate of 0.60, and a put option with a premium of 0.05 and an exercise exchange rate of 0.65. If the actual market rate (*S*) is 0.60, the call option will be at the money. If the market rate is greater than 0.60, the call option will be in the money. However, net profit will be realised only if this rate is greater than 0.63. If the market rate is less than 0.60, the call will be out of the money. On the other hand, if the actual rate is 0.65, the put option will be at the money. At a rate greater than 0.65, the put option will be out of the money. If the exchange rate is less than 0.65, the put will be in the money, but net profit will be made only if the rate is less than 0.60.

Intrinsic and time values

The **intrinsic value** of an option is the extent to which the option is in the money. At any point in time during the life of an option, the greater the difference between the actual exchange rate prevailing then and the exercise exchange rate (or vice versa), the greater the intrinsic value of a call (put) option.

If an option is out of the money, then its intrinsic value is zero. So, why would anyone want to buy an option that is out of the money? Because with the passage of time the market exchange rate may change in such a way as to make the option in the money. The amount paid for the probability that the option will be in the money is called the **time value** of the option. The premium paid to acquire the option reflects both the intrinsic and the time value. If an option is extremely deep in the money or it is very close to expiry, then the premium strictly reflects the intrinsic value.

Example

Consider an Australian-dollar American call option with an exercise exchange rate of 0.60, costing USD0.05. If the spot exchange rate prevailing in the market when the option is bought is 0.55, then the option is out of the money. Thus, it has a zero intrinsic value and the premium reflects the time value only. A trader will buy this option only if the trader thinks that, between the present time and the expiry date, the exchange rate will rise so that it will be not only in the money, but also in the money by an amount that is sufficient to produce net profit. At a rate higher than 0.65, the option will be in the money. At a rate of 0.67, for example, the option will be in the money by

$$0.67 - 0.60 = \text{USD}0.07$$

which produces a net profit of USD0.02.

If, on the other hand, the exchange rate is 0.63 at the time the option is bought, it is already in the money and so it has an intrinsic value of

$$0.63 - 0.60 = \text{USD}0.03$$

The premium in this case reflects both the intrinsic and time values. If, say, one day before the expiry date, the exchange rate is still 0.63, then no one will pay more than the intrinsic value of USD0.03 to buy this option. This is because the probability is very low that, within one day, the exchange rate will rise to a much higher level. Thus, the time value of the option is zero.

OTC and exchange-traded options

OTC options are created by writers to meet the specific requirements of buyers, given that these options are not generally traded on the floor of an exchange. An example is an option to buy AUD242 000 by 12 May at an exercise exchange rate of 0.586 (USD/AUD). These options are obviously non-standardised. On the other hand, **exchange-traded options** are a class of standard options that have predetermined specifications with respect to size, exercise price and expiry date. We examine the currency options traded on the Philadelphia Stock Exchange and the Chicago Mercantile Exchange in the following section.

Assignments

An **assignment** materialises when an option writer receives a notice that the holder of an option has exercised that option, in which case the writer is obliged to deliver the underlying currency in the case of a call or receive the underlying currency in the case of a put. The notice of exercise is originated by the option holder and assigned to the option writer.

Base and underlying currencies

The base currency is the currency in which the option price is expressed. The underlying currency is the currency that is bought and sold. The profit and loss are measured in terms of the base currency.

Margins

A **margin** is the cash or securities required to be deposited by an option writer with his or her brokerage firm or a clearing firm as collateral for the writer's obligation to buy or sell the underlying currency.

Open interest

Open interest is the number of outstanding calls or puts.

Opening and closing transactions

An **opening transaction** is a transaction resulting in opening a new position. A **closing transaction** is a transaction resulting in liquidating or offsetting an existing option position.

Registered options traders

Registered options traders (ROTs) are participants on the exchange, trading for their own or their firm's account. They are responsible for making **two-sided markets** in response to requests. ROT is another term for market makers.

Option quotations

Currency options may be quoted in one of two ways: **American terms** or **European terms** American terms mean that the underlying exchange rate is quoted in terms of the US dollar per unit of the other currency. In European terms it is quoted in terms of the other currency per unit of the US dollar.

7.2 Description of currency options contracts

Options can be traded either on an organised exchange (such as the Philadelphia Stock Exchange and the Chicago Mercantile Exchange) or over the counter (OTC), where dealers contact each other by telephone or other means of telecommunication. The differences between the two modes of trading options resemble the differences between forward and futures contracts. The following points provide a summary of the comparison between trading on an organised exchange and over the counter.

- Both **standardised contracts** and **customised contracts** are available on organised exchanges, but only customised contracts are available over the counter.
- Organised exchanges in the United States are regulated by the **Securities and Exchange Commission (SEC)**, whereas the OTC market is self-regulated.
- The counterparty to every transaction on an organised exchange is the clearing corporation. In the OTC market it is another trader.
- Prices are visible in an organised exchange but are not in the OTC market.
- Margins are required for short positions in the organised exchange but are not in the OTC market.
- Positions must be marked on a daily basis in the organised exchange but this is not the case in the OTC market.

The following is a description of the options contracts traded on the Philadelphia Stock Exchange and the Chicago Mercantile Exchange.

The Philadelphia Stock Exchange

Two kinds of currency options are traded on the Philadelphia Stock Exchange: standardised and customised (tailor-made). Standardised options, where the US dollar is the base currency, are available on six currencies: the Australian dollar, the British pound, the Canadian dollar, the euro, the Japanese yen and the Swiss franc. The following are the specifications of these options:

Currency	AUD	GBP	CAD	EUR	JPY	CHF
Contract size	50 000	31 250	50 000	62 500	6 250 000	62 500
Position limit (contracts)	200 000	200 000	200 000	200 000	200 000	200 000
Base currency	USD	USD	USD	USD	USD	USD
Underlying currency	AUD	GBP	CAD	EUR	JPY	CHF
Premium quotations	Cents/unit	Cents/unit	Cents/unit	Cents/unit	100th of a cent/unit	Cents/unit
Minimum premium change (US cents)	5.00	3.125	5.00	6.25	6.25	6.25

As for **customised options**, any two approved currencies may be matched for trading. Either of the two currencies may be the base currency or the underlying currency. For example, GBP/CHF means that the exercise price is in terms of the pound (the pound being the base currency, whereas the Swiss franc is the underlying currency). Conversely, CHF/GBP means the opposite. These options are available on all the currencies on which there are standardised options, as well as the Mexican peso (MXP). The following are the specifications of customised contracts:

- The contract size for a currency pair is determined by the underlying currency: AUD (50 000), GBP (31 250), CAD (50 000), EUR (62 500), JPY (6 250 000), MXP (250 000), CHF (62 500), USD (50 000).
- The premium may be expressed in the units of the base currency or as a percentage of the underlying currency. For example, the premium of a GBP/EUR contract may be expressed in pence per EUR. If the premium is one penny per euro, the total cost of the option would be 0.01 × 62 500 = GBP625. Alternatively, it can be expressed as a percentage of the contract size. A quote of 2.4 per cent means 0.024 × 62 500 = EUR1500.
- The exercise exchange rate is quoted as the base currency units per unit of the underlying currency. In the GBP/EUR contract, the exercise exchange rate may be 0.62 (GBP/EUR).
- The exercise style is always European (that is, on the expiry date only).
- Customised options may have a standardised expiry date (called a **standard-expiry option**) or a customised expiry date (called a **custom-dated option**). A standard-expiry option conforms to existing exercise and assignments for all standardised contracts. Custom-dated options follow a unique exercise and assignment process on the expiry date.
- There is a 200 000-contract position and exercise limit, except for the Mexican peso option (100 000 contracts).
- There is a minimum limit on the transaction size. Opening transactions may not be less than 50 contracts. Subsequent trades must be at least 50 contracts, unless the position is being closed out.

IN PRACTICE

The growth of long-term currency options in Asian markets

There has been an increased demand in Asian markets for long-term currency options. Three factors can explain this trend:

- Companies having long-dated yen revenue or those looking at reducing funding costs have been trying to take advantage of the interest rate differential between the US dollar and the yen.
- In recent years, investors increasingly have maintained currency mismatch between assets and liabilities (for example, by using short-term liabilities to fund long-term assets) in order to reduce funding costs or improve returns. The risk profile of such positions can be improved with long-term currency options.
- Japanese investors have resorted to the use of long-term options to enhance return. Life insurance companies in particular have found themselves underfunded with a desire for longer-term risk.

The Chicago Mercantile Exchange

Options on futures are traded on the Chicago Mercantile Exchange. These are contracts that give the right to buy or sell futures contracts on the underlying currency at an exchange rate determined in advance. The only difference in this case is that the underlying position is not a cash position but rather a futures contract. When the Australian dollar price is expressed as 1.75 this means 0.0175 × 100 000 = USD1750. The minimum price fluctuation (tick) is USD10/contract.

7.3 Option positions

In this section we describe, using diagrams and graphs, some option positions and the pay-offs on these positions as the spot exchange rate assumes different values. Some of these positions involve one option, whereas others involve more than one option. We start with the single-option positions.

Single-option positions

The pay-off (profit/loss) on option positions can be represented diagrammatically. Let us first consider gross pay-offs by ignoring the premium. Figure 7.5 represents gross pay-offs on long and short calls and puts. In these diagrams, the exercise and actual exchange rates (E and S) are measured on the horizontal axis, whereas the pay-off (which can be positive or negative) is measured on the vertical axis. Note, however, that while the exercise exchange rate, E, is fixed (because it is determined by the contract), the actual exchange rate, S, can be anywhere (because it is determined by the market). The pay-off is determined by the position of the actual exchange rate relative to the exercise exchange rate. These pay-offs are considered from the perspective of the holder and the writer of the option.

Figure 7.5(a) shows the gross pay-off on a long call, which gives the holder the right to exercise the option by buying the underlying currency. As long as the market exchange rate is lower than E (such as S_1), the option is out of the money and will not be exercised, resulting in gross pay-off of zero. If the market exchange rate is higher than the exercise exchange rate (such as S_2), the option will be in the money and the holder will exercise, in which case the gross pay-off will be the difference between S_2 and E, which is indicated by the vertical distance labelled π. The further S_2 is to the right of E, the higher the pay-off will be. Obviously, the gross profit for the holder of a call option cannot be negative. It is like an insurance policy: the worst that can happen is not to make a claim (not to exercise, in the case of an option).

Figure 7.5 Gross pay-offs on single option positions

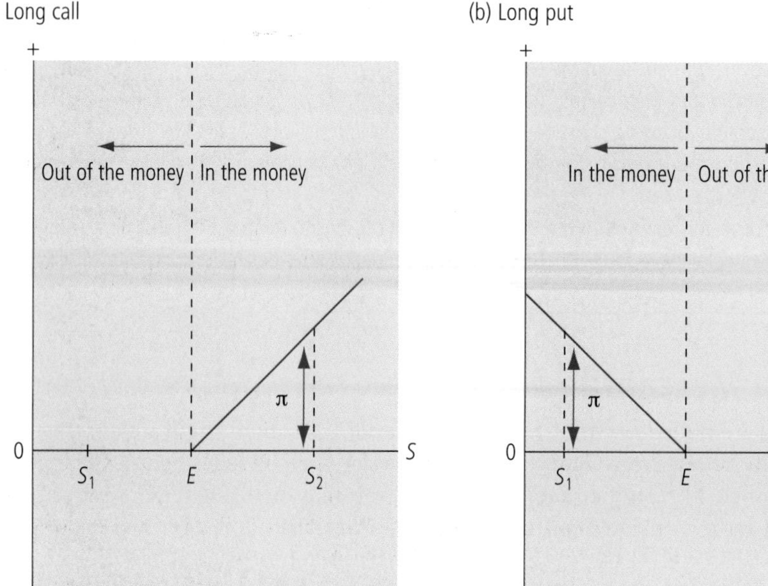

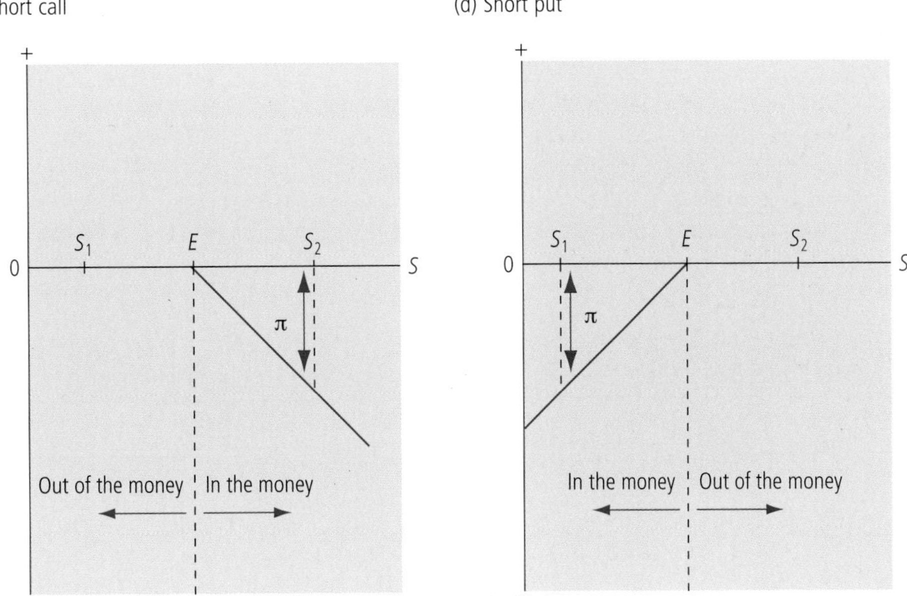

The gross pay-off on a long put position is represented by Figure 7.5(b). If S assumes a value higher than E (such as S_2), the option will be out of the money and will not be exercised, resulting in gross pay-off of zero. If, on the other hand, S assumes a value lower than E (such as S_1), the option will be in the money and will be exercised, in which case the gross profit will be the difference between E and S_1.

In Figure 7.5(c) we find a representation of the gross pay-off on a short call position. As long as the market exchange rate is lower than E (such as S_1) the holder of the option will not exercise and the writer will not lose anything. If the market rate is higher than the exercise exchange rate (such as S_2), the holder will exercise, making profit that is equal to the difference between S_2 and E. This profit is the loss to the option writer (who holds the short call position). Thus, the gross pay-off will be negative (a loss). Similarly, Figure 7.5(d) shows that a short put position will produce a loss when the market exchange rate is to the left of E (such as S_1). Remember that the profit of a long position's holder is the loss of the corresponding short position's holder.

These possibilities can be summarised as follows:

	$S < E$		$S > E$	
Position	**Action**	**Pay-off**	**Action**	**Pay-off**
Long call	Not exercised	$\pi = 0$	Exercised	$\pi = S - E$
Long put	Exercised	$\pi = E - S$	Not exercised	$\pi = 0$
Short call	Not exercised	$\pi = 0$	Exercised	$\pi = -(S - E)$
Short put	Exercised	$\pi = -(E - S)$	Not exercised	$\pi = 0$

Let us now examine the more realistic case of net pay-offs by introducing the premium that has to be paid by the holder to the writer to acquire the option. This is represented in Figure 7.6. It can be seen that the pay-off profiles are shifted downwards or upwards by an amount that is equal to the premium, R. The profiles are shifted downwards for long positions because the premium is a cost and upwards for short positions because the premium is a source of revenue.

Figure 7.6 Net pay-offs on option positions

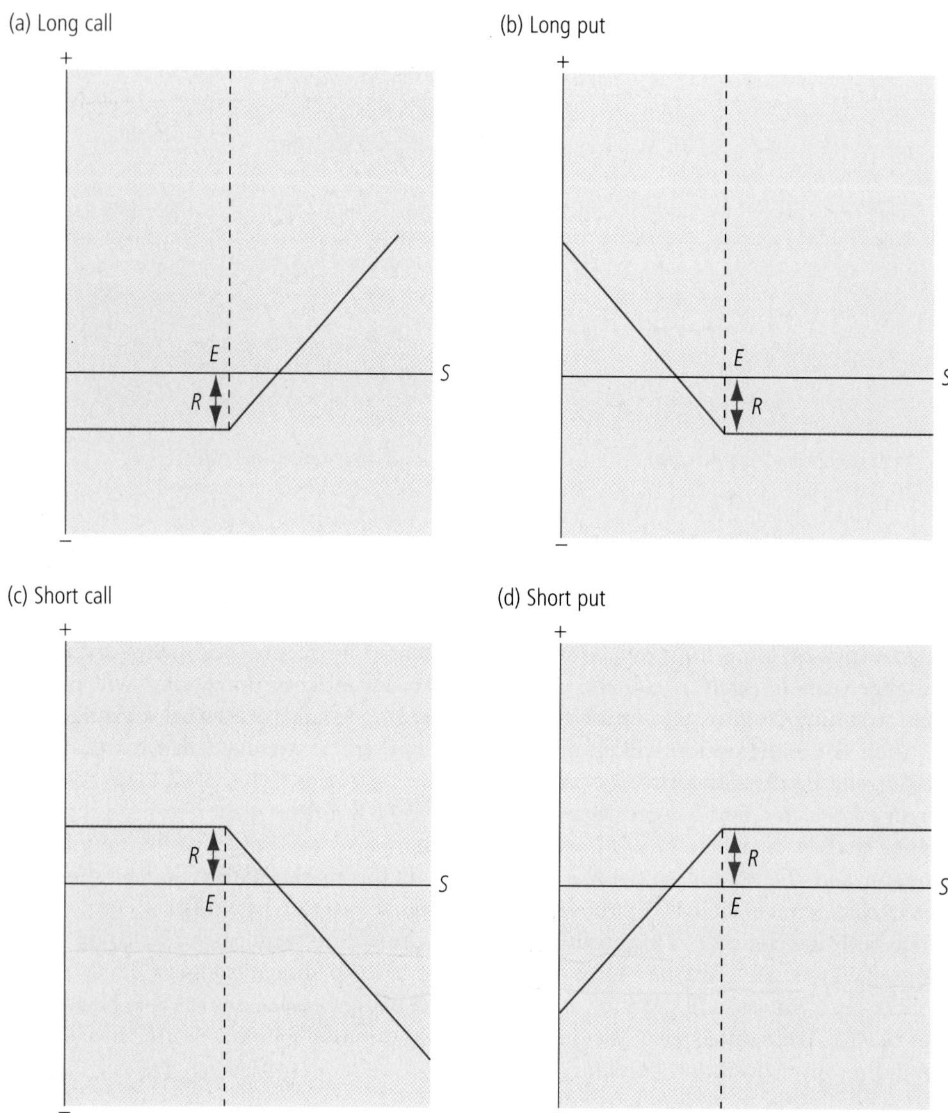

Consider the case of a long call position. If the market rate is lower than the exercise rate, the option will not be exercised and the holder will lose the premium. The pay-off is therefore negative. If the market exchange rate exceeds the exercise exchange rate, the option will be exercised and there are three possibilities here:

- If the market exchange rate exceeds the exercise exchange rate by an amount that is less than the premium, the net pay-off will still be negative because the profit realised by exercising the option is not adequate to cover the cost incurred by paying the premium.
- If the market exchange rate exceeds the exercise exchange rate by an amount that is equal to the premium, the net pay-off will be zero because the profit realised by exercising the option exactly covers the cost incurred by paying the premium.
- If the market rate is greater than the exercise exchange rate plus the premium, the net pay-off will be positive, since the profit realised by exercising the option exceeds the premium.

The other positions exhibit similar possibilities, as shown in Figure 7.6. The following table summarises these possibilities.

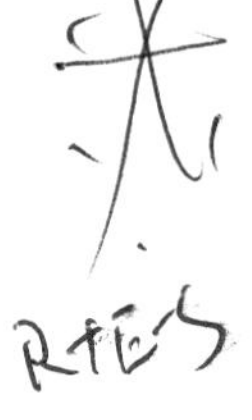

Position	S < E		S > E	
	Action	Pay-off	Action	Pay-off
Long call	Not exercised	$\pi = -R$	Exercised	$\pi = (S - E) - R$
Long put	Exercised	$\pi = (E - S) - R$	Not exercised	$\pi = -R$
Short call	Not exercised	$\pi = R$	Exercised	$\pi = R - (S - E)$
Short put	Exercised	$\pi = R - (E - S)$	Not exercised	$\pi = R$

Combined option positions

Let us now combine some of these positions and see what we come up with. We will describe a number of the combined positions.

Long call and short put

First, we combine a long call with a short put with the same exercise exchange rate, *E*. This combination gives a pay-off represented by an upward-sloping line, as shown in Figure 7.7. This pay-off is similar to the pay-off on a long futures position with a settlement exchange rate (of the futures contract) that is equal to the exercise exchange rate (of the option). The pay-off is positive if the actual exchange rate is higher than the settlement rate. Similarly, if the actual exchange rate is higher than the exercise exchange rate, the long call position will be profitable because the call can be exercised at profit while the put option will not be exercised, in which case the premium is gained. The reverse occurs if the actual exchange rate is lower than the exercise exchange rate. This also means that a **synthetic futures contract** can be created by combining two options. A need for creating a synthetic futures contract may arise because the genuine contract is not available on the market.

Example

Consider Australian dollar call and put options with an exercise exchange rate of 0.60 (USD/AUD) and a premium of USD0.02. As the spot exchange rate varies between 0.45 and 0.75, the net pay-off on a long call, a short put and a combined position are displayed in the following table. You may find it useful to plot the pay-off figures to find out how they resemble the theoretical profiles shown in Figure 7.7.

Exchange rate	Long call	Short put	Combined
0.45	−0.02	−0.13	−0.15
0.50	−0.02	−0.08	−0.10
0.55	−0.02	−0.03	−0.05
0.60	−0.02	0.02	0.0
0.65	0.03	0.02	0.05
0.70	0.08	0.02	0.10
0.75	0.13	0.02	0.15

The combined position also resembles a long spot position on the underlying currency bought at an exchange rate that is equal to the exercise rate of the options. Let us consider such a position when the price of the call is lower than the price of the put. In this case,

Continued...

Figure 7.7 Pay-off on a combined long call and short put position

Figure 7.8 Pay-off on a combined short call and long put position

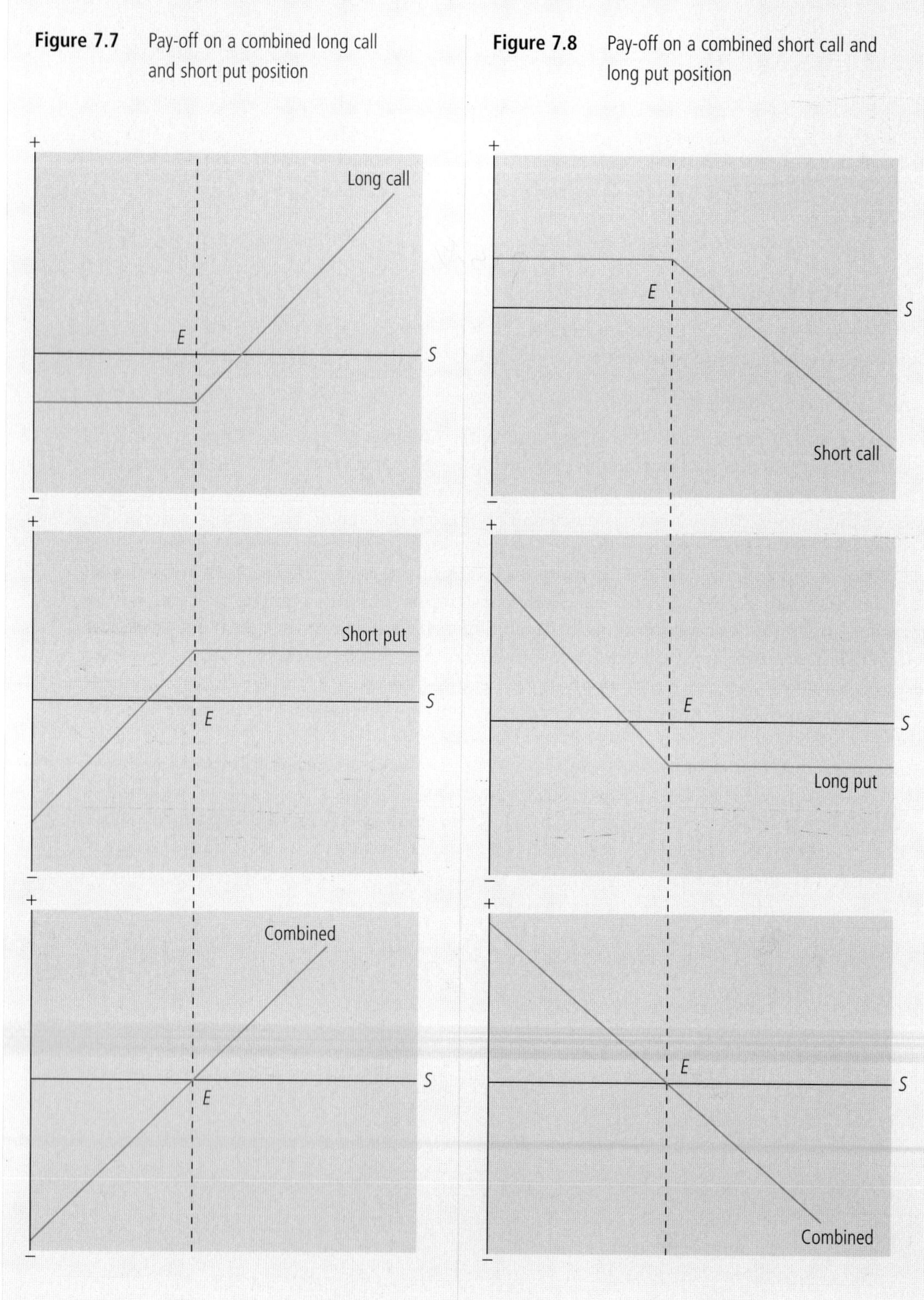

the combined position would give a higher pay-off than a spot position established at an exchange rate that is equal to *E*. Because of the possibility of creating a **synthetic spot position**, the put and call prices cannot diverge from each other without bounds.

Suppose now that the price of the call is USD0.01, the price of the put is USD0.04 and that it is possible to establish a spot position at USD0.60. For any value of the exchange rate between 0.45 and 0.75 the combined position produces a higher pay-off than the spot position. The results are shown below:

Exchange rate	Short call	Long put	Combined	Spot
0.45	−0.01	−0.11	−0.12	−0.15
0.50	−0.01	−0.06	−0.07	−0.10
0.55	−0.01	−0.01	−0.02	−0.05
0.60	−0.01	0.04	0.03	0.0
0.65	0.04	0.04	0.08	0.05
0.70	0.09	0.04	0.13	0.10
0.75	0.14	0.04	0.18	0.15

Short call and long put

Let us now combine a short call and a long put, as represented by Figure 7.8. In this case the pay-off on the combined position resembles the pay-off on a short futures position with a settlement exchange rate that is equal to the exercise exchange rate or a short spot position at the same exchange rate. If the market exchange rate turns out to be lower than the exercise exchange rate, profit will be made on the put option while the call option is not exercised. If, on the other hand, the market exchange rate turns out to be higher than the exercise exchange rate, the put option will not be exercised but a loss will be made on the short call, which will be exercised by the holder. In the case of a short futures or spot position, if the market exchange rate is lower than the settlement or purchase rate, profit will be made because this represents a depreciation of the currency denominating a short position. If the market exchange rate is higher than the settlement or purchase rate, loss will be made because this represents an appreciation of a currency denominating a short position.

Example

Assuming the same information as in the previous example, the net pay-off on a short call and a long put and the combined position are given in the following table. Again, it may be useful to plot the pay-off figures.

Exchange rate	Long call	Short put	Combined
0.45	0.02	0.13	0.15
0.50	0.02	0.08	0.10
0.55	0.02	0.03	0.05
0.60	0.02	−0.02	0.0
0.65	−0.03	−0.02	−0.05
0.70	−0.08	−0.02	−0.10
0.75	−0.13	−0.02	−0.15

INSIGHT

Synthetic and covered option positions

A **synthetic call** and a **synthetic put** can be created (artificially) if they are not available. This can be done as follows (try representing these positions diagrammatically):

- A synthetic call can be created by buying a put option while buying the underlying currency spot. The long spot position provides the feature of unlimited profit from the appreciation of the underlying currency, whereas the long put provides the feature of limited loss from the depreciation of the currency.
- A synthetic put can be created by buying a call option while selling the underlying currency spot. The short spot position provides the feature of unlimited profit from the depreciation of the underlying currency, whereas the long call provides the feature of limited loss from the appreciation of the currency.

Covered call writing and **covered put writing** can be created as follows (again, try to draw diagrams to represent these positions):

- Covered call writing consists of writing a call option while going long on an equivalent amount of the underlying currency. Profit is generated from the appreciation of the foreign currency but it is limited since appreciation to the exercise exchange rate will cause it to be exercised.
- Covered put writing consists of writing a put option while going short on an equivalent amount of the underlying currency. Profit is generated from the depreciation of the foreign currency but it is limited since depreciation to the exercise exchange rate will cause it to be exercised.

Long straddle

A **long straddle** is used when the exchange rate is expected to rise or fall dramatically. Figure 7.9 illustrates a long straddle on the Australian dollar at an exchange rate of USD0.60. The prices of the put and call are equal at USD0.05, which makes the total cost of the position USD0.10. The position will be profitable if the actual exchange rate, *S*, turns out to be higher than or lower than the exercise exchange rate of 0.60 by more than USD0.10. The maximum loss is incurred when the actual exchange rate is equal to the exercise exchange rate at 0.60.

Figure 7.9 Pay-off on a long straddle

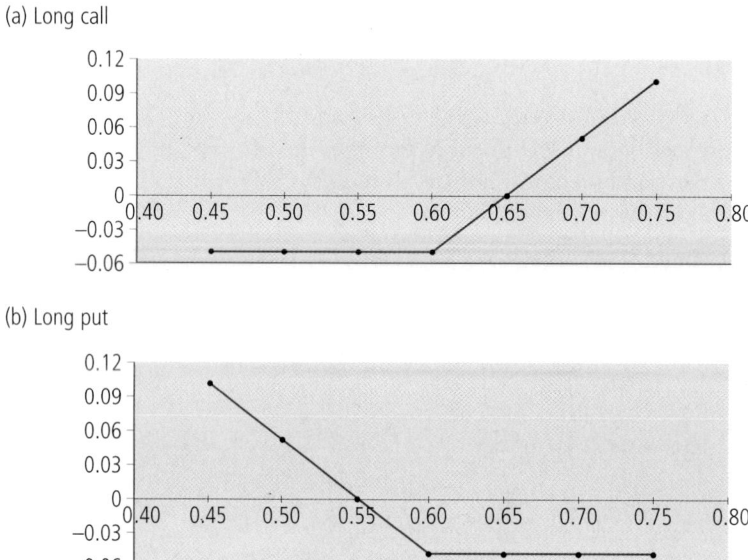

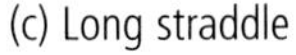

(c) Long straddle

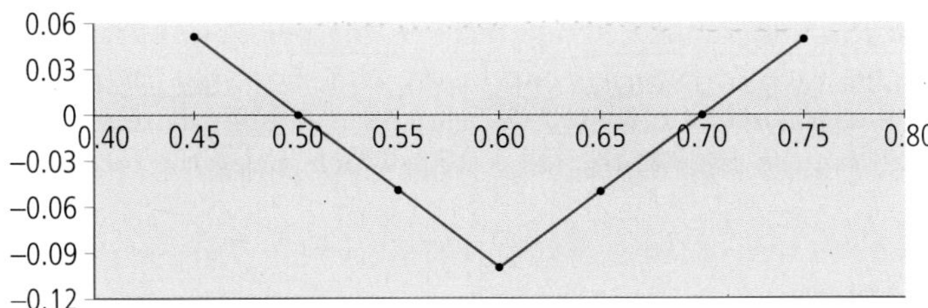

Short straddle

Figure 7.10 illustrates a **short straddle** on the Australian dollar with an exercise exchange rate of 0.60. This position requires writing both the call and the put, earning a total of USD0.10 from option premiums. The position will be profitable if the exchange rate turns out to be higher than or lower than the exercise exchange rate of 0.60 by less than USD0.10. Maximum profit is earned when the exchange rate is equal to the exercise exchange rate at 0.60, because neither of the two options will be exercised in this case.

Figure 7.10 Pay-off on a short straddle

(a) Short call

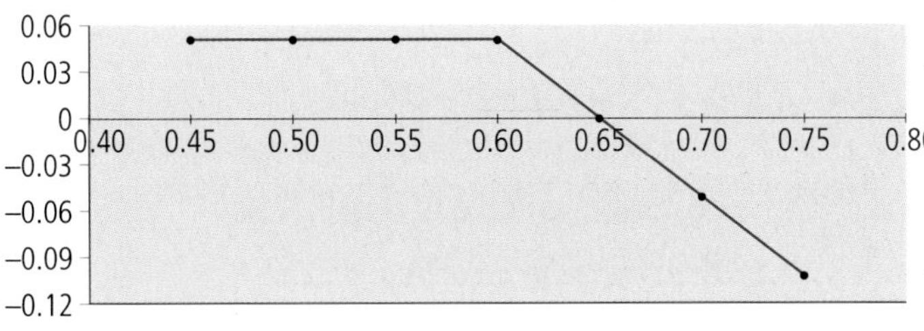

(b) Short put

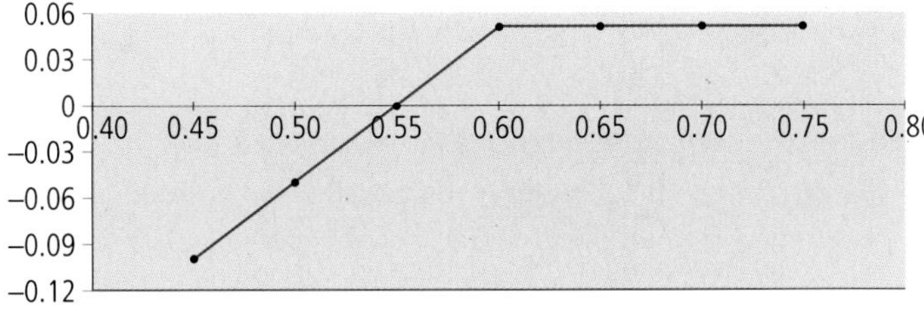

(c) Short straddle

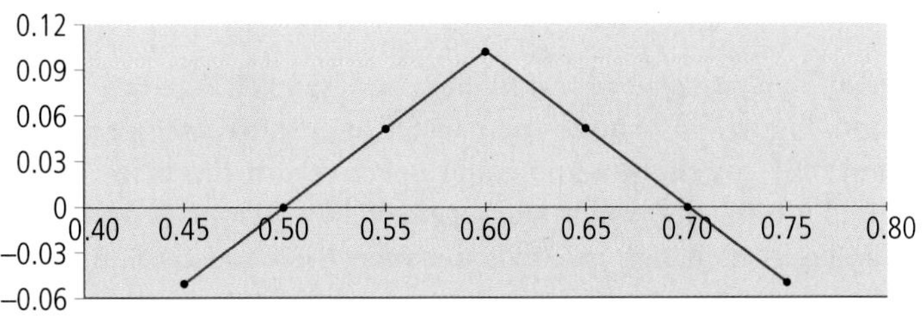

Long strangle

A **long strangle** is similar to a long straddle except that it is cheaper. This is because a cheap call can be bought at a higher exercise exchange rate. Figure 7.11 shows the pay-off on a long strangle with exercise exchange rates of 0.60 and 0.65 for the put and call, respectively. The price of the put is still 0.05 but the price of the call is 0.02, which makes the total cost of the position USD0.07.

Figure 7.11 Pay-off on a long strangle

(a) Long call

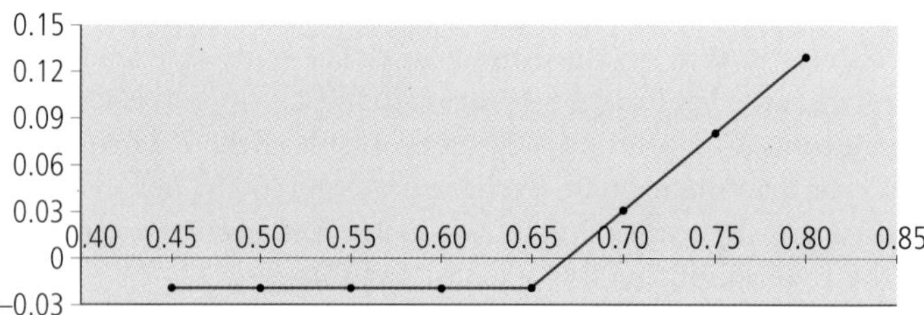

(b) Long put

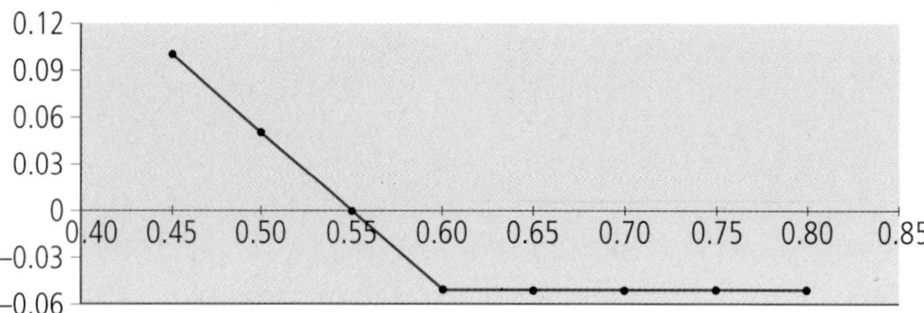

(c) Long strangle

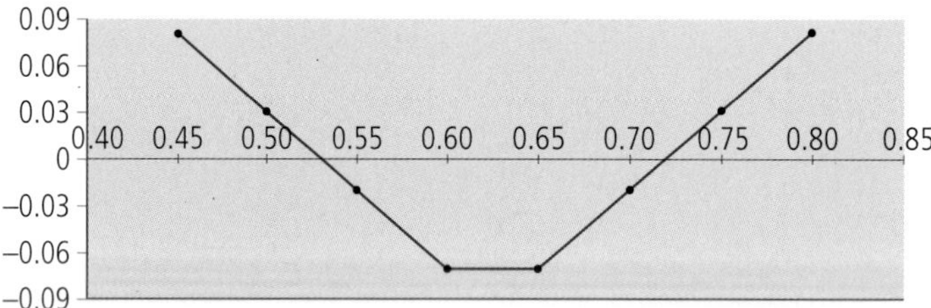

Short strangle

A **short strangle** is obtained by writing a call at a higher exercise exchange rate than the one applicable to the put option. Figure 7.12 shows the pay-off on a short strangle with exercise exchange rates of 0.60 and 0.65 for the put and call, respectively. If the price of the put is 0.05 and the price of the call is 0.02, the writer will receive 0.07 up front. A maximum profit of 0.07 is obtained if the actual exchange rate falls between 0.60 and 0.65, in which case neither of the two options is exercised.

Managing the risk of option trading

IN PRACTICE

The losses incurred by Allfirst (the US subsidiary of the Allied Irish Bank) in 2002 arose from operations involving currency options. It was surprising that those losses were incurred, given that banks have been so cautious about trading derivatives ever since Nick Leeson brought down Barings Bank in 1996.

To monitor and control the risk of trading options, senior management typically imposes various limits on this kind of trading, including the following:

- the instruments and currencies against which options can be written
- positions with counterparties
- the face value of options written and bought, aggregated globally and by country
- expiry concentration
- concentration of exercise exchange rates and settlement dates
- maximum allowable loses from contingent market developments, such as a specified change in rates or volatility.

Most of these risks can be managed specifically. Concentration of settlements with particular non-bank counterparties (which is a combined settlement and counterparty risk) can be reduced either by spreading settlements over several days or by making payment only against confirmed receipt of funds. Concentration of settlements with bank counterparties is handled mainly by imposing restrictions on the number of counterparties or on the amount of options written relative to those purchased from individual bank counterparties. Concern about credit risk is one reason why banks do not often buy options from their non-bank customers. Liquidity risk is dealt with by limiting positions in certain markets, notably in exchange-traded markets where liquidity is vital.

Figure 7.12 Pay-off on a short strangle

(a) Short call

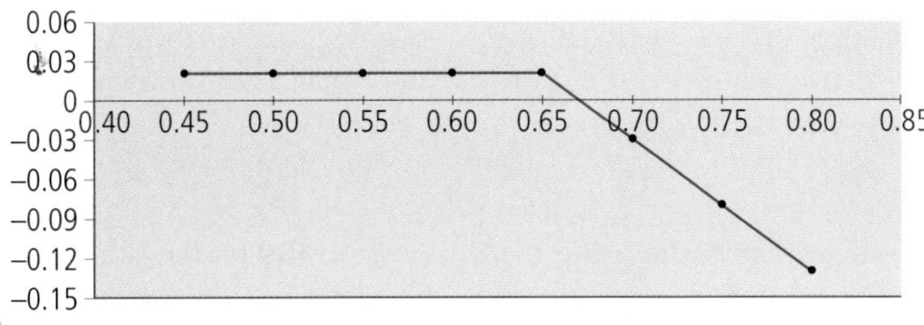

(b) Short put

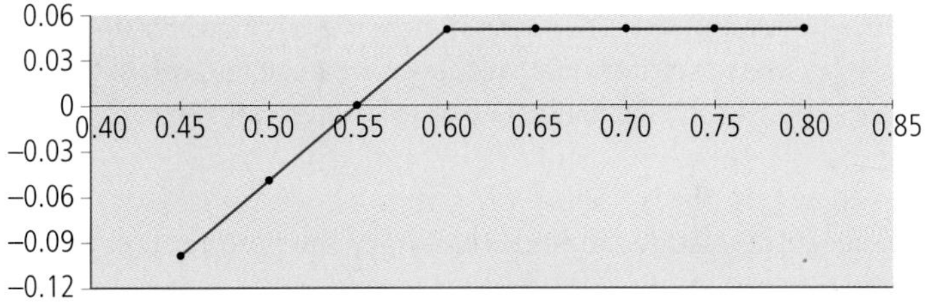

Continued...

(c) Short strangle

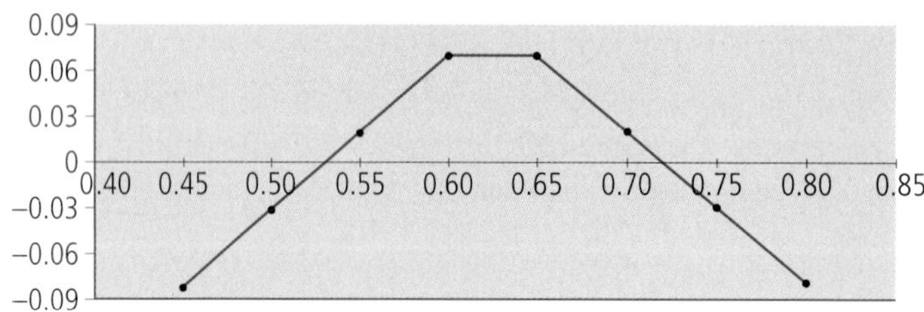

7.4 Determinants of option premiums

Pricing currency options means finding the value of the premium, per unit of the underlying currency, which must be paid by the buyer to the writer of the option. In this section we describe the factors that determine the premium paid to acquire an option. Option dealers quote a **bid premium** and an **offer premium** for each contract: the bid is what the dealer is prepared to pay to buy the option and the offer is what the dealer must be paid to sell. The dealer must state whether the underlying option is a call or a put and whether it is an American or a European option, as well as the exercise exchange rate and the date of expiry.

Exercise exchange rate

The higher the exercise exchange rate, the lower the premium on a call and the higher the premium on a put. This is straightforward. A call option that gives the holder the right to buy a currency at a low exercise exchange rate should be more valuable than when the right can be exercised at a higher exchange rate. The lower the exercise exchange rate, the more likely it is that it will be below the market exchange rate, in which case the holder can exercise the option at a profit. The reverse argument applies to the case of a put option.

Time to expiry

The longer the time to expiry, the greater is the premium. This is because the probability that an out-of-the-money option becomes in the money increases with the time to expiry. On or very close to the expiry date, an out-of-the-money option will be worth nothing because there is a zero probability that it will be in the money. Thus, it has a zero intrinsic value and a zero time value, which means that the premium should be zero.

Intrinsic value

The higher the intrinsic value (that is, the more the option is in the money) the higher the premium. This is because the greater the intrinsic value, the higher is the probability that the option will be exercised at profit.

Exchange rate volatility

An option is like an insurance policy and so it costs more where there is a greater underlying risk, which in currency options arises from exchange rate volatility. Exchange rate volatility is normally measured by the standard deviation of the exchange rate as calculated from historical data.

Type of option

For a given exercise exchange rate, volatility and time to expiry, the premium on an American option should be higher than the premium on a European option.

Interest rate on the base currency

The higher the interest rate on the base currency, the lower is the present value of the exercise price. A higher interest rate, therefore, has the same effect as a lower exercise price. Thus, a higher interest rate is associated with a higher value of calls and a lower value of puts.

The forward spread and the interest rate differential

If the underlying currency is expected to appreciate, then a call option should become more valuable while a put option becomes less valuable (see Chapter 11 on UIP).

INSIGHT

Measures of option price sensitivity

The price of an option depends on several parameters and so it tends to be sensitive to these parameters. The following are measures of sensitivity.

Delta (δ)

Delta measures the change in the premium corresponding to a small change in the spot exchange rate, *S*. It also reflects the probability that the option will expire in the money. Thus, delta ranges in value between zero for far-out-of-the-money options and 1.0 for deep-in-the-money options. A delta of 0.5 means that a one-point change in the spot exchange rate will cause a 0.5-point change in the value of the option. Long calls and short puts have positive deltas, because a rise in the spot exchange rate leads to an increase in the value of the option. Short calls and long puts have negative deltas.

Gamma (γ)

Gamma measures the rate of change of delta with respect to the spot exchange rate. Thus, a low gamma reflects a stable delta. A positive gamma indicates that profits increase when the exchange rate moves in a favourable direction. Long option positions have positive gammas, whereas short positions have negative gammas.

Theta (θ)

Theta measures the anticipated change in the premium resulting from a change in the time to expiry. As the time to expiry declines, so does the time value of the option. Theta quantifies the change in the value of the option as the time to expiry declines. A theta of –1 means that the option's value declines by 1/365 every day. Long option positions have negative thetas, because as time passes the holders lose some value of their investment in terms of the premium. Short option positions have positive thetas for the opposite reason.

Vega (υ)

Vega is a measure of the rate of change of the premium with respect to volatility. Long options have positive vegas, whereas short options have negative vegas.

Rho (ρ)

Rho measures the rate of change of the premium with respect to the interest rate. Remember that the interest rate is used as a discount factor and so rho tends to be higher for options with longer time to expiry. It is also possible to distinguish between ρ and ρ^*, depending on whether the sensitivity is measured with respect to i or i^*.

7.5 Exotic options

Exotic options are European-style options that offer alternative pricing, timing or exercise provisions to those found in the case of 'conventional' options. The pricing of these options is highly complicated. They are mostly produced and sold by the risk-management departments of major multinational banks. The following is a brief description of some of them.

Knockout options

The **knockout option** is also known as the **down-and-out option**, the **barrier option**, the **extinguishable option** and the **activate/deactivate option**. It is designed to offer downside protection but to offer only a limited upside range before crossing a previously specified barrier or knockout level at which it expires automatically.

Path-dependent options

The value of a **path-dependent option** depends on the average value of the spot exchange rate over a specified period. One version of this option is the **average rate option (ARO)**, which is also known as the **Asian option**. This option is exercised at maturity if the average spot rate over the period is less than the predetermined exercise exchange rate. Another version is the **average strike option**, which is exercised if the exercise exchange rate (specified as the average spot rate over the option's life) is greater than the end-of-period spot rate.

RESEARCH FINDINGS

The influence of option trading on the spot and futures markets

The potential effect of option trading on the underlying spot or futures market has been debated extensively. One argument is that option hedging reduces volatility in the spot market. A hedger with the Australian dollar as the base currency having a spot long exposure of USD1 000 000 may choose to cover the exposure by buying the full amount in the forward market or by buying a call option on the amount. To cover the option, the writer will buy the USD in the spot market, but that will not be the full amount. Rather, it will be determined by the sensitivity of the option price to the underlying exchange rate (the so-called delta). If this consideration leads the option writer to buy USD500 000, this applies less pressure on the spot market at the time the option is written than would occur if the original hedger had purchased the full amount forward.

The counterargument is that option trading exacerbates spot market volatility. This happens because the writers of options cover their net option positions by buying the underlying currency when the price is going up and selling it when the price is going down, irrespective of whether call or put options are involved. These purchases and sales reinforce existing exchange rate movements. Some short-term sharp movements in exchange rates have been attributed to large amounts of options written at closely concentrated exercise exchange rates.

Another view is that there is a role for central banks to write options at times when the foreign exchange market is highly volatile. By doing this, the argument goes, central banks can stabilise the market without enforcing or defending a particular level of the underlying exchange rate. Central banks can also signal a desire to reduce overall volatility by selling both puts and calls. The two-sided nature of the operation would indicate that central banks were not taking a view on the level or the direction of exchange rates but only on volatility. Most central banks actually use intervention for this purpose (or at least this is what they claim).

There is also the so-called **lockback option with strike**. This is a European-style option with a predetermined exercise exchange rate, which on maturity is valued against the highest or lowest spot rate reached over the option's life. A **lockback option without strike** has an exercise exchange rate that is set as the lowest or the highest exchange rate achieved over the period for a call and a put, respectively.

Compound options

A **compound option** is an option on an option. It gives the holder the right to buy or sell an option on a specific future date. The compound option has two dates. The near, or first, date is the date on which the holder must decide whether or not to exercise the right pertaining to the underlying option. The last, or second, date is the date on which the underlying option expires.

Chooser options

The **chooser option** allows the buyer to lock in a specific exercise exchange rate, amount and maturity now. At a later date the choice is made between making the option a call or a put.

Summary

- Currency options are contracts that give the holder the right to buy or sell a specified amount of a particular currency on or by a specified date at a predetermined exchange rate.
- A call option can be exercised at gross profit if the spot exchange rate is higher than the exercise exchange rate. A put option can be exercised at gross profit if the spot exchange rate is lower than the exercise exchange rate. Gross profit cannot be negative.
- Net profit realised from an option is the difference between gross profit and the premium paid in advance to acquire the option. The maximum net loss incurred by an option holder is equal to the premium.
- Options are so versatile that a position can be created, by combining two or more options, to bet on almost every possible eventuality. The most common option positions are straddles and strangles.
- Several factors determine the premium on (the price of) a currency option: (i) the exercise exchange rate; (ii) the time to expiry; (iii) the intrinsic value; (iv) exchange rate volatility; (v) the type of option (European or American); (vi) interest rates; and (vii) the forward spread.
- Several parameters measure the sensitivity of the option price with respect to its determining factors. These include delta (the spot exchange rate), gamma (the sensitivity of delta with respect to the spot exchange rate), theta (the time to expiry), vega (volatility) and rho (interest rates).
- Exotic options are European-style options that offer alternative provisions of the product. These are sophisticated risk-management products, some example of which are: (i) knockout options: (ii) path-dependent options; (iii) compound options; and (iv) chooser options.

Key terms

activate/deactivate option 220
American option 202
American terms 205
Asian option 220
assignment 205
at the money 203
average rate option (ARO) 220
average strike option 220
barrier option 220
base currency 196
bid premium 218
call option 196
chooser option 221
closing transaction 205
compound option 221
covered call writing 214
covered option 196
covered put writing 214
credit risk 195
custom-dated option 207
customised contracts 206
customised options 206
deep in the money 203
delta 219
down-and-out option 220
European option 202
European terms 205
exchange-traded options 205
exercise date 195
exercise exchange rate 197
exotic options 220
expiration date 202
expiry date 202
extinguishable option 220
far out of the money 203
gamma 219
gross profit 197
holder (of an option) 195
in the money 203
intrinsic value 204
knockout option 220
lockback option with strike 221
lockback option without strike 221
long call 201
long put 201
long straddle 214
long strangle 216
margin 205
market risk 195
naked option 196
net profit 197
offer premium 218
open interest 205
opening transaction 205
OTC options 205
out of the money 203
path-dependent option 220
premium 195
premium payment date 195
put option 196
registered options traders (ROTs) 205
rho 219
Securities and Exchange Commission (SEC) 206
settlement date 195
settlement exchange rate 200
short call 201
short put 201
short straddle 215
short strangle 216
standard-expiry option 207
standardised contracts 206
strike exchange rate 197
synthetic call 214
synthetic futures contract 211
synthetic put 214
synthetic spot position 213
theta 219
time value 203
two-sided markets 205
underlying currency 196
vega 219
writer (of an option) 195

MaxMARK

MAXIMISE YOUR MARKS! There are 30 interactive questions for this chapter available online at **www.mhhe.com/au/moosa2e**

Review questions

1. Distinguish between a naked option and a covered option.
2. Would you exercise a call option if the spot exchange rate were higher than the exercise exchange rate? Why or why not? Would you exercise a put option in this case?
3. What is the difference between gross and net pay-offs on an option?
4. 'Unlike the case of futures contracts, the pay-offs on options are asymmetric.' Explain.
5. Distinguish between long and short option positions.
6. Why would you pay a higher price to obtain an American option rather than a similar European option?
7. Why would you buy an option that is out of the money?
8. Distinguish between the intrinsic value and the time value of an option.
9. 'If an option is in the money, this does not necessarily mean that net profit can be realised by exercising it.' Explain.
10. Distinguish between an over-the-counter option and an exchange-traded option.
11. Why does the price of a call option decrease as the exercise exchange rate increases for a given expiry date? Why is it the other way round for a put option?
12. Why is it that the prices of similar calls and puts cannot diverge significantly from each other?
13. How would you create synthetic option positions?
14. The gross pay-off for the holder of an option cannot be negative. Why?
15. Explain how a synthetic futures position can be created by combining two option positions. Why would anyone want to do this?
16. 'Options are so versatile that they can be used to create a position to bet on any possible state of the world.' Explain this statement and show why futures, for example, are less versatile.
17. Why does a higher interest rate have the same effect on the price of a currency option as a lower exercise exchange rate?
18. Why do short calls and long puts have negative deltas?
19. How do financial institutions control the risk arising from trading options?
20. Does option trading boost exchange rate volatility?
21. What are exotic options?

Problems

In all the following problems: (i) the underlying currencies to be bought and sold are currencies other than the Australian dollar; (ii) the exchange rates are expressed as units of the Australian dollar per one unit of the underlying currency; and (iii) profit and loss are measured in terms of the Australian dollar.

1 A trader holds a call option to buy EUR100 000 against the Australian dollar at an exercise exchange rate of 1.6500 (AUD/EUR). Determine whether or not the trader will exercise the option and then calculate the gross pay-off at the following spot exchange rates: (a) 1.6630, (b) 1.6900 and (c) 1.6380.

2 A trader holds a put option to sell CHF200 000 at an exercise exchange rate of 1.1360 (AUD/CHF). Determine whether or not the holder will exercise the option and then calculate the gross pay-off at the following spot exchange rates: (a) 1.1420, (b) 1.1510 and (c) 1.1240.

3 A trader holds a call option to buy USD100 000 at an exercise exchange rate of 1.8000 (AUD/USD). If the premium paid is 0.5 Australian cents for each USD, calculate the net pay-off at the following spot exchange rates: (a) 1.8040, (b) 1.8260 and (c) 1.7870. At what exchange rate will the trader break even?

4 A trader holds a put option to sell NOK250 000 at an exercise exchange rate of 0.190 (AUD/NOK). If the premium paid is 0.4 Australian cents for each NOK, calculate the net pay-off at the following spot exchange rates: (a) 0.200, (b) 0.192 and (c) 0.180. At what exchange rate will the trader break even?

5 A trader holds a call and a put on the British pound. The following information is available:

Amount	GBP200 000
Price of call	AUD0.01
Price of put	AUD0.008
Exercise exchange rate of call	2.50
Exercise exchange rate of put	2.50

Calculate the net pay-off on the call, the put and the combined position at the following spot exchange rates: (a) 2.505, (b) 2.540, (c) 2.495 and (d) 2.480.

6 A trader has written a call and a put on the Canadian dollar. The following information is available:

Amount	CAD400 000
Price of call	AUD0.01
Price of put	AUD0.01
Exercise exchange rate of call	0.96
Exercise exchange rate of put	0.94

Calculate the net pay-off on the short call, the short put and the combined position at the following spot exchange rates: (a) 0.99, (b) 0.97, (c) 0.95 and (d) 0.93.

7 Use the information given in Problem 6 to calculate the intrinsic values of the call and the put at various values of the spot exchange rate.

CHAPTER

The Eurocurrency market and international banking

Introduction

The Eurocurrency market is the market for short-term assets and liabilities denominated in Eurocurrencies. The major players in the Eurocurrency market are Eurobanks, mostly branches of international banks, such that the bulk of the activity is accounted for by interbank operations. Hence, international banking encompasses Eurobanking. In this chapter we shed some light on these concepts and discuss related issues.

Objectives

The objectives of this chapter are:

- To define and describe the Eurocurrency market.
- To identify Eurocurrencies and Eurocurrency banking centres.
- To find out the main reasons for the growth of the Eurocurrency market.
- To identify the main features of Eurobanking.
- To illustrate the determination of the bid-offer spread in Eurocurrency rates and the risk premium associated with low-quality borrowers.
- To define international banking and describe international banking activities.
- To describe the organisational set-up of international banking.

8.1 The Eurocurrency market

The **Eurocurrency market** is an integral part of the international financial markets in which transactions involving non-residents or foreign currencies are settled. It is comprised of banks that, *inter alia*, accept short-term deposits and make short-term loans in currencies other than that of the country in which they are located. These currencies are called **Eurocurrencies** and the banks are called **Eurobanks**. The adjective 'short-term' is added to differentiate this market from the Euromarkets for 'longer-term' instruments such as the **Eurobond market** and the **Eurocredit market**. We start with an exposition of the Eurocurrency market because it was the first Euromarket to emerge in the late 1950s.

In the Eurocurrency market, any currency can be a Eurocurrency if it is the denomination of a deposit held with, or a short-term loan granted by, a bank located outside the home country of that currency. Thus, if a bank in London has on its books an Australian dollar deposit, then the deposit is a Eurodeposit (or, to be more precise, a Euro-Australian dollar deposit). The Australian dollar would, in this case, be a Eurocurrency if the bank were located anywhere in the world as long as it was outside Australia. Normally, however, Eurobanks are located in certain financial centres that provide the right environment for the operations of these banks. A Eurobank located in London and dealing in Eurodollar deposits may be a branch of a US bank, a non-US bank or a special offshore banking unit.

The word 'Eurocurrency' combines 'Euro' and 'currency'. The word 'currency' in this sense implies short-term assets and liabilities denominated in various currencies. 'Euro', referring to Europe, is used as a prefix because this market started in Europe, more precisely in London. This is no longer the case: the Eurocurrency market at present spans the globe. Eurocurrency centres now exist outside London and outside Europe. To introduce some distinction, the term **Asian dollars**, for example, is used to refer to US dollar deposits held in Asia, particularly in Hong Kong and Singapore. Moreover, when the Eurocurrency market started in the late 1950s, the currency of denomination was exclusively the US dollar. This is why the Eurodollar market preceded the more currency-diversified Eurocurrency market. It is important to bear in mind that the word 'Euro', used as a prefix here, does not refer to the new European currency. In fact, it is possible to have a Euro-euro deposit if this deposit is held with a bank located outside the euro area.

8.2 Eurocurrencies and Eurocurrency banking centres

As one might expect, the US dollar is the most important Eurocurrency for the same reasons as those making it the most heavily traded currency on the foreign exchange market. On its own, it accounts for more than the other Eurocurrencies put together in terms of the denomination of Eurocurrency bank liabilities (that is, deposits). Other important Eurocurrencies are the euro, the Japanese yen, the British pound and the Swiss franc.

A **Eurocurrency centre** refers to a location where there is a concentration of Eurobanks. There are several prerequisites that make a particular place a Eurocurrency centre. These include the following: (i) political stability and absence of radical government changes; (ii) a favourable environment that is conducive to the smooth conduct of international finance, encompassing a favourable tax treatment of Eurobanks, an absence of exchange and credit controls, and a respect of financial privacy; (iii) good telecommunications with other financial centres; (iv) a favourable time zone; and (v) a high quality of life.

The European centres account for about 60 per cent of the Eurocurrency market. The main centres are London, Luxembourg, Paris, Zurich and Frankfurt. London is the prime Eurocurrency centre in terms of the volume of business and its diversity, with Eurobanking operations conducted in over a dozen foreign currencies. The status of London is attributed to this city's history of financial expertise as well as regulations that have differentiated between banking conducted in the domestic currency and banking conducted in other currencies. The London Eurocurrency market is dominated by US and Japanese banks.

Centres outside developed countries account for about 20 per cent of the global market, including those in the Bahamas, Bahrain, the Cayman Islands, Hong Kong, the Netherlands Antilles, Panama and Singapore. The Cayman Islands is a favoured location for US banks to establish **shell branches**. These shell branches are legally incorporated in the Cayman Islands but the actual 'bank' is a separate set of books in the head office in New York. Several factors make the Cayman Islands attractive as a Eurocurrency centre, including: (i) a low minimum capital requirement; (ii) the absence of restrictions on lending and interest rates as well as reserve requirements on Eurocurrency operations; (iii) the use of the English language; (iv) having the same business hours as New York; and (v) good telecommunication facilities. In the Middle East, Bahrain is the prime Eurocurrency centre, taking over from Beirut, which declined as a Eurocurrency centre due to the civil war in Lebanon. In Asia, Singapore is the prime centre for Asian dollar operations. Eurobanking operations in Singapore started in October 1968 when Bank of America (Singapore) was granted permission to open an international banking facility called an **Asian Currency Unit**. This facility was allowed to accept foreign currency deposits from non-residents and to make cross-border loans.

IN PRACTICE

What makes a financial centre in Asia?

One of the most important factors in making a certain location a successful financial centre is the regulatory requirements and incentives offered by the authorities in that location. Let us consider what the monetary authorities in some Asian countries (including Australia) do in this respect.

Singapore

The Monetary Authority of Singapore offers various concessionary tax incentives for financial institutions looking to set up operations in Singapore. These include incentives offered to banks for banking and capital market services, to financial institutions involved in asset management and insurance, and to multinational firms involved in treasury activities.

Cambodia

There are no financial incentives for banks and finance companies. However, the banking and financial sector enjoys a very liberalised regime that includes: (i) no barriers to entry; (ii) no restrictions on ownership; and (iii) no restrictions on activities.

Australia

The Australian federal government offers no financial incentives to banks and finance companies. State governments offer various tax-based incentives on a case-by-case basis to companies starting or expanding operations in their main cities.

Taiwan

Foreign financial institutions in Taiwan receive the same treatment as local institutions. Other incentives include allowing foreign institutions to acquire or merge with domestic financial institutions, providing tax concessions, relaxing restrictions on capital flows and giving banks more room in foreign exchange operations.

Thailand

The government of Thailand has allowed foreign financial institutions to invest in Thailand, by forming business alliances with domestic financial institutions. The restrictions on foreign ownership have been lifted.

Hong Kong

There are no restrictions on inward and outward investment, no foreign exchange controls and no withholding taxes. Hong Kong has one of the world's highest concentrations of banks.

Malaysia

There are some tax incentives. For example, offshore companies have the option of paying 3 per cent on net audited profits or the sum of 20 000 Malaysian dollars.

Financial centres in North America and Japan account for the other 20 per cent of the global Eurocurrency market. Eurocurrency operations within the United States were made legal in December 1981 when the establishment of **International Banking Facilities (IBFs)** was permitted. An IBF is effectively a set of books kept at US banks. There are, however, no reserve requirements or interest ceilings on deposits booked at the IBFs. In Japan, the government allowed the establishment of the **Japan Offshore Market (JOM)**. Like the IBFs, the JOM exists only in the form of entries in the books of banks with special licences.

The Australian experiment with offshore banking units has not been successful. In 1981, an argument was put forward in the *Final Report of the Committee of Inquiry into the Australian Financial System* for allowing foreign banks to enter general commercial banking operations. The basis for this argument was the belief that adequate and vigorous competition is an essential requirement for the efficient operation of financial markets. In 1988, the establishment of offshore banking units was allowed with the objective of carrying out banking transactions in Australia with non-residents involving foreign currencies. This, however, has not made Sydney and Melbourne important Eurocurrency centres.

IN PRACTICE

Basel II

The **Basel Committee** on Banking Supervision was established by the central bank governors of the Group of Ten countries in 1975, with the objective of devising effective banking prudential regulations and requirements. Since then, the Basel Committee has produced two accords on capital adequacy: in 1988 (**Basel I**) and in 2001 (**Basel II**). The idea behind these accords is to devise a system to calculate the minimum capital requirement as determined by the riskiness of the underlying assets.

Basel II was devised in response to the feeling that Basel I was too broad, making it possible for banks to shift assets to relatively high-risk categories. The Basel II accord, released in January 2001, was intended to replace systems of credit risk weighting by a system that depends on either external rating agencies' credit assessment for determining risk weights or (for sophisticated and/or internationally active banks) the internal credit risk assessments by banks themselves. The new accord rests on three pillars:

- establishing minimum capital requirements, which aims at motivating banks into improving their risk-management and measurement capabilities in market, credit and operational risk
- introducing an enhanced supervisory review process
- providing incentives to strengthen risk-management and internal controls through the forces of market discipline, which requires the detailed disclosure of capital structure, risk exposure and **capital adequacy**.

While the new accord does not change the treatment of **market risk**, it enhances the treatment of credit risk and introduces a capital charge for **operational risk** (that is, higher minimum capital is required for a higher level of operational risk). Of chief concern on the operational risk side is the classification and collection of data consistently across business lines and locations.

While few criticise the objective of developing increased sensitivity to risk, many believe that the new accord is too complicated for institutions to implement and will prove too difficult for regulatory bodies to supervise effectively.

8.3 The evolution and growth of the Eurocurrency market

It is ironic that the Eurocurrency market, a symbol of capitalism, was initiated by capitalism's number one enemy: the former Soviet Union. The Eurocurrency market started as the Eurodollar market in the 1950s in the midst of the Cold War as the Soviets faced the problem of keeping their export-generated dollar balances without running the risk of freezing or confiscation, which would have been possible if these balances had been deposited with US domestic banks. The solution to this problem was for the Soviets to deposit their dollar funds in special accounts with European banks or, in general, banks that were not within the jurisdiction of the US authorities. The Eurodollar market was thus created.

In 1957 and 1958, two developments took place that enhanced the Eurodollar market and subsequently the Eurocurrency market. In 1957, the Bank of England introduced tight controls on pound-denominated transactions between British banks and non-residents. In order to retain their position in the financing of world trade, the British banks started to conduct US dollar-denominated operations with non-residents. This action led to the accumulation of US dollar balances by these banks (that is, the creation of Eurodollar deposits). In 1958, major European currencies were made convertible, allowing European banks to hold dollar accounts rather than being required to exchange dollars with their central banks for domestic currencies. This development led to an increase in the demand for and supply of what had become Eurodollars.

RESEARCH FINDINGS

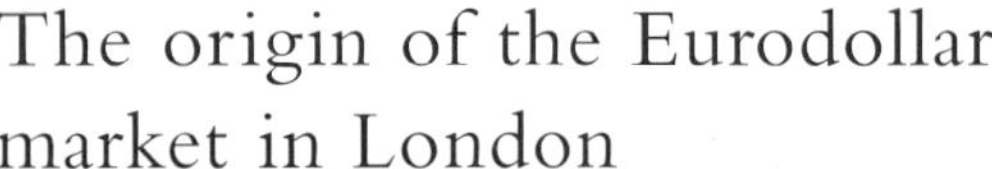

The origin of the Eurodollar market in London

An attempt has been made to seek a non-traditional explanation for the origin of the Eurodollar market. Schenk challenges the idea that the Eurodollar market started in the 1950s as a result of attempts to accommodate US dollar surpluses.[1] Schenk's paper aims to explain why the Eurodollar market emerged and why London kept most of the business. Some archival evidence is presented to show that Eurodollars were accumulated earlier than the 1950s by the Soviets. The major source of London's competitive advantage was the regulatory environment that combined tight money in the domestic economy with relative freedom in the international market.

Schenk claims that the accumulation of foreign currency deposits by London banks was not a new phenomenon in the 1950s, because customers had long been allowed to deposit their US dollar balances or other currencies at banks in London. The interwar period witnessed growth in those deposits, which came to an end with the imposition of exchange controls and the collapse of the gold exchange standard in the 1930s. In the immediate post-war period exchange controls prevented the re-emergence of this practice but by the early 1960s observers became aware of a growth in US dollar deposits from overseas, mainly by Europeans and mainly in London banks.

[1] C. R. Schenk, 'The Origins of the Eurodollar Market in London: 1955–1963', *Explorations in Economic History*, 35, 1998, pp. 221–38.

The Eurocurrency market experienced phenomenal growth following the oil price rise of 1973/1974. Member countries of the Organisation of Petroleum Exporting Countries (OPEC) started, all of a sudden, to accumulate massive dollar balances. These balances were deposited with Eurobanks, resulting in an increase in the liabilities of Eurobanks and therefore the size of the Eurocurrency market. Simultaneously, there was a rapid spread of multinational firms, encouraging banks to make the same move to win the international business of their giant customers.

It seems also that the most important factor behind the spectacular growth of the Eurocurrency market is efficiency in performing financial intermediation between borrowers and lenders. Competitive efficiency of Eurobanks is indicated by the narrowness of the spread between the interest charged to prime borrowers and that paid on deposits, as compared with what is found in domestic money markets. But why are Eurobanks more efficient than domestic banks?

The first of the factors explaining the efficiency of Eurobanks is that, unlike domestic banks, they are not subject to the regulations of the monetary authorities of the countries where they are located. These regulations have historically led US banks to 'migrate' by opening branches in Europe, where they received the privilege of not being subject to regulations, thus enhancing the growth of the Eurocurrency market. An example of these regulations is **Regulation Q**, which limited the interest rate that US banks could pay on US dollar saving accounts. Another example is the 1963 **interest equalisation tax**, which was introduced by the US authorities to protect the balance of payments from capital outflows, making it no longer cheap to raise funds on the New York financial markets. A similar regulation is the 1965 US voluntary foreign credit restraint guideline, which was made compulsory in 1968. This regulation was aimed at limiting the amount of lending to foreigners by US banks.

All these measures increased the degree of imperfection in the US domestic money markets, implying lost business opportunities for US banks. In their endeavours to circumvent these regulations, these banks started to establish branches and subsidiaries outside the jurisdiction of the US banking laws and regulations. It should be mentioned also that **reserve requirements**, which are (or were) applied to domestic banks, are not applied to Eurobanks. Naturally, banks operating without reserve requirements are bound to run a more profitable business than otherwise. Finally, Eurobanks are more efficient because of the utilisation of economies of scale resulting from large-sized operations. For a given level of loans, administrative costs are lower than those of domestic banks, whose business is more on the retail side than that of Eurobanks.

IN PRACTICE

The role of Midland Bank in creating the Eurodollar market

In mid-1955, Midland Bank, a former major British bank that no longer exists due to mergers, indulged in financial innovation that contributed to the creation and growth of the modern Eurocurrency market.[1] Like most cases of financial innovation, it was propelled by the prevailing financial environment.

The first half of 1955 witnessed a tight monetary policy in the United Kingdom, as the Bank Rate (the rate at which commercial banks can borrow from the central bank) was pushed to a post-war high of 4.5 per cent in February to combat inflationary pressures. The growth of the gap between interest rates on bank deposits and the Treasury bill rate in favour of the latter led to a dramatic fall in the deposits of commercial banks.

In response to these conditions, Midland Bank started to bid up to $1\frac{7}{8}$ per cent interest for 30-day US dollar deposits, which was $\frac{7}{8}$ per cent more than the maximum rate payable under US Regulation Q. Midland then sold these dollar funds against the pound and bought them back forward at a premium of $2\frac{1}{8}$ per cent. The resultant pound funds therefore cost Midland 4 per cent, half a percentage point less than the Bank Rate (that is, half a percentage point cheaper than the funds that could have been borrowed from the Bank of England at the Bank Rate).

The Midland deals represented a financial innovation that produced the Eurodollar market. The underlying dollar deposits were not traditional bank liabilities in the sense that they were attracted by Midland to solve a specific liquidity problem that resulted from the policy stance of the British authorities in the 1950s. In June 1955, the Bank of England realised that Midland Bank was attracting foreign currency deposits that were not directly related to its commercial business. However, when approached by the Bank of England for an explanation, an executive manager of Midland asserted that 'nothing out of the ordinary had taken place' and that 'what dollar deposits had been received were in the normal course of business'.

[1] C. R. Schenk, 'The Origins of the Eurodollar Market in London: 1955–1963', *Explorations in Economic History*, 35, 1998, pp. 221–38.

8.4 Some features of Eurobanking

The following are the main features of Eurobanking or Eurobanks:

- Eurobanking is not identical to **international banking**, the distinguishing feature being the currency of denomination. International banking involves operations with non-residents denominated in domestic and foreign currencies as well as operations with domestic residents denominated in foreign currencies. Thus, international banking encompasses Eurobanking.
- The liabilities of Eurobanks are time or call deposits, not demand or checkable deposits. This is why Eurobanks are effectively **non-bank financial intermediaries (NBFIs)**. This is also why the ability of Eurobanks to create money and cause inflation is limited to the effect they have on the velocity of circulation (the speed at which money turns around). It is believed that intermediation by Eurobanks does not necessarily affect aggregate demand, which represents total spending in the economy.
- Unlike domestic banks, Eurobanks cannot create deposits by writing claims against themselves. **Eurodeposits** are created when a Eurobank accepts a term deposit from a party that places the deposit with the bank and passes that deposit on to another Eurobank. The change in the ownership of the original deposit is recorded in the books of a domestic bank. The initial Eurodeposit is created by transferring funds deposited with the domestic bank to a Eurobank.
- Eurobanks accept deposits and make loans in a variety of currencies independently of their physical locations. A Eurobank is often a branch of an international bank located in a Eurocurrency centre.
- There are no formal restrictions on entry into Eurobanking. The Eurocurrency market comprises a large number of banks operating in a highly competitive environment.
- Transactions (borrowing and placement of deposits) are in large sums of a million US dollars and over. Thus, the Eurocurrency market is a wholesale market, a property that gives rise to efficiency in the operations of Eurobanks.
- As we have seen before, the geographical spread of the market is very wide. The Eurocurrency market started in London, but Eurocurrency centres can be found in all corners of the globe at present.
- The Eurocurrency market provides an alternative to domestic banks for conducting large transactions. Since this market is not subject to the regulatory measures of the local monetary authorities, its existence handicaps monetary policy, which depends primarily on the control of the domestic banking system.
- The Eurocurrency market is dominated by interbank operations. About 70 per cent of gross transactions in the Eurocurrency market are conducted among banks, and interbank liabilities amount to over one-half of the Eurobanks' gross liabilities. Funds flow from one bank to another for reasons ranging from **window-dressing** (which can be thought of as a manipulation of accounts to produce a better picture than would be revealed otherwise) to the exploitation of profitable opportunities unidentified by others. Extensive interbank operations have positive and negative implications. The positive implication is that there is an efficient 'invisible hand' shifting funds from net lenders to net borrowers towards an optimum allocation of financial resources. The negative implication relates to contagion: difficulties for one bank could rapidly spread throughout the system.
- Apart from Eurobanks themselves, the principal participants in the Eurocurrency market are multinational firms and central banks.
- Eurobanks do not have to hold reserves against their deposit liabilities. Moreover, they do this without jeopardising their operations because their deposit liabilities are time deposits.

8.5 Interest rate determination

Short-term interest rates (that is, interest rates on short-term assets and liabilities) are determined in the money market, where banks trade short-term assets and liabilities with other banks as well as non-bank customers. Large banks normally act as market makers. Changes in interest rates therefore result from changes in the forces of supply and demand in the money market. We study interest rate determination in the Eurocurrency market because it is closer to being a free market than the domestic money market, as the latter is subject to regulation by the domestic monetary authorities. However, we must bear in mind that the domestic and Eurocurrency interest rates on assets and liabilities denominated in the same currency are closely related (though not equal).

Like exchange rates, interest rates are quoted as bid and offer rates. The bid rate is the rate at which the quoting bank (the market maker) accepts the placement of deposits with it from other parties (the price takers). The offer rate is the rate at which the quoting bank places deposits with other parties. The bid rate is naturally lower than the offer rate. Thus, the quoting bank's demand for funds (deposits) is a decreasing function of the bid rate, whereas its supply of funds to be deposited with other banks is an increasing function of the offer rate. The two functions are represented in Figure 8.1 by the supply and demand by market makers, D^M and S^M, respectively. Price takers have a supply curve that is an increasing function of the bid rate, S^T, and a demand curve that is a decreasing function of the offer rate, D^T. The bid rate, i_b, is determined by the intersection of the D^M curve and the S^T curve, whereas the offer rate, i_a, is determined by the intersection of the D^T curve and the S^M curve.

Figure 8.1 Interest rate determination

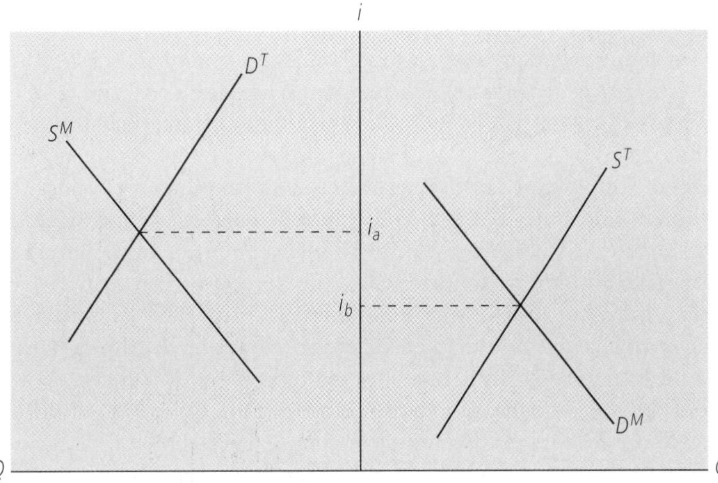

It must be borne in mind that only big banks with high creditworthiness can dictate the bid and offer rates (that is, act as market makers). Moreover, not all other parties can borrow at these banks' offer rates. Banks and non-bank customers with lower creditworthiness can borrow at a higher rate because lending banks add a risk premium as a compensation for the higher credit (or default) risk. This situation is illustrated in Figure 8.2. Customers with high creditworthiness have a demand curve D^H and so they can borrow at i_a. On the other hand, customers with low creditworthiness have a demand curve D^L and so they can borrow at $i_a + \rho$, where ρ is the risk premium required to compensate banks for the credit risk associated with low creditworthiness.

Figure 8.2 Risk premium associated with low-quality borrowers

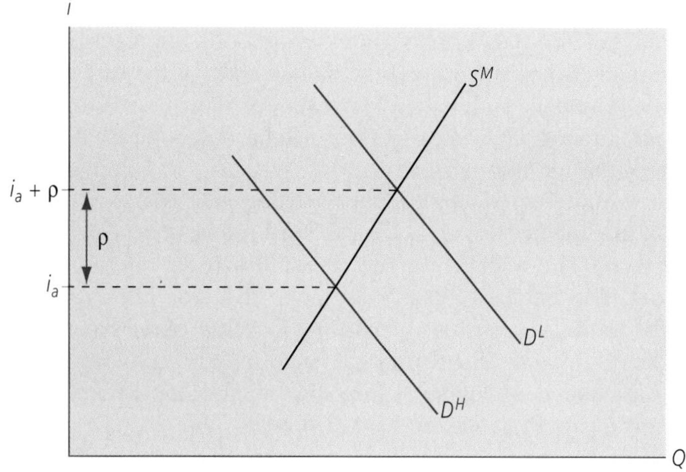

8.6 International banking

International banking operations encompass transactions conducted with non-residents as well as those involving foreign currencies. Thus, international banking encompasses Eurobanking. The origin of foreign-branch banking can be traced back to the nineteenth century. The years since the late 1950s have witnessed remarkable developments in international banking, led by US banks and later bolstered by European, Japanese and other banks. By 1960 there was a significant foreign banking community in London.

Early arrivals (predominantly, if not exclusively, US banks) opened banking offices in London for several reasons. The first reason was to meet the needs of the foreign subsidiaries of domestic corporate customers. In this sense, the spread of international banking was motivated by the spread of non-bank multinational firms. The second reason was to participate in the foreign exchange market. In order to indulge in this activity around the clock, banks found it useful to have branches or representative offices in major foreign exchange centres falling in different time zones. Because London was (and still is) the major foreign exchange centre in the world, physical presence there seemed (and seems) to make a lot of sense. Finally, there was a desire to circumvent capital controls as represented by such measures as Regulation Q.

There are other factors that promoted the emergence of international banking. For example, by opening a foreign branch or a representative office, the task of gathering information can be carried out more effectively. This information pertains to foreign markets (for example, investment opportunities) and to foreign borrowers (that is, assessing creditworthiness). Another factor is the provision of custodial services for customers investing in foreign securities. These services include the safekeeping of securities, the collection of dividends and coupon payments, and the handling of tax matters.

INSIGHT

Types of risk faced by international banks

International banks encounter four types of risk, some of which do not arise from domestic operations. The following are the four types of risk:

- **Credit risk** is the risk of non-payment that arises from the inability or unwillingness of borrowers to generate cash or liquidate other assets to service their loans.
- **Currency risk** (also known as foreign exchange risk) arises from changes in exchange rates between the bank's base currency and other currencies in which loans are denominated. It can be dealt with by lending in the domestic currency only and by balancing assets and liabilities by currency.
- **Country risk** is related to political and economic conditions in the borrower country, which affect the ability of borrowers from that country (government bodies and otherwise) to service their loans.
- **Systematic risk** is related to changes in market conditions or credit quality in an entire sector of financial markets. For example, the syndicated loan market was adversely affected by a series of oil and price shocks in the 1970s and 1980s.

This classification of risk is slightly different from that used in the Basel II accord, which classifies risk into credit risk, market risk and operational risk (see the box on Basel II on page 229). The two classifications are, however, equivalent. Currency risk, country risk and systematic risk have elements of both market risk and operational risk.

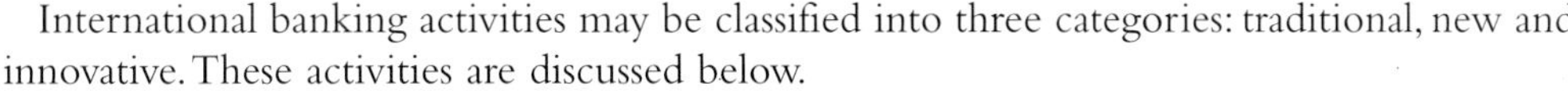

International banking activities may be classified into three categories: traditional, new and innovative. These activities are discussed below.

Traditional activities

Traditional activities are: (i) **trade finance**, including the provision of **letters of credit**; (ii) buying and selling foreign exchange; and (iii) the provision of foreign loans (that is, loans to customers located in other countries).

IN PRACTICE

Explaining international bank loan losses

The Asian crisis alone cost international banks an estimated USD20 billion in losses. Similar losses were experienced through the crises that hit Mexico, Russia and Brazil. How is it that international banks incur these losses when they have sophisticated country risk analysts who closely follow developments in the countries where they have business? Two explanations are possible: (i) while international banks have sophisticated country risk research, they often overlook the causes of political crises; and (ii) because of organisational and managerial problems, banks often fail to act on the basis of their own country risk assessment.

Consider this comparison as an example. Between 1970 and 1995, Italy was swept by 18 government changes, 26 general strikes and 41 political assassinations. By contrast, in the same period Indonesia had no change of government, only one general strike and no political assassinations. Current events, therefore, would have produced misleading indicators of country risk in both cases. On the other hand, it is often claimed that the sophisticated country risk reports produced by economists and political scientists employed by banks are often too long or too abstract to be implemented.

New activities

In the 1970s and 1980s new activities emerged following developments in international financial markets, particularly the growth of the Euromarket. These activities are: (i) dealing in Eurocurrencies; (ii) the provision of **syndicated Eurocredit**; and (iii) merchant or **investment banking** activities (such as Eurobond issues and secondary market trading, as well as mergers and acquisitions).

The impact of e-commerce on trade finance

Banks have traditionally indulged in trade finance (that is, the financing of cross-border exports and imports). Trade finance has historically been a labour- and paper-intensive process. However, the e-commerce revolution brings the opportunity to move from paper-based processing to electronic processing, which means that e-commerce is transforming trade finance. Several set-ups are already in place, including electronic purchase cards, Identrus and Bolero.

Electronic purchase cards (EPCs) facilitate trade-related e-commerce transactions by using a smart card to buy goods and services on the Internet. These cards are hybrid, containing elements of documentary credit/payment orders as well as a debit charge card. EPCs offer a number of benefits for trade facilitation and settlement, as well as faster transaction turnaround and lower transaction costs.

A consortium of international banks (ABN Amro, Bank of America, Chase, Citigroup, Deutsche Bank and Hypovereinsbank) has founded Identrus, which allows the secure exchange of electronic documents within a well-defined legal framework. It also provides digital certification to authenticate the identities of the transacting parties and validate deals on the Internet.

Bolero (Bill of Landing Electronic Registry Organisation) aims to provide an electronic substitute for all types of paper-based trade documentation. Bolero International Limited was founded in June 1998 by the Society for Worldwide International Financial Transactions and the Through Transport Mutual Insurance Association Limited (TT Club). The first task of Bolero is the design of electronic **bills of landing** (which facilitates the transfer of title of the underlying goods). Bolero has already designed electronic templates for some 50 types of trade documents and is apparently working on 50 more. It aims to create a universal standard for electronic trade documentation.

The role of banks in trade finance will evolve as e-commerce and electronic trade documentation create new opportunities. There is already a trend towards supplier financing schemes and open account receivables financing. New hybrid trade finance products can be expected. However, the arrival of unregulated non-bank competitors is threatening the traditional role of banks in trade financing. Trade settlement, trade financing, risk management and credit approach can be expected to undergo radical transformations.

Innovative activities

Innovative international banking activities emerged in the 1980s and 1990s as a result of financial engineering and the need for risk management. These activities are: (i) innovative financing using instruments such as **new issuance facilities (NIFs)**, swaps and other derivatives; (ii) the global money market (24-hour dealing room); (iii) managing the loan portfolios of developing countries; and (iv) **private banking**, which is the provision of financial services to wealthy clients.

The scope for private banking

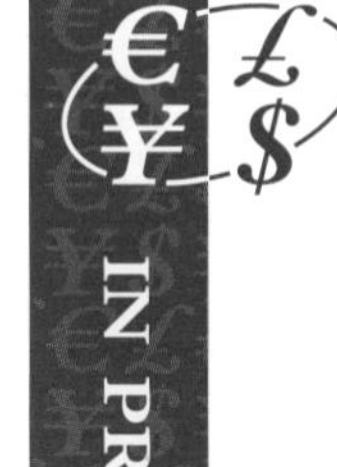

Private banking (or so-called wealth management) is one of the most attractive businesses in financial services as it offers growing revenue for little commitment of capital. This contrasts sharply with the volatile returns and high capital needs of other activities such as securities trading and corporate finance.

The scope for private banking can be judged on the basis of the following figures. In 2000, there were 34 million households worldwide with net investment assets of more than USD40 000 billion, a figure that is expected to rise to USD66 000 billion by 2005. In 2000 these households generated financial services revenue totalling USD506 billion, and this is projected to rise to USD701 billion by 2005. These are obviously huge figures, but we must not forget that they are divided among many providers of private banking services.

8.7 The organisational set-up of international banking

How do banks transfer funds across countries? There are several organisational arrangements between banks involved in cross-border international operations. Some are outlined below.

Correspondent banks

The term **correspondent bank** comes from the mail or cable communications that banks used to settle customers' accounts. Although this is no longer the case, as banks now settle accounts via electronic systems, the term is still used to describe this international banking arrangement. If an international bank does not wish or is not permitted to open a branch in a certain country, a correspondent bank settles customers' payments on its behalf. For example, if the Commonwealth Bank does not have a sufficient volume of business to open a branch in Norway, a Norwegian bank may act as a correspondent bank. The Commonwealth Bank opens an account with the Norwegian bank to facilitate the transfer of funds. If an Australian importer wants to pay for goods imported from Norway in the Norwegian currency, then the amount is debited to the Australian importer's account with the Commonwealth Bank, while the account of the latter with the Norwegian bank is debited to pay for the imported goods.

Representative offices

Banks may choose to open **representative offices** in other countries, with the primary task of providing information to their customers in the home country about business conditions in the foreign country, as well as information about the creditworthiness of actual and potential customers. The representative office is not a bank, in the sense that it does not perform the function of accepting deposits and granting loans. For example, the ANZ's presence in Indonesia started in 1973 when Grindlays Bank established a representative office in Jakarta. This move has enabled the ANZ to learn about the local business culture and build relationships with the government and business. Standard Chartered Bank's acquisition of Grindlays in 2002 illustrates a change in the organisational set-up of ANZ's Indonesian presence.

IN PRACTICE

Two Swiss banking stories

What has happened to the famous Swiss banking industry? It has recently been hit by a series of bad decisions that have resulted in significant losses. The following are two stories of Swiss banking.

On 3 June 2002 it was announced that two Swiss banks, Lombard Odier and Darier Hentsch, had merged. These two banks were traditionally involved in private banking, managing the wealth of wealthy individuals. The merger followed in the wake of the demise of Swiss private banking as it lost its true appeal (its famed secrecy) because of an international drive against **money laundering**. This came at a time when the two banks were having other troubles and showing signs of weakness and loss making. For example, Darier Hentsch suffered a blow in October 2001 when a senior partner, Benedict Hentsch, stepped down because of his involvement (as vice-chairman) in the collapse of Swissair. Lombard Odier, on the other hand, put itself in trouble by venturing into alien territory, trying to ride the equity boom that came to an end in 2000.

The merger came as an attempt by the two banks to reinvent themselves and to find some economies of scale. However, some observers believe that by going for scale the two banks are destroying their traditional attraction, attentive service to (wealthy) clients. This is not a bad business. A study by UBS Warburg suggests that the returns from private banking can be as high as 30 per cent on equity (see the box on private banking on page 237).

The second story is about Credit Suisse, Switzerland's second-largest financial group. In the spring of 1997, Lukas Muhlemann, the chairman and chief executive, is quoted (by *The Economist*) as having made fun of the idea of combining banking and insurance by saying 'why buy a cow when all you want is a glass of milk'. A few months later the man himself decided to buy the cow, in the form of Winterthur Insurance. In 2001 things started to go wrong. In June of that year, Credit Suisse sold the insurance arm that served multinational firms, Winterthur International, at a low price. Then the fall in stock markets hit Winterthur's life business, ending up booking a CHF4 billion fall in shareholders' equity. And in the first quarter of 2002, Winterthur booked a post-tax loss of CHF150 million on its life-insurance business. All this punished the Credit Suisse share price, which declined by over 40 per cent between January 2000 and June 2002.

Bank agencies

Bank agencies are similar to ordinary commercial banks except that they do not handle ordinary deposits. Bank agencies deal in money and foreign exchange markets, arrange loans and clear cheques.

Foreign branches

If the volume of the international business of the customers of a certain bank is large enough, then it may be economically and financially viable to set up a foreign branch. This branch is normally subject to the banking regulations of the home as well as the foreign country, although it is incorporated in the home country. One advantage of this arrangement is the speed with which cheques are cleared, because it becomes an internal operation. Different countries have different attitudes towards the establishment of branches by foreign banks, with some imposing total prohibition.

IN PRACTICE

The end of money laundering in Asia?

The days have gone when a strange character could walk into an Asian bank to deposit a briefcase full of paper money. Suspicious bank customers across Asia are now required to explain themselves, thanks mainly to the tightening up of anti-money laundering measures by the regulators. In the May 2001 meeting of the Asian Development Bank (ADB), which was held in Hawaii, there was a two-hour seminar on money laundering comprising speakers (regulators or administrators) from Japan and Australia and an audience consisting mainly of bankers. The message of the discussion was that bankers had to bear the extra burden imposed by the regulators, requiring more paperwork, particularly by those banks with large retail and private banking businesses.

Standards of anti-money laundering regulations in Asia vary from one country to another. The following are examples:

- Thailand requires holders of non-resident bank accounts to file documentary evidence of the purpose of all transactions of more than USD5000.
- The central bank of the Philippines has introduced measures to tighten up monitoring of bank transactions following the scandals surrounding former president Joseph Estrada's financial dealings.
- In Singapore, a 1999 report called for an urgent review of the anti-money laundering system, advocating an extension of provisions to a range of serious crimes, not just drug trafficking.
- In Hong Kong, however, legislators rejected the proposed Drúg Trafficking and Organised Crimes Bill in March 2001, which would have raised the requirement for reporting suspicious transactions to that of 'reasonable grounds of suspicion'.

Is this the end of money laundering in Asia (or anywhere else in the world for that matter)? Definitely not, as more sophisticated money laundering transactions can prove to be hard to detect.

Foreign subsidiaries and affiliates

While a foreign branch is part of the parent bank, a foreign **subsidiary** or **affiliate** in the banking industry is a bank established in a foreign country and owned solely or jointly with other parties (hence, a **joint venture**). Another difference is that foreign branches have the name of the parent bank, but subsidiaries and affiliates typically do not. The difference between subsidiaries and affiliates lies in the degree of control exerted by the parent bank, as the degree of control is greater in the case of subsidiaries. In the extreme case, the control over a subsidiary is total if it is solely owned by the parent bank. An example of a banking joint venture is the Indonesian-based ANZ Panin Bank, of which the ANZ owns 85 per cent whereas the remainder is owned by Panin Bank, one of Indonesia's largest private commercial banks.

Consortium banks

Consortium banks are joint ventures set up by large international banks. These are giant organisations dealing only with large companies and governments. Their activities include large commercial and investment banking operations, such as arranging loans, underwriting and leading bond issues, as well as arranging mergers and acquisitions.

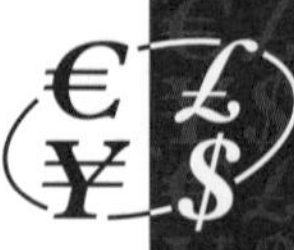

IN PRACTICE

The world's largest banks

The 2001 list of the world's largest 10 banks by total assets included three from the United States, two from Japan and Germany, and one each from the United Kingdom, Switzerland and France. The following is the list of the largest 10 according to their total assets in millions of US dollars.

Mizuho Financial Group	Japan	1 259 498
Citigroup	United States	902 210
Deutsche Bank	Germany	874 706
JP Morgan Chase & Co	United States	715 348
Bank of Tokyo-Mitsubishi	Japan	675 640
HSBC Holdings	UK	673 614
Hypovereinsbank	Germany	666 707
UBS	Switzerland	664 560
BNP Paribas	France	645 793
Bank of America Corporation	United States	642 191

In Asia (including Australia) the largest four banks are from China, but four Australian banks appear in the list of the largest 10:

Industrial and Commercial Bank of China	China	22 797
Bank of China	China	17 086
Agricultural Bank of China	China	18 971
China Construction Bank	China	13 875
National Australia Bank	Australia	8 601
DBS Bank	Singapore	5 891
Commonwealth Bank Group	Australia	5 758
ANZ Banking Corporation	Australia	5 237
Overseas-China Banking Corporation	Singapore	4 749
Westpac Banking Corporation	Australia	4 093

It is interesting to note that a large number of these giant banks appeared as a result of mergers and acquisitions. For example, Midland Bank, which was referred to in an earlier box as a major contributor to the emergence of the Eurocurrency market, is now part of HSBC Holdings, the world's sixth largest bank.

Source: The Banker, July 2001, pp. 133–48.

Global banks

While a conventional international bank takes deposits in one country and make loans in another, a **global bank** takes deposits and offers loans and other banking services within a variety of national markets through local presence. Thus, the difference between international banks and global banks is the way in which these banks finance their foreign assets. International banks concentrate on cross-border business, whereas global banks serve local markets locally.

IN PRACTICE

Why foreign banks are investing in China

In early 2002, Beijing started handing out foreign currency licences, which prompted both Citibank and HSBC to start retail operations in Shanghai and Beijing. In December 2001, HSBC bought a stake in the Bank of Shanghai, with the intention of acquiring another stake in Ping, which is one of China's largest insurance companies. This trend should continue as the Chinese authorities press medium-sized Chinese banks to boost capital, prompting them to approach foreign institutions for equity investment.

But the overall environment in China is not yet ready to receive a mass entry of foreign banks. Steps that need to be taken in this direction, apart from full currency convertibility, are interest rate deregulation and the creation of an interbank market for the renminbi, the Chinese currency. For the time being, the primary opportunities for foreign banks are in niches like trade financing and the foreign currency side of syndicated loans.

HSBC made the first move of its kind when it acquired an 8 per cent stake in the Bank of Shanghai, the primary objective of the move being to learn about the Chinese market through a local partner. This move will most likely be followed by other banks. In May 2002, the *Australian Financial Review* reported rumours about Hong Kong's Bank of East Asia acquiring a stake in the Beijing-based Minsheng Bank. The driving force for these moves has to be the sheer size of the Chinese economy.

Summary

- The Eurocurrency market is the market for short-term deposits and loans denominated in currencies other than the currency of the country where the banks dealing in this market are located. The US dollar is the most important Eurocurrency.
- There are several prerequisites for a particular place to be a Eurocurrency centre, including: (i) political stability; (ii) the absence of exchange and credit controls; (iii) good telecommunication facilities; (iv) a favourable time zone; and (v) a high quality of life.
- The European centres, of which London is the most important, account for about 60 per cent of the Eurocurrency market. Centres outside developed countries account for about 20 per cent of the market. Centres in North America and Japan account for the other 20 per cent.
- Australia's experiment with Eurobanking has not been successful, in the sense that Sydney and Melbourne have not developed as major Eurocurrency centres.
- The Eurocurrency market emerged in the 1950s as the Soviet Union deposited its US dollar holdings with banks located in Europe. Other reasons for the emergence of this market include the controls imposed by the Bank of England in 1957 on pound-denominated transactions with non-residents and the restoration of the convertibility of European currencies in 1958. Factors leading to further growth in the market include the oil price rise in 1973/1974, the spread of non-bank multinationals, and efficiency in performing financial operations.

- Eurobanking has several features, including the following: (i) it is not identical to international banking; (ii) liabilities are time or call deposits; (iii) Eurobanks cannot create deposits by writing claims against themselves; (iv) there are no restrictions on entry into Eurobanking; (v) transactions are very large; and (vi) it is dominated by interbank operations.
- Eurobanks are efficient because (i) they are not subject to the regulations of the domestic monetary authorities and (ii) they enjoy economies of scale.
- The bid and offer interest rates are determined in the Eurocurrency market by the supply and demand (for funds) of market makers and price takers.
- Only big banks with high creditworthiness can dictate the bid and offer rates of the market makers. Borrowers with low creditworthiness can only borrow at a rate higher than the offer rate.
- International banking operations encompass those conducted with non-residents as well as those involving foreign currencies.
- International banking activities are of three types: (i) traditional activities (for example, export-import finance); (ii) new activities (for example, investment banking); and (iii) innovative activities (for example, managing the loan portfolios of developing countries).
- Several organisational arrangements are used to conduct cross-border international operations. These include: (i) correspondent banking; (ii) representative offices; (iii) bank agencies; (iv) foreign branches; (v) foreign subsidiaries; (vi) consortium banks; and (vii) global banks.

Key terms

affiliate 239
Asian Currency Unit 227
Asian dollars 227
bank agencies 238
Basel Committee 229
Basel I 229
Basel II 229
bills of landing 236
capital adequacy 229
consortium banks 239
correspondent bank 237
country risk 235
credit risk 235
currency risk 235
Eurobanks 226
Eurobond market 226
Eurocredit market 226
Eurocurrencies 226
Eurocurrency centre 227
Eurocurrency market 226
Eurodeposits 232
global bank 240
interest equalisation tax 231
international banking 232
International Banking Facilities (IBFs) 228
investment banking 236
Japan Offshore Market (JOM) 228
joint venture 239
letters of credit 235
market risk 229
money laundering 238
new issuance facilities (NIFs) 236
non-bank financial intermediaries (NBFIs) 232
operational risk 229
private banking 236
Regulation Q 231
representative offices 237
reserve requirements 231
shell branches 227
subsidiary 239
syndicated Eurocredit 236
systematic risk 235
trade finance 235
window-dressing 232

MaxMARK

MAXIMISE YOUR MARKS! There are 30 interactive questions for this chapter available online at **www.mhhe.com/au/moosa2e**

Review questions

1. What is the Eurocurrency market?
2. What are Asian dollars?
3. What are the prerequisites that make a particular place a Eurocurrency centre?
4. What are shell branches?
5. What is an Asian Currency Unit?
6. What are Basel I and Basel II?
7. How is the Eurocurrency business carried out in the United States and Japan?
8. Distinguish between Eurobanking and international banking.
9. Distinguish between international banks and global banks.
10. Explain why the crackdown on money laundering has adversely affected Swiss banks.
11. Why are Eurobanks regarded as NBFIs?
12. Why is the Eurocurrency market described as a 'wholesale market'?
13. 'It is ironic that the Eurocurrency market, a symbol of capitalism, was initiated by the Soviet Union, capitalism's number one enemy.' Explain.
14. How did Midland Bank contribute to the creation of the Eurocurrency market in the 1950s?
15. Discuss the factors that have led to the growth of the Eurocurrency market since 1957.
16. Why did US banks start to open branches in London in the period after World War II?
17. What are the types of risk faced by international banks?
18. Banks have traditionally indulged in financing international trade. What is the effect on this activity of the development of e-commerce?
19. What are the new and innovative international banking activities?
20. What is private banking and why is it regarded as a lucrative business?
21. What are the various arrangements used to conduct cross-border international banking operations?

CHAPTER

Purchasing power parity

Introduction

The theory of purchasing power parity (PPP) describes the relationship between prices and exchange rates. Although this theory has been in existence for two (or even four) centuries, it was popularised by a Swedish economist by the name of Gustav Cassel, who started writing about it during World War I. He was motivated by the desire to calculate the 'appropriate' levels of the exchange rates among major currencies, following the advent of the war inflation and the collapse of the gold standard. In fact, it was Cassel who introduced the term 'purchasing power parity' to describe this theory. PPP is important for international business firms because the validity, or otherwise, of this theory implies the possibility, or otherwise, of real currency appreciation and depreciation and hence the presence of exposure to economic risk, as we discuss in Chapter 14. Moreover, PPP can be used as a currency trading rule.

Objectives

The objectives of this chapter are:

- To introduce the law of one price from which the basic version of PPP can be derived.
- To derive PPP from the law of one price.
- To consider PPP in a comparative statistics framework
- To assess the empirical validity of PPP.
- To illustrate how PPP can be used as a trading rule in the foreign exchange market.
- To introduce the monetary model of exchange rates.

9.1 Background

The advent of floating exchange rates, following the collapse of the Bretton Woods system of fixed exchange rates in 1971, resulted in a resurgence of interest in **purchasing power parity (PPP)** for reasons related to policy as well as corporate planning and operations. From a policy perspective, there has been an increasing concern (which is shared by business executives) about the **misalignment** of the exchange rates of major currencies. PPP is relevant in this respect because one way to measure the extent of misalignment is by deviations from the level implied by PPP. Furthermore, economists and policy makers have been searching for alternative exchange rate arrangements (in the process of reforming the international monetary system) because of dissatisfaction with the current system of floating exchange rates (or some of its by-products). One of these alternatives is based on the idea that PPP can be used as a monetary standard. Although these considerations are primarily policy-related, they are of interest to business firms, which are exposed to the risk arising from changes in exchange rates.

There are, however, other considerations of PPP that pertain to business firms. First of all, financial deregulation and the dismantling of capital controls have made exchange rates highly volatile. In their endeavour to make profit from currency trading, corporate foreign exchange dealers resort to using some trading rules, one of which is based on PPP on the assumption that, if the actual exchange rate is different from the level implied by PPP, it tends to converge on that level. Second, PPP is relevant to corporate planning in multinational firms. This is because these firms may adopt the policy of incurring costs in countries where currencies are expected to fall below the level implied by PPP (undervalued) and earning revenue in countries where currencies are expected to rise above that level (becoming overvalued). Third, deviations from PPP imply that real appreciation and depreciation of currencies is possible, which means that there is economic exposure to foreign exchange risk. This is because changes in real exchange rates affect the market shares and competitive positions of business firms.

9.2 The law of one price

The basic version of purchasing power parity can be viewed as a generalisation of the **law of one price (LOP)**. This law stipulates that, in the absence of frictions such as shipping costs and tariffs, the price of a commodity expressed in a common currency is the same in every country. The driving force in this case is **commodity arbitrage**, whereby arbitragers buy the commodity in the market where it is cheap and sell it in the market where it is more expensive. The LOP can be written as

$$P_i = SP_i^* \tag{9.1}$$

where P_i is the domestic price of commodity i, P_i^* is its foreign price and S is the exchange rate expressed as the number of units of the domestic currency per one unit of the foreign currency. Thus, SP_i^* is the domestic currency equivalent of the foreign price of the commodity. Likewise, P_i/S is the foreign currency equivalent of the domestic currency price of the commodity.

We know by now that arbitrage is an activity that is triggered by the violation of an equilibrium condition, which in this case is represented by Equation (9.1). We also know that the process of arbitrage itself restores the equilibrium condition (eliminates arbitrage profit) by changing the forces of supply and demand. In the case of commodity arbitrage, arbitragers buy a commodity in the market where it is cheap and sell it where it is more expensive, making profit as the difference between the selling price and the buying price. This activity leads to a rise in the price of the commodity in the market where it is cheap and a decline in its price in the market where it is expensive until profit is eliminated and the equilibrium condition is restored.

Example

Assume that the price of commodity i in Australia is AUD100 and the exchange rate (AUD/USD) is 1.80. The LOP implies that the equilibrium US price is USD56, because at this price the equilibrium condition represented by Equation (9.1) is not violated and so there is no possibility for profitable arbitrage. This is because the selling price and the buying price measured in the same currency (P_i and SP_i^* respectively) are equal, which produces zero arbitrage profit. If the US price is USD50, then $P_i - SP_i^* > 0$, which means that the no-arbitrage condition is violated and so there is a possibility of profitable arbitrage. Arbitragers make profit by buying the commodity where it is cheap (the United States), paying USD50 (or AUD90) and selling it in Australia at AUD100. Net arbitrage profit is then given by $P_i - SP_i^* =$ AUD10 per unit of the commodity.

Figure 9.1 (on page 249) shows how commodity arbitrage works, starting from the violation of the no-arbitrage condition described by the inequality $P_i > SP_i^*$. Initially, the domestic currency prices of commodity i abroad and at home are SP_{i0}^* and P_{i0}, respectively.

Arbitragers, then, buy the commodity where it is cheaper (in the foreign market), leading to an increase in demand and a shift in the demand curve. They also sell the commodity in the domestic market, leading to an increase in supply. Thus, the price rises in the foreign market and falls in the domestic market, until the former reaches $SP^{\star}_{i1}$ and the latter reaches P_{i1}, which are equal. At this point, arbitrage profit is eliminated and the equilibrium condition is restored.

In reality, however, commodity arbitrage is not as effective as to bring prices into equality and substantial cross-border differences in prices exist. Several reasons can be presented to explain deviations from the LOP, including transportation costs, differences in taste and differences in quality. Remember that for the LOP to work, we must consider exactly similar products in the absence of transportation costs. But even these conditions may not be adequate. Just imagine buying a Big Mac in Melbourne and selling it in New York: by the time it gets there no one would want to buy it, even if it were shipped on Concorde. There are, however, real episodes of commodity arbitrage. In the early 1990s, for example, quantitative restrictions on the imports of alcoholic beverages to the United Kingdom from France were relaxed in the spirit of the European single market. Given that beer was cheaper to buy in France, the English found it profitable to go across the Channel, buy a vanload of French beer and sell it at profit in England. French beer was sold by individuals as far north as Sheffield and Newcastle.

IN PRACTICE

Big Macs and *The Economist* prices

Since 1986, *The Economist* magazine has used the price of a homogenous product, the Big Mac, to show that there are cross-border differences in prices (when measured in the same currency) and to use these prices to calculate the level of exchange rates compatible with the no-arbitrage condition (which *The Economist* calls 'the implied PPP' rate). The idea is very simple. Big Mac prices are recorded in a number of countries, then converted into US dollars and compared. The exchange rate compatible with the LOP or the no-arbitrage rate (per US dollar) is subsequently calculated by dividing the price of a Big Mac in any country by the price in the United States. The deviation of the actual rate from the no-arbitrage rate is calculated and used to indicate the extent of the overvaluation or undervaluation of the dollar (overvaluation is present when the actual rate is higher than the no-arbitrage rate, and vice versa).

In its issue of 27 April 2002, *The Economist* published the following results for some selected currencies (calculations are carried out from a US perspective by assuming that the United States is the home country):

Country	Price (domestic currency)	No-arbitrage exchange rate	Actual exchange rate	Over/under-valuation of USD (%)
United States	2.49			
Australia	3.00	1.20	1.86	+54.4
United Kingdom	1.99	0.80	0.69	−13.7
Canada	3.33	1.34	1.57	+17.4
Indonesia	16 000	6426	9430	+46.8
New Zealand	3.95	1.59	2.24	+41.2

The results show, for example, that the US dollar was overvalued against the Australian dollar by 54.4 per cent, whereas it was undervalued against the pound by 13.7 per cent. The same information can be

Figure 9.1 The effect of commodity arbitrage

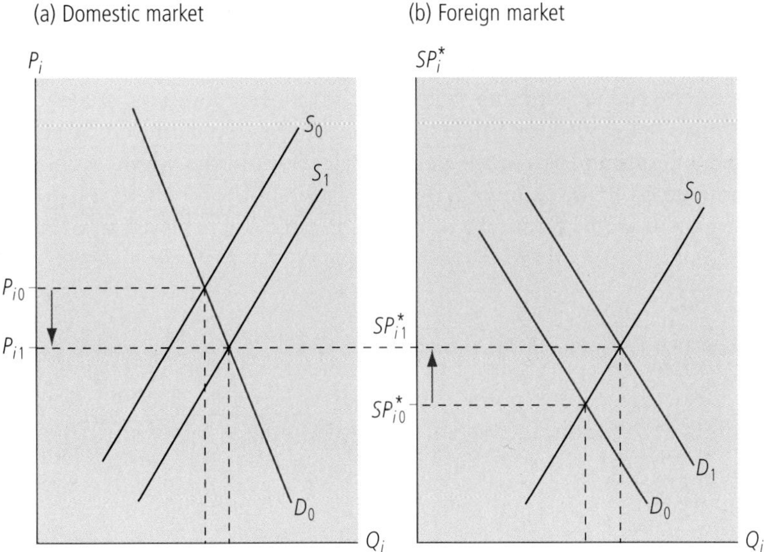

used to calculate the overvaluation or undervaluation of the Australian dollar. For this purpose the no-arbitrage exchange rate (currency/AUD) is calculated by dividing the Big Mac price by the price in Australia. The actual exchange rates against the Australian dollar can be calculated as cross rates from the US dollar rates (you should try this for your self).

The Big Mac is not the only commodity that can be used for this purpose. We could actually use the cover price of *The Economist* itself, as it is a homogenous product (*The Economist* magazine bought in Tokyo is exactly identical to that bought in Melbourne or Auckland). The following table shows the relevant calculations, using the data available in May 2002. We can see that there are significant differences in the prices measured in Australian dollar terms. We can also see that the Australian dollar was undervalued against the Hong Kong dollar and the Japanese yen but overvalued against the currencies of Pakistan, Sri Lanka and Thailand.

Country	Price (domestic currency)	No-arbitrage exchange rate	Actual exchange rate	Over/under-valuation of AUD (%)
Australia	7.95			
Hong Kong	45	5.6604	4.2076	−25.7
India	95	11.95	23.78	+99.0
Japan	920	115.72	68.66	−40.7
New Zealand	9	1.1321	1.2023	+6.2
Pakistan	120	15.09	31.19	+106.6
Philippines	120	15.09	26.08	+72.8
Singapore	9.5	1.1950	0.9783	−18.1
Sri Lanka	200	25.16	44.67	+77.6
Thailand	120	15.09	23.23	+53.9

9.3 From the LOP to PPP

While the LOP applies to the prices of individual commodities (such as a Big Mac and *The Economist*), PPP describes the relationship between the general levels of prices and exchange rates at a particular point in time. What we mean by the general levels of prices here is the price of a basket of commodities or the general price level in the whole economy. PPP can be derived from the LOP by assuming that the latter holds for each and every commodity. Assuming that there are n commodities, the LOP can be generalised to obtain

$$\sum_{i=1}^{n} w_i P_i = S \sum_{i=1}^{n} w_i^* P_i^* \tag{9.2}$$

where w_i and w_i^* are the weights of commodity i in the domestic and foreign price levels, respectively, presumably reflecting consumption patterns. If we assume that the weights assigned to the same commodity are equal across countries (that is, $w_i = w_i^*$ for all i), then

$$P = SP^* \tag{9.3}$$

which is the same as Equation (9.1) except that it is written in terms of the general price levels, P and P^*, and not the prices of individual commodities, P_i and P_i^*. This relationship can be represented diagrammatically by a straight line passing through the origin in the $S-P$ space as shown in Figure 9.2. The line $P = SP_0^*$ represents the PPP relationship when the foreign price level is held constant at P_0^* as measured by the slope of the line. This relationship implies that a rise in the exchange rate from S_0 to S_1 (depreciation of the domestic currency) is associated with a higher domestic price level (a rise from P_0 to P_1). A change in the foreign price level is represented by a shift in the PPP line by rotating around the origin, upwards for an increase ($P_1^* > P_0^*$) and downwards for a decrease ($P_2^* > P_0^*$).

Figure 9.2 Diagrammatic representation of PPP

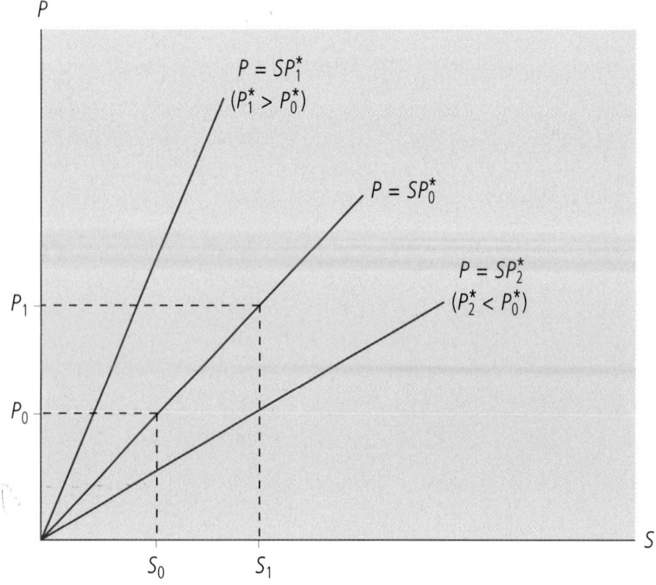

PPP can be viewed as a theory of exchange rate determination because it can be written as

$$S = \frac{P}{P^*} \tag{9.4}$$

Thus, as domestic prices rise relative to foreign prices, S rises (the domestic currency depreciates), and vice versa. For Equation (9.4) to be valid, P and P^* must be measured in terms of the respective currency, being the prices of representative baskets of commodities.

Example

Let us assume that there is a measure of the general price level as a weighted sum of the prices of a basket of commodities as defined by Equation (9.2). If the price of this basket in Australia is AUD1850 and the price of the same basket in the United States is USD1000, the equilibrium exchange rate is calculated by using Equation (9.4) as

$$S = \frac{1850}{1000} = 1.85$$

When P declines to AUD1800, we have

$$S = \frac{1800}{1000} = 1.80$$

which means that when the Australian price level falls from AUD1850 to AUD1800, the exchange rate falls from 1.85 to 1.80.

For PPP (as represented by Equation (9.4)) to hold, there must be no restrictions on the movement of commodities, since any restriction hinders the smooth operation of commodity arbitrage. It is also based on the assumption that there are no transportation costs.

Example

Assume that the cost of shipping the basket of commodities used in the previous example from the United States to Australia is 10 per cent of the price of the basket. If we have the following information, P = AUD1850, P^* = USD1000 and $S = 1.80$, then the exchange rate implied by PPP is

$$\frac{P}{P^*} = \frac{1850}{1000} = 1.85$$

Hence, PPP is violated (at an exchange rate of 1.80) such that $SP^* < P$. Arbitragers will buy the basket of commodities in the United States at USD1000 and ship it to Australia at a total cost of USD1100. Arbitrage will stop when

$$1100S = 1850$$

or when

$$S = \frac{1850}{1100} = 1.68$$

Without transportation costs, arbitrage will stop when $S = 1.85$. In the presence of transportation costs, equilibrium is achieved at a lower exchange rate, such that the PPP equation becomes

$$S = \frac{1.68}{1.85}\left(\frac{P}{P^*}\right) = 0.91\left(\frac{P}{P^*}\right)$$

In the real world, there are transportation costs, trade impediments and extensive product differentiation. Also, there are non-traded goods and there is no simple relationship between the prices of these goods in various countries. In general, the relationship should be taken to imply that the exchange rate 'is determined by', rather than 'is equal to', the price ratio.

INSIGHT

Proportionality, symmetry and exclusiveness in PPP

Three properties of the PPP relationship are often discussed in the literature: **proportionality symmetry** and **exclusiveness**. The following is a brief description of these properties.

Proportionality means that the nominal exchange rate and the price ratio change in a proportional manner. This means that a 10 per cent rise in the domestic price level relative to the foreign price level brings about a 10 per cent depreciation of the domestic currency.

Symmetry implies that changes in the domestic and foreign price levels have equal but opposite changes in the nominal exchange rate. This means that if a 10 per cent rise in the domestic price level brings about a 6 per cent depreciation of the domestic currency, an equal rise in the foreign price level brings about a 6 per cent appreciation of the domestic currency. By definition, proportionality implies symmetry.

Exclusiveness means that only prices affect the nominal exchange rate (that is, other variables such as interest rates do not affect the exchange rate).

These properties do not hold in practice, except under hyperinflation, as shown by Moosa.[1] Tawadros examined the properties using Australian data over the period 1985–1996 and found no evidence for symmetry and proportionality.[2] Furthermore, he could not reject the hypothesis of exclusiveness.

1 I. A. Moosa, 'Testing Proportionality, Symmetry and Exclusiveness in Long Run PPP', *Journal of Economic Studies*, 21, 1994, pp. 3–21.

2 G. Tawadros, 'Purchasing Power Parity in the Long Run: Evidence from Australia's Recent Float', *Applied Financial Economics*, 11, 2001, pp. 1–7.

9.4 PPP as a comparative statics relationship

PPP can be used to describe the relationship between the values assumed by an exchange rate at two points in time under the influence of changes in prices. If PPP holds at two points in time, 0 and 1, then we have $P_0 = S_0 P_0^{\star}$ and $P_1 = S_1 P_1^{\star}$, which gives

$$\frac{P_1}{P_0} = \frac{S_1}{S_0} \frac{P_1^{\star}}{P_0^{\star}} \tag{9.5}$$

or

$$(1 + \dot{P}) = (1 + \dot{S})(1 + \dot{P}^{\star}) \tag{9.6}$$

where a dot represents the rate of change of the underlying variable, and so $\dot{P}$ and $\dot{P}^{\star}$ are the domestic and foreign inflation rates, respectively, whereas $\dot{S}$ is the rate of change of the exchange rate. Equation (9.6) can be manipulated to obtain

$$\dot{S} = \dot{P} - \dot{P}^{\star} \tag{9.7}$$

by ignoring the term $\dot{S}\dot{P}^*$ on the assumption that it is too small. Equation (9.7) is a comparative statics representation of the relationship between the exchange rate and inflation differentials, stipulating that the rate of change of the exchange rate should be equal to the inflation differential. If $\dot{P} > \dot{P}^*$, then $\dot{S} > 0$, which implies domestic currency depreciation, and vice versa. This tells us that if a country had a higher inflation rate than its trading partners, its currency would depreciate.

RESEARCH FINDINGS

Adjusting academic salaries for PPP

Imagine that a US academic is invited to take up a senior lecturer's position in Australia at a salary of AUD65 000, when her present salary in the United States is USD45 000. At an exchange rate of 1.80, the proposed Australian salary would be USD36 111. The academic would thus jump to the conclusion that the offer is not good enough. Is this conclusion necessarily right? The answer is 'not necessarily'.

The problem with this conclusion is that it is based on the assumption that income earned in Australia would be spent in the United States, which is not the case. The most important consideration is whether or not this academic can buy more goods and services for AUD65 000 in Australia than she can buy with USD45 000 in the United States. What should be compared are not the nominal salaries measured in the same currency but rather their purchasing power. This can be done if the Australian salary is converted into US dollars, not at the current exchange rate but rather at the PPP rate.

An interesting study by Ong and Mitchell investigated this issue with the objective of comparing academic salaries in various countries.[1] They compared academic salaries in the United States, Australia and other countries by measuring them at both the current nominal exchange rate and the PPP rate. For a senior lecturer's 1997 salary, the following results were obtained:

Country	Domestic currency salary	USD salary at the nominal rate	USD salary at the PPP rate
United States	49 695	—	—
Australia	59 600	46 202	57 864
United Kingdom	32 487	53 257	43 315
Canada	61 415	44 183	51 609
New Zealand	64 295	44 339	47 981
Singapore	104 695	72 705	84 431
South Africa	96 306	21 740	29 909

The results show that the picture is completely different when the PPP rates are used for converting salaries. Australia was not bad after all, but Singapore is far ahead. The differences are due to the overvaluation of the US dollar. For the same reasons, countries' GDP and GDP per capita are compared on the basis of PPP rates.

1 L. L. Ong and J. D. Mitchell, 'Professors and Hamburgers: An International Comparison of Real Academic Salaries', *Applied Economics*, 32, 2000, pp. 869–76.

Example

Suppose that during a particular period of time the Australian inflation rate was 4 per cent and the US inflation rate was 2 per cent. According to PPP, the percentage change in the exchange rate is given by

$$\dot{S} = 4 - 2 = 2\%$$

If the initial level of the exchange rate was 1.80, the new level of the exchange rate is 2 per cent above the initial level. Hence

$$S = 1.02 \times 1.80 = 1.836$$

The US dollar should have appreciated against the Australian dollar by 2 per cent during this time period, taking the exchange rate to 1.836.

Deriving PPP from the supply and demand model

PPP can also be derived from the supply and demand model of Chapter 4, as shown in Figure 9.3. The right-hand side of the diagram describes supply and demand in the foreign exchange market, whereas the left-hand side describes PPP. If, during the period between points in time 0 and 1, the domestic inflation rate is greater than the foreign inflation rate, the ratio of domestic prices to foreign prices will be higher at time 1 than at time 0. Thus, the price ratio will rise from $(P/P^*)_0$ to $(P/P^*)_1$ and the exchange rate will rise from S_0 to S_1.

The corresponding story in the foreign exchange market goes as follows. If the domestic inflation rate is higher than the foreign inflation rate, the demand for imports rises (and so does the demand for foreign exchange), shifting the demand curve to the right. The demand for exports, on the other hand, falls (and so does the supply of foreign exchange), shifting the supply curve to the left. The exchange rate consequently rises from S_0 to S_1 (that is, the domestic currency depreciates). The relationship between S_0 and S_1 can be written as

$$\frac{S_1}{S_0} = \frac{P_1 / P_1^*}{P_0 / P_0^*} \tag{9.8}$$

or

$$S_1 = S_0\left(\frac{P_1 / P_1^*}{P_0 / P_0^*}\right) = S_0\left(\frac{P_1 / P_0}{P_1^* / P_0^*}\right) \tag{9.9}$$

which can be written as

$$S_1 = S_0\left(\frac{1 + \dot{P}}{1 + \dot{P}^*}\right) \tag{9.10}$$

Equations (9.9) and (9.10) tell us the following: starting from a base time period, 0, with an exchange rate, S_0, the exchange rate at time 1, S_1, will differ from S_0 by a factor reflecting domestic and foreign inflation rates. Thus, Equations (9.9) and (9.10) can be used to calculate the exchange rate consistent with PPP, or what may be called the **PPP exchange rate**. The underlying idea is that if PPP held during the period between 0 and 1, in the sense that relative inflation is the only factor determining the exchange rate, there will be no deviation from the PPP rate. Deviation, however, arises because of the effect of factors other than inflation on the exchange rate.

Figure 9.3 PPP as derived from the foreign exchange market

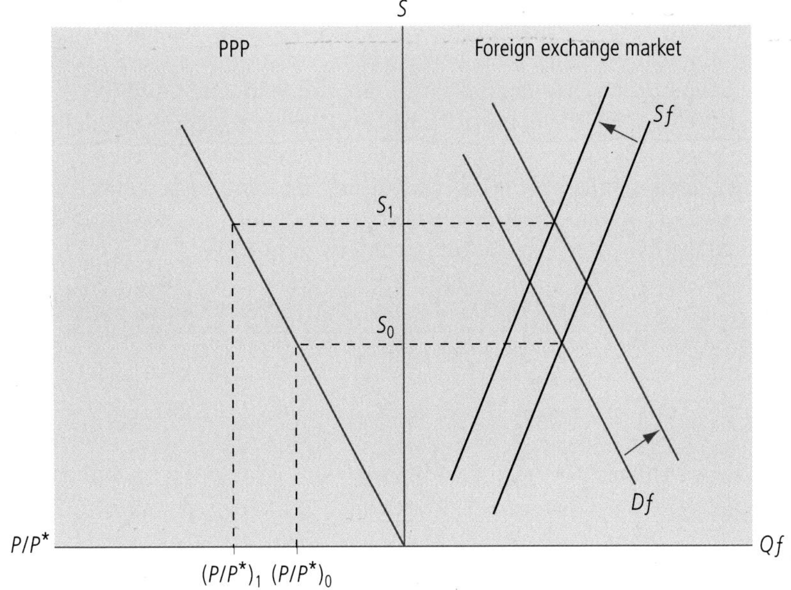

In general, the PPP exchange rate at any point in time, t, starting from a base period 0, is given by

$$\bar{S}_t = S_0\left(\frac{P_t / P_0}{P_t^{\star} / P_0^{\star}}\right) \tag{9.11}$$

The percentage deviation of the actual exchange rate from the PPP rate, D, is calculated as

$$D = 100\left(\frac{S - \bar{S}}{\bar{S}}\right) \tag{9.12}$$

Implications of PPP for the behaviour of the real exchange rate

PPP implies that the real exchange rate does not change because any change in prices will be totally offset by changes in the nominal exchange rate. This proposition can be verified as follows. The real exchange rate at points in time 0 and 1 is given respectively by $Q_0 = S_0(P_0^{\star} / P_0)$ and $Q_1 = S_1(P_1^{\star} / P_1)$. Hence

$$Q_1 = S_0(1+\dot{S})P_0^{\star}(1+\dot{P}^{\star})/[P_0(1+\dot{P})] \tag{9.13}$$

Since PPP implies that $S_0(1+\dot{S}) = P_0(1+\dot{P})/[P_0^{\star}(1+\dot{P}^{\star})]$, it follows that

$$Q_1 = Q_0 \tag{9.14}$$

Example

The following table contains data on nominal exchange rates, prices and real exchange rates as observed in January 1999 and January 2002. By calculating the percentage changes in the nominal exchange rates, prices (that is, inflation rates), real exchange rates and inflation differentials (versus Australia), we find the following results:

- The percentage changes in the nominal exchange rate and the interest rate differential are not close, let alone equal. In one case (the EUR/AUD rate) they have the opposite signs. The Australian dollar should have depreciated against the euro, but it appreciated instead.
- There are significant movements in real exchange rates, which is not what PPP predicts.
- By January 2002, there were significant deviations from PPP.

	January 1999	January 2002	Percentage change/differential
S(JPY/AUD)	71.87	68.08	−5.3
S(USD/AUD)	0.6351	0.5126	−19.3
S(EUR/AUD)	0.5471	0.5808	6.2
P(Australia)	104.41	115.97	11.1
P(Japan)	102.33	99.89	−2.4
P(United States)	107.80	116.20	7.8
P(Europe)	108.80	114.30	5.1
Q(JPY/AUD)	71.87	77.47	7.8
Q(USD/AUD)	0.6351	0.5282	−16.8
Q(EUR/AUD)	0.5471	0.6141	12.2
DIFFERENTIAL (Japan)			−13.5
DIFFERENTIAL (United States)			−3.3
DIFFERENTIAL (Europe)			−6.0
$\bar{S}$*(JPY/AUD)*		63.16	
$\bar{S}$*(USD/AUD)*		0.6165	
$\bar{S}$*(EUR/AUD)*		0.5175	
D(JPY/AUD)		7.69	
D(USD/AUD)		−16.83	
D(EUR/AUD)		12.23	

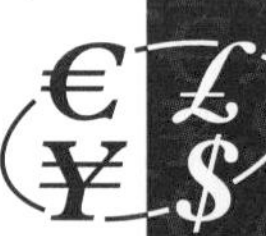

IN PRACTICE

What do foreign exchange traders think of PPP?

In a survey of the views and practices of foreign exchange traders in the US market, Cheung and Chinn asked these traders what they thought of PPP.[1] The following are some of the responses they got:

- A majority of 63 per cent responded by saying that 'PPP is merely academic jargon'.
- Only 11 per cent believed that PPP gave fair exchange rates.
- Most agreed that 'PPP is rarely reached or maintained'.
- Some stated that 'it should work but it does not, perhaps because the basket [of commodities] is wrong or that it excludes capital flows and real interest rates'.
- A dollar overvaluation as indicated by PPP would induce no action by 81 per cent of the traders surveyed. Only 13 per cent would sell the currency.
- Some 93 per cent of the respondents said that PPP has no role at the intraday horizon. About 80 per cent said that PPP was irrelevant at horizons of up to six months.

1 Y. W. Cheung and M. D. Chinn, 'Macroeconomic Implications of the Beliefs and Behavior of Foreign Exchange Traders', NBER Working Paper, No. 7417, November 1999.

9.5 The empirical validity of PPP

While PPP is a plausible theoretical proposition, there seems to be little empirical evidence that supports its validity, particularly in the short run, except under hyperinflation and over long periods of time. To verify this proposition, we examine some data on the exchange rates between the Australian dollar and four currencies going back to 1988.

RESEARCH FINDINGS

Testing the empirical validity of PPP

PPP has been tested extensively in the literature. Formal tests of the theory are based on either the behaviour of the real exchange rate or the relationship between the nominal exchange rate and the price ratio. The following is a summary of the empirical findings:

- There is mixed evidence on PPP during the post-Bretton Woods flexible exchange rates era.
- Most of the studies testing the performance of PPP in countries experiencing high inflation rates (or even better experiencing hyperinflation) have produced supportive evidence.
- Some economists argue that the failure of PPP in the post-Bretton Woods era is a 'dollar phenomenon'. This means that PPP will fail when bilateral exchange rates against the US dollar are used because of its special status. However, tests based on non-dollar currencies have not been highly supportive either.
- Results of empirical testing are sensitive to the data frequency, time horizon and sample size. Most researchers documenting supportive evidence have generally used annual data spanning a century or longer.
- Some studies have found evidence indicating that the validity of PPP is affected by government intervention and announcements concerning exchange rate policies.
- PPP seems to perform better when wholesale prices rather than consumer prices are used. This is probably due to the fact that wholesale prices represent the prices of traded goods.

What matters for business firms is the undisputable conclusion that although PPP may hold over a very long period of time, there are significant and persistent short-run deviations from PPP, which implies that changes in prices are not completely offset by changes in nominal exchange rates. The resulting changes in the real exchange rate affects the competitive positions of firms and hence the rise of economic risk. Moosa and Bhatti have documented the evidence on PPP.[1]

[1] I. A. Moosa and R. H. Bhatti, *International Parity Conditions: Theory, Econometric Testing and Empirical Evidence*, Macmillan, London, 1997.

Figure 9.4 shows the behaviour of the actual exchange rate and the PPP rate as calculated from Equation (9.11) using December 1988 as the base period. We can see that there are significant deviations from PPP. For example, the Australian dollar has been massively undervalued against the US dollar, the Japanese yen and the pound. Figure 9.5 shows the behaviour of the nominal and real exchange rates. It is obvious that there are significant changes in the real exchange rate, which should not be the case if PPP were valid. We can also see that the nominal and real exchange rates are highly correlated, which again is inconsistent with PPP, as it implies that the real exchange rate should not follow the nominal rate. And Figure 9.6 shows scatter diagrams of the percentage changes in the exchange rate on the inflation differential. Not only are they unequal, they are not even highly correlated. Percentage changes in the real exchange rate appear to be more significant than the inflation differential.

Figure 9.4 Actual and PPP exchange rates

(a) AUD/USD

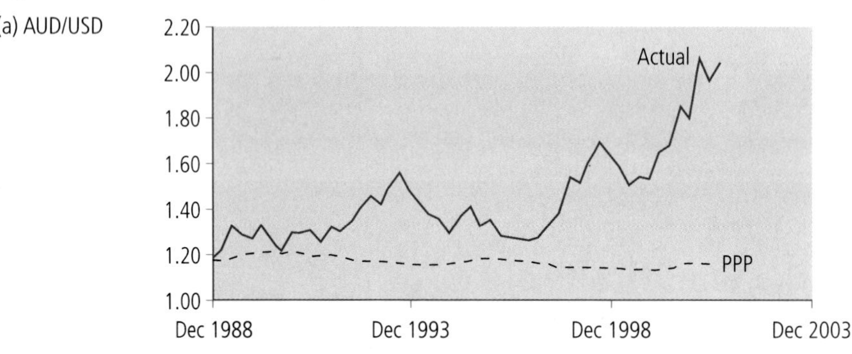

(b) AUD/JPY

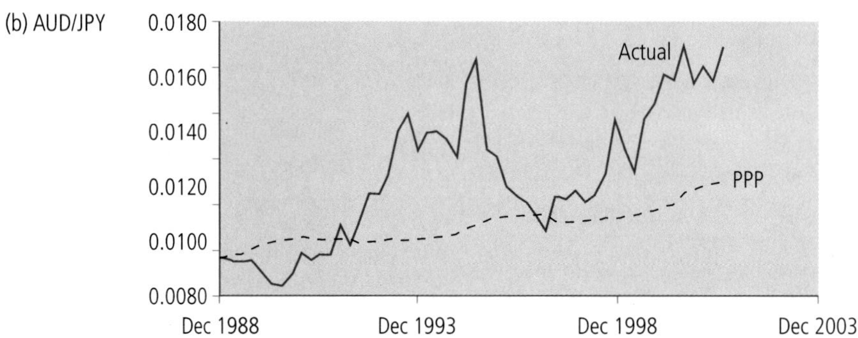

(c) AUD/GBP

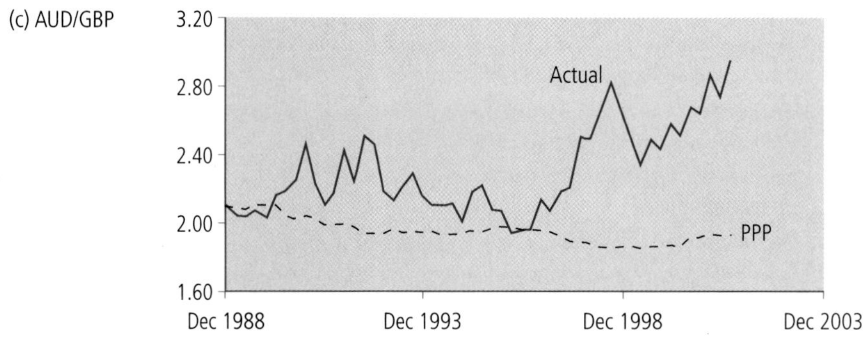

(d) AUD/CAD

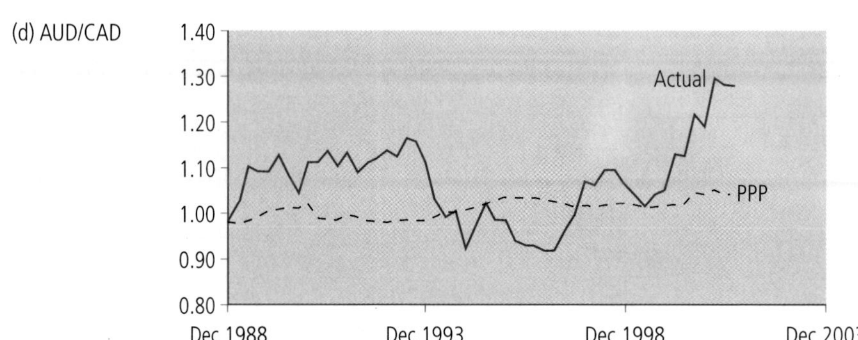

Source: Main Economic Indicators, OECD.

Figure 9.5 Nominal and real exchange rates

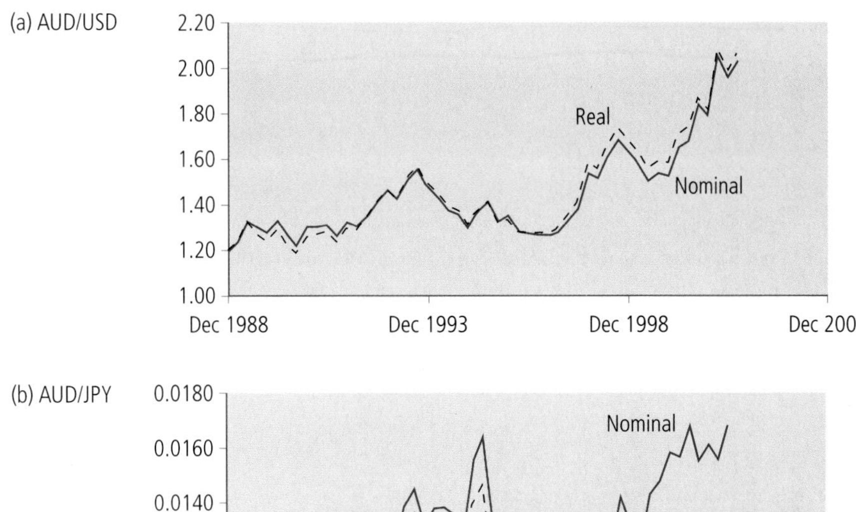

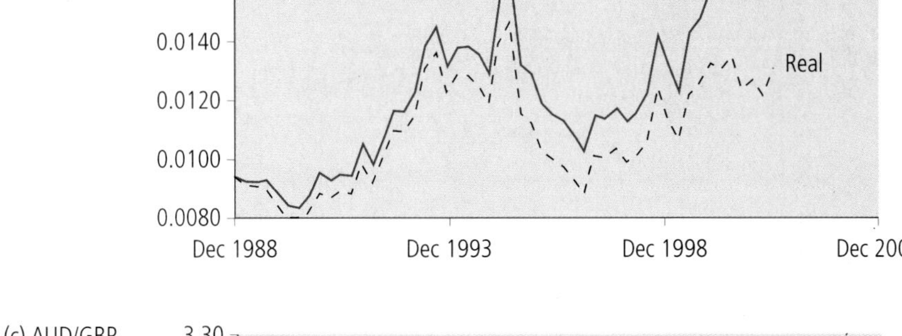

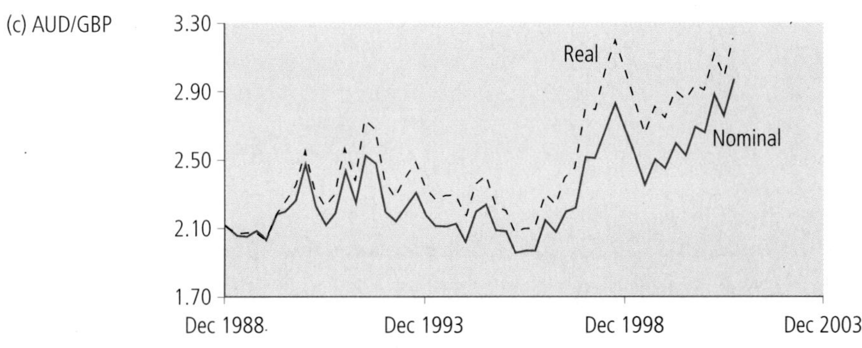

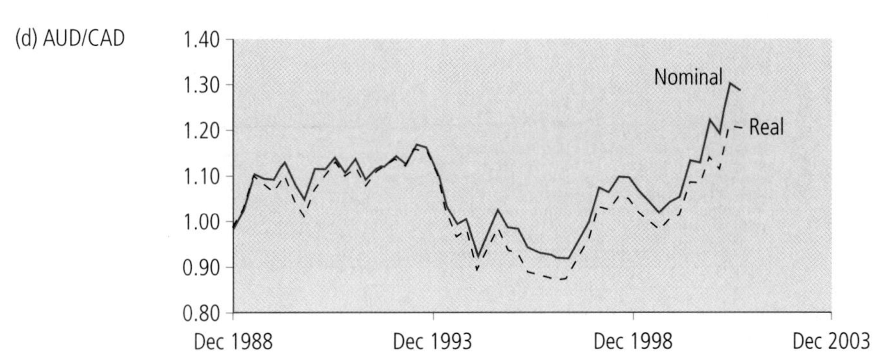

Source: Main Economic Indicators, OECD.

Figure 9.6 Scatter diagrams of percentage changes in exchange rates on inflation differentials

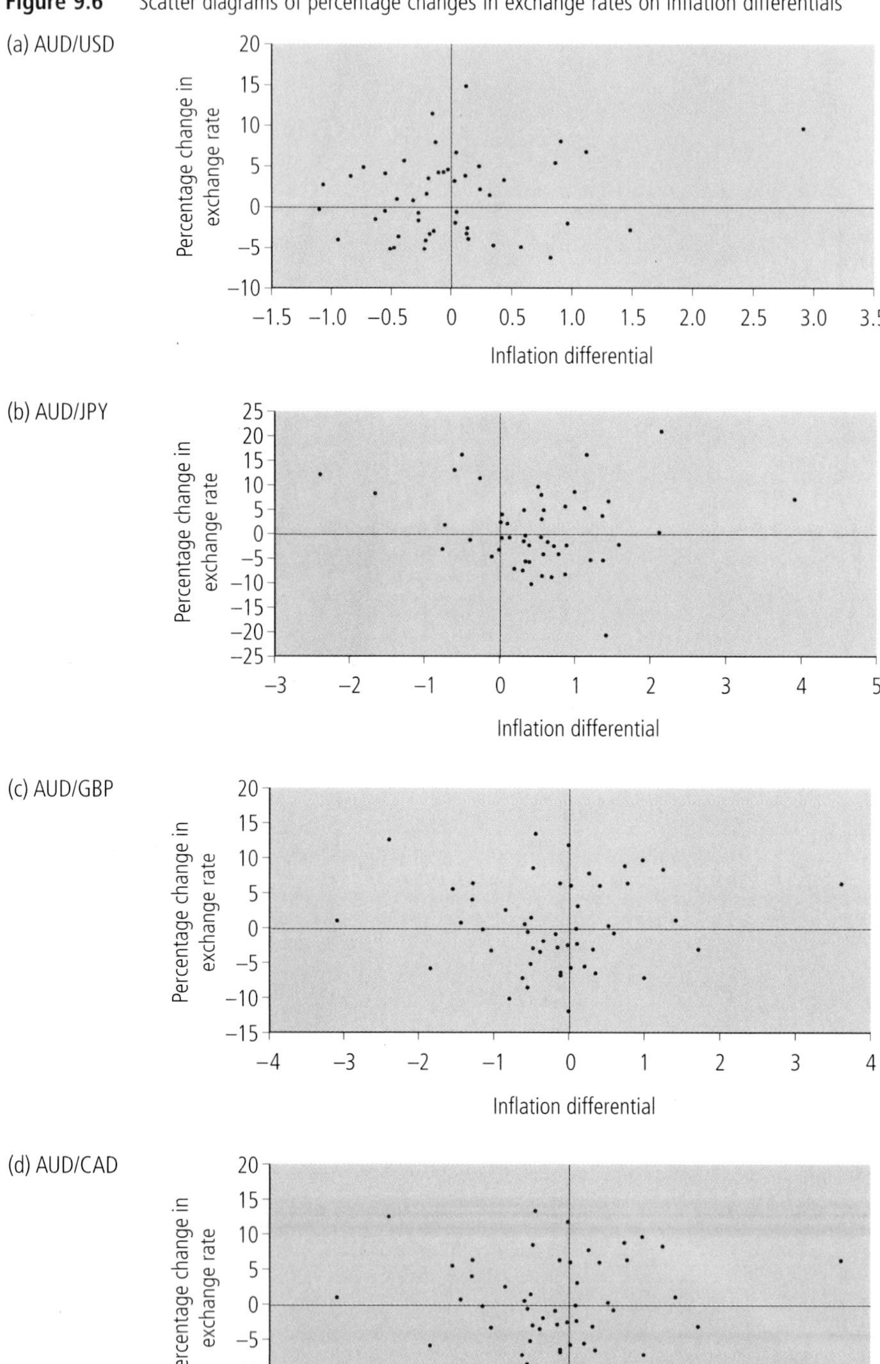

Source: Main Economic Indicators, OECD.

9.6 PPP as a trading rule

Deviations from PPP are most likely due to the effect of factors other than prices on exchange rates. Thus, we may specify the PPP and actual exchange rates as follows

$$\bar{S} = f\left(\frac{P}{P^*}\right) \tag{9.15}$$

and

$$S = F(\bar{S}, X_1, X_2, \ldots, X_n) \tag{9.16}$$

where the Xs are variables other than prices that affect exchange rates (for example, interest rates). Equation (9.15) tells us that the PPP rate, $\bar{S}$, is determined by prices. It is regarded as the long-term equilibrium value of the exchange rate. On the other hand, Equation (9.16) tells us that the current exchange rate, S, is determined in the short run by $\bar{S}$ as well as by other factors that give rise to deviation from PPP. This description of the determination of the exchange rate in the short run and the long run is the basis of using PPP as a trading rule. Figure 9.7 illustrates the behaviour of the price ratio, P/P^*, the PPP exchange rate, $\bar{S}$, and the current exchange rate, S. It shows that while $\bar{S}$ follows the movement of prices closely, S does not because of the effect of other factors, giving rise to deviations of S from $\bar{S}$, although the former turns to go back to the latter with the passage of time.

Figure 9.7 Long-run and short-run behaviour of exchange rates

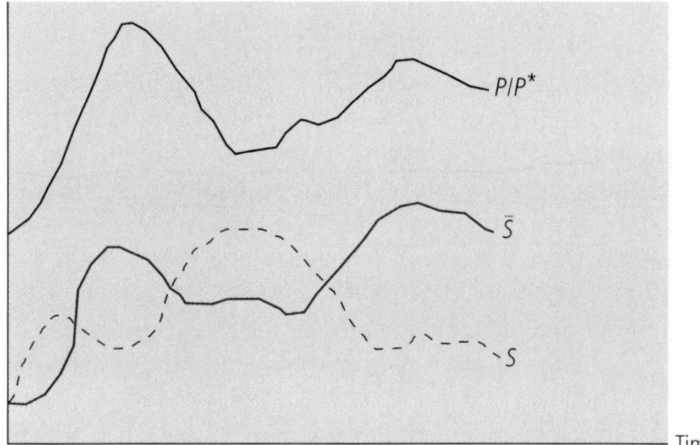

Figure 9.8 shows how the PPP trading rule works. If $S > \bar{S}$, then the foreign currency is overvalued and so it should be sold. If, on the other hand, $S < \bar{S}$, the foreign currency is undervalued and so it should be bought. A trading rule can therefore be the following: sell the foreign currency when the exchange rate is x per cent above its PPP value and buy the foreign currency when the exchange rate is x per cent below its PPP value. It is obvious that this rule does not capture the highs and lows of the exchange rate, but in practice no trader tries to do this because it is a risky endeavour.

Figure 9.8 Buying and selling a foreign currency using a PPP rule

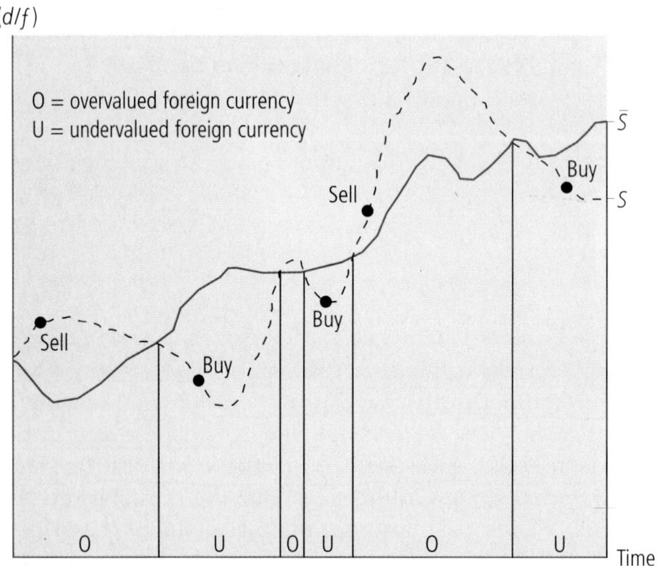

9.7 The monetary model of exchange rates

The **monetary model of exchange rates** combines PPP and the **quantity theory of money** to explain the exchange rate in terms of the money supply, income and prices. The idea behind the model is simple: the exchange rate is the price of one kind of national money in terms of another national money. Hence, when there is too much of one kind of money relative to the other, the price of the first money falls (the underlying currency depreciates). The effects of all the explanatory variables on the exchange rate run through the demand for and supply of money.

Let us assume that there is a stable demand for money function represented by

$$M_d = kPY \tag{9.17}$$

where M_d is the quantity of money demanded, P is the price level, Y is real income and k is a positive constant. Assuming also an exogenous money supply, M, equilibrium in the money market yields

$$P = \frac{M}{kY} \tag{9.18}$$

If PPP holds, then $S = P/P^*$. By substituting (9.18), we obtain

$$S = \frac{M}{kP^*Y} \tag{9.19}$$

where $P^\star$ is the foreign price level. The monetary model, as represented by Equation (9.19), tells us the following:

- A monetary expansion leads to a proportional rise in S (that is, depreciation of the domestic currency).
- A rise in income leads to a fall in S (that is, appreciation of the domestic currency).
- A rise in the foreign price level leads to a fall in S (that is, appreciation of the domestic currency).

Figure 9.9 shows how the model works. A rise in the money supply from M_0 to M_1 causes a proportional increase in the price level from P_0 to P_1, which is a prediction of the quantity theory of money. This change in the price level leads, via PPP, to a proportional increase in the exchange rate from S_0 to S_1.

RESEARCH FINDINGS

The empirical validity of the monetary model of exchange rates

The monetary model of exchange rates in its various forms has been tested extensively. Testing this model amounts to testing several hypotheses about the effect of various variables on the exchange rate.

The weight of the empirical evidence suggests that the monetary model's ability to explain and predict movements in exchange rates is unsatisfactory. However, it has been found that the monetary model works well under hyperinflationary conditions. Frenkel found some evidence for the monetary model, using data from the German hyperinflation of the 1920s.[1] The empirical failure of the monetary model is attributed to the failure of its constituent components (such as PPP), as well as some of its implicit assumptions. Moreover, it has been attributed to the presence of speculative bubbles.

On the other hand, some economists argue that, while the monetary model cannot explain short-run movements in exchange rates, it is an adequate representation of the relationship from which the exchange rate is derived in the long run. This postulation is based on the results of cointegration tests obtained by MacDonald and Taylor[2] and Moosa.[3] MacDonald and Taylor even found some evidence that the monetary model can outperform a random walk model in its predictive power.[4] A full survey of this evidence is found in Taylor.[5]

Although the empirical evidence for the monetary model is not strong, it remains a useful analytical tool for policy purposes and investment strategies. For example, the model correctly warns that pursuing an excessively expansionary monetary policy will lead to a depreciation of the domestic currency. Hence, monetary restraint is required to avoid currency depreciation. Since the monetary model offers useful insights into the way changes in monetary policy influence exchange rates, the currency composition of investment and financing portfolios should be determined by the current and anticipated monetary policy stance in various countries.

1 J. A. Frenkel, 'A Monetary Approach to the Exchange Rate: Doctrinal Aspects and Empirical Evidence', *Scandinavian Journal of Economics*, 78, 1976, pp. 200–4.

2 R. MacDonald and M. P. Taylor, 'The Monetary Approach to the Exchange Rate: Long-Run Relationships and Coefficient Restrictions', *Economics Letters*, 37, 1991, pp. 179–85.

3 I. A. Moosa, 'The Monetary Model of Exchange Rates Revisited', *Applied Financial Economics*, 4, 1994, pp. 279–87.

4 R. MacDonald and M. P. Taylor, 'The Monetary Model of Exchange Rates: Long-Run Relationships, Short-Run Dynamics and How to Beat a Random Walk', *Journal of International Money and Finance*, 13, 1994, pp. 276–90.

5 M. P. Taylor, 'The Economics of Exchange Rates', *Journal of Economic Literature*, 33, 1995, pp. 13–47.

A rise in income, according to this model, leads to a rise in the demand for money, and, given an unchanged money supply, an excess demand for money will emerge. This excess demand for money has the same effect as a reduction in the nominal money supply, which can be traced in Figure 9.9. A reduction in the money supply from M_1 to M_0 reduces the price level from P_1 to P_0 and the exchange rate from S_1 to S_0. Thus, the monetary model predicts that a higher level of domestic income leads to domestic currency appreciation, which is in contrast with the prediction of the model presented in Chapter 4. This is due to a basic difference between the two models.

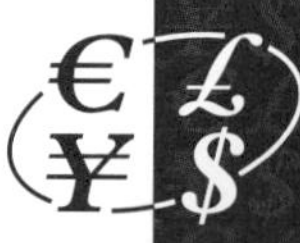

IN PRACTICE

Economic theory and foreign exchange trading

So far we have studied a variety of models that tell us different things about the effect of a change in a macroeconomic variable on the exchange rate. In practice, foreign exchange traders tend to interpret news items in different ways and this is why some of them sell and others buy in reaction to the same piece of news.

Consider the following news items that are relevant to the exchange rate between the Australian and US currencies:

1. 'The RBA announced that the Australian money supply increased by 8 per cent in the previous month.'
2. 'The Australian short-term interest rate jumped from 6.5 to 7.5 per cent.'
3. 'The federal government predicted that the Australian economy would grow by 5 per cent in real terms in the coming fiscal year. Private sector economists seem to agree with this prediction.'
4. 'The federal government announced that public debt as a percentage of GDP would decline by one percentage point in the coming fiscal year.'
5. 'The Treasurer announced that the current account deficit as a percentage of GDP would decline.'

The following is the reasoning why the Australian dollar should be sold in response to each news item:

1. A monetary expansion causes inflation. Both PPP and the monetary model tell us that the domestic currency should depreciate.
2. A higher interest rate depresses economic activity, which is bad for the currency.
3. Growth leads to an increase in imports, which has adverse effects on the current account and the currency.
4. When public debt shrinks, less pressure will be exerted on domestic interest rates. Lower interest rates make domestic assets less attractive, leading to currency depreciation.
5. A smaller current account deficit leads to a smaller budget deficit, lower interest rates and a weaker currency.

On the other hand, the following is the reasoning why the Australian dollar should be bought in reaction to the same news items:

1. The RBA will react by raising interest rates, leading to currency appreciation.
2. Higher interest rates attract capital inflows, leading to currency appreciation.
3. Growth leads to higher profitability and flourishing financial markets. The resulting capital inflows lead to currency appreciation.
4. As public debt shrinks foreign investors will have more confidence in the economy. Capital inflows will increase, leading to currency appreciation.
5. A smaller current account deficit is good for the currency.

Figure 9.9 The monetary model of exchange rates

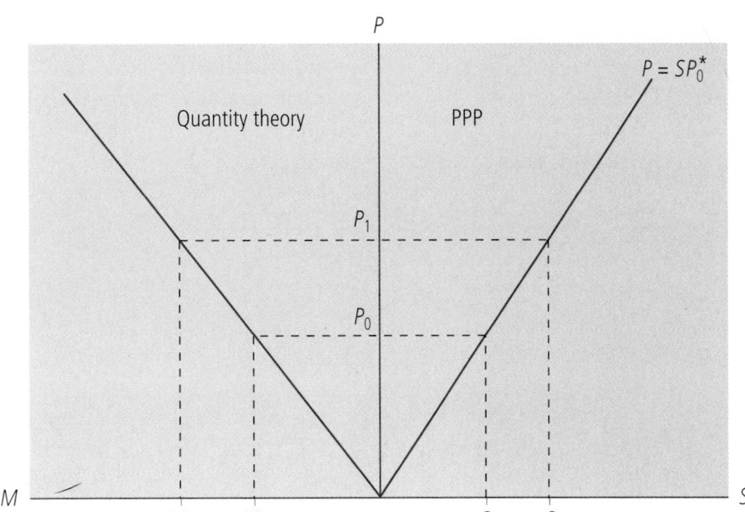

Summary

- PPP theory, which describes the relationship between exchange rates and prices, is important for the operations of international firms. This is because deviations from PPP imply the existence of economic exposure to foreign exchange risk. It is also important because it provides a measure of the long-run equilibrium value of the exchange rate.
- The law of one price (LOP) stipulates that in the absence of shipping costs and tariffs, the price of a commodity expressed in a common currency is the same in every country. Any deviation from this relationship is eliminated by commodity arbitrage.
- PPP stipulates that the percentage change in the exchange rate is determined by the inflation differential. It also implies that the real exchange rate does not change over time.
- The empirical evidence for PPP is rather weak. While there is some evidence for PPP in the long run, there are significant and persistent deviations from it in the short run. However, the hypothesis appears to be valid under hyperinflation and over a long period of time.
- PPP can be used as a trading rule in the foreign exchange market. A currency is bought when it is undervalued and sold when it is overvalued. Undervaluation and overvaluation are indicated by the value of the actual exchange rate relative to what is implied by PPP.
- The monetary model of exchange rates can be derived by combining PPP and the quantity theory of money. It tells us that the exchange rate is determined by the relative money supply.

MAXIMISE YOUR MARKS! There are 30 interactive questions for this chapter available online at **www.mhhe.com/au/moosa2e**

Key terms

Review questions

1. Why did the collapse of the Bretton Woods system lead to a resurgence of interest in the PPP hypothesis?
2. In what sense is PPP relevant to business operations?
3. Explain how the equilibrium condition implied by the LOP is maintained and restored when it is violated.
4. How can we derive PPP from the LOP?
5. Explain how PPP can be derived from the supply and demand model of exchange rate determination.
6. How can the LOP and PPP be used to measure the extent of currency overvaluation and undervaluation?
7. What is the exchange rate consistent with PPP, or the so-called PPP exchange rate?
8. What is wrong with comparing incomes earned in different countries by expressing them in terms of one currency at the current exchange rates?
9. What is the implication of PPP for the real exchange rate?
10. What is the rationale for using PPP as a currency trading rule?
11. Why did the German mark depreciate rapidly during the German hyperinflation of 1919–1923?
12. Select some foreign exchange stories from various issues of the *Australian Financial Review*. Identify the effects of macroeconomic variables (such as inflation and interest rates) on the exchange rate of the Australian dollar. Are there any inconsistencies in these stories?
13. According to the monetary model of exchange rates, explain what happens to the domestic currency if: (i) there is a domestic currency expansion; (ii) domestic income falls; and (iii) the domestic price level rises.
14. The supply and demand model of Chapter 4 predicts that the domestic currency depreciates as domestic income rises. The monetary model predicts that the domestic currency appreciates as income rises. Why does this contradiction arise?

Problems

1. The price of a commodity in New Zealand is NZD10, whereas the price of the same commodity in Australia is AUD6. The current exchange rate (NZD/AUD) is 1.15.
   (a) Is there a violation of the LOP?
   (b) If so, what will happen?

(c) What is the Australian dollar price compatible with the LOP at the current exchange rate?
(d) At the current Australian dollar price, what is the exchange rate compatible with the LOP?

2 At the end of 2002 the exchange rate between *x* and *y* (*x*/*y*) was 1.65. If the expected inflation rates in the countries whose currencies are *x* and *y* are 5 and 7 per cent respectively, what is the exchange rate that is expected to prevail at the end of 2003?

3 The bilateral exchange rates of the domestic currency, *x*, and three foreign currencies (a, b and c) against a numeraire, *k*, at times 0, 1 and 2 are as follows:

	0	1	2
x/*k*	1.50	1.60	1.20
a/*k*	2.10	2.20	2.15
b/*k*	0.60	0.80	0.75
c/*k*	3.20	3.40	3.45

The price levels of the four countries (indicated by upper case letters) are as follows:

	0	1	2
X	100	105	110
A	100	115	125
B	100	102	108
C	100	104	112

(a) Calculate the nominal bilateral exchange rates against *x*, using direct quotation from the perspective of country X.
(b) Calculate the inflation rates in the four countries in periods 1 and 2.
(c) Calculate the percentage changes in the nominal bilateral exchange rates in periods 1 and 2.
(d) Are the results of (b) and (c) supportive of PPP?
(e) Calculate the real bilateral exchange rates and their percentage rates of change. Are the results supportive of PPP?
(f) Compare the percentage changes in the bilateral nominal and real exchange rates. Can you conclude anything about the validity of PPP?
(g) Calculate the nominal bilateral exchange rates compatible with PPP.
(h) Calculate the percentage deviations of the actual rates from the PPP rates and state whether currency *x* is overvalued or undervalued.

4 The following table contains a set of quarterly data on the exchange rates and prices of Australia, Canada and the United States over the period 1996–2001. Use this data set to do the following:
(a) Calculate the nominal bilateral exchange rates in direct quotation from an Australian perspective.
(b) Calculate the quarterly inflation rates in the three countries.
(c) Calculate the percentage changes in the exchange rates.
(d) Plot two scatter diagrams (one for each exchange rate) of the percentage change in the exchange rate on the inflation differential. Are the results supportive of PPP?
(e) Calculate the PPP exchange rates and the percentage deviations of the actual rates from the PPP rates. Plot the actual rates and the PPP rates and also plot the percentage deviations. Are the results supportive of PPP?
(f) Calculate the real exchange rates of the Australian dollar against the two currencies. Plot the real and nominal rates against time. Are the results supportive of PPP?

	CAD/USD	AUD/USD	Australia	United States	Canada
Mar 1996	1.3593	1.2783	101.9	101.7	100.8
Jun 1996	1.3637	1.2698	102.6	102.7	101.5
Sep 1996	1.3620	1.2636	102.9	103.3	101.7
Dec 1996	1.3705	1.2583	103.0	104.0	102.3
Mar 1997	1.3847	1.2723	103.2	104.7	102.9
Jun 1997	1.3810	1.3266	103.0	105.1	103.2
Sep 1997	1.3811	1.3778	102.5	105.5	103.4
Dec 1997	1.4303	1.5378	102.8	106.0	103.4
Mar 1998	1.4195	1.5108	103.0	106.2	103.9
Jun 1998	1.4677	1.6145	103.6	106.8	104.2
Sep 1998	1.5319	1.6855	103.9	107.2	104.3
Dec 1998	1.5303	1.6332	104.4	107.6	104.5
Mar 1999	1.5087	1.5765	104.3	108.0	104.8
Jun 1999	1.4730	1.4981	104.8	109.1	105.9
Sep 1999	1.4680	1.5336	105.7	109.8	106.6
Dec 1999	1.4442	1.5244	106.3	110.4	107.0
Mar 2000	1.4495	1.6474	107.2	111.5	107.5
Jun 2000	1.4795	1.6755	108.1	112.7	108.5
Sep 2000	1.5030	1.8425	112.1	113.6	109.5
Dec 2000	1.4990	1.7900	112.5	114.2	110.3
Mar 2001	1.5762	2.0595	113.7	115.3	110.5
Jun 2001	1.5156	1.9579	114.6	116.5	112.4
Sep 2001	1.5792	2.0356	114.9	116.7	112.5

5 The following table contains data on the exchange rate between two currencies (x and y) and the price ratio (country X/country Y). Use this data set to apply the PPP trading rule.

(a) Calculate the PPP rate.

(b) Plot the actual rate and the PPP rate and identify the buy and sell signals.

(c) Starting with a buy signal and ending with a sell signal, invest 1000 units of currency x in buying and selling currency y. Calculate the final value of the invested amount.

(d) Calculate the final value of the invested amount when a buy and hold strategy is adopted. For this purpose use the first buy signal and the last sell signal. Is the PPP rule more or less profitable than the buy and hold strategy?

x/y	Price ratio	x/y	Price ratio	x/y	Price ratio
1.20	1.00	1.27	1.07	1.29	1.08
1.22	1.01	1.30	1.10	1.28	1.06
1.24	1.00	1.29	1.08	1.27	1.05
1.26	1.03	1.27	1.05	1.24	1.02
1.24	1.04	1.28	1.06	1.25	1.05
1.23	1.02	1.27	1.05	1.28	1.08
1.24	1.01	1.28	1.08	1.26	1.07
1.25	1.03	1.30	1.10	1.27	1.06

CHAPTER

Covered interest parity

Introduction

In Chapter 9 we came across the law of one price (LOP), which was applied to commodity markets. In this chapter we apply the LOP to financial markets, in which case we will be concerned with asset prices and consequently with rates of return. One of the relationships describing the LOP in financial markets is covered interest parity (CIP), which stipulates that once foreign exchange risk is covered by a forward contract, then assets with similar characteristics must offer the same return. CIP, which is the second parity condition we study after PPP, represents an equilibrium condition that is restored and maintained by covered interest arbitrage. CIP has important implications for international financial operations such as hedging, investment and financing, as we will find out in subsequent chapters.

Objectives

The objectives of this chapter are:

- To outline the reasons for interest in CIP.
- To describe the CIP equilibrium condition and how it is violated.
- To describe the effect of covered interest arbitrage.
- To reformulate the CIP relationship by allowing for bid-offer spreads in interest and exchange rates.
- To demonstrate that the consistency of cross forward rates can be maintained by a combination of covered interest arbitrage and three-point arbitrage.
- To explain deviations from CIP.

Background

The **covered interest parity (CIP)** hypothesis describes the equilibrium relationship between the spot exchange rate, the forward exchange rate, domestic interest rates and foreign interest rates. In essence, this theory is an application of the law of one price to financial markets, postulating that, when foreign exchange risk is covered in the forward market, the rate of return on a domestic asset must be the same as that on a foreign asset with similar characteristics. If this is not the case, then **covered interest arbitrage** is set in motion and continues until the resulting changes in the forces of supply and demand (for the underlying assets) lead to a restoration of the equilibrium condition implied by CIP.

Although CIP was originally developed by Keynes in the 1920s as the earliest theory of forward exchange rate determination, the last two decades or so have witnessed a tremendous revival of interest in the theory for several reasons. First of all, CIP may be used to measure the degree of international capital mobility. In this case, lack of mobility is indicated by the extent of the deviation from the equilibrium condition implied by CIP. Second, CIP is also viewed as linking the term structure of interest rates with the term structure of the forward exchange spreads. Third, CIP is important from a policy perspective because it implies that, if market forces are allowed to work freely, financial resources will be allocated around the world in an optimal manner. The empirical failure of CIP would, therefore, imply the failure of market forces in allocating resources, justifying government intervention in capital and foreign exchange markets. Finally, CIP is important from a business perspective because it has some implications for hedging as well as short-term investment and financing decisions.

The practical business implications of CIP

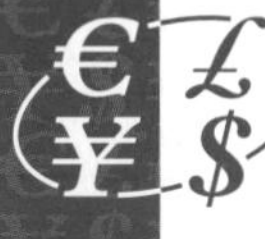

IN PRACTICE

There are two important practical business implications of CIP pertaining to two activities: hedging and short-term investment/financing. If CIP holds then:

- There is no difference between the effectiveness of forward hedging and money market hedging (borrowing and lending in the money market). This is because money market hedging creates a synthetic forward contract with an implicit forward rate that, under CIP, is equal to the forward rate quoted in the market. In this case, money market and forward market hedging produce identical results in terms of the domestic currency values of payables and receivables under the two modes of hedging.
- There is no difference between financing or investing in the domestic currency and in a foreign currency while covering the position in the forward market. This is because the two modes of financing/investment give exactly the same cost of funding/rate of return if CIP holds.

Both of these points are examined in further detail in Chapters 14 and 15, respectively.

10.2 The CIP condition

Consider an investor who has initial capital, K, and faces two alternatives: (i) domestic investment, whereby the investor buys domestic assets, earning the domestic interest rate, i; and (ii) foreign investment, whereby the investor converts the domestic currency into foreign currency to buy foreign assets, earning the foreign interest rate, i^*. Since domestic investment does not involve currency conversion, it does not involve **foreign exchange risk** (the risk arising from changes in the exchange rate). On the other hand, foreign investment produces exposure to foreign exchange risk, but this exposure can be covered by selling the foreign currency (buying the domestic currency) forward. Foreign exchange risk is eliminated because the forward exchange rate is known in advance, although it is used to settle transactions involving delivery of the currencies some time in the future. Thus, the investor knows in advance the domestic currency value of his or her foreign investment. If the position is not covered in the forward market, the investor has to wait until maturity and apply the spot exchange rate prevailing then to determine the domestic currency value of the foreign investment.

Suppose that we are considering a one-period investment starting with the acquisition of a financial asset (for example, a deposit) and ending with the maturity of this asset (see Figure 10.1). When the investor chooses domestic investment, the invested capital is compounded at the domestic interest rate and the investor ends up with the initial capital plus the interest income, that is $K(1 + i)$. If the investor chooses foreign investment, the initial capital is converted to foreign currency at the current spot exchange rate, obtaining K/S units of the foreign currency, where S is measured as domestic currency units per one unit of the foreign currency. If K/S worth of the foreign currency is invested in foreign assets, this capital is compounded for one period at the foreign interest rate such that the foreign currency value of the investment on maturity is $(K/S)(1 + i^*)$. The domestic currency value of this investment is obtained by converting this amount into the domestic currency at the forward rate, F, to obtain $(KF/S)(1 + i^*)$.

Figure 10.1 Return on domestic and foreign investment (with covered position)

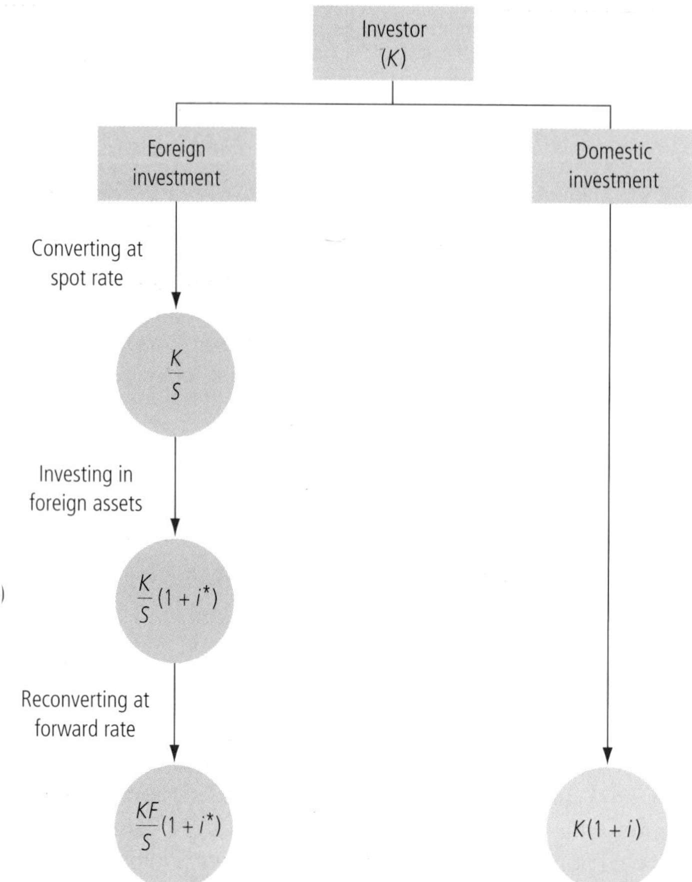

Let us now assume that there are no restrictions on the movement of capital and that there are no transaction costs. We also assume that agents are **risk-neutral**, in the sense that they are indifferent between holding domestic and foreign assets if these assets offer equal returns. The equilibrium condition that precludes the possibility of profitable arbitrage is that the two investments must be equally profitable, in the sense that they provide the same domestic currency amount of capital plus interest. Hence

$$K(1+i) = \frac{KF}{S}(1+i^{\star}) \tag{10.1}$$

By expressing the condition in terms of one unit of the domestic currency, we obtain

$$(1+i) = \frac{F}{S}(1+i^{\star}) \tag{10.2}$$

This equilibrium condition tells us that gross domestic return is equal to gross covered foreign return. The left-hand side of Equation (10.2) is the gross domestic return: it is 'gross' because it includes the amount invested (one unit of the domestic currency) and the interest earned, i.

Since $F/S = 1 + f$, where f is the forward spread, it follows that

$$(1 + i) = (1 + f)(1 + i^*) \quad (10.3)$$

By simplifying Equation (10.3), ignoring the term i^*f (because it is numerically negligible), we obtain the approximate CIP condition

$$i - i^* = f \quad (10.4)$$

which tells us that in equilibrium the interest differential must be equal to the forward spread. Equation (10.4) implies that the currency offering the higher interest rate must sell at a forward discount, and vice versa. This is because if $i > i^*$, then $f > 0$, which means that the foreign currency (offering a lower interest rate) sells at a forward premium whereas the domestic currency (offering a higher interest rate) sells at a forward discount. If, on the other hand, $i < i^*$, then $f < 0$, implying that the foreign currency sells at a discount while the domestic currency sells at a premium.

10.3 The mechanics of covered arbitrage

Covered interest arbitrage consists of going short on (borrowing) one currency and long on (investing in) another currency, while covering the long position via a forward contract (selling the currency forward). Upon the maturity of the investment (and the forward contract) the proceeds are converted at the forward rate and used to repay the loan (covering the short position). The difference between the proceeds from the investment and the loan repayment (principal plus interest) is **net arbitrage profit** or the **covered margin**. For arbitrage to be profitable the covered margin must be positive. This process is illustrated in Figure 10.2.

Depending on the configuration of exchange and interest rates, an arbitrager may choose to indulge in arbitrage from the domestic to a foreign currency (taking a short position on the domestic currency and a long position on the foreign currency), or vice versa. The choice depends on which sequence produces profit or a positive covered margin. For a given configuration of exchange and interest rates, if arbitrage is profitable in one direction it produces a loss in the other direction. In the following descriptions the spot and forward exchange rates are measured in direct quotation as the price of one foreign currency unit (domestic/foreign). Arbitrage, however, does not have to involve the domestic currency, as two foreign currencies may provide a profitable arbitrage opportunity.

Arbitrage from the domestic currency to a foreign currency

Arbitrage in this case consists of the following steps:

- The arbitrager borrows domestic currency funds at the domestic interest rate, i. For simplicity, we assume that the amount borrowed is one domestic currency unit.
- The borrowed funds are converted at the spot exchange rate, S, obtaining $1/S$ foreign currency units. This amount is invested at the foreign interest rate, i^*.
- The foreign currency value of the invested amount at the end of the investment period is $(1/S)(1 + i^*)$.
- This amount is reconverted into the domestic currency at the forward rate, F, to obtain $(F/S)(1 + i^*)$ domestic currency units.
- The value of the loan plus interest is $(1 + i)$ domestic currency units.

Figure 10.2 Covered interest arbitrage

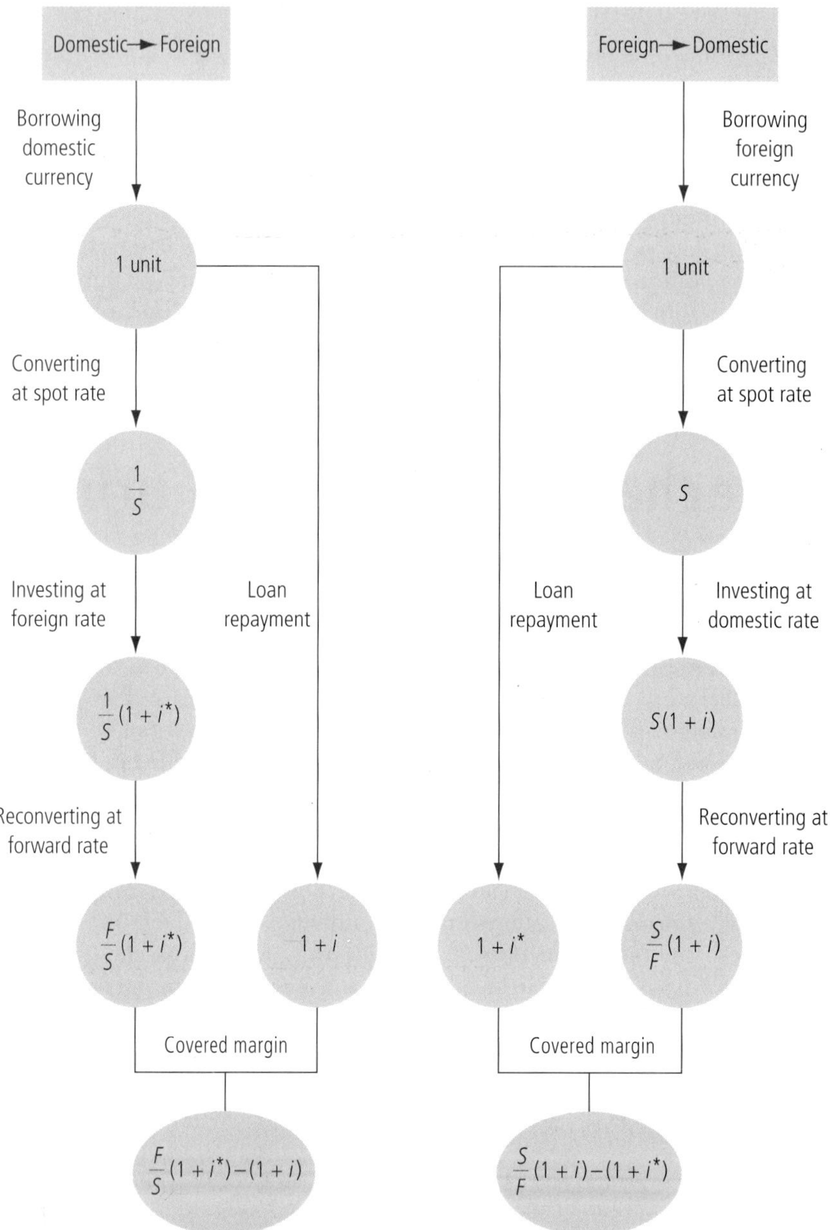

The covered margin, π, is the difference between the domestic currency value of the proceeds and the loan repayment, which gives

$$\pi = \frac{F}{S}(1+i^{*}) - (1+i) \tag{10.5}$$

or approximately

$$\pi = i^{*} - i + f \tag{10.6}$$

Equation (10.6) tells us that the covered margin on arbitrage from the domestic to a foreign currency consists of the interest rate differential (foreign less domestic) and the forward spread.

Arbitrage from a foreign currency to the domestic currency

Arbitrage in this case consists of the following steps:

- The arbitrager borrows foreign currency funds at the foreign interest rate, i^*. For simplicity we again assume that the amount borrowed is one foreign currency unit.
- The borrowed funds are converted at the spot exchange rate, S, obtaining S domestic currency units. This amount is invested at the domestic interest rate, i.
- The domestic currency value of the invested amount at the end of the investment period is $S(1 + i)$.
- This amount is reconverted into the foreign currency at the forward rate, F, to obtain $(S/F)(1 + i)$ foreign currency units.
- The value of the loan plus interest is $(1 + i^*)$ foreign currency units.

The covered margin is again the difference between the foreign currency value of the proceeds and the loan repayment, which gives

$$\pi = \frac{S}{F}(1+i) - (1+i^*) \qquad (10.7)$$

or approximately

$$\pi = i - i^* - f \qquad (10.8)$$

Equation (10.8) tells us that the covered margin on arbitrage from a foreign to the domestic currency consists of the interest rate differential (domestic less foreign) and the negative of the forward spread.

The no-arbitrage condition

The **no-arbitrage condition** is obtained when the covered margin is zero. By substituting $\pi = 0$ in Equation (10.5) or (10.7), we obtain

$$\overline{F} = S\left[\frac{1+i}{1+i^*}\right] \qquad (10.9)$$

where $\overline{F}$ is the **interest parity forward rate**, which is the value of the forward rate that is consistent with the no-arbitrage condition. If CIP holds, then $\overline{F} = F$ (that is, the interest parity forward rate is equal to the actual forward rate).

Suppose that you approach your banker, requesting a quote for the forward rate between the domestic currency and a foreign currency, perhaps because you want to buy the foreign currency forward to cover future payables. The banker may not know what CIP is, but will search in a manual for a formula that provides an expression for the forward rate. This formula would look like Equation (10.9). Why would the banker use this formula to calculate the forward rate? Simply because if the banker chose any other forward rate, you could make (riskless) profit out of your banker by indulging in covered arbitrage. The following example explains the situation.

Example

Suppose that you request your banker to quote a one-year forward rate on the pound, which he or she does, giving you the following information:

One-year forward rate (AUD/GBP)	2.6500
Spot rate (AUD/GBP)	2.7500
One-year AUD interest rate	8%
One-year GBP interest rate	4%

You observe immediately that the pound is selling at a forward discount because the forward rate is lower than the spot rate. Let us see what happens if you try to indulge in covered arbitrage on the basis of the following information, starting with arbitrage from the pound to the Australian dollar:

- Borrow GBP1000 (or any other amount).
- Convert the pound amount spot at 2.75 to obtain AUD2750 (1000 × 2.75).
- Invest the AUD amount at 8 per cent for one year. At the end of the year, you will have AUD2970 (2750 × (1 + 0.08)).
- Reconvert the AUD proceeds at the forward rate back to pounds to obtain GBP1120.8 (2970/2.65).
- The loan repayment that you have to make is GBP1040 (1000 × (1 + 0.04)).
- Net arbitrage profit is GBP80.8 (= 1120.8 – 1040).

Notice that this profit is made without bearing any risk, since all of the decision variables (including the forward rate) are known at the time you decide to indulge in this operation. Now let us see what happens if instead you decide to indulge in arbitrage from the Australian dollar to the pound:

- Borrow AUD1000 (or any other amount).
- Convert the Australian dollar amount spot at 2.75 to obtain GBP363.6 (1000/2.75).
- Invest the GBP amount at 4 per cent for one year. At the end of the year, you will have GBP378.1.
- Reconvert the GBP proceeds at the forward rate back to Australian dollars to obtain AUD1002 (378.1 × 2.65).
- The loan repayment that you have to make is AUD1080 (1000 × (1 + 0.08)).
- Net arbitrage loss is AUD78.0 (= 1002 – 1080).

In this case you make a loss. Now assume that the banker quotes a forward rate of 2.8558. If you indulge in arbitrage from the pound to the Australian dollar at this forward rate, you will, after reconvertion, get GBP1040 (2970/2.8558), in which case your arbitrage profit is zero. If you go from the Australian dollar to the pound you get, after reconversion, AUD1080 (378.1 × 2.8558). Again, your profit is zero. Your banker will always quote you this rate so that you will not make profit out of him or her. This rate is actually calculated from Equation (10.9) as

$$2.75\left[\frac{1.08}{1.04}\right] = 2.8558$$

You make profit if the forward rate is 2.65 because this rate is not consistent with the no-arbitrage condition (but 2.8558 is). If the quoted forward rate is not consistent with the no-arbitrage condition, you will make profit in one direction and loss in the other (exactly as in the case of two-point and three-point arbitrage). How do you know which way to go? Very simply, by calculating the covered margin, which must be positive for arbitrage to be profitable.

We have to be very careful about the **deannualisation** of interest rates when these calculations are carried out. In this example we did not deannualise interest rates because we used a time horizon of one year. If, on the other hand, we used a horizon of six months, the deannualised interest rates on the two currencies would be 4 and 2 per cent, respectively. In general, we deannualise interest rates by dividing by $(12/N)$ where N is the time horizon in months.

10.4 Covered arbitrage with bid-offer spreads

To describe covered arbitrage when there are bid-offer spreads in both exchange and interest rates we have to remember that a price taker in the foreign exchange market (like our arbitrager) buys at the (higher) offer exchange rate and sells at the (lower) bid exchange rate of the market maker (the banker). A price taker in the money market borrows at the (higher) offer interest rate and lends at the (lower) bid interest rate of the market maker. Covered arbitrage in the presence of bid-offer spreads is illustrated in Figure 10.3.

Arbitrage from the domestic currency to a foreign currency

Arbitrage in this case consists of the following steps:

- The arbitrager borrows domestic currency funds (one unit) at the domestic offer interest rate, i_a.
- The borrowed funds are converted into the foreign currency at the spot offer rate, S_a, obtaining $1/S_a$ foreign currency units. This amount is invested at the foreign bid interest rate, $i_b^{\star}$.
- The foreign currency value of the invested amount at the end of the investment period is $(1/S_a)(1 + i_b^{\star})$.
- This amount is reconverted into the domestic currency at the forward bid rate, F_b, to obtain $(F_b/S_a)(1 + i_b^{\star})$ domestic currency units.
- The value of the loan plus interest is $(1 + i_a)$ domestic currency units.

The covered margin in this case is

$$\pi = \frac{F_b}{S_a}(1 + i_b^{\star}) - (1 + i_a) \tag{10.10}$$

Since $F_b/S_a = (1 + f)/(1 + m)$, where f is the forward spread and m is the bid-offer spread, it follows that

$$\pi = i_b^{\star} - i_a + f - m \tag{10.11}$$

Because of the introduction of the bid-offer spreads, which are transactions costs, the no-arbitrage condition is no longer that $\pi = 0$, implying a deviation from CIP. It can be seen from Equations (10.10) and (10.11) that the covered margin is lower if we allow for the bid-offer spreads.

Figure 10.3 Covered interest arbitrage in the presence of bid-offer spreads

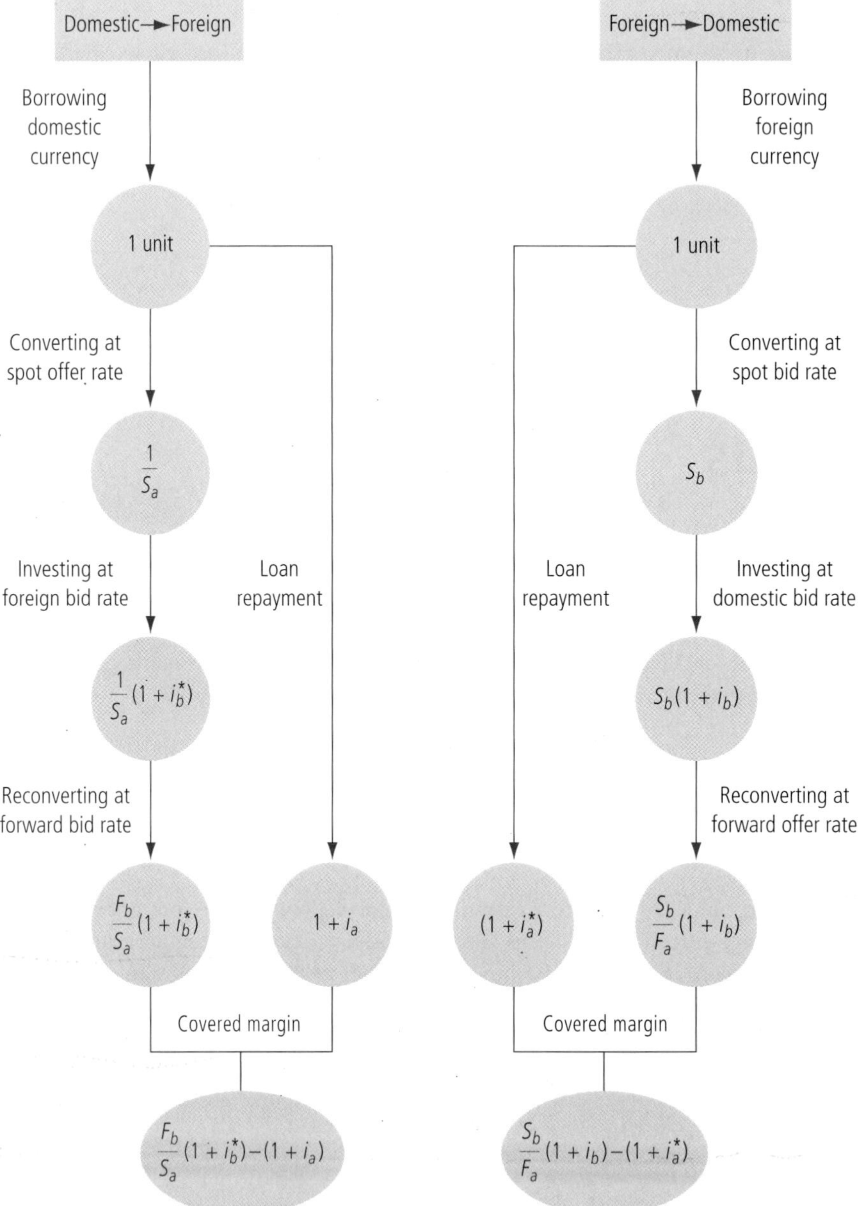

Arbitrage from a foreign currency to the domestic currency

Arbitrage in this case consists of the following steps:

- The arbitrager borrows foreign currency funds (one unit) at the foreign offer interest rate, i_a^*.
- The borrowed funds are converted into the domestic currency at the spot bid rate, S_b, obtaining S_b domestic currency units. This amount is invested at the domestic bid interest rate, i_b.

- The domestic currency value of the invested amount at the end of the investment period is $S_b(1 + i_b)$.
- This amount is reconverted into the foreign currency at the forward offer rate, F_a, to obtain $(S_b/F_a)(1 + i_b)$ foreign currency units.
- The value of the loan plus interest is $(1 + i_a^{\star})$ foreign currency units.

The covered margin in this case is

$$\pi = \frac{S_b}{F_a}(1 + i_b) - (1 + i_a^{\star}) \tag{10.12}$$

Since $S_b/F_a = 1/[(1 + m)(1 + f)]$, it follows that

$$\pi = i_b - i_a^{\star} - f - m \tag{10.13}$$

which again shows that the covered margin is lower if the bid-offer spreads are allowed for.

Example

Consider the profitability of covered arbitrage on the basis of the following information:

One-year forward rate (AUD/GBP)	2.6450–2.6550
Spot rate (AUD/GBP)	2.7450–2.7550
One-year AUD interest rate	7.75–8.25%
One-year GBP interest rate	3.75–4.25%

Let us start with arbitrage from the pound to the Australian dollar:

- Borrow GBP1000 (or any other amount)
- Convert the pound amount spot at 2.7450 to obtain AUD2745 (1000 × 2.7450).
- Invest the AUD amount at 7.75 per cent for one year. At the end of the year, you will have AUD2958 (2745 × (1 + 0.0775)).
- Reconvert the AUD proceeds at the forward offer rate back to pounds to obtain GBP1114 (2958/2.6550).
- The loan repayment that you have to make is GBP1042.5 (1000 × (1 + 0.0425)).
- Net arbitrage profit is GBP71.50 (= 1114 – 1042.50).

which is less than what was obtained in the previous example. Now, let us see what happens if instead you indulge in arbitrage from the Australian dollar to the pound:

- Borrow AUD1000 (or any other amount).
- Convert the Australian dollar amount spot at 2.7550 to obtain GBP363 (1000/2.7550).
- Invest the GBP amount at 3.75 per cent for one year. At the end of the year, you will have GBP377.
- Reconvert the GBP proceeds at the forward bid rate back to Australian dollars to obtain AUD997 (377 × 2.6450).
- The loan repayment that you have to make is AUD1082.50 (1000 × (1 + 0.0825)).
- Net arbitrage loss is AUD85.5 (= 997 – 1082.50)

which is a bigger loss than in the previous example.

10.5 Covered arbitrage and the consistency of cross forward rates

We have seen that three-point arbitrage keeps cross (spot) rates consistent. It is possible to demonstrate that covered arbitrage and three-point arbitrage in the spot market can maintain the consistency of cross forward rates. In this sense, consistency implies that the cross forward rate between two currencies, as calculated from the forward exchange rates of these two currencies against another currency, must be identical to the cross forward rate that is actually quoted in the market.

Assume that there are three currencies (x, y and z) and three forward rates. Consistency of the cross forward rates thus requires the following condition to be satisfied

$$F(x/y) = \frac{F(x/z)}{F(y/z)} \tag{10.14}$$

where $F(x/y)$ is the cross forward exchange rate between x and y, and so on. It can be demonstrated that the condition represented by Equation (10.14) can be established by covered arbitrage and three-point arbitrage. CIP (which results from covered interest arbitrage) implies that

$$F(x/z) = S(x/z)\left(\frac{1+i_x}{1+i_z}\right) \tag{10.15}$$

where $S(x/y)$ is the spot exchange rate between x and z, i_x is the interest rate on x and i_z is the interest rate on z. Likewise, CIP implies that

$$F(y/z) = S(y/z)\left(\frac{1+i_y}{1+i_z}\right) \tag{10.16}$$

and

$$F(x/y) = S(x/y)\left(\frac{1+i_x}{1+i_y}\right) \tag{10.17}$$

Three-point arbitrage in the spot market implies that

$$S(x/y) = \frac{S(x/z)}{S(y/z)} \tag{10.18}$$

By substituting Equation (10.18) into Equation (10.17), we obtain

$$F(x/y) = \frac{S(x/z)}{S(y/z)}\left(\frac{1+i_x}{1+i_y}\right) \tag{10.19}$$

By multiplying and dividing the right-hand side of Equation (10.19) by $1 + i_z$, we obtain

$$F(x/y) = \frac{S(x/z)}{S(y/z)}\left(\frac{1+i_x}{1+i_y}\right)\left(\frac{1+i_z}{1+i_z}\right) \tag{10.20}$$

By rearranging, we obtain

$$F(x/y) = \frac{S(x/z)\left(\frac{1+i_x}{1+i_z}\right)}{S(y/z)\left(\frac{1+i_y}{1+i_z}\right)} = \frac{F(x/z)}{F(y/z)} \tag{10.21}$$

which proves Equation (10.14).

Example

Consider the following information:

Spot exchange rate (AUD/USD)	1.8000
Spot exchange rate (GBP/USD)	0.6500
Three-month interest rate (AUD)	6% p.a.
Three-month interest rate (GBP)	8% p.a.
Three-month interest rate (USD)	4% p.a.

It is possible to calculate the three-month forward exchange rate between the Australian dollar and the British pound by adjusting the spot rate for the interest differential and as a cross rate. Because the interest rates are expressed on a 'per annum' basis, they should be deannualised (divided by 4). Thus, we have

$$S(AUD/GBP) = \frac{1.8000}{0.6500} = 2.7692$$

$$F(AUD/GBP) = 2.7692\left(\frac{1+\frac{0.06}{4}}{1+\frac{0.08}{4}}\right) = 2.7556$$

As a cross rate it is calculated as

$$F(AUD/USD) = 1.8000\left(\frac{1+\frac{0.06}{4}}{1+\frac{0.04}{4}}\right) = 1.8089$$

$$F(GBP/USD) = 0.6500\left(\frac{1+\frac{0.08}{4}}{1+\frac{0.04}{4}}\right) = 0.6564$$

$$F(AUD/GBP) = \frac{1.8089}{0.6564} = 2.7558$$

Hence, the forward AUD/GBP rate is the same whether it is calculated by adjusting the corresponding spot rate or by calculating it as a cross rate (the difference in the fourth decimal place is due to rounding). The cross forward rates are therefore consistent.

Three-point arbitrage in the spot and forward foreign exchange markets

The following four propositions can be put forward:[1]

- Consistency of the forward exchange rates can be established by covered interest arbitrage and three-point arbitrage in the spot market (which is shown here).
- If the forward rates are inconsistent only because the spot rates are inconsistent, then the same profit can be obtained from three-point arbitrage in the spot market or in the forward market.
- In the presence of bid-offer spreads in interest and exchange rates, the consistency of the forward rates condition can be approximately obtained by three-point arbitrage in the forward market.
- In the presence of bid-offer spreads, the profit derived from a violation of the no-arbitrage condition will depend on whether arbitrage is conducted in the spot or forward market.

These propositions show that the bid-offer spreads as transaction costs do affect the results derived from arbitrage in the spot and forward markets.

[1] I. A. Moosa, 'Triangular Arbitrage in the Spot and Forward Foreign Exchange Markets', *Quantitative Finance*, 1, 2001, pp. 387–90.

10.6 Explaining observed deviations from CIP

While CIP has been found to hold almost precisely in the Eurocurrency markets if there are no **measurement errors**, some deviations can be detected if domestic assets (for example, Treasury bills) are used. Deviations from CIP are indicated by a non-zero covered margin.

Let us start by examining the CIP condition for Australia versus four countries: the United States, Japan, the United Kingdom and Canada. Figure 10.4 displays the covered margins against the four currencies resulting from covered arbitrage by taking a short position on the Australian dollar and a long position on the other currencies. Some small deviations from CIP are apparent, but these are mostly due to measurement errors. A precise measurement of deviations from CIP requires actual data that are recorded at the same point in time and obtained from the same source (preferably transaction data).

Figure 10.4 Covered margins in percentage points (short Australian dollar)

(a) AUD/USD

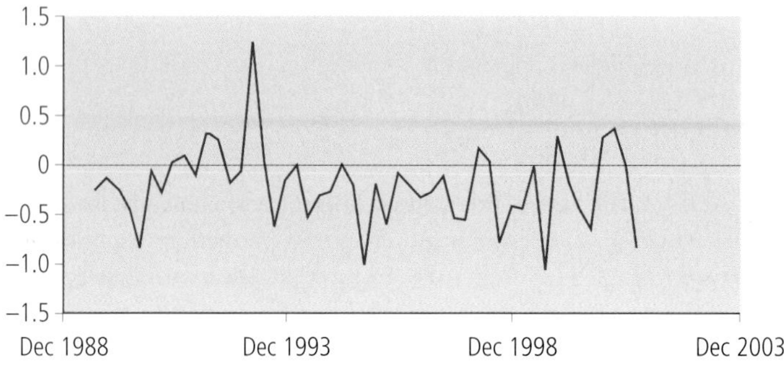

(b) AUD/JPY

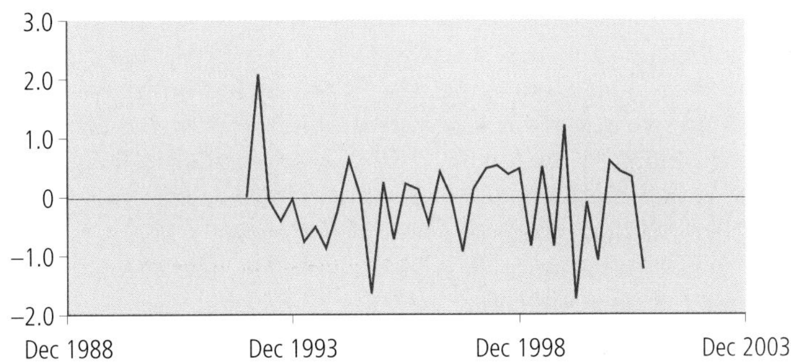

(c) AUD/GBP

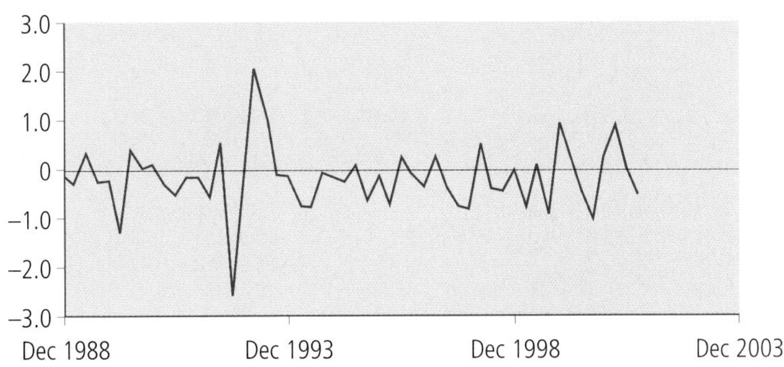

(d) AUD/CAD

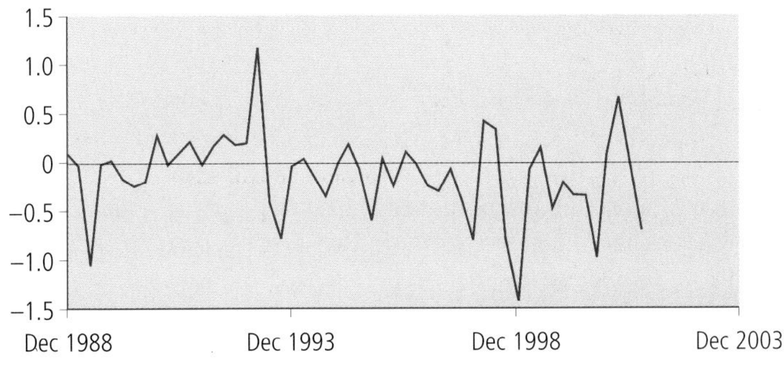

Source: Main Economic Indicators, OECD; Datastream.

If we overlook the possibility of measurement errors, then deviations from CIP must indicate profitable covered arbitrage opportunities. Why is it then that these opportunities are not exploited by arbitragers? The answer is simple: there are a number of factors that make covered arbitrage unprofitable or unattractive. These factors are discussed in turn below.

Transaction costs

Deviations from CIP have been attributed to **transaction costs**, which are represented by the bid-offer spread of exchange rates (the cost of transacting in the foreign exchange market), the bid-offer spread of interest rates (the cost of transacting in the money market) and **brokerage fees.** There are two possible reasons why a minimum covered margin (say, 0.5 per cent) must exist before arbitrage is undertaken: (i) each transaction in financial markets requires a payment of brokerage fees; and (ii) banks may require their foreign exchange departments to earn a higher yield than their domestic departments.

We have already seen the effect of bid-offer spreads on the profitability of covered arbitrage. We will now consider brokerage fees, which are assumed to be t percentage points. In this case, the covered margin on arbitrage from the domestic currency to the foreign currency, and vice versa, are given respectively by

$$\pi = \frac{F}{S}(1+i^{\star}) - (1+i) - t \approx i^{\star} - i + f - t \tag{10.22}$$

$$\pi = \frac{S}{F}(1+i) - (1+i^{\star}) - t \approx i - i^{\star} - f - t \tag{10.23}$$

In the presence of transaction costs, no one would indulge in covered arbitrage unless $i^{\star} - i + f > t$ (domestic to foreign) or $i - i^{\star} - f > t$ (foreign to domestic).

Political risk

Another explanation for deviations from CIP is **political risk**, which refers to the uncertainty that while the funds are invested abroad they may be frozen, become inconvertible or be confiscated. In a less extreme case, they may face new or higher taxes. Thus, a minimum covered margin is required before indulging in covered arbitrage if it is perceived to involve political risk.

RESEARCH FINDINGS

The effect of political risk on covered interest arbitrage across the Tasman

The effect of political risk on CIP can be demonstrated by examining the configuration of the Australian and New Zealand exchange and interest rates during the period 1985–1994.[1] The empirical results revealed no role for speculation in determining the forward rate between the two currencies and that CIP was, on average, valid. However, when CIP was estimated over the period 1985–1990, some statistically significant deviations from CIP appeared. When the relationship was re-estimated by excluding 1985 from the sample period, CIP appeared to be valid.

The study suggested that political risk, as represented by the possibility of re-imposing capital controls, was a possible explanation for the 1985 deviation from CIP. It was also suggested that a fall in transaction costs, resulting from the cumulative effect of financial deregulation, was a possible explanation for the shrinkage of deviations in the post-1990 period.

[1] I. A. Moosa, 'An Empirical Investigation into the Causes of Deviations from Covered Interest Parity Across the Tasman', *New Zealand Economic Papers*, 30, 1996, pp. 39–54.

Tax differentials

Differences between domestic and foreign tax rates may cause deviations from CIP. After all, what is important is not the before-tax returns but the after-tax returns. The covered margin is reduced in the presence of taxes and what may look like a profitable opportunity may not be so if taxes are taken into account.

Liquidity differences

Liquidity differences may also cause deviations from CIP. The liquidity of an asset can be judged by how quickly and cheaply it can be converted into cash. The more uncertainty there is concerning future needs and alternative sources of short-term financing, the higher the premium that should be received before taking a covered position on a foreign currency.

RESEARCH FINDINGS

The effect of speculation on CIP and the forward rate

One explanation that has been put forward for the deviations from CIP is that the forward rate is not determined by arbitrage alone but also by speculation. Moosa and Bhatti investigated the role of speculation in determining the forward exchange rate over the period 1977–1990, producing results showing no role for speculation in determining the forward rates of three currencies against the US dollar.[1] They attributed the results to the proposition that financial deregulation has significantly reduced deviations from CIP.

In another paper, Moosa and Al-Loughani investigated the same proposition in the case of a currency that is pegged to a basket (the Kuwaiti dinar).[2] They found speculation to be the dominant factor determining the forward rate against the US dollar, which is the dominant currency in the basket. The result was explained in terms of the relative stability of this exchange rate. In the case of exchange rates against other currencies, there was a role for speculation, although arbitrage played a more important role.

1 I. A. Moosa and R. H. Bhatti, 'Does Speculation Play Any Role in Determining the Forward Exchange Rate?', *Applied Financial Economics*, 7, 1997, pp. 611–17.

2 I. A. Moosa and N. E. Al-Loughani, 'An Empirical Investigation into the Causes of Deviations from Covered Interest Parity When the Domestic Currency is Pegged to a Basket', *Journal of Financial Studies*, 4, 1997, pp. 29–46.

Other factors

Some other factors have been suggested to explain deviations from CIP because they hinder the movement of arbitrage funds when the possibility for arbitrage arises. One of these factors is the existence of inelastic (or less than perfectly elastic) supply and demand for arbitrage funds, which amounts to a violation of one of the basic assumptions of CIP. A related factor is capital market imperfections, which is not important at the present time, given the increasing degree of market perfection. Another factor is capital controls: this factor has lost importance because of the worldwide tendency to abolish these controls as well as measures of financial deregulation. Finally, it has been suggested that if speculation (as opposed to arbitrage) plays a role in determining the forward rate, deviations from CIP will arise.

RESEARCH FINDINGS

The empirical validity of CIP

Two important studies of the empirical validity of CIP were conducted in the 1980s by Mark Taylor. What was different about these studies was that they were not based on published data, which have some measurement errors. There are certain requirements for a proper testing of CIP, including the following:

- Observations on exchange and interest rates must be recorded at the same points in time.
- They must include bid-offer spreads and transaction costs.
- They must represent the data on which arbitragers take decisions.

Obviously, these three requirements are not satisfied by published data, which were traditionally used to test CIP. Taylor overcame all these problems by collecting the data himself from dealers in the London foreign exchange market. He found no deviations from CIP (that is, the absence of profitable covered arbitrage opportunities).[1] In his subsequent paper, however, he concluded that small but potentially exploitable opportunities of profitable arbitrage emerged occasionally during periods of turbulence in the foreign exchange market but not during periods of tranquillity.[2] He also found that the degree of reduction in the size and persistence of arbitrage increased with the passage of time. Furthermore, he established the notion of the term structure of arbitrage opportunities, indicating that profitable arbitrage opportunities are positively related to the length of the forward contract (the shorter the maturity, the smaller the profitable arbitrage opportunity). One explanation that Taylor presented for observed deviations from covered interest parity was the size and extent of credit limits. If banks impose restrictions on the amounts, maturities and counterparties they deal with, this will operate as a liquidity constraint on covered arbitrage, giving rise to profitable opportunities.

In another study, Committeri, Rosi and Santorelli cast doubt on Taylor's results on the following grounds.[3] First, his analysis was based on data collected in a specific segment of the Eurocurrency market. Second, the data used in his first study did not cover a long period of time. Third, the data did not represent what the dealers were actually prepared to deal on. By doing their own analysis, they found no profitable arbitrage opportunities.

1 M. P. Taylor, 'Covered Interest Parity: A High Frequency, High Quality Data Study', *Economica*, 54, 1987, pp. 429–53.

2 M. P. Taylor, 'Covered Interest Parity and Market Turbulence', *Economic Journal*, 99, 1989, pp. 376–91.

3 M. Committeri, S. Rosi and A. Santorelli, 'Tests of Covered Interest Parity on the Euromarket with High Quality Data', *Applied Financial Economics*, 3, 1993, pp. 89–93.

Summary

- CIP is an application of the law of one price to financial markets. It implies that when the foreign exchange risk is covered in the forward market, then the rates of return on domestic and foreign assets with similar risk characteristics must be equal.
- The revival of interest in CIP can be attributed to the following factors: (i) it can be used to measure the degree of international capital mobility; (ii) it links the term structure of interest rates with the term structure of forward spreads; (iii) it has implications for the optimality, or otherwise, of the allocation of the world's financial resources; and (iv) it has implications for investment and financing decisions.
- A violation of the CIP equilibrium condition triggers covered interest arbitrage. The latter, by changing the forces of supply and demand in the foreign exchange and money markets, restores the equilibrium condition.
- The presence of bid-offer spreads reduces the profitability of covered arbitrage.

- Covered arbitrage and three-point arbitrage can maintain the consistency of cross forward rates.
- While CIP has been found to hold precisely in the Eurocurrency markets, if there are no measurement errors, some deviations can be detected if domestic assets are used. These deviations are attributed to the following factors: (i) transaction costs; (ii) political risk; (iii) tax differentials; (iv) liquidity differences; (v) inelastic supply and demand; (vi) capital market imperfections; (vii) capital controls; and (viii) speculation.

Key terms

MAXIMISE YOUR MARKS! There are 30 interactive questions for this chapter available online at **www.mhhe.com/au/moosa2e**

Review questions

1 What are the reasons for the revival of interest in covered interest parity?

2 What are the practical business implications of CIP?

3 Why is risk neutrality an important assumption for deriving the CIP condition?

4 Why is covered interest arbitrage covered?

5 What is the interest parity forward rate?

6 In equilibrium, the currency offering a lower interest rate must sell at a forward premium, whereas the currency offering a higher interest rate must sell at a forward discount. Why?

7 Explain how covered arbitrage restores the CIP equilibrium condition when it is violated.

8 What is the covered margin?

9 What is the effect of the presence of bid-offer spreads in interest and exchange rates on the CIP equilibrium condition and on the profitability of covered interest arbitrage?

10 Explain how covered arbitrage and three-point arbitrage in the spot market maintain the consistency of cross forward rates.

11 Deviations from the CIP condition involving the Australian and New Zealand dollars were significantly high immediately following the abolition of capital controls by both countries in the mid-1980s. Is there any possible explanation for this phenomenon?

12 'In the presence of transaction costs, the covered margin must exceed some minimum amount before arbitrage becomes profitable.' Explain.

13 'Less than perfectly elastic supply and demand for arbitrage funds, capital controls and market imperfections give rise to deviations from CIP in a similar manner.' Explain.

Problems

1 You are given the following information:

Spot exchange rate (AUD/EUR)	1.60
One-year forward rate (AUD/EUR)	1.62
One-year interest rate on the Australian dollar	8.5%
One-year interest rate on the euro	6.5%

(a) Is there any violation of CIP?
(b) Calculate the covered margin (going short on the AUD).
(c) Calculate the interest parity forward rate and compare it with the actual forward rate.
(d) Calculate the forward spread and compare it with the interest differential.
(e) What would arbitragers do?
(f) If arbitrage is initiated, suggest some values for the interest and exchange rates after it has stopped and equilibrium has been reached.

2 You are given the following information:

Spot exchange rate (AUD/CHF)	1.1500
Three-month forward rate (AUD/CHF)	1.1585
Australian three-month interest rate	10.5% p.a.
Swiss three-month interest rate	6.5% p.a.

(a) Is there any violation of CIP?
(b) Calculate the covered margin (going short on the AUD).
(c) Calculate the interest parity forward rate and compare it with the actual forward rate.
(d) Calculate the forward spread and compare it with the interest differential.
(e) What would arbitragers do?

3 You are given the following information:

Spot exchange rate (CAD/GBP)	2.42
Six-month forward rate (CAD/GBP)	2.46
Canadian six-month interest rate	8% p.a.
British six-month interest rate	10% p.a.

(a) Is there any violation of CIP?
(b) Calculate the covered margin from a Canadian perspective (going short on the CAD).
(c) Calculate the interest parity forward rate in direct quotation from a Canadian perspective and compare it with the actual forward rate.
(d) Calculate the forward spread and compare it with the interest differential from a Canadian perspective.
(e) What would arbitragers do?
(f) Redo all the calculations from a British perspective (going short on the GBP).

4 You are given the following information:

Spot exchange rate (AUD/EUR)	1.5950–1.6050
One-year forward rate (AUD/EUR)	1.6150–1.6250
One-year interest rate on the Australian dollar	8.25–8.75%
One-year interest rate on the euro	6.25–6.75%

(a) Calculate the covered margin (going short on the AUD).
(b) What would arbitragers do?
(c) Compare the results with those obtained by solving Problem 1.

5 You are given the following information:

Spot exchange rate (AUD/CHF)	1.1450–1.1550
Three-month forward rate (AUD/CHF)	1.1535–1.1635
Australian three-month interest rate	10.25–10.75% p.a.
Swiss three-month interest rate	6.25–6.75% p.a.

(a) Calculate the covered margin (going short on the AUD).
(b) What would arbitragers do?
(c) Compare the results with those obtained by solving Problem 2.

6 You are given the following information:

Spot exchange rate (CAD/GBP)	2.4150–2.4250
Six-month forward rate (CAD/GBP)	2.4550–2.4650
Canadian six-month interest rate	7.75–8.25% p.a.
British six-month interest rate	9.75–10.25% p.a.

(a) Calculate the covered margin from a Canadian perspective (going short on the CAD).
(b) Calculate the covered margin from a British perspective (going short on the GBP).
(c) What would arbitragers do?
(d) Compare the results with those obtained by solving Problem 3.

7 The table below shows a set of quarterly data on the spot and three-month forward rates between the Australian dollar and the Canadian dollar, as well as the Australian and Canadian three-month interest rates. On the basis of this data set, you are required to do the following (all calculations are to be carried out from an Australian perspective):
(a) Calculate the interest parity forward rate and plot it against the actual forward rate.
(b) Calculate the percentage deviation of the actual forward rate from the interest parity forward rate and plot it.
(c) Calculate the covered margin and plot it.

	Spot AUD/CAD	**Forward AUD/CAD**	**Australian interest**	**Canadian interest**
Mar 1998	1.0643	1.0692	4.84	4.59
Jun 1998	1.1000	1.1037	4.93	4.87
Sep 1998	1.1003	1.0904	4.85	4.91
Dec 1998	1.0672	1.0520	4.62	4.66
Mar 1999	1.0449	1.0440	4.66	4.63
Jun 1999	1.0170	1.0188	4.70	4.56
Sep 1999	1.0447	1.0398	4.78	4.66
Dec 1999	1.0555	1.0538	5.08	4.85
Mar 2000	1.1365	1.1339	5.78	5.27
Jun 2000	1.1325	1.1295	5.87	5.53
Sep 2000	1.2259	1.2163	6.41	5.56
Dec 2000	1.1942	1.1969	6.03	5.49
Mar 2001	1.3066	1.3165	4.98	4.58
Jun 2001	1.2918	1.2941	4.88	4.30
Sep 2001	1.2890	1.2838	4.30	3.05

8 You are given the following information:

Spot exchange rate (USD/GBP)	1.46
Spot exchange rate (USD/CAD)	0.64
US one-year interest rate	6%
British one-year interest rate	8%
Canadian one-year interest rate	10%

(a) Calculate the one-year forward rate between the Canadian dollar and the British pound (CAD/GBP) by adjusting the spot rate for the interest rate differential.
(b) Calculate the same forward rate as a cross rate. Do you obtain the same answer?

9 You are given the following information:

Spot exchange rate (AUD/EUR)	1.60
One-year forward rate (AUD/EUR)	1.62
One-year interest rate on the Australian dollar	8.5%
One-year interest rate on the euro	6.5%
Transaction costs	0.5%

(a) Calculate the covered margin by going short on one currency and long on the other.
(b) What is the value of transaction costs that makes profitable arbitrage unprofitable?

10 You are given the following information:

Spot exchange rate (CAD/GBP)	2.42
Six-month forward rate (CAD/GBP)	2.46
Canadian six-month interest rate	8% p.a.
British six-month interest rate	10% p.a.

British investors require a risk premium of 1.5 per cent p.a. to invest in Canadian assets, whereas Canadian investors require a risk premium of 1 per cent p.a. to invest in British assets. Find out who will indulge in arbitrage and in which direction.

11 Obtain some recent data on interest rates and exchange rates from newspapers or the Internet. Are there profitable covered arbitrage operations? If so, why is it that they are not exploited?

CHAPTER

Market efficiency, uncovered interest parity and real interest parity

Introduction

This chapter deals with the three related concepts of market efficiency, uncovered interest parity and real interest parity. There are several definitions of market efficiency but the general definition is that, in an efficient market, prices reflect all available information such that it is not possible to make abnormal profit. Uncovered interest parity (UIP) is a condition that is obtained via uncovered interest arbitrage, which is similar to covered arbitrage except that the long position is not covered in the forward market. The real interest parity (RIP) condition is the most stringent of the four international parity conditions studied in this book. This is why it is taken to imply integration of both goods and financial markets. These conditions and concepts have some implications for international financial operations. For example, if the three conditions hold, then there is no need to worry about foreign exchange risk and hence no need to indulge in costly hedging operations.

Objectives

The objectives of this chapter are:

- To explain the concept of market efficiency.
- To describe the UIP condition and explain the effect of uncovered arbitrage.
- To modify the UIP condition to take into account bid-offer spreads in interest and exchange rates.
- To assess the empirical validity of UIP.
- To explain the concept of the real interest rate.
- To derive the RIP condition.

11.1 The concept of market efficiency

The concept of **market efficiency** was initially developed for the stock market, but it is equally valid for the foreign exchange market and indeed for markets in general, financial or otherwise. In an efficient market, prices reflect all available information (hence, this is a definition of **informational efficiency** rather than **allocative efficiency**). The implication of this definition is that it is not possible to predict price movements from available information because this information is already reflected in prices. Since the arrival of information is random and given that new information is reflected in prices very quickly, the period-to-period changes in prices tend to be random. Another implication is that it is not possible to earn **abnormal returns** via active trading as compared to what can be obtained from a passive buy-and-hold strategy.

We actually came across the concept of market efficiency implicitly in Chapter 10, because the implication was that there are no profitable (covered) arbitrage opportunities in an efficient market. Remember that covered arbitrage is based on information pertaining to interest and exchange rates that is available at the time the decision to indulge in arbitrage is taken. If there are profitable arbitrage opportunities, as indicated by the publicly available information, then every market participant will try to make profit from riskless covered arbitrage and the opportunities will thus disappear.

Whether or not markets are efficient has significant implications for the operations of international business firms. The international parity conditions that we have come across so far (PPP and CIP) and those we are going to discuss in this chapter (UIP and RIP) have important implications for the international firm's investment and financing decisions as well as its exposure to risk. These conditions hold only if the underlying markets are efficient. In this sense market efficiency precludes the possibility of earning profit via arbitrage and speculation based on the violation of these conditions.

There are three levels of efficiency, which are defined with reference to the contents of the underlying information set. These concepts are explained with reference to the foreign exchange market.

Weak efficiency

Weak efficiency means that prices reflect all the information contained in the past behaviour of prices (or rather exchange rates). This is obviously a limited set of information as it excludes the effect of other relevant variables that, in the case of the foreign exchange market, affect the exchange rate. If the foreign exchange market is weakly efficient, this means that the future behaviour of exchange rates cannot be predicted from their past behaviour. This proposition casts doubt on the reliability and usefulness of time series and technical forecasting as well as the mechanical trading rules, which we study in Chapter 12.

Semi-strong efficiency

Semi-strong efficiency implies that the information set contains not only the past behaviour of exchange rates, but also all publicly available information. In the case of the foreign exchange market, **public information** pertains to the variables that affect exchange rates, economic and otherwise. Economic news as released by the authorities (the Reserve Bank and Treasury) is publicly available, since it is reported by the media as soon as it is released. This information includes statistics and analysis pertaining to inflation, growth, unemployment, the balance of payments, the money supply, public debt and any other economic variables that may cause changes in the supply and demand forces in the foreign exchange market. Relevant information also includes various reports and analyses prepared by the media and financial institutions and made publicly available. Non-economic factors include such things as cabinet reshuffles and changes in governments. If the foreign exchange market is efficient in this sense, then even research into the fundamental factors affecting the exchange rate will not help us to predict its future behaviour. This level of efficiency casts doubt on the reliability not only of technical and time series forecasting, but also econometric forecasting models, which are built on the basis of some underlying economic theory.

Strong efficiency

Strong efficiency implies that prices reflect all available information, including **private information** and **insider information**. It is normally argued that this level of efficiency does not apply to the foreign exchange market because, unlike the stock market, insider information is not important. However, it is not difficult to come up with examples of insider and private information pertaining to the foreign exchange market. Insider information may be obtained by having dinner with an official of the Reserve Bank who (privately) transmits knowledge of plans for intervention in the foreign exchange market or plans to change the exchange rate arrangement. Insider information can also be transmitted by Treasury officials who are aware of hitherto unreleased information pertaining to changes in macroeconomic policy that are bound to affect the exchange rate. Private information may arise when, for example, an analyst develops a profitable trading rule that is not revealed as public information. If the foreign exchange market is efficient in this sense, then not even insider and private information can help us to predict the future behaviour of exchange rates or to make abnormal profit.

11.2 Spot and forward market efficiency

The efficiency of the spot foreign exchange market implies that spot exchange rates move in a random and unpredictable manner, reflecting the random arrival of new information. This means that it is not possible to make profit by speculating in the foreign exchange market by buying and selling currencies actively. It also means that the exchange rate follows a **random walk**, which means that period-to-period changes in the exchange rate are random and do not follow any pattern and hence are unpredictable. The random walk behaviour may be represented by the equation

$$S_t = S_{t-1} + \varepsilon_t \tag{11.1}$$

where ε_t is a random error term. This equation tells us that the level of the exchange rate today differs from the level yesterday (or last month or whatever) by a random term, ε_t, which can be positive or negative. Equation (11.1) may be rewritten as

$$\Delta S_t = \varepsilon_t \tag{11.2}$$

which says that the period-to-period change in the exchange rate is random and unpredictable.

The concept of **forward market efficiency** encompasses both the spot and forward markets. In this sense, the market is efficient if it reflects all available information, where the information is embodied in the forward rate. The forward rate performs this function because it represents the collective wisdom of many well-informed profit-seeking traders and also because it is revised quickly as new information becomes available.

Consider the following example of speculation on the relationship between the spot and forward rates. If a speculator believes that the one-period forward exchange rate is lower than the spot rate prevailing on the maturity date of the contract, it will be profitable to buy forward and sell spot on the maturity of the forward contract. Let S_1 be the spot rate prevailing at time 1 where 0 is the present time and F be the forward rate agreed upon at time 0 for delivery at time 1. If the speculator is correct, he or she will make profit that is given by

$$\pi = S_1 - F \tag{11.3}$$

If this speculator acts on the basis of public information, there is no reason why other speculators will not take part in this 'feast'. The increase in the demand for forward contracts will raise the forward rate and reduce profit until the latter reaches the level of zero. At time 0, when the decision to speculate is taken, S_1 is not known, which means that speculators have to act on the basis of their expectation with respect to the spot exchange rate. Hence, speculators will buy forward at 0 and sell spot at 1 if the expected value of the spot exchange rate (S^e) is higher than the forward rate. This operation will come to an end if and when the expected value of the spot exchange rate is equal to the forward rate, that is if

$$S^e = F \tag{11.4}$$

The difference between the spot exchange rate at time 1 and the forward rate is also the **forecasting error** when the forward exchange rate is used as a forecaster of the spot rate. Market efficiency will hold in general if the forward exchange rate is an unbiased and efficient forecaster of the spot exchange rate. **Unbiasedness** means that, on average, the forward rate is equal to (and that it does not systematically underestimate or overestimate) the spot exchange rate prevailing on the maturity date of the forward contract. Efficiency of forecasting means that it is not possible to improve the forecast by utilising information other than what is embodied in the forward rate. This is why this kind of efficiency is alternatively known as **unbiased efficiency**.

Example

Suppose that the one-month USD/AUD exchange rate stands at 0.60. If a speculator thinks that on the date of the maturity of the forward contract (in one month's time), the spot exchange rate will be 0.65, he or she will buy the Australian dollar forward. What happens on the maturity of the forward contract depends on the level of the spot exchange rate prevailing then. If the speculator is correct, in the sense that the spot exchange rate turns out to be 0.65, then he or she will take delivery of the Australian dollar bought forward one month ago at 0.60 and sell it spot at 0.65, making profit of USD0.05 per unit. The speculator makes profit as long as the spot exchange rate turns out to be higher than 0.60 and incurs a loss if it turns out to be below this level.

If all market participants indulge in this operation, the spot exchange rate will rise, reducing the expected profit. Hence, speculation will cease. Note that if they all believe that the forward rate is an unbiased and efficient predictor of the spot rate (that is, the market is efficient), then they will think that the spot rate on the maturity of the forward contract will be 0.60, which means that expected profit will be zero. Hence, no one will attempt to make profit by speculating in this way.

Figure 11.1 plots the AUD/GBP spot rate against the forward rate three months earlier (the lagged forward rate). It can be seen that the forward rate follows the spot rate, implying that both the spot rate and the forward rate are determined simultaneously by the same set of factors. For example, if the market turns bullish on the pound, both the spot and forward rates will rise. This means that the forward rate is not a good predictor of the spot rate. Figure 11.2 plots the forecasting error of the forward rate. It is obvious that this error can be substantial.

Figure 11.1 The forward rate as predictor of the spot rate (AUD/GBP)

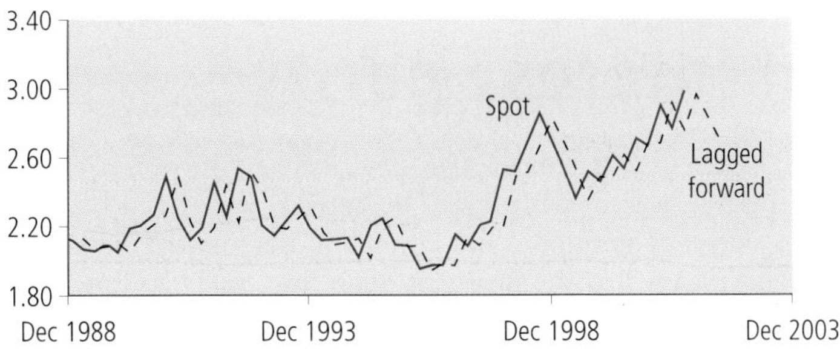

Source: Main Economic Indicators, OECD; Datastream.

Figure 11.2 The forecasting error of the forward rate (AUD/GBP)

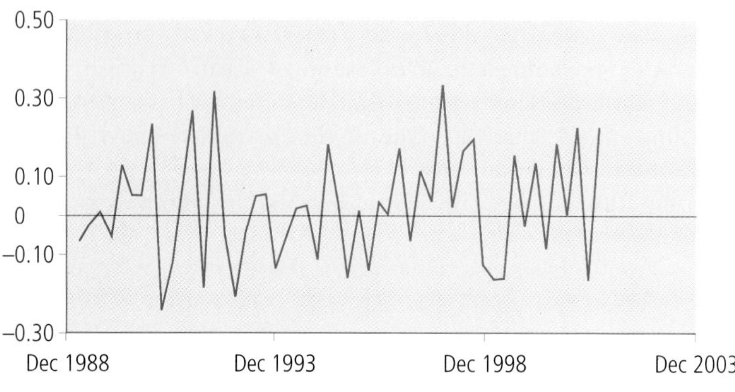

Source: Main Economic Indicators, OECD; Datastream.

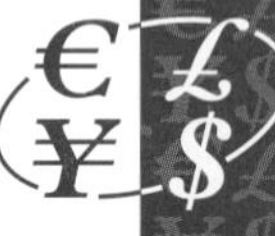

IN PRACTICE

What is the peso problem?

The **peso problem** is a concept that emerged out of a real-life event in Mexico, but it has become a term that is used frequently by applied economists to explain the failure of the unbiased efficiency hypothesis (that is, the inability of the forward rate to predict the spot rate).

Long before its devaluation in 1976, the Mexican peso was consistently selling at a forward discount because market participants were anticipating a sizeable devaluation of the currency. Thus, for a long period of time prior to the actual devaluation of the currency, it looked as though the forward rate was not capable of predicting the spot rate.

Since then, the concept of the peso problem has been generalised to mean the following: if there is a small probability of a large change in the underlying determinants of the exchange rate (market fundamentals), standard statistical tests of the unbiasedness hypothesis may not be valid. This would certainly be the case if the test were conducted using data covering the period prior to the actual devaluation of the currency. The research conducted by Sachsida, Ellery and Teixeira confirms the validity of the peso problem for the Brazilian currency during the period 1995–1998.[1]

[1] A. Sachsida, R. Ellery and J. R. Teixeira, 'Uncovered Interest Parity and the Peso Problem: The Brazilian Case', *Applied Economics Letters*, 8, 2001, pp. 179–81.

11.3 Uncovered interest parity

The **uncovered interest parity (UIP)** condition is described as 'uncovered' because it is restored and maintained by **uncovered arbitrage**. The latter is uncovered because, unlike covered arbitrage, the long currency position is not covered in the forward market but rather left uncovered or open. This means that the proceeds of an investment in foreign currency assets are reconverted into the domestic currency (or vice versa) at the spot exchange rate prevailing on the maturity date of the investment rather than at the forward rate determined in advance. Thus, foreign exchange risk is present.

UIP is an important relationship for several reasons. First, the empirical validity of UIP implies that financial markets are highly integrated despite the presence of foreign exchange risk. Thus, deviations from the UIP equilibrium condition could imply lack of integration between capital markets. Second, UIP can be used to investigate interest rate linkages across countries. Third, this relationship is a component of some exchange rate determination models such as some versions of the monetary model. Thus, the empirical validity, or otherwise, of UIP has implications for the empirical validity, or otherwise, of these models. UIP also has implications for the investment and financing decisions of international firms.

The UIP condition can be derived by combining CIP with the unbiased efficiency condition. Thus, we can obtain UIP if the forward rate (forward spread) in CIP is replaced with the expected spot rate (expected percentage change in the spot rate). This difference in specification reflects the difference between covered arbitrage, which is based on the forward rate (or forward spread), and uncovered arbitrage, which is based on the expected spot rate (or expected change in the spot rate).

Just like CIP, UIP can be derived from the process of uncovered arbitrage. One important difference remains, however. Foreign exchange risk is present in uncovered arbitrage and so it may be perceived to be more like speculation than arbitrage, which is normally defined as a risk-free activity. However, the term 'uncovered arbitrage' is used so that it can be the counterpart of 'covered arbitrage'. Moreover, if arbitragers firmly believe in their exchange rate expectations, then they will behave as if there is no foreign exchange risk. Finally, if the operation involves a pair of currencies with a fixed or highly stable exchange rate, then foreign exchange risk will be absent or minimal, in which case the term 'arbitrage' is appropriate.

Consider an investor with initial capital, K, who is facing two alternatives: (i) domestic investment, whereby the investor buys domestic assets, earning the domestic interest rate, i; and (ii) foreign investment, whereby the investor converts the domestic currency into foreign currency to buy foreign assets, earning the foreign interest rate, i^*. Foreign investment produces exposure to foreign exchange risk, which in this case is not covered, as the investor leaves the position open. Foreign exchange risk is present because, unlike the forward rate, the spot exchange rate used to reconvert the proceeds of foreign investment into domestic currency is not known in advance (that is, prior to the maturity of the investment). In this case, the investor acts upon the spot rate expected to prevail on the maturity date of the investment, not knowing in advance the domestic currency value of his or her foreign investment on maturity.

Suppose that the investor is considering a one-period investment starting with the acquisition of a financial asset (for example, a bank deposit) at time 0 and ending with the maturity of this asset at time 1. When the investor chooses domestic investment, the invested capital is compounded at the domestic interest rate and the investor ends up with the initial capital plus the return, which is $K(1 + i)$, where i is the interest earned by holding the domestic asset between time 0 and time 1. If the investor chooses foreign investment, he or she will convert the initial capital into foreign currency at the current spot exchange rate, S, obtaining K/S units of the foreign currency, where S is measured as domestic currency units per one unit of the foreign currency. If K/S worth of the foreign currency is invested in foreign assets, this capital is compounded for one period at the foreign interest rate, i^*, such that the foreign currency value of the investment on maturity is $(K/S)(1 + i^*)$. The expected domestic currency value of this investment is obtained by reconverting this amount into domestic currency at the expected spot rate, S^e, to obtain $(KS^e/S)(1 + i^*)$. The two alternatives are described in Figure 11.3.

Figure 11.3 Return on domestic investment and foreign investment (with uncovered position)

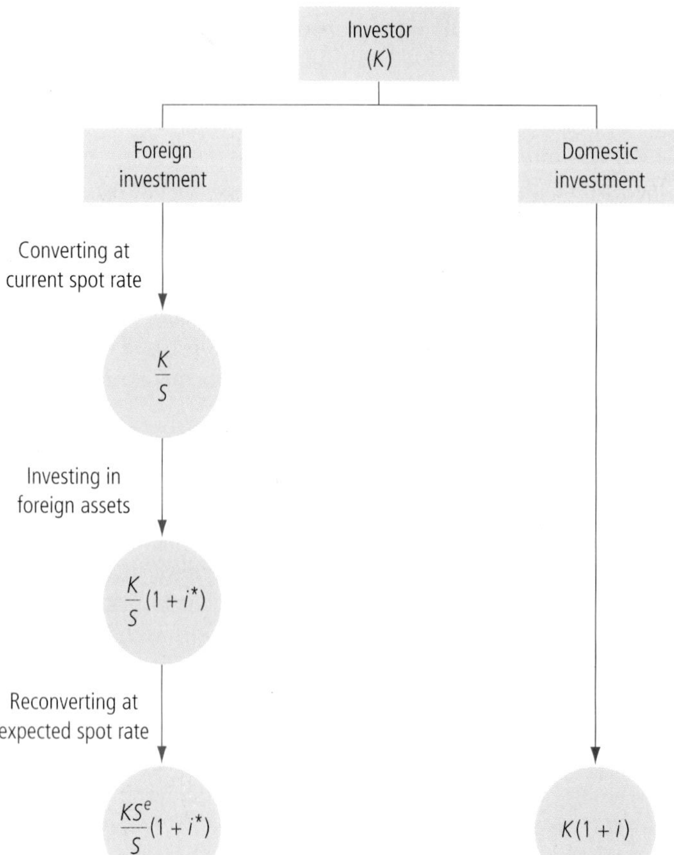

Again, we assume that there are no restrictions on the movement of capital and no transaction costs. Assume also that traders are risk-neutral, in the sense that they are indifferent between holding domestic and foreign assets if these assets offer the same (expected) return. The equilibrium condition that precludes the possibility of profitable arbitrage is that the two investments must be equally attractive, offering the same return. Hence

$$K(1+i) = \frac{KS^e}{S}(1+i^*) \tag{11.5}$$

or

$$1+i = \frac{S^e}{S}(1+i^*) \tag{11.6}$$

which says that the gross domestic return must be equal to the gross foreign uncovered return.

Since $S^e / S = 1 + \dot{S}^e$, where $\dot{S}^e$ is the expected percentage change in the exchange rate, it follows that

$$1+i = (1+\dot{S}^e)(1+i^*) \tag{11.7}$$

Equation (11.7) can be used to derive an approximate UIP condition by ignoring the term $i^{\star}\dot{S}^{e}$ on the assumption that it is too small. The approximate condition is given by

$$i - i^{\star} = \dot{S}^{e} \tag{11.8}$$

Equation (11.8) tells us that the currency offering the higher interest rate must be expected to depreciate, and vice versa. This is because if $i > i^{\star}$, then $\dot{S}^{e} > 0$, which means that the foreign currency (offering a lower interest rate) is expected to appreciate, whereas the domestic currency (offering a higher interest rate) is expected to depreciate. If, on the other hand, $i < i^{\star}$, then $\dot{S}^{e} < 0$, implying that the foreign currency is expected to depreciate, whereas the domestic currency is expected to appreciate. This must be a necessary condition for equilibrium because no investor wants to hold a currency that offers a low interest rate and is expected to depreciate, whereas everyone wants to hold a currency that offers a high interest rate and is expected to appreciate.

Example

Assume that the current exchange rate between the Australian dollar and the US dollar is 1.80 (AUD/USD) and that the three-month interest rates on the Australian and US currencies are 6 and 4 per cent p.a., respectively. If UIP holds, the level of the exchange rate expected to prevail three months from now can be calculated from the (deannualised) interest rate differential as follows:

$$i - i^{\star} = \frac{6}{4} - \frac{4}{4} = 0.5\%$$

The US dollar should appreciate by 0.5 per cent. The level of the exchange rate three months from now should be

$$1.005 \times 1.80 = 1.809$$

11.4 The mechanics of uncovered interest arbitrage

Uncovered interest arbitrage consists of taking a short position on (that is, borrowing) a currency and taking a corresponding long position on (that is, investing in) another currency without covering the long position (see Figure 11.4). One of the two currencies may be the domestic currency and the other a foreign currency (although this is not necessarily the case). We will illustrate uncovered arbitrage by taking time 0 to be the time at which the operation is initiated and time 1 to be the time at which the investment matures and the short position is covered.

Arbitrage from the domestic currency to a foreign currency

Arbitrage in this case consists of the following steps:

- The arbitrager borrows domestic currency funds at the domestic interest rate, i. For simplicity, we assume that the amount borrowed is one domestic currency unit.
- The borrowed funds are converted at the spot exchange rate, S_0, obtaining $1/S_0$ foreign currency units. This amount is invested at the foreign interest rate, $i^{\star}$.

Figure 11.4 Uncovered interest arbitrage

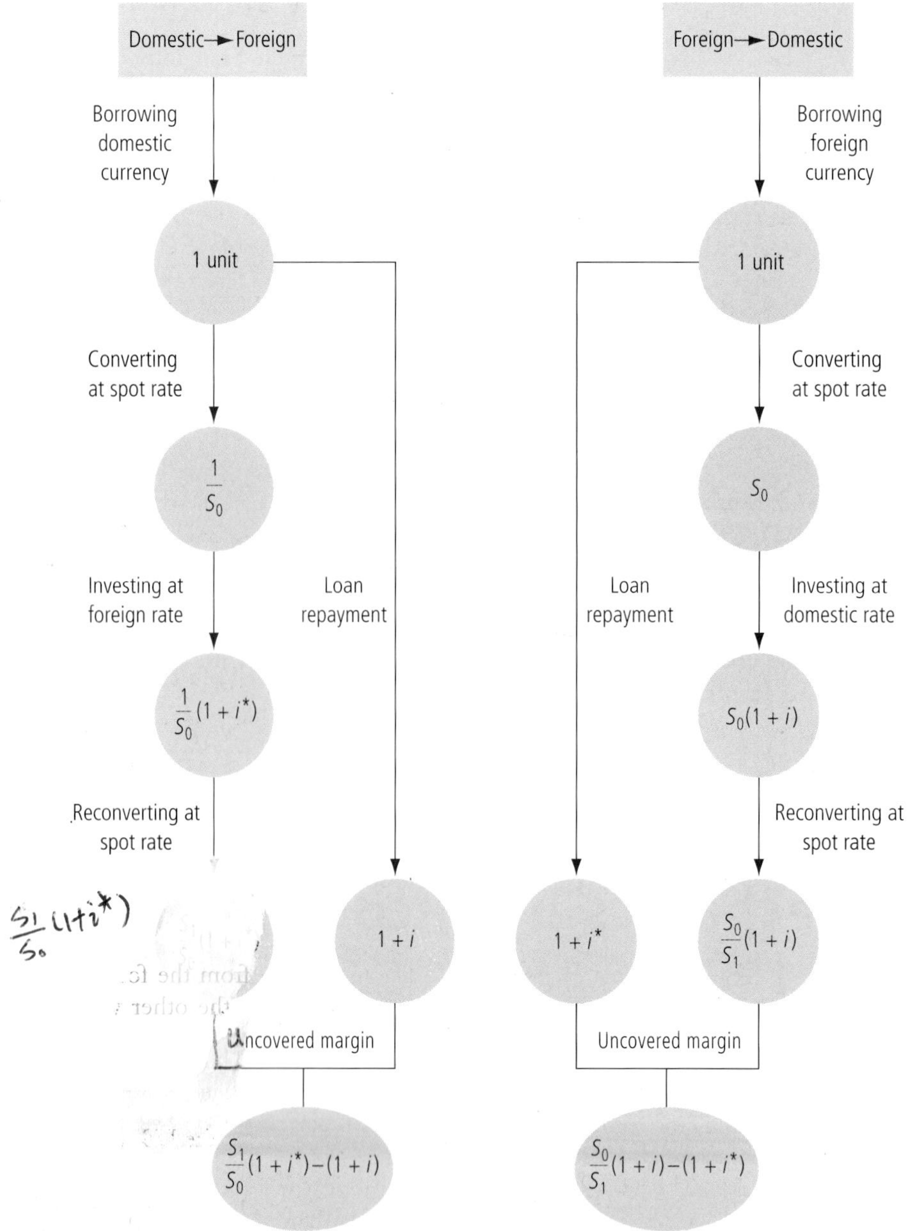

- The foreign currency value of the invested amount at the end of the investment period is $(1/S_0)(1 + i^*)$.
- This amount is reconverted into the domestic currency at the spot exchange rate prevailing at time 1, S_1, to obtain $(S_1/S_0)(1 + i^*)$ domestic currency units.
- The value of the loan plus interest is $(1 + i)$ domestic currency units.

The **uncovered margin**, π, is the difference between the domestic currency value of the proceeds and the loan repayment, which gives

$$\pi = \frac{S_1}{S_0}(1 + i^\star) - (1 + i) \tag{11.9}$$

or approximately

$$\pi = i^\star - i + \dot{S} \tag{11.10}$$

where $\dot{S}$ is the percentage change in the exchange rate between 0 and 1. Equation (11.10) tells us that the uncovered margin on arbitrage from the domestic to a foreign currency consists of the interest rate differential and the percentage change in the exchange rate.

Arbitrage from a foreign currency to the domestic currency

Arbitrage in this case consists of the following steps:

- The arbitrager borrows foreign currency funds at the foreign interest rate, $i^\star$. For simplicity, we again assume that the amount borrowed is one foreign currency unit.
- The borrowed funds are converted at the spot exchange rate, S_0, obtaining S_0 domestic currency units. This amount is invested at the domestic interest rate, i.
- The domestic currency value of the invested amount at the end of the investment period is $S_0(1 + i)$.
- This amount is reconverted into the foreign currency at the spot rate, S_1, to obtain $(S_0/S_1)(1 + i)$ foreign currency units.
- The value of the loan plus interest is $(1 + i^\star)$ foreign currency units.

The uncovered margin is the difference between the foreign currency value of the proceeds and the loan repayment, which gives

$$\pi = \frac{S_0}{S_1}(1 + i) - (1 + i^\star) \tag{11.11}$$

or approximately

$$\pi = i - i^\star - \dot{S} \tag{11.12}$$

Equation (11.12) tells us that the uncovered margin on arbitrage from the foreign to the domestic currency consists of the interest rate differential (measured the other way round) and the negative of the percentage change in the exchange rate.

Example

Assume that the one-year interest rates on the Australian dollar and the US dollar are 4 and 7 per cent, respectively. The current exchange rate (AUD/USD) is 1.80. An investor is considering uncovered arbitrage by taking a short position on (borrowing) the Australian dollar and a long position on (lending) the US dollar. Since the interest rate differential is 3 per cent, this investor will make profit (ignoring transaction costs) as long as the US dollar does not depreciate against the Australian dollar by more than 3 per cent. The following table shows the rate of return or the uncovered margin for various levels of the exchange rate prevailing on the maturity of the investment for arbitrage in both directions (calculations are based on (11.10) and (11.12)).

Continued...

S_0	S_1	AUD→USD	USD→AUD
1.80	1.85	5.8	−5.8
1.80	1.80	3.0	−3.0
1.80	1.75	0.2	−0.2
1.80	1.70	−2.6	2.6
1.80	1.65	−5.3	5.3

Suppose now that the Australian dollar interest rate rises to 9 per cent whereas the US dollar interest rate remains unchanged. The investor will be willing to go long on the US dollar only if it is expected to appreciate by more than 2 per cent. The following table shows the rate of return for various levels of the final exchange rate:

S_0	S_1	AUD→USD	USD→AUD
1.80	1.85	0.8	−0.8
1.80	1.80	−2.0	2.0
1.80	1.75	−4.8	4.8
1.80	1.70	−7.6	7.6
1.80	1.65	−10.3	10.3

11.5 Uncovered arbitrage with bid-offer spreads

Let us now reconsider uncovered arbitrage when there are bid-offer spreads in both exchange and interest rates, as illustrated in Figure 11.5. Remember that a price taker in the foreign exchange market buys at the (higher) offer exchange rate and sells at the (lower) bid exchange rate of the market maker. A price taker in the money market borrows at the (higher) offer interest rate and lends at the (lower) bid interest rate of the market maker.

Arbitrage from the domestic currency to a foreign currency

Arbitrage in this case consists of the following steps:

- The arbitrager borrows domestic currency funds (one unit) at the domestic offer interest rate, i_a.
- The borrowed funds are converted into the foreign currency at the spot offer rate, S_{a0}, obtaining $1/S_{a0}$ foreign currency units. This amount is invested at the foreign bid rate, $i_b^{\star}$.
- The foreign currency value of the invested amount at the end of the investment period is $(1/S_{a0})(1 + i_b^{\star})$.
- This amount is reconverted into the domestic currency at the spot bid rate, S_{b1}, to obtain $(S_{b1}/S_{a0})(1 + i_b^{\star})$ domestic currency units.
- The value of the loan plus interest is $(1 + i_a)$ domestic currency units.

The uncovered margin in this case is

$$\pi = \frac{S_{b1}}{S_{a0}}(1 + i_b^{\star}) - (1 + i_a) \qquad (11.13)$$

Figure 11.5 Uncovered interest arbitrage in the presence of bid-offer spreads

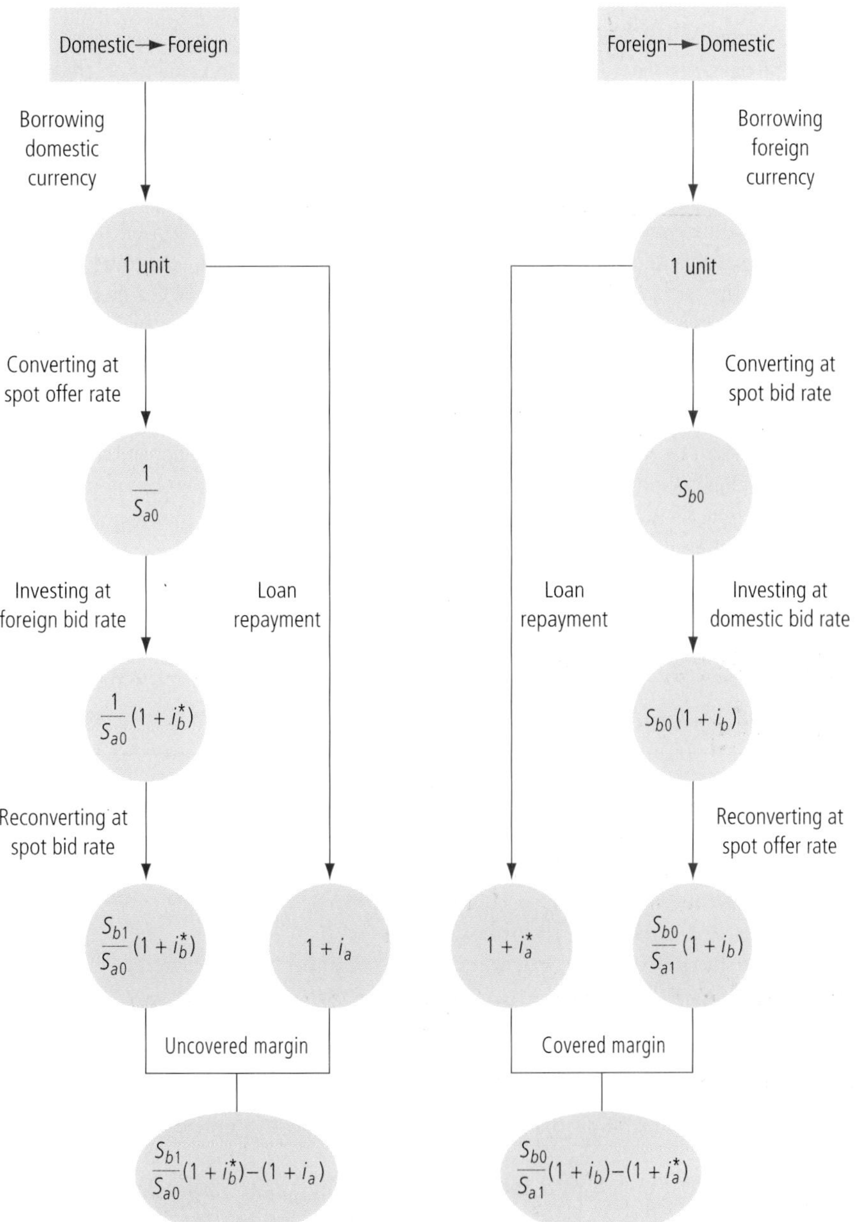

Since $S_{b1}/S_{a0} = (1+\dot{S}_b)/(1+m)$, it follows that

$$\pi = i_b^* - i_a + \dot{S}_b - m \tag{11.14}$$

where $\dot{S}_b$ is the percentage change in the bid exchange rate. It can be seen from Equations (11.13) and (11.14) that the uncovered margin is lower if we allow for bid-offer spreads.

IN PRACTICE

'Innovative' uncovered arbitrage

Uncovered arbitrage is a risky operation, because an adverse change in the exchange rate could wipe out the gains derived from the interest rate differential. Thus, what prevents an arbitrager from going short on a low-interest currency and long on a high-interest currency is the fear that the high-interest currency will depreciate against the low-interest currency. We have seen that one way of eliminating this risk is by covering the long position in the forward market. In practice, this (covered arbitrage) operation would not produce much profit, since covered interest parity tends to hold.

Is there any other way of eliminating or reducing foreign exchange risk in uncovered arbitrage that makes it possible to utilise the interest rate differential without being concerned about adverse movements in the exchange rate? The answer is, surprisingly, 'yes'. This could be done in two cases. The first involves two currencies whose exchange rates against the US dollar are highly correlated. If this is so, the cross exchange rate between the two currencies tends to be stable and hence foreign exchange risk becomes minimal. The second case involves a currency that is pegged to a basket. If the currency components of the basket can be revealed (which would take some research), arbitrage profit can be made by taking short (long) positions on the component currencies and a corresponding long (short) position on the pegged currency. If the structure of the portfolio of the component currencies is similar to the structure of the basket (that is, if the weights are equal), it would be as if the arbitrager is taking a long (short) position on a currency and a short (long) position on the same currency. This is because the exchange rate of the pegged currency against the dollar is a weighted average of the exchange rates of the component currencies against the dollar. A more detailed description of these operations is available.[1]

[1] I. A. Moosa, *International Financial Operations: Arbitrage, Hedging, Speculation, Financing and Investing*, Palgrave, London 2003.

Arbitrage from a foreign currency to the domestic currency

Arbitrage in this case consists of the following steps:

- The arbitrager borrows foreign currency funds (one unit) at the foreign offer interest rate, i_a^*.
- The borrowed funds are converted into the domestic currency at the spot bid rate, S_{b0}, obtaining S_{b0} domestic currency units. This amount is invested at the domestic bid interest rate, i_b.
- The domestic currency value of the invested amount at the end of the investment period is $S_{b0}(1 + i_b)$.
- This amount is reconverted into the foreign currency at the spot offer rate, S_{a1}, to obtain $(S_{b0}/S_{a1})(1 + i_b)$ foreign currency units.
- The value of the loan plus interest is $(1 + i_a^*)$ foreign currency units.

The uncovered margin in this case is

$$\pi = \frac{S_{b0}}{S_{a1}}(1+i_b) - (1+i_a^*) \tag{11.15}$$

Since $S_{b0} / S_{a1} = 1/[(1+\dot{S}_b)(1+m)]$, it follows that

$$\pi = i_b - i_a^* - \dot{S}_b - m \tag{11.16}$$

Example

Consider the previous example with bid-offer spreads. The exchange rates are as shown in the table below, whereas the interest rates are 3.75–4.25 and 6.75–7.25. The uncovered margin (using Equations (11.13) and (11.15)) should now be as in the table.

S_0	S_1	AUD→USD	USD→AUD
1.7950–1.8050	1.9450–1.9550	10.8	−12.0
1.7950–1.8050	1.8950–1.9050	7.8	−9.5
1.7950–1.8050	1.8450–1.8550	4.9	−6.9
1.7950–1.8050	1.7950–1.8050	1.9	−4.1
1.7950–1.8050	1.7450–1.7550	−1.1	−1.4

11.6 The empirical validity of UIP

For UIP to be valid, the uncovered margin must fluctuate around a mean value of zero. Figure 11.6 displays the three-month uncovered margins *vis-à-vis* four currencies (short position on the Australian dollar) over the period 1988–2001. It is obvious that the uncovered margins assume large values (note that the numbers are not annualised) and that they have mean values that are significantly different from zero. This means that there are significant deviations from UIP. Note also that these deviations are greater than those encountered in the case of CIP (see Figure 10.4).

Figure 11.6 Uncovered margins in percentage points (short Australian dollar)

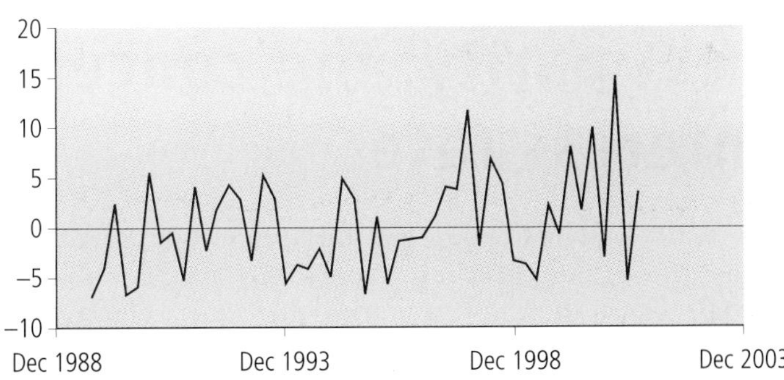

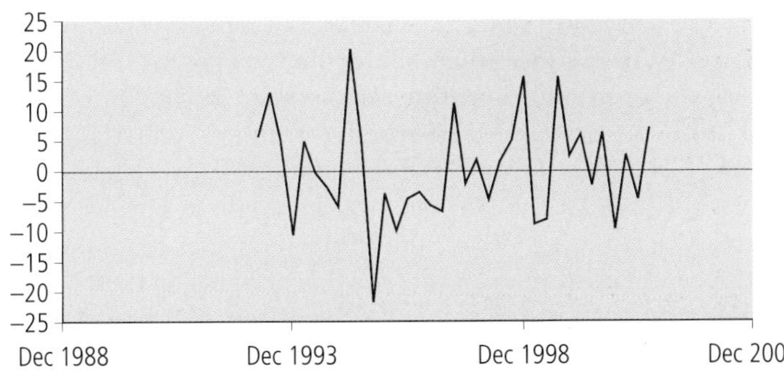

Continued...

(c) AUD/GBP

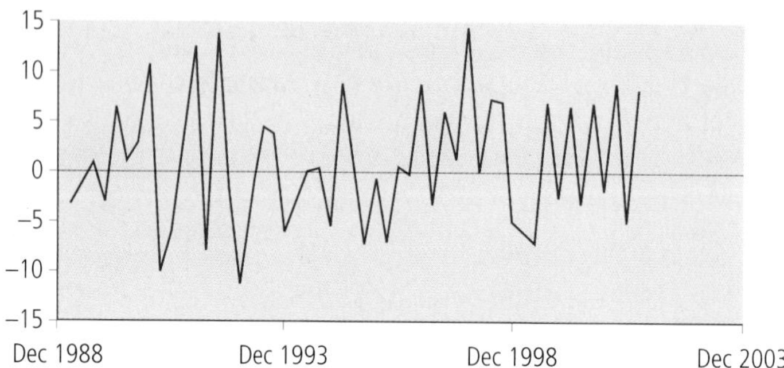

(d) AUD/CAD

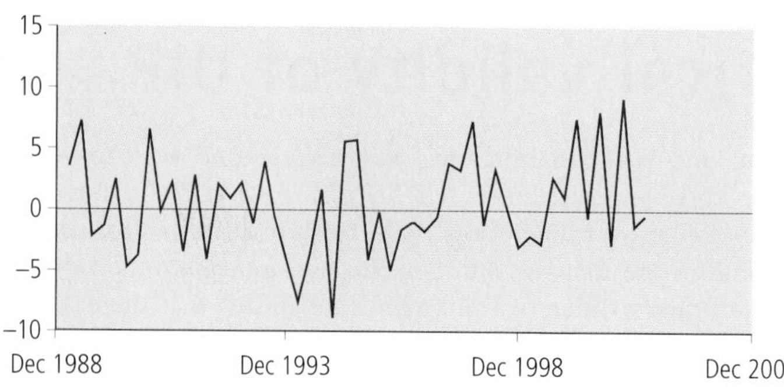

Source: Main Economic Indicators, OECD.

11.7 Real interest parity: the concept of the real interest rate

The **real interest parity (RIP)** hypothesis postulates that, if the world markets for goods, capital and foreign exchange are integrated, real interest rates on perfectly comparable financial assets tend to be equalised across countries over time. Obviously, this has implications for investment and financing decisions in the sense that, if the hypothesis held precisely, currency denomination of investment and financing portfolios would not matter.

We start by defining the **real interest rate**. Suppose that an investor is contemplating buying a financial asset such as a Treasury bill or a certificate of deposit. The investor knows in advance that on the maturity of the investment, he or she will receive the principal and some return measured by the **nominal interest rate**, which is the quoted, inflation-unadjusted interest rate. Thus, if the principal, K, is invested at time 0, and assuming that the investment matures at time 1 and that the underlying (nominal) interest rate is i, then on maturity the investor receives $K(1 + i)$. The real value of this amount, however, depends on the general price level prevailing at time 1. What is meant by the real value is the quantity of goods and services that can be obtained in exchange for this nominal amount.

Let us assume that at time 0, when the investment is undertaken, the general price level is P_0. The real value of the capital invested is obtained by deflating (that is, dividing) the amount

The empirical validity of unbiasedness and UIP

RESEARCH FINDINGS

The unbiased efficiency hypothesis has been tested extensively, with mixed results. While most individual country studies have produced mainly unfavourable results, Ho used panel data covering 17 countries, including Australia, to obtain evidence that was supportive of the hypothesis.[1] Jung, Doroodian and Albarano attributed the failure to find supportive evidence to the model choice.[2] If the relationship is tested by relating the level of the spot rate to the level of the lagged forward rate, the evidence turns out to be mixed. If the model relates the forward spread to the percentage change in the exchange rate, then the tests reject the hypothesis comprehensively. Wolff showed that the rejection of the hypothesis is attributed to the presence of a **risk premium** that varies with time.[3] If the risk premium is modelled such that it is allowed to vary over time, the forecasting power of the equation becomes much greater. Moosa confirmed the presence of this kind of risk premium in six different exchange rates.[4]

Since the unbiasedness hypothesis is a necessary condition for UIP, any evidence against unbiasedness must imply the failure of UIP. Direct tests of UIP have also produced mixed evidence that is influenced by the model used. For example, King found that UIP held strongly between Australia and New Zealand following the removal of capital controls, indicating that the capital markets of these two countries have become highly integrated.[5]

1 T. W. Ho, 'The Forward Rate Unbiasedness Hypothesis Revisited', *Applied Financial Economics*, 12, 2002, pp. 799–804.

2 C. Jung, K. Doroodian and R. Albarano, 'The Unbiased Forward Rate Hypothesis: A Re-Examination', *Applied Financial Economics*, 8, 1998, pp. 567–75.

3 C. C. P. Wolff, 'Forward Foreign Exchange Rates and Expected Future Spot Rates', *Applied Financial Economics*, 10, 2000, pp. 371–7.

4 I. A. Moosa, 'A Test of the News Model of Exchange Rates', *Weltwirtschaftliches Archiv*, 138, 2002, pp. 694–710.

5 A. King, 'Uncovered Interest Parity: New Zealand's Post-Deregulation Experience', *Applied Financial Economics*, 8, 1998, pp. 495–503.

by the prevailing price level. This means that the real value of K at time 0 is K/P_0. At time 1, the real value of the amount $K(1 + i)$ is $K(1 + i)/P_1$. Now, remember that the nominal interest rate is calculated from the nominal amounts (K and $K(1 + i)$), whereas the real interest rate is calculated from the real amounts (K/P_0 and $K(1 + i)/P_1$). Let the real interest rate be r, then

$$1 + r = \frac{K(1+i)/P_1}{K/P_0} \tag{11.17}$$

This equation can be manipulated to produce

$$1 + r = \frac{(1+i)}{P_1/P_0} \tag{11.18}$$

Since $P_1/P_0 = 1 + \dot{P}$, where $\dot{P}$ is the rate of change of the price level between 0 and 1 (that is, the inflation rate), it follows that

$$(1+r)(1+\dot{P}) = (1+i) \tag{11.19}$$

which gives

$$r = i - \dot{P} - r\dot{P} \tag{11.20}$$

If we ignore $r\dot{P}$ because it is small, Equation (11.20) reduces to

$$r = i - \dot{P} \tag{11.21}$$

This tells us that the real interest rate is the nominal interest rate minus the inflation rate over the holding period. If the inflation rate is higher than the nominal interest rate, the real interest rate is negative. This is the case when the amount consisting of the principal and interest received at time 1 buys a smaller quantity of goods and services than could be bought with the principal only at time 0.

Example

Suppose that a principal amount of AUD1000 is invested in a fixed deposit. The deposit is placed on 31 December 2002 at a time when the price of a glass of beer is AUD2. Thus, on 31 December 2002, the nominal value of the principal invested is AUD1000. The real value of this amount (that is, its purchasing power, using beer as a yardstick) is equal to

$$\frac{1000}{2} = 500$$

The deposit matures on 31 December 2003, with the investor receiving AUD1100. This is the nominal amount of the principal and interest, which means that the nominal interest rate is given by

$$1 + i = \frac{1100}{1000}$$

which gives i = 10 per cent. The real value of the principal and interest is determined by the price of beer on 31 December 2003. Let us assume that for some reason the price of a glass of beer rose to AUD2.10. The real value of AUD1100 is

$$\frac{1100}{2.10} = 524$$

This means that on 31 December 2003, AUD1100 can buy 524 glasses of beer, which is its purchasing power or real value. The real interest rate is thus given by

$$1 + r = \frac{524}{500}$$

which gives r = 4.8 per cent. Thus, the real interest rate is lower than the nominal interest rate.

The real interest rate can also be calculated from the approximate formula given by Equation (11.21). Since i = 10 per cent and $\dot{P}$ = 5 per cent, it follows that

$$r = 10 - 5 = 5\%$$

which is slightly different because Equation (11.19) is an approximate formula that ignores the term $r\dot{P}$.

If the price of a glass of beer goes up to AUD2.50, we obtain a negative real interest rate. This is because the real value of the principal and interest earned is

$$\frac{1100}{2.50} = 440$$

Hence, the real interest rate is

$$1 + r = \frac{440}{500}$$

which gives $r = -12$ per cent. In practice, however, we do not measure real values in terms of the price of a single commodity, such as beer, but rather in terms of a basket of goods and services such as the consumer price index.

The real interest rate defined by Equation (11.21) can only be determined at time 1 when the inflation rate over the holding period is known. This rate tells us how well the investor has done after the fact and so it is described as an **ex post real interest rate**. What is important for investment and financing decisions is the real interest rate that is expected at time 0 to prevail over the holding period between 0 and 1, which is the expected or **ex ante real interest rate**. An investor who wants to buy a financial asset at time 0 will contemplate the real interest rate to be obtained on the investment. Obviously, if the expected real interest rate is negative, then the investor may consider another investment, perhaps real estate, if the latter gives a positive expected return. The real interest rate cannot be known at time 0 because the inflation rate is not known then. Thus, the expected or ex ante real interest rate is obtained by subtracting the expected inflation rate from the nominal interest rate, which gives

$$r^e = i - \dot{P}^e \tag{11.22}$$

This relationship is also known as the **Fisher equation** or the **Fisher hypothesis** after its founder, US economist Irving Fisher.

Example

The difference between the ex ante and ex post real interest rates can be illustrated with the help of this numerical example. Suppose that on 31 December 2002 the consumer price index stood at 150. An investor is considering investing AUD1000 as a one-year fixed deposit earning a nominal interest rate of 10 per cent. The investor believes that by 31 December 2003, the consumer price index would have reached a level of 157.5, implying an expected inflation rate of 5 per cent. Thus, this investor expects to earn a real interest rate of

$$r^e = 10 - 5 = 5\%$$

This is the ex ante real interest rate. Whether or not this turns out to be the case depends on whether or not the actual inflation rate turns out to be equal to or different from the expected rate. Only if the expected inflation rate is realised will the ex ante real interest rate be equal to the ex post rate. The following table shows the ex post real interest rate for various actual inflation rates.

CPI (Dec 2002)	Inflation rate	Ex post real interest rate
150.0	0.0	10.0
154.0	2.7	7.3
157.5	5.0	5.0
165.5	10.3	−0.3
170.0	13.3	−3.3

Does the Fisher hypothesis work in Australia?

The Fisher hypothesis would work perfectly if the nominal interest rate changed in proportion to inflation so that the real interest rate remained unchanged. Most of the evidence, however, indicates that real interest rates are not constant because nominal interest rates do not adjust in full to changes in inflation.

At least three studies have investigated the validity of the Fisher hypothesis in Australia. The following are the main findings of these studies:

- Inder and Silvapulle examined the relationship between the nominal interest rate and inflation in Australia over the period 1965–1990. They found that the nominal interest rate did not respond fully to changes in inflation and that real interest rates remained at a high level. Their explanation is that Australian interest rates are determined by foreign interest rates rather than by domestic inflation.[1]
- Mishkin and Simon concluded that the Fisher hypothesis is valid over a long period of time, but not in the short run. They explained their results by postulating that short-run changes in interest rates reflect changes in monetary policy, but the level of the nominal interest rate in the long run reflects inflationary expectations.[2]
- Olekalns obtained results that were highly sensitive to the period under consideration. He found the Fisher hypothesis to be more valid in the post-deregulation (that is, the post-1983) period.[3]

1 B. Inder and P. Silvapulle, 'Does the Fisher Effect Apply in Australia?', *Applied Economics*, 25, 1993, pp. 839–43.
2 F. S. Mishkin and J. Simon, 'An Empirical Examination of the Fisher Effect in Australia', *Economic Record*, 71, 1995, pp. 217–29.
3 N. Olekalns, 'Further Evidence on the Fisher Effect', *Applied Economics*, 28, 1996, pp. 851–6.

11.8 Real interest parity: derivation and empirical evidence

The RIP condition, relating expected real interest rates, can be derived by combining UIP and PPP written in ex ante form (that is, in terms of the expected values of the variables). These two relationships are reproduced below.

$$\dot{S}^e = i - i^\star \tag{11.23}$$

$$\dot{S}^e = \dot{P}^e - \dot{P}^{\star e} \tag{11.24}$$

By combining Equations (11.23) and (11.24), we obtain

$$\dot{P}^e - \dot{P}^{\star e} = i - i^\star \tag{11.25}$$

This can be rearranged to produce

$$i - \dot{P}^e = i^\star - \dot{P}^{\star e} \tag{11.26}$$

or

$$r^e = r^{\star e} \tag{11.27}$$

Equation (11.27) tells us that expected real interest rates must be equalised across countries. RIP can also be derived independently. If investors allocate their funds according to expected real interest rates, this will ensure the equality of these rates. Suppose that there are two financial centres, A and B, such that the real interest rate in A is higher than that in B. Investors shift resources from B to A, causing a fall in the expected real interest rate in A and a rise in the expected real interest rate in B. The flow of funds continues until the expected real interest rates in A and B are equal.

RIP is used as an indicator of: (i) the efficiency of the goods and financial markets; (ii) the degree of integration of capital and goods markets across countries; and (iii) the degree of capital mobility. This can be seen by splitting the real interest differential as follows. Since

$$r^e - r^{\star e} = (i - \dot{P}^e) - (i^\star - \dot{P}^{\star e}) \tag{11.28}$$

By rearranging, we obtain

$$r^e - r^{\star e} = (i - i^\star) + (-\dot{P}^e + \dot{P}^{\star e}) \tag{11.29}$$

By adding and subtracting the expected change in the spot exchange rate, we obtain

$$r^e - r^{\star e} = (i - i^\star - \dot{S}^e) + (\dot{S}^e - \dot{P}^e + \dot{P}^{\star e}) \tag{11.30}$$

The first term on the right-hand side of Equation (11.28) is the **uncovered interest differential**, which reflects deviations from UIP and hence the efficiency of financial markets. The second term is the expected real appreciation or depreciation, which measures deviations from ex ante PPP and hence the efficiency of the goods markets. Note that if both UIP and ex ante PPP hold, then both of the terms on the right-hand side of Equation (11.30) will be zero, which means that the **real interest differential** is zero (that is, RIP holds precisely). By adding and subtracting the forward spread, f, Equation (11.30) can be rewritten as

$$r^e - r^{\star e} = (i - i^\star - f) + (f - \dot{S}^e) + (\dot{S}^e - \dot{P}^e + \dot{P}^{\star e}) \tag{11.31}$$

The first term is now the **covered interest differential**, which implies deviations from CIP, whereas the second term is the **forward rate bias**, which measures deviations from unbiased efficiency. If CIP, unbiasedness and ex ante PPP hold, the expected real interest differential is zero, which means that RIP holds.

Example

The following table contains data on spot and forward exchange rates, as well as prices and interest rates, at the end of March and the end of June 2001:

	Mar 2001	Jun 2001
Australia		
P	113.7	114.6
i	4.98	4.88
United States		
P^*	115.3	116.5
i^*	4.29	3.63
S (versus AUD)	2.0595	1.9579
F (versus AUD)	2.0712	1.9644

Continued...

	Mar 2001	Jun 2001
Japan		
P^*	101.0	101.0
i^*	0.12	0.05
S (versus AUD)	0.01565	0.01571
F (versus AUD)	0.01658	0.01592
United Kingdom		
P^*	115.2	116.7
i^*	5.57	5.06
S (versus AUD)	2.9172	2.7728
F (versus AUD)	2.9388	2.7710
Canada		
P^*	110.5	112.4
i^*	4.58	4.30
S (versus AUD)	1.3066	1.2918
F (versus AUD)	1.3164	1.2941

By using this information we can show that Equations (11.30) and (11.31), which represent the split of the real interest differential, do hold as at the end of March 2001. Notice that by applying these equations to historical data, variables with the superscript e take the time subscript 1 (June 2001), whereas those without the superscript take the time subscript 0 (March 2001). The results are shown in the following table (all figures are annualised).

	Australia	United States	Japan	United Kingdom	Canada
Inflation*	3.17	4.16	0.0	5.21	6.88
Real interest rate	1.81	0.13	0.12	0.36	−2.30
Change in spot rate*		−19.73	1.53	−19.80	−4.53
Forward spread		2.27	23.77	2.96	3.00
Real interest differential		1.68	1.69	1.45	4.11
Deviation from UIP		20.42	3.33	19.21	4.93
Deviation from PPP		−18.74	−1.64	−17.76	−0.82
Deviation from CIP		−1.58	−18.91	−3.55	−2.60
Deviation from unbiasedness		22.01	22.24	22.76	7.53

*Calculated relative to March as the base period (time zero) to represent the expected rates.

The empirical validity of real interest parity

The empirical validity of RIP has been examined extensively, with mixed results depending on the interpretation of the condition. Those studies taking RIP to mean the equality of real interest rates on a period-to-period basis failed to find supportive evidence. However, if RIP is interpreted to mean that the real interest rates of two countries with strong trading and financial links should move together and converge on each other in the long run, then there is plenty of evidence supporting RIP. The following are examples of these findings:

- It has been found that the implementation of Closer Economic Relations (CER) and the deregulation of financial markets have contributed to achieving a higher degree of integration between goods and financial markets in Australia and New Zealand. This evidence is based on the finding of real interest linkages in the post-CER period.[1]
- It has been shown that the property of mean reversion in the real interest differentials versus Germany indicates capital market integration in Europe.[2]
- It has also been shown that RIP is supported when tested for Australia and New Zealand versus Japan. Again, the interpretation is that financial goods markets have become integrated.[3]

[1] I. A. Moosa and R. H. Bhatti, 'Are Australian and New Zealand Markets Integrated? Evidence from RIP Tests', *Journal of Economic Integration*, 10, 1995, pp. 415–33.

[2] I. A. Moosa and R. H. Bhatti, 'Does Europe Have an Integrated Capital Market? Evidence from Real Interest Parity Tests', *Applied Economics Letters*, 3, 1996, pp. 517–20.

[3] I. A. Moosa and R. H. Bhatti, 'Are Pacific Markets Integrated? A Case Study of Australia, New Zealand and Japan', *Journal of International Economic Studies*, 11, 1997, pp. 93–108.

Summary

- In an efficient market, prices reflect all available information. If information pertains to past prices only, then the market is weakly efficient. If the relevant information set contains publicly available information as well, the market is efficient in a semi-strong sense. If the information set includes insider and private information, the market is efficient in a strong sense.
- Spot market efficiency implies that spot exchange rates move in a random and unpredictable way. Foreign exchange market efficiency, or unbiased efficiency, refers to the proposition that the forward exchange rate is an unbiased and efficient forecaster of the spot rate.
- Uncovered interest parity describes the relationship between exchange rates and interest rates. It tells us that a currency that offers a high interest rate must be expected to depreciate, and vice versa.
- UIP is important because: (i) its empirical validity implies that financial markets are integrated; (ii) it can be used to investigate interest rate linkages across countries; and (iii) it is a component of exchange rate determination models.
- The uncovered margin is net profit received from uncovered arbitrage.
- The UIP condition can be adjusted to allow for the presence of bid-offer spreads in interest and exchange rates. Uncovered arbitrage is less profitable if we take into account bid-offer spreads because these spreads are transaction costs.

- Real interest rates are nominal interest rates adjusted for inflation. The relationship between the nominal interest rate and the real interest rate is represented by the Fisher equation or the Fisher hypothesis.
- The real interest parity hypothesis postulates that real interest rates on perfectly comparable financial assets tend to be equalised across countries.
- While there is some evidence for RIP as a long-run equilibrium condition, the evidence is overwhelmingly against the hypothesis. One implication is that capital is not perfectly mobile.

Key terms

abnormal returns 292
allocative efficiency 292
covered interest differential 311
ex ante real interest rate 309
ex post real interest rate 309
Fisher equation 309
Fisher hypothesis 309
forecasting error 295
forward market efficiency 294
forward rate bias 311
informational efficiency 292
insider information 293
market efficiency 292
nominal interest rate 306
peso problem 296
private information 293
public information 293
random walk 294
real interest differential 311
real interest parity (RIP) 306
real interest rate 306
risk premium 307
semi-strong efficiency 293
strong efficiency 293
unbiased efficiency 295
unbiasedness 295
uncovered arbitrage 296
uncovered interest differential 311
uncovered interest parity (UIP) 296
uncovered margin 301
weak efficiency 293

MaxMARK

MAXIMISE YOUR MARKS! There are 30 interactive questions for this chapter available online at **www.mhhe.com/au/moosa2e**

Review questions

1. Distinguish among weak efficiency, semi-strong efficiency and strong efficiency. Why is strong efficiency more applicable to the stock market than to the foreign exchange market?
2. Explain why the forward rate forecasting error is also a measure of speculative profit.
3. What is meant by unbiasedness and efficiency?
4. What is the peso problem?
5. Why is uncovered interest arbitrage uncovered?
6. Explain how it is possible to reduce foreign exchange risk arising from uncovered arbitrage.
7. What is the connection between CIP and UIP?
8. 'The difference between the specification of CIP and UIP reflects the difference between covered and uncovered arbitrage.' Explain.

9 Uncovered interest parity tells us that a currency that offers a higher interest rate is expected to depreciate. Is it possible to reconcile this proposition with the prediction of the supply and demand model pertaining to the effect of the interest rate on the exchange rate?

10 What is the real interest rate and what is its significance?

11 What is the Fisher equation?

12 'RIP is the most stringent of the international parity conditions.' Explain.

13 Explain how RIP can be used to measure commodity and financial market integration.

Problems

1 The current AUD/EUR exchange rate is 1.60, the Australian three-month interest rate is 8.5 per cent p.a. and the three-month interest rate on the euro is 6.5 per cent p.a. Where will the exchange rate be in three months time if UIP holds?

2 Suppose that the exchange rate in three months time turned out to be 1.68. Calculate the uncovered margins obtained by going short on the Australian dollar and long on the euro, and vice versa.

3 The following information is available:

Spot exchange rate (CAD/GBP)	2.32
Canadian six-month interest rate	8% p.a.
British six-month interest rate	10% p.a.

Calculate the uncovered margin obtained by going short on the Canadian dollar if the exchange rate assumes the following values in six months: (a) 2.25, (b) 2.28, (c) 2.32, (d) 2.35 and (e) 2.38. Do the same by going short on the pound.

4 The following information is available:

Spot exchange rate (CAD/GBP)	2.3175–2.3225
Canadian six-month interest rate	7.75–8.25 p.a.
British six-month interest rate	9.75–10.25 p.a.

Calculate the uncovered margin by going short on the Canadian dollar if the exchange rate assumes the following values in six months: (a) 2.2475–2.2525, (b) 2.2775–2.2825, (c) 2.3175–2.3225, (d) 2.3475–2.3525 and (e) 2.3775–2.3825. Do the same by going short on the pound.

5 An investor pays AUD850 for a financial asset with a face value of AUD1000 maturing in one year. The consumer price index assumes the values 115 and 125 on the date of purchase and on maturity, respectively. Calculate the nominal and real interest rates.

6 The following is a set of quarterly data covering the period 1998–2001 on spot and three-month forward rates (AUD/CAD), three-month interest rates and prices for Australia and Canada. Use this data set to:
(a) Calculate and plot the real interest differential.
(b) Calculate and plot the deviation from PPP.
(c) Calculate and plot the deviation from UIP (the uncovered interest differential).
(d) Calculate and plot the deviation from CIP (the covered interest differential).
(e) Calculate and plot the deviation from unbiasedness (the forward rate bias).
(f) Verify that the real interest rate differential is equal to the sum of its components.

	Spot AUD/CAD	Forward AUD/CAD	Australian interest	Canadian interest	Australian prices	Canadian prices
Mar 1998	1.0643	1.0692	4.84	4.59	103.0	103.9
Jun 1998	1.1000	1.1037	4.93	4.87	103.6	104.2
Sep 1998	1.1003	1.0904	4.85	4.91	103.9	104.3
Dec 1998	1.0672	1.0520	4.62	4.66	104.4	104.5
Mar 1999	1.0449	1.0440	4.66	4.63	104.3	104.8
Jun 1999	1.0170	1.0188	4.70	4.56	104.8	105.9
Sep 1999	1.0447	1.0398	4.78	4.66	105.7	106.6
Dec 1999	1.0555	1.0538	5.08	4.85	106.3	107.0
Mar 2000	1.1365	1.1339	5.78	5.27	107.2	107.5
Jun 2000	1.1325	1.1295	5.87	5.53	108.1	108.5
Sep 2000	1.2259	1.2163	6.41	5.56	112.1	109.5
Dec 2000	1.1942	1.1969	6.03	5.49	112.5	110.3
Mar 2001	1.3066	1.3165	4.98	4.58	113.7	110.5
Jun 2001	1.2918	1.2941	4.88	4.30	114.6	112.4
Sep 2001	1.2890	1.2838	4.30	3.05	114.9	112.5

CHAPTER

Exchange rate forecasting

Introduction

Exchange rate forecasting is a crucial element of the decision-making process of international business firms under a system of floating exchange rates. The importance of exchange rate forecasting stems from the fact that the outcome of a decision taken now is contingent upon the value of the exchange rate prevailing some time in the future. These decisions pertain to a variety of activities, including speculation, hedging, investment, financing, pricing and strategic planning. The forecasting techniques include econometric models, time series models, market-based forecasting, judgmental forecasting and composite forecasting. Exchange rate forecasting is also implicit in technical analysis and mechanical trading rules, which are used to generate buy and sell signals.

Objectives

The objectives of this chapter are:

- To outline the reasons why exchange rate forecasting is needed.
- To illustrate various methods and techniques of forecasting.
- To present some empirical evidence on exchange rate forecasting models.
- To explain how to evaluate the performance of exchange rate forecasters.
- To demonstrate how technical analysis is used to generate buy and sell signals.
- To explain how filter rules and moving average rules work.

12.1 What is forecasting?

Forecasting is a formal process of generating expectations. Expectations themselves are implicit forecasts, used as an input in the decision-making process. If you are planning a trip to the United Kingdom in three months time, you may decide to buy a certain amount of pounds now because you expect the pound to appreciate against the Australian dollar by the time you start your trip. This forecast may be based on a chat with some friends in a pub. Another person may believe in this view so firmly that she uses it as the basis for a (risky) decision to convert her cash balances into pounds to capitalise on the expected appreciation of this currency. If the forecast turns out to be correct, at least qualitatively, this person will generate profit by selling the pound at a higher price (or exchange rate). It is obviously useful to be able to forecast, with some degree of accuracy, future movements in exchange rates.

The layperson often questions the validity and efficacy of forecasting, the procedure whereby we attempt to predict the future, because of a failure to recognise the progress that has been made in forecasting in various fields. There are a large number of phenomena that can now be predicted easily, tasks that at one time were believed to be impossible. For example, we can easily predict sunrise, the time it takes a falling object to hit the ground and rainfall. However, the forecasting of economic and financial variables (such as the exchange rate) is more problematical and is sometimes a total failure. Exchange rates in particular are notoriously difficult to forecast. In its 29 January 2003 issue, the *Australian Financial Review* reported the US Federal Reserve Chief, Alan Greenspan, as having said that exchange rates are forecast with less success than almost any other economic variable. He also described exchange rate forecasting as being 'remarkably difficult'.

A large number of forecasting methods are now available, ranging from the most naïve method, using the most recent observation as the forecast for the next period, to highly complex approaches, such as the use of structural econometric models and state-of-the-art time series methods. The fact remains that, whether we do it consciously or not and whether we like it or not, forecasting is an input in the decision-making process.

12.2 Why do we need exchange rate forecasting?

Weather forecasts on Hurricane Floyd, which hit North Carolina in September 1999, persuaded state governors along the US southeastern seaboard to urge more than two million people to move inland. Weather foresting is valuable: it is estimated that each dollar invested in meteorology yields about 15 times as much in terms of casualties avoided, harvests saved, and so on. But that is not all, as weather forecasting is also important for running businesses. There is a close link between temperature and the consumption of cold drinks. An accurate forecast of temperature allows retailers to stock properly, while helping breweries and soft-drink makers to adjust their rates of production.

Just as weather forecasting is important for business, so is exchange rate forecasting. The bad news is that it is much more difficult to forecast exchange rates than to forecast the weather. The question as to why we need exchange rate forecasting can be answered by listing some cases where there is a need to indulge in this exercise.

Spot speculation and uncovered interest arbitrage

A spot speculator buys (goes long on) a currency if a forecast indicates that it will appreciate and sells or short sells a currency if the forecast indicates an impending depreciation. In both cases profit will be made if the expectation or forecast turns out to be correct. Hence, forecasting is important for spot speculation.

Example

A spot speculator forecasts the USD/AUD exchange rate to rise from the current level of 0.55 to 0.60, and buys the Australian dollar at USD0.55. If the actual rate turns out to be as forecast, the speculator will sell at USD0.60 to earn profit of 0.05 for each Australian dollar sold. Another speculator forecasts the rate to fall to 0.50, and short sells the Australian dollar at USD0.55. If the actual rate turns out to be as forecast, the speculator will buy the Australian dollar at USD0.50 to cover the short position. This operation results in profit of USD0.05 for each unit of the Australian dollar sold short. Needless to say, this is a simplified example that ignores interest rates on the two currencies (and bid-offer spreads). The role of interest rates is taken into account in the case of uncovered interest arbitrage. Remember that a decision variable in uncovered interest arbitrage is the expected exchange rate (or the expected change in the exchange rate).

Spot-forward speculation

If a forecast indicates that the spot exchange rate will be higher than the forward rate on the maturity date of the forward contract, a speculator will buy forward and sell spot upon delivery. If the forecast indicates that the spot exchange rate will be lower than the forward rate, a speculator will sell forward and buy spot. If the forecast of the spot exchange rate on the maturity date of the forward contract is correct, profit will be made.

Example

If the current forward exchange rate between the Australian dollar and the US dollar (USD/AUD) is 0.55 and there is a forecast indicating that in three months time the spot rate will be 0.60, a speculator would buy the Australian dollar forward at USD0.55. In three months time, the speculator will take delivery of the currency. If the forecast turns out to be correct, the speculator can sell the Australian dollar at USD0.60, obtaining profit of USD0.05 for each Australian dollar bought and sold.

Option speculation

We have seen that a long call or a short put position will be taken if the underlying currency is expected to appreciate, whereas a short call or a long put position will be taken if the currency is expected to depreciate. Thus, there is a need to forecast the level of the underlying exchange rate on the expiry date in the case of a European option and throughout the life of an American option. It is important to note that forecasting is needed for the decision whether or not to take a position in European options, but in the case of American options forecasting is also needed to determine the optimal time of exercising.

Example

Consider a European call option on the Australian dollar with an exercise exchange rate of 0.55 (USD/AUD) and a premium of USD0.02. If a forecast indicates that the spot exchange rate on the expiry date will be 0.60, how would a speculator react?

A European option can only be exercised on maturity. If the speculator believes in this forecast, he or she will buy the call option. If the forecast turns out to be correct, the speculator will exercise, buying the Australian dollar at USD0.55 and selling it spot at USD0.60. Net profit is calculated as

$$0.60 - (0.55 + 0.02) = \text{USD}0.03$$

Suppose now that the option is an American option that can be exercised on or prior to maturity. A speculator in this case needs to forecast the exchange rate path throughout the period between the present time and the expiry date. Assume that the forecast indicates the following: the exchange rate will rise to a peak of 0.62 prior to the expiry date and then start to decline, reaching a level of 0.56 on the expiry date. The speculator in this case buys the option and exercises before maturity, when the exchange rate reaches 0.62. Net profit is:

$$0.62 - (0.55 + 0.02) = \text{USD}0.05$$

Note that if the speculator acts on the forecast for the expiry date only, he or she will not buy the option because at 0.55 a loss will be incurred. This loss (in USD) is calculated as

$$0.56 - (0.55 + 0.02) = -0.01$$

Hedging

The decision whether or not to hedge exposure to foreign exchange risk resulting from payables or receivables depends on the spot exchange rate expected to prevail when the payables or receivables are due. Remember that risk implies the possibility of good outcomes and bad outcomes. While hedging protects you from the bad outcome, it also deprives you of the good outcome. In the case of receivables, a hedging decision will be taken if the foreign currency is expected to depreciate. In the case of payables, the decision to hedge will be taken if the foreign currency is expected to appreciate. Once the decision has been taken and implemented (by selling or buying the foreign currency forward, for example), the hedger may regret the decision if the forecast is wrong. For example, if the foreign currency appreciates, it will be better not to hedge receivables because their domestic currency value will be greater than under hedging. Similarly, if the foreign currency depreciates, it will be better not to hedge payables because their domestic currency value will be lower than otherwise. In general, good outcomes (+) or bad outcomes (–) may materialise, depending on: (i) whether the decision to hedge or not to hedge is taken; (ii) whether the foreign currency appreciates or depreciates; and (iii) whether hedging involves payables or receivables. Figure 12.1 shows a general framework for the relationship between exchange rate forecasting and hedging.

Figure 12.1 The relationship between exchange rate forecasting and hedging

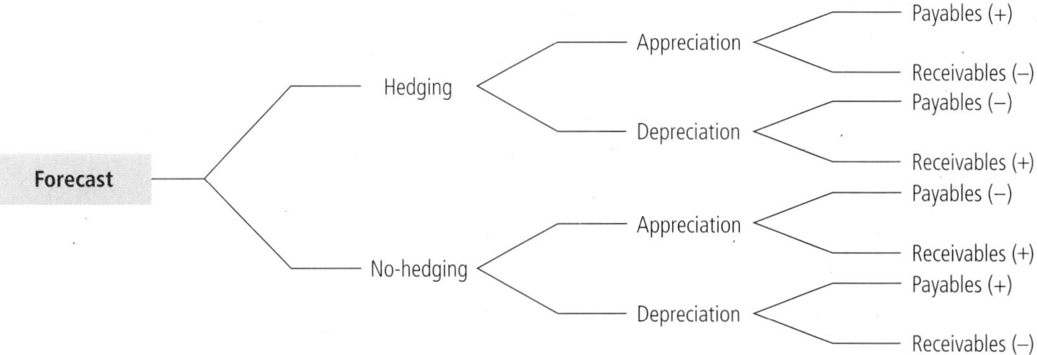

Example

Consider a financial manager who is faced with the decision of whether or not to hedge receivables worth GBP600 000 due in three months, given that the current spot exchange rate (AUD/GBP) is 2.50 and the three-month forward rate is 2.55. If a forecast indicates that in three months the spot exchange rate will rise to 2.60, what will the financial manager do?

A decision to hedge in the forward market implies that the Australian dollar value of the receivables is

$$600\,000 \times 2.55 = \text{AUD}1\,530\,000$$

If the position is left unhedged and the forecast turns out to be correct, then the value of the receivables is

$$600\,000 \times 2.60 = \text{AUD}1\,560\,000$$

A financial manager who is willing to bear risk may be tempted to leave the position unhedged in order to benefit from the expected appreciation of the pound.

Investment and capital budgeting decisions

The choice of the currency for short-term investment depends on the rate of return on assets denominated in this currency and whether or not it is expected to appreciate over the investment horizon. Thus, exchange rate forecasting is important for the decision concerning the choice of the investment currency, whether we are considering short-term investment, long-term portfolio investment or foreign direct investment. In the case of capital budgeting for foreign direct investment, such as the decision to establish a foreign subsidiary, the decision is normally based on a feasibility study involving the estimation of the expected cash flows of the subsidiary. Since the base currency of a foreign subsidiary is different from the currency of the parent company, exchange rate forecasting is needed in order to convert the estimated future cash flows into domestic currency. These decisions are discussed in Chapters 15, 17 and 18.

Financing decisions

A currency will be chosen for financing purposes if it is expected to depreciate. A long-term financing decision involves the choice of the currency to serve as the denomination of a bond issue, for example. In both cases, exchange rate forecasting is required. These decisions are discussed in Chapters 15 and 16.

Pricing decisions

Exchange rate forecasting is important for international business firms selling their products in foreign countries. The foreign currency price of a product could be anything in relation to the corresponding domestic currency price, depending on the level of the exchange rate (see Chapter 3). If a particular domestic currency price is chosen, for example, to implement a **market penetration** objective (that is, to capture a share in the existing market), then exchange rate forecasting is essential. Appreciation of the domestic currency may make the foreign currency price of the product too high to achieve the market penetration objective.

Strategic planning

Exchange rate forecasting is also important for strategic planning, such as the choice of the production location and the foreign markets in which to sell the products. Normally, international firms aim to incur costs in countries where currencies are expected to depreciate and earn revenue in countries where currencies are expected to appreciate.

Macroeconomic conditions

Exchange rate forecasting may be useful not only for its own sake but also because of its by-products. The forecasting process provides an extensive discussion of macroeconomic conditions in each country. Forecasting other macroeconomic variables, such as growth and inflation, may require exchange rate forecasting as an input because exchange rates affect other macroeconomic variables, particularly in open economies.

Central bank intervention

Business firms need exchange rate forecasting, and so do central banks and economic decision-making authorities. For example, the central bank intervenes in the foreign exchange market in order to make the expected path of the exchange rate converge on the desired path. Knowing what the expected path is requires exchange rate forecasting.

12.3 Econometric forecasting models

Econometric models, as the term is used in this book, are models that are specified on the basis of some economic theory and estimated by an econometric method. Econometric models may be classified into **single-equation models** and **multi-equation models**.

Single-equation models

In the case of single-equation models (also called **reduced-form models**), the exchange rate (or its rate of change) is specified to depend on one or more variables. In general, a single-equation model may be specified as

$$S_t = f(X_{1,t}, X_{2,t} \ldots X_{n,t}) \tag{12.1}$$

which tells us that the value of the exchange rate at point in time t depends on the values of the **explanatory variables** $X_{1,t}, X_{2,t} \ldots X_{n,t}$. The exchange rate and the explanatory variables may be measured in natural logarithms. The explanatory variables may include anything that influences the exchange rate, such as prices, interest rates, the money supply and the balance of payments position. The variables may also be **composite variables**, such as the interest rate differential. Moreover, some of these variables may have a different time subscript such as $t + 1$ or $t - 1$. This will be the case if the exchange rate at time t depends on the future or the lagged values of a variable (that is, $X_{1,t+1}$ and $X_{1,t-1}$, respectively). The functional relationship given by Equation (12.1) is invariably specified as a **linear equation**. Therefore, it can be written as

$$S_t = a_0 + a_1 X_{1,t} + a_2 X_{2,t} + \ldots + a_n X_{n,t} \tag{12.2}$$

where $a_1, a_2, \ldots a_n$ are parameters that measure the magnitude and direction of the influence of each explanatory variable on the exchange rate. a_0 is a constant term that reflects the autonomous component of the exchange rate, which is unrelated to any of the explanatory variables. A **random error term** is normally added to the equation to reflect the unexplained variation in the exchange rate, but this term is omitted here for simplicity and convenience. The estimation of Equation (12.2) by a **regression** method (or otherwise) on the basis of historical data produces numerical values for the coefficients $a_0, a_1, \ldots a_n$. Once these estimates are obtained, forecasting is carried out by estimating the value of the exchange rate at time $t + 1$ and beyond, which can only be obtained if we know, or assume, the future values for the explanatory variables. Hence:

$$S_{t+1} = a_1 X_{1,t+1} + a_2 X_{2,t+1} + \ldots + a_n X_{n,t+1} \tag{12.3}$$

We have already come across some single-equation econometric models that are specified on the basis of some theories. These models include purchasing power parity, uncovered interest parity and unbiasedness, which can be written respectively as

$$\dot{S}_t = a_0 + a_1(\dot{P} - \dot{P}^*)_t \tag{12.4}$$

$$\dot{S}_t = a_0 + a_1(i - i^*)_{t-1} \tag{12.5}$$

$$S_t = a_0 + a_1 F_{t-1} \tag{12.6}$$

These models use, as explanatory variables, the inflation differential, the lagged interest differential and the lagged forward rate, respectively. The flow model presented in Chapter 4 uses three explanatory variables: relative growth rates, relative inflation rates and the interest rate differential.

Note that PPP, unbiasedness and UIP are not written as exact relationships showing, for example, equality between the spot exchange rate and the lagged forward rate. Rather, they are written as equations with unknown coefficients that have to be estimated empirically based on historical data. If we consider the exact relationships, then no estimation is required, in which case the forward rate is taken to be the forecast for the level of the spot rate and the interest rate differential is taken to be the forecast for the percentage change in the exchange rate. This is a very simple and cheap form of forecasting as it is based entirely on readily available data on interest rates and forward rates. This is sometimes known as **market-based forecasting**. The simplest form of market-based forecasting utilises the assumption of a random walk, in which case the current level of the exchange rate is taken to be a forecast for next period's value.

Example

This example shows how unbiasedness can be used to forecast the spot exchange rate. Suppose that the estimated relationship using quarterly data over a given period of time for the AUD/USD exchange rate is:

$$S_t = 0.09485 + 0.91307F_{t-1}$$

To forecast the spot exchange rate in the following quarter, we feed in the current forward rate (1.8560) to obtain

$$S_t = 0.09485 + 0.91307 \times 1.8560 = 1.7895$$

Problems with single-equation econometric models

There are several problems associated with forecasting using single-equation econometric models. Other forecasting models can circumvent, or be equally subject to, the same problems.

First, a single-equation econometric model is called a reduced-form model because it explains the value of the exchange rate in terms of other variables without telling us how these explanatory variables are determined. This is like feeding information into a 'black box' and obtaining a forecast without knowing what goes on inside. This property of single-equation models is problematical and can be explained with reference to uncovered interest parity. This model tells us that the domestic and foreign interest rates are determined by factors outside the model and they, in turn, affect or determine the exchange rate. The model implicitly precludes the possibility of the influence running from the exchange rate to interest rates. It is therefore a black box in the sense that it does not readily explain the transmission mechanism whereby interest rates affect exchange rates. It is more plausible to think of exchange rates and interest rates as being determined jointly, an idea that is dealt with by specifying a multi-equation model.

Second, the forecast may be conditional on the future values of the explanatory variables. If this is the case, our forecast of the exchange rate depends on the accuracy of the forecasts of the explanatory variables. If we employ the models based on unbiasedness or UIP, this problem does not arise if we are interested in forecasting the exchange rate for one period ahead only. This is because to forecast the exchange rate one period ahead, we need to know only the forward rate and the interest rate differential prevailing at the present time. On the other hand, forecasting on the basis of PPP requires a knowledge of future prices or inflation rates. We may assume specific values for the explanatory variables on the basis of past behaviour and monetary policy stance or by obtaining an official forecast (such as the forecast implicit in the budget). If a single value of inflation for each future period of time is fed into the equation, we will obtain a **point forecast** of the exchange rate. Alternatively, we may obtain an **interval forecast** by constructing scenarios for the explanatory variables, feeding in a range of values for each time period. For example, we may envisage a low-inflation environment and a high-inflation environment, thus feeding in two values for inflation to obtain a range of forecasts between two extremes for each period.

Example

Assume that a forecaster has estimated the PPP equation (written in terms of percentage changes) for the AUD/USD exchange rate to be the following:

$$\dot{S}_t = 0.52 + 0.92(\dot{P} - \dot{P}^\star)_t$$

where $\dot{P}$ is the Australian inflation rate and $\dot{P}^\star$ is the US inflation rate. Assume that the current AUD/USD exchange rate is 1.80 and that the forecaster is trying to forecast the exchange rate one year from now. The following four scenarios are available for Australian and US inflation rates during the coming year:

Scenario	$\dot{P}$	$\dot{P}^*$	Probability
(1) High inflation in both countries	10	8	0.10
(2) High inflation in Australia	10	2	0.20
(3) High inflation in the United States	3	8	0.15
(4) Low inflation in both countries	3	2	0.55

For each inflation scenario, there is a corresponding exchange rate forecast calculated from the estimated equation. The forecast corresponding to the first scenario is calculated as

$$\dot{S}_{t+1} = 0.52 + 0.92 \times (10 - 8) = 2.36\%$$

The first scenario leads to a forecast telling us that the US dollar will appreciate by 2.36 per cent. Hence, one year from now, the exchange rate will be

$$S_{t+1} = 1.0236 \times 1.80 = 1.8425$$

We can calculate the forecasts corresponding to other scenarios in a similar manner to obtain the following results:

Scenario	$\dot{P}$	$\dot{P}^*$	$\dot{S}_{t+1}$	S_{t+1}	Probability
1	10	8	2.36	1.8425	0.10
2	10	2	7.88	1.9418	0.20
3	3	8	−4.08	1.7266	0.15
4	3	2	1.44	1.8259	0.55

Thus, the forecast exchange rate assumes values ranging between a low of 1.7266 and a high of 1.9418. The expected value of the forecast exchange rate can be calculated as a weighted average as

$$1.8425 \times 0.10 + 1.9418 \times 0.2 + 1.7266 \times 0.15 + 1.8259 \times 0.55 = 1.8359$$

The other problems associated with single-equation econometric models are the following:

- If we want to forecast exchange rates on a daily basis, which is important for day-to-day trading in the foreign exchange market, the explanatory variables must be available on a daily basis to estimate the relationship. This is not always the case. Prices are available only on a monthly basis, whereas national income figures are available only on a quarterly basis. Thus, we cannot use the PPP relationship to forecast exchange rates on a daily basis.
- The underlying assumption is that the relationship as estimated from historical data will remain valid over the **forecasting horizon**, which implies that the estimated coefficients are

constant. These models need to be modified to take into account **structural changes** in the relationship. One way to do this is to re-estimate the models, using only the most recent data.

- There are **measurement errors** in some explanatory variables. For example, the balance of payments position is measured with a significant errors and omissions item. It is argued, however, that decisions affecting exchange rates are taken on the basis of published data even if they involve measurement errors.
- A bigger problem arises when some of the explanatory variables are qualitative in nature, such as market sentiment. This problem can be tackled either by quantitative adjustment of the forecasts derived from an econometric model or by resorting to judgmental forecasting.

Multi-equation econometric models

The first problem associated with single-equation econometric models can be dealt with by specifying a structural multi-equation model. This can be done by specifying equations to explain the explanatory variables $X_1, \ldots X_n$. For example, it is possible to specify an equation explaining X_1 in terms of S and the explanatory variables $X_2, \ldots X_n$. This equation may be written as

$$X_{1,t} = b_0 + b_1 S_t + b_2, X_{2,t} \ldots + b_n X_{n,t} \tag{12.7}$$

which implies the presence of feedback from the exchange rate to the variable X_1. If we assume that X_1 is the interest rate, then Equations (12.2) and (12.5) tell us that while the interest rate affects the exchange rate (via UIP or by attracting capital flows), the exchange rate in turn affects the interest rate. For example, an excessively weak currency may trigger a policy reaction in the form of raising interest rates. While multi-equation models solve the black-box problem of the reduced-form models, they are very costly because they require a much larger amount of data and they are more difficult to estimate. Some of the models used in practice consist of hundreds of equations. There is no evidence, however, to indicate that the forecasting performance of these models is better than that of single-equation models. These models also suffer from the other problems associated with single-equation models.

IN PRACTICE

Why the US dollar frustrated forecasters in the 1980s

In the first half of the 1980s, the US dollar showed remarkable strength against all major currencies, as shown in Figure 5.9 on page 144. While forecasters were constantly predicting the currency's eventual collapse 'in the second half of the year', the dollar steadily climbed to new record highs. In late 1984 the dollar's strength was phenomenal, defying economic fundamentals that warranted its depreciation. Specifically, it rose in the face of declining interest rates and regardless of the performance of the US economy. This is unlike what we saw in 2002 and 2003 when the dollar depreciated as a result of a weak economy and widening current account deficit (between January 2002 and January 2003 the dollar lost 13.3 per cent of its value).

The dollar's outstanding and unpredictable performance in the 1980s stimulated mixed reactions from those involved in forecasting exchange rates, which amounted to justifying why they had gone wrong by predicting the depreciation of the currency. Some observers described the behaviour of the currency as 'irrational'. Others talked about the dollar being a unique currency because of its particular international role, implying that its behaviour cannot be explained by resorting to conventional economic analysis. Forecasters using econometric models based on the relationship between the exchange rate and the external balance attributed the failure of the models to errors of measurement in the balance of payments figures. Forecasters using other econometric models were frustrated by the failure of their models to predict the movement of the dollar and not even judgmental manipulation of the models helped. Some were so frustrated that they abandoned econometric models and resorted to using time series models and technical analysis. But even these did not perform well.

In one week in the second half of 1984, the US dollar appreciated despite two supposedly adverse developments. The first was a half-percentage point reduction in the US prime lending rate (the rate charged by banks on loans to high-quality borrowers). The second was a downward revision of the US economy's growth rate, confirming that it was slowing down. Some foreign exchange dealers, based on the forecasts provided by their economists, took short positions on the US dollar and sustained heavy losses because the currency appreciated and did not depreciate as forecasters said.

This behaviour was surprising, given the consensus view that 'if it were not for high US interest rates and the rapid growth of the US economy, then the dollar would surely depreciate as a result of the current account deficit'. While this argument is generally valid, high interest rates and a booming economy alone are insufficient to explain the movement of the dollar unless other factors remain unchanged. The classical economic assumption of *ceteris paribus* (all other things remain unchanged) does not hold in the complex real world. Thus, the appreciation of the dollar in the face of lower interest rates and a slower economy occurred because the *ceteris paribus* assumption did not hold, in the sense that there were other factors supporting the dollar.

In order to provide the facts and figures to support this line of reasoning, we estimate a simple econometric model based on historical data (covering the period 1981–1984) on the dollar's effective exchange rate (Q), the quarter-to-quarter growth rate of the US economy (g) and the three-month Eurodollar interest rate (i). On the basis of this data, the estimated model is (standard errors in parentheses):

$$\underset{(8.75)}{Q = 136.2} - \underset{(0.65)}{1.98i} + \underset{(0.22)}{0.94g} \qquad R^2 = 0.26 \quad DW = 0.91$$

This equation is then used to forecast the effective exchange rate over the sample period. The following results are obtained:

Year	Quarter	Actual	Forecast
1981	1	94.7	108.3
	2	101.9	100.6
	3	103.0	101.4
	4	100.3	108.0
1982	1	106.7	104.8
	2	111.1	105.2
	3	113.3	113.6
	4	111.3	117.5
1983	1	112.0	117.6
	2	114.3	118.2
	3	116.7	118.7
	4	118.0	117.5
1984	1	115.4	116.9
	2	120.2	113.4
	3	127.3	113.9
	4	129.5	120.0

It can be seen that the model has low explanatory power (low R^2) and exhibits serial correlation (low DW). Both of these indicate missing variables, which otherwise supported the dollar. This is why this model produces inaccurate forecasts, as the table shows.

12.4 Time series forecasting models

What distinguishes time series models from what we call econometric models is that the former are based entirely on the past history of the exchange rate. The level of the exchange rate is postulated to depend on its past levels, in which case the model is written as

$$S_t = f(S_{t-1}, S_{t-2} \ldots S_{t-n}) \tag{12.8}$$

which implies that there is no underlying economic theory. This functional relationship is normally specified in a linear form, which gives

$$S_t = a_0 + a_1 S_{t-1} + a_2 S_{t-2} + \ldots + a_n S_{t-n} \tag{12.9}$$

Once the parameters $a_0, a_1, a_2, \ldots a_n$ are estimated, the exchange rate can be forecast as

$$S_{t+1} = a_0 + a_1 S_t + a_2 S_{t-1} + \ldots + a_n S_{t-n+1} \tag{12.10}$$

Equation (12.9) is a representation of an **autoregressive model**. A simple form is called an autoregressive representation of order 1, because the current level of the exchange rate depends only on its level in the previous period. This model is written as

$$S_t = a_0 + a_1 S_{t-1} \tag{12.11}$$

Another approach is based on the decomposition of the exchange rate time series. Thus, the exchange rate series is conceived to be the following

$$S_t = \mu_t + \gamma_t + \phi_t + \varepsilon_t \tag{12.12}$$

where μ is the **trend**, γ is the **seasonal component**, ϕ is the **cyclical component** and ε is the **random component**. The trend describes the long-term movement of the exchange rate. For example, the US dollar had an upward trend between the second half of 1980 and February 1985 and a downward trend between March 1985 and early 1987 (see Figure 5.9). The total movement of the exchange rate is formed by combining the other components with the trend. This makes the actual exchange rate at any time either above or below the level implied by the trend. Exchange rate forecasting is carried out by decomposing the time series, forecasting the individual components and adding the forecast components to obtain the forecast exchange rate.

The major problem with time series forecasting is the market efficiency hypothesis, if the market is indeed efficient. If the foreign exchange market is weakly efficient, the exchange rate must follow a random walk, which means that we cannot forecast the exchange rate based on its past history. The random walk model implies that, given the level of the exchange rate today, it is as likely to be up tomorrow as it is to be down.

12.5 Judgmental forecasting

Judgmental forecasting takes into account all factors affecting the exchange rate, economic and otherwise, including those that cannot be quantified (such as **market sentiment**). Judgmental forecasts differ from forecasts based on formal models in that they are not generated by an exact numerical formula derived from an estimated model. The forecaster follows the developments pertaining to the foreign exchange market and relates the forecasts to these developments. The forecasts normally take the form of a qualitative description of what may happen and this could pertain only to the direction of the possible change in the exchange rate. Alternatively, a possible range of values may be given.

It is arguable that judgmental forecasting may be used in situations involving dating ('Will my invitation to dinner be accepted?') and football ('Will my team win?'), but not when it comes to business decisions. This is not the case, however, because business forecasts are often made on a judgmental basis. An economist who normally uses formal models to forecast exchange rates may resort to judgmental forecasting on some occasions. For example, the economist could be attending a meeting with his superiors in which he is (unexpectedly) asked to give a view on a certain currency. The economist cannot excuse himself from the meeting to go and generate forecasts from the forecasting model on his computer. Rather, he will respond with a quick (very quick) brainstorming session whereby he comes up with an answer. Naturally, the view must represent a **rational forecast** (based on all available information), because this economist has his job in the balance. In other situations the unavailability of data, measurement problems and other reasons may force this economist to resort to judgmental forecasting.

Forecasters often resort to judgmental modification of formal forecasts. Suppose that an econometric model gives a forecast that intuitively looks either on the high side or on the low side. The forecaster may then 'modify' this forecast to make it look more appealing.

Judgmental forecasting may also be used within the process of formal forecasting by econometric models. A single-equation model based on PPP can be used to forecast the exchange rate only if we can assume some values for the future inflation rates. These values may be determined by judgmental forecasting. In this sense also, judgmental forecasting is used in conjunction with the econometric forecasting of the nominal exchange rate to forecast the real exchange rate.

Judgmental forecasting, daily life and soccer

In a sense, all forecasts are judgmental. Since forecasts pertain to future events, some element of human judgment is always involved in making inductive inferences. Forecasting is a day-to-day activity of the human brain. We generate forecasts continuously through time as we contemplate the outcomes of frequently encountered situations. We often ask ourselves questions such as 'Who will win the World Cup final?', 'Will he/she go out to dinner with me?', 'Will I get the job I was interviewed for yesterday?' and 'Will I get to the station before the train leaves?'. These are only some of an endless list of questions that arise in our daily lives, each of which requires forecasting. In all these situations judgmental forecasts are generated. You do not construct a formal model and use a computer to forecast whether or not your invitation to dinner will be accepted—even if you are a brilliant mathematician and/or a computer wizard. You will, however, process all the available information to generate a forecast, since the decision to accept or decline your dinner invitation (which you are trying to forecast) matters to a considerable extent.

In generating a forecast on whether or not your date is going to materialise, you might deliberately overlook some important pieces of information because they point to a negative outcome that you find hard to contemplate or digest. In this case, what is generated is not a judgmental forecast, but rather wishful thinking or wishful expectation.

This reminds me of the 'prediction' made by the arrogant manager of an unknown team in the 1982 World Cup soccer tournament held in Spain. That manager, whose team qualified for the tournament for the first (and last) time, made the 'forecast' that his team would reach the final, making the additional remark that he did not care which other team joined his team on the occasion (implying, naturally, that the other team would lose anyway). The manager disregarded several pieces of information, including the fact that his team was in a very difficult group in the first round. His forecast cannot be regarded as a judgmental forecast, and not even an irrational forecast. It was wishful thinking. Needless to say, his team was knocked out of the tournament in the first round. Ironically, when the manager was interviewed following his team's exit from the tournament, he made another (long-term) 'forecast'. He declared, 'We will win the World Cup even if we have to wait one million years'! Naturally, he will not be around to be held accountable for an inaccurate forecast.

12.6 Composite forecasting

Composite forecasting is based on two or more forecasts that are derived independently. The basic idea behind composite forecasting is that forecasting accuracy can be increased by pooling different forecasts and deriving some sort of average or consensus forecast. The easiest thing to do is to take the simple average of two forecasts. Suppose, for example, that $\hat{S}_1$ is a forecast based on purchasing power parity, whereas $\hat{S}_2$ is a forecast based on a time series model. A composite forecast based on the simple average of these two forecasts is therefore given by

$$\hat{S}_c = \frac{\hat{S}_1 + \hat{S}_2}{2} \tag{12.13}$$

If, however, we believe that econometric forecasting is more reliable than time series forecasting, we may assign more weight to the former. In this case, the composite forecast is calculated as a weighted average of these two forecasts. Hence

$$\hat{S}_c = w_1\hat{S}_1 + w_2\hat{S}_2 \tag{12.14}$$

where $w_1 + w_2 = 1$ and $w_1 > w_2$. Alternatively, the weights may be estimated as regression coefficients by estimating an equation (based on historical data) in which the dependent variable is the actual exchange rate and the explanatory variables are the various forecasts. For k different forecasts the following equation may be estimated:

$$S = \beta_1\hat{S}_1 + \beta_2\hat{S}_2 + \ldots + \beta_k\hat{S}_k \tag{12.15}$$

where the estimated coefficients can serve as the weights.

Forecasters resort to composite forecasting for at least two reasons. The first is that different forecasters possess different information and forecasting abilities and hence they have different degrees of **forecasting accuracy**. The second reason is that diversification reduces the risk of large **forecasting errors**.

Perhaps some elaboration is needed on the question as to why forecasters differ. The most obvious reason is that they use different forecasting techniques. A forecaster using an econometric model will most likely produce different forecasts from those based on a time series model or another forecasting technique. But even forecasters using econometric models produce different forecasts. Let us for this purpose assume that two forecasters use the following two single-equation models

$$S_t = a_0 + a_1X_{1,t} \tag{12.16}$$

and

$$S_t = a_0 + a_1X_{1,t} + a_2X_{2,t} \tag{12.17}$$

The first model explains the exchange rate in terms of one variable, X_1. This model will be purchasing power parity if the explanatory variable is the price ratio. The second model explains the exchange rate in terms of two variables, X_1 and X_2, where the latter may be the interest rate differential. It is obvious why these two models produce different forecasts: the first model does not account for changes in X_2.

Even two models explaining the exchange rate in terms of the same explanatory variables can produce different forecasts for the following reasons:

- The relationship may be specified differently. A variant of the model represented by Equation (12.16) is the nonlinear equation

$$S_t = a_0 + a_1X_{1,t}^2 \tag{12.18}$$

- The econometric estimation methods may be different, producing different estimates of the coefficients a_0 and a_1.
- The models may be estimated using different samples of historical data, again producing different estimates of the coefficients.
- The models may be estimated using different definitions of the variables. The PPP model, for example, may be estimated on the basis of consumer prices and wholesale prices.
- Even if two forecasters have exactly the same estimated econometric equation, their forecasts will still be different because of differences with respect to the future values of the explanatory variables. For example, suppose that two forecasters using the PPP model agree that a currency will depreciate exactly by a percentage that is equal to the inflation differential. For their forecasts of the exchange rate to be identical, they must have the same opinion with respect to the future values of the domestic and foreign inflation rates. Only if they agreed, for example, that the domestic and foreign inflation rates would be 5 and 2 per cent respectively, would their forecasts become identical, indicating a 3 per cent appreciation of the foreign currency. Given all these factors, it seems that the possibility of two forecasters agreeing on a point forecast is indeed remote. If it is the case, then it must be by pure coincidence.

12.7 Forecasting performance evaluation

Forecasting is a process that produces forecasts. These forecasts are used as input in decision making and these decisions may pertain to a position or an investment that involves millions of dollars. Forecasting accuracy is thus of crucial importance for profitability.

The forecasting function may be carried out internally or externally by subscribing to the services of a forecasting firm. In both cases, the performance of the forecasters must be evaluated against a standard that must be established according to two general principles:

- If the forecasts are based on a model estimated from historical data, then a more meaningful assessment of the model is made by analysing its performance outside, rather than within, the sample.
- The **loss function** is important. The user of the forecasts must be able to specify the purpose for which the forecasts are used and the costs associated with the forecasting errors.

Obviously, accuracy must be a criterion for measuring the performance of forecasters. Accuracy is indicated by the deviation of the forecast from the actual or realised value of the exchange rate. Accuracy, however, must be measured not at a particular point in time but over a period of time to establish a track record. Let us assume that over points in time $t = 1, 2, 3, \dots n$, the actual and forecast values are given by S_t and $\hat{S}_t$, respectively. At a particular point in time, therefore, the deviation or the forecasting error is given by

$$e_t = \hat{S}_t - S_t \tag{12.19}$$

A **perfect forecast** is produced if $\hat{S}_t - S_t = 0$ or if $e_t = 0$. Based on these individual forecasting errors, the following measures of accuracy can therefore be calculated:

- The **mean absolute error (MAE)** is the average of the absolute value of the forecasting error, which is given by

$$MAE = \frac{1}{n}\sum_{t=1}^{n}\left|\hat{S}_t - S_t\right| \tag{12.20}$$

The reason why the absolute value is taken is that negative errors may cancel out positive errors, producing a low or zero MAE, although the forecaster may be far from being accurate.

- The **mean square error (MSE)** is given by

$$MSE = \frac{1}{n}\sum_{t=1}^{n}\left(\hat{S}_t - S_t\right)^2 \tag{12.21}$$

Squaring the errors has two advantages. The first advantage is that it eliminates the effect of negative errors, which is the same advantage obtained by taking absolute values. The second advantage is that by squaring the errors, large errors are penalised more proportionately than small errors.

- The **root mean square error (RMSE)** is the square root of the mean square error. Thus

$$RMSE = \sqrt{\frac{1}{n}\sum_{t=1}^{n}\left(\hat{S}_t - S_t\right)^2} \tag{12.22}$$

In all cases, these measures can be calculated from the percentage rather than the absolute errors. The percentage errors are calculated by dividing the errors derived from Equation (12.19) by the actual level of the exchange rate and multiplying by 100 (that is, $100e_t/S_t$). This is useful if, for example, the forecaster is trying to compare how well a model does in forecasting two different exchange rates. Furthermore, the forecasting power of a particular model can be measured relative to a benchmark (such as the forward rate) by comparing the measures corresponding to the model under consideration with those corresponding to the forward rate.

Example

Three forecasters, A, B and C, have the following track records for forecasting the AUD/USD exchange rate:

Time	Actual	A	B	C
1	1.85	1.87	1.80	1.79
2	1.87	1.88	1.85	1.86
3	1.89	1.86	1.90	1.87
4	1.84	1.88	1.82	1.92
5	1.83	1.84	1.81	1.85
6	1.80	1.79	1.76	1.79
7	1.81	1.76	1.84	1.80
8	1.84	1.85	1.84	1.86
9	1.87	1.90	1.88	1.90
10	1.90	1.95	1.86	1.92

The results of calculating the three measures of forecasting power are as follows:

Criterion	A	B	C
MAE	0.026	0.046	0.036
MSE	0.00092	0.00278	0.00196
RMSE	0.030	0.053	0.044

A has a lower MAE, MSE and RMSE than B and C, whereas B has a higher MAE, MSE and RMSE than A and C. Thus, A is the best forecaster and B is the worst.

The forecasting power of exchange rate models

RESEARCH FINDINGS

The empirical evidence on the forecasting performance of models and forecasting services is not very sanguine. This is not surprising, however. For one thing, there is no consensus view on the factors affecting exchange rates and the direction of this effect. Theoretical models of exchange rate determination, which form the basis for econometric forecasting models, differ greatly with respect to both of these features. This implies that we do not know much about the process of exchange rate determination and so cannot forecast exchange rates accurately. At one time it was difficult to forecast rainfall because the process itself was not understood. There is also a ready explanation for the poor performance of time series models and technical forecasting techniques, which is the efficient market hypothesis. But no matter what, forecasting is an important input in decision making.

In what has become a well-known study, Meese and Rogoff tested the ability of several popular economic models and concluded that, even when these models perform well within the sample, they perform poorly out of the sample.[1] In this respect, these models fail to outperform the random walk model and the forward rate as a forecaster. Levich found that professional forecasters did worse than the forward rate.[2] On the other hand, Boughton showed that some fundamental models outperformed the random walk model in out-of-sample forecasting for the exchange rates of the US dollar against the German mark and the SDR (special drawing rights).[3]

Some economists have tried to enhance the forecasting power of econometric models by introducing some dynamics (lagged variables), by using error correction models and by allowing the estimated model coefficients to vary over time.[4] By using an error correction model, MacDonald and Taylor demonstrated that the monetary model can forecast better than a random walk. Tawadros reported similar results for the exchange rate of the Australian dollar against the US dollar.[5]

It has also been found that there is some value in composite forecasting. Levich estimated a composite model for an in-sample period and reported a track record of 70 per cent correct forecasts.[6] Bilson concluded that an additional forecast (either from a professional service or one based on PPP) can make a significant marginal contribution to forecasting performance.[7]

1 R. Meese and K. Rogoff, 'Empirical Exchange Rate Models of the Seventies: Do They Fit Out of Sample?', *Journal of International Economics*, 14, 1983, pp. 3–24.

2 R. M. Levich, 'Analyzing the Accuracy of Foreign Exchange Advisory Services: Theory and Evidence', in R. M. Levich and C. Whilborg (eds), *Exchange Risk and Exposure*, Lexington Books, Lexington, Mass., 1980.

3 J. M. Boughton, 'Exchange Rate Movements and Adjustment in Financial Markets: Quarterly Estimates for Major Currencies', *International Monetary Fund Staff Papers*, 31, 1984, pp. 445–68.

4 R. MacDonald and M. P. Taylor, 'The Monetary Model of Exchange Rates: Long-Run Relationships, Short-Run Dynamics and How to Beat a Random Walk', *Journal of International Money and Finance*, 13, 1994, pp. 276–90.

5 G. Tawadros, 'The Predictive Power of the Monetary Model of Exchange Rate Determination', *Applied Financial Economics*, 11, 2001, pp. 279–86.

6 R. M. Levich, 'Composite Forecasts', in B. Antl and R. Ensor (eds), *The Management of Foreign Exchange Risk*, Euromoney Publications, London, 1982.

7 J. Bilson, 'The Evaluation and Use of Foreign Exchange Rate Forecasting Services', in R. Herring (ed.), *Managing Foreign Exchange Risk*, Cambridge University Press, Cambridge, 1983.

Sometimes, however, it is more important to predict the direction of the change than its magnitude. That is, it is more important for a forecaster to predict whether the exchange rate is going to rise or fall than to predict by how much it will change. An example will clarify this point. Suppose that the USD/AUD exchange rate is currently 0.55 and that there are two forecasts for the value of this exchange rate in three months time: 0.65 and 0.53.

IN PRACTICE

Internal or external forecaster?

A decision that often arises concerns the choice between generating the forecasts internally by hiring one or more forecasters and the alternative of obtaining the forecasts from external sources by subscribing to one or more forecasting services. The issue eventually boils down to the cost-effectiveness of these two alternatives. Some companies may not need external forecasters because they have sophisticated foreign exchange departments. This is naturally the case if the company believes that an external forecaster is unable to offer anything that cannot be made in-house.

Subscribing to a forecasting service may seem easier and cheaper than hiring one or more forecasters. Forecasting services may be able to offer their forecasts at a low cost because they have a large number of clients, enabling them to exploit the economies of scale. This may be appealing to small companies that find it expensive to run their own forecasting units. Moreover, the personnel of the forecasting services do nothing but forecasting. Over time, they build up significant expertise that may not be available elsewhere. In a competitive market they are forced to keep on developing their forecasting techniques and offer better services. Another reason why hiring the services of an external forecaster is appealing is that this forecaster is more likely to provide independent and objective advice than an internal forecaster who wants to please the boss. While most big companies can utilise their staff to generate the products offered by external forecasters, it is easy to become biased and lose objectivity.

There are reasons, however, why subscribing to a forecasting service may not be appealing. First, the methodology, format and frequency of output may not be suitable for the needs of the client. The

Obviously, the first forecast indicates that the Australian dollar will appreciate, implying that a long position should be taken on the Australian currency. The second forecast indicates the contrary. Suppose, now, that the actual exchange rate in three months time turns out to be 0.57. The absolute forecasting error associated with the first forecast is greater than that associated with the second forecast (0.08 and 0.04, respectively), so can we conclude that the second forecast is better? Perhaps it is more accurate but it is not more useful, since a speculative decision based on the second forecast will lead us to take a short position on the Australian dollar, which would produce a loss. On the other hand, a long position based on the first forecast would be profitable.

Consider also the following example that involves speculation and hedging using the forward rate. Suppose that the three-month forward rate is 0.55. If a forecast indicates that the spot exchange rate prevailing three months from now (on the maturity of the forward contract) will be greater than 0.55, then the following will happen: (i) to speculate, the Australian dollar must be bought forward; and (ii) US dollar payables will not be hedged. Thus, a forecast of 0.65 will support these decisions, whereas a forecast of 0.53 will not. If the actual spot rate turns out to be 0.57, then the less accurate forecast of 0.65 leads to profitable speculation and hedging decisions, whereas the more accurate forecast leads to faulty decisions.

Thus, the usefulness of the forecasts, in the sense that they lead to profitable decisions, may be another criterion for forecasting performance evaluation. What is important in this case is forecasting the direction rather than the magnitude of the change in the exchange rate. A device that detects errors of both magnitude and direction is the **prediction-realisation diagram**, which is shown in Figure 12.2. The diagram is obtained by plotting the actual change in the exchange rate $(S_t - S_{t-1})$ on the vertical axis and the forecast change $(\hat{S}_t - S_{t-1})$ on the horizontal axis. We then plot points representing the combinations of changes in the forecast rate and the corresponding changes in the actual rate. A 45-degree line passing through the origin represents the line of perfect forecast, which satisfies the condition that the forecasting error given by Equation (12.19) is zero. Points A, B and C fall on the line methodology pertains to whether the forecasting service uses **fundamental models** or **technical models**. The format pertains to whether the forecasts are point forecasts or interval forecasts, whether they are short-term or long-term forecasts, and so on. The frequency of output refers to the frequency of receiving the forecasts. This may not sound like a problem because a firm is bound to find a forecasting service with the characteristics that are suitable to its needs. However, it is a problem if the most suitable forecasting service does not have a good track record.

Sometimes, it is argued that external forecasters do not have any responsibility for the advice they give, while huge losses can be incurred by following the wrong advice. However, this argument is equally valid for internal forecasters. Both have something to lose if they provide inaccurate forecasts: the internal forecaster could lose his or her job, whereas the external forecaster could lose a client or clients if the word gets around. But, in either case, faulty forecasts do not constitute a criminal offence for which either the internal or the external forecaster can be prosecuted.

If a satisfactory external forecaster cannot be found, it may be better to generate the forecasts internally, particularly if this proves to be more cost-effective. At least the internal forecaster is always on standby to respond to any need pertaining to forecasting and economic analysis. Sometimes, however, it may be found useful to employ a forecaster as well as subscribing to a forecasting service. This will be the case if the objective is to reach some sort of a consensus forecast. The internal forecaster may also monitor the track record of the forecasting services, providing some recommendation to management on whether subscription is to be maintained or terminated.

because they indicate zero forecasting errors. Points D and E and any other points in the same quadrant represent a forecast of a rising exchange rate when the exchange rate actually rises. Hence, there is no error of direction. Point F and all other points in the same quadrant also indicate no error of direction, but in this case the forecast indicates a falling exchange rate when the exchange rate actually falls. Points H and G and other points in the same two quadrants indicate errors of direction: either that the forecast indicates a rising rate when the rate actually falls (point G) or that it indicates a falling rate when it actually rises (point H).

Figure 12.2 The prediction-realisation diagram

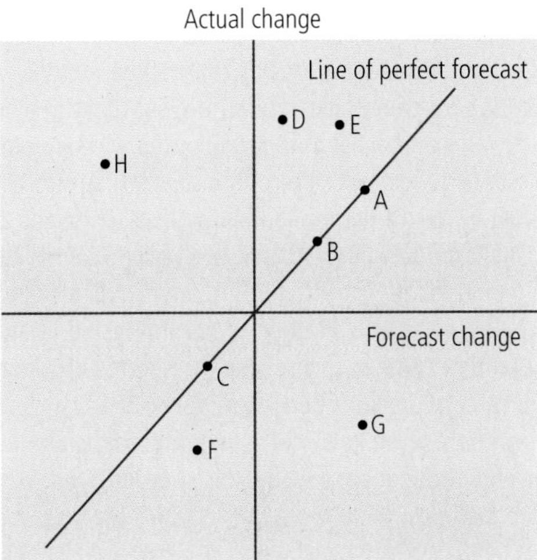

IN PRACTICE

Selecting an external forecaster

Selecting the right external forecaster involves a vital decision that effectively boils down to forecasting the forecasters. The choice can be costly in terms of the fees charged and/or the losses incurred if the forecaster produces excessively erroneous forecasts. It is important to establish beforehand what is expected from a forecaster. After all, we pay for what we need (or what we want) and we do not pay for what we do not need (or want), even if it is extremely cheap.

Clients have different needs, which becomes obvious by considering the following situations:

- A straightforward currency speculator is interested in buy/sell signals.
- A hedger is interested in knowing the direction and magnitude of the change in the exchange rate between the present time and the point in time when the payables or receivables become due.
- A speculator on European options needs forecasts on the level of the exchange rate at a particular point in time (the time of expiry of the option).
- A speculator on American options needs forecasts on the behaviour of the exchange rate between the time a position is taken and the option's expiry date.
- A speculator on combined option positions, like a straddle, is interested only in the magnitude of change (that is, in the volatility of the exchange rate) irrespective of the direction.
- A decision maker addressing a capital budgeting problem involving foreign direct investment needs long-term forecasts over a period of, say, 10 years.

Given these possibilities, the client will be concerned with the methodology, format, timing and frequency of the release of the forecasts. Although forecasters are in the same general business, most of them do not compete head-on because they do not offer the same services and do not cater for the same clientele. Let us now examine what the clients described above need and what kind of product they seek.

- A speculator who is only interested in buy/sell signals may choose a forecasting service using technical analysis. Such a speculator will be trading on a day-to-day basis, which makes daily updates rather important. Forecasts based on technical analysis are more suitable for this kind of client. The speculator will also look for a foreign exchange forecasting service that can deal with his or her needs around the clock.
- A hedger does not require day-to-day updates because the hedger is only interested in where the exchange rate will end up on the date when the payables or receivables are due. Thus, a forecaster who provides monthly or weekly updates may be suitable. The problem here is the timing, as the date on which the payables and receivables are due may not coincide with the date for which the forecasts are prepared. In this case, the frequency of releasing the forecasts does matter. It is more likely that the date on which the payables and receivables are due will be near a date for which forecasts are prepared when the forecasting frequency is weekly rather than monthly.
- A speculator on European options will look for something similar to what a hedger looks for. But a speculator on American options would want a forecast of the level of the exchange rate between the time the position is taken and the date of expiry of the option. Such a speculator would be interested in output showing the forecast values of the exchange rate at discrete and close points in time between the present time and the date of expiry. Otherwise, a description of the time path of the exchange rate during this time period identifying the turning points will also be suitable.
- A speculator on combined option positions, such as a straddle, is not interested in an exact level of the exchange rate by or on a particular date. Rather, this speculator is interested in the absolute magnitude of change in the exchange rate. What this speculator wants to know is whether the exchange rate will be above or below a certain level. In this case, point forecasts are not necessary and interval forecasts will be just as useful. More appropriately, this speculator needs forecasts of several point values with associated probabilities.

- A decision maker considering a foreign direct investment project needs long-term rather than short-term forecasts. Exchange rate forecasts at the end of each year over the next 10 years may be required to evaluate the net present value and the internal rate of return on the project (see Chapter 18).

The criteria used to select an external forecaster can be listed as follows:

The methodology

To start with, the methodology affects the description of the product as explained above. A forecaster using a PPP model cannot provide forecasts on a daily basis, whereas a forecaster using a technical model to generate buy/sell signals cannot provide the long-term forecasts needed to make a capital budgeting decision. The methodology may also affect the choice of the forecaster for 'ideological' reasons. For example, a client who thinks that technical analysis is some sort of 'witchcraft' is unlikely to choose a forecaster who uses technical models. Moreover, a client is more likely to choose a forecaster who uses methodology that sounds familiar or convincing. Other important aspects of the methodology pertain to how up-to-date it is, as well as the quality and the sources of the data used to estimate the model forecasting.

The format

Like the methodology, the format also affects the characteristics of the product. These pertain to such aspects as whether the forecast is given in terms of buy/sell signals, point estimates or interval forecasts, with or without a commentary, and so on.

Timing and frequency of the forecasts

Again, these two criteria affect the characteristics of the product.

Judgmental adjustment

Some clients might believe that judgmental adjustment is subjective and inappropriate. This is why the size of judgmental adjustment may be an important factor in determining the selection of the forecaster.

Means of transmission

Forecasts are transmitted from the forecaster to the client by a number of means, including mail, fax, telephone and computer networks. The means of transmission is important for at least two reasons. First, it makes a difference for the time elapsing between the production and delivery of the forecasts and hence between the availability of the information and the utilisation of this information in decision making. Second, the means of transmission must be conducive to delivery without error and allow for the evaluation of a track record. Thus, mail and telephone delivery do not satisfy these requirements.

Exclusiveness of the forecasts

A client will feel more comfortable if the forecasts are not available to competitors. It may not be possible, however, to have access to information revealing the identity of other subscribers.

The track record

The track record is very important because it shows the accuracy, or otherwise, of the forecasts. Two points must be borne in mind when the track record is considered. First, it is possible to falsify the track record. This can be done fairly easily as all it takes is to change the wrong forecasts when the track record is printed out from the computer. Thus, it is important to find out whether the track record has been audited by an independent body. Second, the track record as such may not be as important as whether or not profits have been generated by following the forecasts.

The cost

The cost comes last because what is important is cost-effectiveness (that is, the value of the service obtained for the subscription paid). The cost factor cannot be considered independently of the other aspects of the contract, including support services.

12.8 Technical analysis

Technical analysis, which comprises a variety of practices and procedures, is the opposite of fundamental analysis implicit in econometric models. It is used to generate buy and sell signals and so it is a forecasting device. This technique is similar to time series forecasting, as the underlying models utilise the exchange rate's past history to forecast its future level, but it tends to be less formal and less rigorous.

Technical analysis ignores (at least explicitly) the role of fundamental determinants of the exchange rate, such as inflation and interest rates. One argument for ignoring information on fundamental variables is that this information contains significant errors. While this is certainly true (particularly with respect to the balance of payments data), it is normally the case that traders take decisions on the basis of published data, irrespective of whether or not they contain measurement errors. Moreover, it can be argued that it is not easy to pinpoint all the fundamental factors affecting the exchange rate over a period of time. Given also that some of these factors are qualitative in nature (and therefore cannot be measured), a combination of market forces (driven by a set of fundamental factors) may cause the exchange rate to make a move that appears contradictory to what is implied by the fundamental information we are exposed to. For example, the US dollar is known to have appreciated in spite of lower interest and growth rates, both of which should have caused its depreciation (see the box on pages 326–7). Thus, while attention may be focused on these two fundamental factors, other determinants of the exchange rate (including non-economic factors) must have moved in such a way as to strengthen the dollar. And while traders believing in fundamental factors would have made a faulty prediction of a depreciating dollar, those who only watched a chart were convinced that the dollar would keep on appreciating. Because of these problems with fundamental analysis, technicians argue that the best thing to do is to watch the past history of the exchange rate and generate forecasts accordingly. In this section, we describe some of the techniques and chart formations that constitute technical analysis.

Technical analysis relies on the study of historical data, normally by plotting them on a **chart**. This is why technical analysis is also known as **charting** and technical analysts as **chartists**. There are three kinds of charts: line charts, bar charts and point and figure charts.

Line charts and bar charts

A **line chart** is a plot against time, normally of daily closing exchange rates. For intraday trading (that is, buying and selling within one day), the frequency of observation could be hourly or by the minute. A **bar chart**, on the other hand, plots not only the closing exchange rates, but also the high and low for each day or period. A typical bar chart is shown in Figure 12.3. A bar is a vertical line whose top end measures the high value of the exchange rate, whereas the bottom end measures the low value. The closing value is represented by a small horizontal line crossing the bar at that value.

Point and figure charts

Point and figure charts are used to highlight major market trends. Unlike line and bar charts, they do not show small exchange rate movements and they are not time-related, to the extent that initially they look very confusing. Entries are made on a point and figure chart only when there is a 'significant change' in the exchange rate. What is significant depends on the underlying exchange rate and on the technical analysts utilising the chart. If the underlying exchange rate is USD/AUD, then a significant change may be 25 points or 50 points.

RESEARCH FINDINGS

How good is technical analysis?

Traditionally, economists have rejected the propositions put forward by technical analysts, since they believe that economic fundamentals are the only determinants of exchange rates. Given the notion of market efficiency, old information (particularly publicly available information) must be useless because it is already incorporated in the current exchange rate. Malkiel put forward the cynical view that 'technical strategies are usually amusing, often comforting, but of no real value'.[1] But if this is the case, why is it that technical analysts are still in demand by financial institutions? Malkiel has a ready answer: they are hired by brokers largely in order to generate trades and hence commissions. Allen and Taylor put forward the counterargument that, even if this is the case, 'the results of this policy manifest themselves as self-fulfilling chartist strategies'.[2] The fact remains, however, that the failure of fundamental models has forced economists to take technical analysis more seriously.

While economists have traditionally regarded technical analysis as 'mumbo jumbo', arguing that it is to fundamental analysis what astrology is to astronomy, a recent paper by Lo, Mamaysky and Wang has come to the defence of technical analysis.[3] They investigated the predictive ability of widely used chart formations, including head and shoulders. Their results showed that various chart formations occurred more frequently than they would have done if they were truly random events. In general, they found chart formations to contain useful information about future financial prices. However, they did not say whether this information was useful enough to make sufficient profit trading on it to justify the extra risk. Moreover, the study did not explore what caused the formations. One possibility is that they reflect changes in investor psychology: the appetite of traders for risk may change in predictable ways in response to particular changes in financial prices.

1 B. G. Malkiel, *A Random Walk Down Wall Street*, 5th edition, Norton, New York, 1990.

2 H. L. Allen and M. P. Taylor, 'Chartist Analysis', in P. Newman, M. Milgate and J. Eatwell (eds), *The New Palgrave Dictionary of Money and Finance*, Macmillan, London, 1993.

3 A. Lo, H. Mamaysky and J. Wang, 'Foundations of Technical Analysis: Computational Algorithms, Statistical Inference and Empirical Implementation', *Journal of Finance*, 55, 2000, pp. 1705–70.

Figure 12.3 A bar chart

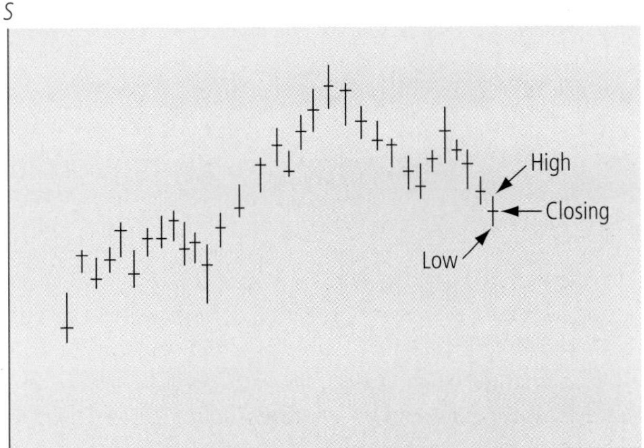

If the significant change is 25 points, then a change in the exchange rate from 0.5550 to 0.5565 does not have a corresponding entry on the chart. However, a change to 0.5575 does have a corresponding entry. Obviously, this implies that the more unstable the exchange rate, the greater the number of entries.

Figure 12.4 is a representation of a point and figure chart for the USD/AUD exchange rate, assuming a significant change of 25 points. Entries are made with Xs when the exchange rate is rising and Os when it is falling. The six Xs in the first column indicate that over some period in time, which could be anything, the exchange rate rose from 0.5250 to 0.5375. Afterwards, the exchange rate started to decline, as shown by the three Os in the second column. A change from a column of Xs to a column of Os indicates a trend reversal after a peak in the exchange rate. Conversely, a change from a column of Os to a column of Xs indicates a trend reversal following a trough. The height of the column indicates the persistence of an upward trend (X) and a downward trend (O). In general, the way the chart looks depends on the choice of the significant change (the sensitivity) and the volatility of the exchange rate. The greater the volatility, the faster the chart is filled. Smaller significant changes are more useful for short-term forecasting and trading.

Figure 12.4 A point and figure chart (USD/AUD, significant change = 25 points)

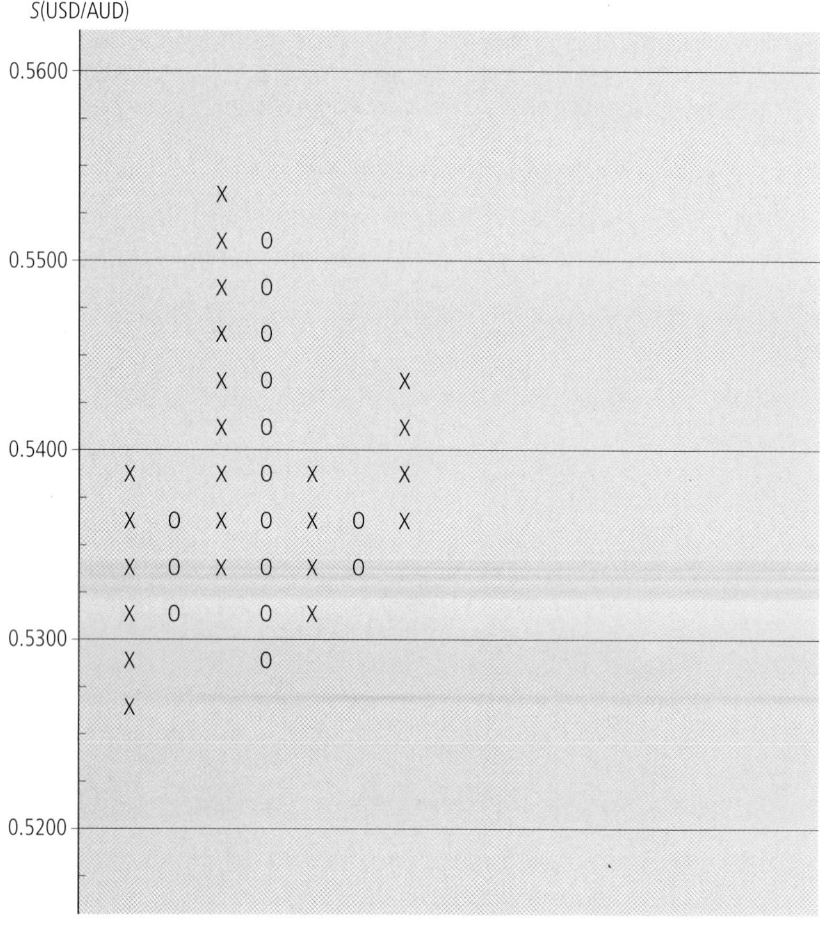

Chart formations

Chartists study charts of movements of exchange rates to identify certain patterns that have specific implications for the future movements of exchange rates. The following patterns and formations attract the interest of technical analysts.

Trendlines and trading ranges

A trend may be upward, downward or sideways. In a bull (rising) market, the trend is upward and so the chart will show a series of ascending bottoms. In a bear (falling) market, the trend is downward, characterised by a series of descending tops. Otherwise, the market moves sideways when the tops and bottoms are at the same level, in which case the market is said to be in a **trading range**. In order to recognise a trend, chartists draw **trendlines** connecting the **tops** and **bottoms** Normally, a trend is not 'confirmed' until three tops or bottoms touch the line. A parallel line is then drawn, creating a **trend channel**. These possibilities are illustrated in Figure 12.5.

Figure 12.5 Trendlines and trend channels

(a) Upward trend (bull market)

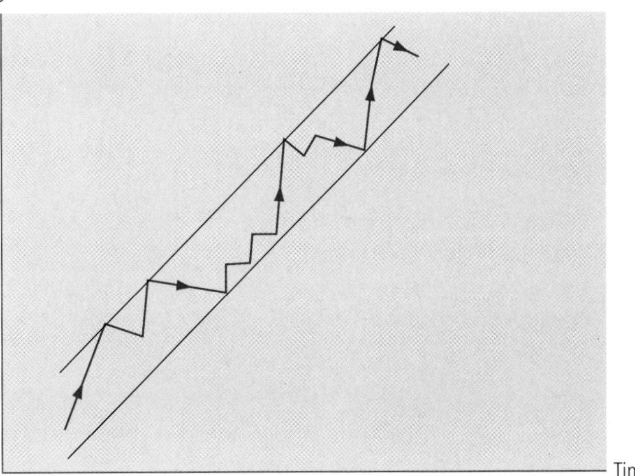

(b) Downward trend (bear market)

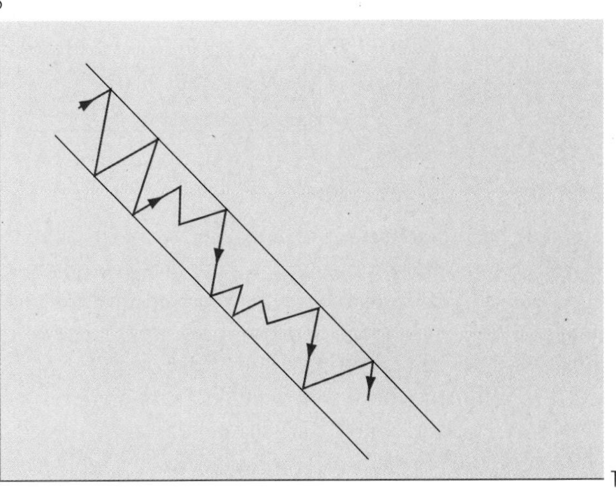

Continued...

(c) Sideways trend (trading range)

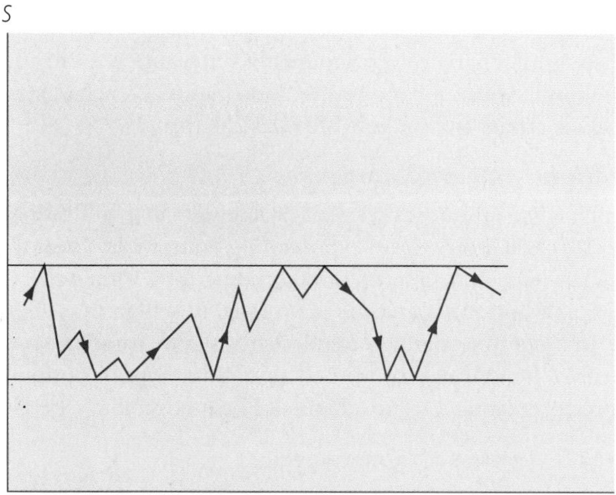

When exchange rates break through the upper line of the channel in a bear market, this indicates that the decline will slow down or that a reversal of the trend is imminent. Another indicator of trend reversal is the changing slope of the trend line or the parallel line. Figure 12.6 shows a change in the slope from negative to positive, indicating a reversal of the trend.

Figure 12.6 Trend reversal

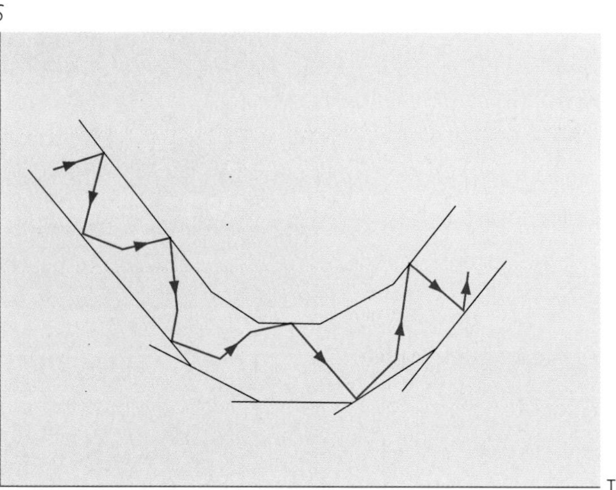

Support and resistance levels

A **support level** is the bottom of a market swing (that is, the point at which the exchange rate reverses a downward move). A **resistance level**, on the other hand, is a point where the market peaks and the exchange rate reverses an upward move. Support levels are created by additional buying or excess demand pressure, whereas resistance levels are created by additional selling or excess supply.

Figure 12.7 illustrates how resistance and support levels are created. Suppose that at point in time t_1 a speculator bought the currency at S_1. At time t_2, the speculator decided to take profit by selling the currency at S_2. The increased supply at t_2 puts downward pressure on the exchange rate and so it starts to decline. When it reaches S_1 again at t_3, the speculator may decide to do the same thing all over again. The increased demand puts upward pressure on the exchange rate, which starts to rise. When the exchange rate approaches S_2, the speculator remembers what happened last time and sells the currency, creating downward pressure, and so on. Therefore, S_1 becomes a support level, whereas S_2 becomes a resistance level.

Figure 12.7 Creation of resistance and support levels

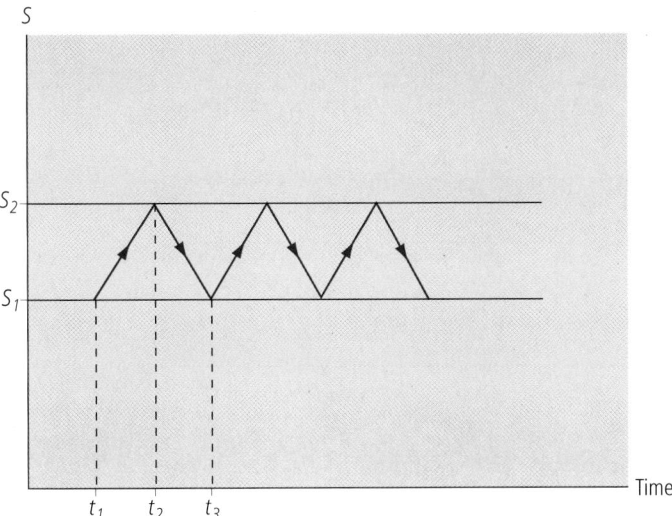

Resistance and support levels are not static: they change over time. Figure 12.8 illustrates how this change may take place. Suppose that, for some reason, the exchange rate breaks through the resistance level indicated by S_2. The speculator then regrets selling the currency at S_2. If the exchange rate turns back to this level, this speculator will buy, putting pressure on the exchange rate to rise. Thus, S_2 becomes the new support level, as shown in Figure 12.8(a). Similar reasoning can be used to explain why S_1 may become the new resistance level when there is a break through the support level, as in Figure 12.8(b).

Figure 12.8 Change of resistance and support levels

(a) A new support level

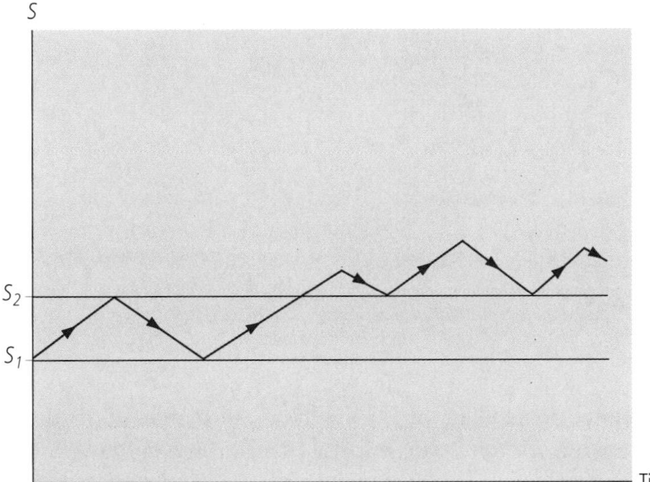

Continued...

(b) A new resistance level

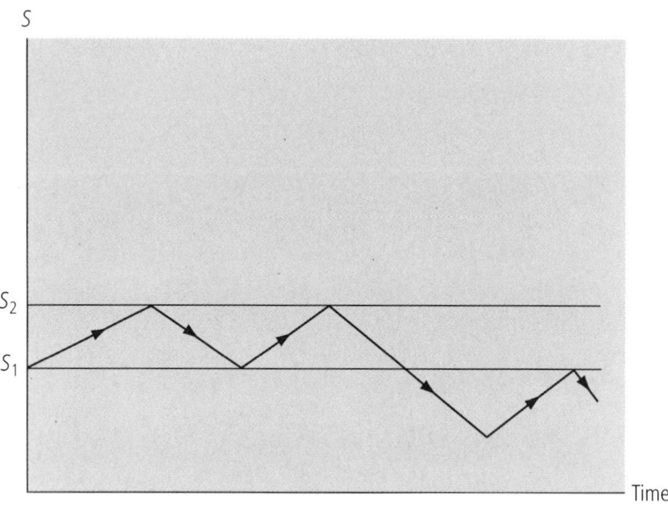

Flags

Flags are **continuation patterns**. Two examples of flags are shown in Figure 12.9. For a pattern to qualify as a flag, the flag's 'pole' has to be a continuation of a previous trend. A break-out from the flag pattern indicates a move of the same magnitude and direction as that leading up to the flag. A flag occurs when major trends are interrupted. When this takes place, some market participants sit and wait for the move to continue, while others consider getting in, thinking that the trend will continue. In a bull market, the increase in buying caused by these participants results in upward pressure and a continuation of the trend.

Figure 12.9 Flags

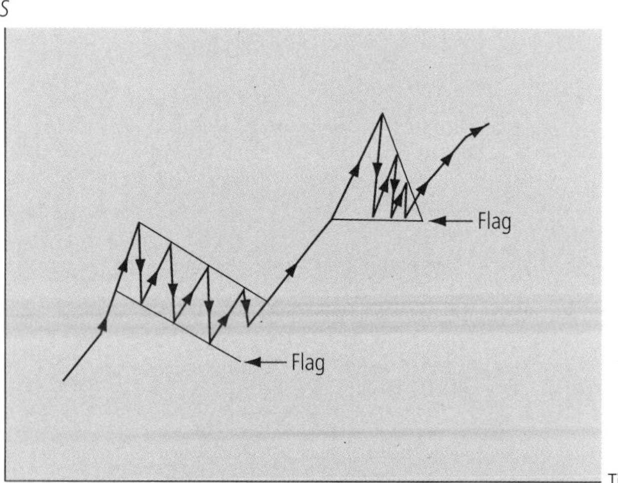

Triangles

Triangles can be ascending, descending or symmetrical, as shown in Figure 12.10. An ascending triangle occurs when buyers come into the market at progressively higher levels while sellers get out at the same level. The buyers put pressure on the exchange rate to rise, causing a continuation of the trend. The reverse happens in the case of a descending triangle. A symmetrical triangle is difficult to interpret and so it does not give a reliable signal until either top or bottom lines are broken.

Figure 12.10 Triangles

(a) Ascending

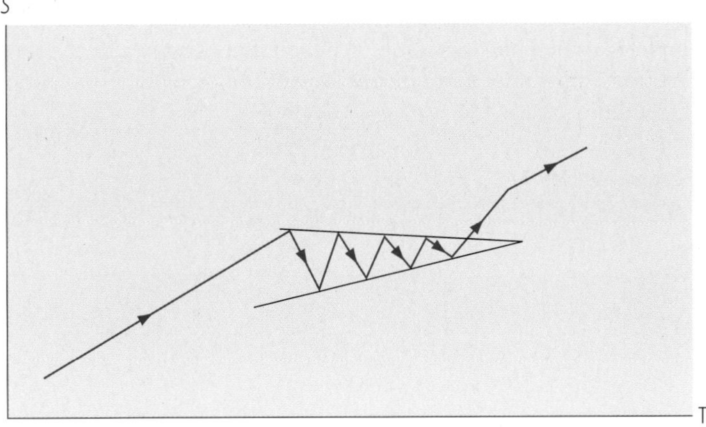

(b) Descending

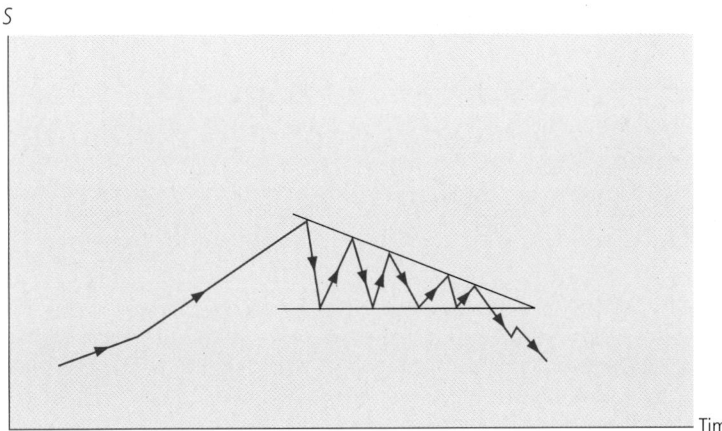

(c) Symmetrical

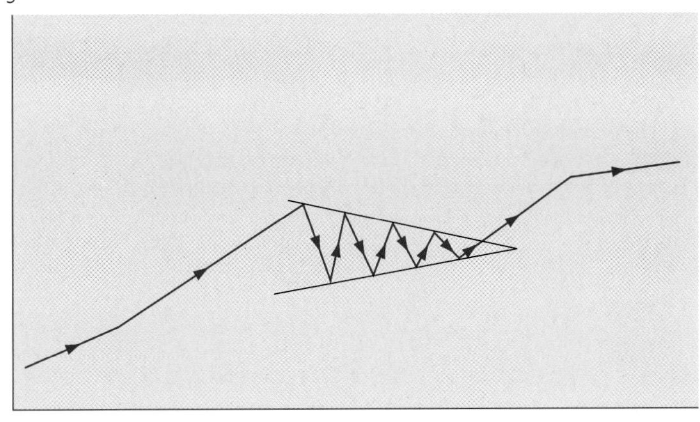

Head and shoulders

A **head and shoulders** formation, which is shown in Figure 12.11, indicates a reversal of an upward trend and the onset of a bear market. It has the following features: (i) it comes after a prolonged upward trend; (ii) the middle top (the head) must be higher than the tops of the shoulders on either side; (iii) the shoulder tops must be at approximately equal levels. A **neckline** is drawn between the two lows that occur between the head and the shoulders. The pattern is completed when the neckline is penetrated downwards. A **reverse head and shoulders** formation comes after a significant downtrend, signalling the end of a bear market. This is shown in Figure 12.12.

Figure 12.11 Head and shoulders

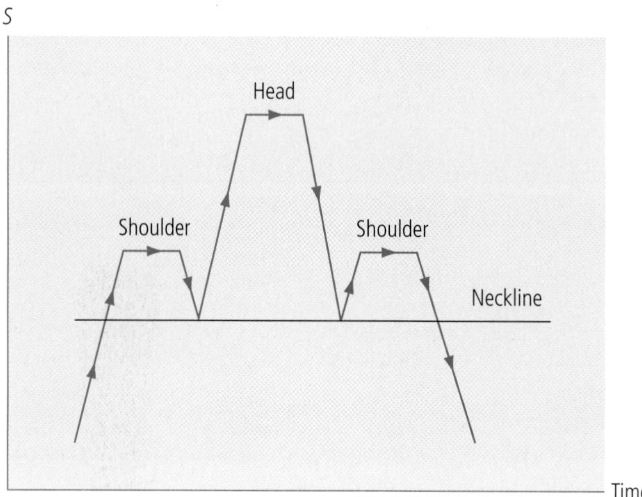

Figure 12.12 Reverse head and shoulders

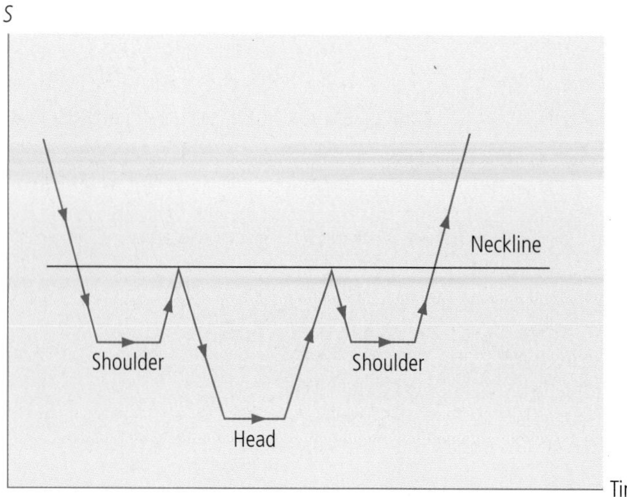

Other formations

Other formations used by technical analysts include **wedges**, **double tops**, **double bottoms**, **triple tops**, **triple bottoms**, **saucers** and **spikes**. It is easy to imagine what these patterns look like. Technical analysis as applied to futures contracts also utilises the concept of a **gap**. A gap is an area of a chart where no entries are made. This occurs, for example, when a futures contract trades up to its permitted limit one day and opens higher the following day.

RESEARCH FINDINGS

Who uses technical analysis?

Studies on the extent of the use of technical analysis have produced results showing extensive use of this technique, particularly for short-term forecasting. Allen and Taylor[1] and Taylor and Allen[2] presented evidence on the use of technical analysis based on a survey of some 240 foreign exchange dealers in London. The survey revealed a broad consensus regarding the weights given to technical analysis at different time horizons. At short horizons, ranging from intraday to weekly, 90 per cent of the participants reported using technical analysis. Some 60 per cent of the participants said that they regarded technical analysis to be at least as important as **fundamental analysis** The results also revealed that at long horizons the weight given to fundamental analysis is greater. There was a very small minority (2 per cent) who claimed never to have used fundamental analysis. The overall conclusion that can be derived from the survey is that technical analysis and fundamental analysis are complementary.

More recently, Lui and Mole conducted a similar survey involving 153 foreign exchange dealers in the Hong Kong market.[3] This survey revealed that a very high proportion of the respondents placed some weight on both technical and fundamental analysis at all time horizons. At shorter horizons, however, there exists a skew towards reliance on technical analysis. Moreover, a view was expressed that technical analysis is only slightly more useful than fundamental analysis in predicting trends, but significantly more useful in predicting turning points.

Oberlechner presented findings of a survey of the perceived importance of technical versus fundamental analysis among foreign exchange traders and financial journalists in four European financial centres.[4] The results confirmed the proposition that most traders use both forecasting approaches and that the shorter the forecasting horizon, the more important technical analysis becomes. Results also indicated that the importance of technical analysis has increased since the 1990s. Financial journalists seem to put more emphasis on fundamental analysis than do foreign exchange traders.

Cheung and Chinn reported findings from a survey of US foreign exchange traders. The results showed that: (i) technical trading best characterises about 30 per cent of traders; and (ii) the importance of fundamental analysis increases at longer horizons.[5]

1 H. L. Allen and M. P. Taylor, 'Chart Analysis and the Foreign Exchange Market', *Bank of England Quarterly Bulletin*, November 1989.

2 M. P. Taylor and H. L. Allen, 'The Use of Technical Analysis in the Foreign Exchange Market', *Journal of International Money and Finance*, 11, 1992, pp. 304–14.

3 Y. H. Lui and D. Mole, 'The Use of Fundamental and Technical Analysis by Foreign Exchange Dealers: Hong Kong Evidence', *Journal of International Money and Finance*, 17, 1998, pp. 535–45.

4 T. Oberlechner, 'Importance of Technical and Fundamental Analysis in the European Foreign Exchange Market', *International Journal of Finance and Economics*, 6, 2001, pp. 81–93.

5 Y. W. Cheung and M. D. Chinn, 'Macroeconomic Implications of the Beliefs and Behavior of Foreign Exchange Traders', NBER Working Paper, No. 7417, 1999.

12.9 Trading rules

Trading rules are mechanical procedures that are used to generate buy and sell signals, which makes them forecasting tools. We have already come across a mechanical trading rule based on purchasing power parity, whereby a currency is bought if it is undervalued, as implied by PPP, and sold otherwise (see Chapter 9). Since the prices of goods and services underlying the PPP relationship change very sluggishly, the relationship between the actual level of the exchange rate and what is implied by PPP varies very slowly, in the sense that if a currency is overvalued it will remain so for a long period of time. Thus, the PPP rule is not useful for short-term (such as day-to-day) trading. For this purpose we resort to using filter rules and moving average rules.

Filter rules

A **filter rule** may work as follows. A currency is bought when it appreciates by x per cent from its most recent trough and sold when it depreciates by x per cent from its most recent peak, where x is any small number. Thus, we could, for example, have 0.5 per cent, 1 per cent, 2 per cent, 5 per cent and 10 per cent filters. Figure 12.13 illustrates how a 5 per cent filter rule works. The exchange rate reaches a peak at point A, after which it starts to decline. Once it has declined by 5 per cent, the underlying currency is sold. The trader then waits until a trough is recognised at B. Once the exchange rate has risen by 5 per cent from this trough, the currency is bought again. In this case, the currency is kept until the exchange rate falls by 5 per cent from its subsequent peak at C, and so on.

Figure 12.13 A 5 per cent filter rule

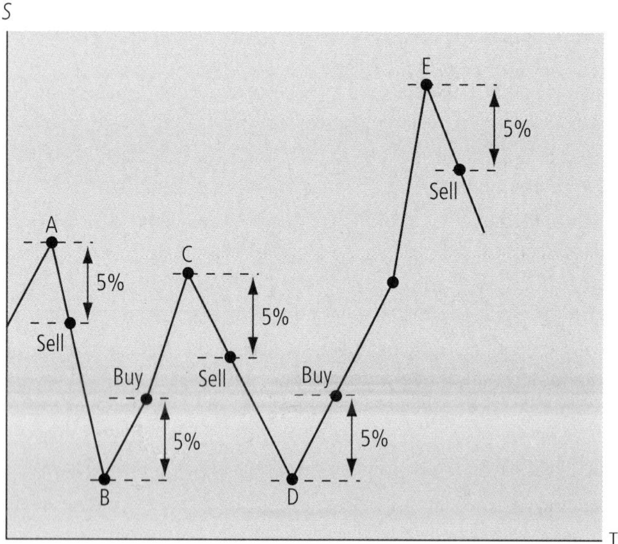

Filter rules are designed to catch a break-out from the bands represented by the dotted lines. Within the band, the currency is assumed to be trading at around its equilibrium value. But as new information is absorbed, the exchange rate breaks out, presumably towards its new equilibrium value. The filter rule is designed to catch the exchange rate at the break-out point as it moves from the old equilibrium value to the new equilibrium value that falls within the following band. The break-out point is represented by the lower dashed line on the downturn and the upper dashed line on the upturn. In an efficient market, this is not possible since the exchange rate would adjust to new information too quickly to allow any trader to capture it.

A problem arises as to the choice of the **filter size**. The larger the filter, the more likely the trader is to trade only on the 'true' break-outs, but to be later in catching the trend. The smaller the filter, the more likely that the trader will catch the trend early enough, but may be misled by false break-outs. Moreover, smaller filters lead to a larger number of transactions and hence they are associated with higher transaction costs.

Example

Suppose that the AUD/USD exchange rate assumes the following values on 14 consecutive trading periods: 1.8000, 1.8907, 1.8423, 1.7495, 1.6445, 1.6858, 1.7701, 1.8679, 1.8198, 1.7610, 1.8258, 1.9202, 1.8411 and 1.7359. In order to detect the buy and sell signals (by using filter sizes of 2.5 per cent and 5 per cent and assuming that the first observation is a trough), the following steps must be followed:

- Identify the troughs (T) and peaks (P).
- Calculate the percentage change from the most recent trough/peak.
- Identify the buy/sell signals according to the filter rules.

The results are displayed in the following table. It is obvious that the smaller filter leads to a larger number of transactions.

Day	Exchange rate	Peak/trough	Percentage change	2.5% filter	5% filter
1	1.8000	T			
2	1.8907	P	5.04	Buy	Buy
3	1.8423		−2.56	Sell	
4	1.7495		−5.04		Sell
5	1.6445	T	−6.00		
6	1.6858		2.51	Buy	
7	1.7701		5.00		Buy
8	1.8679	P	5.53		
9	1.8198		−2.58	Sell	
10	1.7610	T	−3.23		
11	1.8258		3.68	Buy	
12	1.9202	P	5.17		
13	1.8411		−4.12	Sell	
14	1.7359	T	−5.71		Sell

Moving average rules

A **moving average rule** depends on the behaviour of one or two moving averages in relation to the actual exchange rate and to each other. A moving average of order (length) q at time (day) t is the simple average of the daily values over the last q days. Thus

$$M_t(q) = \frac{1}{q}\sum_{i=0}^{q-1} S_{t-i} \tag{12.23}$$

Using the data of the previous example, we may calculate a four-period moving average as follows. The first observation of the four-period moving average (at day 4) is calculated as

$$\frac{1}{4} \times (1.800 + 1.8907 + 1.8423 + 1.7495) = 1.8206$$

The other observations are listed in the following table:

Period	Exchange rate	Moving average
1	1.8000	
2	1.8907	
3	1.8423	
4	1.7495	1.8206
5	1.6445	1.7817
6	1.6858	1.7305
7	1.7701	1.7124
8	1.8679	1.7421
9	1.8198	1.7859
10	1.7610	1.8047
11	1.8258	1.8186
12	1.9202	1.8317
13	1.8411	1.8370
14	1.7359	1.8307

A **single moving average rule** works as illustrated by Figure 12.14, which plots the data displayed in the above table. The currency is bought when the moving average cuts the exchange rate series from above and is sold or sold short when the moving average cuts the exchange rate series from below.

Figure 12.14 A single moving average rule

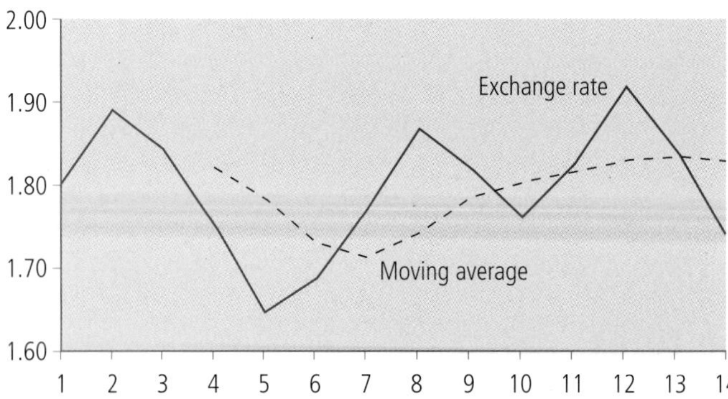

Another alternative is to use the **double moving average rule**, which involves using two moving averages of different orders. A buy signal is indicated when the long moving average crosses the short moving average from above and a sell or short sell signal is indicated when the long moving average cuts the short moving average from below.

RESEARCH FINDINGS

Using trading rules to test market efficiency

Testing market efficiency on the basis of trading rules is straightforward. What is needed is a sample of historical data (preferably daily) on the underlying exchange rate. Suppose that the data cover a period of two years. The sample period is divided into subperiods, say, eight quarters, and two trading strategies are applied over each subperiod. The first strategy is based on a trading rule, whereas the other is a passive buy-and-hold strategy, based on buying at the exchange rate prevailing at the beginning of the subperiod and selling at the rate prevailing at the end. The rate of return on both strategies can then be calculated and compared. If the strategy based on a trading rule can consistently (that is, for all or the majority of subsamples) outperform the buy-and-hold strategy, then this is evidence against market efficiency.

Several studies have been conducted to test the efficiency of the foreign exchange market by measuring the profitability of trading rules. Dooley and Shafer examined the profitability of 1 per cent, 3 per cent and 5 per cent filter rules.[1] They concluded that these rules would have been profitable for all currencies over the entire sample period, but the element of risk was very high. It is important to remember that these rules can only be used if a high degree of volatility, and hence greater risk, is present.

Sweeney analysed filter rules for 10 currencies over the period 1973–1980 and found that small filters tend to produce profitable trading strategies.[2] In many cases, profits were significant in a statistical sense, but not necessarily according to economic risk-return criteria. Goodman examined the performance of the professional advisers who issue buy and sell signals on the basis of technical analysis.[3] He reported large profits in excess of the risk-free rate, but risk was also present.

Martin put forward the proposition that central bank intervention makes trading rules more profitable in the foreign exchange markets of developing countries.[4] By using a moving average rule, she showed that statistically significant profits were generated in most of the markets that were examined.

The evidence is therefore mixed. The general consensus now is that the foreign exchange market is highly but not perfectly efficient. Thus, hard work can produce results in terms of trading profit.

1 M. Dooley and J. Shafer, 'Analysis of Short-Run Exchange Rate Behavior: March 1973 to November 1981', in D. Bigman and T. Taya (eds), *Exchange Rate and Trade Instability*, Ballinger Publishing, Cambridge, Mass., 1983.

2 R. J. Sweeney, 'Beating the Foreign Exchange Market', *Journal of Finance*, 41, 1986, pp. 163–82.

3 S. Goodman, 'Technical Analysis Still Beats Econometrics', *Euromoney*, August 1981.

4 A. D. Martin, 'Technical Trading Rules in the Spot Foreign Exchange Markets of Developing Countries', *Multinational Financial Management*, 11, 2001, pp. 59–68.

Summary

- Forecasting is a formal process of generating expectations. Exchange rate forecasting is needed by international firms for many purposes, including: (i) spot speculation; (ii) uncovered interest arbitrage; (iii) spot-forward speculation; (iv) option speculation; (v) hedging; (vi) investment and capital budgeting decisions; (vii) financing decisions; (viii) pricing decisions; (ix) strategic planning; (x) consideration of overall macroeconomic conditions; and (xi) central bank intervention.
- Econometric forecasting models are based on some underlying economic theory. They can be single-equation models or multi-equation models.

- Market-based forecasting amounts to the use of the current spot or forward rates as forecasters.
- Time series forecasting models are based entirely upon the past history of the exchange rate. The use of these models is incompatible with the efficient market hypothesis. This is because in an efficient market the exchange rate must follow a random walk, which means that it is not possible to forecast the exchange rate on the basis of its past behaviour.
- Judgmental forecasting takes into account all the factors affecting the exchange rate, including those that cannot be quantified. These forecasts, however, are not based on some numerical formula.
- Composite forecasting is based on two or more forecasts that are derived independently. The underlying idea is that the forecasting error can be reduced by pooling forecasts.
- Forecasting accuracy can be measured by a variety of criteria, which are based on the magnitude of the forecasting error. These include: (i) the mean absolute error; (ii) the mean square error; and (iii) the root mean square error.
- The prediction-realisation diagram is a diagrammatic representation of forecasting accuracy, which also identifies errors of direction.
- The empirical evidence on the forecasting performance of models and forecasting services is not impressive. Several studies have shown that most forecasting models cannot outperform the random walk model or the forward rate as a forecaster.
- Technical analysis and forecasting also depend on the exchange rate's past history, but they tend to be less formal. Technical analysis ignores the role of the fundamental determinants of the exchange rate.
- Technical analysis relies on studying charts describing past behaviour. These charts may be: (i) line charts; (ii) bar charts; or (iii) point and figure charts.
- Chartists study movements of exchange rates and identify patterns and formations, including: (i) trendlines and trading ranges; (ii) support and resistance levels; (iii) flags; (iv) triangles; and (v) head and shoulders.
- Trading rules are mechanical procedures that are used to generate buy and sell signals, which makes them forecasting tools.
- A filter rule stipulates that a buy signal is generated when the exchange rate eases above its trough by a given percentage, whereas a sell signal is generated when the exchange rate falls from its peak by a given percentage.
- A moving average rule generates buy and sell signals by the points of intersection of the time paths of the exchange rate and a moving average.

Key terms

MAXIMISE YOUR MARKS! There are 30 interactive questions for this chapter available online at **www.mhhe.com/au/moosa2e**

Review questions

1 Why is it that forecasting the future value of an exchange rate is more difficult than forecasting rainfall? Why is the latter more difficult than forecasting the time it takes a falling object to hit the ground?

2 Despite the fact that exchange rate forecasting has not produced spectacular results, it is still used as an input in decision making. Why?

3 What are the business operations for which exchange rate forecasting is required?

4 Why do central banks need exchange rate forecasting?

5 What are the problems associated with single-equation forecasting models? Which of these problems can be circumvented by using other models?

6 How do multi-equation models solve the black-box problem of the reduced-form models?

7 During the period 1981–1985, the US dollar went through protracted depreciation that took it to its highest value ever in February 1985. Why did forecasters fail miserably to anticipate this move? Why did the dollar strengthen in the face of negative announcements on macroeconomic variables?

8 What is the rationale for using composite forecasting?

9 Is judgmental forecasting useful for business decisions? Why?

10 What determines whether a firm uses an external or an internal forecaster?

11 What factors determine the selection of an external forecaster?

12 Why do forecasters produce different forecasts?

13 Why do forecasters occasionally resort to judgmental forecasting?

14 'Market-watchers are convinced the US dollar's decline will continue for at least the next 12 months, giving the $A plenty of scope to venture above US60c. But doubts are growing about whether the currency will hold on to its gains by the end of the year', *Australian Financial Review*, 29 January 2003. Can you rationalise this judgmental forecast?

15 With reference to the prediction-realisation diagram, explain what is indicated when the points fall in the following positions: (a) the first quadrant to the left of the line of perfect forecast; (b) the first quadrant to the right of the line of perfect forecast; (c) the second quadrant; (d) the third quadrant to the left of the line of perfect forecast; (e) the third quadrant to the right of the line of perfect forecast; and (f) the fourth quadrant.

16 As a consultant, you have been approached by a bank contemplating whether or not to close down its exchange rate forecasting unit. Advise the bank as to the desirability of this action.

17 How do technical analysts justify the overlooking of fundamental factors in exchange rate forecasting?

18 What is the rationale for using technical analysis?

19 What is the major difference between a line chart and a point and figure chart?

20 What indicates a trend reversal in technical analysis?

21 Define support and resistance levels. How are these levels created and how do they change?

22 What is the implication of a flag formation?

23 What is the interpretation of: (a) an ascending triangle; (b) a descending triangle; (c) a symmetrical triangle; (d) head and shoulders; and (e) reverse head and shoulders?

24 What is the difference between a double moving average rule and a single moving average rule?

Problems

1 It is the end of September 2002. The current AUD/USD exchange rate is 1.9230, and the Australian and US three-month interest rates are 6 per cent and 4.5 per cent p.a., respectively. A forecast indicates that the exchange rate at the end of 2002 will be 1.8750.
(a) What would you do on the basis of this information?
(b) If the actual exchange rate turns out to be 1.9370, calculate the percentage forecasting error.
(c) Is there an error of direction in this forecast?
(d) What is the outcome of acting on this forecast?

2 It is the end of 2001 and the following information is available:

Spot exchange rate (AUD/USD)	1.9640
Three-month forward rate	1.9850
Price of a call option expiring at the end of March 2002	AUD0.01
Price of a put option expiring at the end of March 2002	AUD0.01
Exercise exchange rate for the call option	1.9750
Exercise exchange rate for the put option	2.0050

A forecaster has produced the following values for the AUD/USD exchange rate prevailing at the end of March 2002: 1.9900 with a probability of 0.6 and 1.9620 with a probability of 0.4.

(a) What will you do if you act on the basis of the higher forecast?
(b) What will you do if you act on the basis of the lower forecast?
(c) What will you do if you act on the basis of the expected value of the forecast?

3 Use the data set given in Problem 6, Chapter 11 (on page 316), to study the forecasting power of various models over the whole sample period.

(a) Use the random walk model to forecast the spot AUD/CAD exchange rate. In this case, the following quarter's forecast is the current quarter's value. Plot the percentage forecasting error over time. Does it look random?
(b) Use the forward rate as a forecaster. In this case, the following quarter's forecast is this quarter's forward rate. Plot the percentage forecasting error over time. Does it look random?
(c) Estimate the UIP model by regressing the percentage change in the spot exchange rate on the lagged interest rate differential. Use the estimated model to generate forecasts for the percentage change and the level of the spot exchange rate. Plot the percentage forecasting error over time. Does it look random?
(d) Estimate the PPP model by regressing the percentage change in the spot exchange rate on the inflation differential. Use the estimated model to generate forecasts for the percentage change and the level of the spot exchange rate. Plot the percentage forecasting error over time. Does it look random?
(e) Calculate a composite forecast as the simple average of the four different forecasts and the corresponding forecasting errors.
(f) Plot the prediction-realisation diagram for each of the five forecasts and identify the number of turning point errors in each case.
(g) Using various criteria, evaluate the forecasting performance of the various models (including the composite forecast).

4 The following is a data set containing daily observations on the AUD/USD exchange rate in February, March and April 1996 (the observations are arranged vertically):

1.3408	1.3238	1.3080	1.2920	1.2832	1.2695
1.3328	1.3200	1.3099	1.2932	1.2755	1.2726
1.3196	1.3208	1.3179	1.2890	1.2740	1.2718
1.3248	1.3256	1.3111	1.2922	1.2812	1.2724
1.3252	1.3280	1.3087	1.2900	1.2752	1.2673
1.3222	1.3242	1.3055	1.2870	1.2702	1.2719
1.3221	1.3194	1.3028	1.2910	1.2671	1.2658
1.3233	1.3187	1.3006	1.2933	1.2642	1.2702
1.3261	1.3168	1.2923	1.2900	1.2641	1.2732
1.3249	1.3098	1.2887	1.2776	1.2625	

You have AUD1000 to trade by buying and selling the US dollar. Start with a buy signal and finish with a sell signal.

(a) Apply a filter rule, using a filter size of your choice. Calculate the final value of the amount you start with. What is the rate of return?

(b) Calculate the final value of the amount and the rate of return when you adopt a passive buy-and-hold strategy (buy at the first buy signal and sell at the last sell signal). Is this strategy more or less profitable than the filter rule?

(c) Use a single moving average rule by choosing a short moving average. Calculate the final value of the amount you start with and the rate of return.

(d) Calculate the final value of the amount you start with and the rate of return. Compare the profitability of this rule with the profitability of a buy-and-hold strategy.

5 Use the daily time series from Problem 4 above to plot a point and figure chart. For this purpose, use a very small 'significant change' of your choice.

6 Obtain some daily exchange rate data from the Internet and plot them over time. Try to identify any of the technical patterns that you studied in this chapter.

CHAPTER

Foreign exchange risk and exposure

Introduction

Although the terms 'risk' and 'exposure' are sometimes used interchangeably, they are different but related concepts. In this chapter we shed some light on these concepts and identify the different kinds of foreign exchange exposure. One of the important issues that we will come across is the distinction between transaction exposure and economic exposure, which often arise together. Another important issue that we will consider is that while translation exposure does not affect the true economic value of the firm, it still has to be dealt with because it may affect the firm's share prices.

Objectives

The objectives of this chapter are:

- To define risk and exposure and to distinguish between them, concentrating on foreign exchange risk and exposure.
- To introduce the technique of value of risk.
- To measure the extent of risk arising from changes in Australian dollar exchange rates.
- To distinguish among transaction, economic and translation exposures.

13.1 Definition of risk

The Concise Oxford Dictionary defines **risk** to imply something bad. Risk is defined as the 'chance of bad consequence, loss, etc'. *The Oxford English Dictionary* defines risk as 'the possibility of meeting danger or suffering harm or loss'. *Webster's Dictionary* defines risk similarly to imply bad outcomes. Thus, risk is a measure of 'the possibility of loss, injury, disadvantage or destruction'.

The origin of the word 'risk' is thought to be either in the Arabic word *risq* or the Latin word *risicum*. The Arabic *risq* has a positive connotation, signifying anything that has been given to a person (by God) and from which this person can draw profit or satisfaction. The Latin *risicum*, on the other hand, implies an unfavourable event, as it originally referred to the challenge that a barrier reef presents to a sailor. The Greek derivative of the Arabic *risq*, which was used in the twelfth century, relates to chance outcome in general. In his *General Theory*, Keynes defined an entrepreneur's risk as the risk arising 'out of doubts in his own mind as to the probability of him actually earning the prospective yield for which he hopes'.

Risk implies both favourable and unfavourable outcomes with some probability distribution. It is hence associated with variability. Suppose that you were given the following two alternatives: (i) receiving AUD100 with certainty; and (ii) receiving AUD80 with a probability of 0.5 and AUD120 with a probability of 0.5. Your choice depends upon your attitude towards risk, which is inherent in the second alternative but not in the first. This is because the second alternative involves a probability distribution that describes various (in this case, two) outcomes. Thus, if you choose the second alternative, you will be exposed to risk, and you would do this if you were a **risk-lover**. Risk-lovers deliberately bear risk in anticipation of obtaining the favourable outcome, in this case the larger amount of AUD120.

If, on the other hand, you choose the first alternative, then you are **risk-averse**, liking certainty and disliking outcomes described by probability distributions. If you are indifferent between the two options, you are **risk-neutral**.

A question may arise here. What if there is no probability distribution for the outcomes? This case arises if, for example, the second alternative is that you would receive an amount that could be higher or lower than AUD100. What we have in this case is not risk, but rather **uncertainty**. Risk in general implies the availability of a probability distribution and this distribution may be entirely subjective.

In finance, risk is measured by the extent of the dispersion around the mean or average value of the underlying variable. This underlying variable could be the rate of return, the cost of borrowing, the value of assets and liabilities, and so on. Suppose that we are concerned with the rate of return on a certain investment. The rate of return over a holding period extending between t and $t + 1$, R, is calculated as the percentage change of the price of the underlying asset over the holding period. Thus, it is not known at the beginning of the period (that is, at time t). However, we may have a probability distribution for R. Suppose that the probability distribution tells us that there are n possible values for R, such that the ith value (R_i where $i = 1, 2, \dots n$) materialises with a probability p_i. The **expected value** of the rate of return is calculated as a weighted average of all possible values with probabilities serving as weights. Hence

$$E(R) = \sum_{i=1}^{n} p_i(R_i) \tag{13.1}$$

where E is the expected value operator and $E(R)$ is the expected value of R such that the expectation is formed at time t on the basis of the information available then. Risk is measured by dispersion around this expected value (that is, by the **variance** or the **standard deviation** of the expected rate of return). The variance is given by

$$\sigma^2(R) = \sum_{i=1}^{n} p_i\left[R_i - E(R)\right]^2 \tag{13.2}$$

The standard deviation is the square root of the variance, which is hence given by

$$\sigma(R) = \sqrt{\sum_{i=1}^{n} p_i\left[R_i - E(R\ )\right]^2} \tag{13.3}$$

The larger the value of the variance or the standard deviation, the greater is the risk. With reference to the example given earlier, the first alternative has an expected value of AUD100 with zero variance, since the value is known with certainty. The second alternative, on the other hand, has an expected value of AUD100 but a variance of 400 and a standard deviation of 20, meaning that (on average) the final outcome could be above or below the expected value by AUD20. If the second alternative gives either AUD60 or AUD140 with equal probabilities, the same expected value of AUD100 is obtained, but the risk is higher. In this case, the variance is 1600 and the standard deviation is 40.

If no probability distribution is available, risk or the variability of the rate of return may be evaluated on the basis of historical data. If the rate of return over the past n periods assumes the values $R_1, R_2, \dots R_n$, then the expected value of the rate of return can be represented by the average or **mean** value over the n periods. The mean value, $\overline{R}$, variance and standard deviation are calculated respectively as

$$\overline{R} = \frac{1}{n}\sum_{t=1}^{n} R_t \tag{13.4}$$

INSIGHT

What is operational risk?

In this chapter we deal with **foreign exchange risk**, which is a particular kind of **financial risk**, traditionally resulting from forces from outside the firm (for example, an exchange rate going the wrong way). **Operational risk**, which we referred to in Chapter 8, is different in that it results from within the firm. More precisely, it is the risk of loss resulting from internal causes.

King argues that people often do not do what they are supposed to do, either because they cannot or because they do not want to.[1] People act with stupidity when, for example, they hit the wrong keys, plug the wrong numbers into formulae they do not understand and read the wrong lines from displays. On the other hand, people may lie, cheat and steal, which we may call malice. Operational risk, King argues, is the result of both stupidity and malice.

The following is an example of operational risk resulting from the possibility of pressing the wrong button. On 14 May 2001, a trader at London-based Lehman Brothers keyed in the wrong number of shares on his trading screen. This action meant that the sell order on a basket of shares worth some GBP30 million turned into one valued ten times that amount. The FTSE 100 index of the London Stock Exchange fell by 2.2 per cent when the trade was executed. Lehman Brothers lost millions of pounds as a result (and the trader would have been sacked!).

One question remains: was that incident an act of stupidity or malice?

[1] J. J. King, *Operational Risk, Measurement and Modeling*, John Wiley & Sons, New York, 2001.

$$\sigma^2(R) = \frac{1}{n-1}\sum_{t=1}^{n}\left(R_t - \overline{R}\right)^2 \tag{13.5}$$

$$\sigma(R) = \sqrt{\frac{1}{n-1}\sum_{t=1}^{n}\left(R_t - \overline{R}\right)^2} \tag{13.6}$$

Foreign exchange risk arises because of uncertainty about the future spot exchange rate. It refers to the variability of the domestic currency value of certain items resulting from the variability of the exchange rate. These items include assets, liabilities, operating income, rates of return and expected cash flows, whether they are certain (contractual) or uncertain. If an investment in a foreign asset is taken at time t, maturing at time $t + 1$, then the rate of return over the holding period is defined as

$$R = \dot{V} = \frac{V_{t+1}}{V_t} - 1 \tag{13.7}$$

where V is the domestic currency value of the asset. If the exchange rate is expressed in direct quotation as the price of one unit of the foreign currency, then the domestic currency value of the asset is calculated as

$$V = SV^* \tag{13.8}$$

Hence

$$R = \frac{S_{t+1}V_{t+1}^*}{S_t V_t^*} - 1 \tag{13.9}$$

which gives

$$R = (1+\dot{S})(1+\dot{V}^*) - 1 \tag{13.10}$$

where $\dot{S}$ and $\dot{V}^*$ are the percentage changes in the exchange rate and the foreign currency value of the asset, respectively. Foreign exchange risk arises because the level of the exchange rate at time $t + 1$, S_{t+1} (and hence its rate of change between t and $t + 1$, $\dot{S}$) is unknown at time t, when the investment is undertaken. Thus, we can calculate the expected value, the variance and the standard deviation of the percentage change in (or the level of) the exchange rate in the same way as we calculate the same statistics for the overall rate of return, as summarised in the following table:

Statistic	Probability distribution	Historical data
Expected value (mean)	$E(\dot{S}) = \sum_{i=1}^{n} p_i(\dot{S}_i)$	$\bar{\dot{S}} = \frac{1}{n}\sum_{t=1}^{n} \dot{S}_t$
Variance	$\sigma^2(\dot{S}) = \sum_{i=1}^{n} p_i[\dot{S}_i - E(\dot{S})]^2$	$\sigma^2(\dot{S}) = \frac{1}{n-1}\sum_{t=1}^{n} (\dot{S}_t - \bar{\dot{S}})^2$
Standard deviation	$\sigma(\dot{S}) = \sqrt{\sum_{i=1}^{n} p_i[\dot{S}_i - E(\dot{S})]^2}$	$\sigma(\dot{S}) = \sqrt{\frac{1}{n-1}\sum_{t=1}^{n} (\dot{S}_t - \bar{\dot{S}})^2}$

INSIGHT

Two perspectives on risk

There are two perspectives on risk: the top-down or strategic perspective and the bottom-up or tactical perspective.

The top-down (or strategic) perspective is driven by the requirements of senior management whose focus is on medium-term results. Important questions that pertain to this perspective are the following:

- What are the risk levels in the current quarter compared to the previous quarter?
- How has the firm's risk-return performance changed?
- What is the likely range for profit and loss in the next quarter?
- What is the probability of making a quarterly loss?

The bottom-up (or tactical) perspective is driven by the needs of traders and trading management. The focus in this case is shorter and the relevant questions primarily pertain to how to make profit from principal exposures while controlling risk in the midst of constantly changing markets.

Example

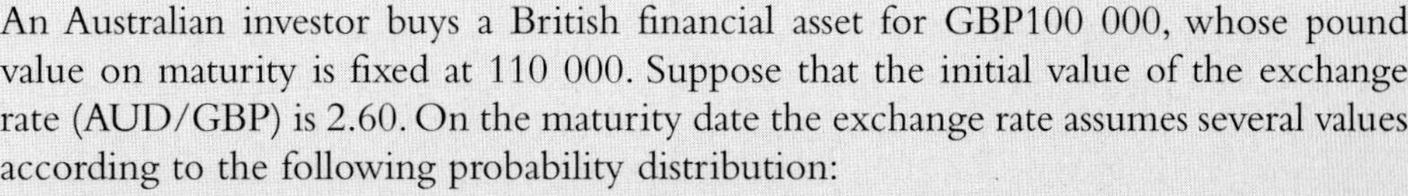

An Australian investor buys a British financial asset for GBP100 000, whose pound value on maturity is fixed at 110 000. Suppose that the initial value of the exchange rate (AUD/GBP) is 2.60. On the maturity date the exchange rate assumes several values according to the following probability distribution:

V^*_{t+1}	S_{t+1}	Probability
110 000	2.55	0.05
110 000	2.60	0.10
110 000	2.65	0.15
110 000	2.70	0.30
110 000	2.75	0.40

Continued...

We can calculate a probability distribution for $\dot{V}$ and $\dot{S}$ as follows:

V_{t+1}	$\dot{V}^*$	$\dot{S}$	$\dot{V} = R$	Probability
280 500	10.00	−1.92	7.88	0.05
286 000	10.00	0	10.00	0.10
291 500	10.00	1.92	12.11	0.15
297 000	10.00	3.85	14.24	0.30
302 500	10.00	5.77	16.35	0.40

As we can see, the rate of return on the asset in pound terms ($\dot{V}^*$) is constant at 10 per cent because the maturity value of the asset is fixed at GBP110 000. Thus, the only market risk to which this investor is exposed is the foreign exchange risk, represented by the variability of $\dot{S}$. The rate of return on the investment in Australian dollar terms can be above or below the rate of return on the asset in pound terms depending on whether the pound appreciates (positive $\dot{S}$) or depreciates (negative $\dot{S}$). We can calculate the expected value and the standard deviation of the percentage change in the exchange rate as

$$0.05 \times -1.92 + 0.10 \times 0 + 0.15 \times 1.92 + 0.30 \times 3.85 + 0.40 \times 5.77 = 3.66$$

$$\sqrt{0.05(-1.92 - 3.66)^2 + \ldots + 0.40(5.77 - 3.66)^2} = 2.27$$

Similarly, the expected value and standard deviation of the rate of return are calculated as

$$0.05 \times 7.88 + 0.10 \times 10 + 0.15 \times 12.11 + 0.30 \times 14.24 + 0.40 \times 16.35 = 14.02$$

$$\sqrt{0.05(7.88 - 14.02)^2 + \ldots + 0.40(16.35 - 14.02)^2} = 2.49$$

The standard deviation of the percentage change in the exchange rate is lower than that of the rate of return because the latter encompasses the former.

INSIGHT

Alternatives to the standard deviation as a measure of risk

The standard deviation as a measure of risk has been criticised for the arbitrary manner in which deviations from the mean are squared and for treating positive and negative deviations in a similar manner, although negative deviations are naturally more detrimental. To meet these criticisms, the **mean absolute deviation (MAD)** and the **downside semi-variance (DSV)** have been suggested as alternative measures of risk. These measures are given respectively by

$$MAD(\dot{S}) = \frac{1}{n}\sum_{t=1}^{n}\left|\dot{S}_t - \bar{\dot{S}}\right|$$

$$DSV(\dot{S}) = \frac{1}{n-1}\sum_{t=1}^{n}X_t^2$$

where $X_t = \dot{S}_t - \bar{\dot{S}}$ if $\dot{S}_t < \bar{\dot{S}}$ and $X_t = 0$ if $\dot{S}_t > \bar{\dot{S}}$.

13.2 Value at risk

Value at risk (VAR) is a new approach to risk management, which has been accepted by practitioners and regulators as the 'right' way to measure risk. For example, the Bank for International Settlements (BIS) has allowed banks to use their own models of VAR to set the capital requirements for market risk.

Essentially, this approach is used to answer the following question: over a given period of time with a given probability, how much money might be lost? The money lost pertains to the decline in the value of a portfolio that may consist of a single asset or a large number of assets. The measurement of VAR requires the choice of: (i) a measurement unit, such as the Australian dollar; (ii) a time horizon, which could be a day, a week or longer, provided that the composition of the portfolio does not change during this period; and (iii) a probability that normally ranges between 1 and 5 per cent.

Implementation of VAR analysis

There are at least three approaches to the implementation of VAR analysis, all of which involve the estimation of the statistical distribution of asset returns: these are the **parametric approach** (or **analytical approach**), the **historical approach** and the **simulation approach**. The first two approaches are based on a sample of observations on the underlying rate of return. The third approach, which we will not discuss here (as it is more demanding technically), is based not on actual values but rather on simulated values of the underlying rate of return.

The main assumption of the parametric VAR is that the distribution of asset returns is normal. Let us, for the purpose of illustration, consider the underlying asset to be the US dollar, in which case the rate of return is the daily percentage change in the AUD/USD exchange rate, whereas the unit of measurement is the Australian dollar. To calculate the one-day VAR of a position of, say, AUD1 million in US dollars, we need to estimate the mean of daily returns and volatility, as measured by the standard deviation. The daily rate of return is measured as the percentage change in the Australian dollar value of the position. If the rate of return is normally distributed, then 95 per cent of the observations will fall within 1.96 standard deviations of the mean and 98 per cent will fall within 2.33 standard deviations of the mean. Let us assume that the mean and standard deviation of the rate of return were estimated to be −0.005 per cent and 0.45 per cent, respectively. If the distribution is normal, then 98 per cent of all returns will fall between −1.0535 and 1.0435 per cent. On a position of AUD1 million, a −1.0535 rate of return is translated into a loss of AUD10 535. This is the value at risk. It implies that the daily loss on this position will exceed this amount no more than one day out of one hundred. It also means that there is a 99 per cent chance that the daily loss could not exceed AUD10 535.

The following table provides some information that is useful for calculating VAR under the assumption of normality, where $\overline{R}$ is the mean value of the rate of return and σ is its standard deviation. The first three columns specify the lowest and highest values of the rate of return falling within a certain percentage of the observations if they are normally distributed. The last column defines VAR for a position of size K with an underlying probability that is listed in the fourth column. Obviously, if $K = 1$ and $\overline{R} = 0$ (which is often the case over a long period of time), then VAR $= 1.65\sigma$ if the underlying probability is 5 per cent, and so on. In this case, VAR is measured as the number of standard deviations.

Per cent of observations	Lowest *R*	Highest *R*	Probability	VAR
68	$\bar{R}-\sigma$	$\bar{R}+\sigma$	16.0	$K(\bar{R}-\sigma)$
90	$\bar{R}-1.65\sigma$	$\bar{R}+1.65\sigma$	5.0	$K(\bar{R}-1.65\sigma)$
95	$\bar{R}-1.96\sigma$	$\bar{R}+1.96\sigma$	2.5	$K(\bar{R}-1.96\sigma)$
98	$\bar{R}-2.33\sigma$	$\bar{R}+2.33\sigma$	1.0	$K(\bar{R}-2.33\sigma)$
99	$\bar{R}-3\sigma$	$\bar{R}+3\sigma$	0.5	$K(\bar{R}-3\sigma)$

If we use $\bar{R} = -0.005$ and $\sigma = 0.45$, we get the following estimates of VAR for a position (K) of AUD1 million. As we can see, VAR increases as the probability decreases and the confidence level increases.

Probability	Confidence level	VAR (AUD)
16.0	84.0	4 550
5.0	95.0	7 475
2.5	97.5	8 870
1.0	99.0	10 535
0.5	99.5	13 550

IN PRACTICE

Microsoft's use of VAR

VAR is widely used by major companies in real life and the VAR figures are often disclosed in annual reports. Microsoft uses VAR as a management tool to estimate its exposure to market risks, reporting the estimated VAR figures in its annual reports. For the purpose of calculating VAR, Microsoft uses a time horizon of 20 days, which is a longer horizon than that typically used by banks. Another difference is that Microsoft uses a confidence level of 97.5 per cent rather than 99 per cent, which is used by banks.

RESEARCH FINDINGS

The mismeasurement of risk

Investors typically measure risk as the probability of a given loss or the amount that can be lost with a given probability at the end of the investment horizon. This view of risk considers only the final result but, according to Kritzman and Rich, investors should perceive risk differently because they are affected by risk and exposed to loss throughout the investment period.[1] They suggest that investors should consider risk and the possibility of loss throughout the investment horizon: otherwise, their wealth may not survive to the end of the investment horizon.

As a result of this way of thinking, Kritzman and Rich suggest two new measures of risk: within-horizon probability of loss and continuous VAR. These risk measures are then used to demonstrate that the possibility of making loss is substantially greater than what investors normally assume.

[1] M. Kritzman and D. Rich, 'The Mismeasurement of Risk', *Financial Analysts Journal*, May–June 2000, pp. 91–8.

One problem with the parametric approach is the assumption of normally distributed returns. It has for a long time been established that this is not the case and that the distributions of financial returns have fat tails and tend to be skewed to the left. Because of this deviation from the normal distribution, the historical method may be preferred. From historical daily data we calculate the daily rates of return and identify the lowest 1 per cent of them. Suppose that the lowest percentile was found to be –1.23 per cent. In this case the daily VAR is AUD12 300 (0.0123 × 1 000 000).

Example

The following are 11 observations on the AUD/USD exchange rate: 1.7900, 1.8500, 1.8180, 1.7870, 1.7750, 1.8045, 1.8338, 1.8400, 1.8080, 1.800 and 1.8442. On the basis of this sample, we can calculate the VAR of an AUD1 million position on the US dollar, using the parametric approach and the historical approach. For this purpose, we will use a time horizon of one day and a probability of 1 per cent.

The daily rate of return on this position is measured by the daily percentage change in the exchange rate. This rate of return has a mean value of 0.314 per cent and a standard deviation of 1.867. Assuming normality, the lowest 1 per cent returns fall 2.33 standard deviations below the mean. Hence

$$0.314 - 2.33 \times 1.867 = -4.036\%$$

Using the parametric approach, VAR is calculated as

$$1\ 000\ 000 \times 0.04036 = \text{AUD}40\ 360$$

This means that the probability that the loss on the position in one day exceeds AUD40 360 is 1 per cent.

Using the historical approach we identify the lowest percentile of the rate of return, which in this case is the lowest value (–1.739 per cent). Hence, VAR is

$$1\ 000\ 000 \times 0.01739 = \text{AUD}17\ 390$$

It is obvious how the two approaches produce significantly different estimates of VAR.

Pros and cons of the VAR methodology

Value at risk has become a widely used method for measuring financial risk and justifiably so. The attractiveness of the concept lies in its simplicity: it measures the market risk of the entire portfolio in one number that is easy to comprehend. It thus conveys a simple message on the risk borne by an institution. The concept is also suitable for risk-limit setting and for measuring performance based on the correlation between the return earned and the risk assumed. It can also take account of complex movements such as non-parallel yield curve shifts.

There are, however, several shortcomings associated with this methodology. First, it can be misleading to the extent of leading to unwarranted complacency. And, as we have seen, VAR is highly sensitive to the assumptions used to calculate it. Moreover, VAR is a number that itself is measured with some error or estimation risk. Thus, the VAR results must be interpreted with reference to the underlying statistical methodology. Finally, this approach to risk management cannot cope with sudden and sharp changes in market conditions.

RESEARCH FINDINGS

Do Australian companies use VAR analysis?

In 1999, a survey was conducted to uncover the practices of Australian public shareholding companies with respect to the use of VAR analysis.[1] The results of the survey revealed significant unfamiliarity with VAR analysis, as half of the respondents indicated that they were unaware of the existence of this technique. Financial institutions, those involved in international operations and those using derivatives tend to be more familiar with the technique. Moreover, not all of the companies with VAR awareness actually use the technique for measuring risk.

The results of the survey produced the following findings:

- Companies that do not use VAR mostly employ **scenario analysis**.
- Companies that do not use VAR claim that it is not relevant to their operations.
- Companies that use VAR predominantly employ the parametric approach.
- The majority of users employ **back testing** and **stress testing**.
- VAR is predominantly used for aggregating risk in particular business units and for providing risk-related information to senior management.
- Reluctance to use VAR is partly attributed to the fact that it is not widely accepted or understood by senior management.
- Financial institutions, companies involved in international operations and those using derivatives are more aware of the existence of VAR analysis and are more inclined to use it.
- Companies that do not use VAR but that intend to use it are predominantly those involved in international operations and those using derivatives.

1 I. A. Moosa and J. J. Knight, 'Firm Characteristics and Value at Risk Analysis: A Survey of Australian Public Shareholding Companies', *Accounting Research Journal*, 16, 2003, pp. 48–57.

RESEARCH FINDINGS

Value at risk of major banks

The daily value at risk from exchange rates of major banks has been reported in a research paper prepared by the Reserve Bank of Australia and published in its monthly bulletin.[1] In 1999, the VAR of major Australian banks was 0.02 per cent of their capital base, much lower than the corresponding figures in other countries (see the table below). In Germany, for example, the corresponding figure was 0.15 per cent.

Country	Foreign exchange risk (% of capital)	Total market risk (% of capital)
Australia	0.02	0.08
Canada	0.02	0.12
Netherlands	0.02	0.20
United Kingdom	0.03	0.16
United States	0.03	0.15
Japan	0.07	0.31
Germany	0.15	0.71

1 'Foreign Exchange Exposure of Australian Banks', *Reserve Bank of Australia Bulletin*, August 2000, pp. 43–9.

It neglects the possibility of discrete, large jumps in prices. Losses resulting from catastrophic occurrences are overlooked due to dependence on symmetric statistical measures that evaluate upside and downside risk equally.

VAR is useful, but it should be handled with care and should be used in conjunction with other measures of risk. For example, it can be complemented by a series of stress tests that account for extremely unfavourable market conditions. It is imperative, however, that VAR should not be viewed as a strict upper bound on the portfolio losses that can occur.

What is stress testing?

Stress testing consists of a series of scenario analyses aimed at investigating the effect of extreme market conditions and/or the effect of violating some of the basic assumptions underlying the risk model. The objective is simply to understand what will happen if the assumptions underlying the model break down.

Stress testing is often suggested as a complementary methodology to VAR analysis, because of the latter's failure to provide reasonable estimates of the probability of extreme losses resulting from the assumptions incorporated in its computation (such as normality). To perform stress testing, hypothetical extreme scenarios are created and corresponding hypothetical profits/losses are computed.

13.3 Definition of exposure

That there is a relationship between risk and exposure is evident from some dictionary definitions of risk. In *The Concise Oxford Dictionary*, risk is defined as 'exposure to mischance', while in *The Oxford Australian Dictionary* it is defined as 'exposure to the possibility of meeting danger or suffering harm or loss'. In finance, risk measures the probability and magnitude of deviations from some expected outcome, and exposure is a measure of the sensitivity of what is at risk to the source of risk. Since the source of foreign exchange risk is changes in the exchange rate, exposure to foreign exchange risk is a measure of the sensitivity of the domestic currency value of foreign currency items (assets, liabilities and cash flows) to changes in the exchange rate. Sometimes, however, exposure is defined as the amount at risk, a definition that we do not adopt here.

Long exposure

A **long exposure** to foreign exchange risk is exposure to foreign assets. The domestic currency value of foreign assets rises when the foreign currency appreciates, and vice versa. If the exchange rate is measured in direct quotation (domestic/foreign), this means that the domestic currency value of foreign assets will rise as the exchange rate rises. Exposure is therefore a measure of by how much the domestic currency value of foreign assets will rise (fall) as the exchange rate rises (falls). This relationship is represented diagrammatically in Figure 13.1, where the percentage change in the exchange rate ($\dot{S}$) is measured on the horizontal axis and the percentage change in the domestic currency value of assets ($\dot{V}$) is measured on the vertical axis. The exposure line has a positive slope to indicate the positive relationship between changes in the exchange rate and changes in the domestic currency value of foreign assets. Foreign currency appreciation (positive $\dot{S}$) implies a gain, and vice versa. The equation of the **exposure line** is

$$\dot{V} = \beta \dot{S} \tag{13.11}$$

where the slope of the line, β, is a measure of exposure. In the case of foreign assets, $\beta > 0$. Thus, the steeper the exposure line (that is, the larger the value of β), the greater the exposure.

Figure 13.1 Foreign assets exposure line

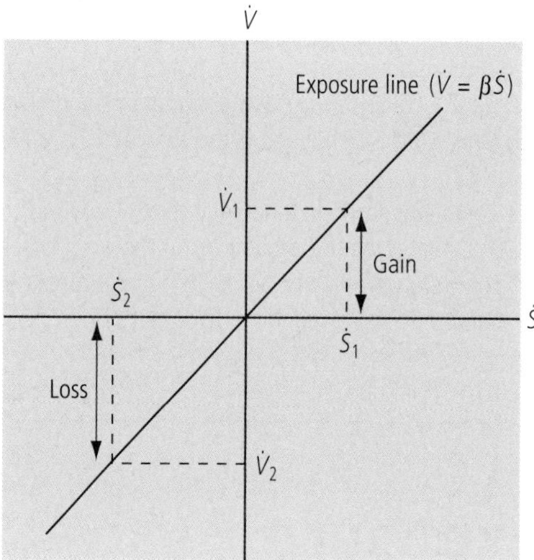

Example

To illustrate the meaning of a long exposure, consider an Australian investor who deposits GBP100 000 with a British bank to earn 10 per cent over one year. The value of the principal and interest earned is GBP110 000. The value of this amount in Australian dollar terms at different exchange rates is given below:

S(AUD/GBP)	GBP value (V^*)	AUD value (V)	$\dot{S}$	$\dot{V}$	$\beta = \dot{V}/\dot{S}$
2.50	110 000	275 000			
2.60	110 000	286 000	4.00	4.00	1.0
2.70	110 000	297 000	3.85	3.85	1.0
2.80	110 000	308 000	3.70	3.70	1.0
2.90	110 000	319 000	3.57	3.57	1.0

These calculations show that the exposure is constant at one because the foreign currency value of the asset is not affected by changes in the exchange rate. Suppose now that the Australian investor bought British real estate worth GBP100 000. As time passes by, both the exchange rate and the pound value of the real estate rise according to the following table. In this case, the exposure is not constant. It is greater than one because the pound value of the investment increases with the exchange rate. The average exposure is the slope of a regression line of $\dot{V}$ on $\dot{S}$.

S(AUD/GBP)	GBP value (V^*)	AUD value (V)	$\dot{S}$	$\dot{V}$	$\beta = \dot{V}/\dot{S}$
2.50	110 000	275 000			
2.60	120 000	312 000	4.00	13.46	3.37
2.70	130 000	351 000	3.85	12.50	3.25
2.80	140 000	392 000	3.70	11.68	3.16
2.90	150 000	435 000	3.57	10.97	3.07

We will now examine a third case in which the foreign currency value of the investment falls proportionately with the exchange rate rise, as shown in the following table. In this case, the exposure is zero even though a position in foreign currency assets is held. Hence, holding foreign currency assets does not necessarily imply exposure to foreign exchange risk.

S(AUD/GBP)	GBP value (V^*)	AUD value (V)	$\dot{S}$	$\dot{V}$	$\beta = \dot{V}/\dot{S}$
2.50	100 000	250 000			
2.55	98 039	250 000	2.00	0	0
2.60	96 154	250 000	1.96	0	0
2.65	94 340	250 000	1.92	0	0
2.70	92 593	250 000	1.89	0	0
2.75	90 909	250 000	1.85	0	0
2.80	89 286	250 000	1.82	0	0
2.85	87 719	250 000	1.79	0	0
2.90	86 207	250 000	1.75	0	0

Short exposure

Short exposure to foreign exchange risk is exposure to foreign liabilities. A rise in the exchange rate induces a rise in the domestic currency value of liabilities. Unlike assets, the rise in the value of liabilities entails a loss, whereas a fall in the exchange rate implies a gain because the domestic currency value of foreign liabilities declines. Hence, the exposure line for foreign liabilities is downward-sloping, as shown in Figure 13.2. The exposure line has the same equation as (13.11) except that the slope is negative ($\beta < 0$).

Combined exposure

Figure 13.3 illustrates what happens if the assets and liabilities exposure lines have similar or different slopes (that is, if assets and liabilities are equally or differently sensitive to changes in exchange rates). In Figure 13.3(a), assets and liabilities are equally sensitive. In this case, an appreciation of the foreign currency produces a gain on the assets side and a loss on the liabilities side. Since the exposures on both sides are equal, the gain and loss are equal. In Figure 13.3(b) assets are more sensitive than liabilities and so the gain on the assets side is greater than the loss on the liabilities side. Finally, Figure 13.3(c) shows that the loss on the liabilities side is greater than the gain on the assets side because liabilities are more sensitive.

Figure 13.2 Foreign liabilities exposure line

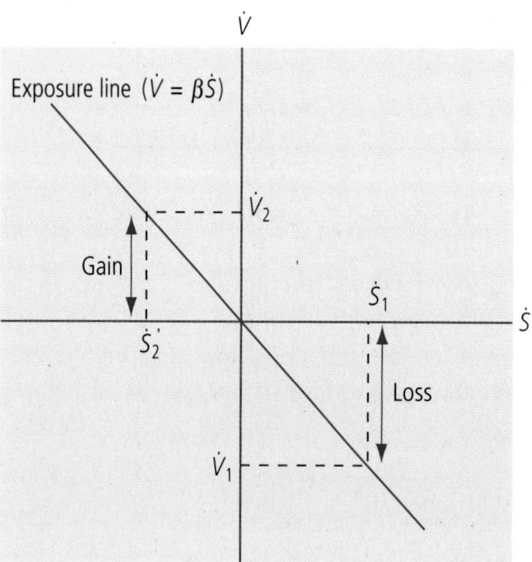

Figure 13.3 The effect of changes in the exchange rate with equal and different slopes of exposure lines

(a) Assets and liabilities are equally sensitive

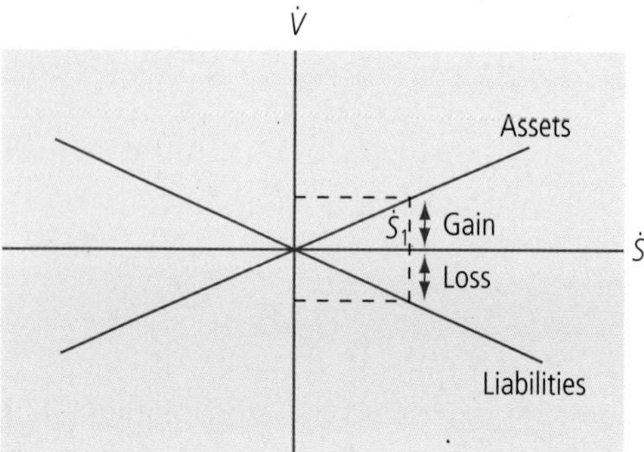

(b) Assets are more sensitive

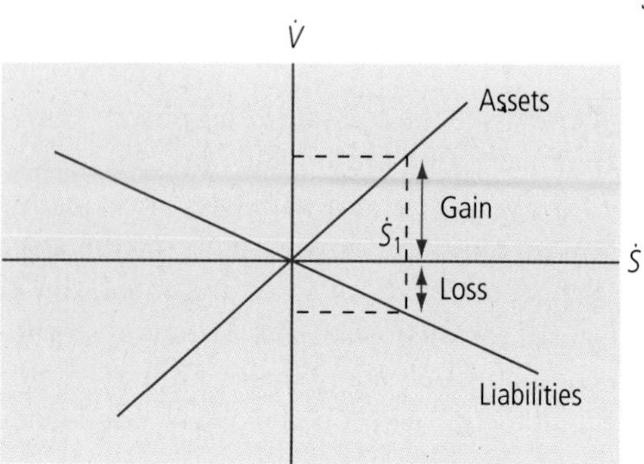

(c) Liabilities are more sensitive

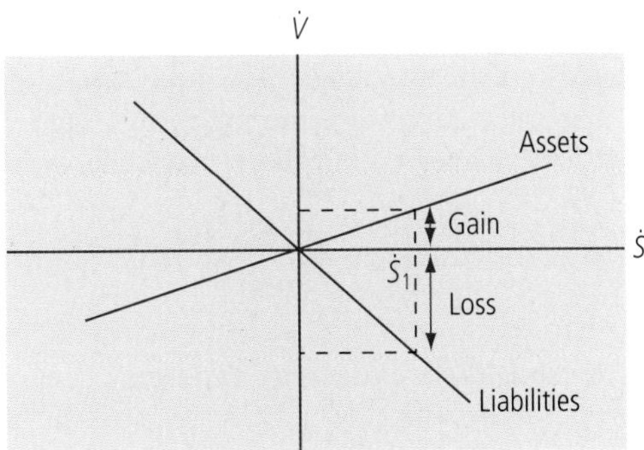

Example

Consider an Australian firm that has the following estimated exposures to British assets and liabilities represented by the equations $\dot{V} = 1.2\dot{S}$ and $\dot{V} = -2\dot{S}$, respectively. The exposure equations imply a greater liability exposure than an asset exposure. A rise in the exchange rate will thus lead to a bigger loss on the liabilities side than the gain on the assets side. The following table shows what happens at various levels of the exchange rate:

S(AUD/GBP)	$\dot{S}$	$\dot{V}$ (assets)	$\dot{V}$ (liabilities)	$\dot{V}$ (total)
2.50				
2.60	4.00	4.80	−8.00	−3.20
2.70	3.85	4.62	−7.70	−3.08
2.80	3.70	4.44	−7.40	−2.96
2.90	3.57	4.28	−7.14	−2.86

The relationship between risk and exposure

The relationship between risk and exposure can be determined from Equation (13.11), which gives

$$\sigma^2(\dot{V}) = \beta^2\sigma^2(\dot{S}) \tag{13.12}$$

Equation (13.12) tells us that the variance of the percentage change in the domestic currency value of foreign assets and liabilities is related to the variance of the percentage change in the exchange rate by a factor that reflects exposure, β^2.

Example

The following table shows the probability distribution associated with changes in the exchange rate and in the domestic currency value of foreign assets:

$\dot{S}$	$\dot{V}$	β	Probability
1.0	1.5	1.5	0.1
2.0	3.0	1.5	0.2
3.0	4.5	1.5	0.3
4.0	6.0	1.5	0.2
5.0	7.5	1.5	0.2

Continued...

The expected value and the variances of $\dot{S}$ and $\dot{V}$ can be calculated from the probability distribution. The calculations give the following results: $E(\dot{S}) = 3.2$, $\sigma^2(\dot{S}) = 1.56$, $E(\dot{V}) = 4.8$ and $\sigma^2(\dot{V}) = 3.51$. By taking the ratio of the variances we get

$$\beta^2 = \frac{\sigma^2(\dot{V})}{\sigma^2(\dot{S})} = \frac{3.51}{1.56} = 2.25$$

Hence $\beta = 1.5$, which is the value of the exposure.

Multiple exposure

So far we have dealt with exposure to a single foreign currency. In practice, exposure to several currencies is normally the case, as international business firms diversify their investment and financing portfolios. Hence, we need a **multiple exposure** model, which may be written as

$$\dot{V} = \beta_0 + \beta_1\dot{S}(x_0/x_1) + \beta_2\dot{S}(x_0/x_2) + \ldots + \beta_n\dot{S}(x_0/x_n) \qquad (13.13)$$

where $\dot{S}(x_0/x_i)$ is the rate of change of the exchange rate between the domestic currency, x_0, and foreign currency i for $i = 1, 2, \ldots n$. The coefficient $\beta_i (i = 1, 2, \ldots n)$ measures exposure to foreign currency i. The coefficient β_0 measures changes in value, which are unrelated to any of the currency exposures. In the case of foreign currency assets, the coefficients are positive, whereas in the case of liabilities they are negative.

13.4 Volatility of the Australian dollar exchange rates

Foreign exchange risk is related to the volatility of the nominal and real exchange rates. In this section, we measure the extent of the volatility of the bilateral exchange rates of the Australian dollar against four currencies over the period 1988–2001. The currencies are: the US dollar, the Japanese yen, the British pound and the Canadian dollar.

The following table reports the basic statistics of the percentage changes in the nominal exchange rates of the Australian dollar against these currencies. Positive (negative) values indicate depreciation (appreciation) of the Australian dollar. The extent of the foreign exchange risk is measured by the standard deviation of these changes. It is obvious that the Australian dollar is more stable against the US and Canadian currencies than against the yen and the pound. This means that positions on the yen and the pound are more risky than those on the US dollar and the Canadian dollar when the Australian dollar is the domestic currency.

Exchange rate	Minimum	Maximum	Mean	Standard deviation
AUD/USD	−6.08	15.06	1.21	4.88
AUD/JPY	−20.22	21.49	0.88	7.81
AUD/GBP	−11.67	13.84	1.47	6.23
AUD/CAD	−8.68	9.41	0.62	4.11

13.5 Transaction exposure

Transaction exposure to foreign exchange risk arises if a firm has foreign currency receivables and payables (cash inflows and outflows). Risk is present because the domestic currency value of these items when they are due varies according to changes in the nominal exchange rate. Transaction exposure is clearly a **cash flow exposure**, which may be associated with trade flows (resulting from exports and imports) and capital flows (for example, dividends and interest payments). It involves an actual conversion of foreign currency receivables and payables into the domestic currency. This kind of exposure arises, for example, from (i) a foreign currency asset or a liability that is already recorded on the balance sheet and (ii) a contract or an agreement involving a future foreign currency cash flow.

Measurement of the transaction exposure of a multinational firm with subsidiaries requires the calculation of the consolidated net amount in currency inflows and outflows for all subsidiaries. If Subsidiary A has a cash outflow in a particular foreign currency, then appreciation of this currency is bad for this subsidiary. If, on the other hand, Subsidiary B has a cash inflow in the same foreign currency, then the appreciation of this currency is good news for this subsidiary. If the cash inflow of Subsidiary B is equivalent to the cash outflow of Subsidiary A, then any change in the value of the foreign currency does not affect the multinational firm, since the favourable effect on Subsidiary B is cancelled out by the unfavourable effect on Subsidiary A. This is also because the net position in this currency is zero.

Example

The following table shows the net exposure to each currency of an Australian multinational firm that has various single currency exposures. The net exposure to each currency is calculated by subtracting the value of receivables in each currency from the value of the payables in each currency. This shows that the net exposure is much less than the exposure of individual subsidiaries.

Currency	Receivables	Payables	Net exposure
US dollar	200 000	150 000	+50 000
Japanese yen	15 000 000	21 000 000	−6 000 000
Euro	350 000	250 000	+100 000
British pound	250 000	460 000	−210 000

Two points are worthy of consideration here. The first is the degree of variability of each exchange rate. An exposure to a foreign currency that fluctuates sharply against the domestic currency is more of a source of concern than an exposure to a currency that is relatively stable. Second, attention should be paid to the **correlation coefficients** of the underlying exchange rates. If the exchange rates between the domestic currency and foreign currencies are strongly and positively correlated, the foreign currencies will all depreciate or appreciate against the domestic currency more or less proportionately. If they are positively but weakly correlated, the foreign currencies will tend to move in the same direction but in different proportions. A negative correlation implies that the foreign currencies move against the domestic currency in different directions, thus providing some sort of a **natural hedge**. However, a natural hedge would arise from two positively correlated exchange rates if a long position is taken on one of the currencies and a short position is taken on the other.

The following table shows the correlation coefficients of the exchange rates of the Australian dollar against four currencies. The highest correlation coefficient is that between the AUD/USD and the AUD/GBP rates. This means that a long position on the US dollar can be more effectively hedged by taking a short position on the pound than on any of the other currencies.

	AUD/USD	AUD/JPY	AUD/GBP	AUD/CAD
AUD/USD	1.00	0.76	0.86	0.71
AUD/JPY		1.00	0.53	0.30
AUD/GBP			1.00	0.68
AUD/CAD				1.00

Example

This example illustrates the first point. Imagine an Australian investor holding US dollar and pound assets worth USD500 000 and GBP250 000 at initial exchange rates of 1.80 and 2.70, respectively. The following table shows the probability distribution of the exchange rates and the Australian dollar values of the investment one year from now. The table shows that the Australian dollar value of the US dollar investment fluctuates within a band of ±5 per cent around the initial value (between a maximum of USD945 000 and a minimum of USD855 000). Because the exchange rate of the Australian dollar against the pound is more volatile than that against the US dollar, the Australian dollar value of the pound investment fluctuates within a wider band of ±10 per cent around the initial value. From the information provided in the table, we can find out that the standard deviation of the rate of change of the Australian dollar value of the US dollar investment is half that of the pound investment (2.92 versus 5.88). The idea here is clear. Because the exchange rate of the Australian dollar against the pound is more volatile than that of the Australian dollar against the US dollar, the pound investment tends to be more risky.

$S(USD)$	$V(AUD)$	$\dot{V}$	$S(GBP)$	$V(AUD)$	$\dot{V}$	Probability
1.71	855 000	−5.00	2.43	607 500	−10.00	0.05
1.76	880 000	−2.22	2.57	642 500	−4.81	0.10
1.80	900 000	0.00	2.70	675 000	0.00	0.15
1.85	925 500	2.78	2.84	710 000	5.19	0.30
1.89	945 000	5.00	2.97	742 500	10.00	0.40

Note: $\dot{V}$ is calculated relative to the initial value.

Example

Assume four currencies, x_0, x_1, x_2 and x_3, where x_0 is the domestic currency, such that the three exchange rates against the domestic currency assume an initial value of 1.00. We will also assume that $S(x_0/x_1)$ and $S(x_0/x_2)$ are perfectly correlated but that $S(x_0/x_1)$ and $S(x_0/x_3)$ are weakly correlated. This means that x_1 and x_2 move in the same proportions against the domestic currency but x_1 and x_3 do not.

Consider first a long position on x_1 and a short position on x_2, each of which is equal to 200 000 currency units, such that the net position is zero. If currency x_1 appreciates against the domestic currency x_0, then x_2 will appreciate by approximately the same percentages. So, if $S(x_0/x_1)$ rises to 1.05, $S(x_0/x_2)$ will rise to the same level, in which case both the long and the short positions rise to 210 000 units of x_0. The net position is still zero and no effect arises out of domestic currency depreciation.

Now, consider a long position on x_1 and a short position on x_3, each worth 200 000 units of the respective currency, which at the initial exchange rates are equal to 200 000 units of x_0. Because $S(x_0/x_1)$ and $S(x_0/x_3)$ are weakly correlated, a 5 per cent appreciation of x_1 will not be matched by a 5 per cent appreciation of x_3 and may even be accompanied by a depreciation of x_3. If $S(x_0/x_1)$ rises by 5 per cent to 1.05, $S(x_0/x_3)$ may rise to 1.08. After these changes in exchange rates, the domestic currency value of the long and short positions become 210 000 and 216 000 respectively, resulting in a net loss of 6000 units of the domestic currency. This means that to take offsetting long and short positions the exchange rates of the two currencies denominating the positions against the domestic currency must be highly (positively) correlated.

IN PRACTICE

The transaction exposure of Foxtel, 1998–2007

In 1998, Foxtel signed a 10-year US dollar contract to buy Hollywood movies. To stop losses from a depreciating Australian dollar, Foxtel arranged a currency hedge for the contract that lasted until 30 June 2001. Thus, Foxtel was safe from currency movements until June 2001, when USD1.12 billion remained due on the contract. But once the currency hedge came to an end, things started to turn nasty.

During the period 30 June 1997 to 30 June 1998 the Australian dollar depreciated from USD0.746 to USD0.614. When the deal was done, the USD1.12 billion liability that Foxtel faced in 2001 was worth AUD1.82 billion. If the deal had been done in 1997, it would have been worth just AUD1.5 billion.

By June 2001, the Australian dollar was down to USD0.506 and the amount still owing on the contract had blown out to AUD2.21 billion. The failure to hedge the contract beyond June 2001 has blown out the Australian dollar cost by between AUD391 million and AUD713 million over the final six years of the contract.

13.6 Economic exposure

Economic exposure arises because changes in exchange rates affect the firm's domestic and foreign cash flows. This may sound like transaction exposure, but the difference lies in the fact that we are in this case concerned with non-contractual or unplanned future cash flows. These cash flows pertain to sales in foreign markets and sales in domestic markets, as well as input costs whether these inputs are domestic or foreign.

While transaction exposure refers to a potential gain or loss arising from transactions that are planned, currently in progress or have already been completed, economic exposure refers to changes in future earning power as a result of changes in exchange rates. In effect, it refers to exchange-rate-induced changes in the competitive position of the firm. It is therefore related to changes in the real, rather than the nominal, exchange rate (recall from Chapter 2 that exports and imports depend on the nominal exchange rate and prices and hence on the real exchange rate). Another difference is that economic exposure, unlike transaction exposure, does not involve any currency conversion of cash flows.

INSIGHT

Related exposure concepts

Sometimes, economic exposure is portrayed as consisting of transaction exposure and **operating exposure**. Operating exposure can be defined as the extent to which the firm's operating cash flows would be affected by changes in exchange rates. Operating exposure has several components because operating cash flows depend on several factors. In all cases, the exposure is a measure of the sensitivity of the underlying factor to changes in the exchange rate. Thus we have:

- **Revenue exposure** and **cost exposure**.
- **Conversion exposure:** pure conversion exposure arises if changes in the exchange rate do not affect the foreign currency price but only the domestic currency price of the product. This may sound like transaction exposure but it is not. Under transaction exposure, the cash flows are contractual and the conversion takes place. Under operating exposure the cash flows are non-contractual and unknown in advance and conversion may or may not take place.
- **Price exposure**.
- **Demand exposure:** changes in the exchange rate lead to changes in demand and hence in domestic currency revenue.
- **Competitive exposure:** demand and price exposures may be the result of a firm's competitive position.
- **Indirect exposure:** a firm that has no direct foreign exchange exposure due to conversion, price, demand or competitive effects could still have an indirect exposure if it is a supplier to firms that have direct exposure.
- **Multimarket exposure:** a firm that derives its revenues by selling in various markets is said to have multimarket exposure. If this firm operates in a foreign market and the domestic market, it will have revenue exposure only to the extent of the revenue derived from the foreign market.

Economic exposure cannot in general be known accurately in advance, but it can be estimated from historical data. One way of doing this is to estimate a regression equation that relates changes in cash flows over a certain period of time to changes in the exchange rate, something like Equation (13.11). A more general version of this regression equation would be like Equation (13.13), which relates changes in cash flows to a number of exchange rates. Another version of this equation involves regressing the percentage change in the share price of the underlying company on the percentage change in a domestic share price index and percentage changes in the exchange rates of the domestic currency against several currencies. The coefficient on each exchange rate thus indicates economic exposure to the underlying currency. Note that the percentage change in the share price is in this case a proxy for changes in the value of the underlying company.

IN PRACTICE

The effect of the Australian dollar appreciation on Australian company valuations

The relative rebound of the Australian dollar in the second half of 2002 from its sub-50 US cents levels has affected Australian companies in different ways. In May 2002, analysts started to reassess the currency sensitivities of locally listed companies and the impact of the dollar appreciation on the company valuations. In general, the sensitivity depends on the percentage of non-AUD income. Thus, resource companies and those with a high currency translation exposure (such as wine producers) were expected to be hit, whereas the beneficiaries were expected to be retail and media stocks.

A report released by Credit Suisse-First Boston in May 2002 shows the following estimates:

Company	Percentage of non-AUD revenue	Percentage valuation impact of a 5% change in the exchange rate
Fairfax	0	0.0
Goodman Fielder	30	6.0
Woolworths	0	0.0
PBL	0	1.0
National Foods	10	5.0
MIM	90	−14.8
BHP	84	−5.6
Foster's Group	40	−2.0
Cochlear	83	−3.0
Rio Tinto	96	−2.8

13.7 Translation exposure

Also called **accounting exposure**, **translation exposure** arises from the consolidation of foreign currency assets, liabilities, net income and other items in the process of preparing consolidated financial statements (balance sheet and income statement) based on the domestic currency.

Translation exposure gives rise to the possibility that the conversion of foreign-currency-denominated items into the domestic currency for the purpose of consolidation may show a loss or gain. It is therefore a function of the accounting system and may have little to do with the true value of the firm in an economic sense. Firms with identical balance sheet and income statement items may show different consolidated results, depending on the **translation method** used.

Translation methods refer to the choice of the exchange rate used for converting (translating) the values of foreign currency items into domestic currency. The balance sheet contains the values of assets and liabilities as at the end of the accounting period, which may be a year, a quarter or a month. The income statement reports items such as revenues, costs and net income realised over the accounting period. The following three rates can be used for conversion:

- The **closing rate** (or **current rate**), which is the rate prevailing at the end of the accounting period (that is, coinciding with the balance sheet date).

- The **average rate**, which reflects the average value of the exchange rate over the accounting period. The simplest procedure is to take a simple average of the closing rate and the rate prevailing at the beginning of the period. Otherwise, a time-weighted average may be used.
- The **historical rate**, which is the rate prevailing on the date when an asset is acquired or a liability is committed. The historical rate may therefore fall outside the current accounting period. In fact, this is invariably the case for long-term assets and liabilities.

In translating the income statement items, either the closing rate or the average rate is used, which means that the amount exposed is net income. The possibility of using the historical rate in translating balance sheet items makes the matter more complicated. For the purpose of translating balance sheet items, the following methods are used.

The current/non-current method

The **current/non-current method** is based on the traditional accounting distinction between current items (such as short-term deposits and inventory) and long-term items (such as real estate and long-term debt). According to this method, current items are translated at the closing rate, whereas long-term items are translated at the historical rate. Obviously, the use of the historical rate precludes foreign exchange risk, but the use of the closing rate does not. Hence, if this method is used, the amount exposed to foreign exchange risk is net current assets. There is an obvious problem with this method, which is that items such as long-term loans are portrayed not to be subject to foreign exchange risk, and this does not make sense. This is why there has been a move away from this method.

The closing (current) rate method

The **closing rate method** is the most widely used worldwide. Assets and liabilities are translated at the closing exchange rate prevailing at the end of the accounting period. When this method is used, the amount exposed is shareholders' equity.

The monetary/non-monetary method

The **monetary/non-monetary method** is based on the distinction between monetary and non-monetary items. Monetary items are those items whose values are fixed in terms of the number of units of the currency of denomination. For example, a bond is a monetary item, since its par (or face) value (the value received by the bondholder on maturity) is fixed by contract and displayed on the face of the bond. Real estate, on the other hand, is a non-monetary item, since its value in the currency of denomination may rise or fall. According to this method, monetary items are translated at the closing rate, whereas non-monetary items are translated at the historical rate. The amount exposed in this case is the value of net monetary items.

The temporal method

According to the **temporal method**, the use of the closing rate or the historical rate is determined by the valuation of the underlying item. The closing rate is used for items stated at **replacement cost**, **realisable value** or **market value**. The historical rate is used for all items stated at **historical cost**. The rationale for this method is that the translation rate should preserve the accounting principles used to value assets and liabilities in the original (foreign currency) financial statements.

Some principles

In general, the following principles are observed in practice:

- The translation of the balance sheet items is based on the closing rate.

- Transaction gains and losses are accounted for in the income statement.
- Non-transaction gains and losses are recorded on the balance sheet as reflected by changes in reserves.
- If a transaction profit or loss arises from foreign currency borrowing designed as a hedge for a net investment in the same foreign currency, then the profit or loss (if less than that on the investment) is accounted for by movements in reserves. Otherwise, the excess is reported on the income statement.

Changing the Australian financial reporting standards

In its issue of 17 May 2002, the *Australian Financial Review* reported that the Australian Accounting Standards Board was considering some proposed changes to financial reporting standards that would give major multinational firms the freedom to lodge their accounts in the currency in which they conduct most of their business. These changes would also reduce the amount of currency hedging conducted by Australian companies, as well as the volatility of profits from foreign operations.

Two of Australia's oil and gas exploration companies, Novus Petroleum and Roc Oil, responded to the news by saying that they would like to report their earnings in US dollars, given that they earn most of their income from foreign operations.

Summary

- Risk refers to the probability of incurring a loss. Foreign exchange risk arises from unanticipated changes in exchange rates that give rise to the probability of incurring a loss.
- In finance, risk is measured by the dispersion around the mean value of the rate of return (that is, by the variance or the standard deviation).
- Foreign exchange risk is measured by the variance or the standard deviation of the exchange rate or its rate change.
- Value at risk is a new approach to risk management that is used to estimate the amount of money that might be lost with a given probability during a given period of time. VAR can be estimated by using the parametric approach, the historical approach or the simulation approach.
- Foreign exchange exposure is a measure of the sensitivity of the domestic currency value of foreign assets, liabilities and cash flows to changes in the exchange rate.
- Transaction exposure to foreign exchange risk arises because of the conversion of anticipated foreign currency payables and receivables into the domestic currency.
- Economic exposure arises because changes in exchange rates affect the firm's domestic and foreign non-contractual and unplanned cash flows.
- Translation exposure arises in the process of converting financial statement items into the domestic currency. Translation can be carried out on the basis of one of the following exchange rates: (i) the closing (current) rate; (ii) the average rate; and (iii) the historical rate.
- Several methods are used in practice to translate balance sheet items. These methods include: (i) the current/non-current method; (ii) the closing rate method; (iii) the monetary/non-monetary method; and (iv) the temporal method.

Key terms

accounting exposure 377
analytical approach 363
average rate 378
back testing 366
cash flow exposure 373
closing rate 377
closing rate method 378
competitive exposure 376
conversion exposure 376
correlation coefficients 373
cost exposure 376
current rate 377
current/non-current method 378
demand exposure 376
downside semi-variance (DSV) 362
economic exposure 375
expected value 359
exposure line 368
financial risk 360
foreign exchange risk 360
historical approach 363
historical cost 378
historical rate 378
indirect exposure 376
long exposure 367
market value 378
mean 359
mean absolute deviation (MAD) 362
monetary/non-monetary method 378
multimarket exposure 376
multiple exposure 372
natural hedge 373
operating exposure 376
operational risk 360
parametric approach 363
price exposure 376
realisable value 378
replacement cost 378
revenue exposure 376
risk 358
risk-averse 359
risk-lover 358
risk-neutral 359
scenario analysis 366
short exposure 369
simulation approach 363
standard deviation 359
stress testing 366
temporal method 378
transaction exposure 373
translation exposure 377
translation method 377
uncertainty 359
value at risk (VAR) 363
variance 359

MaxMARK

MAXIMISE YOUR MARKS! There are 30 interactive questions for this chapter available online at **www.mhhe.com/au/moosa2e**

Review questions

1 What is the origin of the word 'risk'?

2 Distinguish between financial risk and operational risk.

3 'Operational risk is the result of both stupidity and malice.' Explain

4 Why is the standard deviation not totally acceptable as a measure of risk?

5 What is the difference between risk and uncertainty?

6 What are the ingredients required to calculate the VAR of a foreign currency portfolio?

7 What is the difference between risk and exposure?

8 Explain why foreign exchange exposure can be measured by the slope of the exposure line.

9 Why is the exposure line of foreign liabilities downward-sloping?

10 What is the relationship between risk and exposure?

11 What is a multiple exposure model?

12 Why is it that even purely domestic firms can be exposed to foreign exchange risk?

13 'Transaction exposure is a cash flow exposure.' Explain.

14 What is the difference between economic exposure and transaction exposure?

15 Why does transaction exposure arise?

16 Discuss the pros and cons of the foreign currency translation methods.

Problems

1 It is the end of 2002 and the exchange rate between the Australian dollar and the US dollar (AUD/USD) is 1.8550. The exchange rate outlook is very blurred as it is believed that the exchange rate could move either way. The following probability distribution is available for the value of the exchange rate expected to prevail at the end of 2003:

AUD/USD	Probability
1.8000	0.1
1.8500	0.2
1.9000	0.3
1.9500	0.4

(a) Calculate the expected value and the standard deviation of the AUD/USD exchange rate.
(b) Calculate the expected value and the standard deviation of the rate of change of the exchange rate.
(c) Assuming equal interest rates on both currencies would you, on the basis of this probability distribution, invest in Australian or US assets?

2 Using the data set given in Problem 4, Chapter 12 (on page 355), calculate the daily rate of change of the AUD/USD exchange rate. Also calculate the mean and the standard deviation of the rate of change. If the mean is close to zero, what does this imply?

3 Using the data set in Problem 4, Chapter 12 (on page 355), calculate the value at risk of an AUD1 million position in US dollars. For this purpose, use the parametric and historical approaches.

4 An Australian investor buys a US Treasury bill with a face value of USD500 000. Assume that, on maturity, the exchange rate will have the values described by the following probability distribution:

AUD/USD	Probability
1.7900	0.1
1.8100	0.2
1.8200	0.4
1.8300	0.2
1.8400	0.1

(a) What is the probability distribution of the Australian dollar value of the Treasury bill on maturity?
(b) Calculate the expected value and standard deviation of the Australian dollar value of the Treasury bill.
(c) What is the foreign exchange exposure?

5 An Australian company has a loan of USD400 000, obtained when the AUD/USD was 1.8200. Assuming the same probability distribution as in Problem 4 above:
(a) What is the probability distribution of the Australian dollar value of the principal on maturity?
(b) Calculate the expected value and the standard deviation of the Australian dollar value of the principal on maturity.
(c) Calculate the change in value at each level of the exchange rate on maturity relative to the level at the initial exchange rate.
(d) What is the foreign exchange exposure?

6 Using the same information as in Problems 4 and 5 above, calculate the change in value associated with a combined asset-liability position consisting of a loan of USD200 000 and a Treasury bill with a face value of USD500 000. Redo the same calculations for a combined position consisting of a loan of USD500 000 and a Treasury bill with a face value of USD200 000. Comment on your results.

7 Using the data set given in Problem 4, Chapter 9 (on page 268), calculate the means and standard deviations of the nominal and real exchange rates of the Australian dollar. Comment on your results.

8 An Australian company sells its products in Australia and New Zealand. The following information is available on the company's costs, revenues and profit:

Item	Australian business (AUD)	New Zealand business (NZD)
Sales	2 500 000	2 000 000
Cost of goods sold	1 000 000	800 000
Gross profit	1 500 000	1 200 000
Operating expenses	500 000	400 000
Profit before interest and taxes	1 000 000	800 000
Interest payments	100 000	0
Profit before taxes	900 000	800 000
Profit after taxes	675 000	640 000

The exchange rate has the following probability distribution:

NZD/AUD	Probability
1.10	0.2
1.15	0.3
1.20	0.5

Calculate the expected value and the standard deviation of the consolidated cost, revenue and profit items.

9 Eagle Breweries Ltd is a wholly owned New Zealand subsidiary of Greensborough Breweries Pty Ltd. The subsidiary is solely engaged in the production and distribution of canned Eagle beer, which has become popular in New Zealand and neighbouring South Pacific islands. About 30 per cent of the total production is sold in New Zealand, while the rest is exported to other South Pacific islands. The following information is available:

- Eagle Breweries obtains its raw materials and labour locally.
- The tax rate in New Zealand is 25 per cent.
- The annual depreciation charge on plant and equipment is NZD400 000.
- The subsidiary has NZD2 million of debt, carrying an annual interest rate of 5 per cent.
- All sales are invoiced in New Zealand dollars.
- It is expected that the Australian dollar will appreciate by 20 per cent by the end of next year, taking the exchange rate to 1.38.
- Eagle beer is so popular that it has a very low elasticity of demand. It is predicted that Eagle can raise the unit (slab) price to NZD25 without affecting sales.
- The cost of raw materials is expected to increase by 20 per cent. It is possible, however, to import the raw materials from other Pacific islands at roughly the same current cost.
- On the basis of the current exchange rate of 1.15 (NZD/AUD), the following are Eagle Breweries' projected sales, after-tax income and cash flows for the coming year. Also available is Eagle's current balance sheet.

Projected cash flows

	Units (slabs)	Unit price (NZD)	Total (NZD)
Export sales (slabs)	300 000	20	6 000 000
Local sales (slabs)	700 000	20	14 000 000
Total sales (slabs)			20 000 000
Labour (hours)	150 000	18	2 700 000
Raw materials			6 000 000
Total operating expenditure			8 700 000
Net operating income			11 300 000
Overhead expenses			3 000 000
Interest payments			100 000
Depreciation			400 000
Net profit before tax			7 800 000
Income tax			1 950 000
Profit after tax			5 850 000
Plus depreciation			400 000
Net cash flow			6 250 000
Net cash flow in AUD			5 434 783

Balance sheet (NZD)	
Cash	1 000 000
Accounts receivable	4 500 000
Stock	2 000 000
Net fixed assets	10 500 000
Total assets	18 000 000
Accounts payable	2 000 000
Long-term debt	2 000 000
Total liabilities	4 000 000
Shareholders' equity	14 000 000
Total liabilities and shareholders' equity	18 000 000

Given this information, it is proposed that Eagle should increase the unit price to NZD25 and import the raw materials.

(a) If the expected appreciation of the Australian dollar is realised, calculate the translation gains and losses, using both the current rate and the monetary/non-monetary methods of translation.

(b) Calculate the cash flow in Australian dollar terms if the expected appreciation of the Australian dollar is realised under the following two scenarios: (i) the proposals are implemented; and (ii) the proposals are not implemented.

CHAPTER

Foreign exchange risk management

Introduction

Foreign exchange risk management (and financial risk management in general) is a costly activity. Yet firms exposed to this kind of risk tend to hedge it to avoid the consequences of adverse movements in exchange rates. This chapter deals with the instruments and techniques used to hedge exposure to foreign exchange risk. Hedging can be either financial or operational. Financial hedging involves taking positions on other financial assets (such as derivatives) or some other financial operations (such as borrowing and lending). Operational hedging, which is mainly used to hedge economic exposure, involves some restructuring of operations to make costs and revenues less sensitive to changes in exchange rates.

Objectives

The objectives of this chapter are:

- To explain why there is concern about foreign exchange risk.
- To illustrate how to manage short-term transaction exposure using forward hedging, futures hedging, money market hedging and option hedging.
- To illustrate other techniques of managing short-term and long-term transaction exposure.
- To explain how to hedge economic exposure by restructuring operations.
- To explain the means and consequences of hedging translation exposure.

14.1 Why worry about foreign exchange risk?

Hedging, which is the core **risk-management** operation, is a process whereby a firm can protect itself from unanticipated changes in exchange rates. The decision to hedge or not to hedge an uncovered or open foreign currency position is basically a speculative decision. It all depends on the expected spot rate or the movement of the exchange rate between the point in time when the decision is taken and when its effect materialises. Remember that, if the decision to hedge is taken, some costs may be incurred up front, such as the premium paid to acquire an option. If the decision to hedge the position is taken and the exchange rate moves in a favourable direction (for example, the foreign currency appreciates when the position involves receivables), then some possible gain will be lost. This gain would have been made by leaving the position unhedged. On the other hand, if the decision not to hedge is taken and the exchange rate moves in an unfavourable direction (for example, the foreign currency appreciates when the position involves payables), then some losses will be incurred. These losses would have been avoided by taking a decision to hedge.

There are at least three arguments as to why there is no need to worry about foreign exchange risk:

- If international parity conditions hold, then foreign exchange risk will not arise.
- If it is possible to forecast exchange rates accurately, then foreign exchange risk can be controlled and the favourable outcome that is precluded by hedging can be enjoyed.
- Shareholders are naturally hedged through diversification and so there is no need to indulge in costly hedging operations.

Let us start with the first argument by considering the relevance of three conditions: unbiased efficiency, UIP and PPP. Consider first unbiased efficiency in the case of a foreign investment. If unbiased efficiency holds, then the forward rate is an unbiased predictor of the expected spot rate. Covering forward, therefore, is useless in the long run because the same results can be achieved by leaving the position unhedged. Indeed, given that the bid-offer spread in the forward market is wider than the spread in the spot market, leaving the position unhedged may be more profitable. In the short run, however, leaving the position uncovered can be extremely dangerous: a big loss may end the long run altogether. We have in any case seen that there is little support for the hypothesis of unbiased efficiency.

Similarly, if UIP holds, then the foreign currency return is equal to the domestic currency return and hence the former is known with certainty. Any change in the exchange rate is offset by a change in the interest rate differential in such a way as to keep returns at the same level. But we have seen that deviations from UIP are significant and hence the domestic currency value of the foreign return is not known with certainty. Consequently, risk would arise.

Finally, if PPP holds, then real currency depreciation and appreciation will not occur. This is because changes in commodity prices are offset by equivalent changes in the nominal exchange rate. We have seen, however, that deviations from PPP in the short run are large and persistent. But even if PPP were empirically valid, it is unusual for the firm's individual costs and revenues to move proportionately with inflation. Hence, economic exposure would arise.

In general, these conditions may hold, at best, in the long run, if at all, and the long run can be very long indeed, as in the case of PPP. In the short run, deviations from the conditions are significant and persistent, implying the relevance of risk.

The second point pertains to the accuracy of forecasting exchange rates. It has for a long time been established (by both academics and practitioners) that forecasting exchange rates is a rather difficult task and a hazardous endeavour. Some views even point to the near impossibility of forecasting exchange rates because they are driven by unanticipated events, which are unpredictable by definition. The empirical failure of unbiased efficiency and UIP implies that foreign exchange risk cannot be controlled by using the forward rate or the interest differential as forecasters of the future spot rate. Similarly, we cannot control foreign exchange risk by using any other forecaster, since the accuracy of the forecasts is questionable, to say the least.

The third point concerns the desirability of foreign exchange risk management from the viewpoint of the shareholders and managers of a company. Remember that risk management is costly and so shareholders may not find it worthwhile to manage risk, given that shareholders are diversified by virtue of their investments in various companies. Because of this diversification, the amount of exposure at any point in time may be difficult to measure and even small. The problem is that some hedging techniques may not be available for shareholders although they are available for managers (for example, changing the currency of invoicing and other techniques of **operational hedging**).

IN PRACTICE

Australian cotton farmers face a double whammy

In 2002, the Australian cotton industry faced a crisis as cotton farmers defaulted on foreign exchange and cotton forward contracts worth tens of millions of dollars. The farmers found themselves exposed to the double whammy of a depreciating Australian dollar and plunging world cotton prices. While they had hedged the currency risk, they did not hedge the US dollar cotton price, which declined to a 30-year low. As a result, several cotton farmers faced bankruptcy, while cotton merchants (such as the listed companies Namoi Cotton and Queensland Cotton) reacted to these developments by refraining from offering forward cotton contracts in Australian dollars and forward foreign exchange facilities to growers. Namoi Cotton and Queensland Cotton increased their provisions for bad debt from AUD1.84 million to AUD16.35 million and from AUD2.2 million to AUD4.4 million, respectively.

One farmer repeatedly took legal action, alleging that the advice he was given by the cotton merchants was inadequate. This incident brought back memories of the 1980s foreign exchange scandals involving farmers and banks. At that time, the claimants owed foreign currency funds at significantly lower interest rates than the Australian dollar (such as the Swiss franc and the Japanese yen), but claimed that they were not advised on the associated foreign exchange risk.

Apart from the argument that hedging has a positive effect on the value of the firm, it is also desirable because it produces a more stable corporate income stream than otherwise. This may be desirable from a managerial point of view for the following reasons:

- If a progressive tax rate is in operation, more taxes are paid in high-income periods than are saved in periods of low or negative income. Hence, a more stable before-tax income produces a higher average after-tax income than otherwise.
- A more stable income may be conducive to sales in the case of consumer durables and capital goods. This is because a stable income may give the impression that the company will last for long enough to provide after-sale services.
- Volatile earnings may cause a high degree of employee turnover or demands for higher wages if they are interpreted to imply lack of job security.

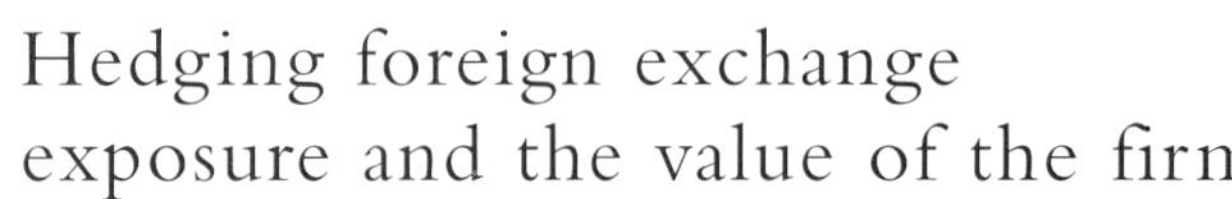

Hedging foreign exchange exposure and the value of the firm

One motive or explanation for why firms hedge is the belief that hedging can increase the value of the firm by reducing the expected costs of financial distress, lowering the expected tax payments and alleviating the underinvestment problem associated with costly external financing. A study conducted by Hagelin examined the question as to why firms hedge by using survey and published data on a sample of Swedish firms.[1]

The results of the study revealed differences between the motives for hedging transaction exposure and those behind hedging translation exposure, since these exposures affect the firm in different ways. It was found that firms hedge transaction exposure to boost their value by reducing the indirect costs of financial distress or alleviating the underinvestment problem. However, no evidence was found to suggest that translation exposure is hedged to increase the value of the firm.

1 N. Hagelin, 'Why Firms Hedge with Currency Derivatives: An Examination of Transaction and Translation Exposure', *Applied Financial Economics*, 13, 2003, pp. 55–69.

14.2 Hedging short-term transaction exposure with forward and futures contracts

Once the amount exposed has been measured, it can be hedged by buying (in the case of payables) or selling (in the case of receivables) foreign currency forward and futures contracts. Basically, both of these hedging instruments give similar results (in terms of the domestic currency value of payables and receivables). However, some quantitative differences will arise because of the standardisation of futures contracts.

Forward hedging of payables

Forward hedging entails locking in the exchange rate at which payables and receivables are converted from the domestic currency into a foreign currency, and vice versa. The result could be unfavourable, *ex post*. If, for example, the foreign currency appreciates, then hedged foreign receivables will be lower than otherwise. If, on the other hand, the foreign currency depreciates, then the value of hedged payables will be higher than otherwise. The idea, however, is that hedging provides stability and certainty. For the purpose of the following illustration we will assume two points in time: 0, when the decision to hedge or not to hedge is taken, and 1, when the payables and receivables become due.

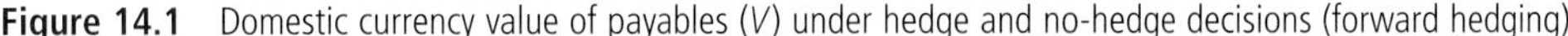

Forward hedging involves buying and selling the foreign currency forward. In the case of payables the foreign currency is bought forward. Thus, if the amount of payables is K foreign currency units, this amount is bought forward at time 0 at a cost of KF_0 domestic currency units. Since this amount is known with certainty at time 0, the exposure is covered. On the other hand, the domestic currency value under the no-hedge decision is KS_1. At time 0, the domestic currency value of the payables is known with certainty under the hedge decision, but the value under the no-hedge decision may be anything depending on the level assumed by the exchange rate at time 1, when the payables are due. This is shown in Figure 14.1, where it is assumed that at time 0, the foreign currency is selling at par (that is, a zero forward spread) so that the spot and the forward exchange rates are equal.

Figure 14.1 Domestic currency value of payables (V) under hedge and no-hedge decisions (forward hedging)

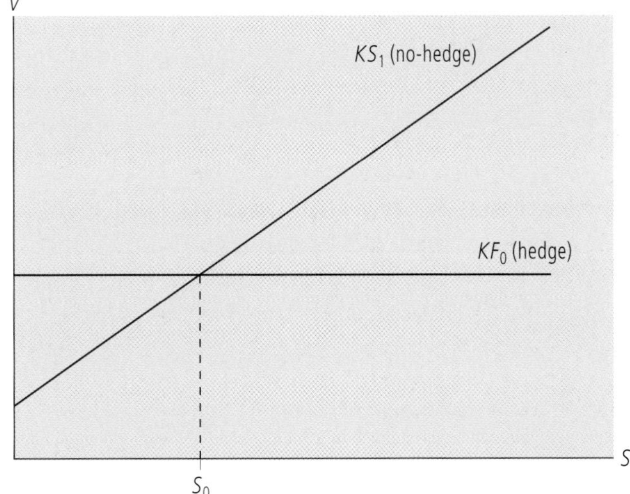

Figure 14.2 illustrates the essence of **financial hedging**: by taking an offsetting position on a hedging instrument (in this case a forward contract), the profit/loss on the unhedged position (exposure) is offset by the loss/profit on the hedging instrument. As the spot exchange rate assumes higher values at time 1, a loss will be incurred on a short exposure (payables). If we take the spot exchange rate at time 0 as a benchmark, then the loss on the exposure can be measured as $K(S_0 - S_1)$. A depreciation of the foreign currency, such that $S_1 < S_0$, means that profit will be made in the sense that a lower domestic currency amount is required to cover the payables. If a long forward position is taken to hedge the position, then the profit/loss on the forward position (the hedge) is given by $K(S_1 - F_0)$, such that an appreciation of the foreign currency brings about profit, and vice versa. Now, if we add up these profits and losses we get $K(S_0 - F_0)$, which is the foreign currency value of the payables multiplied by a factor that is equal to the (negative of) the forward spread. If the foreign currency at time 0 is selling at forward par, the spread is equal to zero and the combined profit/loss is equal to zero, as in Figure 14.2(a). If the forward spread is not equal to zero, the combined profit/loss will not be zero, as shown in Figure 14.2(b) and (c).

Figure 14.2 Offsetting profit/loss on payables and a long forward position

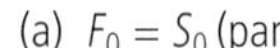
(a) $F_0 = S_0$ (par)

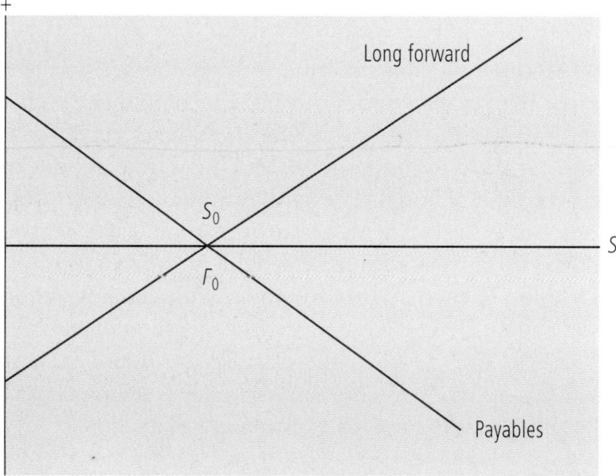

(b) $F_0 > S_0$ (premium)

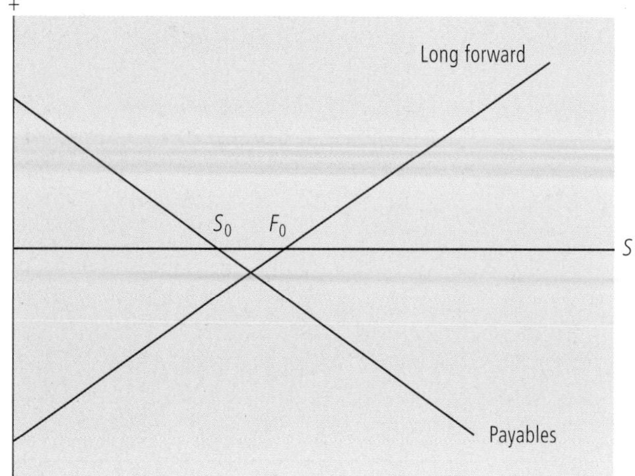

(c) $F_0 < S_0$ (discount)

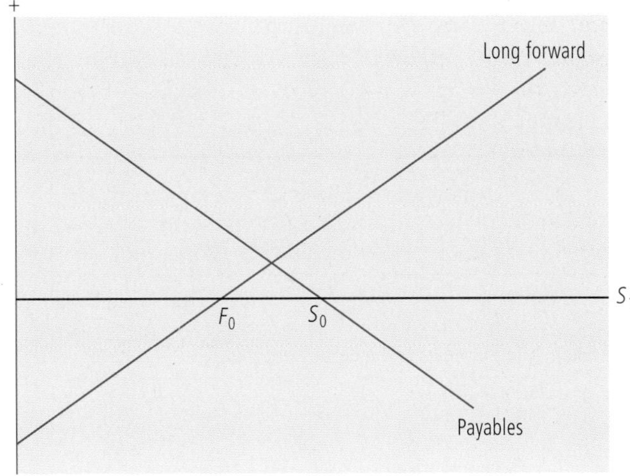

Example

An Australian company owes an amount of GBP300 000, due in one month. The current spot and one-month forward rates are 2.70 and 2.75, respectively. If the company chooses to hedge its position, the domestic currency value of the payables is

$$300\,000 \times 2.75 = \text{AUD}825\,000$$

Under the no-hedge decision, the domestic currency value of the payables may assume any value depending on the spot exchange rate when the payables become due (that is, S_1). The following table shows the value of the payables under the hedge and no-hedge decisions, as well as the profit/loss on the spot and forward positions at various levels of S_1. Figures 14.3 and 14.4 show the same graphically.

S_1	No-hedge	Hedge	Profit/loss (payables)	Profit/loss (long forward)	Net
2.50	750 000	825 000	60 000	−75 000	−15 000
2.60	780 000	825 000	30 000	−45 000	−15 000
2.65	795 000	825 000	15 000	−30 000	−15 000
2.70	810 000	825 000	0	−15 000	−15 000
2.75	825 000	825 000	−15 000	0	−15 000
2.80	840 000	825 000	−30 000	15 000	−15 000
2.85	855 000	825 000	−45 000	30 000	−15 000
2.90	870 000	825 000	−60 000	45 000	−15 000
2.95	885 000	825 000	−75 000	60 000	−15 000

Continued...

Figure 14.3 The AUD value of payables under the hedge and no-hedge decisions

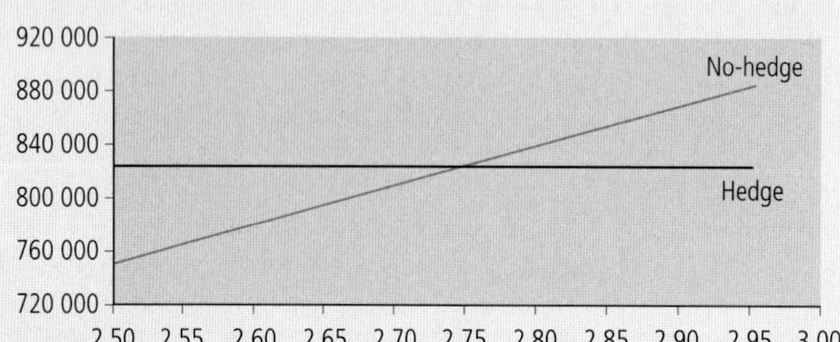

Figure 14.4 Profit/loss on payables and long forward (AUD)

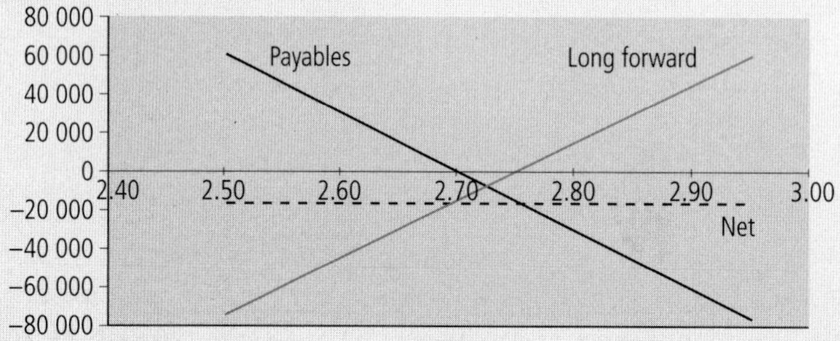

At time 0, when the decision to hedge or not to hedge is taken, the value of S_1 is not known. Thus, the decision must be based on a forecast. If there is a probability distribution for S_1, then the decision to hedge is taken if the expected value of the payables under the hedge decision is less than the value under the no-hedge decision. The following table shows the probability distribution for S_1 and the corresponding domestic currency value of the payables:

S_1	V	Probability
2.50	750 000	0.05
2.60	780 000	0.05
2.65	795 000	0.05
2.70	810 000	0.10
2.75	825 000	0.10
2.80	840 000	0.10
2.85	855 000	0.15
2.90	870 000	0.15
2.95	885 000	0.25

The expected AUD value of the payables is:

$$750\,000 \times 0.05 + 780\,000 \times 0.05 + \ldots + 885\,000 \times 0.25 = 843\,750$$

which means that the decision to hedge would be taken.

Forward hedging of receivables

In the case of receivables, the foreign currency is sold forward. Thus, if the amount of receivables is K foreign currency units, this amount is sold forward at time 0 to receive KF_0 domestic currency units. Since this amount is known with certainty at time 0, the exposure is covered. On the other hand, the domestic currency value under the no-hedge decision is KS_1.

The value of the receivables increases with the appreciation of the foreign currency. As the spot exchange rate assumes higher values at time 1, profit will be made on this exposure. If we take the spot exchange rate at time 0 as a benchmark, then the profit on the exposure can be measured as $K(S_1 - S_0)$. A depreciation of the foreign currency, such that $S_1 < S_0$, means that a loss will be incurred in the sense that a lower domestic currency amount is received. If a short forward position is taken to hedge the position, then the profit/loss on the forward position is given by $K(F_0 - S_1)$, such that an appreciation of the foreign currency brings about a loss, and vice versa. If we add up these profits and losses, we will get $K(F_0 - S_0)$, which is K multiplied by the forward spread. By taking an offsetting position on a hedging instrument (in this case a forward contract), the profit/loss on the receivables is offset by the loss/profit on the short forward position. If the forward spread is not equal to zero, the combined profit/loss will not be zero, as shown in Figure 14.5.

Figure 14.5 Offsetting profit/loss on receivables and a short forward position

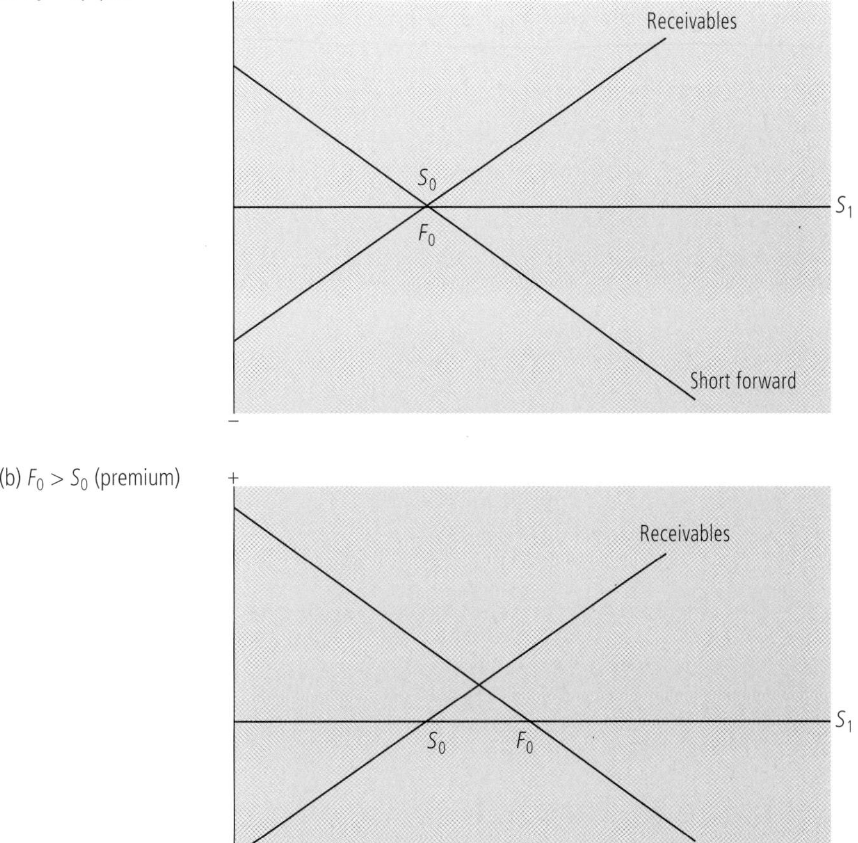

Continued...

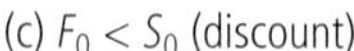

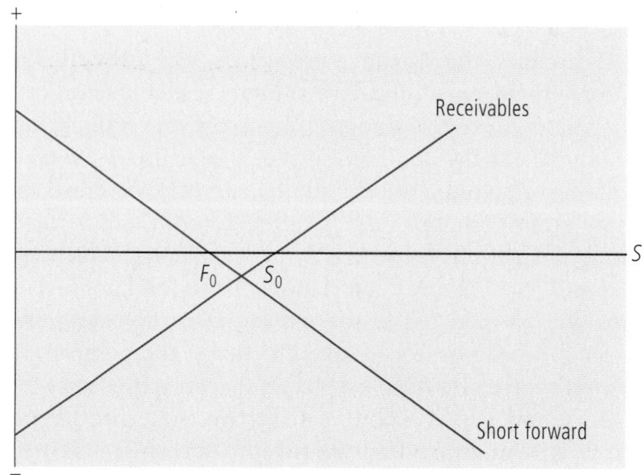

Example

Consider the same figures as in the previous example, but assume now that the GBP amount is receivables rather than payables. As the exchange rate at time 1 assumes various values, there will be profit/loss on the receivables and the short forward position, as reported in the following table. As the exchange rate assumes higher values, profit will be made on the receivables but loss will be incurred on the short forward position, so that the net profit/loss is constant at AUD15 000. This results from selling the US dollar at a forward premium. Figure 14.6 shows the profit/loss graphically.

S_1	No-hedge	Hedge	Profit/loss (receivables)	Profit/loss (short forward)	Net
2.50	750 000	825 000	–60 000	75 000	15 000
2.60	780 000	825 000	–30 000	45 000	15 000
2.65	795 000	825 000	–15 000	30 000	15 000
2.70	810 000	825 000	0	15 000	15 000
2.75	825 000	825 000	15 000	0	15 000
2.80	840 000	825 000	30 000	–15 000	15 000
2.85	855 000	825 000	45 000	–30 000	15 000
2.90	870 000	825 000	60 000	–45 000	15 000
2.95	885 000	825 000	75 000	–60 000	15 000

Figure 14.6 Profit/loss on receivables and short forward (AUD)

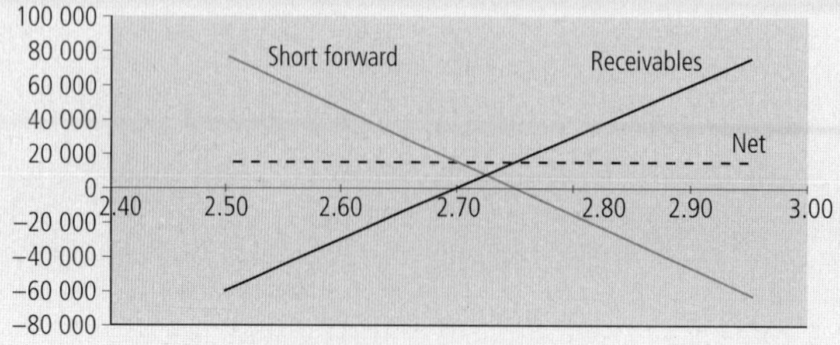

Forward hedging in the presence of bid-offer spreads

In the presence of bid-offer spreads in spot and forward exchange rates, the hedger buys the foreign currency (both spot and forward) at the offer rates and sells the foreign currency at the bid rates. Remember that the hedger buys the foreign currency in the case of payables and sells it in the case of receivables. Thus, the domestic currency value of payables and receivables having a foreign currency of K under the hedge and no-hedge decisions are as follows:

Position	Hedge	No-hedge
Payables	KF_{a0}	KS_{a1}
Receivables	KF_{b0}	KS_{b1}

Example

Consider the previous examples of payables and receivables in the presence of bid offer-spreads by assuming that the current spot and forward rates are 2.6950–2.7050 and 2.7450–2.7550, respectively. The following table shows what happens to the domestic currency values of the payables and receivables as the spot exchange rate at time 1 assumes various values. As we can see, the value of the payables is higher and the value of the receivables is lower than in the absence of bid-offer spreads. This is because bid-offer spreads are transaction costs.

S_1	No-hedge (payables)	Hedge (payables)	No-hedge (receivables)	Hedge (receivables)
2.4950–2.5050	751 500	826 500	748 500	823 500
2.5950–2.6050	781 500	826 500	778 500	823 500
2.6450–2.6550	796 500	826 500	793 500	823 500
2.6950–2.7050	811 500	826 500	808 500	823 500
2.7450–2.7550	826 500	826 500	823 500	823 500
2.7950–2.8050	841 500	826 500	838 500	823 500
2.8450–2.8550	856 500	826 500	853 500	823 500
2.8950–2.9050	871 500	826 500	868 500	823 500
2.9450–2.9550	886 500	826 500	883 500	823 500

Futures hedging

The consequences of using futures contracts to hedge transaction exposure are the same as those of using forward contracts. However, because of the standardisation of futures contracts and because they involve marking-to-market, some quantitative rather than qualitative differences may arise. First, because futures contracts are standardised with respect to size, it may not be possible to hedge the amount of payables or receivables exactly. For example, if the amount of the receivables is GBP85 000 and the size of the pound contract is GBP25 000, then by selling three contracts only, the amount covered is GBP75 000. The uncovered portion (GBP10 000) has to be sold in the spot market when the receivables are realised. Second, because futures contracts are standardised with respect to the settlement date, it is likely that the date on which the receivables are due does not coincide with a settlement date. Even if the size and the settlement dates match what is required, marking-to-market will introduce some variation *vis-à-vis* the forward market. For all these reasons, forward hedging is preferred to futures hedging.

IN PRACTICE

The hedge ratio and the hedging decision: what do Australian companies do?

It seems that the hedging decision is a speculative decision, in the sense that a firm facing foreign exchange exposure may or may not take the decision to hedge, depending on exchange rate expectations. However, the discussion so far implicitly assumes that if a decision to hedge is taken, then the full amount of the foreign currency value of the payables or receivables is covered, which means that a **hedge ratio** of one is always chosen (the hedge ratio is the amount of the hedging instrument relative to the amount of payables or receivables). In reality, companies do not necessarily choose to be fully hedged. It is most likely the case that they will choose a hedge ratio that is different from one. If, for example, a firm is facing payables worth USD400 000, then this firm may choose to cover half this amount by buying a forward contract on USD200 000 (a hedge ratio of 0.5). When the payables become due, the hedger will take delivery of USD200 000 and buy the other USD200 000 on the spot market to meet the payables. A decision like this would be taken if there were an indication that the US dollar might depreciate against the Australian dollar but the decision maker is not really sure about this. In any case, the optimal hedge ratio that eliminates risk completely is not necessarily equal to one: it depends on the correlation between the prices of the asset to be hedged and that of the hedging instrument (such as the spot and forward exchange rates). The attitude towards risk determines whether or not a hedger chooses the optimal hedge ratio.

Australian companies that earn foreign currency revenue from exports behave in different ways, but it is almost universally the case that they do not take a full cover (a hedge ratio of one). Companies like BHP, MIM, AWB, Pasminco, WMC, Santos and Woodside Petroleum, for example, hedge exposure to foreign exchange risk to varying degrees because they would benefit from the depreciation of the Australian dollar to the extent that they are not covered.

Take BHP, for example. Its profit rises by AUD26 million for each cent fall of the Australian dollar against the US dollar. Normally, BHP hedges a minimum of 50 per cent and a maximum of 75 per cent of its annual exposure (hedge ratios of 0.5 and 0.75, respectively). WMC, Australia's largest nickel producer and a significant alumina, gold, uranium and copper producer, is typically around 40 per cent covered. The same story goes for MIM, whose profit would be boosted by AUD100 million for a 10 per cent fall in the Australian dollar against the US dollar if it is unhedged, but the company is normally about 60 per cent hedged.

By mid-2000, Rio Tinto was unhedged and thus enjoyed a healthy rise in its profits as a result of the 15 per cent depreciation of the Australian currency in the first half of the year. Rio Tinto's annual financial review makes it explicit that 'the group does not generally believe that active hedging would provide long-term benefits to shareholders, but in special circumstances currency hedging may be appropriate'.

14.3 Money market hedging of short-term transaction exposure

A **money market hedge** amounts to taking a money market position to cover expected payables or receivables. Taking these positions involves borrowing and lending domestic and foreign currencies, which in effect leads to the creation of a synthetic forward contract.

Money market hedging of payables

Assume that the amount due sometime in the future is K units of the foreign currency. At that time, this amount must be available to make the payment. A money market hedge of payables involves borrowing and lending such that the final product is K units of the foreign currency. The following steps are involved:

- At time 0 an amount equal to $KS_0/(1 + i^*)$ of the domestic currency is borrowed.
- This amount is converted spot into foreign currency at the prevailing exchange rate, S_0, to obtain $K(1 + i^*)$ foreign currency units. This amount is the present value of the payables.
- The foreign currency amount is invested at the foreign interest rate to obtain K units of the foreign currency when the payables are due at time 1. This amount is used to meet the payables.
- At time 1, the domestic currency loan becomes due and so the amount of the principal and interest should be repaid. This amount is equal to $KS_0(1 + i)/(1 + i^*)$.

This operation, which is shown diagrammatically in Figure 14.7, does not involve the exchange rate prevailing at time 1. The domestic currency amount required to meet the payables is $KS_0(1 + i)/(1 + i^*)$, which is known at time 0. Under the hedge decision, therefore, the conversion rate is $S_0(1 + i)/(1 + i^*)$, which is the forward rate consistent with covered interest parity (the interest parity forward rate), $\overline{F}_0$. This is, in effect, creating a **synthetic forward contract** with an **implicit forward rate**, $\overline{F}_0$.

Figure 14.7 Money market hedging of payables

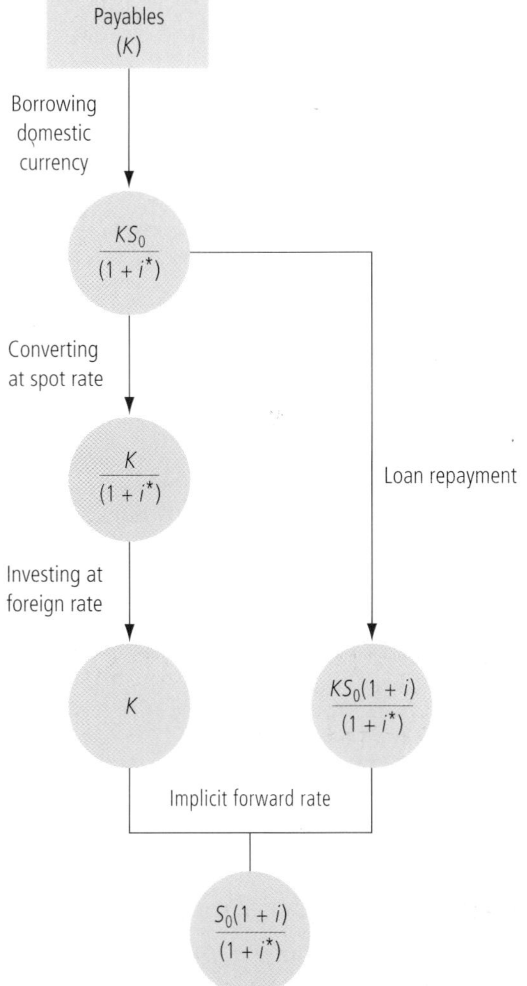

Recall that in forward hedging the conversion rate is the market-quoted forward rate. This means the following:

- Money market hedging of payables will be preferred to forward hedging if $\overline{F}_0 < F_0$.
- If CIP holds then $\overline{F}_0 = F_0$, which means that money market hedging and forward hedging will produce identical results in terms of the domestic currency value of the payables.

In practice, however, it is rarely the case that there is a large deviation from CIP, in which case the hedger should be indifferent between money market and forward hedging. However, the following points must be borne in mind:

- Since money market hedging involves a number of transactions, it is bound to be more costly than forward hedging, which involves one operation.
- Money market hedging may be resorted to if a forward contract is unavailable on the underlying foreign currency.

Example

Consider the previous example on the pound payables, assuming that the Australian and British one-month interest rates are 8 and 4 per cent per annum, respectively. How can the GBP payables be hedged using a money market hedge?

The Australian dollar amount to be borrowed at the present time is

$$\frac{300\,000 \times 2.70}{1+\dfrac{0.04}{12}} = \text{AUD}807\,309$$

This amount is converted into pounds at 2.70 to obtain

$$\frac{807\,309}{2.70} = \text{GBP}299\,003$$

The pound amount is invested for one month at 4 per cent per annum to obtain

$$299\,003 \times \left(1+\frac{0.04}{12}\right) = \text{GBP}300\,000$$

which is paid out when the amount is due. The Australian dollar amount due is

$$807\,309 \times \left(1+\frac{0.08}{12}\right) = \text{AUD}812\,691$$

This is a hedge in the sense that the Australian company would know in advance that no matter what happens to the AUD/GBP exchange rate, the Australian dollar amount to be paid out is AUD812 691. The implicit forward rate is calculated as

$$\frac{812\,691}{300\,000} = 2.7090$$

which is the same result obtained by using the formula for calculating the interest parity forward rate as

$$\overline{F}_0 = 2.70 \times \left(\frac{1+\dfrac{0.08}{12}}{1+\dfrac{0.04}{12}}\right) = 2.7090$$

In this case $\overline{F}_0 < F_0$, which means that CIP does not hold. Under these conditions money market hedging will be preferable.

Money market hedging of receivables

Hedging receivables works the other way round. This time, a foreign currency amount is expected to be received and the hedger is not sure how much this amount will be worth in domestic currency terms when it is received. The following steps are involved:

- At time 0 a foreign currency amount equal to $K/(1 + i^{*})$, which is the present value of the receivables, is borrowed.
- This amount is converted into the domestic currency at the prevailing exchange rate, S_0, to obtain $KS_0/(1 + i^{*})$ domestic currency units.
- This domestic currency amount is invested at the domestic interest rate to obtain $KS_0(1 + i)/(1 + i^{*})$ units of the domestic currency when the receivables are due at time 1.
- At time 1, the foreign currency loan becomes due and the amount of the principal and interest should be repaid. This amount is equal to K, which is covered by the receivables.

Again, this operation does not involve the exchange rate prevailing at time 1 and the conversion takes place at the interest parity forward rate. Money market hedging of the receivables will be preferred to forward hedging if $\overline{F}_0 > F_0$. The operation is illustrated in Figure 14.8.

Figure 14.8 Money market hedging of receivables

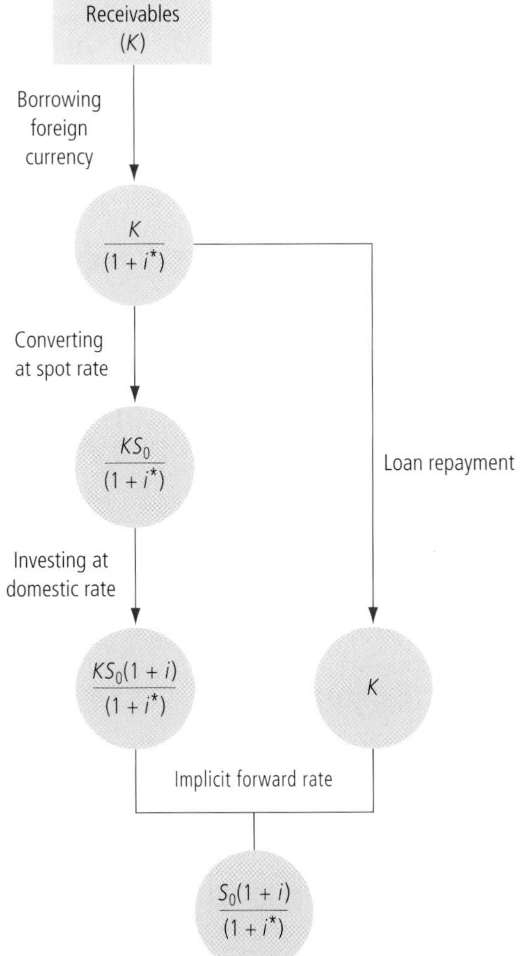

Example

Let us rework the previous example for the case of receivables. The GBP amount borrowed at the present time is

$$\frac{300\,000}{1+\dfrac{0.04}{12}} = \text{GBP}299\,003$$

The pound amount is converted into Australian dollars at 2.70 to obtain

$$299\,003 \times 2.7 = \text{AUD}807\,308$$

The Australian dollar amount is invested for one month at 8 per cent to obtain

$$807\,308 \times \left(1+\frac{0.08}{12}\right) = \text{AUD}812\,690$$

which is the amount received in one month. The pound amount due is

$$299\,003 \times \left(1+\frac{0.04}{12}\right) = \text{GBP}300\,000$$

which is paid out when the receivables are realised. Hence, the hedge results in certainty about the Australian dollar value of the receivables. No matter what happens to the spot exchange rate, the amount received will be AUD812 690. The implicit forward rate is

$$\frac{812\,690}{300\,000} = 2.7090$$

which again can be calculated using the formula for the interest parity forward rate.

Money market hedging in the presence of bid-offer spreads

Let us now see what happens if we allow for bid-offer spreads in interest and exchange rates. The process of hedging payables in the money market changes to the following:

- At time 0 an amount equal to $KS_{a0}/(1 + i_b^*)$ of the domestic currency is borrowed.
- The domestic currency amount is converted into the foreign currency at the prevailing offer exchange rate, S_{a0}, to obtain $K/(1 + i_b^*)$ foreign currency units. This amount is the present value of the payables.
- The foreign currency amount is invested at the bid foreign interest rate, i_b^*, to obtain K units of the foreign currency when the payables are due at time 1. This amount is used to meet the payables.
- At time 1, the domestic currency loan becomes due and so the amount of the principal and interest should be repaid. This amount is equal to $KS_{a0}(1 + i_a)/(1 + i_b^*)$.

The process is shown in Figure 14.9. The domestic currency value under the no-hedge and the hedge decisions is KS_{a1} and $KS_{a0}(1 + i_a)/(1 + i_b^*)$, respectively. The conversion rate under the hedge decision is the offer interest parity forward rate, $\overline{F}_{a0}$. The decision to hedge will be taken if $\overline{F}_{a0} < S_{a1}$.

Figure 14.9 Money market hedging of payables in the presence of bid-offer spreads

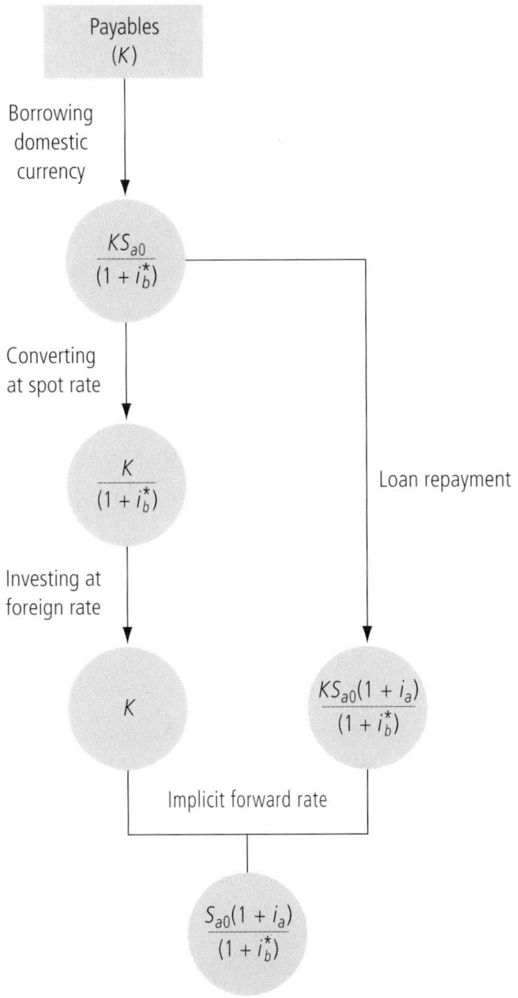

Payables (K)

Borrowing domestic currency

$\frac{KS_{a0}}{(1 + i_b^*)}$

Converting at spot rate

$\frac{K}{(1 + i_b^*)}$

Investing at foreign rate

K

Loan repayment

$\frac{KS_{a0}(1 + i_a)}{(1 + i_b^*)}$

Implicit forward rate

$\frac{S_{a0}(1 + i_a)}{(1 + i_b^*)}$

Let us now consider hedging receivables, which involves the following steps:

- At time 0 an amount of the foreign currency equal to $K/(1 + i_a^*)$, which is the present value of the receivables, is borrowed.
- This amount is converted into the domestic currency at the prevailing bid exchange rate, S_{b0}, to obtain $KS_{b0}/(1 + i_a^*)$ domestic currency units.
- The domestic currency amount is invested at the domestic interest rate to obtain $KS_{b0}(1 + i_b)/(1 + i_a^*)$ units of the domestic currency when the receivables are due at time 1.
- At time 1, the foreign currency loan becomes due and the amount of the principal and interest should be repaid. This amount is equal to K, which is covered by the receivables.

The process is shown in Figure 14.10. The domestic currency value under the no-hedge and the hedge decisions is KS_{b1} and $KS_{b0}(1 + i_b)/(1 + i_a^*)$, respectively. The conversion rate under the hedge decision is the bid interest parity forward rate, $\overline{F}_{b0}$. Therefore, the decision to hedge will be taken if $\overline{F}_{a0} > S_{a1}$.

Figure 14.10 Money market hedging of receivables in the presence of bid-offer spreads

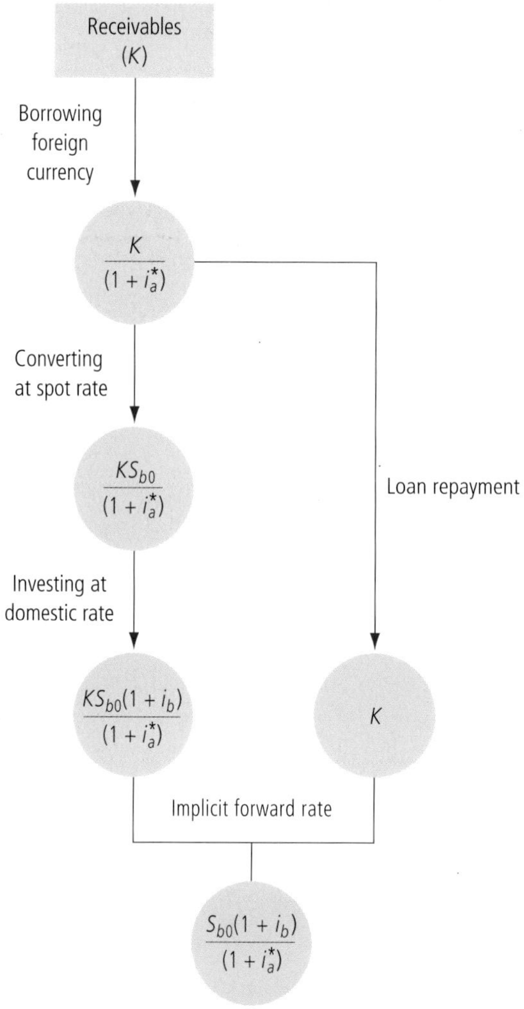

The following table shows the domestic currency value of payables and receivables under the hedge and no-hedge decisions when a money market hedge is used.

Position	Hedge	No-hedge
Payables	$K\bar{F}_{a0}$	KS_{a1}
Receivables	$K\bar{F}_{b0}$	KS_{b1}

Money market hedging as a pricing mechanism

If you approach your banker requesting a quote on the forward rate to buy a particular currency, the banker can use the cost of money market hedging to calculate the forward rate to be quoted. When the banker quotes a forward rate for a future delivery of a particular currency, the banker will be exposed to the risk arising from possible appreciation of the underlying currency. The

Example

Consider the previous examples of payables and receivables in the presence of a 50 basis point bid-offer spread in the interest rates. The following table shows what happens to the domestic currency values of the payables and receivables under money market hedging. These are calculated by converting at the offer and bid interest parity rates (2.6850 and 2.6972, respectively).

S_1	No-hedge (payables)	Hedge (payables)	No-hedge (receivables)	Hedge (receivables)
2.4950–2.5050	751 500	809 160	748 500	805 500
2.5950–2.6050	781 500	809 160	778 500	805 500
2.6450–2.6550	796 500	809 160	793 500	805 500
2.6950–2.7050	811 500	809 160	808 500	805 500
2.7450–2.7550	826 500	809 160	823 500	805 500
2.7950–2.8050	841 500	809 160	838 500	805 500
2.8450–2.8550	856 500	809 160	853 500	805 500
2.8950–2.9050	871 500	809 160	868 500	805 500
2.9450–2.9550	886 500	809 160	883 500	805 500

banker can protect himself or herself by hedging the forward position in the money market, so that on the maturity date he or she receives the amount of the underlying currency to be delivered according to the forward contract. The minimum forward rate that the banker can quote, therefore, is the cost of money market hedging, which is the implicit forward rate on the synthetic forward contract created by money market hedging. In the absence of bid-offer spreads, this rate is $\overline{F}$, which is equal to the interest parity forward rate that is consistent with the no-arbitrage condition (see Chapter 10). In the presence of the bid and offer spreads, the bid rate will be

$$\overline{F}_b = S_{b0}\left[\frac{1+i_b}{1+i_a^{\star}}\right] \tag{14.1}$$

whereas the offer rate quoted by the banker will be

$$\overline{F}_a = S_{a0}\left[\frac{1+i_a}{1+i_b^{\star}}\right] \tag{14.2}$$

It is obvious from Equations (14.1) and (14.2) that the bid rate is lower than the offer rate.

14.4 Option hedging of short-term transaction exposure

Unlike the cases of forward hedging, futures hedging and money market hedging, the outcome of option hedging is not known with certainty, since it depends on whether or not the option used as the hedging instrument is exercised. This, in turn, depends on whether the actual exchange rate when the payables or receivables are due, S_1, is higher or lower than the exercise exchange rate. However, options can be used to ensure that the domestic currency value of payables does not rise above a certain value and that the domestic currency value of receivables does not fall below a certain value. It is also possible, by using over-the-counter non-standardised options, to hedge the exact amount of payables and receivables.

Option hedging of payables

Let us start with the case of hedging foreign currency payables worth K units of a foreign currency. In this case a call option is bought, giving the hedger the right to buy K units of the foreign currency at the exercise exchange rate. For simplicity, let us assume that the option is a European option with an expiry date that coincides with the date when the payables are due. Let us also assume that the exercise exchange rate is equal to the current exchange rate, S_0. The exchange rate prevailing on the expiry date, S_1, will assume any value, and depending on this value we have the following possibilities (see Figure 14.11):

- If $S_1 < S_0$, then the option will not be exercised and the foreign currency will be bought on the spot market. The total cost of covering the payables is the domestic currency value, KS_1, and the option premium lost, which is equal to KR, where R is the premium per unit of the foreign currency. The total cost will thus be $K(S_1 + R)$.
- If $S_1 > S_0$, then the option will be exercised and the foreign currency will be bought at the exercise exchange rate, S_0. The total cost of covering the payables is the domestic currency value, KS_0, and the option premium paid up front, which is equal to KR. The total cost will thus be $K(S_0 + R)$.

Under the no-hedge decision, the domestic currency value of the payables will be KS_1. The decision to hedge will be taken if the expected value of the payables under the hedge decision is less than the expected value under the no-hedge decision. As the exchange rate at time 1 assumes increasing values, losses will be incurred on the payables if $S_1 > S_0$. The loss is equal to $K(S_0 - S_1)$. But, at the same time, profit will be made on the call option equal to $K(S_1 - S_0 - R)$. If we add up these profits/losses, we end up with $-KR$, which is the cost of the option.

Figure 14.11 Domestic currency value of payables when a call option is used as a hedge

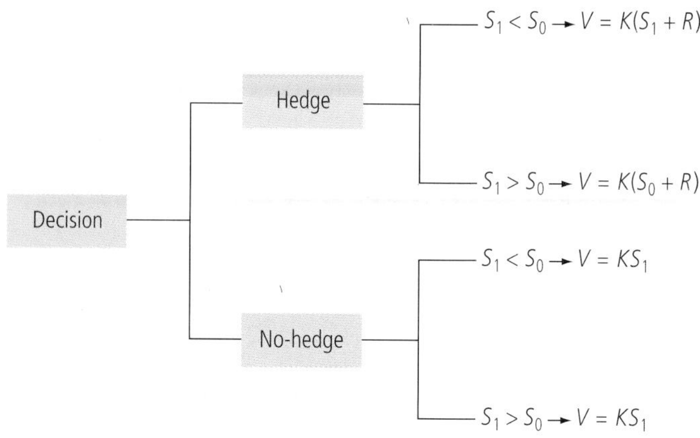

Example

Consider hedging the GBP300 000 payables using a call option with an expiry date coinciding with the date when the payables are due. Assume that the current exchange rate and the exercise exchange rate are equal at 2.80 and that the option premium is AUD0.05. The following table shows the relevant calculations. If the exchange rate values materialise with certain probabilities, we can calculate the expected AUD value of the payables under the hedge and no-hedge decisions. In this case they are equal to AUD838 125 and AUD846 375, respectively. The hedge decision seems to be preferable. Figure 14.12 shows the domestic currency value of the payables under the hedge and no-hedge decisions. Figure 14.13 shows the profit/loss on the option and the payables relative to the initial level of the exchange rate ($S_0 = 2.80$). As we can see, the maximum loss is the option premium.

S_1	No-hedge	Hedge	Probability
2.50	750 000	765 000	0.050
2.55	765 000	780 000	0.050
2.60	780 000	795 000	0.050
2.65	795 000	810 000	0.050
2.70	810 000	825 000	0.075
2.75	825 000	840 000	0.075
2.80	840 000	855 000	0.100
2.85	855 000	855 000	0.100
2.90	870 000	855 000	0.100
2.95	885 000	855 000	0.150
3.00	900 000	855 000	0.200

Figure 14.12 Domestic currency value of payables under the hedge and no-hedge decisions (call option)

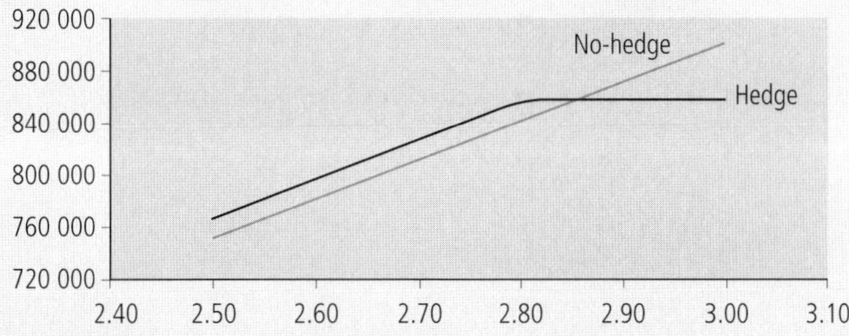

Figure 14.13 Profit/loss on payables and call option

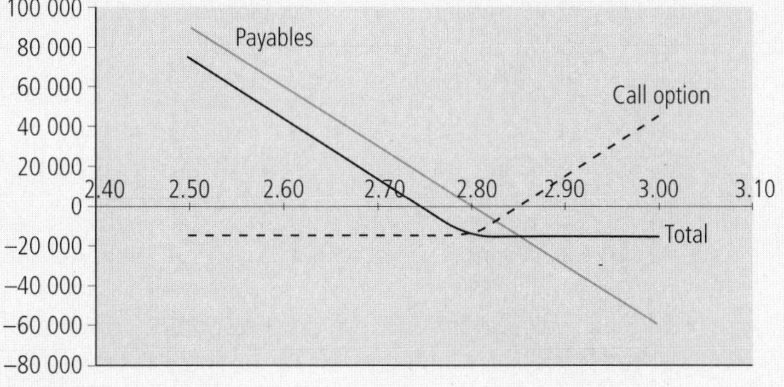

Hedging receivables with a put option

A put option gives the hedger the right to sell K units of the foreign currency at the exercise exchange rate. Making the same assumptions as before, we have the following possibilities:

- If $S_1 < S_0$, then the option will be exercised and the foreign currency will be sold to the option writer at S_0. The net amount obtained will be equal to the domestic currency value, KS_0, minus the option premium paid up front, which is equal to KR. Thus, the net amount is equal to $K(S_0 - R)$.
- If $S_1 > S_0$, then the option will not be exercised and the foreign currency will be sold on the spot market at S_1. The net amount received is therefore $K(S_1 - R)$.

Under the no-hedge decision, the domestic currency value of the receivables will be KS_1, as shown in Figure 14.14. The decision to hedge will be taken if the expected value of the receivables under the hedge decision is greater than the expected value under the no-hedge decision.

Figure 14.14 Domestic currency value of foreign currency receivables when a put option is used as a hedge

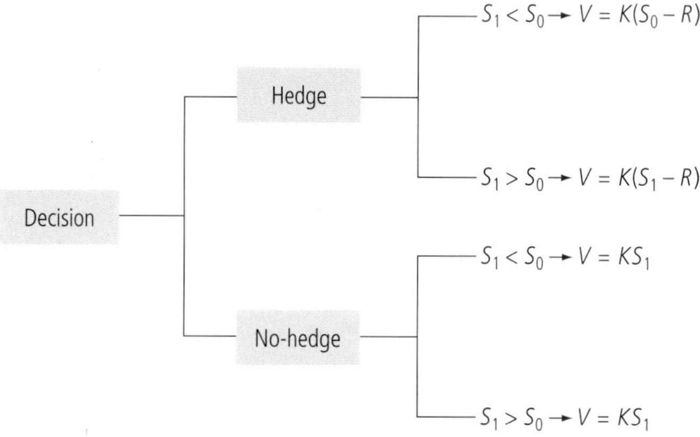

Hedging a contingent exposure

A contingent exposure is an exposure that arises only if a certain outcome materialises, such as winning a contract. In this case, an option hedge is preferable to a forward hedge because the latter can cover all possible eventualities. Let us assume that a firm bids for a contract valued at K units of a foreign currency. Exposure to the foreign currency would arise only if the contract is granted, in which case the firm would face receivables worth the value of the contract. If, in the meantime, the foreign currency depreciates against the domestic currency, the firm would incur some losses.

Let us see what happens when the firm uses forward contracts and options to hedge this contingent exposure. To use a forward contract, the firm takes a short forward position on the foreign currency, by selling K units of the currency forward. In any case (that is, whether or not the contract is won) the firm is committed to come up with K units of the foreign currency on the maturity of the contract. There are then two outcomes:

- The contract is won, in which case the amount of the receivables covers the forward contract. Hence, there is no problem as the hedge works in the sense that the firm locks in the domestic currency value of the receivables.

Example

Consider hedging the GBP300 000 receivables using a put option with an expiry date coinciding with the date when the receivables are due. Assume that the current exchange rate and the exercise exchange rate are equal at 2.80 and that the option premium is AUD0.04. The following table shows the relevant calculations. If the exchange rate values materialise with certain probabilities, we can calculate the expected AUD value of the receivables under the hedge and no-hedge decisions. In this case they are equal to AUD846 375 and AUD851 250, respectively. The hedge decision seems to be preferable. Figures 14.15 and 14.16 show the same results graphically.

S_1	No-hedge	Hedge	Probability
2.50	750 000	828 000	0.050
2.55	765 000	828 000	0.050
2.60	780 000	828 000	0.050
2.65	795 000	828 000	0.050
2.70	810 000	828 000	0.075
2.75	825 000	828 000	0.075
2.80	840 000	828 000	0.100
2.85	855 000	843 000	0.100
2.90	870 000	858 000	0.100
2.95	885 000	873 000	0.150
3.00	900 000	888 000	0.200

Figure 14.15 Domestic currency value of receivables under the hedge and no-hedge decisions (put option)

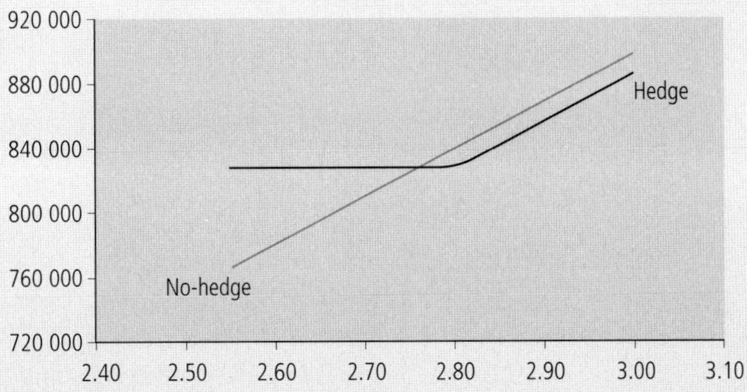

Figure 14.16 Profit/loss on the receivables and the put option

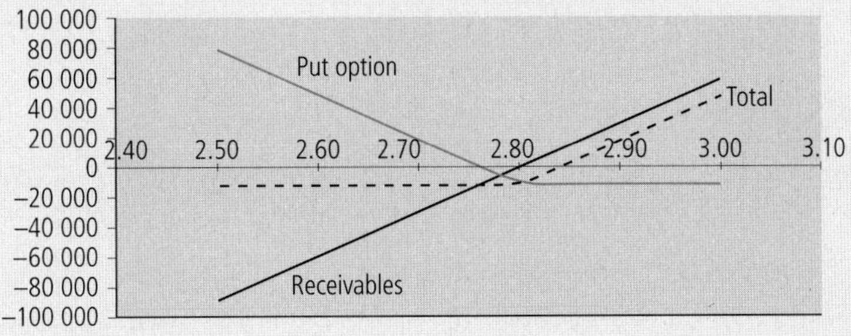

- The contract is not won, in which case the foreign currency amount has to be provided at the pre-specified forward rate. If the spot rate at that time happens to be higher than the forward rate, the firm would incur unlimited loss, proportional to the difference between the spot and forward rates.

Now let us consider what happens if a put option is used to hedge this contingent exposure. In this case, there are four possible outcomes because the option may or may not be exercised. The following outcomes are possible:

- The contract is won and the actual exchange rate turns out to be less than the exercise exchange rate ($S_1 < S_0$). The firm exercises the option, converting the proceeds at the exercise exchange rate and obtaining KS_0 units of the domestic currency.
- The contract is won but the exchange rate turns out to be greater than the exercise exchange rate ($S_1 > S_0$). The firm does not exercise, losing the premium on the option but the proceeds from the contract are converted at the higher rate (KS_1).
- The contract is not won and the actual exchange rate turns out to be less than the exercise exchange rate ($S_1 < S_0$). The firm exercises the option, making profit of $K(S_0 - S_1 - R)$.
- The contract is not won and the exchange rate turns out to be greater than the exercise exchange rate ($S_1 > S_0$). The firm does not exercise, losing the premium on the option.

All of these outcomes are illustrated in Figure 14.17. It is obvious that if a forward contract is used to hedge a contingent exposure, then the loss will be unlimited if the exchange rate rises and the contract is not won. If, on the other hand, a put option is used to hedge this exposure, then the maximum loss is the premium on the option whether or not the contract is won.

Figure 14.17 Hedging a contingent long exposure

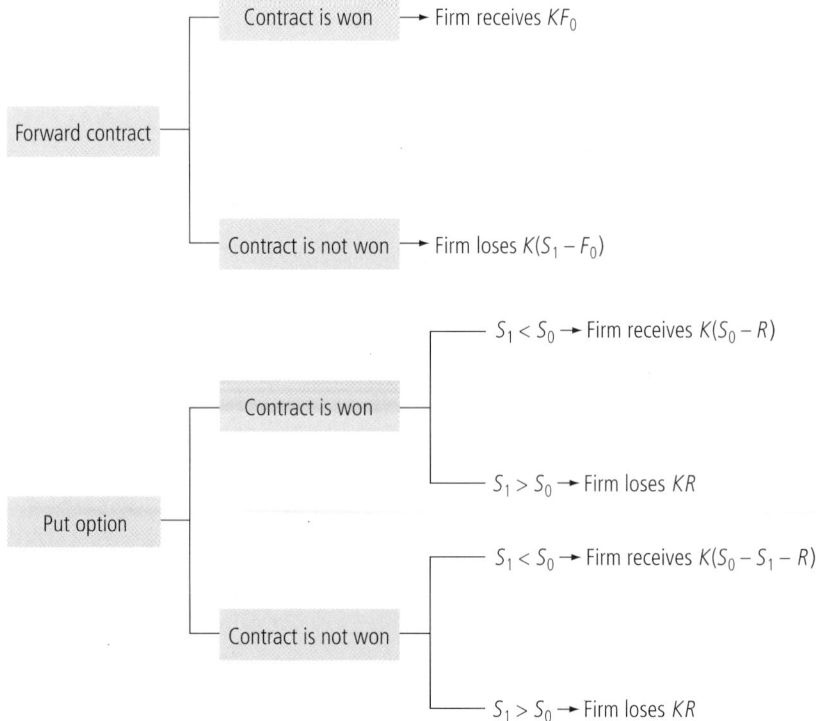

Writing an option in itself creates a contingent exposure, which can be hedged by taking another option position. The only certain way to hedge an option completely is by buying an equivalent option, identical with respect to all attributes of the exercise exchange rate, the face value and the expiry date. The premium cost of an option purchased as a hedge will probably be equal to that received for an option written. Therefore, if the option written is hedged with an identical option bought, trading profit opportunities will, in principle, be limited on average to the bid-offer spread between the two. However, it is likely that the option writer will hedge by buying an option that differs in one or more features, such as the underlying currency, the face value, the exercise exchange rate and the maturity date. For example, the sale of an October AUD2.80 pound call may be hedged by buying an October AUD2.85 pound call. If the pound went below AUD2.80, both calls would expire worthless and the hedger would at most profit by the premium it received from the 2.80 call, less the premium paid for the 2.85 call and transaction costs. If the pound appreciated to above 2.85, then both options would be exercised resulting in the hedger's maximum loss being the difference in the call exercise exchange rates less the net credit received in call premium.

INSIGHT

What is delta hedging?

Delta hedging is a method whereby the writer of an option can hedge his or her position. Since the option pricing formula shows the option price corresponding to the price of the underlying currency, it can be used to calculate the risk exposure of the option to any change in the price of the underlying currency (the spot exchange rate). The common practice is to calculate the change in the value of the option for a given change in the price of the underlying currency. This, as we recall from Chapter 7, is called the delta of an option.

Delta has a value between 0 and 1. A delta of 1 means that the value of the option increases in proportion to the price of the underlying currency. A deep-in-the-money option has a delta close to or equal to 1, since the intrinsic value of the option will increase in proportion close or equal to the increase in the price of the underlying currency, whereas the time value will be very small. A far-out-of-the-money option will have a delta close to 0, since it has no intrinsic value and a low time value owing to the small probability that it will become in the money.

Delta hedging means that the writer of a call option can cover his or her position by buying an amount of the underlying currency (spot or forward) in proportion to the delta, for any given price of the underlying instrument. For example, a call option written on GBP1 000 000 with a delta of 0.7 (at-the-money option) will rise or fall in value by about 0.7 per cent for each one per cent fall or rise in the pound. Therefore, the option writer can buy GBP700 000 in the spot market and in theory the value of the spot position will move in a manner exactly offsetting the value of the option, leaving the financial position of the option writer unaffected by changes in the exchange rate.

The problem with delta hedging is that the value of the delta is not constant, as it varies with the price of the underlying currency, which means that the amount of the spot currency purchased should be adjusted accordingly. The extent of the adjustment depends on the gamma, which is the rate at which the delta changes in response to a change in the price of the underlying currency. The adjustment would then be determined by (or rather equal to) the gamma position, which is the product of the gamma for a specific option and the size of the contract. If gamma is 0.1, the gamma position would be GBP100 000, which is the amount of the adjustment (upwards or downwards to the GBP700 000) for each 1 per cent change in the price of the underlying currency.

14.5 Hedging long-term transaction exposure

Long-term transaction exposure involves payables and receivables materialising over a long time in the future (say, five years). If it is possible to estimate the amount exposed, it can be hedged using three alternative techniques. These techniques are discussed in turn.

Long-term forward contracts

Commercial banks do provide forward contracts in major currencies with long maturities (for example, five or 10 years). However, because of the risk involved, banks only offer these contracts to the most creditworthy customers.

Currency swaps

We described currency swaps in Chapter 6. It may be best to explain how currency swaps are used as a hedging instrument. Suppose that BHP was granted a contract to carry out oil exploration works in the territorial waters of Japan, being paid in yen over a period of five years. At the same time, Kawasaki (a Japanese company) is hired to do some work on the Melbourne docks, paid in Australian dollars over a period of five years. While BHP knows how much it is going to receive over five years in Japanese yen terms, the value of the receivables in Australian dollar terms is not known in advance. Likewise, while Kawasaki knows the value of its receivables in Australian dollar terms, the value of these receivables in Japanese yen terms is not known in advance. In both cases, what will happen depends on the future course of the JPY/AUD exchange rate.

IN PRACTICE

The foreign exchange exposure of Australian banks

A recent study by the Reserve Bank of Australia dealt with the foreign exchange exposure of Australian banks.[1] The study showed that net foreign currency liabilities represent around 13 per cent of Australian banking assets, higher than in any other developed country. Although this may give the impression that Australian banks are vulnerable to foreign exchange risk, the exposure is really negligible because it is predominantly hedged. The study also showed that the daily value at risk (VAR) from exchange rate changes for the major Australian banks is smaller than that of major banks in other countries.

The study pointed out that Australian banks generally hedge their currency exposure in the derivative markets, predominantly using such instruments as currency swaps and foreign exchange forward contracts. These operations, which involve the shifting of risk to other counterparties, are conducted within the Australian banking sector (35 per cent), the Australian corporate sector (35 per cent), other financial institutions (15 per cent) and with the Reserve Bank (15 per cent).

1 'Foreign Exchange Exposures of Australian Banks', *Reserve Bank of Australia Bulletin*, August 2000, pp. 43–9.

Hedging would eliminate this state of unknown domestic currency value of the receivables. This can be done by an agreement between BHP and the Japanese company to exchange the cash flows at a negotiated exchange rate. This is shown in Figure 14.18.

Figure 14.18 Using a currency swap as a hedge

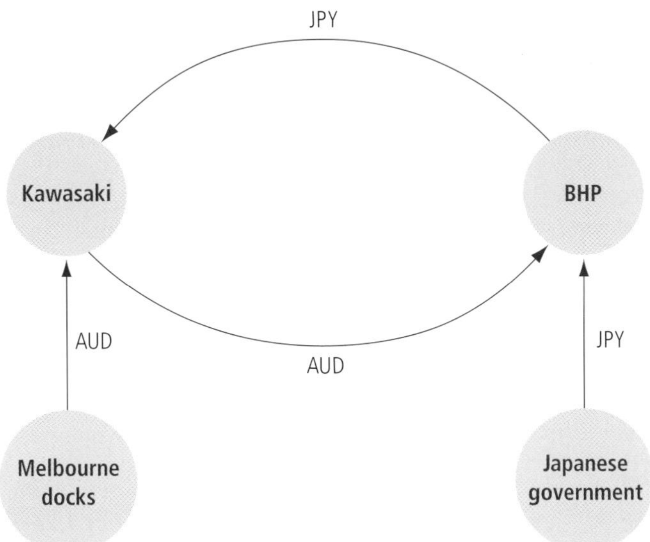

Parallel loans

Parallel loans were also discussed in Chapter 6. They can be used to hedge long-term payables and receivables in exactly the same way as swaps.

Other techniques of managing transaction exposure

It may not be possible to implement the hedging techniques discussed so far because of the unavailability of forward, futures or option contracts for the underlying currency. When this is the case, the following techniques may be considered.

Leading and lagging

Leading and **lagging**, which constitute an operational hedging technique, involve an adjustment in the timing of the realisation of foreign currency payables or receivables. If the foreign currency were expected to appreciate, it would be a good idea to pay the foreign currency dues sooner rather than later: this is called leading. If, on the other hand, the foreign currency were expected to depreciate, it would be a good idea to meet the payables later rather than sooner: this is called lagging. Naturally, it works the other way round in the case of receivables.

Example

Consider an Australian company having US dollar payables worth USD500 000 due in six months time. Suppose now that this company believes that the US dollar will appreciate during the next six months, such that the AUD/USD exchange rate will reach a level of 2.00 (from the current level of 1.80), after which it will depreciate to a level of 1.60 three months later. If the company pays on time, the Australian dollar value of the payables will be AUD1 000 000. With this kind of forecast the Australian company would consider lagging. To do that, it should negotiate an agreement whereby the payables are settled three months after the original date. If this is the case and the forecast turns out to be correct, the Australian dollar value of the payables would be AUD800 000. Even with a penalty or interest charges, the Australian company will be better off by lagging.

Cross hedging

Cross hedging is used when it is not possible to hedge a foreign currency exposure because of the unavailability of hedging instruments (such as forward contracts and options) on this currency. In this case we look for another foreign currency whose exchange rate against the domestic currency is highly correlated with that of the currency to be hedged and then take a forward, futures or an option position on this currency. It is important to bear in mind that strong correlation between the underlying exchange rates is essential for the effectiveness of cross hedging.

Example

An Australian company has payables in Swedish krona worth SEK200 000 due in three months. It is believed that the Swedish currency will appreciate in the coming three months as the exchange rate (AUD/SEK) rises from 0.18 to 0.20. The company wishes to hedge the position but there is a problem: no forward, futures or option contracts are offered on this exchange rate.

One solution to this problem is to resort to cross hedging, given that the exchange rates of the Swedish currency and the euro are highly correlated. The current exchange rate between the Australian dollar and the euro is (AUD/EUR) 1.70. If the Swedish krona appreciates against the Australian dollar, the euro will appreciate by approximately the same percentage and the exchange rate would rise to 1.89. This will keep the cross SEK/EUR rate constant at 9.45.

To hedge the position, the Australian company buys the euro forward. The amount bought should be equivalent to SEK200 000 valued at the cross rate. Hence, the amount bought is

$$\frac{200\ 000}{9.45} = \text{EUR}21\ 164$$

The Australian dollar value of this amount at the forward rate of 1.75 is

$$21\ 164 \times 1.75 = \text{AUD}37\ 037$$

In three months time, the euro amount is converted into Swedish krona to obtain approximately SEK200 000. The Australian dollar value of the payables under the no-hedge decision is

$$200\ 000 \times 0.20 = \text{AUD}40\ 000$$

Another approach to cross hedging does not involve the forward market. In this case a long (short) position on a foreign currency can be hedged by taking a spot short (long) position on another currency. If $S(x/y)$ and $S(x/z)$ are highly correlated, then a firm with a domestic currency x can hedge payables in y by buying currency z. If y appreciates against x, then z will also appreciate, in which case the loss incurred on the short position in y will be offset by the profit on the long position in z. Referring to the previous example, the Australian company can hedge its short position in the Swedish currency by buying the euro spot.

Currency diversification

From an Australian perspective, the depreciation and appreciation of foreign currencies against the Australian dollar is not as harmful if a large number of currencies are involved, provided that the exchange rates of these currencies against the Australian dollar are not highly correlated. For example, the Australian dollar value of foreign currency payables rises when the foreign currencies appreciate against the Australian dollar. If the exchange rates are not highly and positively correlated, then the adverse effect is smaller, because some of these currencies will appreciate only slightly, while others may even depreciate.

Exposure netting

A natural hedge would arise when the firm has both payables and receivables in the same currency, in which case only the net exposure should be covered. **Exposure netting** may involve the same currency or currencies with highly correlated exchange rates. Consider the case of the same currency first by assuming that a firm has both payables and receivables in currency y. If the positions are of equal sizes, then the net position will be zero and there is no need to do anything about it because a natural perfect hedge is in place. If the positions are of different sizes then only the difference should be hedged. For example, if payables are K_1 and receivables are K_2, such that $K_1 > K_2$, then a long forward position of $K_1 - K_2$ should be taken on currency y.

Consider now a position of payables in currency y and receivables in currency z, such that $S(x/y)$ and $S(x/z)$ are highly, but not perfectly, correlated. Profit on one position will be partially offset by loss on the other. Only the residual risk that cannot be eliminated by combining the two positions should be hedged via a forward or futures contract.

Example

An Australian company has payables and receivables of SEK200 000 and EUR30 000, respectively. At the current exchange rate of 9.45 (SEK/EUR) the value of the payables is EUR21 164. Thus, the difference between the two positions is

$$30\,000 - 21\,164 = 8836$$

The company, therefore, can hedge its total position by selling EUR8836 forward at 1.71.

At the current exchange rates of 0.18 (AUD/SEK) and 1.70 (AUD/EUR) the Australian dollar value of the net position (receivables less payables) is

$$30\,000 \times 1.70 - 200\,000 \times 0.18 = +15\,000$$

Let us now calculate the net position when: (i) the Australian dollar depreciates to 0.20 and 1.89; and (ii) the Australian dollar appreciates to 0.171 and 1.615. The calculations are shown in the following table. As we can see, there is little change in the Australian dollar value of the net position, irrespective of what happens to the exchange rates.

	AUD appreciation	AUD depreciation
SEK200 000 (spot)	−40 000	−34 200
EUR21 164 (spot)	+40 000	+34 180
EUR8836 (forward)	+15 110	+15 110
Net	+15 110	+15 090

Price variation and currency of invoicing

Price variation and **currency of invoicing** are techniques that are particularly useful for firms engaged in international trade, say exporting final products and importing raw materials. Price variation is a technique that involves changing prices to contain the effect of unfavourable exchange rate movements. Australian trade transactions are invoiced in either US dollars or Australian dollars. Figures provided by the Australian Bureau of Statistics show that 70 per cent of exports and 50 per cent of imports are invoiced in US dollars. The Australian dollar is the currency of invoicing for 28 per cent of exports and 20 per cent of imports.

Remember that the domestic currency price, which the exporter receives, is the product of the foreign currency price and the exchange rate (that is, $P = SP^{*}$). When the exchange rate falls (the foreign currency depreciates), the domestic currency price received by the exporter declines. To eliminate this effect and maintain the level of the domestic currency price, the foreign currency price is raised. For example, the domestic currency price received by an Australian exporter can be maintained at AUD100 for various levels of the AUD/USD exchange rate by raising the US dollar price to offset the depreciation of the US dollar, as shown in the table below.

Two problems are associated with this technique of hedging. First, it may not be possible to implement it if the foreign currency price is fixed by a contract. Second, the rise in the foreign currency price may reduce demand and hence revenue. This policy will be more successful if foreign demand is inelastic.

S	P(AUD)	P^*(USD)
1.95	100	51.28
1.90	100	52.63
1.85	100	54.05
1.80	100	55.56
1.75	100	57.14
1.70	100	58.82
1.65	100	60.61
1.60	100	62.50

The price may be set completely in domestic currency terms. In this case, the domestic currency price is fixed but the foreign currency price changes with the exchange rate, rising as the exchange rate falls. From the perspective of the exporting firm, however, this method eliminates foreign currency exposure. This means that the risk is passed on entirely to the foreign importer.

Risk-sharing arrangements

An alternative in which both the exporter and the importer bear the risk is **risk sharing**, whereby only part of the shipment is invoiced in domestic currency terms. Risk sharing may be implemented by using a customised hedge contract embedded in the underlying trade contract. The hedge agreement typically takes the form of a price adjustment clause whereby a base price is adjusted to reflect certain exchange rate changes. Formally, risk sharing works as follows. Given the foreign currency value of the contract, the domestic currency value is obtained by using a range of exchange rates. First, a base rate is set, say $\overline{S}$. Then a neutral zone is set around this rate, say between a minimum of $\overline{S}(1-\theta)$ and a maximum of $\overline{S}(1+\theta)$, where $0 < \theta < 1$.

Assume that K is the foreign currency value of the payables due from an importer to an exporter, whose base currencies are the foreign currency and the domestic currency, respectively. Remember that payables from the perspective of the importer are receivables from the perspective of the exporter. Within the neutral zone, the payables are converted at $\overline{S}$, which means that the domestic currency value of the payables is $K\overline{S}$. Formally, if $\overline{S}(1-\theta) < S_1 < \overline{S}(1+\theta)$, then $V = K\overline{S}$. If the exchange rate falls below the lower limit of the neutral zone such that $S_1 < \overline{S}(1-\theta)$, then the payables are converted at a rate that is equal to the base rate less half the difference between the lower limit and the actual exchange rate. This gives

$$V = K\left[\overline{S} - \frac{\overline{S}(1-\theta) - S_1}{2}\right] \tag{14.3}$$

which can be simplified to produce

$$V = K\left[\frac{\overline{S}(1+\theta) + S_1}{2}\right] > KS_1 \tag{14.4}$$

This means that the domestic currency value of the payables is greater than it would be if there were no hedge. The benefit of foreign currency depreciation is shared between the importer and the exporter in the sense that the importer does not enjoy the full extent of the depreciation, whereas the exporter does not suffer to the full extent. The benefit accruing to the exporter, as compared with the no-hedge decision, is given by

$$V - KS_1 > 0 \text{ for } S_1 < \bar{S}(1+\theta) \tag{14.5}$$

On the other hand, if the exchange rate rises above the upper limit of the neutral zone, such that $S_1 > \bar{S}(1+\theta)$, then the payables are converted at a rate that is equal to the base rate and half the difference between the actual exchange rate and the upper limit of the neutral zone. This gives

$$V = K\left[\bar{S} + \frac{S_1 - \bar{S}(1+\theta)}{2}\right] \tag{14.6}$$

which can be simplified to produce

$$V = K\left[\frac{\bar{S}(1-\theta) + S_1}{2}\right] < KS_1 \tag{14.7}$$

This means that the domestic currency value of the payables is lower than it would be if there were no hedge. The result of foreign currency appreciation is shared between the importer and the exporter, in the sense that the importer pays less than under the no-hedge decision, whereas the exporter receives less than otherwise. The benefit accruing to the importer, as compared with the no-hedge decision, is given by

$$V - KS_1 < 0 \text{ for } S_1 > \bar{S}(1-\theta) \tag{14.8}$$

Example

Consider an Australian exporter to Sweden having receivables (payables from the perspective of the Swedish importer) worth SEK200 000. Let $\bar{S} = 0.20$ and $\theta = 0.10$, which means that the neutral zone is 0.18–0.22. Thus:

- If S_1 falls between 0.18 and 0.22, the receivables are converted at $\bar{S} = 0.20$.
- If S_1 falls below 0.18, the receivables are converted at the exchange rate given by Equations (14.3) and (14.4).
- If S_1 goes above 0.22, the receivables are converted at the exchange rate given by Equations (14.5) and (14.6).

The following table shows the Australian dollar value of the receivables at various values of S_1 under a risk-sharing arrangement and in the absence of such an arrangement (the hedge and no-hedge decisions, respectively). The Australian dollar value of the receivables with and without a risk-sharing arrangement is also shown in Figure 14.19. As we can see, the Australian dollar value of the receivables moves with a narrower range under a risk-sharing arrangement than otherwise.

S_1	*V* (risk sharing)	*V* (no risk sharing)	Benefit to exporter	Benefit to importer
0.12	34 000	24 000	10 000	−10 000
0.14	36 000	28 000	8 000	−8 000
0.16	38 000	32 000	6 000	−6 000
0.18	40 000	36 000	4 000	−4 000
0.20	40 000	40 000	0	0
0.22	40 000	44 000	−4 000	4 000
0.24	42 000	48 000	−6 000	6 000
0.26	44 000	52 000	−8 000	8 000
0.28	46 000	56 000	−10 000	10 000

Figure 14.19 Australian dollar value of receivables with and without a risk-sharing arrangement

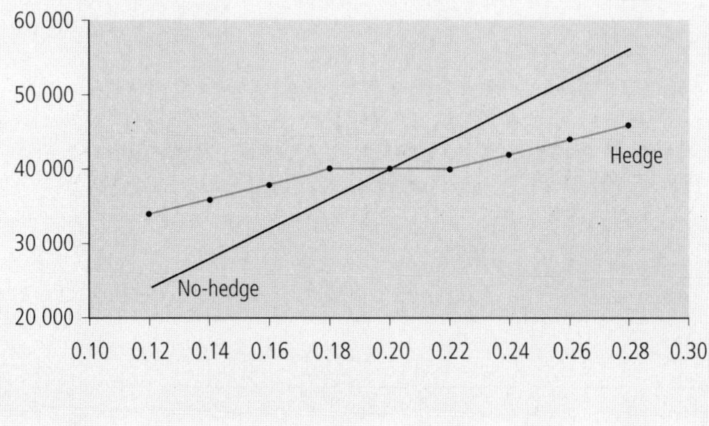

Currency collars

We will now illustrate the use of **currency collars** (also called **range forward**) in hedging receivables (from the perspective of the exporter). A currency collar is used to set a minimum value for the domestic currency receivables at the expense of setting a maximum value. Thus, it involves a trade-off between potential loss and potential gain. A currency collar contains a certain range for the exchange rate extending between a lower limit, S_L, and an upper limit, S_U. The following are the possibilities:

- If the exchange rate falls below the lower limit, the rate used to convert receivables into the domestic currency is the lower limit itself and this is how the minimum value is obtained. Hence, $V = KS_L$.
- If the exchange rate falls within the range, the conversion rate is the current exchange rate, S_1, which means that the domestic currency value of the receivables rises with the exchange rate within this range. Hence, $V = KS_1$.
- If the exchange rate rises above the upper limit, the conversion rate is the upper limit and this is how the maximum value is obtained. In this case, $V = KS_U$.

Example

Consider the previous example of the Australian exporter to Sweden. Let $S_L = 0.16$ and $S_U = 0.24$. The following table shows the Australian dollar value of the receivables at various values of S_1, with and without a currency collar. Figure 14.20 shows the profile of the domestic currency value of the receivables graphically.

S_1	*V* (currency collar)	*V* (no currency collar)	Benefit to exporter	Benefit to importer
0.12	32 000	24 000	8 000	–8 000
0.14	32 000	28 000	4 000	–4 000
0.16	32 000	32 000	0	0
0.18	36 000	36 000	0	0
0.20	40 000	40 000	0	0
0.22	44 000	44 000	0	0
0.24	48 000	48 000	0	0
0.26	48 000	52 000	–4 000	4 000
0.28	48 000	56 000	–8 000	8 000

Figure 14.20 Australian dollar value of receivables with and without a currency collar

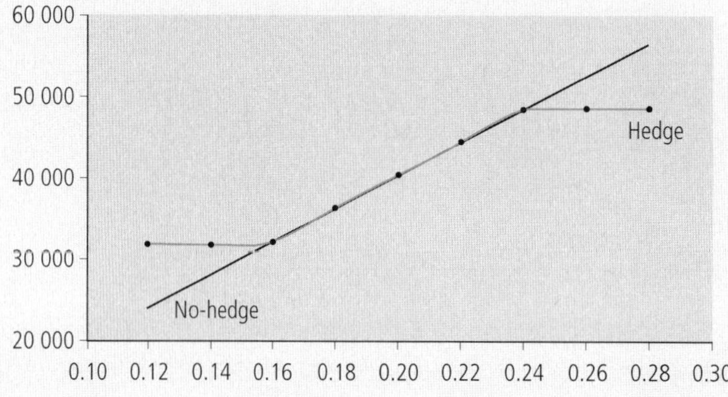

IN PRACTICE

How does Daimler-Benz hedge its exposure to foreign exchange risk?

The 1997 *Annual Report* of Daimler-Benz, the maker of the world-famous Mercedes cars, stated the following:

'The Daimler-Benz group is exposed to market risks from changes in interest rates and foreign currency exchange rates which may adversely affect its results of operations and financial condition. The Group seeks to minimise the risks from these interest rate and foreign currency exchange rate fluctuations through its regular operating and financing activities and, when deemed appropriate, thorough the use of derivative financial instruments.'

The exposure of Daimler-Benz to foreign exchange risk arises because the company generates a substantial portion of its sales revenue in foreign currencies, whereas a major share of the corresponding cost of production is incurred in the domestic currency (the euro at present and the German mark previously). In the passenger car division, sales are denominated in the currencies of

Managing economic exposure

Economic exposure arises because revenues and costs vary with changes in the real exchange rate. Assuming that demand is elastic, real appreciation of a foreign currency will result in the following:

- an increase in domestic sales and, therefore, domestic sales revenue
- an increase in foreign sales revenue
- an increase in the cost of imported raw materials as well as financial costs (for example, the cost of borrowing)

Whether the net result is positive or negative (that is, whether the foreign currency appreciation leads to an increase or a decrease in net operating income) depends on whether revenues or costs are more sensitive to exchange rate changes. If revenues are more sensitive, then real foreign currency appreciation over time will bring about a favourable result because revenues will rise faster than expenses and hence net income will rise over time, as shown in Figure 14.21(a). If, on the other hand, costs are more sensitive, then they will rise faster than revenues and the result will be a declining net income over time, as shown in Figure 14.21(b). Note, however, that these scenarios are conditional upon the crucial assumption that demand and supply are elastic. If the demand for competing foreign products in the domestic market is inelastic, then domestic sales will not rise. If also the demand for domestic goods in the foreign market is inelastic, then foreign demand will not rise and the domestic currency value of foreign sales revenue may actually decline.

We now consider the effect of real depreciation of the foreign currency. Again, assuming elastic demand, this will result in the following:

- a decrease in domestic sales and, therefore, domestic sales revenue
- a decrease in foreign sales revenue
- a decrease in the cost of imported raw materials and financial costs

Whether the net result is positive or negative (that is, leading to an increase or a decrease in net operating income) depends on whether revenues or costs are more sensitive to exchange rate changes. If revenues are more sensitive, then real foreign currency depreciation

the countries in which cars are sold, but manufacturing costs are denominated mainly in the euro, since manufacturing is concentrated in Germany. Likewise, aerospace revenue resulting from the sale of aircraft, engines and parts is denominated in US dollars, but the products are manufactured exclusively in Germany. An additional element associated with the operations of the aerospace division is that the contracts for its products, particularly aircraft, are generally entered into well in advance of the production and delivery of the products. As a result, Daimler-Benz Aerospace is exposed to fluctuations in exchange rates between the date of the contractual order and the date of delivery and payment, which may be a very long period of time.

To provide a natural hedge, the company attempts to increase cash outflows in the same currencies in which it has a net excess inflow. This is accomplished mainly through increased procurement in foreign currencies and by increasing production in those countries that are primary markets for its products. To mitigate further the impact of exchange rate fluctuations, Daimler-Benz assesses on a continual basis its remaining exposure and hedges a portion of the exposure by using derivatives, mainly forward contracts and currency options.

will bring about an unfavourable result because revenues will fall faster than costs and hence net income will decline over time, as shown in Figure 14.22(a). If, on the other hand, costs are more sensitive, then they will fall faster than revenues over time and the result will be a rising net income over time, as shown in Figure 14.22(b).

Figure 14.21 The effect of real foreign currency appreciation

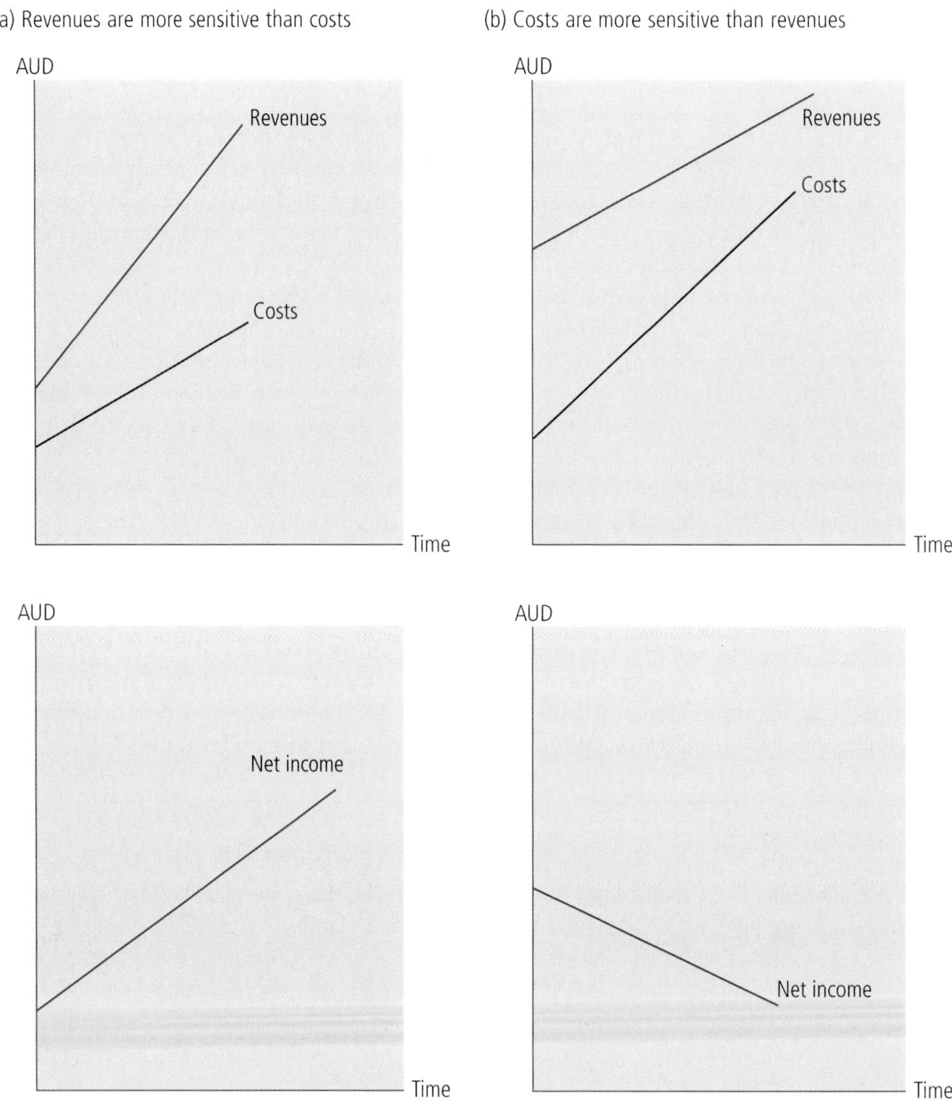

Hedging economic exposure invariably involves the restructuring of operations. Let us examine the case described by Figure 14.21(b), which shows the risk of declining net income resulting from real foreign currency appreciation. Economic exposure could be reduced by increasing the sensitivity of revenues and reducing the sensitivity of costs to real exchange rate movements. The first task requires making demand more elastic, so that any small change in the relative prices of foreign and domestic goods resulting from foreign currency appreciation could bring about a greater increase in both domestic and foreign demand for

Figure 14.22 The effect of real foreign currency depreciation

(a) Revenues are more sensitive than costs (b) Costs are more sensitive than revenues

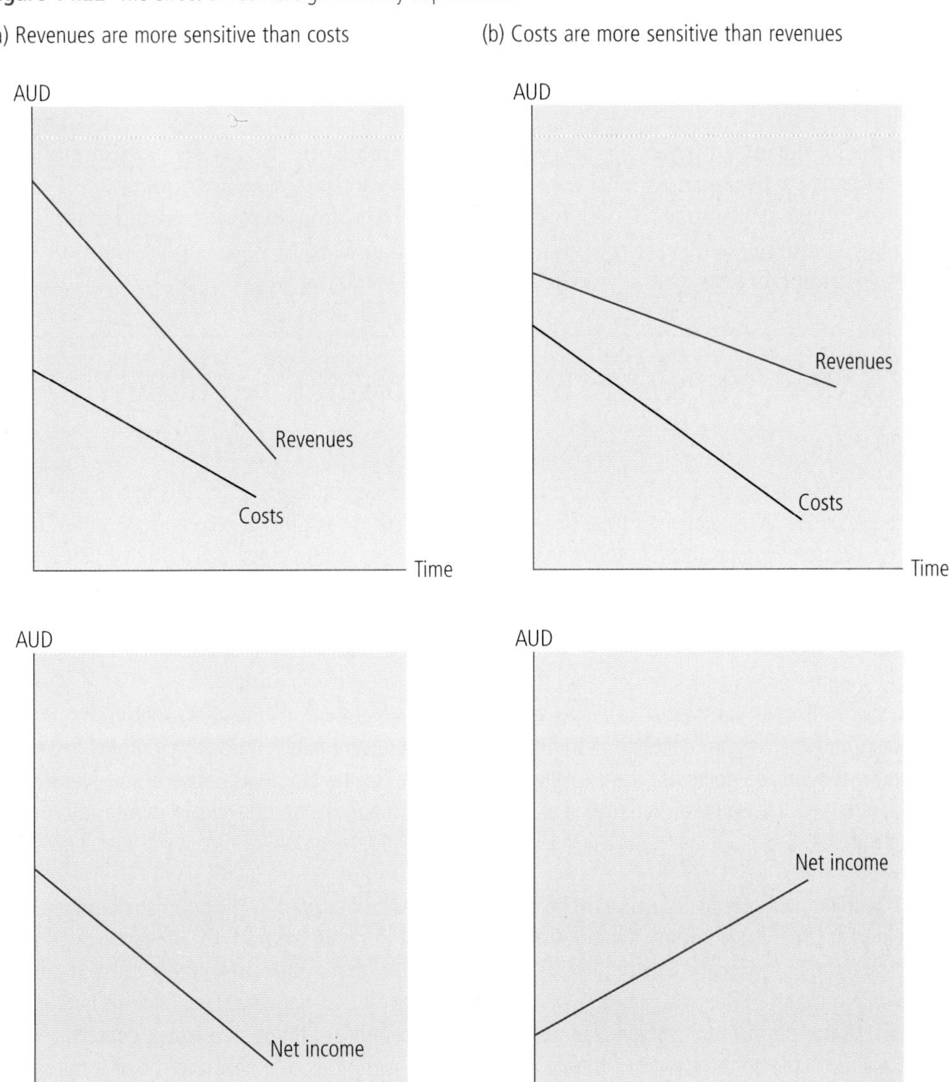

the firm's products. This can be accomplished, for example, by increasing expenditure on advertising. The second task of reducing the sensitivity of costs can be accomplished by changing the source of imported raw materials, preferably to a domestic source, or even negotiating an agreement whereby the invoices are billed in domestic currency terms. If these tasks are executed successfully, the behaviour of net income will change from that described by Figure 14.21(b) to that described by Figure 14.21(a).

Restructuring in order to reduce economic exposure in general involves more than is described above. Depending on the conditions, the following measures may be considered:

- increasing or reducing sales in new or existing foreign markets
- increasing or reducing dependence on foreign suppliers of raw materials and other intermediate products

- establishing or eliminating production facilities in foreign countries
- increasing or reducing the level of foreign currency debt.

The case of Laker Airways, which was described in Chapter 1, is a classic example of a company that collapsed because of both transaction exposure and economic exposure. When the pound depreciated against the dollar in early 1982, the economic exposure adversely affected the company's operations as demand for transatlantic flights by British holiday-makers fell, adversely affecting sales revenues. The transaction exposure took its toll when Laker's US dollar-denominated debt became due. Economic exposure could have been reduced by reducing dollar-denominated expenses and increasing dollar-denominated revenues. Having failed to do this, the company went bankrupt.

IN PRACTICE

How does Microsoft hedge its foreign exchange exposure?

Microsoft uses the currency of invoicing to hedge its foreign exchange exposure. In some regions it uses the US dollar (the company's base currency) to bill its customers. This approach is used in Latin America, Eastern Europe and Southeast Asia. The problem with this approach is that Microsoft becomes exposed to economic risk if the domestic currencies in these areas depreciate against the US dollar. In other parts of the world, Microsoft conducts its business in the local currency. Microsoft's 2000 *Annual Report* states that 'finished goods sales to international customers in Europe, Japan, Canada and Australia are primarily billed in local currencies'.

Microsoft also has substantial expenses in Europe associated with its manufacturing, sales and services. The expenses are denominated in local currencies. Every month Microsoft's profits/losses are converted into US dollars at the average exchange rate for the month. Because of this feature, what matters is the average exchange rate for the month and not the end of the month rate. To hedge this risk, Microsoft makes an extensive use of average rate options, which were described in Chapter 7.

The problem with the policy of using the US dollar as the currency of invoicing in some parts of the world is that a significant depreciation of the local currency against the dollar implies a significant rise in the local currency price of the products, which may adversely affect demand and revenue, particularly if demand is elastic. To soften the impact of a strong US dollar, Microsoft enters a long forward contract to buy the dollar against the local currency. If the local currency depreciates, profit will be made on the forward contract and some of this profit is channelled to the distributors to relieve the pressure on their profit margins. In 1999, Microsoft used this approach to mitigate the impact of the depreciation of the Brazilian real.

14.8 Managing translation exposure

Why do firms worry about translation exposure, given that it does not affect the economic value of the firm? Translation exposure is a source of concern because different translation methods have, as we have seen, different impacts on the reported earnings per share and other vital indicators. It is important, for the prosperity of the firm, how the investment community interprets the published financial statements. The following techniques are used to hedge translation exposure.

Fund adjustment

Fund adjustment involves altering either the amounts and/or the currencies of the planned cash flows of the firm or its subsidiaries to reduce exposure to the currency of the subsidiary. If the currency of the subsidiary is expected to depreciate, direct fund adjustment methods include: (i) pricing exports in hard currencies and imports in the domestic currency; (ii) investing in hard currency securities; and (iii) replacing hard currency borrowings with local currency loans. The indirect methods include: (i) adjusting transfer prices (see Chapter 18); (ii) speeding up the payment of dividends, fees and royalties; and (iii) adjusting the leads and lags of the intersubsidiary accounts.

Forward contracts

Translation exposure can be hedged via forward contracts. If the base currency of a foreign subsidiary is expected to depreciate against the parent firm's base currency, then translation exposure exits. The parent firm may hedge this exposure by selling forward an amount of the foreign currency that is equal to the subsidiary's expected net income. If the expectation materialises and the foreign currency depreciates, the company will make profit on the short forward position that will compensate for the translation loss. The success or otherwise of this operation depends on the accuracy of forecasting the subsidiary's net income. A major problem with this operation is that the forward position results in increasing transaction exposure. If the foreign currency appreciates, the company will be compensated for an actual, realised loss by a translation gain that has no corresponding cash flows.

Example

The French subsidiary of an Australian company is forecasting net income of EUR10 000 000. The plan is to reinvest the entire amount in France without remitting any portion of it to the parent company in Australia. Since there is no currency conversion, transaction exposure is not present.

The current exchange rate (AUD/EUR) is 1.75. It is expected that the euro will depreciate throughout the year, such that the average value of the exchange rate for the year will be 1.70. Let us assume that in the consolidation of the financial statements, the average exchange rate for the year is used to translate net income. The depreciation of the euro will undoubtedly bring about a translation loss, which would be

$$10\,000\,000 \times (1.75 - 1.70) = \text{AUD}500\,000$$

The parent company may consider a forward hedge of the translation exposure. This involves selling EUR10 000 000 forward at the current one-year forward exchange rate, say 1.76. Suppose now that by the end of the year, the exchange rate falls to 1.65. The parent company would buy the euro spot and sell it at the forward rate agreed upon earlier. The gain from this operation would be

$$10\,000\,000 \times (1.76 - 1.65) = \text{AUD}1\,100\,000$$

Hence, the profit made on the hedge more than offsets the translation loss. It is obvious, however, that hedging the translation exposure in this way creates transaction exposure.

Exposure netting and balance sheet hedging

Exposure netting can be used by multinational firms with offsetting positions in more than one foreign currency. A balance sheet hedge eliminates the mismatch between assets and liabilities in the same currency. If these assets and liabilities are equal, then a change in the exchange rate will not matter.

RESEARCH FINDINGS

What do firms do in practice?

Three questions often arise that are related to the behaviour of firms with respect to hedging:

1. Do firms hedge?
2. If they do, which exposure do they hedge?
3. If they do, what hedging instruments and techniques do they use?

These questions can only be answered by surveying the actual practices of firms with respect to hedging. In a survey, Jesswein, Kwok and Folks documented the extent of knowledge and use of foreign exchange risk-management products by 500 US firms.[1] The products considered were forward contracts, currency swaps, currency futures, straight options, futures options, synthetic forward contracts, synthetic options and other more sophisticated instruments such as compound options and lockback options. The results of the survey showed that 93 per cent of the respondents used forward contracts followed by swaps and options. Only 5.1 per cent and 3.8 per cent used lookback options and compound options, respectively.

Joseph obtained a measure of the degree of utilisation of hedging techniques on the basis of a survey of 109 companies from the top 300 category of *The Times 1000*.[2] The following results were obtained:

- British firms utilise a narrow set of techniques to hedge exposure.
- They place much more emphasis on currency derivatives (**external hedging**) than on **internal hedging** techniques (that is, operational hedging).
- Firms place more emphasis on transaction exposure and economic exposure and much less on translation exposure.
- There is strong cross-sectional variation in the characteristics of firms that hedge.

Marshall surveyed the foreign exchange risk practices of 179 large British, US and Asia–Pacific multinational firms.[3] The following results were obtained:

- There are some notable variations between British and US firms and, in particular, respondents from Asia–Pacific multinational firms. Differences pertain to the importance and objectives of foreign exchange risk, the emphasis on translation and economic exposure, the use of internal/external hedging techniques and policies to manage economic exposure.
- The percentage of overseas business is not a significant factor, but size and the industry sector are significant in determining the importance of foreign exchange risk, the emphasis on economic and translation exposure and the methods used for hedging.
- The main objectives of managing foreign exchange risk are minimising fluctuations in earnings and seeking certainty of cash flows.
- Multinational firms place more emphasis on transaction exposure and less emphasis on translation exposure, particularly in the United States.
- For translation exposure, the main internal method used is balance sheet hedging, whereas matching and netting are the predominant internal methods for managing transaction exposure.

- The most popular external method (that is, technique of financial hedging) for managing translation and transaction exposure is the forward contract, although swaps are popular with British firms.
- The majority of multinational firms do not prefer exchange-traded instruments, such as currency futures and options, to currency forward contracts.
- The industry sector is an important determinant of the use of derivatives.
- Reasons for not managing economic exposure include the difficulty of quantifying the exposure and the lack of effective tools to deal with the complexity of this exposure.
- Pricing strategies and the currency of invoicing are the most widely used methods for dealing with economic exposure.

Other studies have found a variety of results. Nance, Smith and Smithson[4] and Dolde[5] used a questionnaire survey, which required respondents to indicate whether or not they used one or more of four currency derivatives: forward contracts, futures, swaps and options. In contrast, Berkman and Bradbury classified forms according to the hedging information contained in firms' audited financial reports.[6] Dolde found that firms may or may not hedge or partially hedge, depending on their perception about the behaviour of exchange rates and/or their confidence in handling derivatives.

It has been found that firms use a wide variety of techniques to hedge exposure to foreign exchange risk. And although newer financial innovations can reduce the demand for traditional types of hedging techniques, empirical evidence shows that firms are not that receptive to complex types of derivatives, as shown by Tufano.[7] This is because firms are concerned about the banks' commitment to those products and their ability to provide real solutions to exposure problems.

Some researchers have found that managers tend to adjust their hedging decisions to reflect their expectations of changes in financial prices. Thus, if the forward rate is a biased predictor of the spot rate, managers can alter their hedging strategies to accommodate this effect. Berg and Moore[8] and Schooley and White[9] argued that in this case a partial, no-hedge or fully hedged strategy can be optimal for both transaction and economic exposure. Khoury and Chan[10] and Joseph and Hewins[11] argued that the use of hedging techniques might reflect the types of exposure (in general, caring more about transaction exposure than about economic or translation exposure).

Giddy and Dufey argued that options are not ideal hedging instruments because the gains/losses arising from their use are not linearly related to changes in exchange rates.[12] But Ware and Winter argued that forward contracts can only hedge economic exposure in an optimal manner if managerial decisions regarding inputs and outputs are fixed, otherwise options are more appropriate.[13] Evidence provided by De Iorio and Faff, based on an analysis of the foreign exchange exposure of the Australian equity market, showed some evidence for asymmetry.[14] De Iorio and Faff attributed asymmetry to the use of currency options, which limit the downside exposure while permitting the potential upside gains.

Another issue that needs to be brought up here is the extent to which firms use operational as opposed to financial hedging. There seems to be a mixture of views on this issue. In its 1995 *Annual Report*, Schering-Plough argued in support of the exclusive use of operational hedging by saying that 'to date, management has not deemed it cost-effective to engage in a formula-based program of hedging the profitability of these operations using derivative financial instruments. Some of the reasons for this conclusion are: the company operates in a large number of foreign countries; the currencies of these countries generally do not move in the same direction at the same time'. On the other hand, it is well known that many corporations with large worldwide networks, such as IBM and Coca-Cola, make extensive use of derivative financial instruments.

Continued...

[1] K. Jesswein, C. Kwok and W. Folks, 'Corporate Use of Innovative Foreign Exchange Risk Management Products', *Columbia Journal of World Business*, Fall 1995.

[2] N. L. Joseph, 'The Choice of Hedging Techniques and the Characteristics of UK Industrial Firms', *Journal of Multinational Financial Management*, 10, 2000, pp. 161–84.

[3] A. P. Marshall, 'Foreign Exchange Risk Management in UK, USA and Asia Pacific Multinational Companies', *Journal of Multinational Financial Management*, 10, 2000, pp. 185–211.

[4] D. Nance, C. Smith and C. Smithson, 'On the Determinants of Corporate Hedging', *Journal of Finance*, 48, 1993, pp. 267–84.

[5] W. W. Dolde, 'The Trajectory of Corporate Financial Risk Management', *Continental Bank Journal of Applied Corporate Finance*, 6, 1993, pp. 33–41.

[6] H. Berkman and M. Bradbury, 'Empirical Evidence on the Corporate Use of Derivatives', *Financial Management*, 25, 1996, pp. 5–13.

[7] P. Tufano, 'Securities Innovation: A Historical and Functional Perspective', *Bank of America Journal of Applied Corporate Finance*, 7, 1995, pp. 90–104.

[8] M. Berg and G. Moore, 'Foreign Exchange Strategies: Spot, Forward and Options', *Journal of Business Finance and Accounting*, 18, 1991, pp. 449–57.

[9] D. Schooley and H. White, 'Strategies for Hedging Translation Exposure to Exchange Rate Changes: Theory and Empirical Evidence', *Journal of Multinational Financial Management*, 5, 1995, pp. 57–72.

[10] S. Khoury and K. Chan, 'Hedging Foreign Exchange Risk: Selecting an Optimal Tool', *Midland Corporate Finance Journal*, 5, 1988, pp. 40–52.

[11] N. L. Joseph and R. Hewins, 'Portfolio Models for Foreign Exchange Exposure', *Omega: International Journal of Management Science*, 19, 1991, pp. 247–58.

[12] I. Giddy and G. Dufey, 'Uses and Abuses of Currency Options', *Bank of America Journal of Applied Corporate Finance*, 8, 1995, pp. 49–57.

[13] R. Ware and R. Winter, 'Forward Markets, Currency Options and the Hedging of Foreign Exchange Risk', *Journal of International Economics*, 25, 1988, pp. 291–302.

[14] A. De Iorio and R. Faff, 'An Analysis of Asymmetry in Foreign Exchange Exposure of the Australian Equities Market', *Journal of Multinational Financial Management*, 10, 2000, pp. 133–60.

Summary

- The decision to hedge or not to hedge a foreign currency position is basically a speculative decision, as it depends on the spot rate expected to prevail on the maturity date of the position.
- There are at least three arguments why there is no need to worry about foreign exchange risk: (i) if international parity conditions hold, then foreign exchange risk will not arise; (ii) foreign exchange risk can be controlled by accurate forecasting of exchange rates; and (iii) shareholders are naturally hedged through diversification. It can be demonstrated that all of these arguments are not valid.
- Transaction exposure can be managed by a forward hedge, a futures hedge, a money market hedge and an option hedge.
- Payables can be hedged by: (i) buying the foreign currency forward; (ii) buying futures contracts on the foreign currency; (iii) borrowing the domestic currency and converting the amount into the foreign currency; and (iv) buying a call option.
- Receivables can be hedged by: (i) selling the foreign currency forward; (ii) selling futures contracts on the foreign currency; (iii) borrowing the foreign currency and converting the amount into the domestic currency; and (iv) buying a put option.

- Hedging becomes a more expensive operation when bid-offer spreads in interest and exchange rates are allowed for.
- The hedging instrument used is the one that produces the smallest domestic currency value of the payables and the largest domestic currency value of the receivables.
- Options are more appropriate than futures and forwards for hedging a contingent exposure.
- Long-term transaction exposure can be hedged by using: (i) long-term forward contracts; (ii) currency swaps; and (iii) parallel loans.
- Other techniques of hedging include: (i) leading and lagging; (ii) cross hedging; (iii) currency diversification; (iv) price variation and currency of invoicing; (v) exposure netting; (vi) risk sharing; and (vii) currency collars.
- Economic exposure arises because revenues and costs vary with changes in real exchange rates. Real appreciation of the foreign currency leads to: (i) an increase in domestic sales revenue; (ii) an increase in foreign sales revenue; and (iii) an increase in the cost of imported raw materials. Real depreciation of the foreign currency leads to: (i) a decrease in domestic sales revenue; (ii) a decrease in foreign sales revenue; and (iii) a decrease in the cost of imported raw materials.
- Hedging economic exposure invariably entails restructuring of operations. Restructuring may involve the following measures: (i) increasing or reducing sales in new or existing foreign markets; (ii) increasing or reducing dependence on foreign suppliers of raw materials; (iii) establishing or eliminating production facilities in foreign countries; and (iv) increasing or reducing foreign currency debt.
- Translation exposure is a source of concern, although it does not involve an actual conversion of currencies, because of the bad impression a translation loss may give to the investment community.
- Translation exposure can be hedged by using fund adjustment, forward contracts, exposure netting and balance sheet hedging. Otherwise, the exposure can be left unhedged while clarifying how the consolidated financial statements are affected by currency movements.

Key terms

contingent exposure 406
cross hedging 412
currency collars 417
currency of invoicing 414
delta hedging 409
exposure netting 413
external hedging 424
financial hedging 390
fund adjustment 423
hedge ratio 396
hedging 386
implicit forward rate 397
internal hedging 424
lagging 411
leading 411
money market hedge 396
operational hedging 387
price variation 414
range forward 417
risk management 386
risk sharing 415
synthetic forward contract 397

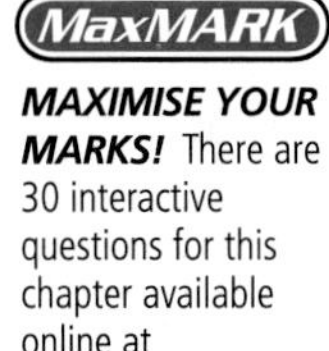

Review questions

1. Hedging is the covering of risk, whereas speculation is the deliberate assumption of risk. Why then is the decision to hedge or not to hedge regarded as a speculative decision?
2. What are the arguments for ignoring foreign exchange risk? Are they valid?
3. Why do deviations from unbiased efficiency, UIP and PPP imply the presence of risk?
4. Does hedging boost the value of the hedging firm?
5. What happens if bid-offer spreads are taken into account in the process of money market and forward hedging of payables and receivables?
6. If CIP holds, which of the following courses of action is preferable: (a) using a money market hedge; (b) using a forward hedge; or (c) remaining unhedged?
7. What are the differences between a forward hedge and a futures hedge?
8. Why is the domestic currency value of payables and receivables unknown with certainty if an option hedge is used? Why is option hedging used if, under forward and money market hedging, this value is known with certainty?
9. Why are options more appropriate than forwards and futures for hedging a contingent exposure?
10. In its issue of 29 January 2003, the *Australian Financial Review* reported an interview with Paul McNee, ANZ's chief foreign exchange dealer, who talked about hedging exposure to the risk of Australian dollar appreciation. In this interview, Mr McNee declared that 'the smarter corporates are using options'. He also said that 'options are a lot more flexible' and that 'it's better than locking in a rate where you can't take advantage of a fall'. Do you agree with these views? Why or why not?
11. What is the hedge ratio?
12. Why is it difficult to hedge payables and receivables with long maturities using forwards, futures and options? What can be done about this problem?
13. How can leading and lagging be used to hedge payables? Is the effect similar to that of a forward hedge?
14. Explain how price variation and currency of invoicing can be used to hedge transaction exposure.
15. Under what conditions is cross hedging resorted to?
16. Distinguish between risk sharing and currency collars as hedging techniques.
17. Show that a currency collar can be replicated by combining options.
18. Why does economic exposure arise?
19. What does managing economic exposure involve?
20. Translation exposure does not affect the value of the firm because it does not involve currency conversion of cash flows, anticipated or otherwise. Why, then, is translation exposure a source of concern?
21. How can translation exposure be hedged?
22. If a decision not to hedge translation exposure is taken, what can be done to alleviate the concern about it?
23. Do firms hedge exposure to foreign exchange risk in practice? If so, what instruments/techniques do they use?

Problems

1 An Australian company owes a Swiss exporter CHF250 000, due in six months. The following information is available:

Spot exchange rate (AUD/CHF)	1.15
Australian six-month interest rate	10.5% p.a.
Swiss six-month interest rate	6.5% p.a.

(a) Calculate the Australian dollar value of the payables under a money market hedge.
(b) Calculate the implicit forward rate.
(c) If the spot exchange rate in six months is expected to be 1.20, will the hedge be taken? What if it is 1.10?

2 A British importer of Australian crocodile meat owes the Australian exporting company a payment of GBP100 000, due in three months. The following information is available:

Spot exchange rate (AUD/GBP)	2.60
Australian three-month interest rate	8% p.a.
British three-month interest rate	10% p.a.

(a) Calculate the Australian dollar value of the receivables under a money market hedge.
(b) Calculate the implicit forward rate.
(c) If the spot exchange rate in three months is expected to be 2.65, will the hedge be taken? What if it is 2.55?

3 An Australian company owes a Swiss exporter CHF250 000, due in six months. The following information is available:

Spot exchange rate (AUD/CHF)	1.1475–1.1525
Australian six-month interest rate	10.25–10.75% p.a.
Swiss six-month interest rate	6.25–6.75% p.a.

(a) Calculate the Australian dollar value of the payables under a money market hedge.
(b) If the spot exchange rate in six months is expected to be 1.1975–1.2025, will the hedge decision be taken? What if it is 1.0975–1.1025?
(c) Compare the results with those obtained in Problem 1.

4 A British importer of Australian crocodile meat owes the Australian exporting company a payment of GBP 100 000, due in three months. The following information is available:

Spot exchange rate (AUD/GBP)	2.5975–2.6025
Australian three-month interest rate	7.75–8.25% p.a.
British three-month interest rate	9.75–10.25% p.a.

(a) Calculate the Australian dollar value of the receivables under a money market hedge.
(b) If the spot exchange rate in three months is expected to be 2.6475–2.6525, will the hedge decision be taken? What if it is 2.5475–2.5525?
(c) Compare the results with those obtained in Problem 2.

5 An Australian company owes a Swiss exporter CHF250 000, due in six months. The following information is available:

Spot exchange rate (AUD/CHF)	1.15
Six-month forward rate	1.17

(a) Calculate the Australian dollar value of the payables under a forward hedge.
(b) If the spot exchange rate in six months is expected to be 1.20, will the hedge be taken? What if it is 1.10?

6 A British importer of Australian crocodile meat owes the Australian exporting company a payment of GBP100 000, due in three months. The following information is available:

Spot exchange rate (AUD/GBP)	2.60
Three-month forward rate	2.62

(a) Calculate the Australian dollar value of the receivables under a forward hedge.
(b) If the spot exchange rate in three months is expected to be 2.65, will the hedge be taken? What if it is 2.55?

7 An Australian company owes a Swiss exporter CHF250 000, due in six months. The following information is available:

Spot exchange rate (AUD/CHF)	1.1475–1.1525
Six-month forward rate	1.1675–1.1725

(a) Calculate the Australian dollar value of the payables under a forward hedge.
(b) If the spot exchange rate in six months is expected to be 1.1975–1.2025, will the hedge be taken? What if it is 1.0975–1.1025?
(c) Compare the results with those obtained in Problem 5.

8 A British importer of Australian crocodile meat owes the Australian exporting company a payment of GBP100 000, due in three months. The following information is available:

Spot exchange rate (AUD/GBP)	2.5975–2.6025
Three-month forward rate	2.6175–2.6225

(a) Calculate the Australian dollar value of the receivables under a forward hedge.
(b) If the spot exchange rate in three months is expected to be 2.6475–2.6525, will the hedge be taken? What if it is 2.5475–2.5525?
(c) Compare the results with those obtained in Problem 6.

9 An Australian company importing French perfumes owes the French exporting company EUR250 000, due in three months. The following information is available:

Current spot exchange rate (AUD/EUR)	1.60
Expected spot exchange rate (AUD/EUR)	1.65 and 1.55 with probabilities of 0.4 and 0.6, respectively
Premium on EUR call option	AUD0.01
Exercise exchange rate	1.61
Time to expiry	3 months

Calculate the expected value of the payables in Australian dollar terms under an option hedge. Will the decision to hedge be taken?

10 A French importer of Australian kangaroo meat owes the Australian exporting company EUR150 000, due in three months. The following information is available:

Current spot exchange rate (AUD/EUR)	1.60
Expected spot exchange rate (AUD/EUR)	1.55 and 1.65 with probabilities of 0.4 and 0.6, respectively
Premium on EUR put option	AUD0.01
Exercise exchange rate	1.60
Time to expiry	3 months

Calculate the expected value of the receivables in Australian dollar terms under an option hedge. Will the decision to hedge be taken?

11 An Australian company has just sold a shipment of live sheep worth KWD100 000 to Kuwait, with the payment due in three months. The company wishes to hedge this exposure, since the Kuwaiti dinar is expected to depreciate against the Australian dollar in the next three months. Australian banks are unwilling to offer forward contracts on the Kuwaiti currency. However, Kuwaiti banks offer forward contracts to trade the currency against the US dollar. The following information is available:

Current spot rate (AUD/KWD)	5.46
Expected spot rate (AUD/KWD)	5.20
Current spot rate (KWD/USD)	0.340
Expected spot rate (KWD/USD)	0.324
Three-month forward rate (KWD/USD)	0.322
Current spot rate (AUD/USD)	1.8564
Expected spot rate (AUD/USD)	1.6848

(a) Explain how cross hedging can be implemented.

(b) Supposing that all expectations are fulfilled, calculate the Australian dollar value of the KWD receivables under the hedge and no-hedge decisions.

12 The following table shows quarterly data for two AUD exchange rates.

(a) Calculate the average Australian dollar value of 100 units of the other currency under the following situations:

- No hedge is taken.
- A risk-sharing arrangement is implemented, such that $\bar{S}$ is the average value of the exchange rate and $\theta = 0.05$
- A currency collar is implemented such that S_U and S_L are above and below the average values by 4.5 per cent.

(b) Comment on the results.

	AUD/USD	AUD/JPY	AUD/GBP	AUD/CAD
Mar 1998	1.5108	0.0113	2.5252	1.0643
Jun 1998	1.6145	0.0116	2.6926	1.1000
Sep 1998	1.6855	0.0123	2.8655	1.1003
Dec 1998	1.6332	0.0144	2.7103	1.0672
Mar 1999	1.5765	0.0133	2.5411	1.0449
Jun 1999	1.4981	0.0124	2.3629	1.0170
Sep 1999	1.5336	0.0144	2.5261	1.0447
Dec 1999	1.5244	0.0149	2.4623	1.0555
Mar 2000	1.6474	0.0160	2.6216	1.1365
Jun 2000	1.6755	0.0158	2.5421	1.1325
Sep 2000	1.8425	0.0170	2.7204	1.2259
Dec 2000	1.7900	0.0157	2.6781	1.1942
Mar 2001	2.0595	0.0163	2.9172	1.3066
Jun 2001	1.9579	0.0157	2.7728	1.2918
Sep 2001	2.0356	0.0170	3.0015	1.2890
Average	1.7057	0.0145	2.6626	1.1380

13 By using the data set in Problem 12, show what happens when exposure to any of the four foreign currencies (USD, JPY, GBP and CAD) can be hedged by taking an opposite spot position on any of the other currencies. Why is this hedging technique not as effective as forward and futures hedging?

14 An Australian company has three separate positions on the Indonesian rupiah: receivables (IDR750 million), payables (IDR960 million) and receivables (IDR870 million). The company wishes to hedge the three positions by buying and selling the rupiah at the current forward rate (IDR/AUD) of 5045–5145. There are also brokerage fees amounting to 1 per cent of the amount bought/sold. Calculate the net AUD position when the individual positions are hedged separately and when the net IDR amount only is hedged.

CHAPTER

International short-term financing and investment

Introduction

The management of working capital in an international environment characterised by integrated financial markets and high capital mobility has two objectives. The first objective is to achieve minimum borrowing costs, whereas the second objective is to allocate short-term investments and cash balances in such a way as to obtain the highest possible rate of return (subject to risk). International short-term financing therefore refers to the activity of borrowing funds for short periods (less than one year) from the international money markets using a variety of currencies for this purpose. International short-term investment is the activity of investing surplus short-term funds. In both cases, there is a paramount role for changes in exchange rates.

Objectives

The objectives of this chapter are:

- To explain why firms may indulge in foreign currency financing and investment.
- To explain how to calculate the effective financing rate of, and the effective rate of return on, foreign currency financing and investment.
- To explain how the choice is made between domestic currency and foreign currency short-term financing and investment.
- To evaluate the return and risk associated with investing and financing in currency portfolios.
- To discuss the issue of centralised versus decentralised cash management.

15.1 International short-term financing

Before resorting to **external financing**, a business firm normally determines whether or not internal funds are available. A multinational business firm with international subsidiaries can, for example, utilise **internal financing** by requesting a transfer of surplus funds from one of its subsidiaries. Another method, which produces the same effect, is to increase mark-ups on supplies sent by the multinational firm to subsidiaries with surplus funds. If internal funds were not available, then the firm would resort to external financing. One source of external financing is borrowing from the Eurocurrency market. To source funds from the Eurocurrency market, direct loans may be obtained from Eurobanks by utilising **credit lines**. **Standby Eurocredits** are of two types: **Eurocurrency lines** and **revolving commitments**. A Eurocurrency line of credit means that a bank promises to lend funds denominated in a Eurocurrency up to the credit limit. A Eurocurrency revolving commitment is an arrangement whereby a bank agrees to lend Eurocurrency funds for a period of three to five years by accepting a series of sequential notes at each maturity. For example, the borrower may renew a series of 180-day notes at each maturity at the interest rate prevailing at the time.

Alternatively, funds can be obtained by issuing **Euronotes**. These are debt instruments that include **note issuance facilities (NIFs)** and **Euro-commercial papers (ECPs)**. NIFs are short-term notes underwritten by banks or guaranteed by bank standby credit arrangements. They are attractive to investors because they offer high liquidity through an active secondary market. In the case of **revolving underwriting facilities (RUFs)**, borrowers use a single bank to place their paper at a set price. Euro-commercial papers are short-term debt obligations of a corporation or a bank. The maturities of these instruments are typically one, three and six months. ECPs are normally sold at a discount and occasionally they offer a fixed interest rate. The ECP market has experienced spectacular growth because borrowers can raise large amounts of funds with maturities suitable to their cash flows. Another reason is that the cost of borrowing in the ECP market is lower than the cost of bank loans.

The growth of the ECP market

IN PRACTICE

Since January 2000 the ECP market has been one of the fastest-growing debt markets. The main reason for this growth has been the rising cost of bank loans. This rise can be attributed to the perception (by lending banks) that companies no longer choose financial advisers or new issues managers on the basis of who offers the cheapest overdraft. As a result, several major European companies, including Volkswagen, British Telecom, CGNU, Deutsche Telekom, SAS and Marks & Spencer, have increased their ECP issuance.

The increase in new ECP issues has not only come from European companies, but from US companies as well. One reason for this is the change in US accounting standards. Until 2000, most US companies financed their European subsidiaries by raising funds in the United States and swapping them into the underlying European currency. The change in accounting standards requires swaps to be marked to market on a daily basis, which makes the ECP market more practical.

Growth of the ECP market is also attributed to demand factors. There has been a surge of investment in money market funds, the main buyers of ECPs, as well as a shift (by lenders) from deposits to ECPs.

Why foreign currency financing?

An immediate question arises here. If **foreign currency financing** creates exposure to foreign exchange risk, why do business firms find it attractive (at least sometimes) to borrow in foreign currency? There are at least two reasons.

The first reason is that foreign currency financing introduces exposure to foreign exchange risk if the business firm does not already have such an exposure. If, on the other hand, the firm already has this kind of exposure, then it may actually be reduced by foreign currency financing. Suppose that an Australian firm has receivables in yen and euro due in three months time. This firm is obviously subject to foreign exchange risk because the Australian dollar values of these receivables are not known until they are realised. This firm can eliminate the exposure completely by borrowing amounts in the same currencies and with the same maturity date as when the receivables are due, such that the amounts borrowed and the interest payments are equal to the receivables. The firm can then utilise the receivables to pay off the loans. No matter what happens to the exchange rate, the firm will not be affected as far as these transactions are concerned.

Example

Suppose that the amounts of receivables are JPY10 000 000 and EUR750 000. Assume that the interest rates on the yen and the euro are 2 and 4 per cent per annum respectively and that the receivables are due in three months time. The exposure can be eliminated by borrowing amounts in the two currencies, such that when these amounts are compounded at the current interest rates for three months, they will yield exactly the amounts of the receivables. The amounts to be borrowed can be calculated by discounting the receivables at the current (deannualised) interest rates. This gives the following:

$$\frac{10\,000\,000}{\left[1+\frac{0.02}{4}\right]} = 9\,950\,249 \text{ yen}$$

$$\frac{750\,000}{\left[1+\frac{0.04}{4}\right]} = 742\,574 \text{ euro}$$

These amounts are converted into domestic currency for whatever purpose is required. When the receivables are realised, they are used to pay off the loans, which mature at the same time. Thus, the foreign exchange exposure is eliminated by foreign currency borrowing.

The second reason is that foreign currency financing may be cheaper. Interest rates on loans in various currencies are different and in many cases foreign currencies offer lower interest rates than the domestic currency. Figure 15.1 displays the three month interest rates on the Australian dollar and four major currencies at selected dates. It can be seen that the interest rate on the Australian dollar has invariably been higher than the rates on the other currencies. From an Australian perspective, therefore, it seems that financing with foreign currencies makes a lot of sense. However, these figures may be misleading because foreign currency borrowing introduces another element to the cost of borrowing, the percentage change in the exchange rate. Thus, to compare the cost of borrowing in the domestic currency with the cost of borrowing in a foreign currency, we need to compare the nominal domestic interest rate, not with the nominal foreign interest rate, but rather with the **effective financing rate** of the foreign currency. This concept is illustrated in a subsequent section.

Figure 15.1 Three-month interest rates on the Australian dollar and four major currencies

(a) AUD

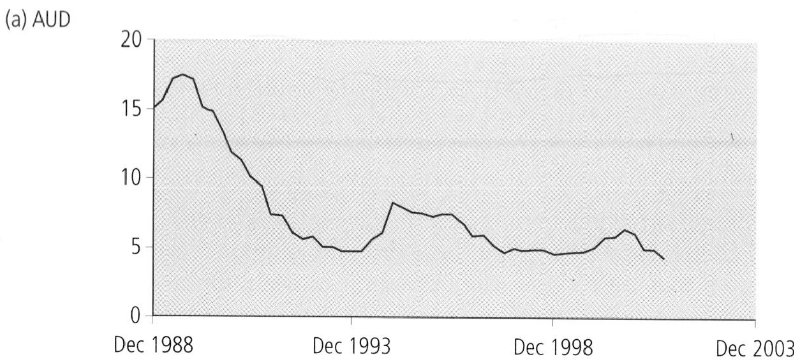

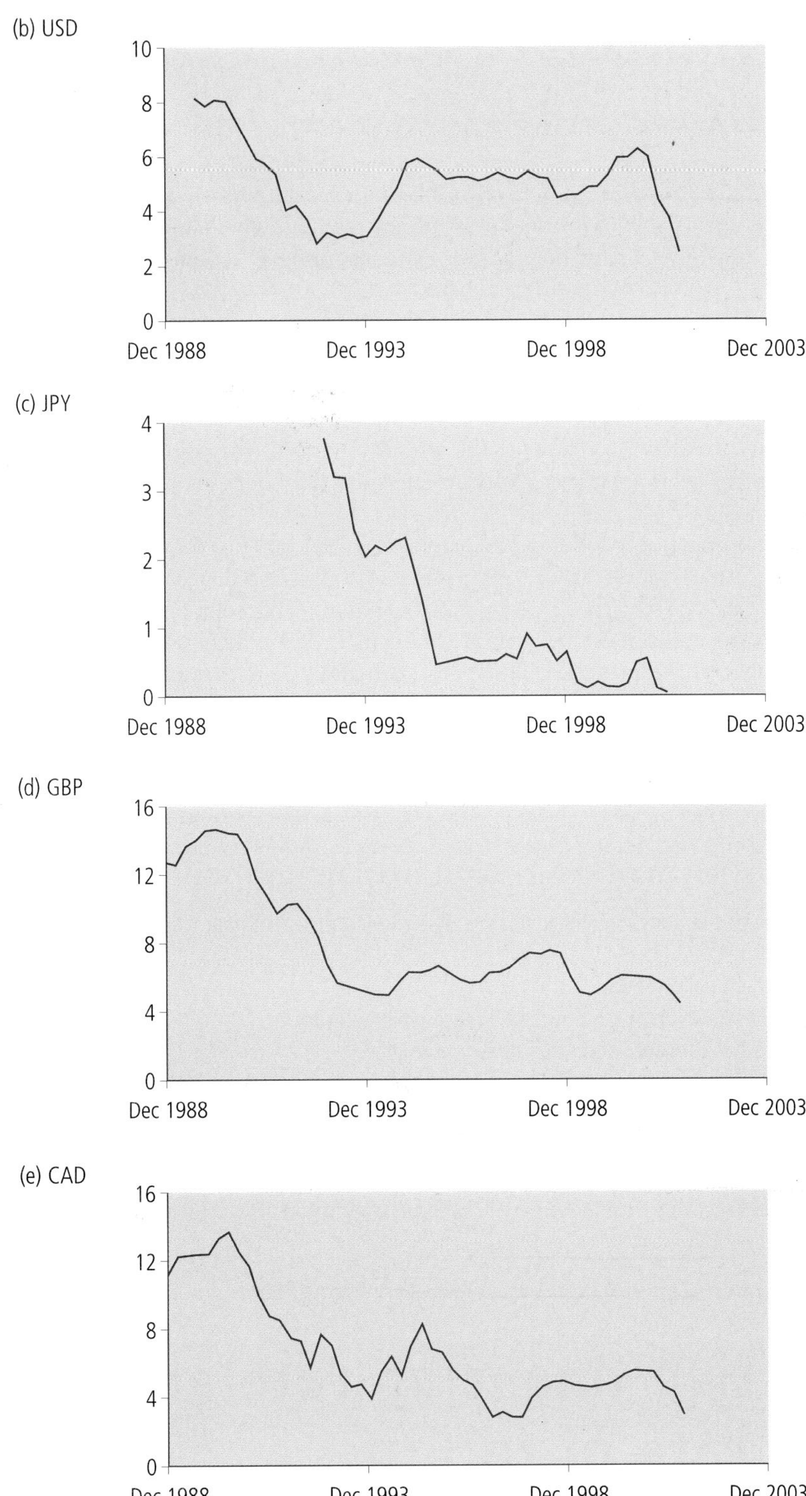

Source: Main Economic Indicators, OECD.

15.2 International short-term investment

International short-term investment is the activity of placing excess funds or cash balances in the short-term instruments available in international money markets, which are denominated in various currencies. The word 'placing' here has the same meaning as 'lending', 'depositing' and 'investing'.

The Eurocurrency market offers two examples of the instruments used for short-term international investment. They are basic types of deposit instruments: **time deposits** and **certificates of deposit (CDs)**. The placement of a Eurocurrency time deposit implies that the depositor commits the underlying funds for a specified period of time at a specified interest rate. On maturity, the depositor receives the amount invested (the principal) and the interest paid on the principal. The maturities of Eurocurrency time deposits range between overnight and 12 months.

Certificates of deposit comprise a smaller percentage of the total value of these instruments than time deposits. The attractiveness of CDs, as compared with time deposits, stems from their property of being negotiable (that is, they can be bought and sold on a secondary market). A CD specifies the amount of the deposit (the principal), the date of maturity and the interest rate applicable to the principal. There are normally three types of CDs: (i) **tap CDs**, which are large-denomination, fixed-term deposits; (ii) **tranche CDs**, which are divided into several portions, making them appealing to smaller investors; and (iii) **rollover CDs**, which are renewed after maturity at an interest rate reflecting market conditions.

Key questions in working capital management

The following are some of the questions that typically arise in the process of improving **working capital management**:

- Is the fund management policy optimal?
- Is there any means of forecasting cash flows with reasonable accuracy?
- Is it possible to make bank reconciliation less time-consuming?
- What would be the effect of reducing the number of the firm's bank accounts? Would such a measure have an effect on the receivables collection process?
- Is there any duplication in the system?
- Are there too many processes that raise issues of internal control?
- What are the means whereby the relationships with suppliers and customers can be improved for the sake of efficiency?

15.3 The effective financing rate and effective rate of return

The effective financing rate in a foreign currency depends on the foreign nominal interest rate and the percentage change in the exchange rate. It can be calculated as follows. Suppose that an amount, K, of the foreign currency is borrowed at time 0 at a nominal interest rate i^*. The domestic currency value of the amount borrowed, L_0, is given by

$$L_0 = KS_0 \tag{15.1}$$

where S_0 is the spot exchange rate prevailing at time 0 (measured in direct quotation as domestic per foreign). When the loan matures at time 1, the domestic currency amount to be repaid (the principal plus interest), L_1, is given by

$$L_1 = KS_1(1 + i^*) \tag{15.2}$$

where S_1 is the spot exchange rate prevailing at time 1. The effective financing rate, e, is therefore given by

$$(1+e) = \frac{L_1}{L_0} \tag{15.3}$$

or

$$(1+e) = \frac{KS_1(1+i^*)}{KS_0} \tag{15.4}$$

which reduces to

$$(1+e) = (1+i^*)(1+\dot{S}) \tag{15.5}$$

where $\dot{S}$ is the percentage change in the exchange rate between 0 and 1. Thus

$$e = (1+i^*)(1+\dot{S}) - 1 \tag{15.6}$$

By ignoring the term $i^*\dot{S}$, an approximate formula for the effective financing rate is

$$e = i^* + \dot{S} \tag{15.7}$$

which tells us that the effective financing rate is approximately equal to the foreign nominal interest rate plus the rate of change of the exchange rate. So, if $e < i$, foreign currency financing would be cheaper than domestic currency financing, and vice versa. The effective financing rate may be negative, implying that the borrower pays back fewer units of the domestic currency than the amount actually borrowed.

Example

An Australian firm borrowed USD100 000 for a year at a nominal interest rate of 4 per cent. The exchange rate (AUD/USD) at the time of the borrowing was 1.85. Calculate the effective financing rate if the exchange rate prevailing on the maturity date assumes the values 1.80, 1.95 and 1.65.

The amount borrowed in Australian dollar terms (Equation (15.1)) is

$$L_0 = 100\ 000 \times 1.85 = \text{AUD}185\ 000$$

The amount due at an exchange rate of 1.80 (Equation (15.2)) is

$$L_1 = 100\ 000 \times 1.80 \times 1.04 = \text{AUD}187\ 200$$

Therefore (Equation (15.4)),

$$1 + e = \frac{187\ 200}{185\ 000} = 1.012$$

Continued...

Hence, $e = 0.012$ or 1.2 per cent. Alternatively, Equation (15.6) can be used directly to get

$$e = (1 + 0.04) \times (1 - 0.027) - 1 = 0.012$$

which gives the same result. In this case, foreign currency financing is better (cheaper) if the interest rate on the Australian dollar borrowing is greater than 1.2 per cent. The effective financing rate is lower than the nominal interest rate on the US dollar because during the period that elapsed between time 0 and time 1 the US dollar depreciated against the Australian dollar.

If, on the other hand, the exchange rate at time 1 was 1.95, implying an appreciation of the US dollar, the effective financing rate will be

$$e = (1 + 0.04) \times (1 + 0.054) - 1 = 0.0962$$

or 9.62 per cent. Suppose now that the exchange rate at time 1 turned out to be 1.65, implying a sharp depreciation of the US dollar. In this case

$$e = (1 + 0.04) \times (1 - 0.11) - 1 = -0.074$$

or −7.4 per cent. A negative effective financing rate is obtained because the foreign currency depreciated by more than its nominal interest rate.

The effective financing rate can be looked upon from an ex ante perspective (before the fact) or from an ex post perspective (after the fact). At time 0, the borrower does not know what the effective financing rate will be, because it depends on the percentage change in the spot exchange rate between 0 and 1: this is unknown at time 0. Decisions taken at time 0 then have to be based on the expected or ex ante effective financing rate. At time 1, however, the change in the spot exchange rate is known and so is the effective financing rate. Hence, the actual or ex post effective financing rate is realised at time 1. The ex post rate tells the borrower whether or not his or her decision at time 0 was right. The right decision is indicated by an effective financing rate that is lower than the domestic interest rate, which is the cost of financing in domestic currency.

Let us now examine some actual figures from an Australian perspective, using historical data. Figure 15.2 shows the behaviour of the three-month (deannualised) effective financing rate in four major currencies from an Australian perspective during the period 1988–2001. The first thing to notice is that the effective financing rates are much more volatile than the corresponding interest rates. This volatility, which results from the volatility of exchange rates, means that foreign currency financing is highly risky. While the effective financing rate may assume positive and negative values, it has been predominantly positive, reflecting the depreciation of the Australian dollar against major currencies. This means that foreign currency financing has been predominantly more expensive from the perspective of an Australian-dollar-based firm.

Because we are not yet making the distinction between bid and offer interest rates, i and i^* may also be considered the lending rates. If this is the case, then the **effective rate of return**, r, can be calculated from the equations

$$r = (1 + i^*)(1 + \dot{S}) - 1 \tag{15.8}$$

and

$$r = i^* + \dot{S} \tag{15.9}$$

Figure 15.2 Effective financing rates from an Australian perspective (quarterly deannualised rates)

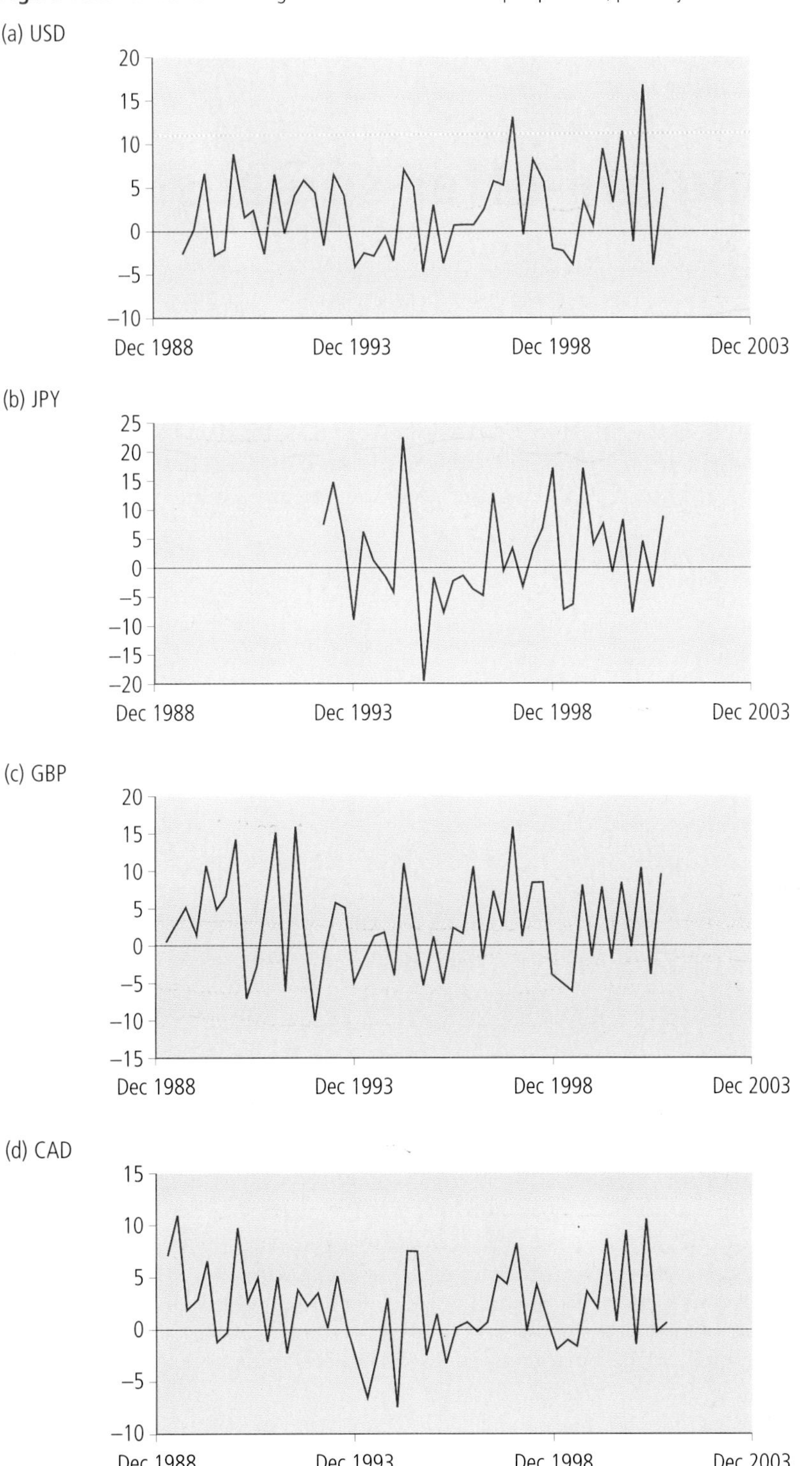

Source: Main Economic Indicators, OECD.

Figure 15.2 may be taken to represent the behaviour of the effective rate of return from an Australian perspective, which in this case gives a favourable outcome (that is, foreign currency investment has been more profitable than domestic currency investment because of the depreciation of the Australian dollar).

15.4 Introducing bid-offer spreads

The equations that are used to calculate the effective financing rate and the effective rate of return will be different if allowance is made for bid-offer spreads in interest and exchange rates. We will now derive these equations in the presence of bid-offer spreads.

The effective financing rate

Suppose that an amount, K, of the foreign currency is borrowed at time 0 at the offer foreign interest rate, i_a^*. The foreign currency amount is converted into domestic currency at the bid exchange rate prevailing at time 0, S_{b0}. Thus, the domestic currency value of the amount borrowed, L_0, is given by

$$L_0 = KS_{b0} \tag{15.10}$$

When the loan matures at time 1, the foreign currency amount to be repaid (the principal plus interest), L_1, is given by

$$L_1 = KS_{a1}(1 + i_a^*) \tag{15.11}$$

where S_{a1} is the offer spot exchange rate prevailing at time 1. The effective financing rate, e, is therefore given by

$$(1+e) = \frac{KS_{a1}(1+i_a^*)}{KS_{b0}} \tag{15.12}$$

or

$$(1+e) = (1+i_a^*)\left(\frac{S_{a1}}{S_{b0}}\right) \tag{15.13}$$

Therefore,

$$e = (1+i_a^*)\left(\frac{S_{a1}}{S_{b0}}\right) - 1 \tag{15.14}$$

which obviously shows that the effective financing rate is higher in the presence of bid-offer spreads than otherwise.

Example

Assuming the same situation as in the previous example, calculate the effective financing rate if the interest rate on the US dollar is 3.75–4.25, the exchange rate (AUD/USD) at the time of the borrowing is 1.8450–1.8550 and the exchange rate when the loan is due is 1.7950–1.8045.

The amount borrowed in Australian dollar terms (Equation (15.10)) is

$$L_0 = 100\,000 \times 1.8450 = \text{AUD}184\,500$$

The amount due (Equation (15.11)) is

$$L_1 = 100\,000 \times 1.8045 \times 1.0425 = \text{AUD}188\,119$$

Therefore

$$1 + e = \frac{188\,119}{184\,500} = 1.020$$

Hence, $e = 0.020$ or 2 per cent. Alternatively, Equation (15.14) can be used directly:

$$e = (1 + 0.0425)\left[\frac{1.8045}{1.8450}\right] - 1 = 0.020$$

or 2 per cent. Note that the effective financing rate turns out to be higher in the presence of bid-offer spreads.

The effective rate of return

Suppose that the foreign currency equivalent of an amount, K, of the domestic currency is available for foreign currency investment at time 0 at the bid foreign interest rate, i_b^*. The domestic currency amount is converted into foreign currency at the offer exchange rate prevailing at time 0, S_{a0}. Thus, the foreign currency value of the amount available for investment is

$$I_0 = \frac{K}{S_{a0}} \tag{15.15}$$

When the investment matures at time 1, the domestic currency equivalent of the foreign currency amount received is given by

$$I_1 = \frac{K}{S_{a0}}(1 + i_b^*)S_{b1} \tag{15.16}$$

where S_{b1} is the spot bid exchange rate prevailing at time 1. This is because the amount of the foreign currency realised from the investment is sold at the lower bid rate. The effective rate of return, r, is therefore given by

$$(1 + r) = \frac{\frac{K}{S_{a0}}(1 + i_b^*)S_{b1}}{K} \tag{15.17}$$

or

$$(1 + r) = (1 + i_b^*)\left(\frac{S_{b1}}{S_{a0}}\right) \tag{15.18}$$

which gives

$$r = (1 + i_b^*)\left(\frac{S_{b1}}{S_{a0}}\right) - 1 \tag{15.19}$$

Example

We can use the previous example to calculate the effective rate of return as follows:
The amount borrowed in Australian dollar terms is

$$I_0 = \frac{185\ 500}{1.8550} = 100\ 000$$

The amount due (Equation (15.16)) is

$$I_1 = \frac{185\ 500}{1.8550} \times 1.0375 \times 1.7950 = 186\ 231$$

Therefore,

$$1 + r = \frac{186\ 231}{185\ 500} = 1.004$$

which gives $r = 0.004$ or 0.4 per cent.
Alternatively, Equation (15.19) can be used directly:

$$r = (1 + 0.0375)\left[\frac{1.7950}{1.8550}\right] - 1 = 0.004$$

or 0.4 per cent. As expected, the rate of return is lower in the presence of bid-offer spreads.

15.5 Implications of international parity conditions

Two international parity conditions have some implications for short-term financing and investment decisions: covered interest parity (CIP) and uncovered interest parity (UIP). The implications of the two parity conditions for short-term financing decisions are discussed in turn. Exactly the same reasoning applies to short-term investment decisions.

Covered interest parity

To assess the implications of CIP for short-term financing decisions, the process used to derive an expression for the effective financing rate is modified by assuming that the borrowing firm wishes to avoid foreign exchange risk. To do this, the foreign currency exposure is covered in the forward market. In this case, the foreign currency is bought forward at time 0, which means that the amount to be repaid is converted into foreign currency at the forward rate prevailing at time 0, F_0. Thus

$$L_1 = KF_0(1 + i^*) \tag{15.20}$$

The effective financing rate is therefore given by

$$(1 + e) = \frac{KF_0(1 + i^*)}{KS_0} \tag{15.21}$$

which reduces to

$$(1 + e) = (1 + i^*)(1 + f) \tag{15.22}$$

where f is the forward spread. Thus

$$e = (1 + i^*)(1 + f) - 1 \tag{15.23}$$

If CIP holds, then $(1 + f) = (1 + i)/(1 + i^*)$, which gives

$$e = i \tag{15.24}$$

Thus, if CIP holds, then the effective financing rate will be equal to the domestic interest rate. Hence, foreign currency financing will be useless in the sense that it will not be cheaper than domestic currency financing. If, however, CIP is violated, then foreign currency financing may be more or less attractive (cheaper or more expensive) than domestic currency financing. The following general rules apply:

- If CIP holds, foreign currency financing (investment) will be identical to domestic currency financing (investment).
- If CIP is violated such that the forward spread is higher than the interest differential, then domestic currency financing (investment) will be more (less) desirable.
- If CIP is violated such that the forward spread is lower than the interest differential, then domestic currency financing (investment) will be less (more) desirable.

Example

We have the following information where the domestic currency is the Australian dollar and the foreign currency is the British pound:

Australian interest rate (i)	4%
British interest rate (i^*)	6%
Current spot exchange rate (AUD/GBP)	2.7015
Current forward exchange rate (AUD/GBP)	2.6505

The forward spread is calculated as:

$$f = \frac{2.6505}{2.7015} - 1 = -0.0189$$

which satisfies CIP because

$$\frac{1 + i}{1 + i^*} - 1 = \frac{1.04}{1.06} - 1 = -0.0189$$

The effective financing rate can be calculated from Equation (15.23) as

$$e = (1 + 0.06) \times (1 - 0.0189) - 1 = 0.04$$

or 4 per cent, which is equal to the Australian interest rate.

Let us now consider two different values of the forward rate, which are inconsistent with CIP: 2.6800 and 2.6200. If the forward rate is 2.6800, then

$$f = \frac{2.6800}{2.7015} - 1 = -0.0080$$

Continued...

Therefore,

$$e = (1 + 0.06) \times (1 - 0.0080) - 1 = 0.052$$

or 5.2 per cent, which makes domestic currency financing more desirable. If the forward rate is 2.6200, then

$$f = \frac{2.6200}{2.7015} - 1 = -0.0302$$

Therefore,

$$e = (1 + 0.06) \times (1 - 0.0302) - 1 = 0.0280$$

or 2.8 per cent, which makes foreign currency financing more desirable.

Uncovered interest parity

If UIP holds, then the percentage change in the spot exchange rate will be equal to the interest rate differential or $(1 + \dot{S}) = (1 + i)/(1 + i^*)$. If this expression is substituted in equations (15.6) and (15.8), we obtain $e = i$ and $r = i$, respectively. The following general rules apply:

- If UIP holds, foreign currency financing (investment) will be identical to domestic currency financing (investment).
- If UIP is violated such that the expected change in the spot rate is higher than the interest differential, then domestic currency financing (investment) will be more (less) desirable.
- If UIP is violated such that the expected change in the exchange rate is lower than the interest differential, then domestic currency financing (investment) will be less (more) desirable.

Example

We have the following information where the domestic currency is the Australian dollar and the foreign currency is the US dollar:

Australian dollar interest rate (i)	6%
US dollar interest rate (i^*)	4%
Current spot exchange rate (AUD/USD)	1.8500
Expected spot exchange rate (AUD/USD)	1.8856

The expected change in the spot exchange rate is calculated as

$$\dot{S} = \frac{1.8856}{1.8500} - 1 = 0.019$$

which satisfies UIP because

$$\frac{1 + i}{1 + i^*} - 1 = \frac{1.06}{1.04} - 1 = 0.019$$

The effective financing rate can be calculated from Equation (15.6) as

$$e = (1 + 0.04) \times (1 + 0.019) - 1 = 0.06$$

which is equal to the domestic interest rate.

Let us now consider two different values of the expected spot rate, which are inconsistent with UIP: 1.9250 and 1.8000. If the expected spot rate is 1.9250, then

$$\dot{S} = \frac{1.9250}{1.8500} - 1 = 0.0405$$

Therefore,

$$e = (1 + 0.04) \times (1 + 0.0405) - 1 = 0.082$$

or 8.2 per cent, which makes domestic currency financing more desirable. If the expected spot rate is 1.8000, then

$$\dot{S} = \frac{1.8000}{1.8500} - 1 = -0.027$$

Therefore,

$$e = (1 + 0.04) \times (1 - 0.027) - 1 = 0.012$$

or 1.2 per cent, which makes foreign currency financing more desirable.

RESEARCH FINDINGS

The implications of CIP for foreign currency financing

Covered interest parity can be tested indirectly by using its implication that foreign currency financing, while covering the position in the forward market, is equivalent to domestic currency financing. Three hypotheses have been tested based on a sample of quarterly data covering three currencies (USD, GBP and CAD) over the period from the first quarter of 1978 to the fourth quarter of 2000.[1] The three hypotheses are:

1. If CIP holds, then financing in a foreign currency, while covering the position in the forward market, produces results that are similar to those obtained from domestic currency financing.
2. If CIP holds and the nominal interest rates on two currencies are equal, then the effective financing rates in the two currencies are equal when their roles are reversed.
3. The effective financing rates in two currencies will be equal even if CIP is violated, provided that the violation follows a certain condition.

The results of the empirical testing indicated that CIP held only for the USD/CAD exchange rate. They further showed that the second and third hypotheses could not be rejected. The observed deviations from CIP for currency combinations involving the pound were attributed to measurement errors and similar factors.

[1] I. A. Moosa, 'The Implications of Covered Interest Parity for Short-Term Financing: Testing Some Underlying Hypotheses', *Journal of Economics and Accounting*, 1, 2002 pp. 23–8.

15.6 Introducing probability distributions

Using the UIP condition as a criterion for foreign currency financing and investment decisions implies that the decision is based on the expected change in the exchange rate, such that foreign currency financing (investment) will be preferred if the exchange rate is expected to change by less (more) than what is implied by UIP. As we have seen, it is sometimes difficult to obtain a point forecast for the exchange rate. In this case, we use a **probability distribution** for the expected change in the exchange rate to arrive at a probability distribution for the effective financing rate and the effective rate of return. The following discussion is based on the effective financing rate.

Suppose that the expected (percentage) change in the exchange rate assumes the values $\dot{S}_1, \dot{S}_2, \ldots \dot{S}_n$ with probabilities $p_1, p_2, \ldots\ p_n$. The effective financing rate has a similar probability distribution (that is, it assumes the values $e_1,\ e_2,\ \ldots\ e_n$ with probabilities $p_1,\ p_2,\ \ldots\ p_n$). The expected value of the effective financing rate is therefore given by

$$E(e) = \sum_{i=1}^{n} e_i p_i \tag{15.25}$$

The measure of risk in this case is the variance or the standard deviation of the effective financing rate, both of which measure the variability of the effective financing rate or the dispersion around the expected value. The variance and the standard deviation are calculated as

$$\sigma^2(e) = \sum_{i=1}^{n} p_i[e_i - E(e)]^2 \tag{15.26}$$

$$\sigma(e) = \sqrt{\sum_{i=1}^{n} p_i[e_i - E(e)]^2} \tag{15.27}$$

Example

Assuming that the US interest rate is 4 per cent and that the percentage change in the spot exchange rate between the Australian and US currencies follows a probability distribution, we can calculate the expected value of the effective financing rate corresponding to each probability as shown in the following table:

$\dot{S}_i$(%)	P_i	e_i(%)
−6	0.05	−2.24
−2	0.10	1.92
0	0.20	4.00
2	0.25	6.08
6	0.40	10.24

The expected value of the effective financing rate is therefore calculated as

$$E(e) = -2.24 \times 0.05 + 1.92 \times 0.10 + 4.00 \times 0.20 + 6.08 \times 0.25 + 10.24 \times 0.40 = 6.50$$

By using Equations (15.26) and (15.27), we find the variance and the standard deviation to be 12.81 and 3.58, respectively.

If no probability distributions are available, we can calculate these statistics from historical data, in which case the expected value is replaced by the mean. Therefore, if we have a sample of observations on the effective financing rate, e_1, e_2, ... e_n, the mean, the variance and the standard deviation of the effective financing rate are calculated respectively as

$$\bar{e} = \frac{1}{n}\sum_{t=1}^{n} e_t \tag{15.28}$$

$$\sigma^2(e) = \frac{1}{n-1}\sum_{t=1}^{n}(e_t - \bar{e})^2 \tag{15.29}$$

$$\sigma(e) = \sqrt{\frac{1}{n-1}\sum_{t=1}^{n}(e_t - \bar{e})^2} \tag{15.30}$$

Example

Calculate the mean, the variance and the standard deviation of the effective financing rate that assumed the following values during the period January–December 2001: 2.28, –0.32, –3.08, –0.71, –0.03, 1.04, 0.35, 2.65, 1.86, 3.47, 4.35 and 4.62.

$$\bar{e} = \frac{1}{12} \times (2.28 + \ldots + 4.62) = 1.37$$

$$\sigma^2(e) = \frac{1}{11} \times \left[(2.28 - 1.37)^2 + \ldots + (4.62 - 1.37)^2\right] = 5.15$$

$$\sigma(e) = \sqrt{5.15} = 2.27$$

It is important to remember that financing or investing in the domestic currency involves no foreign exchange risk, since the cost of financing and the rate of return (which are equal to the domestic interest rate) are known with certainty. When foreign currency financing or investment is chosen, the effective financing rate and the effective rate of return are at best probabilistic, in the sense that they assume a range of values with some probabilities. This, naturally, implies the presence of risk. Therefore, the choice between foreign currency financing (investment) and domestic currency financing (investment) depends on the attitude towards risk.

Suppose that an Australian firm has the following three short-term financing alternatives. The first is domestic currency (Australian dollar) financing, which costs 5 per cent and is known with certainty, since no foreign exchange risk is involved. The second alternative is financing with the euro, which offers the following probability distribution for the effective financing rate: 6 per cent or 4 per cent with equal probabilities of 0.5. The third alternative is financing with the British pound, which offers the following probability distribution: 8 per cent or 2 per cent with equal probabilities. In both cases, the expected value of the effective financing rate is 5 per cent, which is equal to the domestic currency financing rate. However, financing with the British pound is more risky than financing with the euro, because of the greater variability of the effective financing rate of the pound. This is indicated by the fact that the dispersion of the actual values of the effective financing rate around the expected value of 5 per cent is greater in the case of the pound. The standard deviation of the effective financing rate in the case of the euro is 1 per cent, implying that the rate may be higher or lower than the expected value of 5 per cent by 1 percentage point. In the case of the pound, the standard deviation is 3 per cent, implying that the effective financing rate may be higher or lower than the expected value of 5 per cent by 3 percentage points.

The choice of one of the three financing alternatives depends on the attitude towards risk. If the firm is risk-averse (dislikes bearing risk), the choice will definitely fall on domestic currency financing. In this case there are no ifs or buts, as a financing cost of 5 per cent will be incurred. If the firm is willing to bear a reasonable amount of risk, the choice would fall on the euro. The reward for bearing risk is the possibility (only a possibility) that the firm may realise the lower effective financing rate of 4 per cent. However, it is equally possible that the firm will incur the higher effective financing rate of 6 per cent. If, on the other hand, the firm is willing to bear a more significant amount of risk in the hope of obtaining a bigger reward, then the pound would be the choice as the currency of financing. The bigger reward in this case takes the form of a much lower effective financing rate of 2 per cent.

We could use historical data to calculate the mean values and the standard deviations of the effective financing rates and effective rates of return from an Australian perspective. These are reported in the following table, which shows that the most volatile rate is that of the yen and the most stable is that of the Canadian dollar. We could use as a selection criterion (that takes risk into account) the ratio of the mean to the standard deviation. This is a measure of the cost of financing or return per unit of risk. Hence, the objective should be to minimise this measure in financing decisions and maximise it in investment decisions.

	USD	JPY	GBP	CAD
Mean	2.26	1.72	2.86	2.29
Standard deviation	4.97	8.71	6.56	4.13
Ratio	0.46	0.20	0.44	0.55

15.7 Financing and investment with currency portfolios

In the previous example, the firm had to make a choice among three alternatives, each of which involves financing with a single currency. There is no reason, however, why the firm cannot choose to finance with a portfolio of currencies, which may or may not include the domestic currency. In fact, such an operation may be beneficial because it is a well-known principle in finance that diversification reduces risk.

Let us look at the matter in general terms. Assume that there are two foreign currencies, y and z. The effective financing rate in currency y assumes the values e_i^y with probabilities p_i^y for $i = 1, 2, \ldots n$. Similarly, the effective financing rate of currency z assumes the values e_j^z with probabilities p_j^z for $j = 1, 2, \ldots m$. Let us assume that the financing portfolio is formed by assigning weights w_y and w_z to currencies y and z respectively, such that $w_y + w_z = 1$. The effective financing rate of the portfolio is

$$e_{i,j}^p = w_y e_i^y + w_z e_j^z \quad (15.31)$$

which materialises with a joint $p_i^y p_j^z$, such that

$$\sum_{i=1}^{n}\sum_{j=1}^{m} p_i^y p_j^z = 1 \tag{15.32}$$

The expected values, means and standard deviations can be calculated in the usual manner. The same can be done if we have historical data rather than probability distributions.

Example

The following table reports hypothetical probability distributions for the effective financing rate (in percentage points) in the euro and the pound that face an Australian firm considering international short-term financing:

EUR	Probability	GBP	Probability
5.0	0.5	3.0	0.1
7.0	0.2	5.0	0.3
10.0	0.3	8.0	0.6

If the firm is considering a two-currency financing portfolio, then the worst that can happen is that the EUR and GBP effective financing rates assume their highest values (10 and 8 per cent, respectively). This occurs with a joint probability of 0.18 (0.3 × 0.6). The best that can happen is that the two effective financing rates assume their lowest values (5 and 3 per cent) with a joint probability of 0.05 (0.5 × 0.1). The most likely outcome, when the two financing rates assume values independently from each other, is that the EUR effective financing rate turns out to be 5 per cent while the effective financing rate of the GBP turns out to be 8 per cent. This outcome occurs with a joint probability of 0.30 (0.5 × 0.6). The following table shows all possible combinations and the associated joint probabilities. If the firm assigns equal weights to the two currencies in the portfolio, then the portfolio's effective financing rate is simply the average of the effective financing rates for the two currencies.

EUR	GBP	Portfolio	Joint probability
5.0	3.0	4.0	0.05
5.0	5.0	5.0	0.15
5.0	8.0	6.5	0.30
7.0	3.0	5.0	0.02
7.0	5.0	6.0	0.06
7.0	8.0	7.5	0.12
10.0	3.0	6.5	0.03
10.0	5.0	7.5	0.09
10.0	8.0	9.0	0.18

Therefore, the worst that can happen is that the effective financing rate of the portfolio assumes a value of 9 per cent, whereas the best outcome is associated with an effective financing rate of 4 per cent. The most likely value is 6.5 per cent. Note that the joint probabilities in the fourth column add up to 1.

Continued...

We can calculate the expected value of the portfolio's effective financing rate as

$$E(e^P) = 4 \times 0.05 + 5 \times 0.15 + ... + 9 \times 0.18 = 6.75$$

The same value can be calculated as a weighted average (in this case a simple average) of the effective financing rates of the two portfolios. These effective financing rates can be calculated from the first table as follows:

$$E(e^{EUR}) = 5 \times 0.5 + 7 \times 0.2 + 10 \times 0.3 = 6.9$$

$$E(e^{GBP}) = 3 \times 0.1 + 5 \times 0.3 + 8 \times 0.6 = 6.6$$

The expected value of the portfolio's effective financing rate is

$$E(e^P) = 6.9 \times 0.5 + 6.6 \times 0.5 = 6.75$$

15.8 Centralised versus decentralised cash management

In this section we consider the issue of **centralised cash management** versus **decentralised cash management**, which often faces firms with overseas branches or multinationals with subsidiaries in various countries. Centralised cash management implies that receipts and payments in various currencies are managed by a central body, normally in the company's head office. Decentralised cash management implies that these receipts and payments are managed locally by the branches or subsidiaries.

Centralised cash management

Most of the advantages of centralised cash management are associated with economies of scale. The first of these perceived advantages is **netting**, which involves calculating the overall corporate position in each currency by adding up the short and long positions of various branches and subsidiaries. Netting provides a natural hedge when there is a short position in one currency and an equivalent long position in the same currency, as we have seen earlier. It also reduces the cost of hedging in the sense that it is cheaper to hedge the net position than to hedge the individual positions separately.

Example

To illustrate this point consider an Australian-dollar-based firm with six different long and short positions on the US dollar, the pound and the euro. The positions are as follows:

Currency	Receivables (long)	Payables (short)
USD	500 000	300 000
GBP	500 000	300 000
EUR	400 000	600 000

Now assume that the positions have to be settled at the current spot rates:

AUD/USD 1.8025–1.8075
AUD/GBP 2.7025–2.7075
AUD/EUR 1.7925–1.7975

Assume also that there are brokerage fees amounting to 1 per cent of the transaction. To settle the short (long) positions, the firm must buy (sell) the foreign currency. The Australian dollar cash flows arising from the settlement of the individual positions (including brokerage fees) are as follows:

Currency	Position	Amount	Operation	AUD cash flow
USD	Long	500 000	Sell the USD at 1.8025	892 238
USD	Short	300 000	Buy the USD at 1.8075	(547 673)
GBP	Long	500 000	Sell the GBP at 2.7025	1 337 738
GBP	Short	300 000	Buy the GBP at 2.7075	(820 373)
EUR	Long	400 000	Sell the EUR at 1.7925	709 830
EUR	Short	600 000	Buy the EUR at 1.7975	(1 089 285)
Total				482 475

Now, consider what happens when only the net positions are hedged, as shown in the following table:

Currency	Net position	Amount	Operation	AUD cash flow
USD	Long	200 000	Sell the USD at 1.8025	356 895
GBP	Long	200 000	Sell the GBP at 2.7025	535 095
EUR	Short	(200 000)	Buy the EUR at 1.7975	(363 095)
Total				528 895

Obviously, the net Australian dollar amount received is higher when netting is used. The difference results from the reduced transaction costs (bid-offer spread and brokerage fees).

Moreover, netting reduces the costs of transferring funds between subsidiaries and the parent firm. There are, typically, significant fund transfers between a multinational firm and its subsidiaries and among the subsidiaries themselves. These transfers involve some costs such as the cost of transfers and the interest lost while the funds are in transit. Netting reduces these costs because it reduces both the number of payments and the amount involved in each payment. The following example illustrates **bilateral netting**, which involves two companies, and **multilateral netting**, which involves more than two companies.

Example

Figure 15.3 shows that Company A owes Company B AUD500 000, whereas Company B owes Company A AUD300 000. Without netting, there are two payments with a combined value of AUD800 000. With netting only one payment needs to be made: AUD200 000 from A to B.

Continued...

Figure 15.3 Bilateral netting

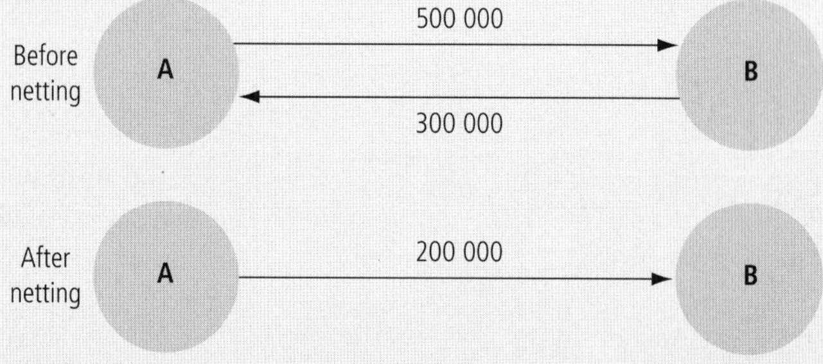

Figure 15.4 shows the situation when four companies are involved in intercompany payments. Without netting there are 12 payments with a total value of AUD8 900 000. The net receipts (receipts minus payments) of each company are as follows

$$A = 1\ 800\ 000 - 1\ 900\ 000 = -100\ 000$$

$$B = 2\ 100\ 000 - 2\ 400\ 000 = -300\ 000$$

$$C = 2\ 800\ 000 - 1\ 800\ 000 = 1\ 000\ 000$$

$$D = 2\ 200\ 000 - 2\ 800\ 000 = -600\ 000$$

where a negative number implies net payment, and vice versa. It is obvious that C's net receipts are equal to the sum of the net payments of A, B and D. Multilateral netting entails A, B and D making payments to C. With netting there are three payments worth only AUD1 000 000. In this way, multilateral netting reduces the costs of transferring funds.

Figure 15.4 Multilateral netting

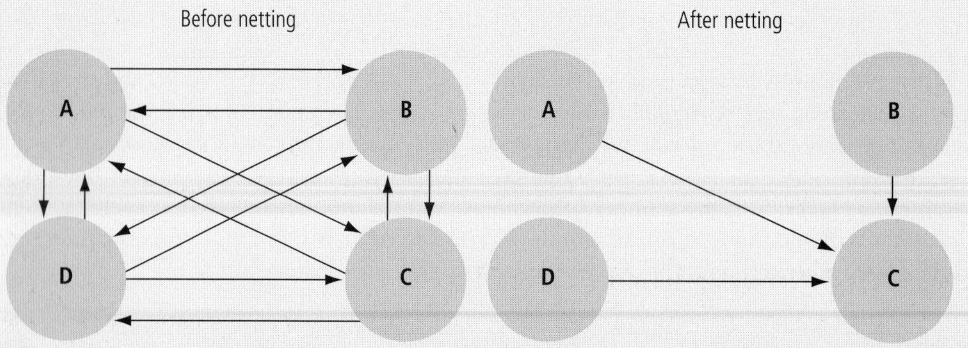

Continued...

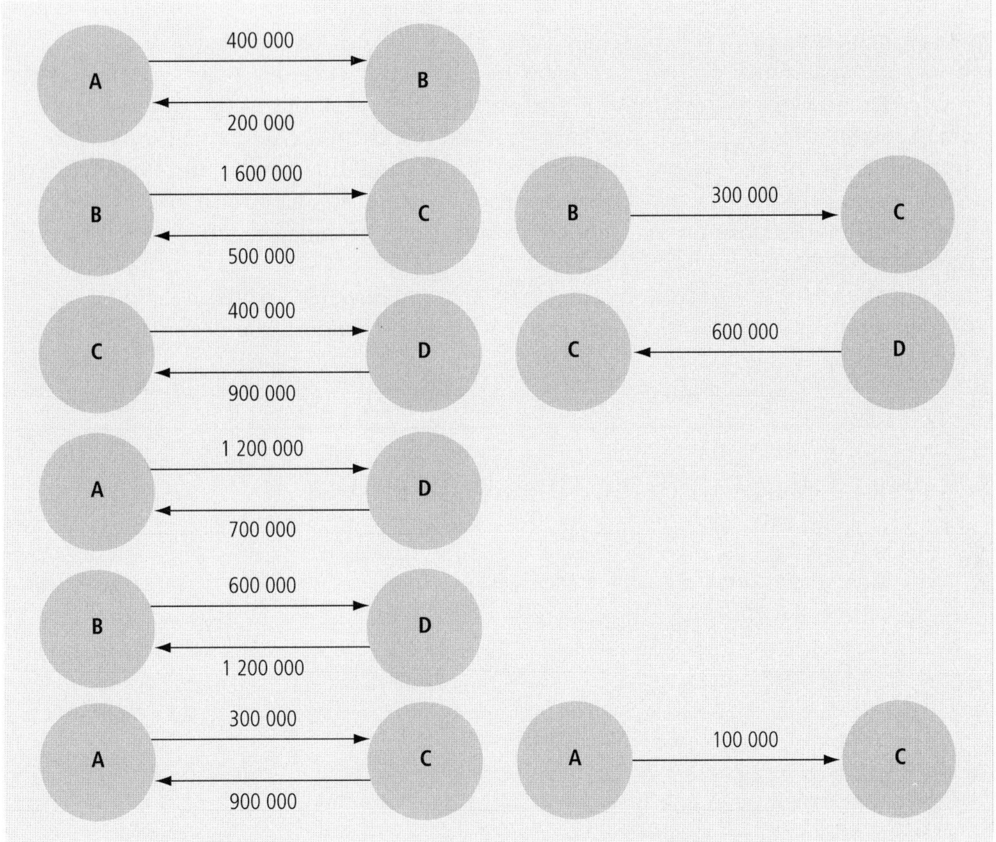

Another advantage of centralised cash management is currency diversification. Even if the combined position is not zero, centralised cash management may result in a combined position that is so diversified that the foreign exchange risk is sufficiently reduced, again removing the need to hedge individual positions. Specifically, if the combined position is well diversified, in terms of currency, and if the exchange rates of these currencies against the base (domestic) currency are not highly correlated, this will effectively provide a natural hedge.

Finally, **pooling** is another advantage. By pooling cash balances in a centralised location, the cash requirements of any branch or subsidiary anywhere can be met without having to keep balances denominated in various currencies in every locality. The requirements of a subsidiary that is short of cash in a certain currency can be met from the central 'pool of resources'.

Decentralised cash management

There are at least two circumstances when decentralised cash management may be preferable. The first is when delays are expected in transferring funds to countries where the banking system is inefficient. The funds may have to be held ready to settle a transaction exposure with unknown timing. The second is when it is felt that local representation is necessary in order to maintain on-the-spot links with clients and banks. This is why this issue is not so much the choice between centralised and decentralised cash management systems, but rather the determination of the extent of centralisation and decentralisation.

If decentralised cash management is preferred, what are the factors that determine where and in which currency cash balances are held? The following are some guidelines:

- If it is anticipated that the received funds in a particular currency will be needed in the future, then transaction costs make it sensible to keep these funds in the same currency.
- The same reasoning applies if there is no forward market in the underlying currency.
- If political risk in one country is high, then funds should be kept in the home country rather than in the country in whose currencies the funds are denominated.
- Liquidity considerations make it sensible to keep funds in the currency in which they are most likely to be needed in the future.
- In the presence of taxes, funds should not be kept in countries with high tax rates.

Obviously, these factors may conflict with each other. Therefore, the decision will involve a trade-off.

IN PRACTICE

Cash management in the aftermath of the Asian crisis

It has been reported that Malaysian companies have begun to pay more attention to cash management in the aftermath of the Asian crisis, which forced these companies to explore means of reducing operating costs. Besides the effect of the Asian crisis, there seem to be other factors that have contributed to this change of heart, including the following:

- the move towards automated accounting packages and resource planning systems, which makes it easier for companies to adopt up-to-date banking technology
- increased awareness by chief financial officers and treasurers of the cash management tools that are made available by a growing number of providers
- infrastructure development in cheque-clearing systems and interbank payment systems

Summary

- Internal financing is normally considered before resorting to external financing. For this purpose, a multinational firm with foreign subsidiaries can (i) request a transfer of funds from a subsidiary and (ii) raise mark-ups on supplies sent to subsidiaries with surplus funds.
- International short-term financing takes several forms including: (i) direct loans from Eurobanks; (ii) note issuance facilities; and (iii) Euro-commercial papers.
- Foreign currency financing is considered for at least two reasons: (i) it may reduce exposure to foreign exchange risk; and (ii) it may be cheaper.
- International short-term investment is the activity of placing excess funds in short-term instruments available in international money markets. Examples of these instruments are time deposits and certificates of deposit.
- The effective financing rate in a foreign currency depends on the foreign nominal interest rate and the rate of change in the exchange rate. Because of the exchange rate factor, this rate is unknown in advance, unlike the financing rate in the domestic currency (which is the domestic interest rate).

- The effective rate of return on a short-term foreign currency depends on the foreign nominal interest rate and the percentage change in the exchange rate. Changes in the spot exchange rate cause the effective rate of return to be different from the nominal interest rate on the foreign currency.
- If CIP holds, the effective financing rate and the effective rate of return will be equal to the domestic interest rate. The same is true for UIP.
- The risk associated with foreign currency financing (investment) is measured by the variability of the effective financing rate (effective rate of return). The means and standard deviations of the effective financing rate and the effective rate of return can be calculated either from a probability distribution or from historical data. The choice between domestic currency and foreign currency financing depends on the attitude towards risk.
- Short-term financing and investment can be carried out by borrowing a portfolio of currencies that may or may not include the domestic currency. Risk in this case is measured by the standard deviation of the effective financing rate (or the effective rate of return) of the portfolio.
- Centralised cash management has the following advantages: (i) netting; (ii) diversification; and (iii) pooling. Decentralised cash management may be preferred when delays are expected in transferring funds to countries where banking systems are inefficient and when it is necessary to maintain personal links with clients.

Key terms

MaxMARK

MAXIMISE YOUR MARKS! There are 30 interactive questions for this chapter available online at **www.mhhe.com/au/moosa2e**

Review questions

1 What are the means whereby a firm with international subsidiaries resorts to internal financing?

2 What are the sources of external short-term financing?

3 Why do business firms use foreign currency financing and investment even though they introduce foreign exchange risk?

4 'If the interest rate on a foreign currency is lower than the domestic interest rate, then it always makes sense to borrow foreign currency funds and convert them into domestic currency funds, rather than to borrow the latter directly.' Is this statement valid?

5 What is the implication of the following values of the effective financing rate and the effective rate of return: (a) negative; (b) zero; (c) positive but lower than the domestic interest rate; (d) positive and equal to the domestic interest rate; and (e) positive and higher than the domestic interest rate?

6 What is the implication of introducing bid-offer spreads into the calculation of the effective financing rate and the effective rate of return?

7 What is the implication of the validity, or otherwise, of CIP for short-term financing and investment decisions?

8 What is the implication of the validity, or otherwise, of UIP for short-term financing and investment decisions?

9 Why do some companies find it useful to finance with a portfolio of currencies that may or may not include the domestic currency?

10 Compare and contrast centralised and decentralised cash management systems.

11 If a decentralised cash management system is adopted, what are the factors determining where and in which currency cash balances are held?

12 Why is multilateral netting more useful than bilateral netting?

Problems

1 An Australian firm borrowed EUR2 000 000 for three months at a nominal interest rate of 6.5 per cent per annum. The exchange rate at the time of borrowing (AUD/EUR) was 1.69. Calculate the effective financing rate if the exchange rate prevailing on the maturity of the loan assumes the following values: (a) 1.75, (b) 1.65 and (c) 1.60.

2 Calculate the effective financing rate of a six-month Swiss franc loan on the basis of the following information (the exchange rate on maturity may assume any of the three values listed below):

Swiss six-month interest rate	3.75–4.25
Initial exchange rate (AUD/CHF)	1.1475–1.1525
Exchange rate on maturity (AUD/CHF)	1.1675–1.1725
	1.1475–1.1525
	1.1275–1.1325

3 The current one-year British interest rate is 8 per cent and the AUD/GBP exchange rate is 2.65. The exchange rate expected to prevail in one year has the following probability distribution:

AUD/GBP	Probability
2.55	0.05
2.60	0.10
2.65	0.15
2.70	0.25
2.75	0.45

(a) Construct a probability distribution for the effective financing rate.

(b) Calculate the expected value and the standard deviation of the effective financing rate in pounds.

4 The following information is available:

Swiss one-year interest rate	4%
Euro one-year interest rate	8%
Current spot AUD/CHF rate	1.10
Current spot AUD/EUR rate	1.60

The exchange rates prevailing one year from now have the following probability distributions:

AUD/CHF	Probability	AUD/EUR	Probability
1.08	0.05	1.54	0.05
1.10	0.10	1.56	0.10
1.12	0.15	1.58	0.15
1.14	0.25	1.60	0.25
1.16	0.45	1.62	0.45

(a) Construct probability distributions for the effective financing rates in Swiss francs and euros.
(b) Calculate the means and standard deviations of the effective financing rates.
(c) Construct a probability distribution for the effective financing rate of an equally weighted portfolio of the two currencies.
(d) Calculate the mean and the standard deviation of the effective financing rate of the portfolio based on the probability distribution obtained in (c).
(e) Comment on your results.

5 Calculate the effective rate of return on a six-month pound deposit on the basis of the following information (the exchange rate on maturity may assume any of the listed values):

British six-month deposit rate	7.75–8.25
Initial exchange rate (AUD/GBP)	2.5975–2.6025
Exchange rate on maturity (AUD/GBP)	2.6475–2.6525
	2.5975–2.6025
	2.5475–2.5525

6 The current one-year Swiss deposit rate is 4.5 per cent and the AUD/CHF exchange rate is 1.17. The exchange rate expected to prevail in one year's time has the following probability distribution:

AUD/CHF	Probability
1.15	0.05
1.17	0.10
1.19	0.15
1.21	0.25
1.23	0.45

(a) Construct a probability distribution for the effective rate of return.
(b) Calculate the expected value and the standard deviation of the effective rate of return on the Swiss franc.

7 The following information is available:

US one-year deposit rate	6%
British one-year deposit rate	8%
Current spot AUD/USD rate	1.75
Current spot AUD/GBP rate	2.60

The exchange rates prevailing one year from now have the following probability distributions:

AUD/USD	Probability	AUD/GBP	Probability
1.72	0.05	2.62	0.05
1.75	0.10	2.60	0.10
1.77	0.15	2.58	0.15
1.79	0.25	2.56	0.25
1.81	0.45	2.54	0.45

(a) Construct probability distributions for the effective rate of return on the US dollar and British pound investments.
(b) Calculate the means and the standard deviations of the effective rates of return.
(c) Construct a probability distribution for the effective rate of return on an equally weighted portfolio of the two currencies.
(d) Calculate the mean and standard deviation of the effective rate of return on the portfolio based on the probability distribution obtained in (c).
(e) Comment on your results.

8 An Australian-dollar-based firm has the following long and short positions on three Asian currencies: the Thai baht (THB), the Singapore dollar (SGD) and the Hong Kong dollar (HKD):

Currency	Receivables (long)	Payables (short)
THB	2 500 000	1 200 000
SGD	300 000	400 000
HKD	700 000	370 000

The current spot exchange rates are as follows:

THB/AUD 25.10–26.10
SGD/AUD 0.98–0.99
HKD/AUD 4.35–4.38

What happens if these positions are settled by buying or selling the foreign currencies at the current spot rates with and without exposure netting? Assume that there are no brokerage fees.

9 Consider the following Australian dollar payments that involve four companies (A, B, C and D):

From	To	Amount (AUD)
A	B	404 000
B	A	188 000
A	C	603 000
C	A	820 000
A	D	710 000
D	A	177 000
B	C	965 000
C	B	774 000
B	D	870 000
D	B	624 000
C	D	919 000
D	C	520 000

(a) Calculate the net payments after (i) bilateral netting and (ii) multilateral netting.
(b) If the cost of transferring funds is 1 per cent of the amount transferred, what is the cost saving resulting from (i) bilateral netting and (ii) multilateral netting?

CHAPTER

International long-term financing

Introduction

In this chapter we consider the international aspects of long-term financing. Since international short-term financing was covered in Chapter 15, long-term financing is defined here to include medium-term financing. Hence, this chapter deals with financing by raising capital via borrowing or issuing medium-term and long-term securities with maturities of more than one year.

Objectives

The objectives of this chapter are:
- To describe international bank loan financing.
- To distinguish among Eurobonds and foreign bonds.
- To demonstrate how the currency denominating a bond issue is chosen.
- To describe the primary and secondary international equity markets.
- To outline other means of international long-term financing.

16.1 International bank loan financing

International bank loans are classified into two categories: **foreign loans** and **Euroloans**. Foreign loans are raised by borrowers who are foreign to the country where the loans are raised. International loans, however, mostly take the form of Euroloans or Eurocredits, which are denominated in a currency other than the currency of the country where the loans are raised. Euroloans and foreign loans are also distinguished as follows. While Euroloans are financed wholly out of Eurocurrency funds, irrespective of whether the borrower is a resident or a non-resident of the country in question, foreign loans are domestic currency credits extended to non-resident borrowers.

Syndicated loans (Euro or foreign) are characterised by being so large in size that it becomes necessary to form a syndicate or a group of lending banks to finance the loan. The advantage of syndication is that it enables banks to spread the risk of very large loans among themselves. This is important because large multinational firms need credit in excess of what a single bank can offer. A syndicated loan is arranged by a lead bank on behalf of a client such as a multinational firm. The lead bank seeks the participation of a group (syndicate) of banks, each providing a portion of the loan.

The interest paid on syndicated loans is usually computed by adding a **spread** to the **London interbank offer rate (LIBOR)** or another **reference rate** such as the US **prime rate** or the **Singapore interbank offer rate (SIBOR)**. The following factors determine the spread:

- Whether the market is a borrower or a lender market (that is, the availability of liquidity or loanable funds relative to demand)—spreads are likely to be higher in a lenders' market, which is characterised by a shortage of liquidity and excess demand for loanable funds.

- The creditworthiness of the borrower, with lower spreads charged to high-quality borrowers—high-quality borrowers include sovereign OECD borrowers (that is, OECD governments), multinationals and major OECD companies and international organisations such as the World Bank.
- The maturity of the loan, with higher spreads charged on long-maturity loans.
- The fees charged—in addition to interest payments, the borrower is expected to pay **management fees, participation fees, commitment fees** and taxes. Management fees are charged by managing banks for their services. These are one-time charges levied when the loan agreement is signed. Participation fees are divided among all banks in relation to their share of the loan. Commitment fees are charged to the borrower as a percentage of the undrawn portion of the loan. There is normally a trade-off between fees and the spread over the reference rates. Banks prefer a combination of high fees and low spreads because they can advertise a low spread (which is good for business) without losing revenue.

RESEARCH FINDINGS

Pricing international loans

International borrowers pay different loan spreads depending on: (i) country risk; (ii) credit risk; and (iii) currency risk. A study by Sargen attempted to explain differences in the loan spreads that borrowers from different countries pay.[1] His findings indicated that borrowers from developing countries paid on average a spread of about 140 basis points over LIBOR, whereas borrowers from developed countries paid on average about 25 basis points less. The study also explained the differences in the spreads paid by borrowers from developing countries, including income, the **debt-service ratio** and inflation.

In another paper Brittain found that borrowers from developing countries with higher debt-to-GDP ratios paid higher spreads than otherwise.[2] Angelini, Eng and Lees managed to identify three variables that determine the loan spread: export growth, growth of per capita income and the ratio of GDP to external debt.[3]

1 N. P. Sargen, 'Commercial Bank Lending to Developing Countries', *Economic Review*, Federal Reserve Bank of San Francisco, Spring 1976, p. 29.

2 W. H. B. Brittain, 'Developing Countries' External Debt and the Private Banks', *Quarterly Review*, Banca Natzionale del Laviro, December 1977, pp. 378–9.

3 A. Angelini, M. Eng and F. Lees, *International Lending, Risk and the Euromarkets*, Macmillan, London, 1979.

16.2 International bond financing

Eurobonds and foreign bonds

International bonds can be **Eurobonds** or **foreign bonds**. Again, the distinction depends on whether the borrower is a domestic or a foreign resident and whether the issue is denominated in the domestic or a foreign currency. A Eurobond issue is underwritten by an international syndicate of banks and other financial institutions and placed (that is, sold) in countries other than the country in whose currency the issue is denominated. A foreign bond, on the other hand, is underwritten by a syndicate consisting of members from a single country, is sold primarily within that country and is denominated in its currency. The issuer (or borrower), however, is foreign. Even if the borrower is not particularly interested in the currency of the issue, the funds raised can be swapped for other currencies. In the early 1960s the volume of foreign bonds dwarfed that of Eurobonds, but this trend has been reversed.

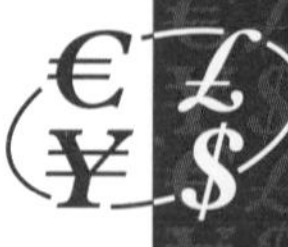

The secret war in the primary market for euro-denominated securities

When the primary market (that is, the market for new issues) for euro-denominated securities began, with the introduction of the new currency in 1999, it was expected that US investment banks, such as Morgan Stanley and Salomon Smith Barney, would dominate it. But this is not what happened, as Deutsche Bank, Paribas, Dresdner Kleinwort Benson and Warburg Dillon Read (all European financial institutions) dominated the market in its first year.

European investment bankers attribute this dominance to familiarity with the needs of European borrowers who provide the business. But US investment bankers disagree, claiming that their European competitors played a combination of relationship and nationalist cards. In its February 2000 issue, *Euromoney* quoted Charlie Berman of Salomon Smith Barney as saying that 'European banks tried to characterise this as a European bond market for European underwriters and investors'. He further claimed that 'many European banks told issuers that there was no need for US investment banks and to exclude them from syndicates'.

Foreign bonds have nicknames: foreign bonds sold in the United States are **Yankee bonds**, in Japan they are **Samurai bonds** and in the United Kingdom they are **Bulldogs**. In April 1992, the Australian government allowed foreign parties to raise funds in the Australian domestic capital market and this market came to be known as the **Matilda bond** market.

The Eurobond market, which is an extension of the offshore or external financial markets, has emerged because of some of the same factors that have led to the emergence of the Eurocurrency market or the market for short-term Eurocurrency funds. These include: (i) the absence of regulatory interference; (ii) less stringent disclosure requirements; and (iii) favourable tax status, as interest income is not subject to income and withholding tax.

IN PRACTICE

The Japanese like Korean issues of yen-denominated bonds

In November 1999, the Korea Development Bank re-opened the yen market for Korean borrowers. Since then, Korean yen issues have been met with enthusiasm by Japanese investors.

One such issue was launched by the Korea Electric Power Corporation in July 2000. This was a JPY30 billion issue of five-year bonds that was priced at par (that is, the price was equal to the par value to be received on the maturity of the bonds). With a coupon interest of 2.6 per cent, the rate of return on the issue was 83 basis points (0.83 percentage points) over the yen-LIBOR.

Types of international bonds

A bond is a fixed income security such that the bondholder (who is a creditor to the issuing firm) receives **coupon** interest payments and/or the **face value** of the bond when it matures.

Unlike dividends, which are paid to shareholders, interest payments to bondholders are contractual and command priority over dividend payments. International bonds can be of the following types.

Straight fixed-rate bonds

The most common type of bond is a **straight bond**, on which coupons are normally paid annually rather than semi-annually, primarily because it is a bearer bond (that is, it is not registered under a particular name). Interest payments are a fixed percentage (determined by the coupon rate) of the par or the face value of the bond. On maturity, the bondholder receives the face value and the last interest payment.

Floating rate notes

Unlike straight bonds, the holder of a **floating rate note (FRN)** receives a variable semi-annual coupon payment. The variable coupon rate is determined by adding a margin to a variable reference rate such as LIBOR. FRNs came to the market as a natural outcome of the increase in interest rate volatility, which caused investors to be reluctant to hold long-maturity straight bonds.

Convertible bonds

Convertible bonds are equity-related bonds. They resemble straight bonds, with the added feature that they are convertible to equity (that is, shares) prior to maturity at a specified price per share. This feature enables the borrower to issue debt instruments with lower coupon rates than the corresponding straight bonds. The lender in this case is willing to accept a lower coupon rate than on a comparable straight bond because of the attractiveness of the feature of convertibility.

Bonds with equity warrants

Bonds with equity warrants are another type of equity-related bond. They give the holder the extra privilege of having the right (which may or may not be exercised) to buy the shares of the same company issuing the bonds. Thus, warrants are like equity options except that the issuers of the bond and the warrant are the same party, unlike the case of options.

Zero-coupon bonds

The holder of a **zero-coupon bond** does not receive coupon payments prior to the maturity date. Upon maturity, the holder receives the full face value of the bond, which is initially purchased at a discount. The attractive feature of zero-coupon bonds is that they are not subject to **reinvestment risk**, which is encountered in the case of straight bonds. With the changing level of market interest rates, the holder of a straight bond is exposed to reinvestment risk because the holder does not know at what rate the coupon payments received prior to the maturity of the bond can be reinvested. Since zero-coupon bonds offer no coupon payments prior to maturity, this kind of risk does not arise.

Multicurrency bonds

The holder of a **multicurrency bond** receives payments in more than one currency. One variant is a **dual currency bond**, which has different currency denominations for coupon payments and face value payments.

Global bonds

The concept of **global bonds** was introduced by the World Bank in 1989. Global bonds are defined as very large issues, which are sold simultaneously in the world's major capital markets. Global bonds may be held and cleared through several different systems in the major geographical regions and the securities can move freely from one system to another. The implication of these characteristics is that these bonds are highly liquid.

Novel bonds

Novel bonds represent financial innovation in the bond market. Examples are **reverse floaters** (on which the coupon rate falls as market interest rates rise), **asset-backed bonds** (which are backed by a specific group of assets), **catastrophe bonds** (whose payments depend upon the materialisation of a certain event) and **indexed bonds** (whose payments are tied to the general price level or the price of a particular commodity).

The choice of the currency of denomination

As with short-term financing, the decision concerning the choice of the currency depends on the relative cost of borrowing in various currencies. Naturally, the (foreign exchange) risk factor is also taken into consideration, but we will for the time being concentrate on the cost of borrowing. In this case, we may say that for the same risk factor the issuer chooses the currency giving the lowest cost of borrowing. Otherwise, it is possible to invoke the assumption of risk neutrality, which implies that the borrower is indifferent between domestic currency and foreign currency issues if they produce the same cost of borrowing.

Suppose that a firm wants to raise an amount, K, of the domestic currency by issuing either domestic currency bonds or foreign currency bonds (which can be Eurobonds or foreign bonds). For simplicity, let us assume that these are zero-coupon bonds, such that all the payments are made on maturity, which we will assume to be n years. If a domestic currency bond is chosen, then the amount to be paid by the firm on maturity is

$$L_n = K(1 + i)^n \tag{16.1}$$

where i is the underlying interest rate. If foreign currency denomination is used, the foreign currency amount raised is K/S_0, where S_0 is the initial exchange rate. On maturity, the domestic currency equivalent of the foreign currency amount due is

$$L_n^* = \frac{KS_n}{S_0}(1 + i^*)^n \tag{16.2}$$

where S_n is the exchange rate prevailing on maturity when the borrowed funds are to be repaid. Equation (16.2) can be rewritten as

$$L_n^* = K(1 + \dot{S})^n(1 + i^*)^n \tag{16.3}$$

where $\dot{S}$ is the annual percentage rate of change of the exchange rate between 0 and n.

Assuming risk neutrality, foreign currency denomination will be preferred if $L_n^* < L_n$ or if

$$K(1 + \dot{S})^n(1 + i^*)^n < K(1 + i)^n \tag{16.4}$$

which can be simplified to give the condition

$$i^* + \dot{S} < i \tag{16.5}$$

If this condition is satisfied, the bond issue should be denominated in foreign rather than domestic currency. Let us assume that, from an Australian perspective, the foreign currency is the Swiss franc. An Australian company should, if the condition represented by (16.5) is satisfied, choose a Swiss franc issue rather than an Australian dollar issue. If the company sells the bonds in Switzerland, this would be a foreign bond issue. If the bonds were sold in any other country, it would be a Eurobond issue. On the other hand, if $i^* + \dot{S} > i$, then the issuing firm should use domestic currency denomination. In the case of the Australian firm, if the bonds were sold in Australia, it would be a domestic (rather than an international) bond issue. If the bonds were sold outside Australia, it would be a Eurobond issue.

IN PRACTICE

Issuing bonds denominated in exotic currencies

In the 1980s, international firms started to tap the Kuwaiti dinar (KWD) bond market to raise US dollar funds. The idea was very simple: the interest rate on the Kuwaiti dinar was six percentage points below that on the US dollar. Because of the exchange rate arrangement of pegging the KWD to a basket of currencies with a dominant dollar component, the exchange rate between the two currencies tended to be rather stable, which eliminated a great part of the foreign exchange risk (see Chapter 5). The following table shows the exchange rates of the Kuwaiti dinar, the Japanese yen, the former German mark and the British pound against the US dollar during the first half of the 1980s. It is obvious that the KWD was much more stable against the USD than the other currencies. Thus, the KWD was called a 'cheap dollar', as the (cheap) funds borrowed by issuing KWD bonds were converted into US dollars.

Year end	KWD/USD	JPY/USD	DEM/USD	GBP/USD
1980	0.27391	214.60	1.94	0.427
1981	0.28210	216.15	2.23	0.514
1982	0.29150	248.11	2.46	0.612
1983	0.29230	233.87	2.70	0.684
1984	0.30360	246.42	3.06	0.826
1985	0.28920	200.65	2.46	0.694

Things have changed, however. The Kuwaiti dinar is no longer a cheap dollar because the interest rate on the KWD has become higher than that on the US dollar and other major currencies. The interest rate hike of the 1990s came as a response to excessive capital outflows. Furthermore, the exchange rate arrangement was changed in January 2003 by pegging the KWD to the USD.

Example

An Australian firm is planning to raise funds by issuing five-year bonds. The firm is considering the choice between an Australian dollar bond issue at an annual interest rate of 6 per cent and a US dollar bond issue at an annual interest rate of 3 per cent. If, in the next five years, the US dollar is expected to appreciate against the Australian dollar by an average of 2 per cent per year, then $i^* + \dot{S} = 5\%$. Hence, the US dollar issue should be preferred since the Australian dollar issue costs 6 per cent.

It must be remembered, however, that the cost of the Australian dollar issue is known with certainty, whereas the cost of the US dollar issue depends on what actually happens to the exchange rate. Hence, the choice depends on the attitude towards risk.

Continued...

In this case, the issuer may want to minimise the cost of borrowing per unit of risk, which is measured by the standard deviation of the cost of borrowing in a foreign currency. It must be borne in mind that both domestic currency and foreign currency issues are subject to the risk (from the perspective of the issuer) of falling interest rates following the launch of the issue. In subsequent years the borrower may have to pay a higher interest rate than what is available in the market. This is why some bond issues have a call option, whereby the issuer can buy back the bonds prior to maturity. Note that the term 'call option' has a different meaning here from what we came across in Chapter 7.

IN PRACTICE

Euro-denominated issues by Asian entities

Some two years after the launch of the euro in January 1999, the amount of euro-denominated bonds issued by Asian sovereigns and corporates remained dismal. Asian borrowers found it rather tough to sell their euro-denominated bonds to Europeans, who are the major buyers of euro-denominated securities.

The main reason for this state of affairs is that European investors tend to buy only high-quality bonds, those rated AA or AAA (see Chapter 17 for bond rating). Asia is perceived to be made up of low credit-rated borrowers. Moreover, investment bankers have identified the fact that there is a cost of entry for non-European borrowers. A premium has to be paid for this purpose.

Another problem is that the weakness of the euro in the aforementioned period made big international (non-European) investors shy away from assets denominated in this currency. With the adverse performance of the currency and the underlying bond market, non-European investors have seen their euro-denominated portfolios underperform. Consequently, the demand for euro-denominated securities remained rather weak. Thus, this state of affairs was created by both supply-side and demand-side factors.

16.3 International equity financing

Unlike loans and bonds, the internationalisation of equities did not take off until about 1983. Privatisation has been a major force behind the volume of international equity issues placed by Germany, France, the United Kingdom and Italy, but not those of the United States. The surge in privatisation worldwide is having a profound impact on capital markets in general and on equity markets in particular. **International equity markets** encompass **primary market** functions (underwriting of new equity issues) and **secondary market** functions (trading of equities outside the issuer's home country). Euronext is an example of an international secondary equity market, accounting for a large portion of international equity trading (see the box opposite).

International business firms operate in international equity markets by listing their shares on foreign stock exchanges (the secondary market function) and by selling new shares to foreigners (the primary market function). We will deal with these functions in turn.

Listing on foreign stock exchanges

One of the objectives of listing on foreign stock exchanges is to improve the liquidity of existing shares by enabling foreign shareholders to trade them in their home markets and currencies. Another objective is to boost the listing firm's commercial and political visibility in foreign countries. A third objective is to support a new equity issue. Finally, a fourth objective is to broaden ownership outside the national frontiers, which may help reduce price fluctuations.

In the United States, foreign shares are traded through **American Depository Receipts (ADRs)**. These are negotiable certificates issued by a US bank in the United States to represent the underlying shares, which are held in trust at a custodian bank. ADRs can be exchanged for the underlying foreign shares, or vice versa, with arbitrage activities keeping foreign and US prices the same. Dividends paid by a foreign firm are passed to its custodial bank and then to the bank issuing the ADRs. The issuing bank converts the foreign currency dividends into US dollars, which are then distributed to ADR holders.

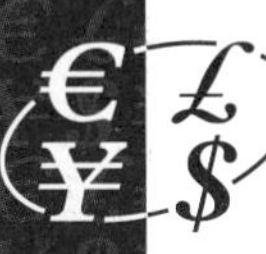

IN PRACTICE

Competition among European stock exchanges

Euronext, the Paris-based European regional stock exchange, initially emerged out of the merger of the Paris, Brussels and Amsterdam stock exchanges. Subsequently, it expanded by merging with LIFFE, the London derivatives exchange. Currently, Euronext, the London Stock Exchange and Frankfurt's Deutsche Borse dominate the European scene, competing with each other, seeking more domination.

In July 2002, Euronext made a big move to outplay its rivals when Euroclear, which settles trades on Euronext, acquired Crest, its opposite number in London. This deal meant that two important pieces of the London financial infrastructure have swung the Paris way. The feeling dominating financial markets is that the London Stock Exchange was not doing enough to stem the tide created by Euronext. The *Financial Times* reported that 'while the LSE may talk global, there is little yet to show for it'.[1]

[1] 'Stock Exchanges Play for a Winning Position', *Financial Times*, 8 July 2002.

The benefits of listing on foreign stock exchanges must be balanced against the cost of the implied commitment to full disclosure. Because the disclosure guidelines of the US Securities and Exchange Commission (SEC) are more stringent than in other countries, it is easier for US firms to list on foreign stock exchanges than for non-US firms to list on US stock exchanges. Once the decision to list on a foreign stock exchange has been taken, the question arises as to where to list. The choice depends on the motive behind foreign listing. If the motive is to support a new equity issue, the target market should be the listing market. If it is to increase the firm's commercial and political visibility, the market should be the one in which the firm has significant physical operations. If the motive is to improve the liquidity of existing shares, then the market should be a major liquid market such as London, New York, Tokyo, Frankfurt or Paris. These markets account for more than half of the total capitalisation of stock markets around the world.

IN PRACTICE

Listing in the US becomes even more difficult

In May 2001, the US Securities and Exchange Commission announced new disclosure rules, requiring companies seeking to sell securities in the United States to disclose their activities in countries subject to US sanctions (such as Cuba, Iraq and Sudan). This requirement changes the way in which the SEC reinforces its requirement to disclose anything that makes an offering risky or speculative. Before the implementation of the new requirement, the disclosure was applicable to environmental risk or lawsuits, but now it applies to political risk and national security.

The new requirement was announced in an unorthodox way—in a letter from the SEC chairman to the chair of the House subcommittee responsible for the SEC's funding. In its issue of 19 May 2002, *The Economist* reported that the chairman of the subcommittee was furious that PetroChina, one of China's oil companies, was able to seek New York listing in 2000 at a time when it was selling oil to Sudan.

Selling new shares in international markets

A firm may sell its newly issued shares to foreign investors in one of the following ways:

- The firm may sell shares in a particular foreign stock market underwritten in whole or in part by institutions from the host country. This may take the form of a private placement.
- The firm may sell Euro-equity issues to foreign investors in more than one country simultaneously. The prefix 'Euro' has the same meaning we came across earlier (not the new European currency). The integration of the world capital markets has led to the emergence of a Euro-equity market.
- The firm may sell a foreign subsidiary's shares to investors in the host country. This can lower a firm's cost of capital if investors in the host country award a higher capitalisation rate on the subsidiary's earnings than on the firm's earnings.
- The firm may sell shares to a foreign firm as part of a strategic alliance. This may involve sharing the cost of developing new technology or pursuing complementary marketing activities.

INSIGHT

Public offerings and private placements

There are two types of offerings of new issues of securities: **public offerings** and **private placements**. In a public offering the issuer offers the issued securities to the public at large, giving any investor the right to buy the newly issued securities, subject to availability. In this case, the entire process of the offering is governed by the regulators, such as APRA in Australia. A private placement, on the other hand, means that the entire issue is sold to a single buyer or a small number (consortium) of buyers.

An issuing firm may resort to private placement because it enables it to avoid the scrutiny of the regulators, thus saving the costs of disclosure. Moreover, a public offering may involve some public disclosure of the firm's business plans, which the firm may want to avoid. From the perspective of the buyers (normally cash-rich institutions such as insurance companies), a private placement is attractive because privately placed securities are cheaper than those sold in a public offering. The problem, however, is that privately placed securities lack liquidity, since they cannot be traded in the secondary market.

16.4 Other sources of financing

There are some other means of long-term financing. These are: (i) parallel loans; (ii) credit swaps; (iii) government lending; and (iv) development institution lending. These are discussed in turn below.

Parallel loans

A **parallel loan** involves an initial exchange of funds between firms in different countries, such that the transaction is reversed at some time in the future. For example, suppose that a subsidiary of an Australian company (say, Rio Tinto) in Japan needs some yen funds, and the subsidiary of a Japanese company (say, Toyota) in Australia needs funds in Australian dollars. The Australian company lends the Japanese subsidiary Australian dollar funds, and the Japanese company lends the Australian subsidiary an approximately equivalent amount in yen. After an agreed period, the Australian subsidiary pays off the yen loan (principal plus interest), and the Japanese subsidiary simultaneously pays off the Australian dollar loan. Obviously, this operation does not involve any foreign exchange risk, because no currency conversion takes place. Figure 16.1 shows how the parallel loan in this example works.

Figure 16.1 A parallel loan

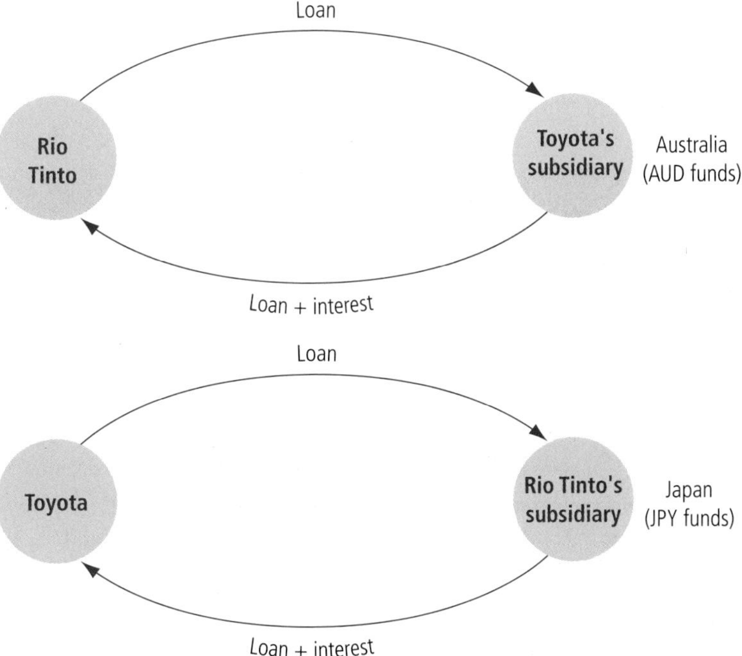

Parallel loans were specifically designed to circumvent foreign exchange controls. However, they have the added advantage over bank lending that the two firms can avoid transaction costs in the form of bid-offer spreads in both interest and exchange rates. The problem with parallel loans arises because of the difficulty of finding two counterparties with exactly matching needs.

Credit swaps

A **credit swap** makes it possible to acquire a loan for a foreign subsidiary without having to send funds abroad. It involves the exchange of currencies between a bank (say, the NAB) and a firm (say, BHP), not between two firms. The procedure is best illustrated with an example. BHP places Australian dollar funds with the NAB in Australia for a certain period. The NAB then instructs its Japanese correspondent bank (or branch or subsidiary) to grant BHP's Japanese subsidiary a yen loan. On the maturity of the loan and the deposit, the correspondent bank receives the loan repayment, whereas BHP receives the matured deposit. This operation is illustrated in Figure 16.2.

Figure 16.2 A credit swap

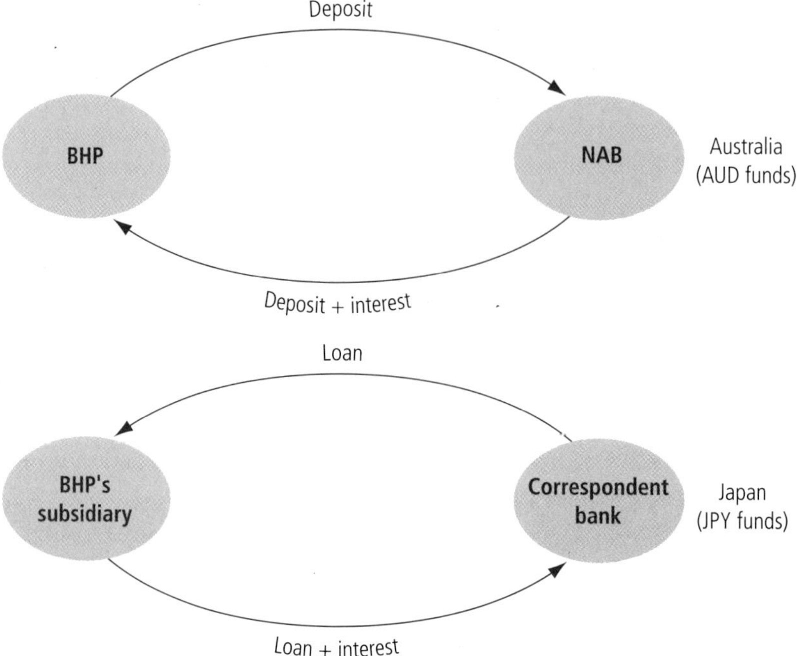

Government lending

Governments of countries acting as hosts to foreign direct investment may provide financing when they believe that the underlying projects will generate jobs, facilitate the transfer of technology and/or provide training for local workers. For example, Australian state governments have used special financing arrangements to attract foreign investors.

Lending by international development institutions

There are a number of development institutions that grant developing countries loans to finance infrastructure projects. While these loans are granted to the host governments, the companies working there are financed indirectly. For example, a development institution may grant Papua New Guinea a **soft loan** (that is, a loan with low or zero interest) to finance a project to build a road to link a gold mine with Port Moresby. If the gold mine is operated by BHP, then the loan is effectively granted to BHP because the project benefits the company's operations.

Summary

- International bank loans can be either foreign loans or Euroloans. Foreign loans are raised by borrowers who are foreign to the countries where the loans are raised. Euroloans are denominated in currencies other than the currency of the country where the loans are raised.
- The spread on syndicated Euroloans over the reference rate is determined by a number of factors including: (i) the state of the market; (ii) the creditworthiness of the borrower; (iii) the maturity of the loan; and (iv) the fees charged.
- International bonds can be Eurobonds or foreign bonds. The distinction depends on whether the borrower is a domestic or a foreign resident and on the currency of denomination.
- International bonds are of several types, including: (i) straight fixed-rate bonds; (ii) floating rate notes; (iii) convertible bonds; (iv) bonds with equity warrants; (v) zero-coupon bonds; (vi) multicurrency bonds; (vii) global bonds; and (viii) novel bonds.
- A foreign-currency-denominated bond issue is preferred to a domestic-currency-denominated bond issue if the sum of the foreign interest rate and the expected appreciation of the foreign currency is lower than the domestic interest rate.
- International equity markets encompass primary market functions (underwriting of new issues) and secondary market functions (trading). International firms operate in international equity markets by listing their shares on foreign stock exchanges and by selling newly issued shares to foreigners.
- A firm may sell its newly issued shares to foreign investors in one of the following ways: (i) selling shares in a foreign stock market; (ii) selling Euro-equity issues; (iii) selling a foreign subsidiary's shares to investors in the host country; and (iv) selling shares to a foreign firm as part of a strategic alliance.
- Other means of long-term financing include: (i) parallel loans; (ii) credit swaps; (iii) government lending; and (iv) lending by international development institutions.

Key terms

American Depository Receipts (ADRs) 469
asset-backed bonds 466
bonds with equity warrants 465
Bulldogs 464
catastrophe bonds 466
commitment fees 463
convertible bonds 465
coupon 464
credit swap 472
debt-service ratio 463
dual currency bond 465
Eurobonds 463
Euroloans 462
face value 464
floating rate note (FRN) 465
foreign bonds 463
foreign loans 462
global bonds 465
indexed bonds 466
international bank loans 462
international bonds 463
international equity markets 468
London interbank offer rate (LIBOR) 462
management fees 463
Matilda bond 464
multicurrency bond 465
novel bonds 466
parallel loan 471
participation fees 463
primary market 468

MAXIMISE YOUR MARKS! There are 30 interactive questions for this chapter available online at **www.mhhe.com/au/moosa2e**

prime rate 462
private placements 470
public offerings 470
reference rate 462
reinvestment risk 465
reverse floaters 466
Samurai bonds 464
secondary market 468
Singapore interbank offer rate (SIBOR) 462
soft loan 472
spread 462
straight bond 465
syndicated loans 462
Yankee bonds 464
zero-coupon bond 465

Review questions

1 Distinguish between foreign loans and Euroloans.

2 What are syndicated loans?

3 What are the reasons for the relative decline of international syndicated loans as a means of raising capital in recent years?

4 What determines the spread over the reference rate in calculating the interest charged on syndicated loans?

5 Distinguish between Eurobonds and foreign bonds.

6 Why has the Eurobond market emerged?

7 What is the difference between straight bonds and FRNs?

8 Why are investors willing to hold convertible bonds although they offer lower coupon interest rates than straight bonds with similar characteristics?

9 What is the difference between a bond with an equity warrant and an equity option?

10 What are novel bonds?

11 What does a firm aim at when it lists its shares on foreign stock exchanges?

12 What are ADRs?

13 What are the means whereby a firm may sell its newly issued shares to foreign investors?

14 What is the difference between a public offering and a private placement?

15 Why has privatisation been a major force behind the growth of international equity issues in recent years?

16 Apart from issuing bonds or equities, what other means are available whereby a firm can raise capital?

CHAPTER

International long-term portfolio investment

Introduction

In this chapter we discuss the issue of international long-term investment in securities or financial assets, mainly bonds and equities. This kind of investment is described as 'long term' because the underlying financial assets either have long maturities of more than one year (bonds) or do not have a defined maturity (equities). It is called 'portfolio investment' because it normally involves a portfolio of securities, such that individual holdings constitute only a small portion of the capital or debt of the underlying firms that issue these securities. This characteristic distinguishes portfolio investment from direct investment, as the latter involves buying big stakes with the objective of exerting some control over the underlying firms by being eligible for membership on the boards of directors. Another characteristic of portfolio investment is the often high turnover of the securities of which the portfolio consists.

Objectives

The objectives of this chapter are:

- To explain how the choice is made between domestic and foreign securities.
- To explain how to determine the risk and return on foreign portfolio investment.
- To consider the effect of taxation on the choice between domestic and foreign portfolio investments.
- To illustrate the effect of international portfolio diversification.
- To extrapolate the capital asset pricing model to internationally diversified portfolios.

17.1 Bond investment

A **bond** is a fixed-income security. It offers fixed contractual payments in the form of periodic coupon interest payments (paid annually or semi-annually) and a **par value** or a **face value** that is paid on the maturity of the bond. These payments are contractual in the sense that they are fixed irrespective of what happens in the market (for example, changes in the level of interest rates) throughout the life of the bond. If the bond is a zero-coupon bond, then there are no periodic interest payments, but the bondholder is entitled to the full face value of the bond upon maturity, having bought it at a discount from the face value.

Let us for simplicity of exposition assume that we are dealing with investment in zero-coupon bonds. If a bond with a face value F and maturity of n years is bought at time 0 at a price P_0 and held until maturity, then the bondholder will at year n receive the face value, F. The annual compound rate of return, r, on this bond investment can be calculated from the equation

$$P_0(1 + r)^n = F \tag{17.1}$$

in which case r is given by

$$r = \left(\frac{F}{P_0}\right)^{1/n} - 1 \tag{17.2}$$

Then, in general, if a domestic currency amount, K, is invested for n years in a domestic bond (or a domestic bond portfolio) offering an implicit rate of return, r, the value of the investment after n years is given by

$$I_n = K(1 + r)^n \quad (17.3)$$

We could derive a similar expression for a foreign currency bond investment. The domestic currency amount, K, is converted into foreign currency at the spot exchange rate prevailing at time 0, S_0, to obtain K/S_0 units of the foreign currency. This amount is then used to buy foreign-currency bonds offering an annual rate of return of r^*. The foreign currency amount accumulated after n years is obtained by compounding the initial amount at r^* to obtain $K/S_0(1 + r^*)^n$. The domestic currency value of this investment at year n, I_n^*, is obtained by converting the foreign currency amount into domestic currency at the spot exchange rate prevailing at year n, S_n, to obtain

$$I_n^* = K(1+r^*)^n\left(\frac{S_n}{S_0}\right) \quad (17.4)$$

We could express the ratio of the exchange rate at year n to the exchange rate at year 0, S_n/S_0, in terms of the average annual rate of change in the exchange rate, $\dot{S}$, as follows:

$$\frac{S_n}{S_0} = (1 + \dot{S})^n \quad (17.5)$$

Therefore,

$$I_n^* = K(1+r^*)^n(1+\dot{S})^n \quad (17.6)$$

Now we are in a position to make a choice between investing in domestic-currency bonds and foreign-currency bonds. Assuming risk neutrality (in the sense that the investor is indifferent between the two investments if they offer the same return), foreign-currency bonds will be preferred if $I_n^* > I_n$ or if

$$K(1+r^*)^n(1+\dot{S})^n > K(1+r)^n \quad (17.7)$$

which can be approximated, by working out the expression and ignoring the small cross products, to

$$\dot{S} > r - r^* \quad (17.8)$$

The condition represented by (17.8) says that investment in foreign-currency bonds will be preferred if the foreign currency is expected to appreciate by more than the difference between the rate of return on domestic-currency bonds and foreign-currency bonds. The condition also implies that foreign-currency bonds will be preferred even if they offer a lower rate of return than domestic-currency bonds, provided that the foreign currency appreciates by more than the differential return, $r - r^*$.

Example

An Australian investor has AUD1 million to invest in five-year bonds. The investor is considering the choice between investing in Australian-dollar bonds that offer a rate of return (yield to maturity) of 8 per cent per annum and British-pound bonds offering a rate of return of 6 per cent. The current exchange rate (AUD/GBP) is 2.70, but the

Continued...

pound is expected to appreciate against the Australian dollar by an average rate of 3 per cent per annum over the next five years. Assuming risk neutrality, what will the investor choose?

If the investor chooses Australian-dollar bonds, the value of the capital invested in year 5 will be

$$1\,000\,000(1 + 0.08)^5 = \text{AUD}1\,469\,328$$

To invest AUD1 000 000 in pound bonds, this amount must first be converted into pounds, to obtain

$$\frac{1\,000\,000}{2.70} = \text{GBP}370\,370$$

When this amount is invested in pound bonds for five years, it produces

$$370\,370(1 + 0.06)^5 = \text{GBP}495\,639$$

If the exchange rate rises by 3 per cent over five years, then at the end of the fifth year, the exchange rate will be

$$2.70(1 + 0.03)^5 = 3.13$$

The Australian dollar value of the pound amount received on maturity is

$$495\,639 \times 3.13 = \text{AUD}1\,551\,350$$

which is greater than the amount received from investing in Australian-dollar bonds.

The same conclusion can be reached by utilising the inequality (17.8). In this case, $\dot{S} = 0.03$, whereas $r - r^* = 0.08 - 0.06 = 0.02$, hence the inequality is satisfied and the investor should choose pound bonds. In general, pound bonds will be preferred if the pound appreciates against the Australian dollar by more than 2 per cent ($\dot{S} > 0.02$).

It is important to bear in mind that at time 0 the two rates of return (r and r^*) are known if the bonds are held until maturity, since the coupon payments and the face values are known in advance. However, the change in the exchange rate is not known in advance, in which case the investor has to act on the basis of the expected change in the exchange rate. At year n, the value of the change in the exchange rate is realised, at which time the investor can determine, ex post, whether or not the right decision was made at time 0.

The effect of taxes

We now compare the after-tax returns on domestic currency and foreign currency bond investments. Two kinds of taxes are relevant to the return on bond investment: **income tax** and **capital gains tax**. Income tax is applied to interest income, whereas capital gains tax is applied to capital gains. If the bonds are held until maturity, then the return on domestic-currency bonds takes the form of interest income, which makes this return subject to income tax only. The return on foreign-currency bonds consists of interest income and the appreciation of the foreign currency, which occurs when the exchange rate rises ($S_n > S_0$). Hence, the return on foreign-currency bonds is subject to capital gains tax in addition to

The market value of a bond investment

Let us consider the value of an investment in a bond with a maturity of n years after k years, such that $k < n$, which means the value of the investment at a particular point in time before maturity. If the bond has annual coupon payments, then the bondholder receives k coupon payments after k years, where each payment is equal to the coupon rate (in per cent) multiplied by the face value of the bond, $C = cF$. The total value of the bond investment consists of (i) the accumulated value of the coupon payments reinvested at the market interest rate, i, and (ii) the market value of the bond (that is, how much it is worth if it is to be sold at that point in time), which is equal to the discounted value of the future cash flows. The future cash flows are the remaining coupon payments and the face value of the bond, which are paid to the holder on maturity. Thus, we can write an expression for the value of the bond investment at k as follows:

$$V = \left[C(1+i)^{k-1} + C(1+i)^{k-2} + \ldots + C\right] + \left[\frac{C}{1+i} + \frac{C}{(1+i)^2} + \ldots \frac{C+F}{(1+i)^{n-k}}\right]$$

where the term in the first square bracket is the value of the reinvested coupon payments and the term in the second square bracket is the market value of the bond. Notice that since C and F are fixed, the value of the bond depends on the market interest rate, i. The equation can be written as

$$V = C\left[(1+i)^{k-1} + (1+i)^{k-2} + \ldots + 1 + \frac{1}{1+i} + \frac{1}{(1+i)^2} + \ldots + \frac{1}{(1+i)^{n-k}}\right] + \frac{F}{(1+i)^{n-k}}$$

In the case of a foreign bond investment, the domestic currency value of the investment after k years depends on what is done with the coupon payments. If the coupon payments are converted into the domestic currency and invested at the domestic interest rate, then the domestic currency value of the bond investment is

$$V = C\left[S_1(1+i)^{k-1} + S_2(1+i)^{k-2} + \ldots + S_k\left(1 + \frac{1}{1+i^*} + \frac{1}{(1+i^*)^2} + \ldots + \frac{1}{(1+i^*)^{n-k}}\right)\right] + \frac{S_k F}{(1+i^*)^{n-k}}$$

Alternatively, if the coupon payments are re-invested at the foreign rate then:

$$V = CS_k\left[(1+i^*)^{k-1} + (1+i^*)^{k-2} + \ldots + 1 + \frac{1}{1+i^*} + \frac{1}{(1+i^*)^2} + \ldots + \frac{1}{(1+i^*)^{n-k}}\right] + \frac{S_k F}{(1+i^*)^{n-k}}$$

In both cases, the domestic currency value of the bond investment depends on the foreign interest rate and the exchange rate.

INSIGHT

income tax. The condition represented by (17.8) can thus be modified, to take into account the effect of taxes, to the following:

$$(1 + \tau_k)\dot{S} > (1 - \tau_y)r - (1 - \tau_y)r^* \tag{17.9}$$

where τ_k is the capital gains tax applicable to foreign exchange gains and τ_y is the income tax rate applicable to interest income. For the time being, we will assume that the domestic and foreign tax rates are identical. By manipulating Equation (17.9) we obtain the following rule: foreign-currency bonds will be preferred if

$$\dot{S} > \left[\frac{1 - \tau_y}{1 - \tau_k}\right](r - r^*) \tag{17.10}$$

Let us now consider what happens if the capital gains tax is less than the income tax rate. If $\tau_k < \tau_y$, then $(1 - \tau_y)/(1 - \tau_k) < 1$, which means that the right-hand side of (17.10) is smaller than the right-hand side of (17.8). Thus, the condition required to prefer foreign-currency bonds can be more easily satisfied on an after-tax basis. For given rates of return on domestic- and foreign-currency bonds, a lower rate of appreciation of the foreign currency is required to prefer foreign-currency bonds on an after-tax basis than on a before-tax basis.

If, on the other hand, $\tau_k > \tau_y$, then $(1 - \tau_y)/(1 - \tau_k) > 1$, which means that, for given rates of return on domestic- and foreign-currency bonds, a higher rate of appreciation of the foreign currency is required to prefer foreign-currency bonds on an after-tax basis than on a before-tax basis. The reason for this is simple. Foreign currency appreciation is taxed at the capital gains tax rate, not at the income tax rate. Thus, a lower capital gains tax rate encourages investing in bonds denominated in currencies that are expected to appreciate.

IN PRACTICE

Online bond trading

Bond traders have for some time lagged behind the rest of the economy in entering the 'new economy' by resisting ventures aimed at **online trading**. In 2000, however, the rush started when leading bond market firms dived in. As a result, dozens of platforms have been launched with the objective of providing buy-side institutions and issuers with the benefits of electronic trading.

The main bond trading platforms can be split into two groups: multiple dealer sites aimed at providing buyers with a range of prices in a limited set of products and single dealer multiproduct sites where one dealer offers access to many kinds of products but with no price comparison. An example of the latter is *Prime Trade*, the platform of Credit Suisse First Boston, which has also taken a position in most of the ventures in the multidealer ventures. It seems, however, that the rush created an oversupply of these sites, which will necessarily bring about consolidation in the form of mergers.

Let us now consider the case when there are different tax rates, assuming that tax is applied only in the country where the investment is undertaken. We assume that there are two different income tax rates but no capital gains tax. In this case, the interest income derived from domestic-currency bonds is taxed at the domestic income tax rate, τ_y, whereas the interest income derived from foreign-currency bonds is taxed at the foreign income tax rate, τ_y^*. Thus, the condition given by (17.9) changes to

$$\dot{S} > (1 - \tau_y)r - (1 - \tau_y^*)r^* \quad (17.11)$$

which says that foreign-currency bonds will be preferred to domestic-currency bonds if the foreign currency is expected to appreciate by more than the after-tax rate of return differential.

Example

Use the information in the previous example and assume a domestic income tax rate of 30 per cent, a foreign income tax rate of 25 per cent and a zero capital gains tax. Will the investor prefer Australian dollar or pound bonds? What is the minimum appreciation required for the Australian investor to prefer pound bonds?

The after-tax rate of return on Australian dollar bonds is

$$(1 - 0.3) \times 8 = 5.6\%$$

The after-tax rate of return on pound bonds is

$$(1 - 0.25) \times 6 + 3 = 7.5\%$$

This means that the investor will prefer pound bonds because they offer a higher rate of return. The final value of the invested capital can be calculated by compounding the initial capital at these two rates for five years. In general, pound bonds will be preferred if the pound appreciates by more than

$$(1 - 0.3) \times 8 - (1 - 0.25) \times 6 = 1.1\%$$

Bond rating

Bond investment is subject to credit risk arising from the possibility that the issuer may default on payments to the bondholders. This is why bonds are rated according to this risk or equivalently according to the quality of the issuers (high-quality issuers have low credit risk, and vice versa). Two US financial services firms, Moody's and Standard & Poor's, rate bonds in four categories according to several financial ratios that measure the profitability, the liquidity and the ability of the issuer to meet debt obligations. The following table shows the symbols used by Moody's and Standard & Poor's in rating bonds. According to Moody's, Aaa represents bonds of the highest rating, whereas D represents bonds with the lowest rating. The corresponding symbols for Standard and Poor's are AAA and D, respectively. The bonds are classified as (i) very high quality, (ii) high quality, (iii) speculative and (iv) very poor.

	Very high quality	High quality	Speculative	Very poor
Moody's	Aaa	A	Ba	Caa
	Aa	Baa	B	Ca
				C
				D
Standard & Poor's	AAA	A	BB	CCC
	AA	BBB	B	CC
				C
				D

17.2 Equity investment

When you invest by buying **equities** (also called stocks or shares) in a company, you become a shareholder of that company. As a shareholder, you are entitled to dividend payments, which are proportional to your equity holdings. These payments, however, are not contractual in the sense that they may or may not be paid even if the company makes profit. The company may simply decide, at the discretion of the board of directors, not to distribute any **dividends** and opt for **retained earnings** or **undistributed earnings** to finance further expansion. But even with this in mind, investors buy shares in anticipation of making profit through **capital appreciation** resulting from the rise in the price or the market value of these shares.

Investment in equities, therefore, provides a return in two forms: dividends and capital appreciation. Let us assume that an equity is bought at time 0, at a price P_0. At time 1, a dividend, D_1, is paid and the market price of the equity rises to P_1. The rate of return on the equity investment between time 0 and time 1 can be written as

$$R = \frac{D_1 + P_1 - P_0}{P_0} \tag{17.12}$$

Equation (17.12) can be rearranged to give

$$R = \frac{D_1}{P_0} + \frac{\Delta P_1}{P_0} \tag{17.13}$$

Equation (17.13) shows the two components of the rate of return on equity investment. The first component, D_1/P_0, is the dividend as a percentage of the purchase price: this is called the **dividend yield**. The second component, $\Delta P_1/P_0$, is the change in the price during the period between 0 and 1 as a percentage of the purchase price. This is the capital appreciation component. The dividend yield can be zero if no dividend is paid out at time 1. The capital appreciation component can be positive, negative or zero, depending on what happens to the equity price between time 0 and time 1. If the price increases, such that $P_1 > P_0$, then $\Delta P_1 > 0$, which means that the capital appreciation component is positive. If the price does not change such that $P_1 = P_0$, then $\Delta P_1 = 0$, which means that the capital appreciation component is zero. And if the price falls such that $P_1 < P_0$, then $\Delta P_1 < 0$, which means that the capital appreciation component is negative.

Example

An investor buys equities of an Australian company at the price of AUD5 per share. By the end of the year, the price of these shares rises to AUD6, while a dividend of AUD0.50 per share is paid. The total rate of return, the dividend yield and the rate of capital appreciation can be calculated respectively as follows:

$$R = \frac{0.50 + 6.00 - 5.00}{5.00} = 0.3 \text{ or } 30\%$$

$$\frac{D_1}{P_0} = \frac{0.50}{5.00} = 0.1 \text{ or } 10\%$$

$$\frac{\Delta P_1}{P_0} = \frac{6.00 - 5.00}{5.00} = 0.2 \text{ or } 20\%$$

Let us write Equation (17.13) as

$$R = d + a \tag{17.14}$$

where d is the dividend yield and a is the rate of capital appreciation, both of which are measured in percentage terms. If a domestic currency amount, K, is invested in equities for n periods (years), and assuming that dividend payments can be reinvested at the same underlying rate of return, then the value of the invested capital at year n, I_n, is given by $I_n = K(1 + R)^n$, or

$$I_n = K(1 + d + a)^n \tag{17.15}$$

Let us now consider what happens if the same amount is invested in foreign equities. The amount K is converted at the spot exchange rate, S_0, to obtain K/S_0 units of the foreign currency. The domestic currency value of the investment after n years, I_n^*, is obtained by compounding the foreign currency amount invested at the rate of return on foreign equities. This amount is then reconverted into the domestic currency at the exchange rate prevailing then, S_n. Thus, we obtain

$$I_n^* = \frac{KS_n}{S_0}(1 + d^* + a^*)^n \tag{17.16}$$

where d^* and a^* are the dividend yield and the rate of capital appreciation associated with foreign equity investment, respectively. By substituting Equation (17.5) into Equation (17.16) we obtain

$$I_n^* = K(1 + \dot{S})^n(1 + d^* + a^*)^n \tag{17.17}$$

Assuming risk neutrality, in the sense that the investor is indifferent between domestic and foreign equities if they offer the same rate of return, foreign investment will be preferred if $I_n^* > I_n$ or if

$$K(1 + \dot{S})^n(1 + d^* + a^*)^n > K(1 + d + a)^n \tag{17.18}$$

This can be approximated by working out the expressions and ignoring the small cross product terms, to obtain

$$\dot{S} > (d - d^*) + (a - a^*) \tag{17.19}$$

which means that foreign equity investment will be preferred even if it offers a lower dividend yield and rate of capital appreciation than domestic equity investment. This would be the case if the foreign currency appreciates by more than the sum of the dividend yield differential and the capital appreciation rate differential. Note, however, that at the time when the decision concerning the choice is made, the values of these variables are unknown and so the decision should be made on their expected or ex ante values. At year n, however, the values of the variables are realised, which enables the investor to find out whether or not the right decision was made at time 0.

Example

An Australian investor has AUD1 million to invest for two years. The choice is between investing this amount in Australian shares or US shares. Australian shares offer an expected dividend yield of 10 per cent per annum and an expected rate of capital appreciation of 15 per cent per annum. The corresponding figures for the US market are 8.5 and 13 per cent, respectively. The current exchange rate (AUD/USD) is 1.80, but the US dollar is expected to appreciate by 5 per cent per annum over the next two years to reach a level of 1.9845 at the end of the second year. Assuming risk neutrality, what will the investor choose and what is the minimum required rate of appreciation of the US dollar that will persuade the investor to choose US shares?

If AUD1 million is invested in Australian shares, the value at the end of the two-year period is

$$1\ 000\ 000(1 + 0.10 + 0.15)^2 = \text{AUD}1\ 562\ 500$$

Continued...

The other alternative is to convert AUD1 million at the current spot exchange rate, to obtain

$$\frac{1\,000\,000}{1.80} = \text{USD}555\ 556$$

If this amount is invested for two years in US shares, the investor will obtain

$$555\ 556(1 + 0.085 + 0.13)^2 = \text{USD}820\ 126$$

The Australian dollar value of this amount is

$$820\ 126 \times 1.9845 = \text{AUD}1\ 627\ 540$$

Therefore, the US investment is preferable. The same conclusion can be reached by using the condition given by (17.19). Since $\dot{S} = 5\%$, $d - d^{\star} = 1.5\%$ and $a - a^{\star} = 2\%$, it follows that the condition is satisfied and hence US investment is preferred. In general, the investor will prefer US investment if the dollar appreciates by more than 3.5 per cent.

The effect of taxes

We now compare the after-tax returns on domestic and foreign equity investments. In this case, income tax is applied to dividends while capital gains tax is applied to capital gains. The after-tax rate of return on domestic equity investment is given by

$$R^{\tau} = (1 - \tau_y)d + (1 - \tau_k)a \qquad (17.20)$$

The after-tax rate of return on foreign equity investment is given by

$$R^{\tau\star} = (1 - \tau_y)d^{\star} + (1 - \tau_k)(a^{\star} + \dot{S}) \qquad (17.21)$$

which shows that the capital gains tax applies to the appreciation component and the foreign exchange gains. Thus, foreign equity investment is preferred on an after-tax basis if $R^{\tau\star} > R^{\tau}$ or if

$$(1 - \tau_y)d^{\star} - (1 - \tau_k)(a^{\star} + \dot{S}) > (1 - \tau_y)d + (1 - \tau_k)a \qquad (17.22)$$

which can be modified to

$$\dot{S} > \left(\frac{1 - \tau_y}{1 - \tau_k}\right)(d - d^{\star}) + (a - a^{\star}) \qquad (17.23)$$

Let us now consider what happens if the capital gains tax rate is lower than the income tax rate. In this case, $(1 - \tau_y)/(1 - \tau_k) < 1$ and so the right-hand side of Equation (17.23) is smaller than the right-hand side of Equation (17.19). Thus, the condition required to prefer foreign equity investment can be satisfied more easily on an after-tax basis. For given domestic and foreign dividend yields and rates of capital appreciation, a lower rate of appreciation of the foreign currency is required to prefer foreign equity investment on an after-tax basis than on a before-tax basis. If, on the other hand, $\tau_k > \tau_y$, then a higher rate of appreciation of the foreign currency is required for the investor to prefer foreign equity on an after-tax basis.

Example

Given the same information as in the previous example and assuming an income tax rate of 30 per cent and a capital gains tax rate of 20 per cent for each currency, will the investor prefer Australian or US equity investment? What is the minimum appreciation of the US dollar required for the Australian investor to prefer US equity investment?

The after-tax rate of return on the Australian equity investment is

$$(1 - 0.3) \times 10 + (1 - 0.2) \times 15 = 19\%$$

The after-tax rate of return on the US equity investment is

$$(1 - 0.3) \times 8.5 + (1 - 0.2) \times (13 + 5) = 20.35\%$$

which obviously means that US equity investment is preferred.

In general, US equity investment will be preferred if the US dollar appreciates by more than the right-hand side of (17.23), which is

$$\left(\frac{1-0.3}{1-0.2}\right) \times (10-8.5)+(15-13)=3.31\%$$

This is less than is required on a before-tax basis.

Assume now that there are different income tax rates and that the capital gains tax applies to capital appreciation in the same currency only—that is, it does not apply to foreign exchange gains. Equation (17.21) becomes

$$R^{\tau\star} = (1-\tau_y^\star)d^\star + (1-\tau_k^\star)a^\star + \dot{S} \tag{17.24}$$

in which case, foreign equity investment is preferred if

$$(1-\tau_y^\star)d^\star + (1-\tau_k^\star)a^\star + \dot{S} > (1-\tau_y)d + (1-\tau_k)a \tag{17.25}$$

This can be rearranged to produce the condition

$$\dot{S} > (1-\tau_y)d - (1-\tau_y^\star)d^\star + (1-\tau_k)a - (1-\tau_k^\star)a^\star \tag{17.26}$$

The condition represented by (17.26) says that foreign equity investment is preferred to domestic equity investment if the foreign currency is expected to appreciate by more than the sum of the after-tax dividend yield differential and the after-tax capital appreciation rate differential.

Example

Use the information in the previous examples, but assume now that the US tax rates are higher, at 32 and 24 per cent, respectively. Assume also that foreign currency gains are not taxed. Will the investor prefer Australian or US equity investment? What is the minimum appreciation of the US dollar required for the Australian investor to prefer US equity investment?

The after-tax rate of return on the US equity investment is

$$(1 - 0.32) \times 8.5 + (1 - 0.24) \times 13 + 5 = 20.66\%$$

Continued...

which obviously means that US equity investment is preferred. In general, US equity investment will be preferred if the US dollar appreciates by more than the right-hand side of (17.26), which is

$$(1 - 0.3) \times 10 - (1 - 0.32) \times 8.5 + (1 - 0.2) \times 15 - (1 - 0.24) \times 13 = 3.34\%$$

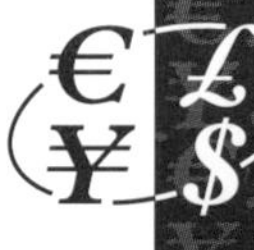

IN PRACTICE

Why foreign investors do not like AMP shares

In its issue of 3 June 2002, the *Australian Financial Review* reported that the AMP share register showed that only 16 per cent of the company is foreign-owned, which is much less than most major Australian companies. The average foreign ownership of the big four Australian banks, according to JP Morgan, is 29 per cent, with Westpac leading the list with 31 per cent, followed by the ANZ (28 per cent).

One reason why foreign investors shy away from AMP shares is the complexity of the company's financial accounts. This complexity arises because two sets of rules are followed to deal with profits from the New Zealand and British operations. The operating profit from its Australian and New Zealand life policies is allocated according to the *Australian Life Insurance Act*, whereas profits from British life business are allocated under British rules. In particular, foreign investors find it difficult to understand the 'margin-on-services accounting' required by the *Australian Life Insurance Act*. In an interview with the *Australian Financial Review*, AMP chief executive, Paul Batchelor, suggested that the provision of more simplistic additional financial data 'will enable the market to have greater understanding of our finances'.

It is interesting to note that the *Australian Financial Review*'s correspondent attributed Batchelor's interest in attracting more foreign investors to the role the share price plays in determining his performance-based options package.

17.3 The benefits of international portfolio diversification

It is a well-known principle in portfolio theory that diversification reduces risk if the rates of return on the assets from which a portfolio is composed are less than perfectly correlated. The economies of various countries are likely to be passing through different phases of the business cycle at the same point in time because they differ in structural composition, institutional arrangements, factor endowments and policy mix. The following are examples of these differences. Differences in the structures of two economies may pertain to the contribution of the manufacturing sector to GDP. An institutional difference is the degree of independence of the central bank. A difference in factor endowments may pertain to oil and mineral reserves. Finally, differences in the policy mix pertain to the relative importance assigned to monetary policy as opposed to fiscal policy.

The implication of these differences for the issue under discussion here is that rates of return in different countries are likely to be less positively correlated than those from different sectors within the same economy. The following table contains a correlation matrix of the quarterly rates of return on equity investment in Australia, the United States, Japan and the United Kingdom over the period 1988–2001. These rates of return are calculated from the share prices exhibited in Figure 17.1. Although the rates of return are positively correlated, the correlation coefficients are adequately low to allow for some benefits from diversification. This is valid whether the rates of return are measured in terms of the currency of investment or in terms of the Australian dollar (in parentheses).

	Australia	United States	Japan	United Kingdom
Australia	1.00 (1.00)	0.61 (0.33)	0.39 (0.26)	0.56 (0.31)
United States		1.00 (1.00)	0.43 (0.32)	0.76 (0.62)
Japan			1.00 (1.00)	0.38 (0.19)
United Kingdom				1.00 (1.00)

Figure 17.1 Share prices (December 1988 = 100)

(a) Australia

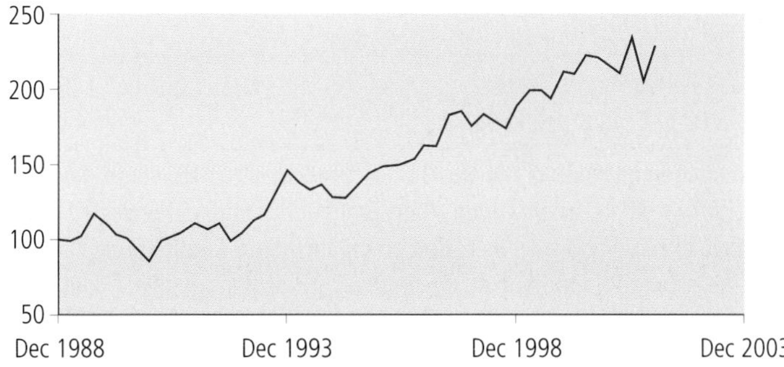

(b) United States

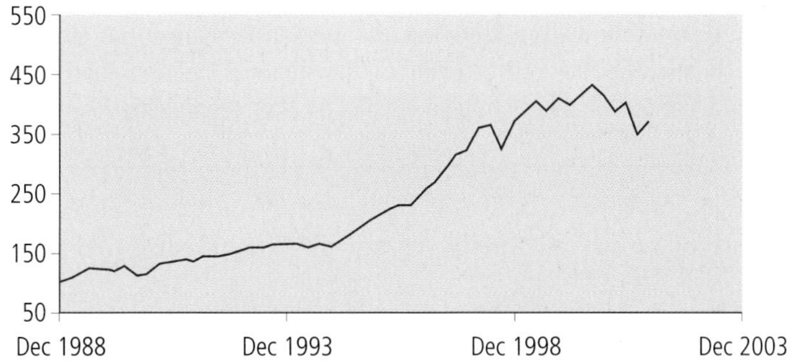

Continued...

(c) Japan

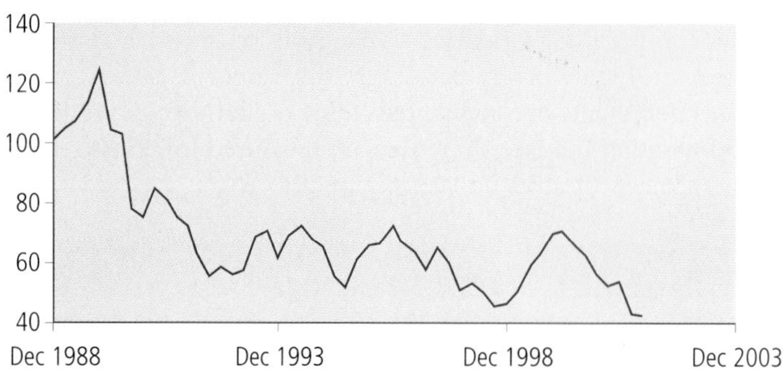

(d) United Kingdom

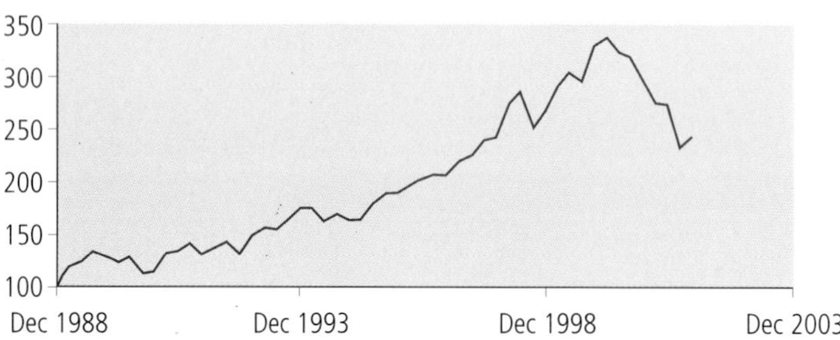

Source: Main Economic Indicators, OECD.

IN PRACTICE

Fund management in Russia

The growth of the fund management industry in Russia has been awaited for some time, but has failed to materialise. As a result, some international fund managers that have invested heavily in marketing their services have either withdrawn or scaled down, including Credit Suisse First Boston. Some analysts attribute the slow development of the Russian fund management industry to the scandals surrounding the 'pyramid schemes' of the mid-1990s, where savers incurred some heavy losses.

By mid-2002 there were signs that the Russian fund management industry was beginning to experience some growth. The main impetus behind this trend was President Putin's economic reforms, which resulted in a transformation of the country's pensions system. This change prompted the Russians, who are traditionally suspicious of financial markets and institutions, to consider channelling their savings to the stock market. Moreover, the Russian Parliament has, after a long delay, approved legislation allowing the restructuring of the national pension fund. This has prompted both Russian and foreign companies to plan for the 'positive eventualities'.

We could write the rate of return on foreign equity investment measured in domestic currency terms as

$$R = A + \dot{S} \tag{17.27}$$

where $A = d + a$ is the total rate of return in foreign currency terms. The variance of R is given by

$$\sigma^2(R) = \sigma^2(A) + \sigma^2(\dot{S}) + 2\sigma(A, \dot{S}) \tag{17.28}$$

where $\sigma^2(.)$ is the variance and $\sigma(.,.)$ is the covariance. This means that the variance of the rate of return can be decomposed into three components: the variance of the rate of return in foreign currency terms, the variance of the percentage change in the exchange rate and (twice) the covariance of these two components. The following table reports the results of this decomposition of the variance for the Australian dollar rates of return on equity investment in the United States, Japan and the United Kingdom over the period January 1988–2001. It is obvious that in all cases the variability of the rate of return in foreign currency terms is a major contributor to the variability of the rate of return in Australian dollar terms. The same composition can be done for the rate of return on bond portfolios.

	$\sigma^2(R)$	$\sigma^2(A)$	$\sigma^2(\dot{S})$	$\sigma(A, \dot{S})$
United States	49.62	33.11	23.81	−3.65
Japan	140.99	93.59	61.00	−6.80
United Kingdom	51.34	49.27	38.81	−18.37

Measuring the performance of multicurrency portfolio managers

The performance of a portfolio manager is typically measured in terms of the rate of return achieved by the portfolio manager in relation to a benchmark, which could be the risk-free interest rate or the rate of return on a market index. Introducing a currency factor into performance evaluation creates three problems:

- It alters the returns.
- A portion of the portfolio may be hedged for currency risk.
- Even if the portfolio is fully hedged, the benchmark may be less than fully hedged.

The traditional approach to evaluating the performance of international portfolio managers focuses on the value added by the portfolio manager (relative to a benchmark), which is attributed to country allocation and security selection. Ankrim and Hensel have suggested an approach to the performance evaluation when there is a currency factor by distinguishing among the following:[1]

- the security selection effect, which measures how much the manager's security selection decisions within each country adds to the manager's differential return
- the allocation effect, which measures the impact on the performance of the manager's decision to invest in certain countries in proportions that are different from those in the benchmark
- the forward premium effect, which measures the return generated by the forward premium in place at the beginning of the period
- the currency management effect, which measures the impact that differential currency exposure (from the benchmark) has on performance
- the interaction effect, which arises from the interaction of the security selection, allocation and currency management effects (the forward premium effect is known in advance).

[1] E. A. Ankrim and C. R. Hensel, 'Multicurrency Performance Attribution', *Financial Analysts Journal*, May–April 1994, pp. 29–35.

Let us see what happens when we combine a domestic security or portfolio, which gives a rate of return R, with a foreign security or portfolio that gives a rate of return $R^\star$ (as defined in Equation (17.27)). If the weights assigned to the two securities are w and $w^\star$, then the expected (or the average) value of the rate of return on the portfolio is given by

$$R^p = wR + w^\star R^\star \tag{17.29}$$

This means that the expected value and the variance of the rate of return on the portfolio are given respectively by

$$E(R^p) = wE(R) + w^\star E(R^\star) \tag{17.30}$$

and the variance is given by

$$\sigma^2(R^p) = w^2\sigma^2(R) + w^{\star 2}\sigma^2(R^\star) + 2ww^\star\sigma(R)\sigma(R^\star)\rho(R,R^\star) \tag{17.31}$$

where $\rho(R,R^\star)$ is the correlation coefficient between the domestic and foreign rates of return. The measure of risk is the standard deviation of the rate of return, which is the square root of the variance. This is given by

$$\sigma(R^p) = \sqrt{w^2\sigma^2(R) + w^{\star 2}\sigma^2(R^\star) + 2ww^\star\sigma(R)\sigma(R^\star)\rho(R,R^\star)} \tag{17.32}$$

Naturally, the mean, the variance and the standard deviation can be calculated from historical data, as we have seen in previous chapters. By using Equation (17.32), we can demonstrate that the reduction in risk via diversification depends upon the correlation coefficient of the rates of return. If the rates of return are perfectly correlated such that $\rho(R, R^\star) = 1$, then the standard deviation of the rate of return on the portfolio is given by

$$\sigma(R^p) = \sqrt{\left[w\sigma(R) + w^\star\sigma(R^\star)\right]^2} = w\sigma(R) + w^\star\sigma(R^\star) \tag{17.33}$$

which is a weighted average of the standard deviations of the individual securities or portfolios. Hence diversification does not lead to a reduction in risk if the rates of return are perfectly correlated. This case is unlikely to arise in practice, even more so if one of the securities is domestic and the other is foreign. It is more likely the case that the rates of return are less than perfectly correlated. If the correlation coefficient is zero we have

$$\sigma(R^p) = \sqrt{w^2\sigma^2(R) + w^{\star 2}\sigma^2(R^\star)} < w\sigma(R) + w^\star\sigma(R^\star) \tag{17.34}$$

which means that the standard deviation of the rate of return on the portfolio is less than the weighted average of the two standard deviations. This means that the portfolio risk is lower when the securities are uncorrelated.

International diversification is most beneficial in terms of risk reduction if the rates of return on the domestic and foreign securities are negatively correlated. In the extreme case, when they are perfectly negatively correlated such that $\rho(R, R^\star) = -1$, the standard deviation of the rate of return on the portfolio is given by

$$\sigma(R^p) = \sqrt{\left[w\sigma(R) - w^\star\sigma(R^\star)\right]^2} = w\sigma(R) - w^\star\sigma(R^\star) \tag{17.35}$$

which is the lowest value that can be assumed by the standard deviation of the rate of return on the portfolio.

Example

The monthly rates of return on equity investment in the Australian and US stock markets in 1995 are given below (both measured in Australian dollar terms). What are the means and the standard deviations of these rates? Construct an equally weighted portfolio of Australian and US equities and calculate the mean and the standard deviation of the rate of return on the portfolio.

Date	Australia	United States
Jan 1995	−1.19	4.46
Feb 1995	−0.40	6.86
Mar 1995	2.01	3.41
Apr 1995	5.35	2.67
May 1995	1.87	5.49
Jun 1995	−1.76	3.68
Jul 1995	4.32	−0.32
Aug 1995	1.86	−1.97
Sep 1995	0.77	2.42
Oct 1995	−2.30	−0.21
Nov 1995	1.42	3.81
Dec 1995	3.73	3.33
Mean	1.31	2.80
Standard deviation	2.42	2.54

The mean of the rate of return on the portfolio is calculated as a weighted average of the means of the rates of return on the two individual rates of return. Hence, it is equal to

$$0.5 \times 1.31 + 0.5 \times 2.80 = 2.06$$

The correlation coefficient between the two rates of return is −0.18. Hence, the variance of the rate of return on the portfolio is

$$(0.5)^2(2.42)^2 + (0.5)^2(2.54)^2 + 2 \times 0.5 \times 0.5 \times 2.42 \times 2.54 \times -0.18 = 2.52$$

which gives a standard deviation of $\sqrt{2.52} = 1.59$. Hence, the portfolio is less risky than the individual investments. This is because the two rates of return are negatively correlated.

The mean and the standard deviation can be calculated by constructing a time series for R^P (as in Equation (17.29)).

For a given value of the correlation coefficient, it is possible to construct a large number of portfolios from domestic and foreign securities by assigning different values to the weights, w and w^*. For each portfolio there is a combination of expected rate of return as given by Equation (17.30) and a standard deviation as given by Equation (17.32). The locus of these points is called the **efficient frontier**, which is the curve AB, as represented in Figure 17.2. It is efficient because points on the curve offer better risk-return combinations than points off (to the right of) the curve. Each point on the curve represents a portfolio of domestic and foreign securities. A is the foreign security that has a high risk and a high return. B is the domestic security that has a low risk and a low return. If we diversify by including foreign securities in the portfolio, we can reduce risk and/or increase return. Portfolio D, for example, offers a higher expected return and a lower risk than the domestic security, B. Portfolio C offers a much higher return and a relatively higher risk than the domestic security.

Figure 17.2 The efficient frontier

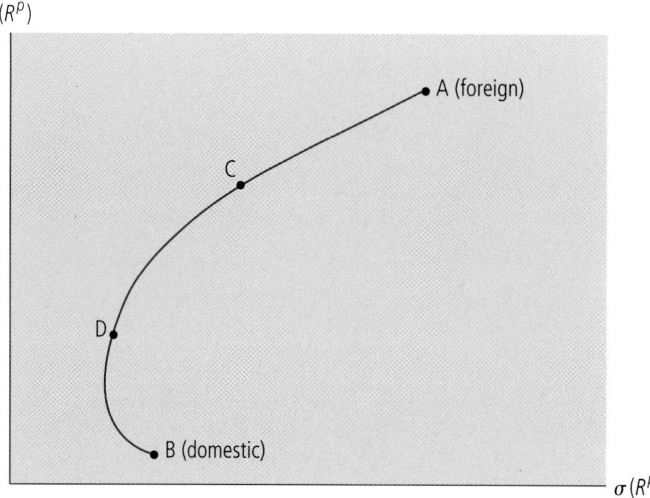

RESEARCH FINDINGS

Dealing with the currency factor in international portfolios

Believing that international portfolio managers do not have sufficient expertise in exchange rates, some institutional investors have turned to specialised 'overlay' managers to manage the currency risk of the portfolio separately. In general, three approaches can be used in situations like these:

- A joint, full-blown optimisation of the underlying securities and currencies: in this case, the manager has the expertise in many securities and can structure a portfolio to account for correlations between security prices and exchange rates.
- A partial optimisation of the currencies, given a predetermined position in the portfolio: in this case, currencies are managed separately, but the manager still controls the total portfolio risk.
- A separate optimisation of currencies: in this case, currencies are managed completely independently of the portfolio such that the currency performance is measured against a separate benchmark.

Philippe Jorion has examined these three alternatives and concluded that the overlay structure is inherently suboptimal because it ignores interactions between security prices and exchange rates, estimating the efficiency loss of about 40 **basis points**.[1]

[1] P. Jorion, 'Mean/Variance Analysis of Currency Overlays', *Financial Analysts Journal*, May–June 1994, pp. 48–56.

The efficient frontier representing domestic securities only falls to the right of an efficient frontier representing international diversification, as shown in Figure 17.3. While diversification among securities produces a similar effect in terms of risk reduction, international diversification has a quantitatively more significant effect. The reason why this is the case is that the rates of return on securities B and A are less strongly correlated than the rates of return on securities B and G.

Figure 17.3 The effect of international diversification

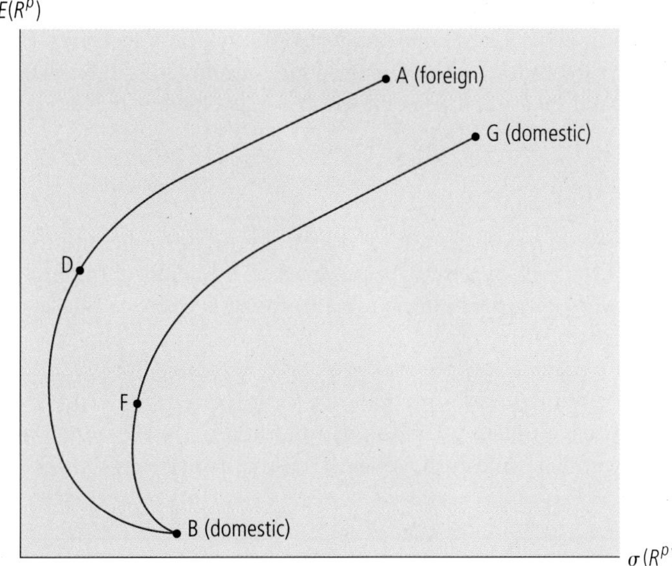

The effects of the US accounting scandals

By mid-2002 the US accounting scandals of Enron, WorldCom, Quest and other companies had wrecked corporate America, bringing US stock prices and those of other major countries to five year lows. Between December 2001, when the Enron scandal became public knowledge, and July 2002, the Dow Jones lost 1023 points, the FTSE lost 784 points and the DAX lost 799 points. Attempts made by some politicians to restore confidence in corporate America failed, because of scepticism about dodgy business dealings by these politicians in the 1990s.

As a result of these scandals, the quality of company accounts emerged as the most important factor influencing the decisions of international investors. In a survey conducted by McKinsey, the consulting firm, published on 8 July 2002 and reported by the *Financial Times*, the majority of some 200 institutional investors in 31 countries called for a single international accounting standard. The survey also showed strong support for including executives' pay share options in the income statement.

It was also revealed that 71 per cent of the participants rated accounting disclosures far higher than any other issue, whereas 43 per cent emphasised the market regulation of the country in which they were considering investing.

17.4 International capital asset pricing model

The conventional or domestic **capital asset pricing model (CAPM)** postulates that the expected return on an asset or a portfolio is positively related to its **systematic risk**, the component of risk that cannot be eliminated by diversification. The relationship can be written as

$$R_j = i + \beta(R_m - i) \tag{17.36}$$

where R_j is the equilibrium or required expected rate of return on a security or a portfolio j, i is the **risk-free interest rate** and R_m is the expected rate of return on the **market portfolio**, such as the portfolio implied by a stock price index. β is a coefficient that is given by

$$\beta = \frac{\sigma(R_j, R_m)}{\sigma^2(R_m)} \tag{17.37}$$

where $\sigma(R_j, R_m)$ is the covariance of the rates of return on the portfolio and the market, and $\sigma^2(R_m)$ is the variance of the rate of return on the market. Equation (17.36) tells us that the expected return on a security or a portfolio is equal to the risk-free rate plus a risk premium that is linearly related to a measure of systematic risk, β, the latter being the risk that the security or the portfolio contributes to the market as a whole. Investors are therefore compensated for bearing systematic risk only (but not for **unsystematic risk**). If the expected return is greater than what is implied by this equation, then the underlying security would be very attractive and investors would rush to buy it, raising its price and lowering its return.

Systematic and unsystematic risk

The total risk resulting from the variability of the rate of return on a security or a portfolio (and measured by the standard deviation) consists of two components: systematic risk and unsystematic risk. Systematic risk, or market risk, is the portion of total variability associated with movements of the market as a whole. This component of risk cannot be eliminated by diversification (it cannot be diversified away). If a portfolio is perfectly diversified, it will behave exactly like the market (it will have a **beta** of 1). The other component of risk, which can be diversified away, is unsystematic or **residual risk**.

The relationship can be represented diagrammatically as in Figure 17.4, with systematic risk, as represented by β, measured on the horizontal axis and the expected return, R_j, measured on the vertical axis. The SML is the securities market line, which is a diagrammatic representation of the relationship between the expected return and systematic risk. The intercept of the line is equal to the risk-free interest rate, i. From Figure 17.4 and Equation (17.36) we can see the following:

- A security with a zero β has a rate of return that is equal to the risk-free interest rate.
- A security with a β of less than 1 (less risky than the market portfolio) has an expected return higher than the risk-free rate but lower than the expected return on the market portfolio. In Figure 17.4, this expected return falls between i and R_m.

- A security with a systematic risk that is equal to that of the market ($\beta = 1$) has an expected rate of return that is equal to the return on the market portfolio.
- If the security is more risky than the market portfolio, ($\beta > 1$), then it will offer an expected rate of return that is higher than what is offered by the market portfolio.

Figure 17.4 The relationship between the expected return and systematic risk

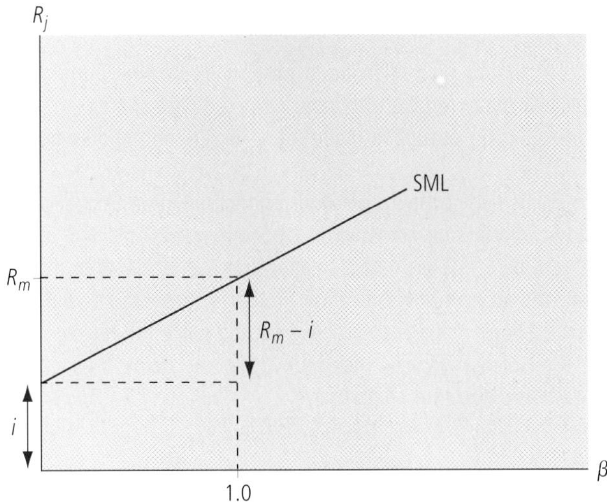

The link between the exchange rate and a firm's share price

Although there are many explanations for the link between the exchange rate and profitability, the link between the exchange rate and a firm's share price is less clear. Dominguez and Tesar have suggested that a test for economic exposure to foreign exchange risk can be carried out by including the change in the exchange rate on the right-hand side of a standard CAPM regression and testing whether its coefficient is significantly different from zero. More specifically, the equation representing the modified CAPM explains the rate of return on a particular firm's shares, R_j, in terms of the market rate of return, R_m, and the percentage change in the exchange rate. By testing this model on a broad sample of firms, they have obtained results indicating a high degree of exposure to foreign exchange risk at both the firm and industry level across eight countries.

[1] K. M. Dominguez and L. Tesar, 'A Reexamination of Exchange Rate Exposure', *American Economic Review*, 91, 2001, pp. 396–9.

The **international capital asset pricing model (ICAPM)** is a relationship between the expected return and systematic risk when assets are priced in internationally integrated financial markets. In this case, the market portfolio is a world market portfolio. If this is the case, then investors cannot obtain abnormal returns by investing in foreign securities: they will only be compensated for systematic risk, which is measured relative to an internationally diversified market portfolio. The difference thus lies in the definition of the market portfolio.

RESEARCH FINDINGS

The benefits of international diversification in bonds

Most of the research on international portfolio diversification has focused on equity portfolios, perhaps because data on equity returns are more readily available than data on bond market returns. Levy and Lerman addressed three questions pertaining to this issue:[1]

- To what extent can international diversification in bonds produce returns in excess of those available from investment in domestic bonds only?
- Is it possible to construct internationally diversified bond portfolios that will outperform share portfolios, despite the relatively low mean returns of bonds compared with shares?
- What is the impact of diversification on portfolios made up of bonds and shares from various markets?

They found that internationally diversified portfolios of bonds dominated internationally diversified share portfolios, because the low correlations across world bond markets allowed investors to increase their domestic currency returns at the price of a smaller increase in risk than that required to achieve the same incremental returns from diversification in shares. They also found that a US investor who diversified across world bond markets could have earned twice the rate of return on a US bond portfolio at the same level of risk. Finally, they found that the gains from international diversification in bonds and shares were even more impressive.

[1] H. Levy and Z. Lerman, 'The Benefits of International Diversification in Bonds', *Financial Analysts Journal*, September–October 1988, pp. 56–63.

The implication of this analysis is that international diversification can produce abnormal returns if markets are segmented and the securities are priced according to the domestic CAPM using a domestic market portfolio as a benchmark. If, on the other hand, markets are integrated, securities are priced according to the international ICAPM using an internationally diversified portfolio as a benchmark.

There are several reasons for **market segmentation**:

- *Legal barriers to foreign investment:* these barriers may take the form of an outright restriction on investment by foreigners or other forms such as the imposition of higher tax rates on foreigners investing in domestic assets.
- *The difficulty of finding and interpreting information about foreign securities:* this difficulty may be due to the use of different accounting standards.
- *Foreign exchange risk:* the problem with foreign exchange risk is that it may not be possible to hedge, perhaps because of the unavailability of forward contracts with long maturities or in certain currencies. Moreover, foreign exchange risk does not conform to the positive risk return trade-off. Bearing more foreign exchange risk does not necessarily mean expecting a higher return.
- *Purchasing power risk:* segmentation can arise because the prices of what investors consume, relative to the returns they earn, change differently in different countries.
- *Political and country risk:* political risk pertains to changes in the rules governing foreign investment by the host government. Country risk encompasses all of the factors that can adversely affect the country's economic performance.
- *Transaction costs:* these costs are higher when they involve foreign transactions. Some of these costs include the bid-offer spread in foreign exchange, settlement costs and custodial costs associated with buying and selling foreign securities.
- *Taxation:* in the absence of double taxation agreements, investment returns may be taxed twice in the foreign and home countries.

- *Domestic regulations:* some countries impose restrictions on the ability of their citizens to invest in foreign securities. Recently, however, some measures of financial deregulation have been taken to abolish these restrictions.

RESEARCH FINDINGS

Investing in emerging markets

In a study based on 24 years of data, Conover, Jensen and Johnson showed that emerging market equities are a worthy addition to a US investor's portfolio of developed market equities.[1] Their estimates showed that portfolio returns increased by approximately 1.5 percentage points per year when emerging market equities were included in the portfolio. However, they also found that the benefits of investing in emerging markets materialised almost exclusively during periods of restrictive US monetary policy (otherwise, they were trivial).

During the first four months of 2002, emerging markets were buoyant at a time when markets in advanced economies were very weak. For example, the Russian market was up 47.9 per cent compared with the end of 2001, while the Indonesian market was up 36.6 per cent. This compares with 1.1 per cent for the United States, and 0.1 per cent for the United Kingdom and Australia. At least two reasons could explain the disparity:

- Overvaluation of shares in advanced markets. For example, the US Nasdaq technology shares were trading at 46 times earnings. This prompted expectation of further downward correction.
- In relative terms, emerging markets are viewed as cyclical or growth-oriented, which means that they tend to benefit from improved global outlook.

[1] C. M. Conover, G. R. Jensen and R. R. Johnson, 'Emerging Markets: When are they worth it?', *Financial Analysts Journal*, March–April 2002, pp. 86–95.

Summary

- A bond is a fixed income security that offers fixed contractual interest (coupon) payments as well as the payment of the face value.
- Foreign currency bonds are preferred to domestic currency bonds if the foreign currency is expected to appreciate by more than the difference between the rate of return on domestic currency bonds and foreign currency bonds.
- If the capital gains tax rate is lower than the income tax rate, bonds denominated in currencies that are expected to appreciate will be more attractive.
- Bonds are rated according to the degree of credit risk assigned by Moody's and Standard & Poor's. Several financial ratios are used to determine the rating.
- Equities offer variable returns consisting of dividend payments and capital appreciation.
- Foreign equity investments will be preferred, even if they offer lower dividend yields and rates of capital appreciation, if the foreign currency is expected to appreciate by a sufficient amount.
- If the capital gains tax rate is lower than the income tax rate, foreign equities denominated in currencies that are expected to appreciate will be more attractive.
- International diversification is beneficial because it reduces risk. This is the case only if markets are segmented.

- The international capital asset pricing model is a relationship between expected return and systematic risk where assets are priced internationally.
- The total risk resulting from the variability of return on a security or a portfolio consists of systematic risk (the risk associated with the whole market) and unsystematic risk, which can be diversified away.
- Market segmentation arises because of the following factors: (i) legal barriers to foreign investment; (ii) information asymmetry; (iii) foreign exchange risk; (iv) purchasing power risk; (v) political and country risk; (vi) transaction costs; (vii) taxes; and (viii) domestic regulations.

Key terms

basis points 492
beta 494
bond 476
capital appreciation 481
capital asset pricing model (CAPM) 494
capital gains tax 478
dividend yield 482
dividends 481
efficient frontier 491
equities 481
face value 476
income tax 478
international capital asset pricing model (ICAPM) 495
international diversification 490
market portfolio 494
market segmentation 496
online trading 480
par value 476
residual risk 494
retained earnings 481
risk-free interest rate 494
systematic risk 494
undistributed earnings 481
unsystematic risk 494

MaxMARK

MAXIMISE YOUR MARKS! There are 30 interactive questions for this chapter available online at **www.mhhe.com/au/moosa2e**

Review questions

1 Under what conditions are foreign-currency bonds preferred even if they offer a lower rate of return (in foreign currency terms) than domestic bonds?

2 Distinguish between the value of reinvested coupon payments and the market value of a bond. How do they change as the interest rate rises?

3 Why does a low capital gains tax encourage investing in bonds denominated in currencies that are expected to appreciate?

4 Why are rates of return on equity investments in different countries likely to be less positively correlated than those on different sectors within the same country?

5 What is the efficient frontier? What does international diversification do to the efficient frontier?

6 Why is it more difficult to evaluate the performance of multicurrency portfolio managers than that of domestic currency portfolio managers?

7 What is the difference between systematic risk and unsystematic risk?

8 What is the securities market line? What does the slope of the line measure?

9 International diversification is beneficial only if markets are segmented. Why, then, do portfolio managers diversify internationally in practice?

10 Is diversification in bonds as useful as diversification in equities?

11 What are the reasons for market segmentation?

Problems

1 An Australian investor wishes to invest AUD250 000 in bonds. The investor is considering the choice between three-year Australian bonds offering an annual rate of return (yield to maturity) of 7.5 per cent and three-year Swiss bonds offering an annual rate of return of 4 per cent. The current (year 0) and expected exchange rate in year 3 are as follows:

Year	AUD/CHF
0	1.15
3	1.26

(a) Assuming risk neutrality, what will the investor choose?
(b) If the expected values of the exchange rates are realised, what is the extra gain achieved by making this choice?

2 Using the same information as in Problem 1 above and assuming an income tax rate of 20 per cent and a capital gains tax rate of 40 per cent in both countries, find out whether the investor prefers Australian bonds or Swiss bonds.

3 An Australian investor has AUD400 000 to invest in either Australian or German shares over a period of three years. The following information is available:

Expected annual dividend yield (Australia)	10%
Expected annual dividend yield (Germany)	2%
Expected annual capital appreciation rate (Australia)	10%
Expected annual capital appreciation rate (Germany)	14%
Current exchange rate (AUD/EUR)	1.65
Expected annual rate of change of the exchange rate	3%

(a) Assuming risk neutrality, what will the investor choose?
(b) Calculate the minimum required rate of change in the exchange rate that will persuade the investor to choose German shares.

4 Use the same information as in Problem 3 above and assume an income tax of 20 per cent and a capital gains tax of 40 per cent in both countries.
(a) Assuming risk neutrality, what will the investor choose?
(b) Calculate the minimum required rate of change in the exchange rate that will persuade the investor to choose German shares.

5 Use the same information as in Problems 3 and 4 above, but assume now that the German tax rates are higher, at 25 and 45 per cent respectively, and that foreign exchange gains are not taxed.

(a) Assuming risk neutrality, what will the investor choose?

(b) Calculate the minimum required rate of change in the exchange rate that will persuade the investor to choose German shares.

CHAPTER

Foreign direct investment and international capital budgeting

Introduction

In Chapter 17, we dealt with portfolio investment in securities. In this chapter we deal with direct investment, which is another form of long-term investment. It differs from portfolio investment in some aspects, the most important of which is the degree of control exerted by the investor over the firm invested in. Foreign direct investment refers to the process of buying and controlling (in whole or in part) a firm in one country (the host country) by the residents of another country (the source country). Thus, instead of talking about the choice among securities, as in the case of portfolio investment, we now switch to a consideration of the choice among competing investment projects. A typical decision-making situation is the choice between serving a foreign market by exporting or by establishing a subsidiary or a production facility in the foreign (host) country.

Objectives

The objectives of this chapter are:

- To discuss the basic characteristics and development of foreign direct investment.
- To outline the theories that have been devised to explain foreign direct investment.
- To describe the techniques of international capital budgeting.
- To examine the implications of taxation, country risk and transfer pricing for international capital budgeting.

18.1 Background

An investment project is classified as direct investment if the investor acquires **significant control** over a firm. Thus, **foreign direct investment (FDI)** implies the acquisition and exertion of a significant control over a foreign firm. The International Monetary Fund's *Balance of Payments Manual* defines direct investment as referring to 'an investment that is made to acquire a lasting interest in an enterprise operating in an economy other than that of the investor, the investor's purpose being to have an effective voice in the management of the enterprise'. The direct investment enterprise is a **branch** or a **subsidiary** in which direct investment is made.

It is not clear, however, what constitutes 'significant control' of a firm. For the purpose of preparing the balance of payments statistics, countries in general classify as FDIs those enterprises in which the percentage of foreign ownership is between 10 and 25 per cent. In the United States, Japan and Australia, a 10 per cent equity threshold is used to define direct investment. In other countries (including France, Germany and the United Kingdom) a higher threshold is used. Some countries (such as Belgium and the Netherlands) use no specific threshold but treat each case on its merits. Thus, what is regarded as direct investment by some countries may be considered portfolio investment (or something else) by other countries.

Reasons for interest in FDI

Interest in FDI is attributed to the following reasons. The first is the rapid growth in global direct investment and the change in its pattern, particularly since the 1980s. These developments have motivated attempts to come up with theories and hypotheses that explain the phenomenon of FDI. The second reason is the concern it raises about the causes and consequences of foreign ownership. The views on this issue are diverse: at one extreme, FDI is regarded as symbolising new colonialism; at the other, it is viewed as something without which the host economy cannot survive. The third reason is the possibility offered by FDI for channelling resources to developing countries. Thus, FDI is becoming an important source of funds at a time when access to other means of financing is dwindling, particularly in the aftermath of the international debt problem. Finally, FDI is thought to play a potentially vital role in the transformation of the former communist countries. This is because FDI complements domestic saving and contributes to total investment in the economy. It is also because FDI brings with it advanced technology, management skills and access to export markets.

History of FDI

In the nineteenth century foreign investment was prominent, but it mostly took the form of lending by Britain to finance economic development in other countries. This was the case until the outbreak of World War I. In the interwar period, foreign investment declined, but direct investment rose to about one-quarter of the total. Another important development that took place between the world wars was that Britain lost its status as the major creditor, with the emergence of the United States as a major economic and financial power. In the period after World War II, FDI started to grow for two reasons. The first reason was technological: the improvement in transport and communications, which made it possible to exercise control from a distance. The second reason was the need of European countries and Japan for US capital to finance reconstruction following the destruction inflicted by the war. This was propelled by the US tax laws, which favoured FDI. By the 1960s, these factors were weakening to the extent of giving rise to a reversal of the trend. First, various host countries started to show resistance to US ownership and control of local industry, which led to a slowdown of outflows from the United States. Second, host countries started to recover, initiating FDI in the United States. As a result, the net outflow from the United States started to decline. The 1970s witnessed lower FDI flows, but the United Kingdom emerged as a major player in this game as a result of the North Sea oil surpluses and the abolition of foreign exchange controls in 1979.

The 1980s witnessed two major changes. The first was that the United States became a net debtor country and a major recipient of FDI, with a negative net **international investment position**. One of the reasons for this development was the low saving rate in the US economy, which made it impossible to finance the widening budget deficit by resorting to the domestic capital market, giving rise to the need for foreign capital that came primarily from Japan and Germany. The second reason was the restrictive trade policy adopted by the United States. The other development was the emergence of Japan as a major supplier of foreign direct investment to the United States and Europe. Motivated by the desire to reduce labour costs, Japanese direct investment also expanded in Southeast Asia.

The surge in FDI in the 1980s is attributed to the globalisation of business and to the growing concern over the emergence of managed trade. Moreover, it is often argued that FDI benefits both multinational firms and the host country and this is why there has been tolerance towards FDI. A factor that accounts for the surge in FDI is the increase in FDI inflows to the United States as a result of the depreciation of the US dollar in the second half of the 1980s. The total flows of FDI from industrial countries more than quadrupled between 1984 and 1990.

In the period 1990–1992, FDI flows fell as growth in industrial countries slowed, but a strong rebound took place subsequently. This rebound is attributed to three reasons: (i) FDI was no longer confined to large firms, as an increasing number of smaller firms became multinational; (ii) the sectoral diversity of FDI broadened with the share of the service sector rising sharply; and (iii) the number of countries that were outward investors or hosts of FDI rose considerably. Moreover, the 1990s brought considerable improvements in the investment climate, triggered in part by the recognition of the benefits of FDI. The change in attitudes, in turn, led to a removal of direct obstacles to FDI and to an increase in the use of FDI incentives. Continued removal of domestic impediments through deregulation and privatisation has also been widespread.

Another important feature of the 1990s was the decline in the importance of Japan as a source of FDI, which was due to the bursting of the Japanese bubble economy. The late 1990s were characterised by the rising popularity of cross-border **mergers and acquisitions (M&As)**. Moreover, the trend towards the liberalisation of regulatory regimes for FDI continued. Some changes have been introduced to (host) government policies on FDI, strengthening the trend towards the liberalisation, protection and promotion of FDI. It seems that this trend will continue for a long time to come, which means that the growth of FDI will be robust in the foreseeable future.

Some statistics

Figures 18.1 and 18.2 show the growth of Australian FDI flows and stocks. A negative outflow in 1999 implies net divestment by Australia in foreign countries (a negative inflow would imply net divestment by other countries in Australia). FDI flows comprise the capital provided (either directly or through related enterprises) by a foreign direct investor to an FDI enterprise or the capital received from an FDI enterprise by a foreign direct investor. From the perspective of a particular country, FDI flows may represent **inward FDI** (when a foreign country invests in the country in question) or **outward FDI** (when the home country invests abroad). FDI flows consist of the following items:

- Equity capital, which is the foreign investor's purchases of shares in an enterprise in a foreign country.
- Reinvested earnings, which comprise the investor's share of earnings not distributed as dividends by subsidiaries or remitted to the home country, but rather reinvested in the host country.
- Intracompany loans, which refer to short-term or long-term borrowing and lending of funds between the parent company and its affiliates.

FDI stocks, on the other hand, represent the value of the capital and reserves (including retained earnings) attributable to the parent firm, plus the net indebtedness of its subsidiaries. Like FDI flows, stocks can also be inward or outward when viewed from a particular country's perspective. FDI stocks are estimated by cumulating FDI flows over a period of time.

Figure 18.3 shows the growth of cross-border mergers and acquisitions, which have become the dominant form of FDI, particularly in developing countries. For the European Union, however, M&As were dominant. Whether FDI takes the form of **greenfield investment** (that is, starting a new project) or M&As depends in part on the level of development in the host country, since this factor determines the supply of target firms.

Figure 18.1 Australian FDI flows (USD billion)

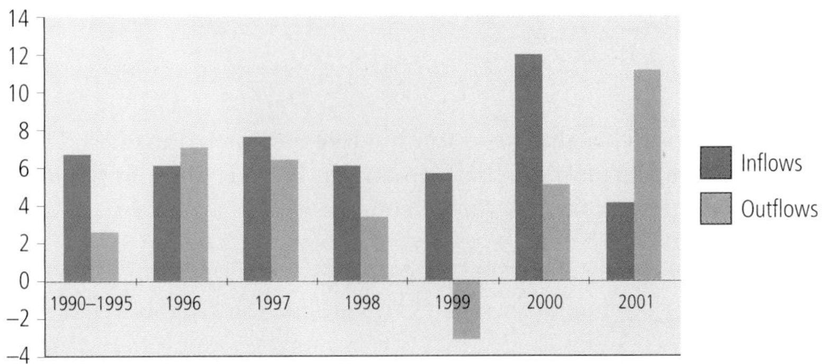

Source: UNCTAD, *World Investment Report*, 2002.

Figure 18.2 Australian FDI stocks (USD billion)

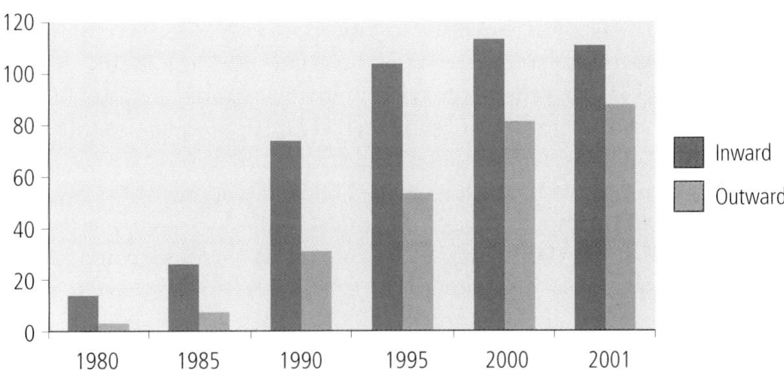

Source: UNCTAD, *World Investment Report*, 2002.

Figure 18.3 Cross-border mergers and acquisitions (USD billion)

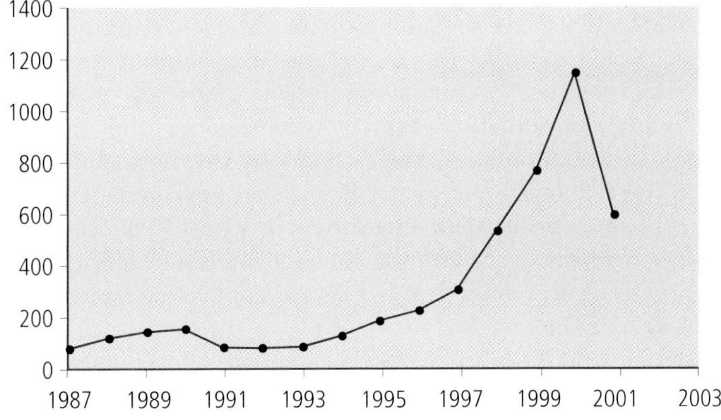

Source: UNCTAD, *World Investment Report*, 2002.

18.2 Approaches to international business

FDI is one of several approaches that firms can use to enter foreign markets. The following is a common sequence that firms use to develop foreign markets for their products:

1. Export of the goods produced in the source country.
2. **Licensing** a foreign company to use a process or product technology.
3. Foreign distribution of products through a subsidiary.
4. Foreign (international) production, which is the production of goods and services in a country that is controlled and managed by firms headquartered in other countries.

Steps 3 and 4 involve FDI. Moving from Step 1 to Step 4 requires larger commitments of resources and in some respects greater exposure to risk. While this sequence may be a chronological path for developing foreign sales, it is not necessary that all four steps are taken sequentially, as some firms jump immediately to Step 3 or Step 4.

The choice between exporting and FDI depends on the following factors: profitability, opportunities for market growth, production cost levels and economies of scale. For example, multinational firms have traditionally invested in Singapore and Hong Kong because of the low production costs in these countries. For the same reasons, these countries have traditionally exported goods to other countries. Initially, exports precede FDI, but after having become familiar with factor and output markets in the foreign country, a firm will establish a production facility there. FDI allows a firm to circumvent actual or anticipated barriers to trade. Another motive for indulging in FDI is the appreciation of the domestic currency, which reduces the competitiveness of exports.

Step 2 is licensing, which may be defined as the supply of technology and know-how or may involve the use of a trademark or a patent for a fee. It offers one way to circumvent entry barriers to FDI. Under these circumstances licensing offers an opportunity to generate revenue from foreign markets that are otherwise inaccessible. Furthermore, the licence owner often may not have the capital, experience or risk tolerance associated with FDI. Firms prefer FDI to licensing in the case of complex technology or when the risk of leakage of technological advantage to competitors exists.

Franchising is another form of entering a foreign market under contractual agreements. Companies with brand name products (such as KFC and Burger King) move offshore by granting foreigners the exclusive right to sell their products in a designated area. The parent company provides the technical expertise pertaining to the production process as well as marketing assistance for an initial fee and subsequent royalties that are related to turnover.

FDI may take one of three forms: greenfield investment, cross-border mergers and acquisitions, and joint ventures. Greenfield investment occurs when the investing firm establishes new production, distribution or other facilities in the host country. This is normally welcomed by the host country because of the job-creating potential and value-added output. Sometimes the term **brownfield investment** is used to describe a situation where an investment that is formally an acquisition resembles greenfield investment. This happens when the foreign investor acquires a firm but almost completely replaces plant and equipment, labour and the product line.

FDI may occur via an acquisition of, or a merger with, an established firm in the host country (the vast majority of M&As are indeed acquisitions rather than mergers). This mode of FDI has two advantages over greenfield investment: (i) it is cheaper, particularly if the acquired project is a loss-making operation that can be bought cheaply; and (ii) it allows the investor to get quick access to the market. Firms may be motivated to engage in cross-border acquisitions to bolster their competitive positions in the world market by acquiring special assets from other firms or by using their own assets on a larger scale.

Whether a firm would choose M&As or greenfield investment depends on a number of firm-specific, host country-specific and industry-specific factors, including the following:

- Firms with lower research and development (R&D) intensity are more likely to indulge in M&As than those with strong technological advantages.
- More diversified firms are likely to choose M&As.
- Large multinational firms are more inclined to indulge in M&As.
- Cultural and economic differences between the home country and the host country reduce the tendency for M&As.
- Multinational firms with subsidiaries in the host country prefer acquisitions.
- The tendency towards M&As depends on the supply of target firms.
- Slow growth in an industry encourages M&As.

IN PRACTICE

Who's who in Australian M&As?

In its issue of 4 April 2002, the *Australian Financial Review* announced the top players in the Australian market for M&As during the first quarter of 2002. The ranking was based on the value (not the number) of the deals and was as follows:

Player	Market share
JP Morgan	28.5
Macquarie Bank	26.3
UBS Warburg	18.1
Citigroup/Salomon Smith Barney	16.7
Cranegie Wylir & Co	13.2
Credit Suisse First Boston	13.2
Goldman Sachs and Co	12.5
Ernst & Young Corporate Finance	4.5
Deutsche Bank AG	4.3
Gresham Partners	4.0

It was reported that both the number and the value of the deals were lower compared with the first quarter of 2001. The slack activity led to a reduction in the staffing of financial institutions. Credit Suisse First Boston, for example, announced that it would slash 300 investment banking positions.

Cross-border acquisition of businesses is a politically sensitive issue, as most countries prefer to retain local control of domestic firms. It follows that although countries may welcome greenfield investment, foreign firms' bids to acquire domestic firms are often resisted and sometimes even resented.The underlying argument here is that M&As are less beneficial than greenfield FDI, and may even be harmful, because they do not contribute to productive capacity and may be accompanied by lay-offs or the termination of some beneficial activities. If mergers and acquisitions take place in some sensitive areas (such as the media), then it may seem (perhaps justifiably) like a threat to the national culture or identity.

Whether or not cross-border acquisitions produce synergetic gains and how such gains are divided between acquiring and target firms are important issues from the perspective of shareholders' welfare and public policy. Synergetic gains are obtained when the value of the combined firm is greater than the stand-alone valuations of the individual (acquiring and target) firms. If cross-border acquisitions generate synergetic gains, both the acquiring firm and the target firm's shareholders gain wealth at the same time. Synergetic gains may or may not arise from cross-border acquisitions depending on the motive of acquiring firms. In general, gains will result when the acquiring firm is motivated to take advantage of market imperfections such as mispriced factors of production or to cope with trade barriers.

FDI can also take the form of **joint ventures** either with a host country firm or a government institution, as well as with another company that is foreign to the host country. One side normally provides the technical expertise and its ability to raise finance whereas the other side provides valuable input through its local knowledge of the bureaucracy as well as local laws and regulations.

18.3 Theories of foreign direct investment

A number of theories or hypotheses have been put forward to explain FDI. Moreover, a number of factors that influence the FDI decision have been identified. These theories, hypotheses and factors are dealt with in turn below.

The differential rates of return hypothesis

The **differential rates of return hypothesis** postulates that capital flows from countries with low rates of return to countries with high rates of return move in a process that eventually leads to the equality of real rates of return. The rationale for this hypothesis is that firms considering FDI behave in such a way as to equate the marginal return on capital and its marginal cost. The hypothesis is obviously based on the assumption of risk neutrality, making the rate of return the only factor upon which the investment decision is made.

The diversification hypothesis

When the assumption of risk neutrality is relaxed, risk becomes another factor upon which the FDI decision is made. According to the **diversification hypothesis**, the choice among various projects is guided not only by the expected rate of return but also by risk, as represented by the variability of the rate of return. The same idea of reducing risk via diversification that is relevant to portfolio investment is used here. Because of **risk aversion**, a rate of return differential will not induce capital flows in one direction until the differential disappears via arbitrage.

The output and market size hypothesis

According to the **output and market size hypothesis**, the volume of FDI in one host country depends either on the output (or sales) of a multinational firm in this country or on the market size as measured by its GDP.

The industrial organisation hypothesis

According to the **industrial organisation hypothesis**, when a firm conducts business in another country, it faces several disadvantages in competing with local firms. These disadvantages emanate from differences in language, culture, legal systems and other intercountry differences. If, in spite of these disadvantages, the firm engages in FDI, it must have some advantages arising from a well-known brand name, patent-protected technology, managerial skills and other firm-specific factors. It is these firm-specific advantages that explain why a firm can compete successfully in a foreign market. One problem with this hypothesis, however, is that it fails to explain why the firm does not utilise its advantages by producing in the home country and exporting, which is an alternative to FDI as an entry mode (as we have seen).

The internalisation hypothesis

According to the **internalisation hypothesis**, FDI arises from efforts by firms to replace **market transactions** with **internal transactions**. For example, if there are problems associated with buying oil products on the market, a firm may decide to buy a foreign refinery. The advantages of internalisation are the avoidance of time lags, bargaining and uncertainty.

The location hypothesis

According to the **location hypothesis**, FDI exists because of the international immobility of some factors of production, such as labour and natural resources. This hypothesis is used to explain US FDI in Australia and Canada.

The eclectic theory

The **eclectic theory** postulates that three conditions must be satisfied if a firm is to engage in FDI. First, it must have a **comparative advantage** over other firms arising from the ownership of some **intangible assets**. These are called **ownership advantages**, and include the right to a particular technology, monopoly power and size, access to raw materials and access to cheap finance. Second, it must be more beneficial for the firm to use these advantages rather than to sell or lease them. These are the **internalisation advantages**, which refer to the choice between accomplishing expansion within the firm or by selling the rights to the means of expansion to other firms. Third, it must be more profitable to use these advantages in combination with at least some factor inputs located abroad. If this is not the case, then exports would do the job. These are called **locational advantages**, and pertain to the question as to whether expansion is best accomplished at home or abroad.

Suppose that there is demand for a particular product in which a particular domestic firm has some ownership advantage. What happens (that is, how the firm responds) depends on the internalisation and locational advantages. So, there are the following possibilities:

- If there are no internalisation gains, the firm will license its ownership advantage to another firm, particularly if locational factors favour expansion abroad.
- If there are internalisation gains and if locational factors favour domestic expansion, the firm will expand at home and export.
- If there are internalisation gains and if locational factors favour foreign expansion, FDI will take place and a multinational firm will emerge.

The product life cycle hypothesis

The **product life cycle hypothesis** postulates that most products follow a life cycle in which they first appear as innovations in the home country (which is more technologically advanced than other countries) but ultimately they become standardised. FDI results from the reaction of firms, by expanding overseas, to the possibility of losing markets as the product matures.

The process goes like this. The product is initially produced at home and any foreign demand (from developed economies initially) is satisfied by exports. Rival producers, who can make the product more cheaply, will eventually emerge in these foreign markets. At this stage, the innovator will examine the possibility of setting up a production unit abroad. When the product is standardised, the innovator may decide to invest in developing economies to obtain some cost advantages, such as cheaper labour.

The oligopolistic reaction hypothesis

In an oligopolistic environment, FDI by one firm triggers similar investments by other leading firms in the industry in an attempt to maintain their market shares. An implication of the **oligopolistic reaction hypothesis** is that the process of FDI is self-limiting, since the invasion of each other's home market leads to an increase in competition and a decline in the intensity of oligopolistic reaction. This implication, however, is incompatible with stylised facts. While direct investment has led to increased competition in many industries, this increase has not resulted in a corresponding reduction in FDI.

The internal financing hypothesis

In this sense, internal financing refers to the utilisation of profit generated by a subsidiary to finance expansion of FDI by a multinational firm in the same country where the subsidiary operates. The **internal financing hypothesis** postulates that multinational firms commit a modest amount of their resources to their initial direct investment, whereas subsequent expansions are financed by reinvesting profits obtained from operations in the host country. This hypothesis therefore implies the existence of a positive relationship between internal cash flows and investment outlays, which is plausible because the cost of internal financing is lower. This hypothesis seems to be more appropriate for explaining FDI in developing countries, for at least two reasons: (i) the presence of restrictions on the movement of funds; and (ii) the rudimentary state and inefficiency of financial markets.

The currency areas hypothesis

The **currency areas hypothesis** postulates that firms of a country with a strong currency tend to invest abroad, whereas firms belonging to a country with a weak currency do not have such a tendency. In other words, countries with strong currencies tend to be sources of FDI and countries with weak currencies tend to be host countries or recipients of FDI.

Diversification with barriers to international capital flows

Investors demand diversification and multinational firms supply diversification services. For international diversification to be carried out through multinational firms, two conditions must hold: (i) there must exist barriers or costs to portfolio flows, which are greater than those associated with direct investment; and (ii) investors must believe that multinational firms provide diversification opportunities that are unavailable otherwise.

Political instability and political risk

Lack of political stability discourages inflows of FDI. **Political risk** arises because unexpected modifications of the legal and fiscal frameworks in the host country may change the economic outcome of a given investment in a drastic manner. For example, a decision by the host government to impose restrictions on capital repatriation to the investor's home country will adversely affect the cash flows received by the parent firm from the foreign subsidiary located in the host country.

Tax policies

Domestic and foreign tax policies affect the incentive to engage in FDI and the means whereby it is financed. There are three channels through which tax policies affect the decisions taken by multinational firms. First, the tax treatment of income generated abroad has a direct effect on the net return on FDI. Second, the tax treatment of income generated at home affects the net profitability of domestic investment and the relative profitability of domestic and foreign investment. Third, tax policies affect the relative cost of capital of domestic and foreign investment. Thus, an increase in the domestic corporate tax rate leads to an increase in the outflow of FDI.

Government regulations

Government regulations may give rise to incentives or disincentives to FDI. Incentives include, in addition to fiscal benefits such as tax credits and exemptions, some financial benefits such as grants and subsidised loans. Disincentives include a number of impediments, from the slow processing of the required authorisation to the outright prohibition of foreign investment in specific regions or sectors.

RESEARCH FINDINGS

Determinants of FDI in Australia

Yang, Groenewold and Tcha used an econometric model to pinpoint the factors that determined FDI flows into Australia over the period 1985–1996.[1] They suggested a model in which FDI flows are determined by the interest rate, the effective exchange rate of the Australian dollar, GDP, wages, openness, industrial disputes and inflation. They found the following results:

- FDI inflow is positively related to the interest rate in Australia, reflecting the fact that higher interest rates in the host country make FDI more attractive (the differential rates of return hypothesis).
- FDI flow is negatively related to the degree of openness of the economy, which is a reflection of the proposition that FDI is a way of circumventing trade barriers.
- A high inflation rate discourages FDI inflows.
- Wage changes, openness and industrial disputes also determine FDI flows.

1 J. Yang, N. Groenewold and M. Tcha, 'The Determinants of Foreign Direct Investment in Australia', *Economic Record*, 76, 2000, pp. 45–54.

Strategic and long-term factors

Some strategic and long-term factors are considered as being instrumental to the decision to indulge in FDI. These factors are as follows:

- the desire on the part of the investor to defend existing foreign markets and foreign investments against competitors
- the desire to gain and maintain a foothold in a protected market or to gain and maintain a source of supply that may prove useful in the long run
- the need to develop and sustain a parent–subsidiary relationship
- the desire to induce the host country into a long commitment to a particular type of technology
- the advantage of complementing another type of investment
- the economies of new product development
- competition for market shares among oligopolists and the concern for the strengthening of bargaining positions.

A summary of the motives for FDI

Multinational firms indulge in FDI for a variety of reasons, which can be summarised as follows:

- *Extending markets:* when the growth of sales is limited in the home market, a firm considers expanding overseas. Under special circumstances, expansion takes place by establishing production facilities abroad. This allows the exploitation of economies of scale.
- *Entering markets where profit margins are higher:* under conditions of market segmentation, firms move into the markets that offer high profit margins.
- *Availability of raw materials:* to avoid the transportation costs associated with importing raw materials that are unavailable at home, a firm will set up a production facility close to the source of raw materials in the foreign country, particularly if the foreign country is a market for the finished products.
- *Using foreign technology:* firms establish plants in foreign countries to learn and utilise foreign technology.
- *Using foreign factors of production:* setting up production facilities in foreign countries is conducive to reducing the costs of production if the costs of labour and land are lower overseas than at home.
- *Integrating operations:* vertical integration is achieved when a firm indulges in various stages of production. For example, vertical integration is achieved in the oil industry when a firm engages in operations ranging from exploration and extraction to retailing. It is beneficial because it results in assured delivery between various stages of production. If different stages can be carried out more efficiently in different locations, then expansion in foreign countries will take place.
- *Non-transferable knowledge:* if a firm develops expertise in the production of a certain commodity and if it is difficult to transfer this knowledge, the firm will be better off expanding overseas.
- *Protecting knowledge:* a firm may have expertise that can be transferred but may not wish to transfer this knowledge. In this case the firm will take production overseas itself.
- *Protecting reputation:* to protect a brand name or product quality, a firm may decide to carry out production abroad.
- *Capitalising on reputation:* firms with a good international reputation may capitalise on it by expanding overseas. Internationally well-known banks, for example, can attract deposits when they set up branches in foreign countries.
- *Avoiding tariffs and quotas by establishing production facilities abroad.*
- *Exchange rate considerations:* firms move into countries with weak currencies because the initial set-up cost is low.
- *International diversification:* this is the same argument put forward for portfolio diversification.
- *Relationships with other multinationals:* some multinationals expand overseas because they follow other multinationals.

18.4 Evaluating direct investment projects

Several methods involving different criteria are used to evaluate direct investment projects, the so-called **capital budgeting**, but things get more complicated when we try to use the same methods to evaluate FDI projects. In this section we review these methods, while the problems associated with evaluating FDI projects are considered in the following section.

Project evaluation criteria

Four project evaluation criteria are discussed in turn below.

The accounting rate of return

The **accounting rate of return** is the percentage return on capital invested in the project, normally the average annual percentage profit before tax relative to the average amount of capital invested in the project. This method is criticised because it is based on profit, which is an accounting concept, rather than on cash flows, which are more appropriate for a resource allocation decision like investment. Another problem with this technique is that it takes no account of the size of the project or the **time value of money**. The latter arises from the fact that a dollar next year is less valuable than a dollar today, because a dollar today can be invested at the market interest rate to get more than one dollar next year.

The payback period

The **payback period** measures how quickly the initial outlay is paid back from after-tax cash flows that are generated from the investment. Only projects that are paid back within a period of time that is acceptable to the investor will be undertaken. The payback period method is preferable to the accounting rate of return method because it is based on cash flows. However, it ignores both the time value of money and the cash flows that occur after the initial investment has been paid back.

Example

Two projects, A and B, give the following cash flows over a period of six years. Which one of these projects will be selected on the basis of the payback period?

	Year						
	0	1	2	3	4	5	6
A	−100	20	30	50	10	10	0
B	−100	10	20	30	40	70	80

The costs of the two projects are equal at 100. Project A generates 100 in the first three years, thus it has a payback period of three years. Project B, on the other hand, has a payback period of four years. Thus, project A will be preferred because it has a shorter payback period. Note that this method does not take into consideration the cash flows of Project A arising after year 3 and the cash flows of Project B arising after year 4.

Net present value

The **net present value (NPV)** method is based on cash flows and takes account of the time value of money by discounting cash flows at an appropriate discount rate. The **discount rate** is the minimum required rate of return, which is normally the **cost of capital**. NPV measures the absolute financial benefit of a project, which is found acceptable if the NPV is positive. To choose between two projects, the one that is picked must have a higher NPV. The NPV is calculated as

$$NPV = -C_0 + \sum_{t=1}^{n} \frac{C_t}{(1+r)^t} \tag{18.1}$$

where C_0 is the initial investment outlay or the capital cost of the project, C_t is the cash flow arising at time t and r is the discount rate. r may be calculated as the weighted average cost of capital as

$$r = \left(\frac{E}{E+D}\right) r^E + \left(\frac{D}{E+D}\right) r^D \tag{18.2}$$

where E is the market value of equity capital, D is the market value of debt, r^E is the **cost of equity capital** and r^D is the **cost of debt capital**. If we take an explicit account of taxes, then the NPV is given by:

$$NPV = -C_0 + \sum_{t=1}^{n} \frac{C_t(1-\tau)}{(1+r)^t} \tag{18.3}$$

where τ is the tax rate. Similarly, the cost of capital is given by

$$r = \left(\frac{E}{E+D}\right) r^E + \left(\frac{D}{E+D}\right) r^D (1-\tau) \tag{18.4}$$

The adjustment of the right-hand side of Equation (18.4) by a factor of $(1 - \tau)$ is required to calculate the effective cost of debt because a fraction, τ, of interest payments is saved on taxes.

If the project has a **salvage value** or a **liquidation value** (that is, if the project is still worth something at the end of its life), then the NPV is given by

$$NPV = -C_0 + \sum_{t=1}^{n} \frac{C_t(1-\tau)}{(1+r)^t} + \frac{V}{(1+r)^n} \tag{18.5}$$

where V is the salvage value at period n.

Example

Assuming that the cost of capital is 10 per cent, calculate the NPV of Projects A and B described in the previous example (assume a tax rate of 20 per cent). If the two projects are mutually exclusive, which one will be preferred? Assume that the two projects are financed exclusively by equity.

Given the assumption about financing, there is no need to adjust the discount rate for taxes. In the absence of taxes, the NPVs are calculated as follows:

$$NPV(A) = -100 + \frac{20}{1.1} + \frac{30}{(1.1)^2} + \frac{50}{(1.1)^3} + \frac{10}{(1.1)^4} + \frac{10}{(1.1)^5} + \frac{0}{(1.1)^6} = -6.42$$

$$NPV(B) = -100 + \frac{10}{1.1} + \frac{20}{(1.1)^2} + \frac{30}{(1.1)^3} + \frac{40}{(1.1)^4} + \frac{70}{(1.1)^5} + \frac{80}{(1.1)^6} = 64.10$$

Project A cannot be accepted because it has a negative NPV. Thus, Project B would be accepted. It is obvious that the payback period could lead to the wrong choice.

If the tax rate is 20 per cent, the after-tax cash flows are:

	Year						
	0	1	2	3	4	5	6
A	–100	16	24	40	8	8	0
B	–100	8	16	24	32	56	64

In the presence of taxes the NPVs are:

$$NPV(A) = -100 + \frac{16}{1.1} + \frac{24}{(1.1)^2} + \frac{40}{(1.1)^3} + \frac{8}{(1.1)^4} + \frac{8}{(1.1)^5} + \frac{0}{(1.1)^6} = -25.14$$

$$NPV(B) = -100 + \frac{8}{1.1} + \frac{16}{(1.1)^2} + \frac{24}{(1.1)^3} + \frac{32}{(1.1)^4} + \frac{56}{(1.1)^5} + \frac{64}{(1.1)^6} = 31.28$$

The results are qualitatively unchanged in that Project A cannot be accepted. However, Project B has a lower NPV in the presence of taxes than otherwise.

Example

Project B in the previous examples is financed by 40 per cent equity and 60 per cent debt. Assuming a tax rate of 30 per cent, what is the NPV of this project if the cost of equity financing is 8 per cent and the cost of debt financing is 5 per cent?

The cost of capital is calculated by using Equation (18.4) as a weighted average of the cost of debt and equity financing. Thus

$$r = \frac{40}{100} \times 8 + \frac{60}{100} \times 5 \times (1 - 0.3) = 5.3\%$$

The after-tax cash flows are:

	Year						
	0	1	2	3	4	5	6
B	–100	7	14	21	28	49	56

Therefore:

$$NPV = -100 + \frac{7}{1.053} + \frac{14}{(1.053)^2} + \frac{21}{(1.053)^3} + \frac{28}{(1.053)^4} + \frac{49}{(1.053)^5} + \frac{56}{(1.053)^6} = 38.96$$

Example

What is the NPV of Project B described in the previous example if it has a salvage value of 5?

With a salvage value of 5, the NPV can be calculated by using Equation (18.5) as

$$NPV = -100 + \frac{7}{1.053} + \frac{14}{(1.053)^2} + \frac{21}{(1.053)^3} + \frac{28}{(1.053)^4} + \frac{49}{(1.053)^5} + \frac{56}{(1.053)^6} + \frac{5}{(1.053)^6} = 42.63$$

The internal rate of return

The **internal rate of return (IRR)** is the discount rate that makes the NPV of a project equal to zero. The IRR can be calculated by solving for r in the equation

$$-C_0 + \sum_{t=1}^{n} \frac{C_t}{(1+r)^t} = 0 \qquad (18.6)$$

If we take an explicit account of taxes, then the IRR is given by

$$-C_0 + \sum_{t=1}^{n} \frac{C_t(1-\tau)}{(1+r)^t} = 0 \qquad (18.7)$$

If the project has a salvage value, then the IRR can be obtained by solving for r in the equation

$$-C_0 + \sum_{t=1}^{n} \frac{C_t(1-\tau)}{(1+r)^t} + \frac{V}{(1+r)^n} = 0 \qquad (18.8)$$

Thus, the IRR on a project with a zero NPV is equal to the discount rate or the cost of capital. A project has a positive NPV if the IRR is greater than the cost of capital, and vice versa. The problem with the IRR, however, is that its calculation is based on the assumption that cash flows can be reinvested at the same rate, and this is not necessarily the case. Hence, it may be in conflict with the NPV when competing projects have different sizes or time horizons.

The cost of capital

The cost of capital is used as a discount rate for future cash flows. It is defined as the minimum risk-adjusted rate of return required in order for the investment to be accepted. The overall cost depends on the type of capital employed and the degree of risk associated with the investment project. The discount rate for new projects should reflect the risk of the project itself and each project may require an individual estimate of its own risk-adjusted discount rate.

The cost of capital can be calculated from Equation (18.2). The cost of debt capital can be measured easily, based on the current market interest rate payable on the debt. The problem is how to determine the cost of equity capital for a multinational firm. The cost of equity capital is the minimum rate of return necessary to induce investors to buy or maintain their holdings of shares. There are two models whereby the cost of equity capital can be determined. The first is the CAPM, which we came across in Chapter 17. The second is the

dividend valuation model. According to this model, the required rate of return is determined by the expected level of dividends. The constant dividend growth model can be written as

$$P = \frac{D}{r^E - g} \tag{18.9}$$

where P is the share price, D is the dividend and g is the growth rate of the dividend. Hence

$$r^E = \frac{D}{P} + g \tag{18.10}$$

Adjusting project assessment for risk

When the NPV or the IRR method is used for project evaluation, a problem is typically encountered as to the accuracy of the cash flows that are expected to materialise in the future as a result of operating the project. Risk means that cash flows generated by the project may fluctuate far away from the expected value that would normally be used to calculate the NPV and the IRR. If it is felt that this is the case, then some adjustment may be made to account for risk. There are five methods to deal with risk in situations like these.

The risk-adjusted discount rate

As we have seen, the greater the risk associated with future cash flows, the greater should be the discount rate used to calculate the present value of the future cash flows. This is why the discount rate may differ from the cost of capital. This is also the reason why different rates may be used to discount cash flows with different degrees of risk. For example, cash flows associated with tax saving from depreciation and interest payments to creditors are less risky than operating cash flows and this is why the latter may be discounted at a higher rate.

This approach to the adjustment for risk is easy to implement but it is criticised as being somewhat arbitrary. Furthermore, it does not take into account changes in the riskiness of cash flows from one time period to another, since the discount rate is assumed to be constant across time for a class of cash flows with a particular degree of risk. Despite these shortcomings, the **risk-adjusted discount rate** is used because of its simplicity.

Risk-adjusted cash flows

For some analysts, adjusting the cash flows is more appropriate than adjusting the discount rate, particularly if the project involves market risk. **Risk-adjusted cash flows** (or **certainty-equivalent cash flows**) are obtained by reducing risky future cash flows to a lower level. This adjustment is made separately for each period of the project's life. The adjusted risk-free cash flows are then discounted at the risk-free discount rate to estimate the NPV of the project. The difference between this method and the adjusted discount rate method is that the former considers time and risk separately, whereas the latter treats them jointly. Although this method is theoretically more appealing, it is not widely used because there are practical problems in identifying the equivalent risk-free cash flows.

Sensitivity analysis

Sensitivity analysis entails the use of 'what if' scenarios, which are implemented by changing the input variables, including the exchange rate. If the NPV remains positive for several scenarios, then the firm should become more comfortable with the project. Sensitivity analysis can be applied to the discount rate or rates as well.

Simulation

Simulation can be used to generate a probability distribution for the NPV based on various combinations of the values of input variables. A large number of iterations are performed: in each iteration, the values of input variables are changed. Each iteration produces a value for the NPV and after a large number of iterations we end up with a probability distribution for the NPV. From the probability distribution it is possible to estimate the probability with which the NPV will be positive.

Break-even analysis

In **break-even analysis**, focus is placed on the point at which the NPV switches from positive to negative.

18.5 Evaluating foreign direct investment projects

Of the four methods of evaluating direct investment projects outlined in the previous section, the NPV method is the only one that consistently leads to absolute financial gains. There are problems in using the NPV formula to evaluate FDI projects and these problems are associated with the measurement of cash flows and the definition or choice of the discount rate.

The problem of estimating cash flows arises because the net after-tax cash inflows of the subsidiary can differ considerably from those of the parent firm. The difference may be due to a number of reasons. The first reason is the existence of different tax rates. If the foreign tax rate is low and the domestic tax rate is high, then the project may be attractive from the subsidiary's perspective but not from the perspective of the parent firm. The second reason is the imposition by the host government of restrictions on remittances from the subsidiary to the parent firm. Funds that cannot be repatriated to the home country can be used by the subsidiary to finance an expansion in the project. Again, such an expansion may be attractive for the subsidiary but not for the parent firm. The third reason is excessive remittances by the subsidiary to the parent firm. This may be the case when the parent firm charges the subsidiary excessively high administrative fees or high prices for the intermediate products supplied by the former to the latter (the so-called transfer prices). While these charges are revenue for the parent firm, they are costs for the subsidiary. Hence, a project may be unattractive for a subsidiary faced with this situation but attractive for the parent firm. Finally, changes in the exchange rate between the base currencies of the subsidiary and the parent firm may result in completely different cash flows realised by each of them. In general, a strong foreign currency (the base currency of the subsidiary) makes the investment more attractive for the parent firm than for the subsidiary, and vice versa.

Example

A project has the following cash flows:

Year			
0	1	2	3
−100	60	80	100

Assume a foreign tax rate of 20 per cent, a domestic tax rate of 20 per cent (no tax credit is given), that only 60 per cent of after-tax cash flows are allowed to be remitted to the parent firm and a discount rate of 8 per cent. Calculate the NPV from the perspective of the subsidiary and the parent firm if the exchange rate (domestic/foreign) assumes the following values:

Year			
0	1	2	3
1.25	1.22	1.20	1.15

We start by calculating the following cash flows:

Cash flow	0	1	2	3
Before-tax cash flows of subsidiary	−100	60.00	80.00	100.00
After-tax cash flows of subsidiary	−100	48.00	64.00	80.00
Remitted to parent (foreign currency)	−100	28.80	38.40	48.00
Remitted to parent (domestic currency)	−125	35.14	46.08	55.20
Remitted to parent (after-tax)	−125	28.11	36.86	44.16

Therefore:

$$NPV(subsidiary) = -100 + \frac{48}{1.08} + \frac{64}{(1.08)^2} + \frac{80}{(1.08)^3} = 62.82$$

$$NPV(parent) = -125 + \frac{28.11}{1.08} + \frac{36.86}{(1.08)^2} + \frac{44.16}{(1.08)^3} = -32.31$$

The results show that, although the project is attractive from the perspective of the subsidiary, it is not so from the perspective of the parent firm.

The appropriate evaluation measure is normally considered to be the funds flowing back to the parent firm. Cash flows remitted to the parent firm usually form the basis of dividends, reinvestment and other decisions. Because of this disparity, problems are encountered when an attempt is made to estimate cash flows for the purpose of calculating the NPV.

The first problem pertains to **blocked funds**, which arises when the host government requires a percentage of the subsidiary's earnings to remain in the host country. If these funds can be utilised in a foreign investment, there is a gain that should be deducted from the capital cost of the project (C_0). This gain is the difference between the face value of the blocked funds and the present value of the funds if the next best thing is done with them. There is also the problem arising from the effects on the sales of other divisions of the multinational firm. If FDI is undertaken in a country in which sales are already taking place, only the increment in income is relevant.

Furthermore, there is the problem of **remittance restrictions**. When the remittances are legally restricted, the restrictions can sometimes be circumvented to some extent by using internal transfer pricing. So, it may be plausible to add to the cash flows the income that is remittable via other means. Different levels of taxation may prove to be problematical. The tax rate used to calculate the NPV must be the higher of the domestic rate and the foreign rate. In reality, taxes are often reduced to levels below the nominal tax rate via transfer prices, royalty payments, and so on. For example, a multinational firm may attempt to reduce the tax paid by its subsidiary in a high-tax country by charging high prices for the intermediate products it sells to the subsidiary (that is, higher transfer prices). Another complication arises from concessionary loans, which may command a lower interest rate.

The role of forecasting

Since cash flows arise in the future, they can only be estimated. Hence, forecasting is an important component of the capital budgeting decision. The process is more complicated in international capital budgeting, since the future cash flows are affected by more variables than in domestic capital budgeting (such as the exchange rate and foreign variables). In general, forecasts of the following variables are required in international capital budgeting:

- Demand for the product, which depends on such factors as the price of the product, prices of competing products, taste and other factors. Typically, demand is estimated statistically from historical data.
- The price of the product, which is determined by several factors. If, for example, the objective is market penetration, the price should be lower than those of competing products. Over time, the price will be affected by inflation, production costs and prices of competitors.
- **Variable costs**, which consist of the costs of labour, fuel and factors of this nature. Variable costs per unit of the product rise with the inflation rate of the host country.
- **Fixed costs**, which are easier to forecast than variable costs because they do not depend on consumer demand.
- Project lifetime, which is difficult to assess and is sometimes beyond the control of the investing firm. Political events may force the liquidation of the project prematurely.
- Salvage value, which again is difficult to forecast because it partly depends on the attitude of the host government.
- Remittance restrictions, which pertain to political risk. The host government may change the regulations at any time, thus affecting the value of the cash flows received by the parent firm.
- Tax rates and laws, which also pertain to political risk and again determine the amount received by the parent firm.
- Exchange rates, which are required to estimate the domestic currency value of the cash flows received by the parent firm from the subsidiary.

A typical evaluation process consists of the following steps:

- estimating the incremental cash flows in the foreign country, taking account of any foreign tax effects
- estimating remittable cash flows to the parent firm and translating these cash flows into the domestic currency at the expected exchange rates for the relevant periods
- incorporating into the parent firm's remitted cash flows any indirect costs and benefits that arise directly as a result of undertaking the project—all parent firm tax effects must be considered at this stage
- discounting the parent firm's incremental cash flows at a rate that reflects the risk of the project to produce the expected NPV of the project.

The cost of capital for multinational firms and across countries

The cost of capital for multinational firms may differ from that of domestic firms for several reasons. The first reason is size. Since multinational firms are normally big (for example, in terms of assets), they receive preferential treatment from creditors. Thus, the cost of capital for multinational firms should be lower for this reason. The second reason why the cost of capital for multinational firms should be lower is that they have better access to international capital markets, which provide the possibility of obtaining cheap funds. Since the cost of capital depends in part on the probability of bankruptcy, any factor that affects this probability also affects the cost of capital. Hence, the international diversification of multinational firms reduces the cost of capital, whereas their exposure to country risk raises it. This is because international diversification reduces, whereas country risk raises, the probability of bankruptcy. Finally, since multinational firms are exposed to foreign exchange risk, their cash flows tend to be volatile and hence the cost of capital would be higher than otherwise.

Understanding cross-country differences in the cost of capital can explain why multinational firms based in some countries may have a competitive advantage over firms based in other countries. Furthermore, understanding the differences between the cost of debt capital and the cost of equity capital can explain why multinational firms based in certain countries have more debt-intensive capital structures.

We begin by explaining that the cost of debt capital is determined by the risk-free rate and the **risk premium**. It is higher in some countries than in others because the risk-free rate and/or the risk premium are higher. Differences in the risk-free rate are due to several factors that affect the supply of and demand for loanable funds and hence the level of the interest rate. For example, the interest rate varies with the state of the economy, tending to rise when the economy is booming and decline when the economy is in a slump. There is also a direct relationship between the level of the nominal interest rate and expected inflation, as represented by the Fisher equation, which we came across in Chapter 11. This is the reason why interest rates could reach triple figures in countries experiencing hyperinflation. In general, the level of interest rate is higher in countries with extremely high inflation rates. Other factors that affect the level of interest rates are the stance of monetary policy (tight or expansionary), tax laws (whether or not these laws encourage saving) and demographical factors (age composition of households affects saving).

The risk premium is meant to compensate creditors for the risk of default by the borrower. This risk varies across countries because of differences in economic conditions, relationships between firms and creditors, government intervention and the degree of **financial leverage**. The risk premium tends to be lower in countries where economic conditions are more stable. The risk of default increases as the economy moves into recession and so we should expect the risk premium to increase as economic activity slows down. The risk premium is also lower in countries where the relationship between creditors and companies is so close that creditors stand ready to extend credit in the event of financial distress (in Japan, for example—or at least this is what used to be the case). The risk premium is higher in countries where the government is not prepared to be called to the rescue. Finally, the risk premium should be higher in countries where companies are allowed high degrees of financial leverage (for example, Japan and Germany).

Now we turn to cross-country differences in the cost of equity capital. Recall that the cost of equity capital is an opportunity cost: what shareholders can earn on investment with similar risk if the equity funds were distributed to them. This return consists of the risk-free interest rate and a risk premium. Differences in the risk-free rate lead to differences in the cost of equity capital, which also depends on investment opportunities in the underlying country. Countries with abundant investment opportunities have higher cost of equity capital than countries with limited investment opportunities.

The adjusted present value

Because there are many problems associated with the measurement of a unique discount rate for cash flows arising from an FDI project, the NPV method may not be suitable for evaluating these projects. An alternative method is the **adjusted present value (APV)** technique. The starting point is to evaluate the project as if it were all equity-financed (as in the NPV method) and then introduce some adjustments by taking into account the side effects, which are discounted at separate rates reflecting their own systematic risk. Thus, the APV of a foreign direct investment project can be estimated as the capital cost plus the present values of the following items: (i) remittable operating cash flows; (ii) tax savings from depreciation or capital allowances; (iii) subsidies to the project; (iv) other tax savings; (v) the project's effect on corporate debt capacity; and (vi) other cash inflows and outflows that result directly from the project.

18.6 More about taxation

International taxation refers to the taxation of cross-border transactions. Such transactions invariably give rise to tax problems because consideration must to be given to two or more different tax systems.

Types of taxes

The impact of taxation on a multinational firm depends on whether or not the tax is considered an income tax, since the tax credit applies to income tax only. In this section the taxes that a multinational firm and its subsidiaries face are discussed briefly.

Corporate income tax

Corporate income tax is a direct tax in the sense that it is paid directly by the taxpayer on whom it is levied. The tax is levied on **active income**, which results directly from the production of goods and services. Corporate income tax rates range between zero per cent in Bahrain, Bermuda and the Cayman Islands to well over 40 per cent in many countries.

There are two approaches to taxing corporate income: the **classic approach to taxation** and the **integrated approach to taxation**. Under the classic approach, the income received by each taxable entity is taxed. Thus, the earnings of a company could be taxed twice: when they are earned and when they are received as dividends by shareholders. The integrated approach aims at eliminating this kind of double taxation by considering both the company and its shareholders, and this can be done in two different ways. The first is to tax undistributed earnings at a higher rate than that used to tax distributed earnings. The second is the so-called **imputation tax system** whereby the portion of income tax paid by a company is imputed when shareholders are taxed on their dividends.

Withholding taxes

A **withholding tax** is levied on passive income earned by a firm within the tax jurisdiction of another country. **Passive income** includes dividends and interest payments as well as income from royalties, patents and copyrights. A withholding tax is an indirect tax that is borne by a taxpayer who did not directly generate the income that serves as the source of the passive income. Countries levy withholding taxes on payments to non-resident investors.

Indirect taxes

The most important form of **indirect tax** is the **value added tax (VAT)**, which in Australia is known as the **Goods and Services Tax (GST)**. The basic idea behind VAT is that the tax is applied at each stage of the production process for the value added by a firm to the goods purchased from other firms.

Import duties

Import duties (also called **customs duties** and **tariffs**) are imposed on imports. Since goods entering a country are shipped to specific ports where policing can be intensive, import duties are a good source of revenue when income or sales records are poor. This partly explains why the governments of some developing countries depend on tariffs as a source of revenue. Tariffs also explain why a car can cost five times as much in some countries as in others. Finally, tariffs explain why some firms move production facilities abroad. Tariffs, and even the threat of imposing tariffs, provide one explanation for FDI.

Taxation of foreign exchange gains

When cross-border transactions are conducted, foreign exchange gains and losses will typically be present. The tax treatment of these gains and losses is very complex and varies from one country to another. In many countries, foreign exchange gains and losses are taken into account in the overall trading profit. If these gains and losses relate to capital transactions, they are recognised in some countries but not in others.

The avoidance of double taxation

Many countries have **bilateral tax treaties** with other countries, mainly to avoid **double taxation**. In 1921 the League of Nations commissioned a report that concluded that double taxation interfered with 'economic intercourse and ... the free flow of capital'. The report put forward some rules for determining when tax should be paid to the country in which income is generated and when it should be paid to the taxpayer's home country. The outcome of this exercise was a model treaty that was subsequently adopted and modified by the OECD to become what is known as the **OECD Model Tax Convention**.

Double taxation of the same funds is invariably detrimental to international trade and investment. One way of avoiding double taxation is **tax credits**, which allows a firm to claim tax relief against the tax paid by its foreign subsidiaries. A subsidiary may be required to pay income tax and withholding tax in the host country. If the income received by the multinational firm is also subject to income tax in the home country, then there will be double taxation. A key point to realise here is that a tax must be considered to be income tax as a precondition for the underlying taxpayer becoming eligible for tax credit. Unlike income tax, VAT is eligible for deduction, not for credit. The problem is that what is considered as income tax in one country may not be so in another.

IN PRACTICE

Reviewing international taxation in Australia

In mid-2002, the Australian Board of Taxation was asked to conduct a review of international taxation, with emphasis on the following aspects of the Australian tax system:

- the bias created through the imputation tax system against Australian companies with substantial foreign sources of income
- simplifying the rules governing foreign income that inhibit companies from operating offshore
- creating an environment that is conducive to attracting firms wishing to locate their regional head offices in Australia
- revising the policy on double tax agreements with other countries
- removing obstacles for multinational firms seeking to invest in Australia.

One of the problems has been that foreign income is taxed twice or more, prompting some Australian multinationals to relocate their head offices offshore. The review came at a time when a decision was taken to shift tax law drafting from the ATO to the Treasury. The move, presumably intended to allow the ATO to concentrate on its core business of tax administration, went against the recommendation of the Tax Commissioner who told a Senate inquiry in February 2002 that the ATO should retain some responsibility for drafting tax legislation.

Differences in philosophy on how income should be taxed have given rise to treaties between countries to minimise the effect of double taxation on the taxpayer, protect each country's right to collect taxes and provide ways to resolve jurisdictional issues. Tax treaties specify the classes of income that are not subject to tax, can reduce the rate on income and/or withholding taxes, and can specifically deal with the issue of tax credit. They may also deal with particular types of taxes that could be considered creditable. Tax treaties specify such issues as the taxes covered, the persons and organisations covered, relief from double taxation, the exchange of information between the authorities of the contracting countries and the conditions under which a treaty may be terminated.

IN PRACTICE

The OECD Model Tax Convention

In an attempt to achieve uniformity in the treaties concluded by the members of the OECD, model treaties have been adopted. Treaties concluded on a bilateral basis invariably follow the OECD Model Tax Convention (originating from the League of Nations' model). However, since each treaty has to take into account differences in the tax systems and fiscal policies, deviations from the model typically arise. The OECD Model and the worldwide network of tax treaties based upon it help to avoid double taxation by providing clear consensual rules of taxation.

For most types of income, particularly business profits and investment income, double taxation is avoided in treaties based on the OECD Model by allocating taxing rights between the resident and source countries and by requiring the former to eliminate double taxation where there are competing taxing rights. Most bilateral tax treaties follow both the principles and the detailed provisions of the OECD Model. Since 1997, the Model has been presented in two volumes. *Volume I* includes the introduction, the text of the articles of the Model and the commentary thereon. *Volume II* includes the new section on the positions of non-member countries, reprints of 16 previous reports dealing with tax conventions that the Committee on Fiscal Affairs has adopted since 1977, the list of tax conventions concluded between member countries and the text of the *Council Recommendation on the Model Tax Convention*.

Tax havens

In recent years there has been a significant increase in the number of centres offering **tax haven** facilities, such as the islands of Malta and Madeira. So, what makes a country or a territory a tax haven? The following are the key factors: (i) a high degree of investor protection; (ii) willingness to prevent money laundering; (iii) political and economic stability; (iv) low or zero taxes; (v) the existence of tax treaties with other countries; (vi) the absence of exchange controls; (vii) the presence of developed legal, banking and accounting systems; (viii) good transport and communication facilities; and (ix) the ability to form a company easily and cheaply.

A tax haven is defined as a 'place where foreigners may receive income or own assets without paying high rates of tax on them'. According to the OECD's *Forum on Harmful Tax Practices*, the main features of a tax haven are: (i) zero or only nominal effective tax rates; (ii) lack of effective exchange of information; (iii) lack of transparency; and (iv) absence of a requirement of substantial activity.

Tax havens offer a variety of benefits, such as low or zero taxes on certain classes of income. Some tax havens impose tax on income from domestic sources but exempt income from foreign sources. And some of these havens allow special privileges. For example, the Bahamas, Bermuda and the Cayman Islands are free from tax for overseas companies (including corporate income tax, capital gains tax, withholding tax and securities turnover tax). Others, such as the British Virgin Islands, offer low tax rates. Some tax havens, such as Luxembourg, specialise in facilities for establishing holding companies. Because of these benefits, thousands of so-called mailbox companies have appeared in places like Liechtenstein, Vanuatu and the Netherlands Antilles. As a result of this variety, tax havens fall into two specific categories: (i) pure tax havens, which impose zero or low tax rates; and (ii) hybrid tax havens, which offer specific tax incentives.

British betting firms migrate to Gibraltar

An example of the ability of tax havens to attract FDI and to internationalise business can be found in the case of British bookmakers, which have migrated to Gibraltar to avoid a 9 per cent tax on bets in the United Kingdom. This move was started by bookmaker Victor Chandler, whose business has now moved entirely to Gibraltar. Other betting firms followed suit, including Coral, Ladbroke's and William Hill. These firms currently operate 24 hours a day, taking tax-free bets by phone and via the Internet. As a result, Victor Chandler has become Gibraltar's largest private sector employer, accounting for 7 per cent of its GDP.

In international tax planning, there is obviously a clear theoretical advantage in arranging for profits to accrue to a company that is located in a tax haven because the tax imposed may be less than what would otherwise accrue to an entity in a high-tax country. To take advantage of a tax haven, a multinational firm would normally set up a subsidiary there through which different forms of income would pass. The subsidiary is then used as an intermediary for the purpose of shifting income from high-tax countries to the tax haven. For example, a multinational firm could sell its products at cost to a subsidiary located in a tax haven and when the subsidiary sells these products to a third party, the profit will be concentrated in the tax haven. Of course, the alternative would be to sell the products directly, in which case the profit will be concentrated in the high-tax home country.

Bill Gates and international taxation

William Woods, the chief executive of the Bermuda Stock Exchange, has been quoted (by *The Economist*) as saying that Bill Gates would have been even more wealthy if he had started Microsoft in Bermuda, and that he (Gates) may have known a lot about computer programming when he started the company (Microsoft), but his ignorance about tax cost him a fortune.[1] It seems, however, that Gates has learned the trick, as he has co-founded Teledesic in Bermuda. This company offers broadband Internet access by satellite.

[1] *The Economist*, 29 January 2000, Survey, p. 11.

18.7 Foreign direct investment and country risk

Although the term **country risk** is sometimes used interchangeably with political risk and **sovereign risk**, these terms do not mean exactly the same thing. Country risk is broader than political risk and sovereign risk, encompassing both of them.

Country risk arises because of the possibility of losses due to country-specific economic, political and social events. Sovereign risk, on the other hand, involves the possibility of losses on claims on foreign governments and government agencies. The risk mostly pertains to bonds issued by and loans granted to these bodies, whereby losses will be incurred when they default. Hence, this kind of risk is not relevant to FDI. Political risk refers to the possibility of incurring losses due to changes in the rules and regulations governing FDI and also to adverse political developments.

Country risk is normally measured by giving each country a score calculated as a weighted average of the values of some indicators. The country risk rating of *Euromoney* magazine, for example, is based on three sets of indicators. The first is the analytical indicators that include: (i) economic indicators, which measure the country's ability to service its debt (including the size of debt, the balance of payments position and the debt service ratio); (ii) economic risk; and (iii) political risk. The second set is the credit indicators, which measure the country's ability to reschedule payments and its performance in servicing its debt in the past. The third set is market indicators, which measure the risk premiums that financial markets place on bonds and securities issued by parties belonging to the underlying country.

Political risk is of special importance for FDI. This category of risk includes the possibility of **confiscation**, whereby the host government assumes ownership of assets belonging to a multinational firm without proper compensation. If compensation is granted, then what we have is the risk of **expropriation**. Political risk also involves the possibility of losses resulting from changes in the rules governing currency convertibility and remittance restrictions that affect the value of cash flows received by the parent firm. Finally, it includes the possibility of losses resulting from such events as riots, civil unrest and military coups.

How can multinational firms reduce political risk? The first method is to keep control of some crucial elements of the firm's operations. If the operations cannot be run properly without these elements, then a would-be confiscator would think twice before trying something. Another way to reduce the possibility of confiscation is by promising divestment, turning over ownership to local parties in the future. An alternative is to share ownership with foreign parties right from the beginning, by forming joint ventures. The multinational firm can also protect itself by borrowing in the country where the investment takes place. In the event of confiscation, the firm can react by defaulting on the loans it has been granted.

The Asian crisis and sovereign ratings

Despite the economic recovery that has followed the Asian crisis of 1997–1998, Asian countries are struggling to regain their pre-crisis ratings. The agencies preparing these ratings, such as Moody's and Standard & Poor's, have as a result of the crisis moved away from a narrow definition of sovereign ability or the willingness of a country to pay its debt. These agencies claim that the Asian crisis has highlighted a number of new risks that are now given greater consideration in a wider definition of sovereign risk. Much emphasis is now based on the contingent assets and liabilities of governments.

It is estimated that Malaysia will not receive a single-A credit rating until about 2005 (the top rating is AAA). The rating agencies apparently want to see how countries like Malaysia go through a cycle and respond to a downturn before they raise their ratings back up again.

Using country risk analysis in capital budgeting

Once the degree of country risk has been determined, the next step is to decide whether or not the risk is tolerable. If it is felt that the risk is too high, then the firm does not need to analyse the feasibility of a project to be undertaken in that country. Of course, it may be argued that no risk is too high if the rate of return on the underlying project is high enough to compensate for the risk. However, in some cases the risk is considered to be so high that the country is deemed to be off limits. This would be the case if, for example, the country has a tendency to experience civil war or kidnapping of foreign personnel for ransom. This would also be the case if the probability of confiscation were too high as judged from historical experience.

Country risk analysis can be incorporated into capital budgeting analysis by adjusting the discount rate or the cash flows, as we have seen before. The higher the country risk, the higher the discount rate applied to the project's cash flows. If, for example, blocked funds are anticipated, then the discount rate may be raised from 8 per cent to 10 per cent. The problem with this procedure is that there is no precise formula for adjusting the discount rate for country risk, which makes adjustment rather arbitrary. The use of a shorter payback period can be used for the same purpose. However, neither of these two methods provides a detailed examination of the risk involved or a true reflection of the investor's fear. This is why it may be preferable to incorporate country risk analysis by adjusting the cash flows.

Suppose that a project is analysed under three scenarios derived from country risk analysis: (i) that nothing will happen; (ii) that the host country will block a certain percentage of the funds to be transferred to the parent firm; and (iii) that the project will be confiscated after a few years. Suppose also that these scenarios produce three net present values (NPV_1, NPV_2

and NPV_3, respectively) with probabilities p_1, p_2 and p_3, respectively. The NPV of the project in this case should be calculated as the expected NPV, which is the weighted average of NPV_1, NPV_2 and NPV_3, where the weights are the probabilities. Hence

$$NPV = \sum_{i=1}^{3} p_i NPV_i \tag{18.11}$$

In general, there are three approaches to the integration of country risk into capital budgeting:

- Adjusting the expected cash flows to account for losses due to country risk.
- Measuring the effects of country risk on the outcome of investment as the value of an insurance policy that reimburses all losses resulting from an event.
- Using option valuation theory to derive the pricing of country risk, particularly the risk of expropriation. If the likelihood of expropriation depends on project outcomes, then the only proper valuation technique is contingent claims analysis. It is arguable that standard valuation approaches, such as the adjustment of future cash flows, are adequate only when the probability of expropriation is independent of the value of the project.

18.8 Transfer pricing

Transfer pricing, also known as **internal pricing**, refers to the pricing of goods and services that are bought and sold (transferred) between members of a corporate family. In other words, transfer pricing is the process of determining the prices of (intermediate and finished) goods and services sold by the parent multinational firm to a subsidiary, sold by the subsidiary to the parent firm and sold by one subsidiary to another. The level of transfer prices affects the attractiveness of payments from the perspectives of the subsidiaries and the parent firm. In setting transfer pricing policies, many factors are considered. Some of these factors are discussed below.

Tax considerations

Multinational firms use transfer pricing to move profit out of countries with high taxes to countries with low taxes. Suppose that there are two subsidiaries, one in a high-tax country and the other in a low-tax country. To reduce the combined tax liability of the two subsidiaries (that is, to increase the combined after-tax profit), the subsidiary that is located in the high-tax country will sell goods to the other subsidiary at lower than normal prices and buy from it at higher than normal prices.

Global regulation

No one group has the authority to establish international transfer pricing standards of taxation because each country establishes rules for companies operating within its boundaries. However, many factors are now causing greater interest in the establishment of international standards for taxing intercompany transactions. For example, the United States, Canada, Germany and the United Kingdom require transfer prices to be 'arm's length' (that is, the price that would be used if the two companies were unrelated). Although growth in international transactions between related companies has led to a need for international standards, there is still no agreement on what constitutes an 'arm's length' price.

Double taxation and transfer pricing: Glaxo versus the IRS

The case raised by the US Internal Revenue Service (IRS) against British-based pharmaceutical company Glaxo is a brilliant illustration of how hard it has become to enforce tax laws in an era where business is global and the most valuable assets are intangible. It is also an illustration of how transfer pricing can be used to avoid taxes.

During the period 1989–1999 Glaxo's revenue from selling its products in the United States, particularly the heartburn drug Zantac, amounted to USD29.5 billion. In December 1999, Glaxo formally requested tax relief from the IRS under the US–UK Convention for the Avoidance of Double Taxation, which resulted in negotiations between the British and US tax authorities to resolve the issue. By mid-2002 it had become clear that the IRS wanted to take the case to court, claiming that Glaxo's US subsidiary, GlaxoSmithKline, overpaid its British parent for drugs, thus artificially reducing US profit and paying less taxes as a result. The IRS argued that the royalties paid by the subsidiary were excessive owing to the overvaluation of the R&D costs in the United Kingdom. Glaxo, as expected, denied the IRS claims.

Management incentives and performance evaluation

If the transfer price set by the parent firm is not acceptable to the management of the subsidiary, managerial disincentives may arise. Transfer pricing policies that are designed to minimise global taxes often produce aberrations in multinational performance evaluation and control systems. The overall results are achieved only at the cost of what seems to be a poor performance of some subsidiaries resulting from tax-reducing transfer pricing policies.

Fund positioning

Transfer pricing is one of the techniques used by multinational firms to transfer funds from one part of the total business to another. This procedure is used particularly in conjunction with short-term investment and financing decisions, where it is normally the case that a business firm checks the availability of internal funds before resorting to external financing. A multinational firm can utilise internal financing by resorting to funds available at its subsidiaries.

If the firm wants to remove funds from one of its foreign subsidiaries, it can charge this subsidiary a higher price for the products it provides the subsidiary with as part of intrafirm trade. If a subsidiary is short of funds, it will be charged a lower transfer price. Transfer pricing can also be used to channel profit into a particular subsidiary to raise its credit rating and boost its ability to borrow funds.

Marketing considerations and competition

There are a number of reasons why a multinational firm may depend on its foreign subsidiaries for the sale of finished goods. One reason is the desire to control the distribution facilities when there is a lucrative market. Another reason is the desire to provide specialised after-sale services. There is also the need to convey information to and from customers. And there may be a need to retain direct representation in order to maintain contacts with foreign governments. All of these marketing considerations can be built into transfer pricing policies.

INSIGHT

FDI and multinational firms: the arguments for and against

The effects of FDI and multinational firms operating in foreign countries constitute a highly controversial issue. The arguments for are as follows:

- FDI flows are less volatile than portfolio investment flows.
- FDI is an important source of funds for developing and transition countries.
- FDI involves the transfer of financial capital, technology and other skills.
- FDI raises income and social welfare in the host country.
- FDI boosts growth in the host country through technology diffusion and the transfer of capital.
- FDI can boost employment in the host country.
- FDI boosts the skills of local workers through training.
- FDI helps provide local firms with increased opportunities by establishing links with local suppliers for locally produced goods.
- FDI encourages competition in the host country's markets.

The arguments against are as follows:

- FDI symbolises new colonialism.
- FDI results in the loss of sovereignty and compromises national security.
- Multinational firms are often in a position to obtain incentives (from the host country) in excess of their needs and perhaps in excess of the benefits they bring to the host country.
- FDI creates enclaves and a foreign elite in the host country.
- FDI introduces adverse cultural changes.
- It is invariably the case that subsidiaries operating in the host country are wholly owned by the parent firm. The host country has no control over the operations of these subsidiaries.
- FDI can reduce employment through divestment and closure of production facilities.
- Outward FDI destroys jobs at the source country because output of foreign subsidiaries becomes a substitute for exports from the home country.
- FDI leads to an increase in wage inequality in the host country.
- Multinational firms worsen income distribution in the host countries and worldwide.
- Multinational firms abuse transfer pricing, depriving host countries of tax revenue.
- Multinational firms form alliances with corrupt elites in developing countries.

What is the verdict? Well, it seems that the jury is still out!

If this is the case, then the marketing objective will influence transfer pricing. For example, initial transfer prices should be lower if the subsidiary is expected to pursue the objective of market penetration (obtaining a foothold in and then a big share of a market) than if the underlying marketing objective is market skimming (targeting customers who are willing to pay a high price for the underlying product).

Risk and uncertainty

Foreign operations are subject to several kinds of risk, including foreign exchange risk, purchasing power risk and political risk. Transfer pricing may be used to reduce exposure to these kinds of risk. A response to the risk of blocked funds could, for example, take the form of increasing transfer prices. By changing transfer prices, funds can effectively be moved from high-inflation countries to low-inflation countries and from countries with weak currencies to countries with strong currencies.

Government policies

There is often some conflict, pertaining to intrafirm trade, between the wishes of the home country's government, which deals with the multinational firm, and the wishes of the host country's government, which deals with the subsidiary. The home country's government likes the multinational firm to use the domestic facilities to supply foreign subsidiaries. The host country's government, on the other hand, wants to see an increase in the use of local inputs by the subsidiary at the expense of imports from the parent firm (in the form of intrafirm trade). This conflict leads to a restriction of the ability to indulge in intrafirm trade with some consequences for transfer pricing.

The interests of joint venture partners

Transfer pricing can be used to preserve the multinational firm's share in the profit generated by a joint venture. To accomplish this objective, the multinational firm charges the joint venture high transfer prices. Of course, this kind of practice would create conflict between the multinational firm and the foreign partner in the joint venture, because the foreign partner prefers low transfer prices. This is why the transfer pricing policy should be agreed upon prior to the establishment of a joint venture.

The negotiating power of the subsidiary

A subsidiary's foreign currency profit is boosted by low transfer prices on its input and high transfer prices on its output. If this is the case, then the subsidiary will be considered to be a good risk by foreign financial institutions and thus the negotiating power of the subsidiary with these financial institutions will be greater. On the other hand, high transfer prices on input and low transfer prices on output will reduce the reported profit of the subsidiary and this may improve its ability to negotiate wages with the trade unions.

Summary

- Foreign direct investment is the acquisition and exertion of a significant control over a foreign firm. Generally speaking, FDI is indicated by a percentage ownership ranging between 10 and 25 per cent.
- Interest in FDI is due to at least four reasons: (i) its rapid growth and changing pattern; (ii) concern about its causes and consequences; (iii) the possibility it offers for channelling resources to developing countries; and (iv) the role it is conceived to play in the transformation of the former communist countries.

- The rapid growth of FDI in the 1990s is due to: (i) the fact that it is no longer confined to large firms; (ii) its increased sectoral diversity; and (iii) the increase in the number of countries acting as outward investors or recipients of FDI.
- FDI is one of several approaches that business firms can use to enter foreign markets. The alternatives include exporting, licensing and franchising.
- FDI may take one of three forms: greenfield investment, cross-border mergers and acquisitions, and joint ventures.
- A large number of theories and hypotheses have been proposed to explain FDI.
- Several methods involving various criteria are used to evaluate direct investment projects, including: (i) the accounting rate of return; (ii) the payback period; (iii) the net present value; and (iv) the internal rate of return. The first two do not take into account the time value of money. The NPV seems to be the most consistent of the four methods.
- Things get more complicated in evaluating FDI projects using the NPV technique. One problem is that the cash flows realised by the subsidiary are likely to be different from the cash flows realised by the parent company. The appropriate evaluation measure is normally based on the cash flows realised by the parent company.
- Calculating the NPV of an FDI project requires forecasting a number of variables, including the following: (i) demand for the underlying product; (ii) its price; (iii) variable costs; (iv) fixed costs; (v) project lifetime; (vi) salvage value; (vii) remittance restrictions; (viii) tax rates and laws; and (ix) exchange rates.
- The cost of capital is used as a discount rate to calculate the NPV. It can be calculated as a weighted average of the cost of debt and equity capital.
- Cross-country differences in the cost of capital can explain why multinational firms based in some countries may have a comparative advantage over others.
- The adjusted present value technique has been suggested as a more suitable alternative for evaluating FDI projects. The APV is equivalent to NPV if all the complexities are taken into account.
- International taxation refers to the taxation of cross-border transactions. Double taxation arises if income earned abroad is taxed by both the home government and the host government. Many countries have bilateral tax treaties with other countries designed to avoid double taxation. These treaties are typically based on the OECD Model Tax Convention.
- Country risk arises because of the possibility of losses resulting from country-specific economic, political and social events. It encompasses political risk and sovereign risk. Political risk is more important for FDI.
- Political risk includes the possibility of confiscation or expropriation, as well as changes in the rules governing FDI. Multinational firms can reduce political risk by: (i) keeping control of some crucial elements of the firm's operations; (ii) promising divestment; and (iii) borrowing in the country where the investment takes place.
- Country risk can be incorporated in capital budgeting analysis by adjusting the expected cash flows or the discount rate. Scenario analysis can be used for the same purpose.
- Transfer pricing policies are determined by: (i) tax considerations; (ii) global regulation; (iii) management incentives; (iv) performance evaluation; (v) fund positioning; (vi) marketing considerations; (vii) risk; (viii) government policies; (ix) the interests of joint venture partners; and (x) the negotiating power of the subsidiary.

Key terms

accounting rate of return 513
active income 522
adjusted present value (APV) 522
bilateral tax treaties 523
blocked funds 519
branch 502
break-even analysis 518
brownfield investment 506
capital budgeting 512
certainty-equivalent cash flows 517
classic approach to taxation 522
comparative advantage 509
confiscation 526
cost of capital 513
cost of debt capital 514
cost of equity capital 514
country risk 526
currency areas hypothesis 510
customs duties 523
differential rates of return hypothesis 508
discount rate 513
diversification hypothesis 508
dividend valuation model 517
double taxation 523
eclectic theory 509
expropriation 526
financial leverage 521
fixed costs 520
foreign direct investment (FDI) 502
franchising 506
Goods and Services Tax (GST) 523
greenfield investment 504
import duties 523
imputation tax system 522
indirect tax 523
industrial organisation hypothesis 508
intangible assets 509
integrated approach to taxation 522
internal financing hypothesis 510
internal pricing 528
internal rate of return (IRR) 516
internal transactions 509
internalisation advantages 509
internalisation hypothesis 509
international investment position 503
inward FDI 504
joint ventures 508
licensing 506
liquidation value 514
location hypothesis 509
locational advantages 509
market transactions 509
mergers and acquisitions (M&As) 504
net present value (NPV) 513
OECD Model Tax Convention 523
oligopolistic reaction hypothesis 510
output and market size hypothesis 508
outward FDI 504
ownership advantages 509
passive income 523
payback period 513
political risk 510
product life cycle hypothesis 509
remittance restrictions 519
risk aversion 508
risk premium 521
risk-adjusted cash flows 517
risk-adjusted discount rate 517
salvage value 514
sensitivity analysis 517
significant control 502
simulation 518
sovereign risk 526
subsidiary 502
tariffs 523
tax credits 523
tax haven 525
time value of money 513
transfer pricing 528
value added tax (VAT) 523
variable costs 520
withholding tax 523

MAXIMISE YOUR MARKS! There are 30 interactive questions for this chapter available online at **www.mhhe.com/au/moosa2e**

Review questions

1. Direct investment implies that the investor exerts 'significant control' over the enterprise. What does 'significant control' mean?
2. What are the reasons for interest in FDI?
3. What are the alternatives to FDI as a means of entering foreign markets?
4. What is the difference between greenfield investment and brownfield investment?
5. Why does the differential rates of return hypothesis fail to explain the actual behaviour of FDI?
6. Why can a firm compete successfully in a foreign market despite the disadvantages emanating from differences in language, culture and other factors?
7. What is the meaning of 'internalisation'? How can it be used to explain FDI?
8. According to the eclectic theory, three conditions must be satisfied if a firm is to engage in FDI. What are these conditions?
9. What is the life cycle of a product? How can the life cycle be used to explain FDI?
10. 'The process of FDI is self-limiting, since the invasion of each other's home market leads to an increase in competition and a decline in the intensity of oligopolistic reaction.' Is this statement valid?
11. What is the relationship between internal cash flows and investment outlays? Can this relationship explain FDI?
12. How do tax policies and government regulations determine the pattern of FDI?
13. What are the strategic and long-term factors that determine whether or not to indulge in FDI?
14. Why are the accounting rate of return and the payback period unacceptable as criteria for evaluating direct investment projects?
15. What is the net present value of a project?
16. What is the relationship between the net present value and the internal rate of return?
17. What are the problems associated with evaluating FDI projects that are different from those associated with the evaluation of domestic direct investment projects?
18. How is the cost of capital calculated? Why does it differ across countries?
19. What is the adjusted present value of an FDI project?
20. What is double taxation? How does double taxation affect FDI?
21. What is the difference between confiscation and expropriation?
22. What are tax havens?
23. What is transfer pricing? How do tax considerations affect it?
24. How does transfer pricing affect management incentives and performance evaluation?

Problems

1 Two projects, A and B, generate the following cash flows over a period of five years (capital cost is incurred at year 0):

Project	Year					
	0	1	2	3	4	5
A	−150	40	50	60	70	90
B	−110	20	30	40	50	70

Assuming that the cost of capital is 8 per cent, calculate the net present values of the two projects. If the two projects are mutually exclusive, which one will be chosen?

2 Assuming a tax rate of 20 per cent and total equity financing, calculate the net present values of Projects A and B described in Problem 1. If the two projects are mutually exclusive, which one will be chosen?

3 Use the information in Problems 1 and 2, but assume now that the two projects, A and B, have salvage values of 20 and 45, respectively. Calculate the net present values of the two projects and determine which one will be chosen if they are mutually exclusive.

4 Assume now that Project A from Problem 1 is financed by 70 per cent equity and 30 per cent debt, whereas project B is financed by 40 per cent equity and 60 per cent debt. If the cost of equity financing is 8 per cent and the cost of debt financing is 5 per cent, calculate the net present values of the two projects, assuming the same salvage values and tax rates as previously. Which project will be chosen if they are mutually exclusive?

5 Assume that Project A from Problem 1 is a domestic project subject to a 20 per cent tax rate, whereas project B is a foreign project subject to a foreign tax rate of 15 per cent, for which full tax credit is given. The cash flows and the salvage value of Project B are expressed in foreign currency terms. The current value of the exchange rate (domestic/foreign) is 0.95 and the foreign currency is expected to depreciate by 5 per cent per year over the next five years. Calculate the net present values of the two projects. Which project will be chosen if they are mutually exclusive?

6 A project that is run by a subsidiary generates the following cash flows over a period of five years:

Year					
0	1	2	3	4	5
−200	20	70	90	110	150

The following information is also available:

Foreign tax rate	20%
Domestic tax rate (full tax credit is granted)	30%
Remitted cash flows allowed	75%
Current exchange rate (domestic/foreign)	0.80
Expected annual depreciation of foreign currency	4.5%
Discount rate	6.5%

Calculate the net present value of the project from the perspectives of the subsidiary and the parent firm.

7 Consider Project A from Problem 1. Calculate the net present value of the project by using the following values of the discount rate: (a) 4, (b) 5, (c) 6, (d) 7, (e) 8, (f) 9 and (g) 10. Plot the net present value against the discount rate.

8 Assume that the values of the discount rate in Problem 7 are associated with probabilities of 0.05, 0.10, 0.15, 0.20, 0.25, 0.10 and 0.15, respectively. Calculate the expected net present value.

9 Consider Project B from Problem 1 under three scenarios: (i) the cash flows are as given; (ii) the cash flows are 20 per cent higher; and (iii) the cash flows are 20 per cent lower. Using a discount rate of 10 per cent, calculate the net present value under these three scenarios. If these scenarios materialise with probabilities of 0.1, 0.3 and 0.6 respectively, what is the expected net present value?

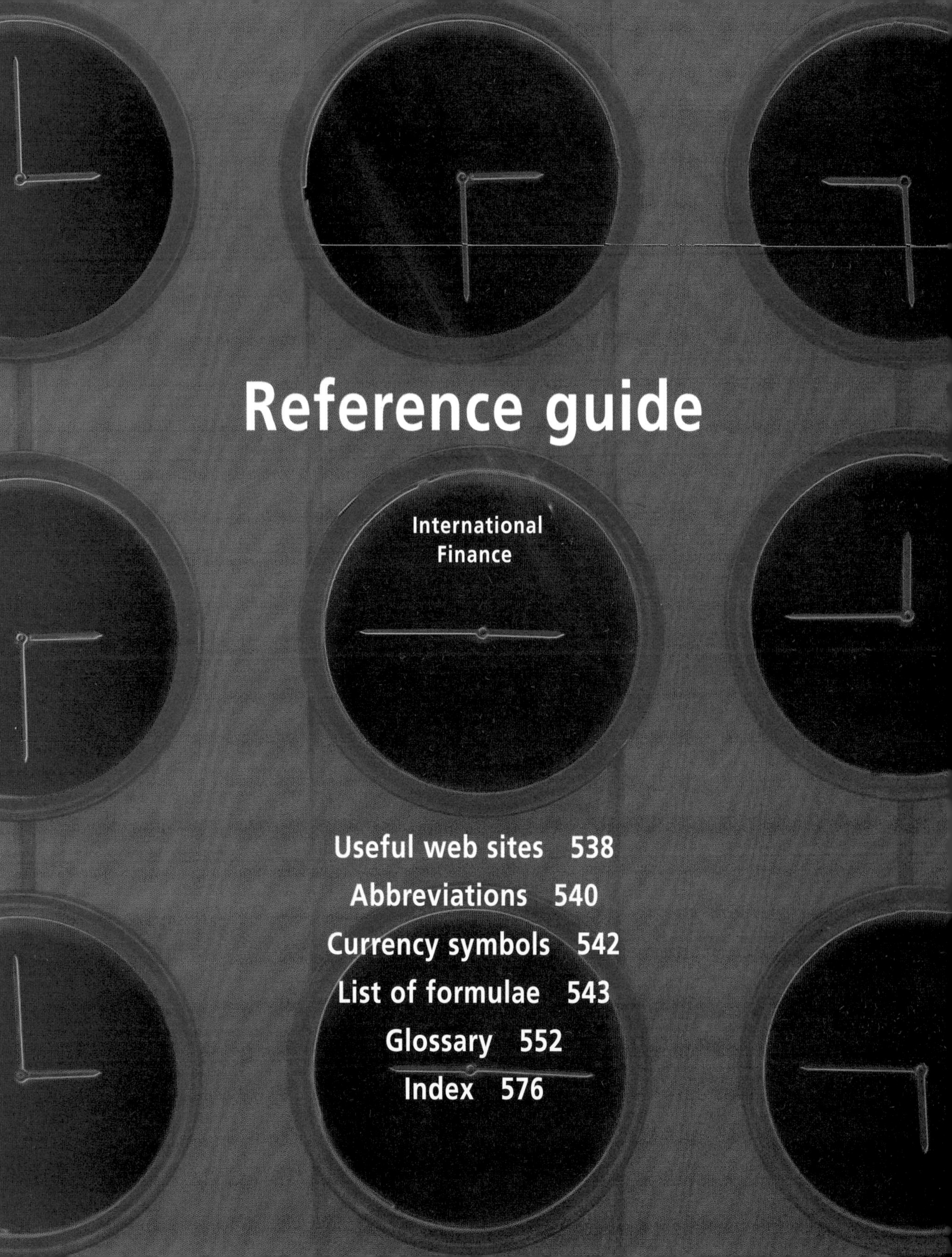

Reference guide

International Finance

Useful web sites

Organisation	Web site	Contents
ABS	www.abs.gov.au	Data and analysis on the Australian economy
APRA	www.apra.gov.au	Information and analysis on prudential regulation in Australia
Bank of England	www.bankofengland.co.uk	Information, data and analysis
Bank of Ireland	www.bankofireland.ie	Information on major money markets
Barchart.com	www.barchart.com/sample/mricur.htm	Charts and statistics of major exchange rates
BIS	www.bis.org/cbanks.htm	Links with various central banks
	www.bis.org/publ/index.htm	BIS *Annual Report*
	www.bis.org/review/index.htm	Articles and speeches by central bankers
Bloomberg	www.bloomberg.com	Data on financial markets
Bureau of Census	www.census.gov/ipc/www/idbnew.html	Economic and demographic data on over 200 countries
CME	www.cme.com	Currency futures and options
Commerzbank	www.commerzbank.com	Exchange rate data
The Dismal Scientist	www.dismal.com	Economic and financial analysis
ECB	www.ecb.int	Analysis and data on the euro area
The Economist	www.economist.com	Economic, financial, business and political developments and data
Federal Reserve Bank of New York	www.ny.frb.org	Current and historical exchange rate data
	www.ny.frb.org/pihome/statistics/forex12.shtml	Daily noon exchange rates
	www.ny.frb.org/pihome/statistics/vrate.shtml	Implied volatilities of currency options
Federal Reserve Bank of St Louis	www.stls.frb.org/fred/	Current and historical exchange rate data
Federal Reserve USA	www.federalreserve.gov/releases/H10/hist/	Historical foreign exchange data
The Financial Times	www.ft.com	Financial news and data. Short-term Eurocurrency interest rates and links to exchange rate data

Florin.com	www.florin.com/v4	Foreign exchange risk management
Forexvoice.com	www.forexvoice.com	Real-time exchange rates
IMF	www.imf.org/external/fin.htm	Exchange rate quotes for selected currencies
ISDA	www.isda.org	Information on swaps and other derivatives
JP Morgan	www.adr.com	Data on ADRs
	www.jpmorgan.com	Historical data on real and nominal exchange rates
KPMG	www.kpmg.com	Information on international taxation and transfer pricing
Moody's	www.moodys.com	Country risk ratings
Oanda.com	www.oanda.com	Current and historical exchange rates, as well as analysis
OECD	www.oecd.org	News, analysis and data on international finance and economics
	www.oecd.org/std	Data on PPP exchange rates
Ohio State University Finance Department	www.cob.ohio-state.edu/dept/fin/fdf/osudata.htm	Links to web sites related to economics and finance
Philadelphia Stock Exchange	www.phlx.com	Currency options
RBA	www.rba.gov.au	Information, analysis and data on the Australian economy and financial system
Reportgallery.com	www.reportgallery.com	Links to the annual reports of over 2000 companies
SFE	www.sfe.com.au	Information on Australian derivatives
Standard & Poor's	www.standardandpoors.com	Country risk ratings
Systems Modelling	www.sysmod.com/eurofaq.htm	Answers to frequently asked questions about the euro
The Wall Street Journal	www.wsj.com	Business and financial news
The World Bank	www.worldbank.org	Economic and demographic data on more than 200 countries as well as forecasts and links to data sources
WTO	www.wto.org	News, information and statistics on international trade

Abbreviations

ABS	Australian Bureau of Statistics
ADB	Asian Development Bank
ADR	American Depository Receipt
ANZAC	Australia–New Zealand Currency
APEC	Asia–Pacific Economic Cooperation Council
APRA	Australian Prudential Regulatory Authority
APV	adjusted present value
ARO	average rate option
ATO	Australian Taxation Office
BCCI	Bank of Credit and Commerce International
BFTA	Baltic Free Trade Area
BIS	Bank for International Settlements
BOLERO	Bill of Landing Electronic Registry Organisation
CAPM	capital asset pricing model
CD	certificate of deposit
CEFTA	Central Europe Free Trade Area
CER	Closer Economic Relations (Agreement)
CIP	covered interest parity
CLS	continuous linked settlement
CME	Chicago Mercantile Exchange
COMEX	Commodities Exchange
CSFB	Credit Suisse First Boston
DS	downside semi-variance
ECB	European Central Bank
ECHO	Exchange Clearing House
ECP	Euro-Commercial Paper
ECU	European Currency Unit
EEC	European Economic Community
EMH	efficient market hypothesis
EMS	European Monetary System
EMU	European Monetary Union
EPCs	electronic purchase of cards
ERM	Exchange Rate Mechanism (of the EMS)
EU	European Union
FDI	foreign direct investment
FOX	forward with optional exit
FRN	floating rate note
FX	foreign exchange
GATT	General Agreement on Tariffs and Trade
GDP	gross domestic product
GNP	gross national product
GST	Goods and Services Tax
IBF	International Banking Facility
IBM	International Business Machines
ICAPM	international capital asset pricing model
IPFM	international portfolio flow monitor

IMF International Monetary Fund
IMM International Money Market
IMS International Monetary System
IRR internal rate of return
IRS Inland Revenue Service
ISDA International Swaps and Derivatives Association
JOM Japan Offshore Market
LCPI Liquidity and Premia Index
LIBOR London Interbank Offered Rate
LIFFE London International Financial Futures Exchange
LOP law of one price
LSE London Stock Exchange
M&As mergers and acquisitions
MAD mean absolute deviation
MAE mean absolute error
MNC multinational corporation
MSE mean square error
NAB National Australia Bank
NAFTA New Zealand–Australia (or North American) Free Trade Agreement
NBFI non-bank financial intermediary
NIF net issuance facility
NPV net present value
OECD Organisation for Economic Cooperation and Development
OPEC Organisation of Petroleum Exporting Countries
OTC over-the-counter (market)
p.a. per annum
PPP purchasing power parity
PSFM Price Specie Flow Mechanism
R&D research and development
RBA Reserve Bank of Australia
RIP real interest parity
RMSE root mean square error
ROT registered options trader
RUF revolving underwriting facility
SDR special drawing rights
SEC Securities and Exchange Commission
SFE Sydney Futures Exchange
SFI sentiment and flow index
SIBOR Singapore Interbank Offer Rate
SML securities market line
STP straight through processing
SWIFT Society for Worldwide Financial Telecommunication
TWI trade-weighted index
UIP uncovered interest parity
VAR value at risk
VAT value-added tax
VB Victoria Bitter
WTO World Trade Organisation

Currency symbols

Currency	Symbol
Australian dollar	AUD
Canadian dollar	CAD
European Union euro	EUR
Fijian dollar	FJD
Hong Kong dollar	HKD
Indian rupee	INR
Indonesian rupiah	IDR
Japanese yen	JPY
Korean won	KRW
Kuwaiti dinar	KWD
Malaysian ringgit	MYR
Mexican peso	MXP
New Zealand dollar	NZD
Norwegian krone	NOK
Philippine peso	PHP
Russian rouble	SUR
Saudi Arabian riyal	SAR
Singapore dollar	SGD
Solomon Islands dollar	SBD
South African rand	ZAR
Swedish krona	SEK
Swiss franc	CHF
Thai baht	THB
United Kingdom pound	GBP
United States dollar	USD

List of formulae

Formula	Remarks
$\dot{S}(x/y)=\dfrac{S_1(x/y)}{S_0(x/y)}-1$	The percentage change in the exchange rate between two points in time, when the exchange rate is measured as the price of one unit of *y*
$S(y/x)=\dfrac{1}{S(x/y)}$	The exchange rate as the price of one unit of *x* (the reciprocal exchange rate)
$\dot{S}(y/x)=\dfrac{S_1(y/x)}{S_0(y/x)}-1$	The percentage rate of change of the reciprocal rate
$\dot{S}(y/x)=\dfrac{1}{1+\dot{S}(x/y)}-1$	The percentage change in the value of *x* as calculated from the percentage change in the value of *y*
$S(d/f)=\dfrac{1}{S(f/d)}$	The exchange rate in direct quotation is the reciprocal of the exchange rate in indirect quotation
$m=S_a-S_b$	The bid-offer spread as the difference between the offer and bid rates
$m=\dfrac{S_a}{S_b}-1$	The bid-offer spread as a percentage of the bid rate
$S=\dfrac{1}{2}(S_b+S_a)$	The mid-rate as the simple average of the bid and offer rates
$S_b(y/x)=\dfrac{1}{S_a(x/y)}$	The bid rate (y/x) is the reciprocal of the offer rate (x/y)
$S_a(y/x)=\dfrac{1}{S_b(x/y)}$	The offer rate (y/x) is the reciprocal of the bid rate (x/y)
$S(x/y)=\dfrac{S(x/z)}{S(y/z)}$	The cross exchange rate, representing the condition precluding three-point arbitrage
$S_a(x/y)=\dfrac{S_a(x/z)}{S_b(y/z)}$	The offer cross exchange rate

Formula	Remarks
$S_b(x/y) = \dfrac{S_b(x/z)}{S_a(y/z)}$	The bid cross exchange rate
$m = \dfrac{F(x/y) - S(x/y)}{S(x/y)} \times 100 \times \dfrac{12}{N}$	The forward spread (in per cent per annum)
$Df = P_m^\star Q_m$	The demand for foreign exchange is equal to import expenditure
$Q_m = a - bP_m$	The quantity of imports demanded is a negative function of the domestic currency price of imports
$P_m = SP_m^\star$	The relationship between the domestic currency and the foreign currency prices of imports
$Sf = P_x^\star Q_x$	The supply of foreign exchange is equal to export revenue
$Q_x = c - dP_x^\star$	The quantity of exports demanded is a negative function of the foreign currency price of exports
$P_x^\star = \dfrac{P_x}{S}$	The relationship between the domestic currency and the foreign currency prices of exports
$B^\star = P_x^\star Q_x - P_m^\star Q_m$	The current account in foreign currency terms
$E_t = \sum_{i=1}^{m} w_i V_{i,t}$	The effective exchange rate as a weighted average of the bilateral exchange rate relatives
$V_{i,t} = \dfrac{S_{i,t}}{S_{i,0}}$	Definition of the exchange rate relative
$w_i = \dfrac{X_i}{\sum_{i=1}^{m} X_i}$	Definition of export weights
$w_i = \dfrac{M_i}{\sum_{i=1}^{m} M_i}$	Definition of import weights
$w_i = \dfrac{X_i + M_i}{\sum_{i=1}^{m} X_i + M_i}$	Definition of trade weights

Formula	Remarks
$w_i^\star = \dfrac{w_i}{\sum_{i=1}^{m} w_i}$	Definition of normalised weights
$E_t = \prod_{i=1}^{m} \left(V_{i,t}\right)^{w_i} = \left(V_{1,t}\right)^{w_1}\left(V_{2,t}\right)^{w_2}\ldots\left(V_{m,t}\right)^{w_m}$	The effective exchange rate as a geometric weighted average of the relatives
$Q(x/y) = S(x/y)\left[\dfrac{P_y}{P_x}\right]$	Definition of the real bilateral exchange rate
$Q_t = \sum_{i=1}^{m} w_i \left(\dfrac{Q_{i,t}}{Q_{i,0}}\right)$	The real effective exchange rate as an arithmetic weighted average
$Q_t = \prod_{i=1}^{m} \left(\dfrac{Q_{i,t}}{Q_{i,0}}\right)^{w_i}$	The real effective exchange rate as a geometric weighted average
$S_A(x/y) = S_B(x/y)$	The condition preçluding two-point arbitrage
$\pi = S_A(x/y) - S_B(x/y)$	Profit from two-point arbitrage
$S(x_1/x_2)S(x_2/x_3)S(x_3/x_4)\ldots$ $\ldots S(x_{n-1}/x_n)S(x_n/x_1) = 1$	The condition precluding multipoint arbitrage
$\left.\begin{array}{l} S_{b,A}(x/y) = S_{a,B}(x/y) \\ S_{a,A}(x/y) = S_{b,B}(x/y) \end{array}\right\}$	The condition precluding two-point arbitrage in the presence of bid-offer spreads
$P_i = SP_i^\star$	The law of one price
$\dot{S} = \dot{P} - \dot{P}^\star$	Purchasing power parity written in percentage terms
$\overline{S}_t = S_0\left(\dfrac{P_t / P_0}{P_t^\star / P_0^\star}\right)$	The PPP exchange rate relative to a base period, 0
$S = \dfrac{M}{kP^\star Y}$	The monetary model of exchange rates
$\left.\begin{array}{l} (1+i) = \dfrac{F}{S}(1+i^\star) \\ i - i^\star = f \end{array}\right\}$	The CIP no-arbitrage condition

Formula	Remarks
$\pi = \frac{F}{S}(1+i^*) - (1+i)$ $\pi = i^* - i + f$	The covered margin when a short position is taken on the domestic currency
$\pi = \frac{S}{F}(1+i) - (1+i^*)$ $\pi = i - i^* - f$	The covered margin when a short position is taken on the foreign currency
$\bar{F} = S\left[\frac{1+i}{1+i^*}\right]$	The interest parity forward rate
$\pi = \frac{F_b}{S_a}(1+i_b^*) - (1+i_a)$ $\pi = i_b^* - i_a + f - m$	The covered margin in the presence of bid-offer spreads (short on the domestic currency)
$\pi = \frac{S_b}{F_a}(1+i_b) - (1+i_a^*)$ $\pi = i_b - i_a^* - f - m$	The covered margin in the presence of bid-offer spreads (short on the foreign currency)
$\pi = \frac{F}{S}(1+i^*) - (1+i) - t \approx i^* - i + f - t$	The covered margin in the presence of transaction costs (short on the domestic currency)
$\pi = \frac{S}{F}(1+i) - (1+i^*) - t \approx i - i^* - f - t$	The covered margin in the presence of transaction costs (short on the foreign currency)
$S_t = S_{t-1} + \varepsilon_t$	The random walk model
$S^e = F$	The forward rate as an unbiased predictor of the spot rate
$1+i = \frac{S^e}{S}(1+i^*)$ $i - i^* = \dot{S}^e$	Uncovered interest parity
$\pi = \frac{S_1}{S_0}(1+i^*) - (1+i)$ $\pi = i^* - i + \dot{S}$	The uncovered margin (short on the domestic currency)

Formula	Remarks
$\pi = \frac{S_0}{S_1}(1+i)-(1+i^\star)$ $\pi = i - i^\star - \dot{S}$	The uncovered margin (short on the foreign currency)
$\pi = \frac{S_{b1}}{S_{a0}}(1+i_b^\star)-(1+i_a)$ $\pi = i_b^\star - i_a + \dot{S}_b - m$	The uncovered margin in the presence of bid-offer spreads (short on the domestic currency)
$\pi = \frac{S_{b0}}{S_{a1}}(1+i_b)-(1+i_a^\star)$ $\pi = i_b - i_a^\star - \dot{S}_b - m$	The uncovered margin in the presence of bid-offer spreads (short on the foreign currency)
$(1+r)(1+\dot{P})=(1+i)$ $r = i - \dot{P}$	Definition of the (ex post) real interest rate
$r^e = i - P^e$	Definition of the (ex ante) real interest rate
$r^e = r^{\star e}$	Real interest parity
$r^e - r^{\star e} = (i - i^\star - \dot{S}^e) + (\dot{S}^e - \dot{P}^e + \dot{P}^{\star e})$	Splitting the real interest differential into deviations from UIP and deviations from PPP
$r^e - r^{\star e} = (i - i^\star - f) + (f - \dot{S}^e) + (\dot{S}^e - \dot{P}^e + \dot{P}^{\star e})$	Splitting the real interest differential into deviations from CIP, deviations from unbiasedness and deviations from PPP
$MAE = \frac{1}{n}\sum_{t=1}^{n}\left\|\hat{S}_t - S_t\right\|$	The mean absolute error
$MSE = \frac{1}{n}\sum_{t=1}^{n}\left(\hat{S}_t - S_t\right)^2$	The mean square error
$RMSE = \sqrt{\frac{1}{n}\sum_{t=1}^{n}\left(\hat{S}_t - S_t\right)^2}$	The root mean square error
$M_t(q) = \frac{1}{q}\sum_{i=0}^{q-1} S_{t-i}$	A moving average of order q

Formula	Remarks
$R = (1+\dot{S})(1+\dot{V}^{\star})-1$	The domestic currency rate of return on a foreign currency asset
$E(\dot{S}) = \sum_{i=1}^{n} p_i(\dot{S}_i)$	The expected value of the percentage change in the exchange rate (probability distribution)
$\sigma^2(\dot{S}) = \sum_{i=1}^{n} p_i[\dot{S}_i - E(\dot{S})]^2$	The variance of the percentage change in the exchange rate (probability distribution)
$\sigma(\dot{S}) = \sqrt{\sum_{i=1}^{n} p_i[\dot{S}_i - E(\dot{S})]^2}$	The standard deviation of percentage change in the exchange rate (probability distribution)
$\bar{\dot{S}} = \frac{1}{n}\sum_{t=1}^{n} \dot{S}_t$	The mean value of the percentage change in the exchange rate (historical data)
$\sigma^2(\dot{S}) = \frac{1}{n-1}\sum_{t=1}^{n}(\dot{S}_t - \bar{\dot{S}})^2$	The variance of the percentage change in the exchange rate (historical data)
$\sigma(\dot{S}) = \sqrt{\frac{1}{n-1}\sum_{t=1}^{n}(\dot{S}_t - \bar{\dot{S}})^2}$	The standard deviation of the percentage change in the exchange rate (historical data)
$\dot{V} = \beta\dot{S}$	The percentage change in the domestic currency value of a foreign item; the exposure line
$\sigma^2(\dot{V}) = \beta^2\sigma^2(\dot{S})$	The variance of the percentage change in the value of a foreign currency item
$\dot{V} = \beta_0 + \beta_1\dot{S}(x_0/x_1) + \beta_2\dot{S}(x_0/x_2) + \ldots + \beta_n\dot{S}(x_0/x_n)$	A multicurrency exposure model involving currencies $x_1, x_2, \ldots x_n$.
$V = K\bar{F}_0$	The domestic currency value of payables/receivables under a money market hedge
$V = KF_0$	The domestic currency value of payables/receivables under a forward hedge
$V = KS_1$	The domestic currency value of payables/receivables under the no-hedge decision
$V = K\bar{F}_{a0}$	The domestic currency value of payables under a money market hedge in the presence of bid-offer spreads

Formula	Remarks
$V = KS_{a1}$	The domestic currency value of payables under the no-hedge decision in the presence of bid-offer spreads
$V = K\overline{F}_{b0}$	The domestic currency value of receivables under a money market hedge in the presence of bid-offer spreads
$V = KS_{b1}$	The domestic currency value of receivables under the no-hedge decision in the presence of bid-offer spreads
$\overline{F}_b = S_{b0}\left[\dfrac{1+i_b}{1+i_a^{\star}}\right]$	The bid interest parity forward rate in the presence of bid-offer spreads
$\overline{F}_a = S_{a0}\left[\dfrac{1+i_a}{1+i_b^{\star}}\right]$	The offer interest parity forward rate in the presence of bid-offer spreads
$V = K\left[\overline{S} - \dfrac{\overline{S}(1-\theta) - S_1}{2}\right]$ $V = K\left[\overline{S} + \dfrac{S_1 - \overline{S}(1+\theta)}{2}\right]$	The domestic currency value of payables/receivables under a risk-sharing agreement
$V = KS_L$ $V = KS_1$ $V = KS_U$	The domestic currency value of payables/receivables under a currency collar
$e = (1+i^{\star})(1+\dot{S}) - 1$ $e = i^{\star} + \dot{S}$	The effective financing rate
$r = (1+i^{\star})(1+\dot{S}) - 1$ $r = i^{\star} + \dot{S}$	The effective rate of return
$e = (1+i_a^{\star})\left(\dfrac{S_{a1}}{S_{b0}}\right) - 1$	The effective financing rate in the presence of bid-offer spreads

Formula	Remarks
$r = (1+i_b^\star)\left(\dfrac{S_{b1}}{S_{a0}}\right) - 1$	The effective rate of return in the presence of bid-offer spreads
$e_{i,j}^p = w_y e_i^y + w_z e_j^z$	The effective financing rate of a portfolio
$L_n = K(1 + i)^n$	The value of a domestic bond issue
$L_n^\star = K(1+\dot{S})^n(1+i^\star)^n$	The domestic currency value of a foreign bond issue
$I_n = K(1 + r)^n$	The value of a domestic bond investment
$I_n^\star = K(1+r^\star)^n(1+\dot{S})^n$	The domestic currency value of a foreign bond investment
$R = \dfrac{D_1}{P_0} + \dfrac{\Delta P_1}{P_0}$	The rate of return on equity investment
$I_n = K(1 + d + a)^n$	The value of a domestic equity investment
$I_n^\star = K(1+\dot{S})^n(1+d^\star + a^\star)^n$	The domestic currency value of a foreign equity investment
$R^\tau = (1 - \tau_y)d + (1 - \tau_k)a$	The rate of return on a domestic equity investment in the presence of taxes
$R^{\tau\star} = (1-\tau_y)d^\star + (1-\tau_k)(a^\star + \dot{S})$	The domestic currency rate of return on a foreign equity investment in the presence of taxes
$R = A + \dot{S}$	Components of the domestic currency rate of return on a foreign equity investment
$\sigma^2(R) = \sigma^2(A) + \sigma^2(\dot{S}) + 2\sigma(A,\ \dot{S})$	The variance of the domestic currency rate of return on a foreign equity investment
$R^p = wR + w^\star R^\star$	The rate of return on a portfolio

Formula	Remarks
$E(R^p) = wE(R) + w^{\star}E(R^{\star})$	The expected value of the rate of return on a portfolio
$\sigma^2(R^p) = w^2\sigma^2(R) + w^{\star 2}\sigma^2(R^{\star}) + 2ww^{\star}\sigma(R)\sigma(R^{\star})\rho(R, R^{\star})$	The variance of the rate of return on a portfolio
$R_j = i + \beta(R_m - i)$	The capital asset pricing model
$\beta = \dfrac{\sigma(R_j, R_m)}{\sigma^2(R_m)}$	Definition of beta (a measure of systematic risk)
$NPV = -C_0 + \sum_{t=1}^{n} \dfrac{C_t}{(1+r)^t}$	The NPV of a project
$r = \left(\dfrac{E}{E+D}\right) r^E + \left(\dfrac{D}{E+D}\right) r^D$	The weighted average cost of capital
$NPV = -C_0 + \sum_{t=1}^{n} \dfrac{C_t(1-\tau)}{(1+r)^t}$	The NPV in the presence of taxes
$r = \left(\dfrac{E}{E+D}\right) r^E + \left(\dfrac{D}{E+D}\right) r^D(1-\tau)$	The weighted average cost of capital in the presence of taxes
$NPV = -C_0 + \sum_{t=1}^{n} \dfrac{C_t(1-\tau)}{(1+r)^t} + \dfrac{V}{(1+r)^n}$	The NPV in the presence of taxes and a non-zero salvage value
$-C_0 + \sum_{t=1}^{n} \dfrac{C_t}{(1+r)^t} = 0$	The IRR on a project
$-C_0 + \sum_{t=1}^{n} \dfrac{C_t(1-\tau)}{(1+r)^t} = 0$	The IRR in the presence of taxes
$-C_0 + \sum_{t=1}^{n} \dfrac{C_t(1-\tau)}{(1+r)^t} + \dfrac{V}{(1+r)^n} = 0$	The IRR in the presence of taxes and a non-zero salvage value

Glossary

Although some of the terms contained in this glossary are generic, they may be defined in reference to the foreign exchange market or exchange rates. More terms can be found in the appendixes to Chapter 2.

abnormal returns Above-average returns on investment.
accounting exposure *see translation exposure.*
accounting rate of return A criterion for evaluating a project based on the accounting profit it generates.
activate/deactivate option *see knockout option.*
active income Income that results directly from the production of goods and services.
adaptive expectations An expectation formation mechanism whereby if the exchange rate rises in at least two of the last three periods, then it should be expected to rise in the coming period.
adjustable peg A fixed exchange rate that can be adjusted when necessary.
adjusted present value (APV) A criterion for evaluating projects based on discounting different cash flows at different discount rates.
affiliate A company established in a foreign country and owned solely or jointly with other parties.
allocative efficiency Market efficiency in achieving an optimal allocation of resources.
American Depository Receipts (ADRs) Negotiable certificates issued by US banks in the United States to represent the underlying foreign shares, which are held in trust at a custodian bank.
American option An option that can be exercised on or before the expiry date.
American terms An exchange rate is quoted in terms of the US dollar per unit of the other currency.
amortising swap A currency swap with a principal that declines over time.
analytical approach *see parametric approach.*
ANZAC A proposed name for the common currency of Australia and New Zealand when the idea was contemplated.
appreciation The rise in the value of a floating currency against other currencies.
arbitrage A profit-seeking operation based on profiting from discrepancy in quoted prices.
arbitragers Participants in financial and commodity markets who try to generate profit from price anomalies.
Asian crisis The 1997–1998 financial crisis that hit countries in Southeast Asia, starting in Thailand.
Asian Currency Unit An Asian-based facility of a foreign bank that is allowed to accept foreign currency deposits from non-residents and to make cross-border loans.
Asian dollars US dollar deposits held with Asian banks.
Asian option *see average rate option.*
Asia–Pacific Economic Cooperation Council (APEC) An economic forum whose members are Pacific countries from various continents, including Australia.
ask rate *see offer rate.*
asset market approach An approach to exchange rate determination postulating that exchange rates are determined by the supply of and demand for financial assets.
asset-backed bonds Novel bonds that are backed by a specific group of assets.
assignment An assignment materialises when an option writer receives a notice that the holder of an option has exercised that option, in which case the writer is obliged to deliver the underlying currency in the case of a call or receive it in the case of a put.
at the money An option is at the money if the exercise exchange rate is equal to the market exchange rate.
Australian Bureau of Statistics (ABS) A government agency in charge of collecting and publishing economic data.
automatic order matching system A network of terminals where foreign exchange dealers enter orders in the form of buying and/or selling prices for a given amount of a currency.
autoregressive model A model in which the exchange rate is a linear function of its past values.

average rate In a sequence of foreign exchange transactions, the average rate is the average of the exchange rates used to settle these transactions. In translation accounting, it is the average exchange rate prevailing over the accounting period.

average rate option (ARO) An option that is exercised at maturity if the average spot rate over a specified period is less than the predetermined exercise exchange rate.

average strike option A version of the average rate option that is exercised if the exercise exchange rate (specified as the average spot rate over the option's life) is greater than the end of the period exchange rate.

back office An office that is responsible for settling the foreign exchange transactions conducted by foreign exchange dealers by making and receiving payments.

back testing Some kind of testing that is used in conjunction with the value at risk measure.

back-to-back loans *see parallel loans.*

balance of indebtedness A statement showing the balance of foreign assets and liabilities of a country.

balance of payments A systematic record of all economic transactions between the residents of one country and the rest of the world.

balancing item An entry on the balance of payments that accounts for or represents missing information and errors in recording trade and financial flows.

Baltic Free Trade Area (BFTA) A free trade area comprising the Baltic European countries.

bank agencies Banking institutions that do not handle ordinary deposits.

Bank for International Settlements (BIS) Based in Basel, Switzerland, it acts as the central bank of central banks. It also conducts a survey of the global foreign exchange market every three years.

banking crises A banking crisis occurs when there is an actual or potential bank run/failure, inducing banks to suspend the convertibility of their liabilities or compelling the government to extend assistance on a large scale.

bar chart A chart in which the high, low and closing values of the exchange rate are represented by a vertical bar.

barrier option *see knockout option.*

base currency In foreign exchange quotation, this is the currency whose unit is being priced. It also means the domestic or the functional currency of a company (that is, the currency in which the company's financial statements are presented). In options, it is the currency in which profit/loss is measured.

Basel Committee A committee that was established by the central bank governors of the largest 10 industrial countries to devise effective banking regulation.

Basel I The 1988 accord on capital adequacy and banking regulation.

Basel II The 2001 accord on capital adequacy and banking regulation.

basis point One hundredth of one per cent (interest rates).

basis swap An interest rate swap that involves two variable interest rates, such as the deposit rate and the rate on Treasury bills.

bear market A declining market.

beta The beta of a security is a measure how closely the price of the security is related to the general market price.

bid premium The price at which a dealer is willing to buy an option.

bid rate The exchange (interest) rate at which the quoting dealer is willing to buy (accept) a currency (deposit).

bid-offer margin *see bid-offer spread.*

bid-offer spread The difference between the offer and the bid rates. It can also be measured as a percentage of the bid rate.

big number Exchange rates are normally quoted to four decimal places, with the big number including the first two decimal places.

bilateral exchange rate The price of one currency in terms of another.

bilateral netting Calculating the net payment due from one company to another.

bilateral tax treaties Treaties between two countries aimed at avoiding double taxation.

bills of landing Documents that facilitate the transfer of title of goods in international trade.

blocked funds Funds generated by a subsidiary operating in a host country that cannot be remitted to the parent firm.

blotter A schedule that is used by foreign exchange dealers to record the details of their individual transactions sequentially.

bond A fixed-income security that offers fixed contractual payments in the form of periodic interest payments and a face value that is paid on the maturity of the bond.

bonds with equity warrants Bonds that give the holder the extra privilege of having the right to buy the shares of the issuing company.

bottoms The low values of the exchange rate over a period of time.

branch An extension of an international firm operating in a different location or country than that in which the head office operates.

break forward contract A forward contract that can be terminated at a predetermined rate, thus providing protection against adverse exchange rate movements.

break-even analysis In project evaluation, the objective of break-even analysis is to determine the point at which the NPV or the APV switches from negative to positive.

Bretton Woods system A system of fixed but adjustable exchange rates that was in operation between 1944 and 1971.

broken date A maturity date (length) of a forward contract that includes a fraction of a week or a month.

brokerage fees A form of transaction costs, normally determined as a percentage of the size of the underlying transaction.

brokers Participants in the foreign exchange market whose function is to bring together buyers and sellers by matching up buy and sell orders.

brownfield investment Direct investment when the foreign investor acquires a firm but almost completely replaces plant and equipment, labour and the product line.

bubbles Movements in financial prices away from their equilibrium values without corresponding movements in fundamental factors.

bull market A rising market.

Bulldogs Foreign bonds sold in the United Kingdom.

call option An option that gives its holder the right to buy a currency. In bonds, it means that the issuer has the right to redeem bonds prior to maturity.

capital account *see financial account*

capital account transactions Transactions involving the buying and selling of financial assets and capital flows.

capital adequacy A requirement that banks maintain a certain capital to assets ratio, taking into account the riskiness of various kinds of assets.

capital appreciation The rise in the market value of a security.

capital asset pricing model (CAPM) A model relating the expected rate of return on a security or a portfolio to its systematic risk.

capital budgeting The procedures used to evaluate direct investment projects.

capital controls Restrictions on the cross-border movement of capital.

capital gains tax A tax levied on the realised increase in the market value of assets.

capital mobility The ability of capital to move from one country to another, seeking investment opportunities.

cash flow exposure The sensitivity of the domestic currency value of foreign currency cash flows with respect to changes in the exchange rate.

cash transaction A foreign exchange transaction that involves instantaneous delivery of the currencies.

catastrophe bonds Novel bonds whose payments depend on the materialisation of a certain (adverse) event.

catch-up hypothesis A hypothesis postulating that low-income countries tend to grow faster than high-income countries, eventually catching up with them.

central bank intervention The buying and selling of currencies by the central bank with the objective of stabilising exchange rates.

Central Europe Free Trade Area (CEFTA) A free trade area comprising central European countries.

central rate In some exchange rate arrangements, the exchange rate is allowed to move within a band around a central rate.

centralised cash management An arrangement whereby the function of cash management is performed by a central body at the head office.
certainty-equivalent cash flows Adjusted (reduced) cash flows to take into account uncertainty.
certificates of deposit (CDs) Fixed-term deposits that can be bought and sold on a secondary market.
chart A graphical representation of the movement of the exchange rate over time.
charting *see technical analysis.*
chartists Technical analysts, or those using charts to generate buy and sell signals.
chooser option An option that allows its holder to lock in the exercise exchange rate, amount and maturity, and subsequently choose to make it a call or a put.
classic approach to taxation Under the classic approach to taxation, income received by each taxable entity is taxed. Thus, the earnings of a company could be taxed twice: when they are earned and when they are received as dividends by shareholders.
clearing corporation A body that is normally owned by a futures exchange, acting as the opposite counterparty to all contracts.
Closer Economic Relations (CER) An agreement for economic cooperation between Australia and New Zealand. It was implemented in 1983 and upgraded in 1990.
closing rate The exchange rate prevailing at the end of the accounting period.
closing rate method A translation method according to which foreign currency items are converted to the domestic currency at the exchange rate prevailing at the end of the accounting period.
closing transaction A transaction that results in liquidating or offsetting an existing position (for example, in options).
commission fees Fees charged by brokers for their services in financial markets.
commitment fees Fees that are charged to the borrower as a percentage of the undrawn portion of the loan.
commodity arbitrage Making profit by buying a commodity where it is cheap and selling it where it is expensive.
comparative advantage A country has a comparative advantage in the production of a commodity if it can produce that commodity relatively more efficiently than other countries.
competitive exposure Exposure to foreign exchange risk resulting from exchange rate-induced changes in the competitive position of a firm.
composite forecasting Generating a single forecast by combining the individual forecasts derived from various models.
composite variables Variables that consist of more than one variable, such as the interest rate differential.
compound option An option that gives its holder the right to buy or sell an option.
confiscation Taking over projects or assets without compensation.
consortium banks Joint ventures set up by large international banks.
contagion Financial contagion means that a financial crisis that hits one country is likely to spread to other countries.
contingent exposure Exposure that arises only if a certain outcome materialises.
continuation patterns In technical analysis, these are chart patterns that indicate the continuation of a trend.
continuous linked settlement (CLS) Settling foreign exchange transactions through a central service provider.
contract date The date on which a foreign exchange transaction is concluded.
contrarian expectations Market participants form contrarian expectations if they hold views opposite to those of the majority of participants.
conversational dealing systems *see screen-based automated dealing systems.*
conversion exposure Exposure to foreign exchange risk resulting from the effect of changes in the exchange rate on the domestic currency value of converted foreign currency cash flows.
convertibility A currency is convertible if it can be converted freely to other currencies.
convertible bonds Bonds that can be converted into equity.
correlation coefficient A statistical measure of the degree of association between two variables (for example, two exchange rates).
correspondent bank A bank located in a foreign country with which a domestic bank holds an account to make and receive payments in that currency.

cost exposure Exposure to foreign exchange risk resulting from exchange rate-induced changes in the domestic currency value of foreign currency costs (for example, the cost of imported raw materials).

cost of capital A weighted average of the cost of debt capital and equity capital.

cost of debt capital The interest paid on borrowed capital.

cost of equity capital The minimum rate of return necessary to induce investors to buy or maintain their holdings of shares in the underlying firm.

country crises Crises that engulf a single country.

country risk The risk arising from the economic and political factors of a particular country.

coupon The fixed-interest payment paid periodically to bondholders.

covered call writing Writing a call option while covering the position by going long on the underlying currency.

covered interest arbitrage A profit-seeking operation consisting of going short on one currency and long on another while covering the long position by selling the underlying currency forward. It is triggered by the violation of covered interest parity.

covered interest differential The interest rate differential adjusted for the forward spread.

covered interest parity (CIP) A condition postulating that no profit can be made by going short on a currency and long on another while covering the long position by selling the underlying currency forward. It also tells us that once foreign exchange risk is covered in the forward market, similar assets should offer the same return.

covered margin Net profit from covered arbitrage, which is equal to the covered return on the long position minus the cost of the short position.

covered option An option with a corresponding spot position on the underlying currency.

covered put writing Writing a put option while covering the position by going short on the underlying currency.

crawling bands An arrangement whereby the exchange rate is maintained within a certain band around a central rate that is adjusted periodically at a fixed, pre-announced rate or in response to changes in some indicators.

crawling peg An arrangement whereby the exchange rate is adjusted periodically at a fixed, pre-announced small rate or in response to changes in some quantitative indicators.

credit lines Loans provided by a bank up to a certain limit.

credit risk The risk arising from the possibility of default.

credit swap The exchange of funds between a bank and a firm. The firm places a deposit with the bank, which in turn instructs its correspondent bank abroad to grant a loan to the firm's subsidiary.

cross exchange rate The exchange rate between two currencies calculated from their exchange rates against another currency.

cross hedging Hedging a spot position on one currency by taking an opposite spot or forward position on another currency.

cross trading Buying a currency against another via a third currency.

cross transactions *see cross trading.*

cross-currency interest rate swap A swap involving the exchange of fixed and variable interest payments denominated in two different currencies.

currency areas hypothesis A hypothesis postulating that countries with strong currencies tend to be sources of FDI, while countries with weak currencies tend to be host countries or recipients of FDI.

currency board An arrangement that is based on an explicit legislative commitment to exchange the domestic currency for a specified foreign currency at a fixed exchange rate, combined with restrictions on the issuing authority to ensure the fulfilment of its legal obligation.

currency collars An agreement whereby a range of exchange rate values between a minimum and a maximum is used to determine the domestic currency value of foreign currency payables and receivables.

currency crises A currency crisis occurs when a speculative attack on the exchange rate results in devaluation (depreciation) or forces the central bank to defend the currency by spending a large amount of reserves.

currency futures Contracts to buy or sell a fixed amount of a currency for delivery at a future date. The amounts and delivery date are standardised.

currency of invoicing The currency in which exports and imports are invoiced.
currency risk *see foreign exchange risk.*
currency swap A transaction in which two counterparties exchange cash flows denominated in two different currencies at a pre-specified exchange rate.
currency union An arrangement whereby two or more countries use the same currency (for example, the European Monetary Union).
current account The part of the balance of payments that records current transactions in goods and services as well as current transfers.
current account transactions Transactions that are recorded on the current account of the balance of payments, including exports, imports and transfers.
current rate *see closing rate.*
current transfers Payments made by foreigners to local residents, and vice versa.
current/non-current method A translation method whereby current items on the balance sheet are translated at the current (closing) rate, while non-current items are translated at the historical rate.
custom-dated option An option with a customised (tailor-made) expiry date.
customised contracts Financial contracts (such as options) that are tailor-made for specific needs.
customised options Tailor-made options that are available on some organised exchanges and over the counter.
customs duties Taxes on imports.
cyclical component The time series component showing the cyclical behaviour of a variable.
daily price limits Limits on the movements of the prices of futures contracts.
dealers Individuals who conduct foreign exchange (and other financial) transactions.
dealing date *see contract date.*
dealing desk *see dealing room.*
dealing room The operational quarters where dealers conduct foreign exchange transactions with each other.
dealing spread *see bid-offer spread.*
deannualisation The process of adjusting interest rates, which are expressed on a per annum basis, to cover the underlying investment horizon.
debt-equity swaps A process whereby debt is swapped for equity. For example, there has been a tendency to swap the debt of highly indebted developing countries for equity in projects in those countries.
debt-service ratio The ratio of debt service payments to some indicator, such as export revenue.
decentralised cash management An arrangement whereby the function of cash management is performed by each individual subsidiary.
deep in the money An option is deep-in-the-money if it can be exercised at significant profit resulting from a significant difference between the market and exercise exchange rates.
delayed-start swap A swap that starts after more than two days but within one year.
delivery date The date on which the currencies involved in a foreign exchange transaction are exchanged.
delta A measure of the change in the option premium corresponding to a small change in the spot exchange rate.
delta hedging A method whereby the writer of an option can hedge his or her position. It amounts to taking an opposite spot position on the underlying currency with a hedge ratio that is equal to the delta of the option.
demand exposure Exposure to foreign exchange risk resulting from exchange rate-induced changes in demand.
depreciation The fall in the value of a floating currency against other currencies.
derived demand Demand for a particular commodity resulting from the demand for another commodity.
destabilising speculation Buying when a currency is strong and selling when it is weak, thus accentuating exchange rate fluctuations.
determination puzzle The perceived phenomenon that exchange rate movements are virtually unrelated to fundamentals.
devaluation A reduction in the value of a currency that has a fixed exchange rate.

differential rates of return hypothesis A hypothesis postulating that capital flows from countries with low rates of return to countries with high rates of return.

direct quotation Expressing the exchange rate as the domestic currency price of one unit of the foreign currency.

dirty floating A system of flexible exchange rates with central bank intervention.

discount rate The rate used to calculate the present value of future cash flows.

diversification hypothesis A hypothesis postulating that the choice among various projects is guided not only by the rates of return but also by risk as measured by the variability of the rates of return.

dividend valuation model A model showing that the value of equity is determined by the present value of the future dividends.

dividend yield Dividends as a percentage of the price of the underlying security.

dividends Payments to equity holders.

done date *see contract date.*

double bottoms A chart formation showing two lows.

double moving average rule A mechanical trading rule whereby buy and sell signals are generated by the intersection of two moving averages of different orders.

double taxation Double taxation occurs when the income of a subsidiary is taxed by the host government and then the funds remitted to the parent firm are taxed by the home government.

double tops A chart formation showing two consecutive highs.

down-and-out option *see knockout option.*

downside semi-variance (DSV) A measure of risk that is arguably superior to the standard deviation.

dual currency bond A bond with two different currency denominations for coupon payments and face value payments.

dual exchange rates An arrangement whereby a fixed exchange rate is used to settle current account transactions and a flexible rate is used to settle financial transactions.

eclectic theory A theory of FDI postulating that if a firm is to engage in FDI, it must have certain advantages over others.

econometric models Models that are specified on the basis of economic theory and estimated by some econometric method.

economic exposure Exposure to foreign exchange risk resulting from changes in exchange rates on the firm's cash flows, market share and value.

economic transactions Transactions that involve the exchange of value, such as exports and imports.

effective exchange rate The exchange rate of a currency against the currencies of its trading partners calculated as a weighted average of the bilateral exchange rates.

effective financing rate The cost of borrowing funds in a currency adjusted by a factor that reflects changes in the exchange rate against the domestic currency.

effective rate of return The interest rate on a currency adjusted by a factor that reflects changes in the exchange rate against the domestic currency.

efficient frontier A curve representing a set of portfolios that maximise expected return at each level of risk.

end/end rule A rule that is used to determine the delivery date in a forward contract. If the value date is the last business day of the current calendar month, maturity will be the last business day of the final calendar month.

equities Shares or stocks of a company.

errors and omissions *see balancing item.*

Eurobanks Banks dealing in short-term assets and liabilities denominated in currencies other than those of the countries where they are located.

Eurobond market The market for bonds that are denominated in currencies other than those of the country in which they are issued.

Eurobonds Bonds denominated in a currency other than that of the country where they are issued.

Euro-commercial papers (ECPs) Short-term debt obligations of a company or a bank.

Eurocredit market The market for loans denominated in currencies other than those of the countries where they are issued.

Eurocurrencies Short-term assets and liabilities denominated in currencies other than those of the countries where they are held.

Eurocurrency centre A financial centre where there is a concentration of Eurobanks.

Eurocurrency lines Loans denominated in Eurocurrencies and provided by banks to their corporate customers.

Eurocurrency market The market for short-term assets and liabilities that are denominated in currencies other than those of the countries where they are held.

Eurodeposits Deposits denominated in currencies other than those of the countries where they are held.

Eurodollar market The market for short-term US dollar assets and liabilities held outside the United States.

Euroloans Loans denominated in a currency other than that of the country where they are raised.

Euronotes Short-term debt instruments denominated in a Eurocurrency.

European currency unit (ECU) The unit of account under the European Monetary System.

European Economic Community (EEC) An economic cooperation forum that was established in 1957 as the nucleus of the current European Union.

European Monetary System (EMS) A system of fixed but adjustable exchange rates that was in operation between 1979 and the creation of the European Monetary Union.

European Monetary Union (EMU) A system whereby the participating European countries have a single currency and a unified monetary policy.

European option An option that can be exercised on the expiry date only.

European terms An exchange rate is quoted in terms of the other currency per US dollar.

European Union (EU) An economic and monetary union comprised of 15 countries, 12 of which have adopted the new European currency, the euro.

ex ante real interest rate The expected real interest rate (the nominal interest rate adjusted for expected inflation).

ex post real interest rate The realised real interest rate (the nominal interest rate adjusted for realised inflation).

excess volatility puzzle The phenomenon that exchange rates are excessively volatile relative to fundamentals.

Exchange Rate Mechanism (ERM) The mechanism governing the process of adjusting exchange rates in the European Monetary System.

exchange rate overshooting The rise/fall of exchange rates above/below their long-run equilibrium values.

exchange rate pass-through The effects of changes in exchange rates on the domestic-currency prices of exports and imports.

exchange rate relative The value of a bilateral exchange rate at a certain point in time relative to its value in a base period.

exchange rate volatility Short-term variation of exchange rates around their mean values.

exchange-traded options Options that are only available on organised exchanges such as the Sydney Futures Exchange.

exclusiveness A property of PPP implying that exchange rates are determined only by prices.

exercise date The date on which an option is exercised.

exercise exchange rate The exchange rate at which the holder of an option can buy and sell the underlying currency.

exotic currencies Currencies that are traded almost entirely on a local basis.

exotic options European-style options that offer alternative pricing, timing or exercise provisions to those found in conventional options.

expected value When a variable assumes several values with associated probabilities, the expected value is a weighted average of the individual values, with the probabilities being the weights.

expiration date *see expiry date.*

expiry date The date on which an option contract expires.

explanatory variables The variables that determine the exchange rate in an econometric model.

export revenue The amount received in return for exports (the quantity of exports multiplied by the unit price).

export-weighted effective exchange rate A weighted average of the bilateral exchange rates of a currency where the weights are export shares.

exposure line A graphical representation of the relationship between the percentage change in the domestic currency value of foreign currency assets and liabilities and that of the exchange rate.
exposure netting Calculating the net value of payables and receivables.
expropriation Taking over a project or an asset by the host government with proper compensation.
external account The current account or the balance of payments.
external financing Borrowing from an external party as opposed to relying on internal funds.
external hedging Hedging foreign exchange risk by using financial instruments such as futures and options.
extinguishable option *see knockout option.*
extrapolative expectations An expectation formation mechanism whereby the exchange rate is expected to rise if it rises in the current period, and vice versa.
face value The value of a bond or the amount that a bondholder will receive on maturity.
far out of the money An option that is far away from being exercisable at profit because of a significant difference between the market and exercise exchange rates.
Federal Reserve System The central bank of the United States.
filter rule A mechanical trading rule whereby the buy and sell signals are generated by pre-specified movements above a trough (buy) and below a peak (sell).
filter size In a filter rule, this is the percentage by which the exchange rate must rise above a trough or fall below a peak to generate buy and sell signals, respectively.
financial account The part of the balance of payments that records capital flows.
financial crises A financial crisis occurs when there are severe disruptions of financial markets, while the ability to function effectively is impaired, exerting an adverse effect on the real economy.
financial deregulation Relaxing the measures used to regulate the financial system.
financial engineering The process of producing sophisticated financial instruments.
financial hedging Covering an open position by taking an opposite position on a hedging instrument.
financial innovation The creation of new financial instruments and the recreation of old instruments in a new form.
financial leverage The extent of debt in corporate/capital structure.
financial liberalisation A set of measures that includes, among others, abolishing capital and credit controls, deregulating interest rates and privatising banks.
financial risk The risk arising from unanticipated changes in financial prices such as interest rates and exchange rates.
Fisher equation A relationship postulating that the observed interest rate consists of the real interest rate (the rate of return on real capital) and the inflation rate.
Fisher hypothesis *see Fisher equation.*
fixed costs Production costs that do not change with output.
fixed dates *see round dates.*
fixed exchange rates Exchange rates that are determined by a central authority rather than market forces.
fixed-for-floating swap A transaction involving the exchange of cash flows calculated by applying a fixed and a variable interest rate to a notional principal.
flags In technical analysis, a flag is a continuation pattern.
flexible exchange rates Exchange rates that are determined by market forces.
floating exchange rates *see flexible exchange rates.*
floating rate note (FRN) A bond with variable interest payments.
flows Economic and financial variables that are measured over a period of time such as trade flows and capital flows.
forecasting A formal process of generating expectations.
forecasting accuracy The degree of closeness of the forecasts to the actual realised values. It may also refer to a correct prediction of the direction of change.
forecasting error The difference between the actual and predicted values. It may also refer to a wrong prediction of the direction of change.
forecasting horizon The time period in the future for which forecasts are generated.
foreign bonds Bonds that are issued by parties who are foreign to the country where the bonds are placed.

foreign currency financing Financing by borrowing funds denominated in foreign currencies.
foreign debt crises A foreign debt crisis occurs when a country cannot service its foreign debt.
foreign direct investment (FDI) Investment in projects located in other countries with the objective of having influencing control.
foreign exchange market The market where currencies are bought and sold.
foreign exchange risk The risk arising from unanticipated changes in exchange rates (also known as *currency risk*).
foreign exchange swap A foreign exchange transaction involving a spot purchase against a matching outright forward sale, or vice versa.
foreign loans Loans that are raised by borrowers who are foreign to the country where the loans are raised.
forward bias puzzle The phenomenon that excess returns in the foreign exchange market are predictable and inexplicable.
forward discount A currency sells at a forward discount when its forward rate is lower than its spot rate.
forward exchange rate The exchange rate applicable to foreign exchange transactions involving the delivery of currencies more than two business days in the future.
forward margin *see forward spread.*
forward market efficiency A notion postulating that the forward rate is an unbiased and efficient predictor of the future spot rate.
forward pickup/markdown *see forward spread.*
forward premium A currency sells at a forward premium when its forward rate is higher than the spot rate.
forward rate bias The difference between the forward rate and next period's spot rate.
forward spread The difference between the forward rate and the spot rate.
forward swap A foreign exchange swap that starts on the spot value date and ends on a forward value date. A forward currency swap starts after more than one year of the verbal agreement.
forward transaction A foreign exchange transaction involving the exchange of traded currencies more than two business days in the future.
forward value date The date on which the currencies involved in a forward transaction are exchanged.
forward with optional exit *see break forward contract.*
forward-forward swap A foreign exchange swap that starts on a forward value date and ends on a later forward date.
franchising Granting foreigners the exclusive right to sell the product of the underlying firm in a designated area in return for an initial fee and subsequent royalties.
fund adjustment Altering either the amounts and/or the currencies of the planned cash flows of a firm or its subsidiaries to reduce exposure to the currency of the subsidiary.
fundamental analysis As opposed to technical analysis, it examines the fundamental factors that affect the exchange rate.
fundamental equilibrium effective exchange rate The effective exchange rate that is compatible with fundamental macroeconomic equilibrium.
fundamental models Models whereby exchange rates are explained in terms of macroeconomic fundamentals, such as growth and inflation.
futures contracts Contracts to buy or sell currencies, assets and commodities for delivery at a future date.
gamma A measure of the rate of change of the delta of an option with respect to the spot exchange rate.
gap In technical analysis, this is an area of a chart where no entries are recorded. For example, a futures contract may trade up to its permitted limit one day and open higher the following day.
Genoa Conference A conference held in 1922, recommending the adoption of the gold exchange standard.
global banks Banks that take deposits and offer loans and other services within a variety of national markets through local presence.
global bonds Very large bond issues sold simultaneously in the world's capital market.
global currency A currency that is acceptable worldwide.

globalisation The process of market integration to form global markets in goods and financial assets.

gold export point The upper limit on an exchange rate under the gold standard.

gold import point The lower limit on an exchange rate under the gold standard.

gold points The upper and lower limits on a fixed exchange rate under the gold standard.

gold standard A system of fixed exchange rates that was in operation worldwide between around 1870 and 1914.

Goods and Services Tax (GST) A consumption tax imposed on goods and services.

goods market approach An approach to exchange rate determination whereby the exchange rate is determined by the demand for and supply of goods.

Great Depression A severe recession that engulfed the world in the 1930s.

greenfield investment Direct investment that takes the form of initiating a new project rather than acquiring an existing one.

gross capital flows The sum of capital inflows and capital outflows.

gross profit In options, this is the difference between the market and exercise exchange rates.

head and shoulders In technical analysis, this is a pattern that indicates impending weakness of the underlying currency.

hedge ratio The value of the position in a hedging instrument as a ratio of the value of the exposed position.

hedgers Participants in the foreign exchange market who strive to cover the risk arising from open foreign exchange positions.

hedging The covering of foreign exchange risk in order to eliminate or reduce the variability of the domestic currency value of a foreign currency position.

Herstatt risk The risk arising from the possibility that one party to a foreign exchange transaction will fail to deliver on the value date.

heterogeneous expectations Market participants form heterogeneous expectations when they hold the same view as the majority of participants.

historical approach A method for calculating the value at risk associated with a certain position based on the historically observed rates of return.

historical cost The original cost of obtaining an asset that appears on the balance sheet.

historical rate The exchange rate prevailing when an asset or a liability is first obtained.

holder (of an option) The counterparty who has the privilege to buy or sell the underlying currency at the exercise exchange rate.

hyperinflation Very rapid rise in the general price level.

immediate delivery Settling a foreign exchange transaction by delivering the underlying currencies within two business days.

implicit forward rate The forward rate associated with a synthetic forward contract arising from money market hedging.

import duties *see customs duties.*

import expenditure The amount spent on imports (the quantity of imports multiplied by the unit price).

import-weighted effective exchange rate A weighted average of the bilateral exchange rates of a currency where the weights are import shares.

imputation tax system A tax system whereby the portion of income tax paid by a firm is imputed when shareholders are taxed on their dividends.

in the money An option is in the money if it can be exercised at profit because of the difference between the exercise and market exchange rates.

income tax Tax on income such as dividends and interest payments.

independent floating A system of flexible exchange rates with central bank intervention aimed at curbing exchange rate volatility rather than defending a particular value or a range of values for the exchange rate.

indexed bonds Novel bonds whose payments are tied to the general price level or the price of a particular commodity.

indirect exposure Exposure to foreign exchange risk resulting from the effect of exchange rate changes on other firms that the underlying firm deals with.

indirect quotation Expressing an exchange rate as the price of one unit of the domestic currency.

indirect taxes Consumption taxes, such as the value-added tax and the Goods and Services Tax.

industrial organisation hypothesis A hypothesis postulating that if a firm engages in FDI despite the disadvantages it faces in foreign markets, it must have some advantages arising from firm-specific factors.

informational efficiency A market is informationally efficient if prices reflect all available information.

initial margin In futures trading, this is the amount deposited in the margin account to open a futures position.

insider information Information that is not publicly available and that can be used for (illegal) profitable trading.

intangible assets Things like goodwill.

integrated approach to taxation An approach to taxation that aims at the elimination of double taxation by considering both the company and its shareholders.

interbank market In the foreign exchange market, this comprises transactions conducted among banks.

interbank transactions Foreign exchange transactions that involve banks only.

interest equalisation tax A tax imposed by the US authorities in 1963 to protect the balance of payments from capital outflows, making it no longer cheap to raise funds on the New York financial markets.

interest parity forward rate The forward rate compatible with the absence of profitable covered arbitrage opportunities. It is calculated by adjusting the spot rate by a factor reflecting the interest differential.

interest rate swap A transaction involving the exchange of cash flows calculated by applying two interest rates to a notional principal.

internal financing Financing by resorting to internal funds (undistributed profit or funds provided by subsidiaries).

internal financing hypothesis A hypothesis implying the existence of a positive relationship between internal cash flows and investment outlays.

internal hedging Hedging exposure to foreign exchange risk by using internal techniques, such as the restructuring of operations or changing the currency of invoicing.

internal pricing *see transfer pricing.*

internal rate of return (IRR) The discount rate that makes the NPV of a project equal to zero.

internal transactions Transactions conducted within a firm or between a firm and its subsidiaries.

internalisation advantages Advantages that refer to the choice between accomplishing expansion within the firm or selling the rights to the means of expansion to other firms.

internalisation hypothesis A hypothesis postulating that FDI arises from efforts by firms to replace market transactions with internal transactions.

International Bank for Reconstruction and Development The World Bank as it used to be known.

international bank loans A collective term encompassing foreign loans and Euroloans.

international banking Operations that encompass those conducted with non-residents as well as those involving foreign currencies.

International Banking Facilities (IBFs) Banking units that are allowed to accept foreign currency deposits from non-residents and make cross-border loans.

international bonds A collective term encompassing foreign bonds and Eurobonds.

international capital asset pricing model (ICAPM) A relationship between the expected return on a security or a portfolio and systematic risk when the market portfolio is an international portfolio.

international debt problem A term that emerged in the early 1980s, following Mexico's announcement that it could no longer service its debt, to describe the problems encountered by indebted developing countries and their inability to meet their debt commitments.

international diversification Diversification by holding securities belonging to various countries.

international equity markets The primary and secondary markets for international equities.

international firms Firms that indulge in cross-border operations.

international investment position The net asset position of a country (the difference between foreign assets and foreign liabilities).

International Monetary Fund (IMF) An international organisation established in 1944 to supervise the working of the Bretton Woods system.

international monetary system (IMS) The framework of rules, regulations and conventions that govern the financial relations among countries.

international operations Cross-border operations, including trading, production, investment and financing.

international reserves International assets held by central banks.

interval forecast A forecast that gives a range, rather than single forecast values, of the underlying variable.

intervention points Upper and lower limits, the breach of which triggers central bank intervention.

intrinsic value The intrinsic value of an option is the difference between the exercise and market exchange rates at a particular point in time.

investment banking Operations such as bond issues, secondary market trading, and mergers and acquisitions.

inward FDI From the perspective of an individual country, inward FDI is direct investment by other countries in that country.

Jamaica Accord A 1978 agreement that ratified the worldwide shift to flexible exchange rates following the collapse of the Bretton Woods system in 1971.

Japan Offshore Markets (JOM) Banking units established in Japan to deal in offshore operations. They take the form of entries in the books of banks with special licences.

J-curve effect Deterioration followed by improvement in the balance of payments following devaluation or depreciation of the domestic currency.

joint venture A business partnership with a host country firm or a government institution, or with a firm that is foreign to the host country.

judgmental forecasting Generating forecasts without using an exact numerical formula derived from an estimated model. The forecasts normally take the form of a qualitative description of what may happen and this could pertain only to the direction of the possible change in the exchange rate.

knockout option An option that is designed to offer downside protection, but offers only a limited upside range before a previously specified barrier or a knockout level at which it expires automatically.

lagging Delaying the realisation of payables (receivables) in anticipation of foreign currency depreciation (appreciation).

law of one price (LOP) The proposition that there should be no cross-country differences in the price of a commodity when it is expressed in the same currency.

leading Bringing the realisation of payables (receivables) forwards in anticipation of foreign currency appreciation (depreciation).

letters of credit Documents issued by banks to finance international trade.

licensing The supply of technology and know-how or the use of a trademark or a patent for a fee.

limit down A limit down occurs when the price of a futures contract hits its lower daily limit.

limit move A limit move materialises if the price of a futures contract hits a predetermined price limit.

limit up A limit up occurs when the price of a futures contract hits its upper daily limit.

line chart A graphical description of the exchange rate (normally the closing values) over time.

linear equation An equation in which the dependent variable (the exchange rate) is a linear function of one or more explanatory variables.

liquidation value *see salvage value.*

liquidity risk The risk arising from the possibility that a counterparty to a foreign exchange transaction will fail to deliver because of an operational or system problem that leaves it with insufficient liquidity.

location hypothesis A hypothesis stipulating that FDI arises because of the international immobility of some factors of production, such as labour and natural resources.

locational advantages These advantages arise when it is more profitable to locate production near the supply of at least some factor inputs abroad.

locational arbitrage *see two-point arbitrage.*

lockback option with strike A European-style option with a predetermined exercise exchange rate, which on maturity is valued against the highest or lowest spot rate reached over the option's life.

lockback option without strike A European-style option with an exercise exchange rate that is set as the lowest or the highest exchange rate achieved over the period for a call and a put, respectively.

London interbank offer rate (LIBOR) The offer interest rate on various currencies in the London interbank market.
long call A long call position is obtained by buying a call option.
long exposure Exposure to foreign exchange risk resulting from the effect of changes in exchange rates on the domestic currency value of foreign currency assets.
long position A long position is created when a dealer buys a currency because it is expected to appreciate.
long put A long put position is obtained by buying a put option.
long straddle A long straddle consists of a long call and a long put at the same exercise exchange rate.
long strangle A long strangle consists of a long call and a long put at different exercise exchange rates.
loss function In forecasting, this is a measure of the costs associated with forecasting errors.
Louvre Accord A 1987 agreement among major industrial countries to stabilise exchange rates.
Maastricht Treaty The treaty that has led to the creation of the European Monetary Union.
macroeconomic fundamentals Macroeconomic variables that affect the exchange rate, such as interest rates and inflation.
maintenance margin In futures trading, this is the lowest level allowed before the trader is asked to pay in more money into the margin account.
managed floating A system of flexible exchange rates with active central bank intervention.
management fees Fees charged to borrowers by the banks for arranging and managing loans.
margin In option trading, this is the cash or securities required to be deposited by an option writer with a broker as collateral.
margin account An account established by a trader of futures contracts with the broker who initiates the trader's order in the exchange.
margin call A margin call arises when a futures trader is required to pay more money into the margin account when the maintenance margin is reached.
market efficiency A market is efficient if prices reflect all available information.
market integration Financial markets are integrated if capital is free to move from one market to another and assets are close substitutes.
market makers Large commercial banks are market makers in the sense that they stand ready to buy and sell currencies at the exchange rates they declare, acting via their foreign exchange dealers. The same applies to accepting and placing deposits.
market participants Buyers and sellers in the foreign exchange market.
market penetration A marketing objective of capturing a share in an existing market.
market portfolio In the capital asset pricing model, this is a portfolio that represents the movement of the whole market (for example, a share price index).
market risk The risk arising from fluctuations in market prices.
market segmentation The separation of national markets from each other.
market sentiment The general consensus on the state of the market and where it is heading.
market transactions As opposed to internal transactions, these are transactions conducted with other firms.
market value The current market price of an asset.
market-based forecasting A cheap form of forecasting that utilises readily available market data.
marking to market In spot foreign exchange transactions, marking to market is the process of comparing the average rate with the current market rate to measure unrealised profit/loss. In futures transactions, it is the process of crediting/debiting the margin account following changes in spot exchange rates.
marking-to-market risk The risk arising from fluctuations in the margin account.
Marshall–Lerner condition A condition requiring the sum of the elasticities of demand for exports and imports to be greater than unity for devaluation to have a positive effect on the current account.
Matilda bonds Foreign bonds issued in Australia.
mean The average value of a variable over a period of time.
mean absolute deviation (MAD) A measure of risk that is arguably superior to the standard deviation.

mean absolute error (MAE) A measure of forecasting accuracy based on the absolute errors.
mean square error (MSE) A measure of forecasting accuracy based on the squared errors.
measurement errors Errors representing the mismeasurement of economic and financial variables.
merchandise account The part of the balance of payments that records the imports and exports of goods.
mergers and acquisitions (M&As) Forming a new business by merging with or acquiring an existing firm.
microstructure approach An alternative approach to exchange rate determination focusing on the process and outcomes of exchanging currencies under explicit trading rules.
mint parity The central value of the fixed exchange rate under the gold standard.
misalignment The deviation of the exchange rate from its long-term equilibrium value.
misquote A situation that arises when a dealer makes a mistake in quoting exchange rates.
mixed standards Monetary standards under which reserves consist of currencies and commodities.
modified following business day convention A rule whereby the maturity date of a forward contract is set to be the value date, but if it falls on a non-business day, the date would be moved to the following day.

monetary model of exchange rates The proposition that exchange rates are determined primarily by the relative national money supplies.
monetary/non-monetary method A translation method whereby monetary items are translated at the closing rate, while non-monetary items are translated at the historical rate.
money laundering Unlawfully legalising illegal funds such as those obtained from drug trafficking.
money market hedge Hedging by determining in advance the domestic currency value of foreign currency payables or receivables by borrowing and lending.
money market swap A swap with a maturity of three years or less.
moving average rule A mechanical trading rule whereby buy and sell signals are generated by the intersection of the time paths of the exchange rate and a moving average or two moving averages of different orders.
multicurrency bonds Bonds whose payments are denominated in more than one currency.
multi-equation models Econometric models that consist of more than one equation explaining exchange rates in terms of its determining variables.
multilateral exchange rate *see effective exchange rate.*
multilateral netting Calculating the net payments due from one company to another when a number of companies have bilateral payments due to each other.
multimarket exposure Exposure to foreign exchange risk faced by a firm that sells its products in a number of foreign markets.
multinational firms Firms that have cross-border presence to carry out the functions of production and distribution.
multiple bands An arrangement whereby the exchange rates of the domestic currency are allowed to move within several bands of different widths.
multiple exposure Exposure to foreign exchange risk resulting from changes in more than one exchange rate.
multipoint arbitrage Arbitrage involving more than three currencies.
naked option An option that has no corresponding spot position in the underlying currency.
natural hedge A natural hedge exists when the effects of changes in the exchange rate on two foreign exchange positions are equal and opposite.
neckline In technical analysis, this is the level that, if penetrated, represents the completion of a head and shoulders or reverse head and shoulders position.
net arbitrage profit In covered and uncovered arbitrage, this is equal to the covered and uncovered margins, respectively. In other kinds of arbitrage, it is the difference between the selling and buying rates.
net capital flows Capital inflows less capital outflows.
net income In balance of payments accounting, this is the income received by factors of production working in other countries minus income received by foreign factors of production operating in the reporting country.
net present value (NPV) The difference between the present value of the future cash flows to be generated by a project and its capital cost.

net profit In option trading, this is gross profit less the option premium.
net services Exports minus imports of services.
netting *see exposure netting.*
new issuance facilities (NIFs) Short-term financing instruments issued by banks and used by firms to borrow funds.
New Zealand–Australia Free Trade Agreement (NAFTA) An agreement that was in operation between 1966 and 1983 when it was replaced by the Closer Economic Relations Agreement.
next-day transaction A transaction involving the exchange of currencies on the business day following the transaction date.
no-arbitrage condition A condition that precludes the availability of profitable arbitrage operations. For example, covered interest parity is the no-arbitrage condition for covered arbitrage.
noise traders Traders who do not pay attention to fundamental factors.
nominal exchange rate The quoted exchange rate without adjustment for prices.
nominal interest rate The quoted interest rate without adjustment for inflation.
non-bank financial intermediaries (NBFIs) Financial intermediaries that do not indulge in conventional banking operations such as accepting demand deposits.
normal quotation *see direct quotation.*
normalised weights Export, import or trade shares adjusted by taking into account the shares of major trading partners only.
North American Free Trade Agreement (NAFTA) A free trade agreement comprising the United States, Canada and Mexico.
nostro account An account that is held at a correspondent bank in a foreign country for the purpose of making and receiving payments in the currency of that country.
note issuance facilities (NIFs) Short-term notes underwritten by banks or guaranteed by bank standby credit arrangements.
notional principal The amount used to calculate the exchanged cash flows in an interest rate or a currency swap.
novel bonds Unconventional bonds that represent financial innovation in the bond market.
odd date *see broken date.*
OECD Model Tax Convention A model treaty designed by the OECD and used by countries as the basis of bilateral tax treaties.
offer premium The price at which a dealer is willing to sell an option.
offer rate The exchange (interest) rate at which the quoting dealer is willing to sell (place) a currency (deposit).
oligopolistic reaction hypothesis A hypothesis stipulating that FDI by one firm triggers similar investment by other leading firms in the industry in an attempt to maintain their market shares.
online foreign exchange trading Trading via Internet-based multidealer foreign exchange services.
online trading Electronic trading, such as that conducted over the Internet.
online trading systems Internet-based trading systems.
open interest The number of outstanding futures or option contracts.
open positions Foreign exchange positions that give rise to foreign exchange risk.
opening transaction A transaction resulting in opening a new position (for example, in options).
operating exposure Exposure to foreign exchange risk resulting from the effect of changes in the exchange rate on operating cash flows.
operational hedging Operational measures aimed at reducing the adverse effects of changes in exchange rates on the domestic currency value of foreign currency cash flows.
operational risk The risk arising from the execution of operations, in which case it is internal to the firm.
option on a swap A contract allowing the holder to exercise, or otherwise, the right to engage in a specified swap.
organised exchange A market, such as the Sydney Futures Exchange, that has a physical location where buyers and sellers can meet face to face. Brokers act on the floor of the exchange.
OTC options Tailor-made options that are available over the counter (that is, they are not traded on organised exchanges).
out of the money An option is out of the money when it cannot be exercised at profit.

output and market size hypothesis A hypothesis stipulating that the volume of FDI in one host country depends either on the output (or sales) of a multinational firm in this country or on the market size as represented by its GDP.

outright forward contract A contract to buy or sell a currency forward without an offsetting spot transaction.

outright operation *see outright forward contract.*

outright rate A forward rate expressed exactly like a spot rate with two numbers representing the bid and offer rates.

outward FDI From the perspective of one country, outward FDI is investment in other countries by that country.

overnight swaps Foreign exchange swaps that end on or before the spot value date.

over-the-counter (OTC) market A market that has no physical location, consisting of a network of buyers and sellers who are connected via means of telecommunication.

ownership advantages Things like the right to a particular technology, monopoly power and size, access to raw materials and access to cheap finance.

par value The value of a fixed exchange rate. For the par value of a bond, *see face value.*

parallel loan A transaction involving an initial exchange of funds between firms in different countries that is reversed at some time in the future.

parametric approach A method of measuring value at risk based on the assumption that the rate of return on the underlying position is normally distributed.

participation fees In syndicated loans, these are fees that are charged to the borrower and divided among participating banks in relation to their shares of the loan.

passive income Income derived from dividends and interest payments as well as royalties, patents and copyrights.

path-dependent option An option whose value depends on the average spot exchange rate over a specified period of time.

payback period The length of time taken for a project to generate enough cash flows to cover its capital cost.

peg *see par value.*

pegging to a basket of currencies A system whereby the exchange rate of the domestic currency against another currency is determined by the exchange rates of a basket of currencies.

pegging to a single currency A system whereby the exchange rate is fixed against a particular currency and allowed to move against other currencies.

perfect forecast A forecast with a zero forecasting error.

peso problem A concept that emerged out of a real-life event in Mexico, but that has become a term that is frequently applied by economists to explain the failure of the unbiased efficiency hypothesis, which is the inability of the forward rate to predict the spot rate.

pip The fifth decimal place in an exchange rate quote. It is one-tenth of a point.

Plaza Accord A 1985 agreement among major industrial countries to intervene in the foreign exchange market to stem the rise of the US dollar.

point The fourth decimal place of an exchange rate quote. It is one-hundredth of a cent.

point and figure charts In technical analysis, these charts are used to highlight major market trends. Unlike line and bar charts, they do not show small exchange rate movements and they are not time-related.

point forecast A single forecast for a particular point in time.

political risk The possibility of incurring losses due to changes in the rules and regulations governing FDI and also to adverse political developments.

pooling Assigning the cash balances of a multinational firm and its subsidiaries to a centralised location, from which the cash requirements of any subsidiary can be met.

portfolio investment Investment in financial assets without buying big stakes of companies with the purpose of exerting some control.

position keeping The monitoring of positions in each currency.

position limit The maximum size of a position in a particular contract.

position squaring The realisation of profit/loss on a foreign exchange position by buying or selling at the current exchange rate.

PPP exchange rate The exchange rate that is compatible with PPP.

prediction-realisation diagram A graphical device that is used to measure forecasting accuracy.
premium (of an option) The price paid to obtain an option (normally expressed per unit of the underlying currency).
premium payment date The date on which the premium of an option is due and payable.
price discovery In spot transactions, this means judging the exchange rate at which a transaction can be executed. When used in reference to futures markets, it means the ability of these markets to indicate the market price.
price exposure Exposure to foreign exchange risk resulting from the effect of changes in the exchange rate on the domestic currency price.
price quotation *see direct quotation.*
price takers Market participants who deal on the basis of the prices (interest and exchange rates) quoted by market makers.
price variation A process whereby the adverse effects of changes in exchange rates are contained by changing prices.
primary markets The markets for new issues of bonds and equities.
prime rate In the United States, this is the lending rate charged by banks to their most favoured corporate customers.
private banking Managing the banking needs of wealthy individuals.
private information Information that is not publicly available, but unlike insider information it is not illegal to trade on private information. An example is the knowledge of a profitable trading rule.
private placements Selling an entire issue of securities to a single buyer or a small number of buyers.
probability distribution A schedule showing the values that can be assumed by a variable with the associated probabilities.
product life cycle hypothesis A hypothesis stipulating that most products follow a life cycle and that FDI arises from the reaction of firms, by expanding overseas, to the possibility of losing markets as the product matures.
proportionality A property of PPP implying that changes in the money supply lead to proportional changes in the exchange rate.
protectionism A policy of imposing restrictions on imports to protect national industries from foreign competition.
public information Information that is publicly available such as that provided in media releases.
public offerings Offering the issued securities to the public at large.
purchasing power parity (PPP) A relationship between exchange rates and prices postulating that a country with a high inflation rate relative to those of its trading partners tends to have a depreciating currency.
pure commodity standards Monetary standards in which reserves take the form of commodities such as gold and silver.
pure fiat standards Monetary standards in which reserves are foreign currencies.
put option An option that gives the holder the right to sell the underlying currency at the exercise exchange rate.
quantity quotation *see indirect quotation.*
quantity theory of money The proposition that the general price level is proportional to the money supply in the long run.
quotas Quantitative restrictions on imports.
quoted currency The currency doing the pricing in an exchange rate quotation.
random component The component of a time series that is unrelated to secular, cyclical or seasonal variation.
random error term A term that is added to the right-hand side of an equation representing an econometric model to show that the equation does not represent a precise relationship. It accounts for the effect of missing and unquantifiable variables.
random walk The proposition that period-to-period changes in exchange rates are random and unpredictable.
range forward *see currency collars.*
rational expectations Expectations based on collecting and processing all available information.
rational forecast A forecast that is based on collecting and processing all available information.

real exchange rate The nominal exchange rate adjusted for domestic and foreign prices. It reflects the purchasing power of a currency.
real interest differential The difference between two real interest rates.
real interest parity (RIP) The equality of real interest rates across countries.
real interest rate The nominal interest rate adjusted for inflation.
realignment A series of devaluations and revaluations in the European Monetary System.
realisable value The value that can be realised by disposing of an asset.
reciprocity In foreign exchange dealing, this means quoting back to other dealers.
reduced-form model A single equation econometric model.
reference rate The rate used to determine the interest rate charged on a loan by adding a spread.
registered option traders (ROTs) Market participants trading on the exchange for their own firm's account.
regression A statistical technique that is used to estimate economic and financial functional relationships.
regressive expectations An expectation formation mechanism whereby the exchange rate is expected to rise if it falls in the current period, and vice versa.
Regulation Q A regulation introduced by the US authorities in the 1960s to limit the interest rate that US banks could pay on US dollar saving accounts.
reinvestment risk The risk arising from changes in interest rates on the value of reinvested coupon payments.
remittance restrictions Restrictions imposed by the host government on the funds that can be remitted by a subsidiary to its parent firm.
replacement cost The cost of replacing an asset.
representative offices Establishments that are used by banks to have a physical presence in other countries.
reserve requirements Obliging banks to hold reserves as a percentage of total assets.
resident A concept used in the construction of the balance of payments statistics as the record of transactions between foreigners and residents.
residual risk *see unsystematic risk.*
resistance level In technical analysis, this is the level at which the exchange rate finds it difficult to penetrate on the up side.
retained earnings The portion of corporate profit that is not distributed to shareholders as dividends.
revaluation Raising the value of a currency with a fixed exchange rate.
revenue exposure Exposure to foreign exchange risk arising from the sensitivity of domestic currency revenue to changes in the exchange rate.
reverse floaters Novel bonds on which the coupon interest rate falls as market interest rates rise.
reverse head and shoulders In technical analysis, this is a pattern that indicates the impending appreciation of the underlying currency.
revolving commitment An arrangement whereby a bank agrees to lend funds for a period of three to five years by accepting a series of sequential notes at each maturity.
revolving underwriting facility (RUF) An arrangement whereby borrowers use a single bank to place their notes at a set price.
rho A measure of the rate of change of the option premium with respect to the interest rate.
risk A measure of the probability and magnitude of deviation from some expected outcome.
risk aversion Requiring a risk premium to take on risky assets or projects.
risk management The techniques and instruments used to mitigate risk.
risk premium The spread required to persuade risk-averse investors to take on risky assets and projects.
risk sharing An operational hedging technique whereby only part of a shipment is invoiced in domestic currency terms or by using a predefined range of exchange rates.
risk transfer The ability of futures contracts to perform the function of allowing traders to transfer risk to others (the hedging function).
risk-adjusted cash flows Cash flows whose values are reduced to allow for the effect of some perceived risk.

risk-adjusted discount rate A higher than usual discount rate to reflect the effect of some perceived risk.

risk-averse A market participant who likes certainty and dislikes outcomes described by probability distribution.

risk-free interest rate The rate of return on a risk-free asset, such as a Treasury bill.

risk-lover A market participant who bears risk deliberately in anticipation of a favourable outcome.

risk-neutral A market participant who is indifferent between equivalent certain and probabilistic outcomes *or* a participant who is indifferent among assets denominated in various currencies if they offer the same rate.

rollover A term used to describe a foreign exchange swap when the forward and spot transactions take place on adjacent days.

rollover CDs Certificates of deposit that are renewed after maturity at an interest rate reflecting market conditions.

root mean square error (RMSE) A measure of forecasting accuracy that is based on the squares of the forecasting errors.

round dates Terms to maturity of forward contracts with a whole number of months

salvage value The market value of a project at the end of its lifetime.

same-day transaction A foreign exchange transaction in which the delivery of currencies takes place on the same day.

Samurai bonds Foreign bonds sold in Japan.

saucers A chart formation in technical analysis.

scenario analysis Consideration of the outcome of a future event based on a series of scenarios with the associated probabilities.

screen-based automated dealing systems Networks that connect terminals used by dealers to call other dealers for the purpose of conducting foreign exchange transactions.

screen-based information systems Information systems providing news and prices from other banks. The first was Reuters Monitor Service, which was introduced in 1973.

seasonally adjusted Adjustment of the balance of payments (and other economic indicators) for seasonal fluctuations.

seasonal component The component of a time series that represents seasonal variation.

secondary markets The markets where existing issues of securities are traded.

Securities and Exchange Commission (SEC) A US agency that is in charge of regulating financial markets and transactions.

securitisation The tendency to raise capital by issuing securities rather than borrowing directly from banks.

seigniorage The difference between the face value of a unit of currency and its production cost.

semi-strong efficiency Market efficiency, implying that prices reflect all available information when the information set encompasses all publicly available information.

sensitivity analysis The application of 'what if' analysis.

settlement In foreign exchange transactions, this means completing the transaction by making and receiving payments.

settlement date In option trading, this is the date on which delivery of the underlying currency is required. It is also the date on which a futures contract is settled.

settlement exchange rate The exchange rate implicit in a futures contract.

shell branches Legally incorporated units representing US banks in places like the Cayman Islands. Each unit is effectively a separate set of books in the head office.

short call A short call position is obtained by writing a call.

short dates Forward contract maturities of one month or less.

short exposure Exposure to foreign exchange risk resulting from the effect of changes in exchange rates on the domestic currency value of foreign currency liabilities.

short position A short position on a particular currency is created when a dealer borrows an amount of that currency and sells it.

short put A short put position is obtained by writing a put.

short straddle A short straddle consists of a short call and a short put at the same exercise exchange rate.

short strangle A short strangle consists of a short call and a short put at different exercise exchange rates.

signalling effect The buying and selling of currencies resulting from the deliberate transmission of information by the central bank about the desirability or otherwise of a certain level of the exchange rate.

significant control An investment is defined as direct investment if the investor has a significant control over the underlying project, which results from some minimum shareholding. This minimum lies between 10 and 25 per cent.

simulation A technique involving the running of a large number of iterations to generate a probability distribution for the underlying variable.

simulation approach A method of calculating the value at risk based on the simulated values of the rate of return.

Singapore interbank offer rate (SIBOR) The offer interest rate on various currencies in the Singapore interbank market.

single moving average rule A mechanical trading rule whereby buy and sell signals are indicated by the intersection of the time paths of the exchange rate and a moving average.

single-equation models Econometric models that consist of one equation describing the relationship between the exchange rate and its determining variables.

Smithsonian Agreement An agreement among the 10 major industrial countries that aimed (but failed) to salvage the Bretton Woods system.

smoothing Smoothing transactions conducted by the central bank aim to ease the volatility of the currency's path in reaction to news to prevent exchange rate overshooting.

Snake in the Tunnel A system of fixed exchange rates adopted by European countries during the period between the collapse of the Bretton Woods system and the advent of the European Monetary System in 1979.

Society for Worldwide Financial Telecommunication An electronic settlement system that connects banks in various countries and whereby foreign exchange transactions are settled.

soft currencies *see exotic currencies.*

soft loan A loan with a zero or low interest rate and easy repayment terms.

soft-edged band In a system of target zones the exchange rates are kept within a band without commitment to central bank intervention should the limits be reached.

sovereign risk The possibility of losses on claims on foreign governments and government agencies.

spatial arbitrage *see two-point arbitrage.*

special drawing rights (SDRs) A composite currency created by the IMF in the 1960s and used mainly as a unit of account.

speculation Buying and selling on the basis of certain expectations with the objective of making profit if the expectations are realised.

speculative attacks Selling or short selling a currency in massive amounts because of a perceived impending weakness.

speculators Participants in financial markets buying and selling on the basis of certain expectations with the objective of making profit if these expectations are realised.

spikes A chart formation in technical analysis.

spot exchange rate The exchange rate applicable to a transaction involving an immediate delivery of the currencies.

spot transaction A foreign exchange transaction involving an immediate delivery of the currencies.

spot-forward spread *see forward spread.*

spot-forward swap *see foreign exchange swap.*

spot-start swap A swap that starts two days after the verbal agreement.

spread In international lending, this is the margin added to the reference interest rate to determine the interest rate on a loan.

stabilising speculation Buying a currency when it is weak and selling it when it is strong, thus reducing exchange rate volatility.

standard deviation A measure of the dispersion around the mean or the expected value of a variable.

standard-expiry option An option with a standardised expiry date.

standardised contracts Financial contracts (such as futures and options) that have standardised features, such as the size and the maturity date.

standby Eurocredits Short-term Eurocurrency loans provided by banks for their corporate customers.

sterilised intervention Central bank intervention that may take the form of buying the domestic currency while replenishing cash in the banking system, thereby leaving interest rates unchanged.

Sterling Area A group of currencies that used to be pegged to the British pound.

stocks Economic and financial variables that are measured at a point in time. It also means equities.

straight bonds Conventional bonds with fixed coupon interest payments.

straight dates *see round dates.*

straight through processing (STP) End-to-end automation of the trading process from order to settlement.

stress testing A series of scenario analyses aimed at investigating the effect of extreme market conditions and/or the effect of violating some of the basic assumptions underlying a risk model.

strike exchange rate *see exercise exchange rate.*

strong efficiency Market efficiency, implying that prices reflect all available information when the information set encompasses all publicly available information as well as private and insider information.

structural changes Permanent changes in economic and financial relationships.

subsidiary A company located abroad that is owned in whole or in part by the parent firm.

support level In technical analysis, this is the level at which the exchange rate finds it difficult to penetrate on the downward side.

swap buyout Closing a swap by settling at current prices.

swap operations Foreign exchange transactions involving forward and spot operations.

swap rate A forward exchange rate expressed in terms of the points of discount/premium.

swaption A contract allowing its holder to alter the underlying swap.

symmetry A property of PPP implying that changes in domestic prices have the same effect on the exchange rate as changes in foreign prices.

syndicated Eurocredits Eurocurrency loans that are provided jointly by a group of banks (a syndicate).

syndicated loans Large loans that are provided by a group (a syndicate) of banks.

synthetic call A position that can be created by buying a put option while buying the underlying currency spot.

synthetic forward contract An implicit forward contract created by borrowing and lending in two currencies.

synthetic futures contract A position with a pay-off similar to that of a futures contract, which can be created by combining two options.

synthetic put A position that can be created by buying a call option while selling the underlying currency spot.

Synthetic spot position A position that can be created by combining the pay-offs on a long call and a short put on the underlying currency.

Systematic risk The portion of total variability of the rate of return that is associated with the whole market.

systemic crises Financial crises that engulf more than one country at the same time.

tap CDs Large-denomination negotiated deposits.

target range A range within which central banks may aim at keeping exchange rates.

target zone An exchange rate arrangement whereby major countries establish a set of mutually consistent targets for real effective exchange rates.

tariffs *see customs duties.*

tax credits Credits given to a company for the taxes paid by one of its subsidiaries in another country.

tax haven A place where foreigners may receive income or own assets without paying high rates of tax on them.

technical analysis A variety of practices and procedures that are used to generate buy and sell signals by examining the past history of the financial prices.

technical models Models that are based only on the analysis of the past history of the financial prices.

temporal method A translation method whereby the closing rate is used to translate items stated at replacement cost, realisable value, market value or expected future value, while the historical rate is used for all items stated at historical cost.

term swap A currency swap with a maturity of more than three years.

terms of trade The prices of exports relative to the prices of imports.

testing An action by the central bank designed to discern market volatility from trends.

theta A measure of the anticipated change in the option premium resulting from a change in the time to expiry.

three-point arbitrage An arbitrage operation triggered when the cross exchange rates involving three currencies are inconsistent.

time deposits Funds that are committed for a specified period of time at a specified interest rate.

time value The time value of an option arises from the possibility that if it is out of the money, it may turn out to be in the money with the passage of time.

time value of money The value resulting from the fact that money can be invested at the market interest rate, making a dollar today more valuable than a dollar tomorrow.

Tobin tax A tax on foreign exchange transactions proposed by James Tobin.

tom/next swaps *see overnight swaps.*

tops In technical analysis, these are the peaks in the time path of the exchange rate.

trade balance *see merchandise account.*

trade date *see contract date.*

trade finance The financing of cross-border exports and imports.

trade-weighted effective exchange rate A weighted average of the bilateral exchange rates when the weights are trade shares.

trade-weighted index (TWI) An index of the trade-weighted exchange rate.

trading range In technical analysis, the exchange rate moves in a trading range when there is no upward or downward trend.

trading rules Mechanical procedures that are used to generate buy and sell signals.

tranche CDs Certificates of deposit that are divided into several portions to make them appealing for small investors.

transaction costs The costs associated with buying and selling in financial and commodity markets. They include brokerage fess and the bid-offer spread.

transaction exposure Exposure to foreign exchange risk resulting from the sensitivity of the domestic currency value of contractual cash flows to changes in the exchange rate.

transfer pricing Pricing of goods and services that are bought and sold (transferred) between members of a corporate family.

translation exposure Exposure to foreign exchange risk resulting from the effect of changes in the exchange rate on the domestic currency values of foreign currency balance sheet and income statement items.

translation methods The methods that determine which exchange rate is used to translate foreign currency items to the domestic currency.

transnational firms Firms that do not have obvious home countries.

trend The component of a time series that represents the long-term secular movement.

trend channel In technical analysis, a trend channel is formed by lines connecting the tops and bottoms.

trendlines In technical analysis, trendlines connect tops in an upward trend and bottoms in a downward trend.

triangles A chart formation in technical analysis.

triangular arbitrage *see three-point arbitrage.*

Triffin Dilemma Named after Robert Triffin, this arose in the 1960s. To avoid a liquidity shortage, the United States had to run a balance of payments deficit, thus undermining confidence in the US currency. And to avoid speculation against the dollar, the deficit had to be reduced.

Triffin Paradox *see Triffin Dilemma.*

triple bottoms A chart formation in technical analysis.

triple tops A chart formation in technical analysis.

twin deficit problem The phenomenon of having big deficits in the current account and the government budget simultaneously.

two-point arbitrage An arbitrage operation triggered when an exchange rate has two different values in two financial centres.
two-sided markets Markets in which both buying and selling orders are available.
two-way quote Quoting exchange rates as bid and offer rates.
two-way rate *see two-way quote.*
unbiased efficiency The notion that the forward rate is an unbiased and efficient predictor of the future spot rate.
unbiasedness *see unbiased efficiency.*
uncertainty The possibility of deviations from some expected outcome without the associated probabilities.
uncovered arbitrage A profit-seeking operation that consists of going short on one currency and long on another without covering the long position.
uncovered interest differential The interest rate differential adjusted for the percentage change in the exchange rate.
uncovered interest parity (UIP) The condition that precludes the availability of profitable uncovered arbitrage operations. It tells that any return that can be derived from an observed interest differential will be completely offset by changes in the exchange rate.
uncovered margin Net profit on uncovered arbitrage.
underlying currency The currency bought and sold according to an option contract.
undistributed earnings *see retained earnings.*
unsystematic risk The component of total risk that cannot be diversified away.
valuation In foreign exchange transactions, this means the calculation of unrealised profit/loss.
value added tax (VAT) A consumption tax levied on the incremental value of goods and services as they pass through different stages of production.
value at risk (VAR) An approach to the measurement of risk that determines the maximum loss that can be incurred over a given period of time with a given probability.
value date *see delivery date.*
value-today transaction *see same-day transaction.*
value-tomorrow transaction *see next-day transaction.*
variable costs Costs that depend on the level of output.
variance A measure of the dispersion around the mean or the expected value of a variable.
variation margin An additional amount that has to be paid into a margin account associated with futures trading in order to bring it to the initial margin level.
vega A measure of the rate of change of the option premium with respect to volatility.
volume quotation *see indirect quotation.*
vostro account An account held by a bank on behalf of a foreign dealer.
weak efficiency Market efficiency, implying that prices reflect all available information when the information set is restricted to the past history of prices.
wedges A chart formation in technical analysis.
wholesale market *see interbank market.*
window-dressing Deliberate actions designed to make financial statements look more appealing than otherwise.
withholding tax A tax that is levied on passive income earned by a firm within the tax jurisdiction of another country.
working capital management Management of short-term assets and liabilities.
World Bank An international organisation created in 1944 to deal with international development problems.
Worm The name given to the narrowest band under the multiple band system of the Snake in the Tunnel.
writer (of an option) The counterparty selling an option in return for a premium.
Yankee bonds Foreign bonds sold in the United States.
zero-coupon bonds Bonds that offer zero-coupon payments sold at discount from the face value that is realised in full on maturity.
zero-coupon swap An interest rate swap that involves the exchange of cash flows on the maturity of the contract only.

Index

A

B

C

E

G

H

I

J

K

L

M

S

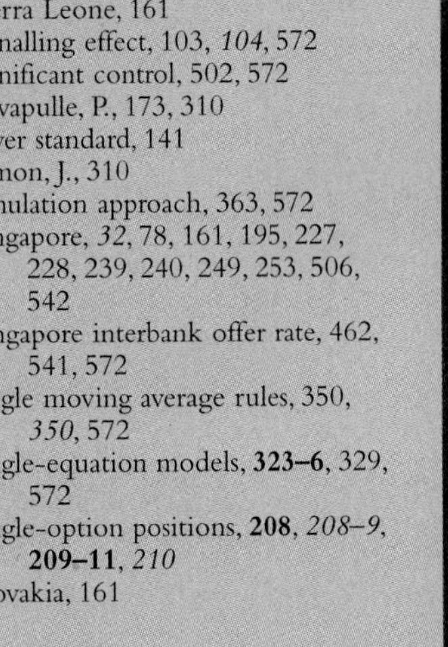

T

U